The Achievement of David Novak

The Achievement of David Novak

A Catholic-Jewish Dialogue

EDITED BY
Matthew Levering
AND
Tom Angier

PICKWICK *Publications* · Eugene, Oregon

THE ACHIEVEMENT OF DAVID NOVAK
A Catholic-Jewish Dialogue

Copyright © 2021 Wipf and Stock Publishers. All rights reserved. Except for brief quotations in critical publications or reviews, no part of this book may be reproduced in any manner without prior written permission from the publisher. Write: Permissions, Wipf and Stock Publishers, 199 W. 8th Ave., Suite 3, Eugene, OR 97401.

Pickwick Publications
An Imprint of Wipf and Stock Publishers
199 W. 8th Ave., Suite 3
Eugene, OR 97401

www.wipfandstock.com

PAPERBACK ISBN: 978-1-7252-7709-0
HARDCOVER ISBN: 978-1-7252-7710-6
EBOOK ISBN: 978-1-7252-7711-3

Cataloguing-in-Publication data:

Names: Levering, Matthew, 1971–, editor. | Angier, Tom P. S., editor.

Title: The achievement of David Novak : A Catholic-Jewish dialogue / edited by Matthew Levering and Tom Angier.

Description: Eugene, OR: Pickwick Publications, 2021 | Includes bibliographical references and index.

Identifiers: ISBN 978-1-7252-7709-0 (paperback) | ISBN 978-1-7252-7710-6 (hardcover) | ISBN 978-1-7252-7711-3 (ebook)

Subjects: LCSH: subject Novak, David, 1941–. | Catholic Church—Relations—Judaism. | Judaism—Relations—Catholic Church. | Judaism—Relations—Christianity—1945–. | Christianity and other religions—Judaism—1945–. | Natural law.

Classification: BM535 L48 2021 (print) | BM535 (ebook)

Manufactured in the U.S.A.   02/16/21

Contents

Preface by Tom Angier | vii
Acknowledgments | xv
List of Contributors | xvii

Introduction: A Master of Jewish-Christian Dialogue | 1
—Matthew Levering

A Conversation between David Novak
and Robert P. George (March 28, 2019) | 22

1. David Novak and Jewish Natural Law: How a Theistic Believer Engages a Pluralistic and Secular Milieu | 40
   —Melanie Susan Barrett

   Response by David Novak | 63

2. A Christian Account of Why David Novak Is Right about the Same-God Question | 67
   —Francis J. Beckwith

   Response by David Novak | 85

3. In the Beginning: The Primordial Character of the Problem of Suicide in David Novak's Scholarship | 90
   —John Berkman

   Response by David Novak | 115

4. The Divine Commandments in Moral Theology | 120
   —David Elliot

   Response by David Novak | 142

5. Natural Law: Having It Both Ways | 146
 —Tom Angier

   Response by David Novak | 160

6. David and Goliath | 164
 —Douglas Farrow

   Response by David Novak | 177

7. The Pedagogy of *Dabru Emet*: How a Catholic Professor Teaches a Jewish Document to Multireligious Students | 181
 —Rita George-Tvrtković

   Response by David Novak | 195

8. Pope Pius IX and the Mortara Case: A Catholic Critique | 199
 —Matthew Levering

   Response by David Novak | 220

9. Giving Justice More Than Its Due | 225
 —Daniel Philpott

   Response by David Novak | 248

10. Reason's Revelation and Revelation's Reason: Reading Apuleius's *De Deo Socratis* and Augustine's *De Civitate Dei* through the Lens of Novak's *Athens and Jerusalem* | 252
 —Thomas Slabon

    Response by David Novak | 288

11. David Novak, Natural Law, and the Sanctity of Human Life | 292
 —Christopher Tollefsen

    Response by David Novak | 308

12. On Good Supersessionism: Jews, Christians, and the Covenant That Binds and Divides Us | 313
 —Thomas Joseph White, O.P.

    Response by David Novak | 328

Index | 333

Preface

Tom Angier

I FIRST MET DAVID Novak while studying for a Diploma at the Oxford Centre for Hebrew and Jewish Studies. He had come to Oxford to give a series of lectures that, two years later, went to make up *Natural Law in Judaism* (1998). I found these not only highly stimulating but also novel, since—given my background in Anglo-analytic philosophy—natural law theory had hardly grazed my intellectual consciousness. This whetted my appetite for more, and soon I found myself working for a PhD in the University of Toronto's "Collaborative Programme in Ancient and Mediaeval Philosophy." Here I was fortunate enough to take David's graduate course on natural law, a magisterial conspectus covering the whole tradition. David's range of reference was hugely impressive, something to which the essays in this volume bear (only partial) witness. In summarizing their content—without here summarizing David's magnificent Responses to the essays (each essay concludes with a Response by David)—I wish to pay homage to David's monumental intellectual achievement, especially in its relevance to Catholic thought. Both Catholic philosophy and theology stand irrevocably in his debt.

After Matthew Levering's Introduction to David as a master of Jewish-Christian dialogue, the volume begins with a conversation, as befits David's gift for friendship. Professor Robert George, a Princeton jurisprudent and old friend of David, skillfully navigates David's long career, and probes his views on topics both personal and professional. Beginning with the resurgence in Orthodox Jewish life since David's youth, Prof. George touches on the challenges facing religious Jews in the academy. This brings him to the analogous challenges facing practicing Catholics, who increasingly also find themselves marginalized in the academy and beyond. For David, natural law can protect and unite Jews and Catholics against the depredations of secularism, without wholly insulating them from its beneficial aspects. David then turns to his time at Georgetown under Germain Grisez, the founder of the "new" natural law theory. Grisez was a powerful influence, who nonetheless accepted that David would never be his disciple. This leads Prof. George to reflect on the public role of natural law, and how it provides, along with biblical sources, a "double-barreled shotgun" against secularism—one wielded by figures as diverse as Martin Luther King and Roy Moore. This intellectual "shotgun," David adds, is needed more than ever, especially when it comes to life issues. Natural law reasoning, in particular, has an explanatory power—and hence power of advocacy—that remains unrivalled.

Melanie Barrett builds on the idea that natural law thought is peculiarly well-suited to engaging our "pluralistic and secular milieu." While militant secularists maintain that Jews can be only particularistic or imperialistic when arguing in the public square, Jewish natural law thought supplies, Barrett contends, the "lower limit" for justice. Beyond this, both Jews and Christians have an ambitious conception of the transcendent, which lays heavy responsibility on all citizens for the stewardship of creation. True, it is this ambition that threatens the (sometimes contrary) ambitions of the totalizing State. Nonetheless, there is real and universal benefit to practices like public prayer, along with traditional marriage. Barrett argues that Jewish and Christian support for such practices constitutes a genuine public service; Jews and Christians should therefore never retreat to a purely self-serving posture, campaigning only in defense of religious liberty. Religious liberty is, nevertheless, vital, and often dovetails with the public good. Barrett takes as an example the debacle over the Obama administration's contraceptive mandate, which showed the need for a chastened, limited State, and a deeper understanding of sex as ordered to the rearing of children. The stark alternative is "liberal illiberalism," which *de facto* aims at establishing a secular religion, and brings about the effective demise of deliberative democracy.

Francis Beckwith tackles a key theological question, namely, whether Jews and Christians worship the same God. In light of *Dabru Emet* (2000), and the scandal at Wheaton College over whether Christians and Muslims worship the same God, this theological question clearly has great practical significance. For some, Christian doctrines such as the Trinity and the Incarnation mean that Jews and Christians do *not* refer to the same (personal) entity when using the name "God." But according to Beckwith, this view is mistaken. What Jews, Christians, and indeed Muslims share is the "merely theistic" conception of God: that is, they agree on what constitutes God's metaphysical nature. That nature is to have ultimate and underived existence, to mention but two of its essential features. While, to borrow Frege's terms, different monotheistic religions ascribe different *senses* to "God," they agree nonetheless on its *reference*, which is determined by (and only by) God's nature. On the one hand, the specifically Christian component of belief in God—regarding His "internal life"—is revealed; on the other, the generically theistic component is accessible to and affirmable by all monotheists. Were this common reference not in place, moreover, St. Paul could not have spoken intelligibly of "God" at the Areopagus, nor could Arians and Athanasians have understood each other at Nicaea.

John Berkman treats a topic of immediate practical import, viz., suicide—which was also the subject of David's first book. According to David, and Jewish tradition more widely, life belongs to God, and we are merely its stewards. Given the self-evident good of life, our natural inclination to it, and the long-standing warrant of tradition, the taking of one's own life seems unaccountable and indeed pathological. No suicide can, therefore, be judged (definitively) as freely and rationally chosen. By contrast, modern liberalism, with its entrenched notions of autonomy, privacy and individual rights, has no adequate basis on which to reject suicide as irrational. For David, this amounts to a capitulation to the ravages of loneliness. A genuinely caring society would not abandon people to loneliness and hence to their desire for suicide. But in response to this, Berkman enters some sharp criticisms. According to him, David's argument *begins* with a refusal to judge suicide as freely chosen—on pain of its incurring guilt—and *ends* with the claim that all suicides are (likely) grounded in psychosis, or at least in delusion. But no evidence is offered for this. Furthermore, that suicide (likely) stems from psychosis not only belies cultural variations in suicide rates, it also makes a nonsense of laws against suicide, which assume that suicide is a type of act from which people can rationally refrain.

David Elliot's chapter is a subtle and historically erudite reflection on the role of divine commandments (*mitzvot*) in Catholic moral theology. Elliot points out that critiques of the Catholic manualist tradition as one of "suffocating rigidity" often verge on a Marcionite (and hence anti-Jewish) hostility to divine commands. It is here that David Novak's notion of the *mitzvot* as vital to human dignity and flourishing can be seen as a much-needed corrective. While the divine commandments should inspire fear, lest we break them and hence damage what they protect, such salutary fear complements and is indicative of the love of God, who we do not wish to offend. Drawing on Aquinas, Elliot adds that the commandments are coordinate with the virtues, which, when we embody them in action, contribute to our flourishing. It remains the case, however, that given our general peccability, the law aspect of morality remains essential, importing as it does a curb on human pride and our tendency to concupiscence. The fear of transgression is nonetheless "born of love," and as a *timor filialis*, or filial fear—rather than *timor servilis*, or servile fear—constitutes one of the gifts of the Holy Spirit. The end of the *mitzvot* remains not law-abidingness *per se*, but rather charity towards our neighbor and maintaining our loving relationship with God. Catholic moral theology can, in sum, learn much from the idea that obedience is a form of love.

My chapter concerns the relation between philosophical approaches to natural law—which typify the Catholic scholastic tradition—and David's "theologically formulated" approach. David's case for the inadequacy of the philosophical approach is, I maintain, threefold. First, what I call his argument from the history of ideas; second, his argument from metaphysics; and third, his argument from the nature of law. The argument from the history of ideas holds that the Greek philosophers rarely refer explicitly to a law or laws of nature. It is only with Philo, and later Christian philosophers, that such terms gain wide currency. Hence the idea of natural law is properly theological. The argument from metaphysics holds that philosophical natural law "depends on the ontological assumption of universal teleology." But since Darwin, this assumption has been rendered defunct. So, the deliverances of philosophical natural law have, in turn, been rendered defunct. Lastly, the argument from the nature of law holds that law is necessarily something promulgated (here David agrees with Aquinas). But in the case of natural law, the only promulgator available is God. Hence, natural law is, once more, an essentially theological notion. I contend that each of these arguments is defeasible and that philosophical natural law continues to be a robust and much needed ethical and political resource.

Douglas Farrow returns to Barrett's theme of how Jews and Christians are called to act in the public square. For Farrow, Canada provides a paradigm case of how State law can become a "deracinatory giant," fostering a "tyrannical democracy" in which traditional communities are increasingly marginalized. This is evidenced by, for example, legal redefinitions of the "family unit," along with State intervention in sex education and religious education. As opposed to the "savior State," and its attempt to legitimize all resentment at limits, Farrow advocates a respect for the limits imposed by an "enclosing nature." And here he finds David's work has its greatest salience. For David has challenged the legal and cultural prominence of individual autonomy, replacing it with the value of personal dignity, and called into question the amorphous notion of "society," finding value instead in the idea of community. For David, communal covenant precedes individual contract and acts as a bulwark against the pseudo-liberty (or license) of "secular space." In short, David's scholarship issues a rallying cry to those resisting the unravelling of a theistically based culture. That scholarship is thus of great moment not only for Jews, but also for Catholics, and indeed all those of good will. According to Farrow, the *mitzvot* cannot be overturned without overturning genuine community—so David's rallying cry should be heeded.

Rita George-Tvrtković teaches at Benedictine University in Chicago and is concerned primarily with interreligious dialogue. She notes that the debate over whether monotheists share the same God is often confined to Christians and Muslims, since it is assumed by many—especially since *Dabru Emet* (2000), in which David played a leading role—that Christians and Jews clearly do. There are, nonetheless, dissenting voices. She refers, for instance, to the Orthodox Jewish classification of Christian worship as *avodah zarah*, or "foreign worship," i.e., idolatry. This is comparable to how Latin Christians conceived of Muslim belief and practice in the mediaeval period. Both Orthodox Jews and mediaeval Latin Christians are responding to what they take to be a later, deficient form of faith. By contrast, *Dabru Emet* and Vatican II's *Nostra Aetate* give far more generous interpretations of their Christian and Jewish counterparts (respectively). The question remains, however, whether such calls to dialogue and reciprocity paper over and sideline key issues. Is reciprocity always good, or even possible? Perhaps not, if the power imbalance between the dialogue partners is strong enough. "Reciprocity pressures," such as the Muslim call that Muhammad be recognized as a prophet, can be injurious, especially when most Muslims continue to view the Jewish and Christian scriptures as corrupted.

Matthew Levering addresses the Edgardo Mortara case in mid-nineteenth century Italy. This woeful episode concerns the removal of a Jewish child from his family by papal police after his nurse-maid allegedly baptized him. Levering navigates the treacherous theological and political waters here with skill. His overall argument is that Pius IX was not justified in his actions. Those actions were, at the very least, imprudent, and they gave scandal. It is doubtful, moreover, whether Anna Morisi, Edgardo's nurse-maid, was telling the truth. Granted, there is a distinction between an illicit and an invalid baptism. But even if a valid baptism took place, it does not follow that papal authorities had the right to forcibly engineer the education of a baptized child, especially where this meant removing him from the jurisdiction and care of his parents. The preponderance of evidence suggests that Aquinas, for his part, also opposed such actions. And this because the supernatural order cannot overrule the natural order, where the latter incorporates duties of natural justice (including the rights of parents). Invoking the notion of "sacramental realism" in this context does not, Levering maintains, alter these facts. He concludes that, even though Pius IX acted wrongly and imprudently, the sins of the Popes, and of the Catholic faithful more widely, need not and should not dissuade people from faith in the Church.

Daniel Philpott critically engages David's view that justice, in its Jewish and covenantal acceptation, is about giving others their due. On the contrary, Philpott argues, the biblical idea of justice is much wider and includes promoting both right relationship and the goal of human flourishing. Here he cites manifold evidence about *tzedakah* from the Tanakh (viz., Hebrew Bible) and about *dikaiosunē* from the New Testament. Justice, on these conceptions, is not merely about respecting and promoting rights. Rather, it anticipates Kant's notion of an "imperfect duty," which goes beyond rights to embrace a general beneficence. Such beneficence is embodied in almsgiving and other works of mercy and is seen wherever compassion and forgiveness are practiced. God's saving justice, for its part, also stretches the bounds of rights-based justice. God can save and deliver, even though these are not deserved as of right; likewise, His purifying retribution and restorative acts of mercy need not be a function of what is due by right. (Take, for instance, the "superabundant" sacrifice of Christ, which, although it did in some sense "pay a debt," was not owed as a matter of right.) Philpott further challenges David's view that, just as rights entail duties, so duties entail rights. This, Philpott adjures, goes against the biblical evidence, which shows that duties can exist without concomitant rights.

Thomas Slabon's is an historically rich, highly scholarly chapter which draws on David's Gifford Lectures (published as *Athens and Jerusalem* (2019)). Central to these lectures is the notion that the Greek and Jewish inheritance is not a matter of reason meeting revelation, but rather of two different kinds of revelation. For although philosophy does not consist in reflection on miracles or unique, revelatory events, like theology it displays faith in the existence and intelligibility of the world, methodological axioms which it cannot itself justify. Where theology departs from philosophy, according to David, is in its claim to offer a superior and perfective revelation. Slabon affirms this interpretative schema and corroborates it by appeal to Apuleius's *De Deo Socratis* and Augustine's *De Civitate Dei*. Apuleius thinks of philosophy as a way of life, seen at its highest in the life of Socrates; this life is then made complete by theistic revelation, together with the virtues it inspires. This is, at least, the view of Augustine, who argues that Christianity preserves Plato's insights better than Plato did himself. While Plato and his heirs may partake of revelation, they also propound false revelations, and reason incorrectly about those that are genuine. By contrast, Christians have received only true revelation, and hence profess the true mediator. This Augustinian account, Slabon holds, is formally the same as David's, even if it differs in content.

Christopher Tollefsen focuses on the sanctity of life. Whose lives are sacred, exactly? According to Tollefsen, non-human animals do not share humanity's "horizon of basic goods," and so their lives fail to qualify as sacred. But even within the human family, some lives can legitimately be taken. Tollefsen countenances the different rationales for this: self-defense, the principle of double effect, and God's delegation of the (properly divine) power to take life. David seems to adopt the third rationale, since he defends capital punishment on scriptural grounds. But Tollefsen argues against this position. While God is, he agrees, the Giver and Lord of life, and could in principle mandate intentional killing, in fact neither suicide (self-killing) nor capital punishment (judicial killing) is ever justified. At most, God permissively wills death, rather than intending that others intend it. Why so? For two reasons. First, because the significance of being made in the "image" of God, *b'tselem elokhim*, is both irrevocable and practically overriding. And second, because God's gift of life—which embodies a profound and basic good, on which numerous other goods depend—cannot be rescinded or treated as at our disposal. Here Tollefsen disagrees not only with David but also with Catholic defenders of capital punishment (such as Feser and Bessette).

Finally, Thomas Joseph White, O.P. explores the vexed topic of supersessionism. He outlines five different versions of this concept. First, there is the supersessionism agreed on by both Jews and Christians, to the effect that monotheistic revelation overturns pagan belief and practice. Second, there is supersessionism *qua* the fulfilment of the Old Testament by the New. Third, there is the idea that the Trinity unfolds Jewish monotheism, intensifying and extending the moral precepts of the Hebrew Bible. Fourth, there is the "incoherent" notion that the Church, as *Verus Israel*, simply supersedes and renders defunct the post-biblical Jewish community. And fifth, there is the supersessionism of *Nostra Aetate*, which, although it did not innovate doctrinally, set a new ethical and spiritual tone for Jewish-Catholic relations. Where Jews and Christians can agree, White maintains, is not only in affirming the first version of supersessionism, but also in denying the supersessionism of both Islam and liberal secularism. Liberal secularism is, in effect, the old paganism *redivivus*, while Islam repudiates Jewish and Christian revelation as (at the very least) systematically unreliable. White concludes that the figure of Jesus the Messiah, Yeshua ha-Mashiach—together with the "good supersessionism" he represents—serves, to this day, not only to divide, but also to unite Jews and Christians.

Acknowledgments

THIS BOOK BEGAN AS a conference held at Mundelein Seminary of the Archdiocese of Chicago in Spring 2019, under the aegis of the Center for Scriptural Exegesis, Philosophy, and Doctrine directed by Matthew Levering. The idea for the conference arose during a conversation between the co-editors in Spring 2018, while at the University of Notre Dame for a conference on the work of Servais Pinckaers. We owe a special debt to James and Molly Perry for a generous financial grant that made the conference possible. We also are indebted to Mundelein Seminary's Provost, Fr. Thomas Baima, for his gracious hospitality, as well as to the Rector of Mundelein Seminary, Fr. John Kartje, who supported the conference. Many thanks as well to the estimable Mary Bertram, who oversaw much of the nuts-and-bolts planning for the event, and to the staff of the Conference Center. Caitlyn Trader prepared the manuscript for publication in accord with the standards of Wipf & Stock. Michael Thomson, my editor at Wipf & Stock, lent his support to the publication, for which we are grateful. Above all, we thank David Novak for his participation at the conference and his acceptance of this Festschrift as a token of the esteem in which all the authors herein hold him.

In 2006, Matthew Levering met Karen Chan, then a Notre Dame doctoral student working at the Center for Ethics and Culture. Karen became a dear friend and she presented a paper at the conference honoring David Novak. She planned to move to Texas with her husband and family, after spending some years as Dean of St. Patrick's Seminary in San Francisco. Karen was a joyful, brilliant, and wise human being. Not long after our conference, to our immense shock and grief, Karen died in a car accident. In sure hope of meeting again, we dedicate this book to the memory of Karen Chan, scholar and friend.

Contributors

Tom Angier is Senior Lecturer in Philosophy at the University of Cape Town.

Melanie Susan Barrett is Professor of Moral Theology at Mundelein Seminary.

Francis J. Beckwith is Professor of Philosophy and Church-State Studies, Affiliate Professor of Political Science, and Associate Director of the Graduate Program in Philosophy, at Baylor University.

John Berkman is Professor of Moral Theology at Regis College, University of Toronto.

David Elliot is Assistant Professor of Moral Theology at Catholic University of America.

Douglas Farrow is Professor of Theology and Ethics at McGill University.

Robert P. George is McCormick Professor of Jurisprudence and Director of the James Madison Program in American Ideals and Institutions at Princeton University.

Rita George-Tvrtković is Associate Professor of Theology at Benedictine University.

Matthew Levering holds the James N. and Mary D. Perry Jr. Chair of Theology at Mundelein Seminary.

David Novak holds the J. Richard and Dorothy Shiff Chair of Jewish Studies as Professor of the Study of Religion and Professor of Philosophy at the University of Toronto.

Daniel Philpott is Professor of Political Science at the University of Notre Dame.

Thomas Slabon is a Doctoral Candidate in Philosophy at Stanford University.

Christopher Tollefsen is Professor of Philosophy at the University of South Carolina.

Thomas Joseph White, O.P. is Professor of Theology and Director of the Thomistic Institute at the Angelicum in Rome.

Introduction

A Master of Jewish-Christian Dialogue

MATTHEW LEVERING

IN THE NEARLY TWO millennia over which the relationship between Jews and Christians has unfolded, polemics and persecution have been the norm. Thus the argument could be made, although the modesty of the man precludes it, that David Novak is the greatest master of Jewish-Christian dialogue who has ever lived. For more than a half century, David has participated in and reflected upon Jewish-Christian dialogue as part of the core of his own philosophical and theological work, without thereby ceasing to address his fellow Jews as his primary audience. Consistently, he has sought to help Jews learn from and develop friendships with Christians, while seeking to help Christians learn from the Jewish tradition and develop friendships with Jews.

David Novak has been able to do all this because of his extraordinary mind and his fluent pen. He has also been able to do this because of an unusually broad education that included some of the preeminent Jewish and Catholic teachers of the twentieth century, among them Abraham Joshua Heschel, Leo Strauss, Yves Simon, Louis Dupré, and Germain Grisez. It helped that he grew up in a Chicago that had vibrant Jewish and Catholic communities. It also helped that, in his career of teaching at the University of Virginia and at the University of Toronto, he has taught in the company of eminent Christian scholars. His collaboration with Richard John Neuhaus in the project of *First Things* provided yet another congenial context for learning and teaching serious dialogue between Jews and Christians. Most important, however, was his sheer attentiveness to the topic—and therefore the practice—of Jewish-Christian dialogue. This attentiveness spans the entirety of his career. The purpose of this Introduction is to reflect a bit on his accomplishments in this regard, by attempting to sketch the arguments of a selection of his most notable writings and, occasionally, to add my own perspective in response.

The Early Writings

David's doctoral dissertation in philosophy, completed in 1971 at Georgetown University, flows in significant part from his experience as Jewish chaplain to St. Elizabeth's Hospital in Washington, DC. The dissertation was written while he served as a rabbi in Oklahoma City in 1970. In his dissertation, he philosophizes about the morality of suicide, with the aid of Plato, Thomas Aquinas, and Immanuel Kant. In each of these thinkers he finds resources of the first importance, which he places implicitly into the service of his theological outlook as a Jewish scholar.[1] Here we find the beginnings of his abiding interest in Aquinas and Kant (both of whom he reads as Christian philosophers) in light of his own constructive ethical inquiry.

In the 1970s, David published a series of halakhic essays that take up central matters of Jewish philosophical theology, ethics, and ritual, under the title of *Law and Theology in Judaism*.[2] Here we see him deepening his mastery of Maimonides, Saadiah Gaon, Gersonides, and the classical rabbinic sources of Judaism, as well as more recent figures such as Baruch Spinoza, Martin Buber, and Franz Rosenzweig—along with the Written Torah (Scripture). Eight years later, still while working as a rabbi, he published a work on Jewish-Christian dialogue from the Jewish side, investigating how Christians were understood in central Jewish sources. This book appeared in 1983 as *The Image of the Non-Jew in Judaism: An Historical and Constructive Study of the Noahide Laws*.[3] Some portions of that book were reworked in his 1989 monograph published by Oxford University Press—indicative of his academic stature as the Edgar M. Bronfman Professor of Modern Jewish Thought at the University of Virginia—under the title *Jewish-Christian Dialogue: A Jewish Justification*.[4] It will become clear that while some of David's positions in the domain of Jewish-Christian dialogue have changed over the decades (as his interactions with Christian theologians have deepened), the foundations of his standpoint have remained constant.

The "justification" that David defends is sketched in the book's preface by way of a personal story. As a young boy in the 1940s, he had a conversation with an old man

---

1. For references to his theological outlook, see Novak, *Suicide and Morality*, 126–27.

2. See Novak, *Law and Theology in Judaism*, first series; Novak, *Law and Theology in Judaism*, second series.

3. See Novak, *The Image of the Non-Jew in Judaism*.

4. See also Sacks, "Jewish-Christian Dialogue," 161–81. Originally published in 1988, a year prior to the publication of Novak's book, this essay does not cite Novak. He seems to be moving toward something like Novak's own solutions (though not yet in terms of natural law) when he argues that ethics always is embedded within a tradition but nonetheless entails concern for people outside one's tradition. He states, "Ethics sets boundary conditions for theology. If the unredeemed are not, at some level, objects of moral concern, possessing independent integrity and rights, then faith itself becomes morally untenable" (Sacks, "Jewish-Christian Dialogue," 177). He is aware, too, that "[o]ne of the regular discoveries of dialogue is that each faith is itself more internally diverse than it seems to an outsider. Often it is easier to find agreement between religious liberals, or conservatives, across faiths, than it is for the two wings to agree within a single faith community" (Sacks, "Jewish-Christian Dialogue," 163).

on a train, who turned out to be a retired Methodist minister. Young David told the old man that his favorite book was the Bible and his favorite person in the Bible was Abraham, "the first Jew."[5] The old man responded positively. David reports discovering a unity grounded in a shared yearning for the God of Abraham: "We began talking about Abraham, and I sensed that he too was Abraham's son, that we both saw ourselves coming from father Abraham.... I discovered that our trip was not at all in truth that of our fellow passengers. Our trip, like father Abraham's, was to that unknown destination. Then and there, we were equals; each of us accepted the other exactly as he was."[6] This sense of eschatological journeying—as Jews and as Christians—to the God of Abraham, to the New Jerusalem, to the unfathomably glorious Messianic consummation that will go beyond all our expectations has remained with David, at the very heart of his thought. He has never been a mere academic.

In the constructive final chapter of *Jewish-Christian Dialogue*, David urges that the core of biblical morality consists in openness to hearing God's voice, addressed to us personally. This insistence upon hearing God's voice does not locate Jews or Christians in the past. Rather, God's voice calls Jews and Christians to an eschatological future. All moral claims, for Judaism and Christianity, "must ever bear in mind the eschatological horizon, the respective hope for each faith community for final redemption"—not a flight from this world, but precisely the glorious redemption of this world.[7] If Jews and Christians are anything, says David, they are people who have heard the God of Abraham's voice and sought to obey it in faithfulness. Insofar as they are such peoples, they may not easily be able to converse with secular neighbors who think God's voice to be a delusion. But surely they should be able to converse with each other. David puts it with his typical rhetorical flair: "Indeed, it is precisely because they have faith that the Lord hears and speaks that they can speak and hear the words of one another."[8]

Not surprisingly, the final two pages of *Jewish-Christian Dialogue* have to do with "the final redemption."[9] He cites Isaiah 64:4, as well as a rabbinic comment on this text and its reaffirmation in 1 Corinthians 2:9, to show that this redemption will be beyond any imagining. Whatever else they are, Jews and Christians are people who have not yet arrived and cannot fully apprehend the arrival for which they yearn. In the present valley of tears, both Jews and Christians know themselves to be journeying rather than aimlessly wandering. They know that the starting point of their journey is the Creator God of Abraham, and they believe that they (and the entire human race) "will meet at the all-mysterious end."[10] Can we conclude, then, that what we have here

5. Novak, *Jewish-Christian Dialogue*, viii.
6. Novak, *Jewish-Christian Dialogue*, viii.
7. Novak, *Jewish-Christian Dialogue*, 148.
8. Novak, *Jewish-Christian Dialogue*, 155.
9. Novak, *Jewish-Christian Dialogue*, 155.
10. Novak, *Jewish-Christian Dialogue*, 155.

are two parallel tracks to the same endpoint, and so Jewish-Christian dialogue can merely be a matter of recognizing the validity of the other's track? In David's view, it certainly is the case that the tracks are different and must remain so in this life. But the purpose of Jewish-Christian dialogue does not consist in adjudicating the relationship of the tracks, beyond being willing to grant a legitimate—even if (relatively speaking) inferior—theological space to the track of the other. Rather, the purpose of Jewish-Christian dialogue prior to the final consummation is primarily an ethical one, though not an ethical one in the Kantian sense of building up the kingdom of God on earth together. It is instead a shared witness to real hope, hope not in human powers or in the unfolding of the cosmos, but in the God of Abraham, the Creator and Redeemer God. David concludes, "Our dialogue might be able to show the world that the hope it needs for its very survival can only be the hope for its final redemption. Neither nature nor history nor the self can supply hope these days."[11]

In drawing this conclusion David makes clear that a central task—even *the* central task—of his work in Jewish-Christian dialogue is to better understand his Judaism. This is as it should be. He holds that liberal Judaism made crucial mistakes. While admiring in certain respects the turning of the tables accomplished by the great Jewish philosopher Hermann Cohen—who argued for "Judaism's universalism as superior to Christian particularisms" and who refused (much like Philo) to accept "capitulation to the inauthentically universalistic majority culture"—David observes with dismay that "Cohen sees a reconciliation between Judaism and Christianity, not on the infinite Messianic horizon, but on the horizon of the secular German state founded by Bismarck after 1871."[12]

In thinking through Jewish-Christian dialogue from the Jewish perspective, David finds important resources in the work of Moses Maimonides. For David, Maimonides's theology grounds two ways of thinking about Jewish-Christian dialogue, the first of which is not acceptable but the second of which (though not taken up by Maimonides himself) will bear much fruit.

Let me sketch these two paths, beginning with the first. Maimonides affirms that Judaism, Christianity, and Islam are each related to the coming Messianic fulfillment. Importantly—and here David strongly agrees with Maimonides—none of them can claim to be the fulfillment, since only the Messiah can bring about the eschatological fulfillment. According to Maimonides, Judaism has the highest degree of "potentiality" (in Aristotelian terms of potency-act) toward the Messianic fulfillment, because Judaism "has the full Mosaic Torah along with its most authentic traditional interpretation

---

11. Novak, *Jewish-Christian Dialogue*, 156.

12. Novak, *Jewish-Christian Dialogue*, 122–23. Specifically, "Cohen saw the liberal Protestantism of his time—best exemplified by his Marburg colleague, the Christian theologian Wilhelm Herrmann—and his type of liberal or 'prophetic' Judaism coming together in an idealistic neo-Kantian socialist (as opposed to a materialist Marxist) constitution for the new German state, with its claims to universalism" (Novak, *Jewish-Christian Dialogue*, 123). Novak notes that Rosenzweig criticized Cohen's perspective sharply in this regard.

and application in Halakhah and Aggadah."[13] Christianity has less potentiality, but it still has the Torah, and therefore it has a degree of potentiality and is related to the Messianic fulfillment and to Judaism. On this view, Christianity is a lesser, partial (and distorted) form of Judaism that nonetheless still is related to the Messianic fulfillment.

David prefers not to follow this first Maimonidean path, even though it gives some theological place to Christianity. As he sees it, the problem is that this path undermines real dialogue by making Christians into a (much) lesser form of Judaism. Namely, although Christians have the Torah and thus are ordered in a certain way toward Judaism and toward the Messianic fulfillment, Christians misunderstand the Torah, misunderstand the Messiah, and misunderstand God. Dialogue with Christians, then, would primarily be aimed at bringing them to Judaism, or at least bringing them closer to Judaism. David does not consider this to be true "dialogue." Rather, here we have a relationship in which the Jewish participant in the dialogue would be the teacher and the Christian participant the student. The Jewish participant would "dialogue" with the Christian in order to show the Christian that Christianity does have some "potential" toward the full actuality that God intends (known to Judaism). The Jewish participant would then be calling upon the Christian to enter more deeply into this potential, by converting to Judaism. Such a dialogue, David thinks, is built on the unacceptable premises of proselytism.

David is aware that this first Maimonidean path, as he describes it, is the one that Christians have generally followed in their discussions with Jews. On this view, Christianity is the fulfillment of Judaism because the Messiah (Jesus) has come. Jews have the Torah and the covenants, but they are in a state of potency that needs to be actualized. They need to recognize that the fulfillment of their own religion—namely, the Jewish Messiah promised by God—has in fact come in Jesus of Nazareth. From this perspective, Christians undertake dialogue with Jews in order to bring them closer to Christianity, by enabling them to recognize that Jesus is in fact the Messiah of Israel and that all people (Jews and gentiles) are to await the eschatological consummation as members of his inaugurated kingdom, the Church.

David warns that this perspective, whether Maimonidean or Christian, makes dialogue impossible: it is merely a covert proselytism. He states that true "dialogue presupposes a true mutuality based on a duality that is not to be overcome in the process of the dialogue itself."[14] In his view, dialogue cannot proceed if Jews aim to bring Christians back to "their primordial Judaism" (which is an advance over the lesser and distorted form of Judaism that they profess) while Christians aim to draw Jews into Christianity (which Christians consider to be the Messianic community that Israel's Messiah has established, and that therefore is in certain respects a fulfilled or perfected Judaism, even if not yet eschatologically consummated).[15]

---

13. Novak, *Jewish-Christian Dialogue*, 127.
14. Novak, *Jewish-Christian Dialogue*, 129.
15. Novak is also consistently worried about syncretism between Judaism and Christianity. This

Maimonides's second path is the one that David not only articulates but also adopts. A core insight of *Jewish-Christian Dialogue* is found in David's argument that in addition to Maimonides's Aristotelian potency-act logic (the first path), Maimonides also offers a "possibility-realization logic."[16] Instead of "potency," which implies an internal teleology (a teleology of Christianity to be fulfilled in a return to its pure source, Judaism, or a teleology of Judaism to be fulfilled in Christianity), Maimonides envisions a "possibility" that arises not from internal resources but from a (transcendent) source that "is external and can never be seen as an internal factor within the realized entity itself."[17] We do not have an internal "potency" to generate revelation but we do have a "possibility" for revelation to be given to us. Metaphysically, Maimonides considers that "potency-act logic better explains more ordinary issues, whereas possibility-realization logic is used to explain more metaphysically significant issues."[18] Although Maimonides uses potency-act logic in explaining the relationship of Christianity to Judaism, David argues that in fact possibility-realization logic should be used. This is so because "possibility, unlike potentiality, entails more than one outcome" and also because "when a phenomenon is seen in terms of possibility-realization logic as opposed to potency-act logic, there is a greater role for God's direct and free action and a greater number of imaginable outcomes."[19]

For David, the result of possibility-realization logic in Jewish-Christian dialogue is that each side (Jews and Christians) can recognize that Judaism and Christianity instantiate diverse possibilities but not *competitive* possibilities. Neither side has to judge the revelation of the other; rather, the one can recognize that the other may have

---

syncretism, in his view, can either take a partial form or a complete form. In the partial form, Christians celebrate the Passover Seder in order to remind themselves of Jesus's Jewishness, and Christians invite Jews to celebrate (or lead) this "Christian" Passover Seder. Novak comments, "Such services, from the points of view of both normative Judaism and normative Christianity, are quite problematic. They suggest the constitution of a new religious reality, the celebration of syncretism itself. Maimonides summarized the tendency of the tradition when he cautioned against gentiles performing Jewish rites without the full faith commitment of conversion to Judaism. In other words, the commandments of the Torah are to be performed in the context of the historic covenant between God and Israel. On the Christian side, the Church Fathers warned against 'Judaizing,' namely Christians practicing Jewish rites. For such practices clearly imply that the historic rites of Judaism and Christianity, respectively, are insufficient for a full relationship with God. When this happens, the dialogue is no longer the relationship of Jews and Christians, in which each one faces the other *from* a distinctive point of origin, one that always transcends the point of meeting *between* them. Rather, the dialogue becomes an encompassing reality in which the Judaism and the Christianity of the participants become moments that are then overcome in a reality whose dynamic is its own momentum" (Novak, *Jewish-Christian Dialogue*, 22). In the complete form of syncretism, some form of Messianic Judaism emerges. In this regard Novak observes, "when the dialogue itself leads to the actual constitution of a religious *tertium quid* . . . it can no longer receive an authentic endorsement from either faithful Jews or faithful Christians" (Novak, *Jewish-Christian Dialogue*, 23).

16. Novak, *Jewish-Christian Dialogue*, 133.
17. Novak, *Jewish-Christian Dialogue*, 134.
18. Novak, *Jewish-Christian Dialogue*, 134.
19. Novak, *Jewish-Christian Dialogue*, 135.

received from God a revelation that constitutes its own domain, its own community. David puts this in Kantian terms: "Thus although the prior conditions of possibility (a priori) compose one unified and universalizable standard, the experienced objects themselves that presuppose them are varied and not covered by one unified and universalizable standard. Each of them in its subsequent singularity (a posteriori) has its own unique and nonuniversalizable standards."[20]

On this view, then, Jews cannot judge Christianity, and Christians cannot judge Judaism, except to affirm the possibility—rooted in God's freedom—that revelation has been received by the other, i.e., that the other's faith could be a valid realization of the human possibility of being spoken to by God. Jews and Christians share this "border" of possibility, "the human precondition for God's revelation to singular faith communities."[21] Anything that pertains to the revelation given to the faith community can be assessed only from within the faith community's relationship with the God who speaks to it and cannot be assessed by outsiders.

According to David, Jews and Christians are thus able to recognize that from the shared realm of human "possibility" there can come more than one revelatory outcome, due to the action of the free God. This means that the reality of true "revelation" cannot be claimed by either Jews or Christians as solely their own prerogative. Instead, Jews must live by the revelation to which they are accountable, and Christians must live by the revelation to which they are accountable, without trying to subsume each other within the framework of one determinative revelation. David explains, "Revelation is univocal only if one posits that God spoke to only one people, or that if God did speak to other peoples, what they received can be ultimately understood only within the context of the one, true, actual revelation, of which their revelation is at best the potential."[22]

Given this perspective, David argues that Jewish-Christian dialogue should not be focused within the specificities of Judaism and Christianity as such but rather should "be constituted on the common anthropological border between Judaism and Christianity," and thus primarily in the domain of ethics.[23] But this should not deprive the dialogue of its theological (specifically "Jewish" and "Christian") character. For a dialogue to be truly a dialogue between Jews and Christians as such, it must be rooted in Jewish and Christian theology. David's argument in this regard is that morality is

---

20. Novak, *Jewish-Christian Dialogue*, 137. Novak adds, "Kant himself, of course, would not apply his own experiential scheme to religious experience of revelation. His theory of experience—in which external transcendence is affirmed—is confined to the experience of the objects of sense.... However, just as Maimonides appropriated the categories of Aristotelian teleology and applied them to history, whereas Aristotle confined them to nature, so I am here appropriating categories of Kantian epistemology and applying them to revelation as a real event, which Kant himself was most unwilling to do" (Novak, *Jewish-Christian Dialogue*, 137).

21. Novak, *Jewish-Christian Dialogue*, 137.
22. Novak, *Jewish-Christian Dialogue*, 138.
23. Novak, *Jewish-Christian Dialogue*, 141.

always tradition-constituted; there is no neutral ground of ethics, because our human nature is always shaped by membership in specific communities that shape our moral reasoning. At the same time, Jewish and Christian morality presumes created human nature and thus has philosophical as well as theological intelligibility. David thinks that it suffices for Jewish-Christian dialogue to be able to share with each other, as Jews and as Christians, our philosophical "theories about human nature and its capacity for concern with fellow humans" and our theological "theories about the human capacity for a relationship with God."[24] Jews and Christians in dialogue can gain from each other's philosophical reflections on human nature and theological reflections on the fact that humans are created for relationship with the free Creator God.

It follows that for David there is a reality to the "Judeo-Christian ethic," rooted in a set of shared theonomic affirmations, including affirmations about creation, commandments, covenant, revelation, covenantal community, and eschatological fulfillment through God's free action. These shared affirmations suffice for grounding a dialogue between Jews and Christians that is not missionary or proselytizing (as it would be if either side claimed to know the truth about the other's revelation, within the one sufficient revelation that accounts for all others), but that is also a specifically *Jewish-Christian* dialogue. As a Jewish-Christian dialogue, one shared premise is that the voice of God, obeyed by the covenant community, leads into a future of consummation that will freely be accomplished by God and that cannot be anticipated by earthly action on the basis of human resources. This cuts against secular utopian dreams as well as against efforts to build the kingdom in ways that exclude and marginalize the religious other.

David's interest in a "Jewish justification" for Jewish-Christian dialogue, therefore, is in significant respects a way of carving out ground for his particular account of Jewish ethics as a contemporary philosophical and theological project engaging the fundamental questions of the public square in modern pluralist democracies, including the nature of rights, the structure of political life, particular moral questions such as abortion and same-sex marriage and nuclear weapons, the status of natural law, and so on. He has never ceased to do the kind of halakhic work found in the 1970s in his two-volume *Law and Theology in Judaism* and in 1985 in a similar volume of essays, *Halakhah in a Theological Dimension*.[25] These volumes of halakhic essays gradually show increasing engagement with Christian thinkers—in part due to his ongoing interest in natural law theory, and in part, no doubt, due to the growing number of invitations that he received to speak under the aegis of Jewish-Christian dialogue. For example, his 1992 volume of halakhic essays, published by Oxford under the title *Jewish Social Ethics*, contains fascinating essay-length engagements with the Protestant theologian Paul Tillich and the Catholic theologian John Courtney Murray. His halakhic essays focus on providing a Jewish response to specific ethical issues: for instance, the AIDS epidemic, human

24. Novak, *Jewish-Christian Dialogue*, 141.
25. Novak, *Halakhah in a Theological Dimension*.

sexuality, the threat of nuclear war, technology and the environment, violent crime and capital punishment, economic justice, and the relationship of American Jews to the state of Israel.[26] A more recent volume, published by Baylor University Press in 2017 under the title *Jewish Justice*, shows that his halakhic work has continued. The volume includes essays on capital punishment, torture, marriage (with an eye to refuting advocates of same-sex marriage), and human rights. It also continues to engage in Jewish-Christian dialogue, as for example in "Defending Niebuhr from Hauerwas" and "Is Natural Law a Border Concept between Judaism and Christianity?"[27]

Works Since 1995

In the period between 1992 and the present, David has written fewer halakhic essays than he did earlier in his career because he has focused on writing a series of significant monographs, taking up both foundational themes (such as election, revelation, the land of Israel, and the knowability of God) and ethical themes (such as secularity, rights, natural law, and religious liberty). These monographs commenced with *The Election of Israel: The Idea of the Chosen People* (1995), and continued with *Natural Law in Judaism* (1998), *Covenantal Rights: A Study in Jewish Political Theory* (2000), *The Jewish Social Contract: An Essay in Political Theology* (2005), *In Defense of Religious Liberty* (2009), *Zionism and Judaism: A New Theory* (2015), and *Athens and Jerusalem: God, Humans, and Nature* (2019).[28] In these seven books, we find David deepening and extending his engagement with sources and authors already significant in his *Jewish-Christian Dialogue*. For example, in *The Election of Israel*, his main interlocutors are Spinoza, Cohen, Rosenzweig, Scripture, the Rabbis, Judah Halevi, and Moses Maimonides—with Maimonides occupying a crucial place toward the end of the volume. David is strongly critical of Maimonides for placing "little emphasis on the doctrine of election," and he finds in Maimonides an example of a Jewish philosophy that, by taking for granted that all societies are religiously constituted, leaves itself open to the Spinozist contention that Judaism, as a political reality, is no longer necessary.[29] In *Natural Law in Judaism*, similarly, the central chapter is devoted (in a critical fashion) to Maimonides, with other chapters engaging Scripture, the Rabbinic tradition, and insights from various figures such as Cohen, Saadiah Gaon, and Rosenzweig.

---

26. See Novak, *Jewish Social Ethics*.

27. See Novak, *Jewish Justice*.

28. See Novak, *The Election of Israel*; Novak, *Natural Law in Judaism*; Novak, *Covenantal Rights*; Novak, *The Jewish Social Contract*; Novak, *In Defense of Religious Liberty*; Novak, *Zionism and Judaism*; and Novak, *Athens and Jerusalem*. In the Preface to *Natural Law in Judaism*, Novak expresses his gratitude to Edward Oakes, S.J., who in a review of *Jewish Social Ethics* challenged Novak to undertake writing projects that would be more theoretically unified. This challenge appears to have stimulated Novak to do exactly that.

29. Novak, *The Election of Israel*, 225.

Covenantal Rights, *The Jewish Social Contract*, and *In Defense of Religious Liberty* are strongly theoretical in their internal structure, rather than being organized around chapters on central figures such as Maimonides. In *Covenantal Rights*, we find a rich account of the God who grants rights to humans (who otherwise would be too terrified and awed to stand before God), as also of the *imago Dei* and our right to depend upon God's justice. David discusses such themes as the Noahide laws, God's covenantal love for Israel, the claims made upon the covenanted community (e.g., justice, compassion, public worship, and martyrdom if necessary), self-love and love of neighbor, procreation and family, and various rights such as the right to protection from harm and the right to social inclusion. Throughout the book, the Rabbinic literature has a primary place in David's adjudications, and Maimonides is present as well, especially through his *Mishneh Torah*.

David's *The Jewish Social Contract* examines democracy, secularity, and pluralism in light of divine and human covenants (and contracts), with attention also to kingship and to the great Jewish thinkers of modernity, above all Spinoza and Moses Mendelssohn. *The Jewish Social Contract* also contains a significant chapter on Jewish-Christian relations, in which David rightly points out that while the Holocaust was for the Jewish people nearly a "physical annihilation," the Holocaust for Christians was nearly a "moral annihilation."[30] As a result, Christians moved to discover Judaism more deeply, and this has resulted in political cooperation between Christians and Jews as well as a recognition by the Catholic Church that it is not necessary to pursue arrangements in which the state's official religion is Catholicism. Equally importantly, David argues, the historical-critical discovery of the significance of Second Temple Judaism has taught Christians that ongoing Judaism cannot be "dismissed as a historical relic, a mere proto-Christianity" and has taught Jews that Christianity has in fact developed "in a trajectory continually parallel to that of Judaism."[31] On both sides, then, there is an emerging recognition that the other cannot be simply ignored in the process of self-understanding.

In Defense of Religious Liberty draws amply on rabbinic sources, particularly in chapters 5 and 6, which treat human rights. At the same time, David enters fully into contemporary philosophical and theological discussions, as well as into issues such as same-sex marriage and how Jews and Christians ought to relate to an expanding state. He also reprises his earlier discussions of natural law and natural rights.

---

30. Novak, *The Jewish Social Contract*, 190.

31. Novak, *The Jewish Social Contract*, 190. In light of post-9/11 politics, Novak adds, "Jews and Christians should be wary of having Judaism or Christianity or even the commonality between them—what is best called 'biblical religion'—become the religious frosting on somebody else's ideological cake. If opposition to a shared enemy is all that unites Jews and Christians politically, they risk slipping into all the usual political paranoia—that is, the *need* for a common enemy. Because of this inevitability, Jews and Christians must discover a mutuality that is more positive and enduring, one that does not need a common enemy" (Novak, *The Jewish Social Contract*, 194).

David's *Zionism and Judaism* returns to themes found in *The Election of Israel*. In *Zionism and Judaism*, his basic point is that God has elected Israel and has commanded his people Israel to live in the land that he has chosen for them. This raises a number of practical questions now that the state of Israel has been established, including whether a state can be both a "Jewish state" and democratic, the status of non-Jews in a Jewish state, and the kinds of Messianism that have arisen in Israel due to the conjunction of the Holocaust and the establishment of the state of Israel. Rabbinic sources remain central, although one chapter is devoted to responding to Spinoza.

At the same time, during these years David has continued to contribute explicitly to Jewish-Christian dialogue. Let me circle back to the arguments of his book *Jewish-Christian Dialogue*, by examining how he has refined them in essays over the past three decades. Many of these essays can be found in his 2005 collection *Talking with Christians: Musings of a Jewish Theologian*.[32] A key essay in this volume is his "From Supersessionism to Parallelism in Jewish-Christian Dialogue," originally published in 2003.

In this essay, David first outlines Christian supersessionism and Jewish counter-supersessionism. The Christian supersessionist view is that "God has exchanged the Jewish people for the Church, thus canceling the election of Abraham and his progeny."[33] Moreover, since the Jewish people do not worship God the Trinity, they therefore cannot and do not worship the true God. The Jewish counter-supersessionism is that Christianity, originating in "a group of renegade Jews," now (post-Nicea) "do not worship the Lord God of Israel as do the Jews but, rather, another god altogether."[34] In short, supersessionist Christians hold that Jews are utterly cut off from the God of Abraham, while supersessionist Jews hold that Christians are utterly cut off from the God of Abraham. Each side condemns the other as idolaters who are even worse than pagans.

In David's view, with which I agree, the breakthrough comes when Christians "acknowledge that *their* God's covenant with the Jewish people is perpetual."[35] Although Christians continue to affirm that Jesus is the Messiah of Israel and that God is Trinity, Christians now do so in a manner that gives theological space to the Jewish people. The Jewish people are still God's elect people; they have not been simply replaced, in God's eyes, by the Church. Indebted to Karl Barth, David puts it this way: for Christians it is the case that "[t]he promises God made through Jesus presuppose

---

32. Novak, *Talking with Christians*.

33. Novak, "From Supersessionism to Parallelism," 8.

34. Novak, "From Supersessionism to Parallelism," 9.

35. Novak, "From Supersessionism to Parallelism," 10. I agree also with Novak's points that "the renunciation of supersessionism has been carried on by Christian theologians committed to the truth of Christianity, over and above Christian diplomats interested in better political relations with Jews" and that "[s]ince supersessionism has been a leitmotif of Christian theology from patristic times to this day, the renunciation of supersessionism by Christian theologians has required not only great theological ingenuity but moral courage as well" (Novak, "From Supersessionism to Parallelism," 10).

that God has already been keeping his promises to Israel."[36] One of these promises to Israel was that God would enable Israel to live, not to die or be destroyed as a people. If the people of Israel—the literal descendants of the Jewish people of Jesus's day—ceased to exist as a distinct people, then it seems to David, as to Barth, that God would have failed to keep his promises.[37]

As an aside, let me note that I think that in the eschatological age both Judaism and Christianity will cease to exist in a certain sense, while continuing to exist in another sense. The eschatologically consummated people of God will be in recognizable continuity with Judaism and Christianity, not least because the Messiah of Israel, a Jew, will reign gloriously. But both Judaism and Christianity, as such, will be fulfilled (and "superseded" in a sense) by the glorious consummation—a point that is central to David's own eschatological expectations. As a Christian, I hold that the Messiah, Jesus, fulfilled Israel's covenants and reconfigured them around himself. In permitting the majority of the Jewish people *not* to recognize Jesus as the Messiah, however, God acted not simply in the mode of his permissive will but for the purpose of willing a particular good in the world. Augustine advanced a version of this view, arguing that God positively willed that the Jewish people according to the flesh continue after Jesus's coming, in order to ensure that the gentiles do not forget or disbelieve the covenantal matrix of the fulfillment brought by Jesus. Yet Augustine's view of the Jewish people is nonetheless deeply negative, because he charges them with being culpable unbelievers.[38] For a variety of reasons—including the scandal caused by Christians—I recognize that the Jewish people are not culpable in the way that Augustine supposes. I believe that as an actual historical matter, God's promises to Israel mean that the Jewish people and Judaism will continue until the final consummation, and that God wills this as a positive good.

This does not mean that I grant that some people are *not* called to acknowledge Jesus as the Christ. A Christian perspective holds that all are called to acknowledge Jesus ultimately. But God has good purposes in allowing some—for reasons that entail lack of culpability—not to recognize Jesus as the Christ in the present.[39] Historically speaking, this means that it is God's will that visible Judaism remain. In fidelity to God, the Jewish people continue to obey God's commandments and to await the Messiah.

36. Novak, "From Supersessionism to Parallelism," 11.

37. Novak cites Sonderegger, *That Jesus Christ Was Born a Jew: Karl Barth's "Doctrine of Israel,"* 131–33.

38. For centuries, Christians assumed that Jews who do not become Christians are thereby in a state of sin. This tragically mistaken belief on the part of generations of Christians helped to fuel constant persecution of the Jewish people by Christians. Through their hate-filled actions, these Christians made it difficult to believe that Jesus had fulfilled the covenant. Paul already foresaw this situation of scandal, warning the gentiles, "do not boast over the branches [the Jewish people]" (Rom 11:18) and teaching that "God has consigned all men [Jews and gentiles] to disobedience, that he may have mercy upon all" (Rom 11:32).

39. I explain my position in much greater detail in my forthcoming *Engaging the Doctrine of Israel: A Christian Israelology in Dialogue with Ongoing Judaism* (Eugene, OR: Cascade).

In a certain sense, appreciated by David, Christians yearn for the end of both Christianity and Judaism in the eschatological consummation. But this end will come about in God's time and not through human acts, whether good acts of evangelizing or repulsive acts of persecution. Recognizing God's will that Judaism continue, Christians can embrace Jewish converts[40] while also firmly supporting God's Jewish people in following their covenants.[41] David is quite right that "the bad behavior of the Jews can only impede the covenant, not lose it."[42] Jews will always be God's chosen people, and their sincere act of obeying the covenant is deeply praiseworthy.[43]

Let me now return to surveying the position David takes in "From Supersessionism to Parallelism in Jewish-Christian Dialogue." He emphasizes that both Christianity and Judaism came out of Second Temple Jewish readings of the Scriptures. It is a mistake to suppose that Christianity came out of "Judaism." Indeed, just as Judaism has a Written Torah and an Oral Torah (the latter interpreting the former), so also Christianity has an Old Testament and a New Testament. It is a mistake for Christians to think of the New Testament as superseding or replacing the Old, and it is a mistake for Jews to think of Christians as mere renegade Jews. David observes that Christians

---

40. Recognizing that Jews should "be attractive to the gentiles because of our public teaching of the Torah and our observance of its commandments," Novak points out that Jews "have never ceased to accept converts from the gentiles" ("From Supersessionism to Parallelism," 14). This does not mean that Novak approves of proselytism, either in its Christian or its Jewish forms. But welcoming converts is something that Novak supports from the Jewish side.

41. Novak states, "The minimal claim Jews have to make on the world is to allow us room to live our life as God's covenanted people. . . . Therefore, the question is: Which members of which communities/traditions can understand, let alone respect, the minimal Jewish claim on the world for our communal survival, which is in essence a theological claim?" ("From Supersessionism to Parallelism," 14). Catholics can and must understand, respect, and support this claim. As Novak points out, Muslims traditionally supported it, but "because of contemporary Jewish claims to national sovereignty in the land of Israel, which is seen as being within Islamic territory (*daar al-Islam*), almost all contemporary Islamic territory is a place from which most Jews have chosen to flee" (Novak, "From Supersessionism to Parallelism," 15). Novak also observes that "most Jews have bitter memories of our marginalization and vulnerability, both communal and individual, in the *ancien régime*, formerly known as 'Christendom'" (Novak, "From Supersessionism to Parallelism," 15). In Novak's view, the basis for Christian interest in Jewish-Christian dialogue is partly that Christians now realize that Christian identity cannot easily survive the liberal-democratic state, which forcefully claims primary allegiance over against the claims of religious identity. Now that Christians are in a vulnerable cultural situation, Christians recognize that Jews can help to promote "Judeo-Christian morality" (Novak, "From Supersessionism to Parallelism," 16). In turn, Jews can call upon Christians to combat the incursions of the liberal-democratic state against Judaism, as for example when Canada sought to outlaw circumcision. As Novak says, "Christians who have truly overcome the errors of supersessionism . . . can certainly understand, respect, even actively support the right of the Jews to remain faithful to God's irrevocable covenant with us. That is the case because Christians have the only communal tradition in the world which, like that of the Jews, requires them to understand themselves covenantally" (Novak, "From Supersessionism to Parallelism," 18–19).

42. Novak, "From Supersessionism to Parallelism," 11–12.

43. I agree with Novak that "Jewish adherence to the commandments is not law in place of grace but, rather, a faithful Jewish response to God's most gracious commandments" (Novak, "From Supersessionism to Parallelism," 19).

do not read the Old Testament and then presume that the New Testament is simply the sequel demanded by logic and reason. Rather, Christians grant primacy to Jesus Christ, and they read the Old Testament through this lens. Faith perceives Christ in the Old Testament, rather than supposing that Christ is merely a logical extension. It follows, says David, that "the 'Old Testament' is 'old' retrospectively, not as earlier 'potential' or as a prior 'cause'"; the Old Testament is "the set of conditions that made acceptance of the Christological revelation possible," but mere logic does not compel any rational reader of the "Old Testament" to reason his or her way to what the New Testament describes.[44] A further revelation, indeed a revelation that has primacy for Christians, is necessary to spark a re-reading of the Scriptures of Israel that then are seen as making sense in light of Christ.

Since this is so, Christianity does not need to be viewed (by Christians) as what all reasonable Jews must accept as the logical sequel of Israel's Scriptures. The logic of supersessionism is one of logical sequence, and this logic does not apply. What in fact has precedence for Christians is "Christological revelation."[45] The same point can be made about Oral Torah. It is known by faithful Jews to be necessary for interpreting Israel's Scriptures, but it is known in this way on the basis of faith, not on the basis of logic that must compel all rational persons. Much as Christians hold with regard to the New Testament, for Jews it is the divinely revealed Oral Torah that governs the interpretation of the Written Torah, rather than the Oral Torah being understood as the logical extension of the Written Torah. The later revelation (Christ, Oral Torah) is actually the one that has priority, insofar as the later revelation provides the lens through which the earlier revelation is read and is understood to be the foundation of the later revelation.

David concludes that theological reflections such as these will enable Jews and Christians to see each other less as competitors (over the meaning of "Judaism") and more as "two traditions, related to the same sources [Israel's Scriptures as mediated by the late Second Temple Pharisaic school], which have developed, often in the same worldly locations, with a striking parallelism."[46] This is better than Jews seeing Christians as a renegade distortion of "Judaism" and Christians seeing Jews as an unfaithful form of "Judaism." Instead, "Judaism" and "Christianity" are both ways of responding to late Second Temple events. They are competitors insofar as they differ over Jesus of Nazareth, including whether he rose from the dead, but they are not competitors in the sense of possessing an original "Judaism" that one or the other then distorts. Christians cannot respond to "Judaism" by arguing that the fullness of "Judaism" is Christianity; and Jews cannot respond to "Christianity" by arguing that the fullness and source (or home) of Christians is Judaism. The linear logic of supersessionism (described by David

---

44. Novak, "From Supersessionism to Parallelism," 22.
45. Novak, "From Supersessionism to Parallelism," 22.
46. Novak, "From Supersessionism to Parallelism," 24.

as "causal" or "teleological"),[47] with its radical mutual critique, is not theologically or historically adequate to the reality of either Judaism or Christianity.

Does this mean that for David, Jewish-Christian dialogue has thereby advanced beyond desiring conversion on either side? On the contrary, David affirms that Jews will always be glad when Christians (or others) become Jews. He states that among other things, Jews value converts to Judaism because converts "remind us that being chosen is best appreciated when our chosenness is what we would want for ourselves over and above the necessity of our birth to a Jewish mother."[48] Likewise, David grants that Christians, in order to be Christians, "must hope that everyone will accept Christ."[49] In Jewish-Christian dialogue, there is an inevitable undercurrent of invitation: either toward acceptance of Oral Torah as "original" for the understanding of Written Torah, or toward acceptance of Christ as "original" for the understanding of Israel's Scriptures. This is a risk that David considers worth taking, now that Christians have renounced the supersessionism that allowed no theological space for Jews to practice Judaism in good conscience. David sees the tension as a fruitful one, recalling both sides to the fact that the eschatological consummation may be more than what either side imagines, since surely God has the power "to make the truly final demonstration of an end that will include us all, making our presently parallel lines converge in eternity."[50] Although David does not say it, surely Paul makes a somewhat similar appeal, shrouded in mystery, in Romans 11.

"Supersessionism Hard and Soft"

One more contribution by David Novak to Jewish-Christian dialogue deserves careful examination here: his 2019 *First Things* essay "Supersessionism Hard and Soft." He begins by distinguishing between "hard" and "soft" supersessionism. According to "hard" supersessionism, the Jews are no longer God's chosen people. They have been completely replaced by Christians, and they are in mortal sin—utterly alienated from God—unless and until they repent and become Christian. According to "soft" supersessionism, God's covenant with his people Israel remains "forever valid."[51] The majority of the Jewish people rejected their Messiah (Jesus), but this does not mean that the people are utterly cast aside by God. They remain elect; they still possess the covenants and promises that God has given them. Thus, their Jewishness is still recognized as having positive theological significance.

David observes that Jews likewise possess forms of "hard" and "soft" supersessionism. For "hard" Jewish supersessionists, Christianity is a retreat to the idolatrous

47. Novak, "From Supersessionism to Parallelism," 24.
48. Novak, "From Supersessionism to Parallelism," 24.
49. Novak, "From Supersessionism to Parallelism," 24.
50. Novak, "From Supersessionism to Parallelism," 25.
51. Novak, "Supersessionism Hard and Soft," 28.

paganism (worship of a man, worship of multiple gods) that Judaism superseded once and for all. Such "hard" Jewish supersessionists reject Christianity, deny that it has any connection to Judaism, and seek to ignore it. Jewish "soft" supersessionists, among whom David includes himself, consider that Christianity, in its self-understanding at least, is not tritheistic and seeks to uphold truths contained in Israel's Scriptures. But Jewish "soft" supersessionists do affirm that Judaism is better—truer in every way—than Christianity.

David allows that some form of "soft" supersessionism is necessary for both Jews and Christians. He rightly remarks, "Without some kind of supersessionism, Christians have no cogent reason for not going back to their Jewish origins. Without some kind of supersessionism on our part, Jews like me would have no cogent reason for not going forward into what Christians regard as Judaism's fulfillment."[52] Christianity has to proclaim that Jesus is the long-awaited Messiah of Israel; Jews deny this and think that Christians have instead gone astray in certain ways, with regard to their claims about Jesus's divine nature as the incarnate Son and about his resurrection and with regard to the notion that God is a Trinity of Persons.

In David's view, however, this "soft" supersessionism need not form the basis of a public disputation, let alone a mutual condemnation. It is instead a matter of what a Christian would tell another Christian who was thinking of converting to Judaism, or what a Jew would tell another Jew who was thinking of converting to Christianity. "Soft" supersessionism pertains to the community's self-understanding, but it does not require denying all theological space to the other community. Jews, for example, can appreciate that Christians proclaim the Scriptures of Israel and uphold the unity of God, the reality of the God of Israel, and the truth of the Decalogue. By contrast, "Christian hard supersessionism tells Jews that they must become Christian in order to be in covenant with God, and Jewish hard supersessionism tells Christians that they must renounce Christianity to avoid being idolatrous pagans."[53] One easily sees the significant difference between hard and soft forms.

Yet, for Christians, has not the Messiah come? And, insofar as Jews have rejected the Messiah of Israel, is this not a sin against the God of Israel and a choice to remain in the covenant with Moses that has been broken by sin (paradigmatically by the worship of the Golden Calf and by the idolatrous and wicked kings prior to the Babylonian exile)? Has not God, through the prophets, promised a "new" covenant, and would it not be a sin to reject the Messiah who inaugurates this new covenant?

David does not raise this question, but he would not be afraid of it. Certainly, it would be a sin to reject the Messiah; just as it would be a sin for his followers to proclaim him the Messiah if he really were not. My view is that after (and even during) the intense conflict of the first century—in which both sides accused each other of sin and did what they could to oppose, vilify, and persecute the other side—the

---

52. Novak, "Supersessionism Hard and Soft," 28.
53. Novak, "Supersessionism Hard and Soft," 29.

gospel proclamation was obscured in the communication between Christianity and Judaism. The general experience of Jews was marked not by Christian witness to Christ's self-sacrificial love, but by Christian boasting, invective, and persecution. The scandal that this caused has only grown over the centuries due to the regularity and intensity of the persecutions. Christians believe that all sinners (not only a few Roman administrators and soldiers or a few Jewish leaders and disciples of Jesus) are responsible for Jesus's death. Indeed, the Catechism of the Council of Trent teaches that we Christians bear by far the weightiest culpability.[54] Christians do not have standing to accuse the Jewish people of sinning in denying that Jesus (especially as witnessed to by Christians in Jewish experience) is the Messiah.

Recognizing that Christians must affirm that Jesus brings a "fulfillment" of Israel's covenants, David proposes that Christian "soft supersessionism can mean accepting the historical fact that Jews have remained with the 'un-supplemented' ancient covenant while Christians have been called by God to a higher level by their affirmation of Jesus as the Christ."[55] This is not the way that I would describe "fulfillment," because, as noted above, I conceive the fulfillment that Christ brings as reconfiguring Israel's covenantal life around himself, rather than merely adding a supplement or establishing a "higher level" by addition to the earlier level. But I agree with David that Christians should affirm that Jews have sincerely sought to remain faithful to their covenantal obligations. Surely this is deeply praiseworthy, once we remove the accusation of sin.

David is understandably concerned about Christian evangelization that directly targets Jews. He does not deny Christians the right to hope that particular Jews will become Christian. But direct Christian evangelization toward Jews, as a matter of historical fact, has generally been undertaken with the aid of explicit or implicit threats—not simply eschatological threats about hell, but threats regarding property, wellbeing, and even life. Given this history, it seems right that Christians, without denying their universal evangelizing mission, should be sensitive enough to avoid any hints of the kind of "aggressive" evangelization that David has in view.[56] This is different from holding out an invitation in sincere friendship. Christians are expected to do this, just as David does toward Christians whose conversion to Judaism he welcomes.

Yet, David again raises the concern that soft supersessionism is difficult to reconcile with a real dialogue in which the partners each respect the other as equal in dignity. When Jews and Christians are soft supersessionists, they do not think of each other as religious equals. Christians assume that at the eschatological consummation, Jews will recognize Jesus Christ (see Romans 11:25–26). Jews assume that when the Messiah truly comes, Christians will realize the mistake they made about Jesus. David describes the second-century Rabbi Joshua ben Hananiah "who thought that unconverted Gentiles

---

54. See *Catechism of the Catholic Church*, 598.
55. Novak, "Supersessionism Hard and Soft," 29.
56. See Novak, "Supersessionism Hard and Soft," 29.

(who at present are living according to what Judaism teaches is universally binding divine law [i.e., the Noachide law]) will be made 'honorary' Jews in the world to come."[57] This leads David to press the question of whether soft supersessionists on both sides are actually capable of genuine dialogue with each other: "can there be an authentic relationship—one that is truly 'dialogical'—when the parties do not look upon each other as they see themselves, both now and in the eschatological future?"[58]

In my view, the answer is that there can be an authentic dialogue between such parties, even if *fullness* of communion will not be achievable since there will remain significant religious differences (until a Christian becomes a Jew, he or she likely will not feel *fully* or *in every way* welcomed by the Jewish community as such, and vice-versa). David agrees, but he adds that there are different modes of soft supersessionism, and dialogue proceeds best when it has identified the best such mode. Returning to the points he sketched in "From Supersessionism to Parallelism in Jewish-Christian Dialogue," he proposes that Judaism and Christianity should see themselves as similarly positioned vis-à-vis "the Old Testament/Hebrew Bible as interpreted by Second Temple Jewish theology."[59] The role played by the New Testament in Christianity is played by Oral Torah in Judaism. David points out that these similarities form a real basis for commonality. In dialoguing with each other, then, Jews and Christians should begin by appreciating this commonality.

Of course, there are significant differences as well. Far from brushing this under the rug, David urges that differences must not be denied or downplayed. He rightly insists that "we must respect the essentially different existential decisions we make as to *who* Jesus of Nazareth *is* and *what* he means for the covenant between God and his people, Israel."[60] He knows that these different existential decisions constitute a stark "*either/or*."[61] Both sides cannot be right; one side must be seriously wrong. Against forms of Messianic Judaism as well as liberal Christian proposals, David emphasizes that "either the Jewish people or the Christian Church is the fullest, most complete location for that ultimate relationship, the final purpose for humans created in the

---

57. Novak, "Supersessionism Hard and Soft," 29. Novak adds, "A soft Jewish supersessionism, unlike hard Jewish supersessionism, does not equate Christianity with the idolatrous past superseded by the Torah. Instead, it somewhat grudgingly accepts Christianity (and Islam) as monotheistic and not polytheistic, though demoting Christianity (and Islam) to the status, in effect, of a watered down version of Judaism for the Gentiles. The great twelfth-century theologian-jurist Maimonides agreed with Rabbi Joshua's inclusivism. . . . He argued that, if Christians could be weaned of some of their erroneous theological interpretations of the Hebrew Bible, they could be persuaded to return to their true origin in Judaism" (Novak, "Supersessionism Hard and Soft," 29–30). At the same time, Novak admits that, contrary to Maimonides's positions, "[m]ost traditional Jews, though, tend toward hard supersessionism" and do not seek gentile converts (Novak, "Supersessionism Hard and Soft," 30).

58. Novak, "Supersessionism Hard and Soft," 30.

59. Novak, "Supersessionism Hard and Soft," 30.

60. Novak, "Supersessionism Hard and Soft," 30.

61. Novak, "Supersessionism Hard and Soft," 31.

image and likeness (*tselem u-demut*) of God."⁶² In seeking to share in the ultimate covenantal relationship with God, one must choose either Judaism or Christianity; one cannot choose both. One of the two must be correct, if either are—since the only *covenantal* religions are Judaism and Christianity.

Yet, David's point is that in making this choice, soft supersessionists must be very attentive to the commonalities, so as to avoid falling into stark antitheses. Although the decision regarding Jesus has crucial import and is an either/or, nonetheless it is not the kind of either/or that must divide absolutely. On the contrary, much commonality still remains, and both sides therefore can allow the other theological space. Given the commonalities, moreover, the dialogue partners can bracket the "*either/or*" and truly appreciate the other *as the other is*, so long as this bracketing is not a cover for denying the significance of difference. The domain of commonality can be expanded, too, by realizing that "neither Jews nor Christians can anticipate what God will do at the end of the world's time. The end time can only be hoped for, bringing another universe altogether, a universe that cannot be imagined by us."⁶³ Even if Jews and Christians believe certain non-negotiable things about the world-to-come, there remains a vast and irreducible mystery about it.

In light of this mystery, David, as is his wont, expresses the hope that the inevitably somewhat competitive relation of Judaism and Christianity in the present world—competitive because both cannot be right—will in the eschatological consummation be revealed to be non-competitive, in a manner that we cannot now imagine. He asks, "What if God's final judgment, ushering in the world-yet-to-come, supersedes our human triumphalism that looks at the final judgment as an either/or proposition? What if God's final verdict is *beyond* our expectations, and thus displaces all of them, replacing them with what our eyes and minds cannot imagine?"⁶⁴ Surely this is a real possibility, even if Christians (for example) believe with the certitude of faith that all the blessed will see Jesus Christ glorified. Even if the all the blessed do see this, as I believe they will, Christians can agree that its mode of occurrence, and its full context, will exceed every expectation, every conception that we can imagine. Christians can admit that God may bring together Judaism and Christianity in a manner beyond our earthly imagining.

Conclusion

David's vision of a soft supersessionism that, without veering into syncretism or downgrading the importance of God's covenants, looks upon the other with the greatest possible appreciation—an appreciation rooted in real commonalities—represents an extraordinarily hopeful and faithful form of Jewish-Christian dialogue. Given the

---

62. Novak, "Supersessionism Hard and Soft," 31.
63. Novak, "Supersessionism Hard and Soft," 31.
64. Novak, "Supersessionism Hard and Soft," 31.

presence of hard supersessionists within his own community, David Novak did not have to follow this path. He could have simply focused on intra-Jewish discussions, especially given the horrible history of the persecution of Jews by baptized Christians, including by the paganized Nazis whose deadly work had been deeply prepared for, tragically, by a steady and virulent stream of Christian anti-Jewish rhetoric and oppressive laws over the centuries.

Given his political, natural-law, and ethical interests, however, it makes some sense that David Novak would dialogue with Christians, especially since eminent Christians were among his teachers. But even so, the extent to which David has advanced Jewish-Christian dialogue is truly amazing. His charitable spirit, which recognizes difference but seeks to engage others' positions with generosity and with real appreciation of shared elements, shines forth in his scholarly work and in personal conversation. His mature vision of Jewish-Christian dialogue allows for soft supersessionism on both sides (and thus rejects syncretism) while highlighting the need for appreciating our extensive areas of theological commonality. It is a vision in which Jews and Christians can be true friends—not yet brothers and sisters in the very fullest sense, but real friends bound tightly by what we share and also by mutual care and support for each other as covenantal people.

That such a great Jewish scholar, in the decades after the Holocaust, would go out of his way to be such a friend of Christians is frankly almost a miracle. For Christians, David Novak has been a wonderful interlocutor as we have sought to develop a new relationship with the Jewish people, away from our hard supersessionist and aggressively oppressive history vis-à-vis God's Jewish people. David has helped us to see how this can be done without abandoning or betraying our Christian faith in Jesus as the Messiah.

The extraordinary extent of Christian indebtedness to David Novak is already apparent. I predict it will be even more apparent in future decades, as Christian communities address the spread of anti-Jewish attitudes under the cover of (even legitimate) opposition to the state of Israel's policies. To show how David's work will be of help in these areas, I would need to attend here to *Dabru Emet*, which he drafted and spearheaded (on which see Rita George-Tvrtković's essay below), as well as more fully to *Zionism and Judaism*. This would take me beyond the limits of the present essay.

Let me conclude on a personal note. As a young professor, I read *Natural Law in Judaism* and realized that I had found in David Novak a distinctive model of how to do theology. He brings together profound attention to biblical and rabbinic texts, with deep understanding of the medieval Jewish masters, modern philosophical developments, and more recent Jewish thought. He freely engages important strands of Christian theology and philosophy. He writes from a perspective of unapologetic, non-syncretistic Jewish faith, but without limiting his sources or his audience solely to the Jewish people. He demonstrates the ability to care for and be a friend to people from other traditions and perspectives.

After reading *Natural Law in Judaism*, I thought to myself, this is how I wish to be a Catholic theologian. I count it as one of the great graces of my life that I have come to know this extraordinary Jewish theologian and to count him as a friend and, even more, a mentor. Not only does he have the gifts of a great scholar, but also he has a joyful spirit. He is a man of real prayer, real love of God, and real compassion. May David Novak be blessed, now and in the world-to-come.

Bibliography

Catechism of the Catholic Church. 2nd ed. Vatican City: Libreria Editrice Vaticana, 1997.

Novak, David. *Athens and Jerusalem: God, Humans, and Nature*. Toronto: University of Toronto Press, 2019.

———. *Covenantal Rights: A Study in Jewish Political Theory*. Princeton, NJ: Princeton University Press, 2000.

———. *The Election of Israel: The Idea of the Chosen People*. Cambridge: Cambridge University Press, 1995.

———. *Halakhah in a Theological Dimension*. Chico, CA: Scholars Press, 1985.

———. *In Defense of Religious Liberty*. Wilmington, DE: ISI Books, 2009.

———. *The Image of the Non-Jew in Judaism: An Historical and Constructive Study of the Noahide Laws*. Toronto: Edwin Mellon, 1983.

———. *Jewish-Christian Dialogue: A Jewish Justification*. Oxford: Oxford University Press, 1989.

———. *Jewish Justice: The Contested Limits of Nature, Law, and Covenant*. Waco, TX: Baylor University Press, 2017.

———. *The Jewish Social Contract: An Essay in Political Theology*. Princeton, NJ: Princeton University Press, 2005.

———. *Jewish Social Ethics*. Oxford: Oxford University Press, 1992.

———. *Law and Theology in Judaism*. First Series. New York: KTAV, 1974.

———. *Law and Theology in Judaism*. Second Series. New York: KTAV, 1976.

———. *Natural Law in Judaism*. Cambridge: Cambridge University Press, 1998.

———. *Suicide and Morality*. New York: Scholars Studies Press, 1975.

———. "Supersessionism Hard and Soft." *First Things* 290, February 2019, 27–31.

———. *Talking with Christians: Musings of a Jewish Theologian*. Grand Rapids: Eerdmans, 2005.

———. *Zionism and Judaism: A New Theory*. Cambridge: Cambridge University Press, 2015.

Sacks, Jonathan. "Jewish-Christian Dialogue: The Ethical Dimension." In *Tradition in an Untraditional Age: Essays on Modern Jewish Thought*, edited by Jonathan Sacks, 161–81. London: Valentine, Mitchell, 1990.

Sonderegger, Katherine. *That Jesus Christ Was Born a Jew: Karl Barth's "Doctrine of Israel."* University Park, PA: Pennsylvania State University Press, 1992.

A Conversation between David Novak and Robert P. George

(March 28, 2019, Mundelein Seminary, Mundelein IL)

RG: It's a special privilege and an honor to be conducting this conversation with my very, very dear friend, really one of my oldest and dearest friends in academic life, Rabbi Novak. We were just going over our history together and David reminded me that we first met in my very first year as an academic when I arrived in Princeton in 1985–86. And we've been very close friends and part of a network of close friends ever since. I've learned an enormous amount, not only from David's books and articles, but just in personal private conversations over many years. He's a mentor as well as a friend. And I also should take this opportunity to thank him for what I assume must have been a rather nice a letter to the tenure committee at Princeton when I was coming up for tenure. I'm not supposed to know about that letter.

DN: Well, the tenure letter was very interesting. I first met Robby when he was a freshly minted D.Phil. from Oxford, and I got a call from my late revered teacher, Germain Grisez, saying John Finnis has got an awfully bright student who is coming to Princeton; you should really get to know him. And I said, well, I will be in Princeton in a few weeks. And we just hit it off in every way and we've been close friends ever since. But when Robby was up for tenure at Princeton (which he didn't think he was going to get), the two outside people who were asked to write for him were Mary Ann Glendon of Harvard law school and me. *My* job in writing was to answer the question: why is a professor of Jewish studies at the University of Virginia (where I was teaching at the time) writing on behalf of a Catholic political theorist at Princeton. The point was basically to defuse the accusation of Robby's enemies at Princeton, i.e., his being a narrow-minded, bigoted Catholic who doesn't talk to anybody outside his little circle, etc.

Robby's rise at Princeton, overcoming the considerable odds against him, reminds me of a famous rabbinic debate. One of the Rabbis in the Talmud, at a time of great persecution, said that basically there is no reward for the righteous in this world. There is no reward for them at all in this world. Whatever reward they're going to get will be gotten somewhere else. One of the medieval glossators—apparently he was living under better circumstances—says, well, that's usually the case, but it's not always so! Robby's great success at Princeton is a prime example of "it's not always so." Here is a man who has been swimming with the barracudas and has not only survived, he has flourished in those often treacherous waters, which is certainly refreshing. What he has done, in terms of his personal career and in terms of what he has established at Princeton, is a model and an inspiration for all of us.

RG: Well David, thank you. But we're here to honor you, not me, and whatever I've been able to accomplish has been largely on the basis of dear, wonderful friends like you and Mary Ann. We only have an hour and David's an authority on just about everything, and he's written about everything. So, I had to narrow it down to a few topics and I'm hoping to cover five that are of particular interest to me. Not that David isn't equally important as a scholar of many, many more, but I want to cover five. And if David will indulge me, I know this is really a conference where we're going to be talking about a Catholic appreciation of David. But let's go back to the roots and let's begin by talking about Judaism and the condition of Judaism today. As I see it, and it's for you to say, but as I see it, there are a couple of very, very big challenges to Jewish faith. One is secularism. The other is antisemitism. And still another might be termed fundamentalism. Here in the United States, at least as I understand it, it continues to be the case that the majority of people who identify as Jewish are not very observant—more toward the secular end of the spectrum—but the growth is all on the other side, on the observant side, and especially on the Orthodox side. You yourself have come from one denomination within Judaism and helped to found another denomination in response to some of these currents and challenges. So looking at the situation today, what do you think the condition of Judaism here in America is and the condition of Judaism worldwide is? Obviously, the issue that I haven't mentioned that's also deeply relevant is the issue of Israel.

DN: Yes. What you say is quite true, when you look at the United States (Canada is a little bit different). When you look at the United States, those Jews who identify as Orthodox or traditional are between, at least according to the polls, 15 to 18 percent of the Jewish population. But when you talk about those people who identify as Jews religiously, who are under age fifty, it doubles; it becomes 35, close to 40 percent. To give you an example, my sister who lives here in Chicago is a member of the largest Reform congregation, where I grew up. (I moved in another direction rather early in life.) This congregation has approximately 2,000 families. For their main service on a Friday night, unless they have something special, the attendance is about eighty to ninety people. On Saturday morning, which is supposed to be the main service, they don't even go into the main sanctuary. On the other hand, my daughter and son-in-law belong to a synagogue of 400 families, an Orthodox synagogue in suburban Skokie, where between the three services for adults (which are not liturgically different by the way), and the two services for young people, on an ordinary Saturday morning there can be close to 1,000 people in the Synagogue. It tells you something. Now, when I was growing up in Chicago, Orthodox Judaism was considered something that was only for old people and foreigners. People thought all that it needed was a decent burial. If I had told somebody when I was growing up that there was going to be an Orthodox synagogue like my daughter's in a suburb like Skokie, they would have said, "Yes, and I'm Napoleon!" They would have said that I am hallucinating.

When you look at the non-Orthodox and non-traditional Jews in terms of their political orientation, it has remained (and I'm not saying they necessarily have to be Republicans) with the Democratic Party—even with the radicals there who've taken a decidedly anti-Israel stand. And I think that one of the disaffections of many liberal American Jews with Israel is that Israel has become much more religious in the sense that the Orthodox population has grown, primarily because Orthodox Jews are having more kids. Also, there are people, especially Jews who came from North Africa and places like that, who themselves might not be consistently observant, but who, nevertheless, are not part of some kind of counter-cultural group.

Now, when virtually all of the anti-Semitism is coming from the political Left, there is a great deal of cognitive dissonance (that's the only way I can describe it) among many American Jews. That is very much the problem. And to give you an idea of this, when Senator Joseph Lieberman (with whom I have a lot of political differences, but he's a practicing Orthodox Jew) said in the 2000 election (when he was the Democrats' candidate for Vice-President) that he would not campaign on the Sabbath, I know a number of Evangelical Protestants who would have never voted for a Democrat candidate, who were so impressed by his Jewish piety that they voted for him anyway. The only opposition came from the head of the B'nai B'rith anti-defamation league who said that Lieberman is injecting religion into American politics. Yet Lieberman didn't say, "Vote for me because I'm keeping the Sabbath." He said, "I'm not going to campaign on the Sabbath." That's it. So, this is where we stand, and as I say, there's a lot of cognitive dissonance there.

But I can tell you that, especially in terms of the youth phenomenon in the Orthodox Jewish community, I think they've gotten to a point where they don't even take liberal, secular Jews seriously anymore. They don't regard them seriously, which is too bad. Orthodox and traditional Jews have mostly given up on them. This very much becomes the factor. There is a story you told me when you first came to Princeton; it was something about public prayer and a Jewish student said, "Jews don't pray in public." Well, where do they pray? I suspect she wasn't praying in private either. So that's where we're at. Or the wonderful story, Robby, of when the Orthodox Jewish students at Princeton asked you to be their advisor, and you said, if I have the story right, "Well, why don't you go to Jewish faculty?" and they said, "we basically don't trust them."

RG: David is telling a story that happened early on in my time at Princeton; it must've been just as I was going back over to Oxford for my first leave, so it would have been 1988–89. I got a telephone message from an Orthodox Jewish student of mine, I believe his name was Daniel Feigelson, if I remember correctly. He asked to come and see me. I got back in touch and said I'd be happy to see him. He came to my office and he said, "I'm here on behalf of Yavneh, our Orthodox Jewish student association, and we would like you to be our faculty advisor." And at first, I wondered whether he had confused something about my marriage. My wife is Jewish, and I wondered if he thought that I was the Jewish spouse and I was married to a Catholic lady. But no, that wasn't it. I said, "Well, I'm very honored that you would ask me, but wouldn't it be better if you had a Jewish member of the faculty?" And he said, "Well, there really isn't anybody on the faculty—any Jewish member of the faculty—who is really sympathetic to what we're all about and you are so we'd like you to do it." I was very flattered by this. I went home and I told my wife about it and she said, "Well, what are you going to do?" And I said, "Well, gee, they were kind enough to give me the honor of inviting me; shouldn't I accept?" And she said, "Of course not! Your Jewish colleagues will never forgive you if you accept that position. They'll be insulted that the orthodox Jewish students thought they weren't good enough and that you were." So I ended up being an informal advisor to Yavneh.

So, David, just consider Judaism as a living faith. Now I know being Jewish is a complex bunch of things, but just now consider the specifically religious component. Given the demographics, are you optimistic about the future of Judaism now?

DN: I don't know whether optimism is the word, but I believe in the promises of God and God said he's not going to let the Jews disappear.

RG: Well, that's hope. That's the theological virtue of hope.

DN: That's the theological version of hope. But I'm certainly much more optimistic than when I was a student. When I was a student, to be an observant Jew on the campus of the University of Chicago, where there were a lot of Jewish students, was to be considered something like a being from outer space, like a Martian. In fact, there was a joke about the University of Chicago when I was a student there, which was still in the kind of Neo-Thomist revival led by Robert Maynard Hutchins. The joke was that the University of Chicago, which is actually officially a Protestant university (founded by the Baptist John D. Rockefeller in 1892), is the Protestant university where atheist professors teach Catholic theology to Jewish students.

So, in that way, it was a very, very, very lonely type of thing. Now, the situation is quite different. Now what you see in places like Princeton is that the better the university, the more likely you are to find Orthodox Jewish students there. That means that despite the losses due to assimilation of various kinds, we're keeping more of the best and the brightest. And I suspect that with more traditional forms of Catholicism or more traditional forms of Evangelical Protestantism, it's the same story. So, in terms of quantity, we can worry; in terms of quality, there's a good chance to be guardedly optimistic.

RG: Well, even on the quantity issue, it sounds as though the direction things are going is one in which a higher percentage of Jews in Israel will be observant and devout and a higher percentage of Jews in America will be observant and devout.

DN: Yes, in Israel you have the phenomenon of Sephardic Jews, i.e., Jews from North Africa or similar Islamic countries, who on Saturday morning will be in the synagogue and on Saturday afternoon they will go to the soccer game. But this person is not identifying with something anti-traditional. He knows that he's not living up to the full Jewish life, if you asked him. But he's not endorsing something countercultural. One of the things about the Sephardic Jews, who are now the majority of Jews in Israel, is how they differ from Ashkenazic Jews, i.e., Jews who came (or their parents or grandparents came) from Europe. In western and central Europe, there was the phenomenon of Reform Judaism, which most Orthodox or traditional Jews viewed as being antinomian. In eastern Europe, there was Communism. In the countries the Sephardic Jews hailed from, some Jews were fully observant; some Jews were less observant. The general attitude, though, was live and let live. That is because there was no counter-cultural movement challenging the validity of traditional belief and practice and advocating freedom from what the ancient Rabbis called "the yoke of the commandments." There was nothing there claiming to be Judaism or "Jewishness" that was clearly non-traditional. So, they have an entirely different perspective there. And of course, in the founding of Israel, it was clearly decided by David Ben Gurion (himself a quite secular Ashkenazic Jew, though not an atheist interestingly enough) that religious Jews would indeed be totally marginalized. However, what happened was when Menachem Begin became the Prime Minister—supported by the Sephardic Jews who felt that they'd been discriminated against by European Jews—it became an entirely different thing.

Now, one of the things in Israel that's interesting is that you also have people on the extreme right who also have a problem with the state. There's a wonderful story that Menachem Begin, who was the first observant Jew to be a prime minister of Israel, visited a group at B'nei Brak, a place near Tel Aviv which is a center of the most right-wing Orthodoxy. He was to visit a group of rabbis there, and there was the question: Should they stand up when he came in the room or not? And there was a heated debate. There was no debate, however, the week before when they were visited by the King of Sweden. The rabbis had no question about the King; of course he is a legitimate monarch. There's no question; of course, you stand for him. So, you have that phenomenon. Some of us and, and there are parallels, certainly in the Catholic community, who want to be faithful to tradition, but who also want to live in the real world, have problems with those on the left who want to be not only in the world, but of it, and with those on the right who don't want to be of or in the world.

I mean, you see it at Princeton, where Orthodox Jewish students are much more self-confident in terms of interacting with Christians and others. It's an amazing phenomenon. There's a young man who was one of the best interns we ever had at *First Things*, Nathaniel Peters, who runs the Morningside Institute at Columbia University. He wanted to bring some of his students to meet with the Orthodox Jewish students at Columbia. Now this was on a rainy morning in November, midterm exams going on, and I brought him to a morning service. He brought ten of his students and he found fifty kids—fifty kids! (about fifteen women and more men, you know, men and women in Orthodox services sit separately). And he was absolutely floored by this phenomenon. And then we had a marvelous group of his students interacting with the Jewish students at breakfast following the service. I led a discussion on what it means to be a religious person in a secular—often militantly secularist—environment like that at Columbia. These are very hopeful signs. This wasn't the case when I was a student, and it probably wasn't the case when you, Robby (a younger man), were a student either.

RG: Certainly when I was a student, now we're going back into the mid 1970s, one would have predicted increasing secularization in the Jewish community, rather than the reverse. And of course, it's the reverse that has happened.

DN: Yes, although there's still a decidedly older, secularist group.

RG: So that's a group of people who identify being Jewish with being politically liberal and progressive and so forth.

DN: Yes. I mean, it's Bernie Sanders. That's very much a fact. Now some people in the Orthodox community still have this kind of siege mentality. And you know, I can tell them, the people that were putting you down a generation or so ago, they're not a threat any longer. So loosen up a little, maybe not the older ones, but certainly the younger ones. Like look at your star student Daniel Mark. We were at his wedding in Lakewood, which is a citadel of Orthodoxy. I mean, look at how he has operated.

RG: People like Daniel and you yourself and others have opted to be observant. I don't know if you accept the label that Daniel would, "Orthodox Jews" but not "Benedict Option" people. Right. So you're not Lakewood.

DN: No.

RG: You're not setting yourself off so that you will be insulated from the culture. People like you, people like Daniel, engage the culture.

DN: Yes. Yes, and engage the culture critically. I remember I had a Bible teacher when I was a teenager and he explained a passage that says that the windows of the Temple were like a cone, with a small opening on the inside and a wide opening on the outside. Now the usual interpretation is the world needs the light of the Sanctuary; the Sanctuary doesn't need the light of the world. But this teacher of mine said the following just as I was ready to enter the University of Chicago: "You're going to see that outside world. Don't close it off, but filter it. Accept what you can accept as a Jew; don't accept what you can't accept." That means critically engaging the outside world, neither rejecting it nor swallowing it whole, but filtering it.

RG: I think there's a parallel there with the true spirit of Vatican II for Catholics. I think the true spirit was one of critically engaging the culture, being willing to learn from it, but also criticize what was wrong. The label "spirit of Vatican II" came to represent something quite different, something more like a capitulation to modern progressive secularism.

DN: Speaking of Vatican II, and I say this as a friend, I think there were two problems with Vatican II, which maybe couldn't have been foreseen. One, I think that it was a mistake giving up the Latin Mass. You could have done like Jewish congregations did; you could have a prayer book with the translation on the side. Because I can go to any synagogue in the world and participate in the service.

RG: Because it's in Hebrew.

DN: Yes, because it's in Hebrew. On the other hand, I remember as a young rabbi in the midst of the 1960s—as a very young rabbi officiating at a burial—there was this little Irish lady who came up to me and she said to me (this was right after Vatican II), "Oh, rabbi, it was so wonderful hearing the old language again." It was unintelligible so it must be holy.

But the other thing about Vatican II is (and I think this is why a number of Catholics got a wrong message) there were too many changes introduced too quickly. And when you change laws and rules too quickly, people get the impression that it's all up for grabs.

RG: Now, that certainly happens. A lot of Catholics came to believe everything was up for grabs.

DN: But I have another connection to Vatican II. And that was that in the mid-1960s, my theological mentor (at the Jewish Theological Seminary of America) Abraham Joshua Heschel, who was the main Jewish spokesperson at the Council, had a secret meeting with Pope Paul VI. When the Pope died in his sleep, on his night table was Professor Heschel's great work in English, *God in Search of Man*. Yet my teacher was severely criticized in the Jewish community. Many said: "Why should you be interfering in their affairs? Do you want them interfering in ours?" Nevertheless, he clearly recognized that this was a major turning point for both Jews and Catholics, especially with the publication of *Nostra Aetate*, the statement on the Jews and Judaism. And it's interesting how this whole matter was dealt with. Before that time, those who dealt with the Vatican or the Catholic Church were basically political people, public relations types. In selecting Rabbi Heschel, the Jewish leadership were so smart in sending in a heavyweight theologian. His first meeting with Cardinal Bea, who was a biblical scholar, was a discussion of comparative Jewish and Christian interpretations of Song of Songs. That is the high theological level that it began at. And some of the Dulles Symposia that Richard John Neuhaus, of blessed memory, used to conduct were theological dialogues between Jews, Catholics, and some Protestants as well, and were likewise at the highest level. Thus, it trickled down to more popular levels; it trickled down because Professor Heschel (whom Richard Neuhaus was very close to) began at the truly theological level. It was much more than a question of public relations and goodwill and all that had been theretofore.

RG: So, David, do I then understand correctly that what Rabbi Heschel represented was a view opposite to that of the view of Rabbi Joseph Soloveitchik, who believed that there should be good relations between Christians and Jews and cooperation, but not theological engagement? He drew the line at theological engagement. Do I get that right?

DN: Well, he drew the line at theological engagement. Actually, it was very interesting because, in his great essay *Halakhic Man*, the first reference is to Karl Barth. Yes, and I think what Rabbi Soloveitchik was saying, and I think what we are dealing with here as well, is yes, we should deal with moral and political issues. But without the theological component, secularism wins the day. Secularists have said something like this: "Let's do an end run around all this stuff, and let's just talk about goodwill and whatever. And why do you have to bring in this? What do you need all these theological premises for?" So that was the point of Rabbi Soloveitchik. Actually, in my 1989 work, *Jewish Christian Dialogue*, I have a critique of Rabbi Soloveitchik on that point. And, of course, his great *The Lonely Man of Faith* began as an address to a Catholic Hospital Association, where he was certainly discussing faith. Until recently, this [reluctance regarding theological engagement] was the case. But now there are a number of people in the Orthodox community, especially Rabbi Jonathan Sacks, who clearly don't take that line. He's been a tremendous force for good.

RG: I can certainly understand Rabbi Soloveitchik's concern in context. My sense is that he did not want a replay of the great medieval disputations. My guess is that he feared that's what theological engagement would become. Now in practice as it had been conducted by you and by Jonathan Sacks and by others at the highest levels, it's been anything but that. No one has tried to win a grand victory. They've tried to learn from each other.

DN: The difference between the medieval disputations and what we have now, which they didn't have then, is a pretty much even political playing field. You're not going to have much of a dialogue where one group, which has the power, asks the other group to justify itself. But now we have a very, very different situation. And one of the things that Jews and Christians understand, is that at the levels of high culture—the universities, the media, the courts—we're both minorities. We're both marginalized minorities. I remember when I was teaching at the University of Virginia, I used to have Evangelical Christian students come to me (and don't forget the University of Virginia was the first officially secular university, founded by Thomas Jefferson) and pour their hearts out about how they were being ridiculed, how their professors were ridiculing them. And after they would come up for air, I would say, "Well, you sound like Jews." And they said, "We feel like Jews." And I said, "Now we can start talking." But the relationship has to be more than just having a common enemy.

RG: This gets me to where I wanted to go next, which is the sense that what we have here are sister religions. The thesis of yours that I find so fascinating came out very well in the recent piece on supersessionism you had in *First Things* and in the dialogue and the letters to the editor of the issue that came after that one. What I'm talking about here is the idea that the dramatic events of the first century resulted in two religions with common roots in biblical revelation and in and what Christians call the Old Testament, the Hebrew Scriptures, but obviously in different directions and with different doctrines and commitments. But nevertheless, a common root. Have I understood you correctly?

DN: There is a common root. It's not that Christianity came out of Judaism. Both Christianity and Judaism came out of the Hebrew Bible and some developments of Second Temple, which we wouldn't even call Judaism at that point. So that becomes very much a factor. But I mean it's a fact that we worship the same God and share the same book, the Hebrew Bible, and there's no statement in the New Testament that doesn't have a reference to the Old Testament, and the same thing with the Talmud and rabbinic literature. But there's one thing that I've been working on and will be discussed in *Athens and Jerusalem: God, Humans, and Nature,* the book that my 2017 Gifford Lectures were based on, coming out later this year [see Novak, *Athens and Jerusalem: God, Humans, and Nature* (Toronto: University of Toronto Press, 2019)]. It's that in the second century, when the communities were splitting, there was a missed opportunity—and I can understand the missed opportunity—in that both Judaism and Christianity were under attack by pagan philosophy. In Origen's *Contra Celsum,* he had to defend *both* Christianity and Judaism from the charge of Roman pagans that they were inferior, intellectually and morally, to pagan philosophies. Origen, and Tertullian for example, who are otherwise very critical of Judaism because the two communities are still in the process of separation from each other, nevertheless were defending the Hebrew Bible and even Judaism against pagan onslaughts. Today, we see a similar attack on both Judaism and Christianity from secularist ideology, challenging the intellectual and moral legitimacy of both Judaism and Christianity. However, not being in the throes of a divorce as we were in the second and third centuries, we no longer need to primarily emphasize our differences (which are now more clearly the fact). We can now face our common enemy working together. We can recognize that this is an attack on both of us, forcing us to not just be opposed to it, but to rethink, our positions by taking the secularist challenge seriously, and coming out the better for it.

And I think that clearly natural law becomes one factor there, which probably couldn't happen in the second century, but can happen at this point as well. It was a different scene there. And I often wonder what would have happened. I can understand why it didn't happen, but it could happen now because we're not threatened by each other any longer.

RG: So, is this a unique opportunity for Jewish Christian engagement, one whose conditions have never been in place before? At least not for 2,000 years?

DN: Yes, this type of opportunity is basically like Psalm 137:4, which says, "How do we sing the Lord's song on strange ground?" We're living on strange ground. Therefore, it's not just defending ourselves against those who would marginalize us both, but understanding that because of that challenge, we must think more deeply and not just repeat old answers that need to be rethought and recontextualized.

RG: I think it was Irving Kristol, correct me if I'm wrong, it might've been Milton Himmelfarb, but it was one of them that said there's something special about America: The issue between Christians and Jews in Europe was that so many Christians hated Jews and wanted to kill them. The problem in the United States is different. So many Christians love Jews and want to marry them.

DN: Yes, that becomes, I suppose, a problem.

RG: Assimilation, intermarriage. I mean, I'm one of the perpetrators here, of course.

DN: Yes (laughter). Let's put it this way: if you don't ask for my blessing, you don't get my curse. (laughter)

RG: Is that a threat though? Does assimilation, even with the new demographics, remain a threat?

DN: Of course it does, because with most people who are intermarried, usually their children frequently follow one or the other or become "nones." A lot of the "nones" are really the products of mixed marriage couples. It is either "your religion or my religion or both religions, since we're kind of Jewish and kind of Christian or whatever. So, let's avoid the problem altogether, and leave all that. Let's have no religion." But, if parents simply make the only thing that they convey to their children is "don't marry out," but they're making no other religious claims upon them, it becomes rather hollow. But tell your children from the start, "This is the way we live, this is the way we brought you up. We're not asking you to do anything we don't ask of ourselves, and part of it is that we want you to have a marriage where you can have a Jewish home and Jewish children."

RG: Even apart from a marriage, there's tremendous pressure to assimilate to whatever culture you happen to be in. And I think Christians are now learning—serious Christians, believing Christians—are now learning this lesson because it is so difficult for Christian parents to bring up their children as Christians in this culture. I mean, the tendency is just to move with the popular culture. All the institutions bear down on kids in that way. The media, entertainment, the arts, everything is pushing kids toward assimilation. And it makes the job of devout parents of any faith, whether they're Jewish, Christian, Muslim, whether they're Catholic, Protestant, Eastern Orthodox, it makes it hard to be a parent.

DN: It does make it hard to be a parent. And that's why so much that was taken for granted in the past now cannot be taken for granted, which is challenging and dangerous. On the other hand, it means that you really have to think about what your religious commitment is and what it means and what it requires of you as opposed to just saying, "Well, this is the way we've always lived."

RG: I think that's right. And I think here, a big part of the challenge is just mass culture. We no longer live in communities like this Jewish community, this largely Catholic community, this Evangelical community in West Virginia where I grew up, or anything like that. It's a national culture. It's a mass culture. Everybody's hearing the same things. I think of the challenges in say the New York Jewish community in the early part of the twentieth century. There were divisions about things like whether you read *The Forward* or *Der Tog*. If you were socialist, you read *The Forward*. If you were an anti-socialist, you read *Der Tog*. But you're not listening to CNN. You're getting something different from what the Evangelicals in West Virginia are getting, and what the Catholics in Milwaukee are getting, and so forth.

DN: That very much becomes the problem. Let me give you an interesting analogy. In Toronto, I still feel like a rabbi when teaching my Tuesday night Talmud class for the past twenty-two years, where we've been learning the tractate *Sanhedrin*, it seems forever. It's fascinating because this tractate was written two centuries after the Sanhedrin actually functioned. Maimonides discusses the demise of the Sanhedrin. You get the impression, well, when there was a Sanhedrin there was a centralized authority and everything else like that, and now we're all split up. But the interesting thing is that the Sanhedrin had seventy members. When the Sanhedrin voted, basically as something came up to the Sanhedrin, one person had to argue pro, another person had to argue con. And the rest of the sixty-eight members could vote any way for no reason whatsoever. And then when they issued their final ruling, they issued the ruling unanimously in the name of everybody with no reason attached. But Maimonides says, now all we have are individual authorities who have to argue for their position. Even though they have authority, they still have to justify what they're doing. So the political decentralization may have been politically questionable, but it's certainly raised the intellectual level. Now people have to argue and persuade people, even though in any community the people are supposed to follow the practical ruling of the local rabbi. But when the local rabbi's not justifying what he's doing, people are going to start not following him.

RG: So his charismatic authority depends on him giving reasons.

DN: Yes, the effectiveness of his authority depends on him giving reasons. So the political dissolution led to a much higher intellectual level. Bernard Lonergan, who was a great Jesuit philosopher and theologian (who did most of his work at Regis College of the University of Toronto) has a wonderful line I like to quote. He talks about ideas that are passed from book to book to book without any evidence of having gone through a mind. And that is the point—I mean, you just cannot repeat the old answers. You've got to rethink them and reformulate them. And that takes effort. So, on the one hand, yes, but, but on the other hand, it's dangerous. Yet more people who are remaining within the community have good reasons for remaining there and are continually looking for the intelligibility of it as opposed to "I'm doing it because my mother and grandmother did that."

RG: David, turning to your own intellectual biography, we have you engaging with Catholicism very early on. Before you become a professional academic, you deliberately pick a Catholic university to do your doctorate on natural law. And to study with a Catholic thinker on the subject, if I recall correctly.

DN: A first-rate Catholic thinker.

RG: If I recall correctly, you went to Georgetown originally to study with Heinrich Rommen.

DN: Right, I went to Georgetown. Actually, it's quite interesting. When I finished my rabbinical training at the Jewish theological seminary in 1966, my theological mentor, Abraham Joshua Heschel, gave me very good advice. He said, "first of all, don't take off a year. Go right into a graduate program because I've known people to take a year and then it becomes two years. You get out of the habit of being a student." And he told me to get a degree in regular philosophy even if you don't write on a Jewish theme. He said the problem with so many of these Jewish thinkers is they have no philosophical method, no philosophical ability.

I was admitted to a program at Harvard, but I couldn't find a rabbinical position within commuting distance. So I just went to Washington and got a rabbinical position there. I went to Georgetown, which some of my Jewish friends said, "my God, what are you going to do there?"

RG: It was a Catholic university.

DN: It was a Catholic university. It was Catholic in those days. And Heinrich Albert Rommen was this man who wrote the famous work, *The Eternal Return of Natural Law*. The thing that impressed me about him was that he was working on natural law, but even more so, he was expelled by Hitler in 1937. This is figuratively speaking, putting his money where his mouth was.

I came to see Rommen and he said he's heard that the Jewish tradition has so many riches in it, and he would love to have me as a student. So I came to Georgetown, but I didn't realize he was dying of cancer and he died within a few months of my coming there. Well, Germain Grisez was just kind of coming into his own, and I discovered we had something in common, that he had gotten his PhD with Richard McKeon at the University of Chicago, and McKeon was my teacher of Aristotle. So we hit it off. The interesting thing with my relationship with Germain Grisez was that Grisez made considerable emotional demands on the students to be his disciples. And of course, Joseph Boyle, my late University of Toronto colleague (and fellow Georgetown graduate student), was his most devoted disciple. But because I wasn't a Catholic, Grisez couldn't quite make the same demand on me. And by a kind of analogy, he liked my Jewish traditionalism, and he was convinced that I was fighting against the same type of people in my community that he was fighting within his. I think I got the best from him because we had this kind of relationship. He was a marvelous mentor. I would submit a chapter of my dissertation and he would critique a point. My first reaction was, "Well, this guy is going to pass me. So, okay, do as he says." But he would say, "Don't say, 'Okay!' You make a better argument if that's what you think." I mean, that's a good mentor.

RG: So you went to study natural law. Whence the interest in natural law?

DN: Well, the interest in natural law came because when I was an undergraduate at the University of Chicago, there was the late great Leo Strauss, and I began seeking him out. He only taught graduate courses, but he let me sit in some of his graduate courses. And in fact, his daughter (who was my colleague at the University of Virginia) and I did a book together, called *Leo Strauss and Judaism*, about him. I also evinced an interest in natural law when I first read John Courtney Murray's *We Hold These Truths*. And I thought to myself, why can't we Jews write a book like that? And I said to Leo Strauss, "My interest is in natural law," and he said, "I am not a natural law theorist." He said, "If you're interested in natural law, go study with Yves Simon." Yves Simon was a great man who died in the middle of the seminar. He was dying of cancer. I remember him even being propped up on pillows in the seminar. He was a great man, Jacques Maritain's leading disciple. Unlike Maritain, though, who gives the impression of being a poet who wrote in tremendous spurts of inspiration, Yves Simon was a much more careful kind of constructive thinker. His work of political philosophy, *A General Theory of Authority*, is just magnificent. So that was the origin of my interest in natural law. It seemed to me that if Jews could make any statements about public issues, it couldn't be because of the authority of the Jewish tradition. It had to be because the Jewish tradition recognized something that was a necessary but not sufficient condition. It is necessary for us to have this universalism, but clearly not as a substitute for the particularities of the tradition (its "singularity"), which at some level are higher than that.

RG: Now, David, for Catholics, you're officially not allowed to be a fideist. For Protestants, you get to decide what you are, whether you are, whether you aren't. I believe the same is true for Jews, right? So if you talk to some Jewish philosophers of law, they're clearly fideists, you talk to others, and most notably you, they're clearly not. Would you make the claim that the Jewish tradition resolves that question against fideism and that people who do adopt a fideistic view within the tradition are not being faithful to the tradition? Or is it really just that the tradition is agnostic on the point and you've got to choose one or the other?

DN: I don't think it's agnostic. There are different streams within the tradition. I think that the way you argue for a natural law perspective in Judaism is for internal and external reasons. Internally, one can show that a natural law perspective has better explanatory power to explain the inherent rationality of the Torah than legal positivism or fideism, which is virtually the same thing. Externally, a natural law perspective enables Jews to bring insights from the tradition into public discourse, in a way that of course implies that you want to be part of the society. But it seems to me when the fideists get involved, it becomes all special pleading, you know, we're a special group or whatever. So those people argue for religious liberty as an exemption. Well, that becomes difficult. We had a case in Toronto recently where a young Ultra-Orthodox Jewish man was declared brain dead, which would normally allow him to be ruled legally dead (and thus have his body removed from the hospital as a corpse). However, his community has a very, very negative—and I think overly negative—view of brain death, because the traditional sources don't recognize it. So, his parents and their rabbis insisted on a religious exemption from this general public policy. But how can you have a patient in, let us say, room 301 who is to be considered dead, and a patient in room 302 who is to be considered alive, when both patients are in the same physical state? You just can't operate that way in a hospital treating patients of different religions or no religion. So I think that a natural law perspective enables Jews to advocate in good faith for a consistent policy of dealing with medical issues that are issues concerning all human beings equally. This perspective enables us to be in the world, but not of it. So, I'm not saying that the fideist or legal positivist position is outside the tradition. I only think that one perspective has better explanatory power and better advocacy power than the other.

RG: And for Jews like yourself who do wish to engage the culture critically, you've got a double-barreled shotgun. It's the resources of the specifically theological tradition, and philosophical arguments, and even the former have some purchase because the basic civilization was formed by the biblical worldview, the biblical understanding.

DN: Yes, the biblical understanding, I mean, Thomas Aquinas regards that aspect of the Hebrew Bible, which is still normative for Christians, as the moral teaching. And if you look at the *Prima secunda* of the *Summa theologiae*, the so-called treatise on law (Aquinas never called it "The Treatise on Law") is really an introduction to the treatment of the Old Law. And you can see it in Aquinas, where usually there are three or four objections—when you get to the Hebrew Bible (and all he knew was the Hebrew Bible and Maimonides's *Guide of the Perplexed*, the only two Jewish books he knew) there were like twelve or thirteen objections; and he generally agrees with Maimonides and refers to him as "Rabbi Moses." Also, it's never a question of a Christian versus a Jew or vice-versa. (In fact, in this section of the *Summa*, Aquinas almost always agrees with Maimonides's interpretations of biblical law.) Even when he disagrees with Maimonides in the first part of the *Summa* on questions of the attributes of God, Aquinas is always treating him with the same respect that he would treat one of the doctors of the Church or Aristotle. Truth is truth.

RG: What I mean by the double-barreled shotgun is that you do, and I certainly try to do, what Martin Luther King does. King doesn't hesitate to use religious language in the public square. He doesn't regard it as out of bounds. And he won't accept anybody who says, you're not allowed to talk that way in the public square. And yet at the same time, look at the letter from Birmingham jail, for example. He's making natural law arguments. So, to the extent that Heschel, for example, represents a view similar to King's, you find that at least in modern Jewish thought in the period of your own formation.

DN: That was very much the thing. Professor Heschel was very close to Martin Luther King. One of the two things that my grandchildren are most impressed about is that I shook Martin Luther King's hand. And number two is that when we moved to Canada, in order to become citizens, we had to get a letter from the sheriff of our last residence, the sheriff of Henrico County, Virginia, stating that we don't have criminal records. My grandchildren are impressed that I shook Martin Luther King's hand and that I don't have a criminal record.

I was once a witness in the trial of Judge Roy Moore of Alabama. (Let's forget, for the time being, what he's been accused of lately.) It was about when he put up the Ten Commandments in the lobby of the court house in Montgomery. I was witness for the defense. I saw Roy Moore, who comes from a racist southern culture, sitting in front of the court, being cheered on by black preachers with their bibles in their hands, and I heard Moore say that Martin Luther King taught all Christians, black or white, that it is sinful to discriminate against another human being created in the image of God. What Martin Luther King's great achievement was, was convincing southerners that they've got to choose between being Christians and being racists.

RG: Yes, that's right.

DN: That they can't have both. And most of the southerners opted for that. And that was never recognized by social scientists, who just thought that the racism was absolutely foundational, and that Christianity was just some kind of rationalization for it. But that was the achievement of Martin Luther King. Now the interesting thing was that in the debate with Roy Moore is that people objected to the Ten Commandments being publicly displayed, but nobody objected to the "Letter from Birmingham" jail being publicly displayed. And one of the arguments was, "What's the difference?"

RG: Now, David, one of the many areas, but a very important one in which you have engaged the culture from both a Jewish perspective and a natural law perspective, is on issues in the area of bioethics, life issues, and human dignity issues. And that work and witness goes all the way back to the beginning of your career. It's in this area that you have made common cause with people like those in the Dulles and Ramsey colloquiums under Father Neuhaus, that is Protestants, Jews, and Catholics—and to some extent Jews across a certain spectrum, Protestants across a certain spectrum, some Evangelical, some mainline. What are your reflections now looking back on all that work over all those years? In some ways, things are looking worse. We now have CRISPR technology. We've got a Chinese scientist who's literally crossed the germline doing CRISPR work on human embryos. How do you see things now?

DN: It's a very distressing type of situation. It's especially distressing to see people in the Jewish community, how they've distorted the Jewish tradition on questions like abortion. (Stem cell research really became a moot point when you can get stem cells from placentas.) One just has to speak the truth and make common cause with whomever one can. Professor Heschel, who was a great, great phrase maker, once said that our task in this world is to conquer evils one by one by one, until the One comes and conquers all evil. That is the point, and I'll discuss some of this in May at Princeton, how we need to be saved from despair. Natural law itself cannot do that for you, but your commitment to it is not negligible.

RG: When our friend Chief Rabbi Jonathan Sacks talks about the contributions of Judaism to the world, he puts at the top of the list the principle of the sanctity of human life. And if you look at cultures across history and across time, that has not been a constant. We can correctly say that we can reach the core of the judgment of the sanctity of human life on the basis of philosophical reflection, on the basis of natural law. Yet, as a hard reality, most cultures that have not had the witness of the Hebrew Bible, man made in the very image and likeness of the divine Creator and ruler of the universe, have not embraced the sanctity of human life view. And to take somebody at the opposite extreme—Peter Singer—he thinks it's very clear that we get this doctrine of the sanctity of human life (which he is determined to overthrow quite explicitly) from the Jewish and Christian religions. Do you agree?

DN: Well, yes, it comes from them, to be sure. But it's talking about all human beings. It's not only saying that Jews or Christians are created in the image of God, although there are some in both of our communities who've tried to argue that in that way. But regarding Singer, interestingly enough—which is really shocking, as the child of Holocaust survivors—there is one country where he cannot lecture and that is Germany. The Germans say, "We've heard that before. We've heard that before." There's actually one funny story about Peter Singer. One day, I was waiting for a train at the Princeton train station. I saw Rabbi Eitan Webb, who for years has been the Chabad rabbi in Princeton, talking to Peter Singer, and Singer was backing up to what I guess is the equivalent of the third rail, and I hear him saying to the Rabbi, "No, I'm not interested in keeping the Sabbath!"

So, anyway, in Canada, there is the Morgentaler decision—which is even worse than Roe v. Wade—that says that abortion can be done at any time, without any restrictions. Henry Morgentaler was also a Holocaust survivor. I mean his point of view is very close to the philosophy that denies that some people are human. This is what is incredibly shocking.

RG: It's hard for us human beings, and maybe here's the evidence of original sin, to really not only accept but act upon the proposition of the radical equality and fundamental dignity of every member of the human family. We can think of a million reasons to slide away from it, but it's the tradition that calls us back. If human beings are made in the image and likeness of God, then whatever our differences—some are stronger, some are weaker, some are pretty, some are not so pretty—in the most fundamental sense, we are equal and our dignity is inherited. It's not something we achieve or earn. We have it simply in virtue of our humanity.

DN: Yes, is the basic human right to life an entitlement or given to us? An entitlement from whom? Or is it something innate? Kant argues that, but I think it is problematic. In a way, that means natural law theory works very well as a theory of practical reason, but it requires some kind of metaphysical background. And the question is who supplies that metaphysical background? We can talk about practical reason, treating people as equals, but if we want to know the source of it, we have to do metaphysical work. And then the question becomes, how is it done? That is very much the question.

Chapter 1

David Novak and Jewish Natural Law

How a Theistic Believer Engages a Pluralistic and Secular Milieu

MELANIE SUSAN BARRETT

IN THEIR VOLUME *Tradition in the Public Square: A David Novak Reader*, co-editors Randi Rashkover and Martin Kavka characterize Novak's writing as "a response to the primary issue confronting modern Judaism," namely "what it means to be a part of Western culture yet separate from its secularized form of life."[1] We Catholic Christians, despite key theological differences, share this mission in common with our Jewish brothers and sisters. For us as Catholics, this mission typically is framed within the Gospel mandate *to be in the world but not of it*. Our theological rationale for existing within this tension is threefold. First, Jesus's kingdom "does not belong to this world" (John 18:36)—as Jesus himself tells Pilate—and the world naturally hates those who do not live according to its own standards (John 15:19). Accordingly, not only will Christians never feel entirely at home in the world; inevitably, they will be persecuted for their beliefs (John 15:20; 2 Tim 3:12; Matt 5:10–12).

Second, because our true citizenship "is in heaven" (Phil 3:20–21), we must assiduously avoid being "conformed to this world" (Rom 12:2)—to its "folly" masquerading as wisdom (1 Cor 3:19), to its evil works (John 7:7), and to its manifold "temptations to sin" (Matt 18:7; cf. 1 John 2:15–17)—so that we might be interiorly transformed and correctly discern what is "good, acceptable, and perfect" according to God's will (Rom 12:2). Third, because the world is essentially good—insofar as it has been created by God, "who wills everyone to be saved and to come to knowledge of the truth" (1 Tim 2:4)—Christians are duty-bound, as Jesus's disciples, not to isolate themselves entirely from the world, but rather to continue Jesus's mission of seeking out those who are lost (Luke 15:1–7 and 19:10) and actively reconciling the world to God (2 Cor 5:18–20).

---

1. Rashkover and Kavka (eds.), *Tradition in the Public Square*, xi.

How ought we Catholics live out this Gospel mandate, practically speaking, within the confines of a contemporary culture characterized not only by religious pluralism but also by secularism: a secularism that is not merely non-religious but is increasingly hostile to religion?[2] I contend that the writings of Rabbi David Novak, a conservative Jewish theologian, offer important guideposts for us Catholics to follow. In particular, Novak sets forth Jewish natural law as a political compass, with which he deftly navigates the philosophical tension between universalism and particularism, in order to protect Jews—and indirectly other religious communities as well—from the danger of a totalizing state that seeks their marginalization (at best) and their annihilation (at worst), while also empowering Jews to contribute productively to the modern democratic project. I will illuminate this trajectory in part one of my paper. In part two, I will consider what Catholics can learn from Novak's paradigm, given our own recent struggle in the American public square with the HHS contraceptive mandate.

David Novak's Political Compass

Jewish Natural Law

At first glance, the very term "natural law" might seem out of place in a Jewish ethic, given Judaism's pervasive emphasis on divine law: special revelation by God to the people of Israel. As Novak himself acknowledges, Torah—God's law as revealed in both Scripture and rabbinic tradition—is not only the most comprehensive explication of God's law available to human beings; it is regarded by Judaism to be "fully sufficient for every question of human praxis and thought."[3] So why would Judaism even have need of a purely philosophical construct? Why seek mere silver "when gold is readily at hand"?[4] And yet, by his own admission, Novak has been "formulating and reformulating a theory of natural law" for over thirty years.[5] So why so much work for something seemingly so non-essential?

2. David Novak helpfully defines "secularism" as "the ideological matrix that regards human-made law not only as necessary for modern life—a point which Jews and Christians who have not retreated to sectarian enclaves can readily accept—but also as sufficient for human fulfillment. It is the modern embrace of the view of the ancient sophists that 'man is the measure of all things.'" According to this definition, "secularists" are "those people who see the total public sufficiency of the secular realm." This is problematic because "at best, [secularists] would so privatize religions that religions become sects: neither of the world nor even in it. At worst, they would see no place at all for religions in any democratic polity. Needless to say, Judaism and Christianity as covenantal religions, which are essentially political entities, are mortally threatened (collectively even if not individually) by such secularism, for it would deny them their worldly place" (Novak, *Talking with Christians*, 206 and 192–93).

3. Novak, "Natural Law and Judaism," 18.

4. Novak, "Natural Law and Judaism," 18.

5. Novak, "Natural Law and Judaism," 4. Prior to this 2014 essay, Novak's conception of natural law was developed in three books—*The Image of the Non-Jew in Judaism* (2011), *Covenantal Rights* (2000), and *Natural Law in Judaism* (1998)—and a number of articles, especially those collected in the volumes, Rashkover and Kavka (eds.), *Tradition in the Public Square: A David Novak Reader* (2008), and Novak, *Talking with Christians* (2005).

Novak provides several justifications, both philosophical and theological. Philosophically, natural law is necessary to dialogue and act in concert with others in an international and multicultural world.[6] It is discovered through the exercise of practical reason when it reflects philosophically on what human nature is—for example, that it is rational and free—and how to act in accord with it, rather than being led by one's sub-rational appetites and inclinations alone (as are animals).[7]

Theologically, Novak contends that divine law itself is twofold: that which God has "revealed in history to a particular people," and that which "all people can discover for themselves through ratiocination."[8] Both types of law are grounded ontologically in God's creative commandment, but the former (revealed law) presupposes the latter (natural law) for historical reasons. Prior to the Jews' being invited into a special covenant with God at Sinai, they resided in a world with the rest of humanity and all were subject to the same general morality.[9] Those moral norms were (and continue to be) epistemically accessible through "discursive human reason," and they oblige human beings universally: "throughout all historical time and all political space."[10] The new law given to the Jews at Sinai—the Mosaic law—did not eliminate this obligation; rather, it replaced the "minimal" version of God's law with the "maximal" version.[11] The natural law thus remains an intrinsic part of Judaism; it is not salvific—for practical reason cannot discover the fullness of the good without the supplementary assistance of revelation—but it establishes the lower bar for justice: that which is minimally required for an act to be just.[12]

Furthermore, although Novak readily admits that "those Jewish thinkers who [regard] natural law [as operative] within . . . Jewish tradition . . . are a minority," especially today when "most scholars of Jewish law . . . are legal positivists," he contends that "enough of a tradition of natural law thinking [exists] in Judaism for any contemporary Jewish thinker to continue it and even develop it."[13] To substantiate this claim, Novak points specifically to "Noahide law": those laws given by God to Noah, after he and his family survived the flood. According to the ancient rabbinic sages, seven precepts are morally binding on all human beings created in God's image:

---

6. Novak, "Natural Law and Judaism," 19.

7. Novak, "Natural Law and Judaism," 8–9.

8. Novak, "Natural Law and Judaism," 6. Notably, this distinction corresponds largely to Thomas Aquinas's division of eternal law (God's blueprint for the universe) into divine law (revelation) and natural law (the rational creature's participation in God's eternal law through the exercise of reason) (Aquinas, *Summa Theologiae* I-II, q. 91).

9. Novak, "Natural Law and Judaism," 19; and "Is Natural Law a Border Concept," 247.

10. Novak, "Is Natural Law a Border Concept," 246.

11. Novak, "Natural Law and Judaism," 19.

12. Novak, "Is Natural Law a Border Concept," 250. Because natural law clarifies only the lower limit, philosophy must be supplemented by theology so that human beings can learn the "upper limit" as well (Novak, "Natural Law and Judaism," 19–20).

13. Novak, "Natural Law and Judaism," 33.

1. the positive injunction to set up courts of law to apply justice
2. the prohibition of blasphemy
3. the prohibition of idolatry
4. the prohibition of sexual license (specifically, incest, homoeroticism, adultery, and bestiality)
5. the prohibition of homicide (including the prohibition of abortion)
6. the prohibition of robbery
7. the prohibition of eating a limb torn from a living animal.[14]

The first six are not explicitly mentioned in Scripture, but Novak affirms Maimonides's claim that reason naturally inclines toward them, so additional revelation was not needed. Only the seventh was specifically mentioned, though it too may be accounted an example of the more general prohibition—naturally accessible to reason—against cruel abuse of nature, especially of those domesticated animals who live in close proximity to human beings.[15]

Novak's identification of natural law with Noahide law enables him to conclude that natural law lies in Judaism's background, not just historically, "not just [as] a *chronological* precondition for revelation," but as a *logical* precondition.[16] Furthermore, he underscores the fact that these laws are morally binding not *because* Jewish authorities proclaimed them (which would constitute an argument from authority). Rather, Jewish authorities proclaimed them because they considered such norms to be *already* universally binding on all human beings (an argument from reason), and deemed it advantageous to apply these universally valid moral norms to their current political context. Given their inherent rationality, Novak muses, Jews should not be surprised to see such norms "being formulated and applied in many other locations in the world" today.[17]

Notwithstanding the Noahide version of natural law articulated and promulgated within Jewish tradition, both oral and written, what versions of natural law could be constituted in today's modern world, given its diverse array of languages and cultures? Although traditions aside from Judaism and Christianity do not possess a dignified view of human nature as made in the image of God, Novak expresses optimism that they can exercise practical reason so as to generate an alternate basis for defending basic human rights. Such reasons will be objectively inferior to those rooted in a truthful recognition of human nature as *imago Dei*, but he asserts that even inferior reasons are preferable to none at all: or to acting merely on the basis of intuition, feeling, or

---

14. Novak, "Natural Law and Judaism," 30.

15. Novak, "Natural Law and Judaism," 32–33. The seventh is derived from the scriptural prohibition in Genesis 9:4: "Indeed, flesh whose life-blood is still in it, you shall not eat."

16. Novak, "Natural Law and Judaism," 33. Italics added for emphasis.

17. Novak, "Natural Law and Judaism," 31.

passion. As it stands, our secular interlocutors already "accept the indispensability of human rights for our political health," and we can fruitfully dialogue with them regarding such rights, in a non-threatening manner, without requiring them to accept our own particular philosophical-theological justifications.[18]

Universalism and Particularism

Novak insists repeatedly not only that Jews *can* articulate a theory of natural law—because it is theologically warranted within Jewish tradition—but also that they *ought* to become skilled at utilizing natural law reasoning in public debates concerning moral issues. His insistence stems not from optimism regarding the likelihood of widespread consensus on controversial topics, but from a realistic appraisal of the tense, harmful, and even destructive relationship that Jews have experienced from non-Jews in the past. "After the Holocaust, especially," he cautions, "no Jew, no matter how rich or powerful, feels totally safe, even when relying upon the most benevolent non-Jews."[19]

Although Jews in the United States currently reside there comfortably as citizens with equal rights—rather than as captives in need of rescue—secularism is on the rise, and "some secularists would like to see Judaism totally privatized or even totally eliminated" so that secularism might triumph definitively.[20] Even if such privatization were to begin slowly, removing "religious Jews *qua religious Jews* from public moral debates" he speculates, eventually "would even remove . . . those nonreligious or secular Jews *qua Jews* who still have some historical attachment to the Jewish ethical tradition" out of suspicion that their ethical standards are inherently particularistic and thus antithetical to the interests of others.[21]

As Novak astutely observes, not only Jews but *anyone* who advocates for a specific public policy "in a secular political climate, because of what [their own] religious tradition teaches, [opens themselves] to the charge of imperialism."[22] Accordingly, religious citizens who seek to defend their claims without utilizing universally accessible reasons, will be suspect of "trying to ram *their* religious morality down everyone else's throat."[23] Whereas in pre-modern times most people believed that morality *required* religious justification, now the tables have turned and religion *itself* requires moral justification.[24] Failure to do so adequately leaves religious adherents vulnerable to being written off as particularists whose minority self-interest only can be advanced at the majority's

---

18. Novak, "Natural Law and Judaism," 38.
19. Novak, "Toward a Jewish Public Philosophy in America," 212.
20. Novak, "Toward a Jewish Public Philosophy in America," 213; and Novak, "The Universality of Jewish Ethics," 142.
21. Novak, "The Universality of Jewish Ethics," 142.
22. Novak, "The Universality of Jewish Ethics," 143.
23. Novak, "The Universality of Jewish Ethics," 143.
24. Novak, "The Universality of Jewish Ethics," 145–46.

expense. During those special instances when Jews (or even Christians) request specific religious exemptions from the laws and procedures governing other citizens, the likelihood of being accused of particularism increases even more.[25]

The great irony here, Novak contends, is that religions like Judaism are intrinsically more universal in their ethics than a purely secular state, whose overemphasis on egalitarianism easily can tend toward radical particularism. His logic is as follows. To begin with, both Judaism and Christianity emphatically defend the norm of "benevolence to all" (positively, to treat others as one would want to be treated) and "malevolence to none" (negatively, to do no harm to others).[26] Novak maintains that this norm is both universal in scope, and universally accessible to reason; so, in principle it can be held by everyone, both religious and secular.

However, Jews and Christians also hold a second principle—which not all secularists share—namely that "one has a more maximal moral obligation to benefit the members of one's own family or clan."[27] This does not mean that the first norm (of universal, egalitarian reciprocity) may be dispensed with: for example, that one's neighbor across the street legitimately could be harmed if doing so would benefit one's own kin. But it does mean that a second set of moral obligations co-exists alongside the first: prescribing additional care, attention, time, and energy to helping one's friends, family members, co-religionists, and so on. In such cases, the universal and the particular exist in tension with each other. However, this tension need not be problematic. As Novak explains, it is "only when particularistic norms *contradict* the universal norms (e.g., 'benefit your own people, *but* harm foreigners') that we have to opt for *either* universal norms, *or* particularistic norms."[28]

Not only do Jews (and Christians) unflinchingly support this two-part universal norm—of benevolence to all, and malevolence to none—they do so with a specific goal in mind: to pursue constructive peace and avoid destructive violence. Because this goal (promoting peace and avoiding violence) is universally accessible to reason (in principle), it too is held by many secularists. However, religious adherents further conceptualize this goal as "infused teleology": promoting peace as part of advancing God's broader purposes for the world.[29] This broader, divine project transcends the world; it cannot be derived from the world, so its additional moral demands will not be grasped as obligatory by everyone.

For example, Novak points out that those non-religious adherents who subscribe to a Kantian framework will conceptualize the moral universe as populated by autonomous agents, so "only those who are conscious, rational, and capable of exercising their free will" are the bearers of rights and duties. He queries,

25. Novak, "The Universality of Jewish Ethics," 146.
26. Novak, "The Universality of Jewish Ethics," 146–47, 151.
27. Novak, "The Universality of Jewish Ethics," 151.
28. Novak, "The Universality of Jewish Ethics," 148.
29. Novak, "The Universality of Jewish Ethics," 156–57.

> What about those who do not possess these essential attributes, temporarily or even permanently? What prevents us from treating them with no genuine respect, at best condescendingly tolerating them, at worst eliminating them when they become too burdensome to us? Are they not part of humankind as well? Do we not have responsibilities to them too? That could only be the case when the claims for respect and care these unconscious or irrational or determined lives make upon us are seen as the claims made upon us by those created in the image of God.[30]

The discrepancy arises not because Kantians are inherently selfish, but because practical reason unassisted by divine revelation simply does not apprehend human nature in its authentic fullness. As Novak explains, "Human beings *qua imago Dei* are unlike the autonomous members of Kant's moral universe who create themselves by the exercise of their autonomy and who can only recognize those who are able to exercise that same capacity."[31] Viewed from a religious standpoint, therefore, the Kantian framework is insufficiently universal because it is not wholly inclusive.

A second example concerns our moral duties to the rest of creation. Novak commends those who acknowledge the current ecological crisis as imperiling not only the nonhuman world but ourselves as well. Yet here again, a purely secular worldview cannot sustain a thoroughgoing commitment to responsible stewardship. Viewed from within the world rather than above it, humans appear to be mere parts of an earth on which they reside alongside both plants and animals. But if humans are mere parts of the whole, then why should they inconvenience themselves in order to care for non-humans? After all, "no other 'part' seems to be assuming responsibility except for its own species."[32]

For religious believers, by contrast, God created "*both* us *and* the world [around] us," and commands us to care for it as a shepherd cares for his flock.[33] From this transcendent perspective, human beings are not radically equal to everything else—they are superior to it—but with this privileged position comes the added duty to be its stewards. Plants and animals cannot be responsible for us, but we can—and should be—responsible for them: a divine command that we are motivated to abide by precisely because of our religious adherence.

The moral inclusiveness that Jews and Christians are duty-bound (by God) to recognize thus extends beyond autonomous, fully rational agents to include human beings who are physically or mentally challenged as well as non-human creatures. Neither group possesses the capability of enacting the universal norm "to do to others what they would have done to them," but they remain objects of our respect and care nonetheless. This is a substantial contribution that religious believers make to the common good:

30. Novak, "The Universality of Jewish Ethics," 159.
31. Novak, "The Universality of Jewish Ethics," 159.
32. Novak, "The Universality of Jewish Ethics," 160.
33. Novak, "The Universality of Jewish Ethics," 160.

broadening the secular notion of universalism to include these groups precisely on account of their own particularism. Not only is religious particularism not antithetical to universalism; it actively promotes it resulting in "a more universal universe."[34]

However, not all secularists will affirm the positive value of this contribution. Novak contends that among secularists who bespeak a commitment to universalism, some are "partial egalitarians," who prescribe equality for some areas of human social interaction, whereas others are "total egalitarians," for whom "egalitarianism is infinite" and as such "should pervade all our interhuman relations."[35] This latter group poses a problem (for religious believers), because their insistence on radical equality in every sphere of human interaction makes them zealous to dismantle traditional religious communities and families because of the political hierarchies that tend to permeate them (such as male versus female, and parents versus children).[36] Even if the community in question neither advocates nor permits overt harm to its own members (or to others around them), it still is regarded with deep suspicion.[37]

Such a project—of dismantling traditional religious groups and families—could only be carried out effectively by the state. Might this ever take place? Possibly. Novak conjectures that as state power increases, competing claims to legitimacy within civil society could be viewed as an existential threat to the state's survival, leading the state down the path toward totalitarianism. For if even the right to privacy (which guarantees a space within society for free religious activity) is regarded merely as a civil right created by the state—not as a natural right, based upon transcendent human dignity, which precedes the state—then the state can choose to remove that right to privacy at any time, and repress religious exercise altogether.[38]

Even if the state does not become totalitarian, the more its totalizing power increases, Novak avers, "the more citizens are hierarchically ranked according to how valuable or invaluable they are to the ruling powers of the state in their never-ending, elitist drive for total power over all aspects of 'their' society."[39] The more this happens, the less inclusive—and the less universal—secular morality becomes. For if "usefulness" becomes "the defining characteristic of persons in this world of human interaction," then "everything and everybody" will be reduced to the status of a commodity.[40] In such a context, physically and mentally handicapped human beings, as well as non-human creatures, justifiably can be exploited at will.

And this is where the great irony may be found. Novak reasons, perceptively, that

---

34. Novak, "The Universality of Jewish Ethics," 159.
35. Novak, "The Universality of Jewish Ethics," 148.
36. Novak, "The Universality of Jewish Ethics," 151.
37. Novak, "The Universality of Jewish Ethics," 148.
38. Novak, "The Universality of Jewish Ethics," 152.
39. Novak, "The Universality of Jewish Ethics," 152.
40. Novak, "The Universality of Jewish Ethics," 162.

universality needs to be in dialectical tension with particularity, lest unchecked universality swallow up particularity and then breed a maximal particularity of its own. For that reason, precisely because religious communities look to One who is greater than the state in every way conceivable . . . they are thereby providing a moral service to the state by being able to cogently limit its totalizing power.[41]

By so doing, they protect not only members of their own religious communities from an overbearing state; they protect everyone else in the society as well.[42]

Jewish Public Philosophy: A Constructive Proposal

Against the backdrop of this philosophical optimism and political realism, Novak proposes a threefold approach to Jewish public philosophy in the United States. According to this proposal, Jewish advocacy of specific policy positions should always be theologically grounded (based on Torah), practically useful (promoting Jewish self-interest), and effective (by adopting the language of general morality).[43]

He offers several examples. One of them is whether public prayer should be permitted by the state. At first glance, Jews might wish to oppose public prayer, because many such prayers inevitably will include Christian content (given that Christians are in the majority). But on Torah grounds, Novak declares, "Jews ought to encourage non-Jews to pray in public in order to show how much they believe the world, including the political order, is dependent upon God."[44] Indeed, it would be beneficial for all citizens to occasionally offer prayers from their particular religious traditions, especially if God is addressed simply as "creator of the universe and giver of natural law," without explicitly mentioning special revelation to one community.[45] Novak readily acknowledges that Jews sometimes have felt like second-class citizens when attending public events where Christians pray in public. However, he insists that a broad practice of public prayer could actively promote Jewish self-interest, by expanding the public space in which Jews can express their own religious beliefs.[46]

41. Novak, "The Universality of Jewish Ethics," 153.

42. Novak, "The Universality of Jewish Ethics," 153.

43. Novak, "Toward a Jewish Public Philosophy in America," 209. Elsewhere Novak explains that utilizing the language of general morality is preferable to either: (1) "simply [reiterating] in public the classical moral teaching of one's own tradition," which would constitute proselytism and could lead to authoritarianism—if persuasion were not successful—resulting in a harmful backlash of public animosity toward religion; or (2) "simply [abdicating] any religious voice in the area of morality and politics, [remaining] content with 'spiritual' matters of belief, ritual, and what could be termed 'private' morality, which is usually the cultivation of 'inner' attitudes," an approach that "is inappropriate because it is essentially other-worldly," abandoning "the moral and political role that Judaism and Christianity must play in the world" (Novak, *Talking with Christians*, 193–96).

44. Novak, "Toward a Jewish Public Philosophy in America," 221.

45. Novak, "Toward a Jewish Public Philosophy in America," 221.

46. Novak, "Toward a Jewish Public Philosophy in America," 222.

As to the general morality, some have argued that public prayer would constitute an illegitimate endorsement of religion by the secular state. However, Novak maintains that public displays of religion do not offend the general morality; they actively promote it, for "the United States has always looked to a transcendent source for its foundational morality and law."[47] He specifically mentions Abraham Lincoln and Martin Luther King, whose public advocacy to end slavery and promote human rights was strengthened precisely because they appealed to God's justice.[48]

Defending the traditional idea that marriage should take place between one man and one woman constitutes a second example in which Novak utilizes this threefold approach to public policy. Theologically, despite attempts of some Jewish groups to publicly defend same-sex marriage, the Torah is "unambiguously negative" on this question, for it is "unilaterally opposed to homosexual acts, whether between men or between women."[49] Because God created human nature "male and female" (Gen 5:1–2 and 1:27), and commanded them to marry (2:24) and to "be fruitful and multiply" (1:27–28), "marriage for the sake of procreation is a positive duty" owed both to the community and to God.[50] Although human sexual acts are practiced not just for procreation but also for pleasure and to ameliorate loneliness, procreation is sex's primary purpose according to God's plan.[51]

Because homosexual unions preclude procreation *by design*, they meet neither the theological definition of family life—"the intended permanent union of a man and a woman [that] intends the conception, birth and parenting of children"—nor the needs of the community, which flourishes when new members are "born, cared for, and raised to responsible adulthood in a home founded on a permanently intended heterosexual union."[52] Given the natural view of marriage set forth in the Torah's creation account, sexual acts that deviate from this framework are prohibited: not just homosexuality (Gen 9:20–27; 19:5), but also incest (Gen 9:20–27; 19:30–35), adultery (Gen 39:6 20), bestiality (Gen 2:18–24), and rape (Gen 6:4; 12:10–20; 20:2–11; 34:1–31).[53]

When a marriage is not only natural but also Jewish, it takes on even deeper spiritual significance as a means to maintain and perpetuate the covenant of Sinai.[54] Accordingly, in the rabbinic tradition, all Jews are expected to marry and have a family, and to engage in sexual activity regularly with their spouses: even when the

---

47. Novak, "Toward a Jewish Public Philosophy in America," 222.
48. Novak, "Toward a Jewish Public Philosophy in America," 222.
49. Novak, "Toward a Jewish Public Philosophy in America," 218–19.
50. Novak, *Covenantal Rights*, 170–73.
51. Novak, *Covenantal Rights*, 168–69.
52. Novak, *Covenantal Rights*, 169 and 171.
53. Novak, "Jewish Marriage," in *Jewish Justice*, 108. Such acts also were forbidden to Israel in Leviticus (18:1–24), along with some additions (p. 109).
54. Novak, "Jewish Marriage," in *Jewish Justice*, 113.

likelihood of conception is remote due to infertility.[55] Voluntary celibacy is not an option, although the tradition does acknowledge that some individuals "are incapable of initiating or sustaining a marriage" for physical or emotional reasons and thus are to be treated with compassion.[56]

Given the Torah's comprehensively robust stance *against* both homosexual acts and same-sex marriage, what would be practically useful to promote Jewish self-interest in the public square? Novak acknowledges that publicly promoting same-sex marriage would further the interest of *some* Jews, those whose homosexual lifestyle previously alienated them from communal life. But he also insists that Jewish self-interest, broadly construed, requires the continuity of the Jewish community which already is threatened by intermarriage between Jews and non-Jews.[57] These two issues (same-sex marriage and intermarriage) are connected because

> our opposition to intermarriage is only cogent if we argue that all forms of sexual desire cannot receive the communal endorsement of Jews because all forms of sexual desire are not in the best interests of the Jewish community. The only form of sexual desire that can be encouraged to the point of being institutionalized is the desire between a Jewish man and a Jewish woman to build a family whose primary (although not exclusive) purpose is the conception, birth, and rearing of children together.[58]

Only by taking a strong stance publicly against same-sex marriage, can Jews credibly maintain their strong stance against intermarriage (and other prohibited unions) and thus preserve the continuity of the Jewish community in the long-term.[59]

How can the language of general morality be utilized to defend this position in the public square? Novak suggests a political argument, focused on the state's role in fostering the common good. He argues as follows. All societies must prohibit at least some sexual practices: either maximally through punishment, or minimally through non-endorsement. The minimal path is appropriate "for sexual acts committed in private by consenting adults," given the high value that our democratic society places upon privacy.[60] For the state to radically change course and *actively endorse* a sexual practice, it must be in the state's interest. Only heterosexual unions are worthy of thoroughgoing endorsement, Novak argues, because only those can produce children (and most do in practice). After all, "how children are brought into the world and how they are raised is very much in the interest of the state to provide for the future

---

55. Novak, "Jewish Marriage," in *Jewish Justice*, 114.
56. Novak, *Covenantal Rights*, 178. Novak also cites "a simple lack of opportunity" as a reason why some Jews legitimately are not married.
57. Novak, "Toward a Jewish Public Philosophy in America," 219.
58. Novak, "Toward a Jewish Public Philosophy in America," 219.
59. Novak, "Toward a Jewish Public Philosophy in America," 219.
60. Novak, "Toward a Jewish Public Philosophy in America," 220.

of its society."[61] To formalize same-sex unions, which *by design* preclude producing children, would not be in the state's interest, just as other human relationships, such as friendship, are of no concern to the state. Hence, all such unions ought to remain in the private sphere, outside the state's jurisdiction.[62]

Unfortunately, same-sex marriage already has been legalized in both Canada (in 2005) and the United States (in 2015). Given this development, Novak recommends some form of civil disobedience on the part of religious clergy who support traditional marriage, such as not signing *any* civil marriage license unless the parties to the marriage meet all of the religious requirements.[63]

Appropriating and Extending Novak's Paradigm: Recent Catholic Debates

What can we as Catholic Christians learn from Novak's analysis? I contend that we share Novak's philosophical optimism regarding the possibility of using reason to generate universal moral claims with which non-religious adherents can agree, as evidenced by our own rich natural law tradition. We also share Novak's political realism regarding the possible threat that a growing secularism poses to the freedom to actively exercise our own religious beliefs and practices. Novak recalls having marched as a Jew (wearing his *kippa*) on behalf of civil rights in the 1960s; many Catholics did as well. In recent decades, Catholics have waged public legal battles over many other moral issues, including abortion, assisted suicide, and traditional marriage.

However, we have not always waged those battles prudently and effectively with our long-term interest in view. As the esteemed Catholic law professor, Helen Alvaré, has argued, in many recent legal battles, Catholics have relied too heavily on religious freedom claims to defend our public policy positions, without also seeking to explain our positions by reasons that could be accessible to non-Catholics.[64] Invoking Novak's threefold framework, our public advocacy has limited itself to the first two criteria—(1) Catholic Scripture and tradition, and (2) Catholic self-interest—with very little reference to the third: (3) the general morality. This limited strategy of "hands-off, this involves religious reasons, which we won't bother explaining to you because they're religious and thus outside your scope" has provided us with some short-term wins but also has set us up for some long-term losses.[65] For as Alvaré cautions, our unwillingness to even *try* to explain the *reasons* undergirding our minority positions—limiting ourselves instead to the claim that such objections are necessary to avoid moral

61. Novak, "Toward a Jewish Public Philosophy in America," 220.
62. Novak, "Toward a Jewish Public Philosophy in America," 220.
63. Novak, "Toward a Jewish Public Philosophy in America," 219.
64. Alvaré, "Free Exercise/Non-Establishment Law and its Implications for the Church."
65. See Alvaré, "Free Exercise/Non-Establishment Law and its Implications for the Church." This is a paraphrase of Alvaré's comments.

cooperation with evil—constitutes a profound missed opportunity by deepening the (false) perception among secularists that the Catholic Church is both anti-women and anti-gay, thereby emboldening their resolve to promote policies that altogether delegitimize the Catholic Church as an institution.[66]

So, if instead, we Catholics were to heed Alvaré's warning, and develop our public discourse along the lines that Novak has proposed, what might that look like? I suggest the following dual strategy. First, we invoke a straightforward defense of religious freedom, coupled with a political argument for its ongoing importance. In his book, *In Defense of Religious Liberty*, Novak states that religious believers must "understand *how* we are to argue for our religious liberty in a secular society," for example, by showing that the "privatization of religion is essentially undemocratic, both in terms of the idea of democracy and in terms of the experience of democracy."[67] Second, rather than just waving the "religious liberty" flag in the air and stopping there, we must set forth the theological rationale undergirding the issue at hand and then endeavor to defend it (as much as possible) through reasoned argument that is accessible to the general morality. According to Novak, our secularist opponents assume that our reasons "can only be *either* religious *or* secular, but never *both* religious *and* secular in tandem."[68] It is our job to disabuse them of that false assumption.

Catholic Doctrine on Religious Freedom

In our Catholic tradition, religious freedom as a basic human right was articulated and defended most vigorously in the Vatican II document entitled *Dignitatis Humanae*, also known as the *Declaration on Religious Freedom*. There the council asserted the following: All human beings have dignity—intrinsic value. This dignity is attested to not only by revelation (the *imago Dei* and the Paschal Mystery) but also by human reason which recognizes that we are beings endowed with both rationality and free will and thus are personally responsible for our actions. To live according to our nature (as rational and free beings), we require the freedom both to hold our own beliefs and to act in accord with them. Consequently, we must be immune from any kind of coercion of our beliefs or actions. Neither individuals nor social groups should coerce us, within due limits. Accordingly, governments ought to acknowledge the basic human right to religious freedom and codify it in constitutional law as a civil right (DH.2).

The council then sets forth a second, supplementary justification for religious freedom. Human beings are naturally inclined and morally bound "to seek the truth, especially religious truth. They are also bound to adhere to the truth, once it is known, and to order their whole lives in accord with the demands of truth. However, men cannot discharge those obligations in a manner in keeping with their own

---

66. Alvaré, "Free Exercise/Non-Establishment Law and its Implications for the Church."
67. Novak, *In Defense of Religious Liberty*, 86.
68. Novak, *In Defense of Religious Liberty*, 86.

nature unless they enjoy immunity from external coercion as well as psychological freedom" (DH.2). Free *inquiry* about the truth requires existential space for "teaching or instruction, communication and dialogue" so that people can explain to each other what they believe to be true and why. Personal *adherence* to the truth requires existential space for acting in accord with one's beliefs. This is especially important because it is by following one's conscience that one comes to God, who is "the end and purpose of life." The Council thus proclaims,

> [The human person] is not to be forced to act in a manner contrary to his conscience. Nor, on the other hand, is he to be restrained from acting in accordance with his conscience, especially in matters religious. The reason is that in the exercise of religion, of its very nature, consists before all else in those internal, voluntary and free acts whereby man sets the course of his life directly toward God. No merely human power can either command or prohibit acts of this kind" (DH.3).

The Council goes on to declare that "if the free exercise of religion is denied in society" then "injury . . . is done to the human person and to the very order established by God for human life" (DH.3).

The only situation in which religious freedom legitimately could be constrained would be providing for "the just demands of public order" (DH.3–4). People must act responsibly, by dealing justly and civilly with one another. If, however, people commit certain abuses—citing freedom of religion as a pretext—then society has the right to defend itself against these, for government is morally obliged to protect the rights of all citizens, to settle peacefully all conflicts of rights, and to guard public morality (DH.7). Aside from this need to preserve the public order, the council declares unequivocally that "the freedom of man is to be respected as far as possible and is not to be curtailed except when and insofar as is necessary" (DH.7).

Defending a Religious Freedom Claim: The HHS Contraceptive Mandate as Test Case

In 2012, the Obama administration's Department of Health and Human Services imposed a mandate that required health-insurance plans to cover both contraceptives (including the controversial emergency contraceptives Plan B and Ella) and sterilizations, under the auspices of the 2010 Patient Protection and Affordable Health Care Act. Although religious employers who objected on religious grounds were given an exemption, the category "religious employer" initially was defined in an extremely narrow way; for example, it included houses of worship but not "religiously affiliated hospitals, universities, and social service agencies" who either employ or serve a fair number of people who do not share their religious beliefs. In response to public outcry on the part of such institutions, and following a successful lawsuit in 2014 against the government by Hobby Lobby (who maintained that "providing coverage for drugs that could cause early abortions violated their Christian beliefs"), the administration offered an accommodation: shifting the responsibility for covering contraception from objecting employers to their insurance companies. However, the terms of this compromise ultimately were deemed insufficient by many religious organizations, such as Little Sisters of the Poor, who (along with some for-profit companies) persisted in suing the federal government.

The issue was resolved in 2017, under the Trump Administration. According to the final rules, issued by the federal Departments of Health and Human Services, Treasury, and Labor, "entities that object to services covered by the mandate on the basis of sincerely held *religious beliefs*" may receive an exemption from the contraceptive mandate.[69] Significantly, the exemption also extends to "nonprofit organizations and small businesses that have *non-religious moral convictions* opposing services."[70]

Prior to this resolution, proponents of the HHS mandate acknowledged the constitutional right to free exercise of religion but also contended: (1) that free exercise claims must be balanced against compelling public interests, (2) that widespread access to no-cost contraception is a compelling public interest, and (3) that the HHS mandate (along with the accommodation) utilized the least restrictive means to further this interest. Those who opposed the mandate maintained that maximizing access to contraception does not constitute a sufficiently compelling government interest to justify restricting free-exercise claims, and/or that the least restrictive means were not utilized.[71]

---

69. HHS Press Office, "Trump Administration Issues Final Rules Protecting Conscience Rights in Health Insurance." Italics added for emphasis.

70. HHS Press Office, "Trump Administration Issues Final Rules Protecting Conscience Rights in Health Insurance." Italics added for emphasis. The rules further specify that "institutions of education, issuers, and individuals" may receive an exemption, but not "publicly traded businesses" or "government entities." Although New Jersey and Pennsylvania subsequently challenged the exemption for employers with religious or moral objections, on July 8, 2020 the Supreme Court upheld it (in Little Sisters of the Poor Saints Peter and Paul Home v. Pennsylvania et al), contending that the federal HRSA (Health Resources and Services Administration) possesses the discretion "to identify and create exemptions from its own Guidelines." Jess Bravin and Brent Kendall, "Supreme Court Expands Religious Rights," *The Wall Street Journal* (July 9, 2020), p. A1.

71. See for example, Helen M. Alvaré, "No Compelling Interest," 379–436. Alvaré argues (on p. 380) that the government's reasoning "does not work nearly as well as its proponents suggest when contraception is promoted on a *social* scale . . . due both to the unique qualities of the sexual transaction, and to the way contraception affects the 'marketplaces' for sex and marriage. In simple terms, contraception has the effect of lowering the 'price' of sex, by separating sexual intercourse from the understanding that sex makes children who, in order to flourish, need their parents' commitment to one another and to the children, over a long period of time. This effect, in turn, tends to increase the demand for sex outside of marriage, which leads to more nonmarital pregnancies and abortions. Consequently, over the long run, large-scale contraception programs are not generally associated with steady declines in unintended pregnancy. . . . Further, it seems likely that a legal Mandate will fail to accomplish its goal of closing the small gap between the current availability and use of contraception, and universal use by women at risk of unintended pregnancy. This is so because the group of women with the highest unintended pregnancy rates (the poor) are not addressed or affected by the Mandate,

In my opinion as a Catholic moral theologian, the general principle of balancing free exercise claims with compelling public interests is a good one. A government would be forfeiting its duty as protector of the common good if it did not consider compelling interests like public health or safety. As political philosopher Jean Bethke Elshtain has argued, governments are obliged to exercise such responsibility.[72] However, Elshtain further contends—in her book on *Augustine and the Limits of Politics*—that governments must *also* be careful not to overreach for we are sinful human beings whose "God-given reason and . . . capacity for love" are coupled with a "lust for dominance" that "cuts across [all] levels . . . of human existence" and all human institutions.[73] Because earthly power is always "tied to the temptations inherent [in] that form of power we call dominion," we must remain circumspect when exercising it.[74] With Augustine, "any human institution can be turned into an idolatry—whether of family or of state or of anything else" if it is driven to become "superordinate" rather than "chastened or limited."[75]

How does this apply to the case at hand? I would suggest that just as we need to be circumspect, lest religions misuse their power in ways that harm others (either intentionally or unintentionally), so we need to be equally circumspect about other institutions, including the federal government. In the recent case, the Obama administration maintained that providing contraceptive services and elective sterilization for women was such an important public good—on the level of public health and safety—that it compelled them to limit free exercise rights in order to provide it.

Drawing upon Novak's political-ethical strategy (for religious believers doing public philosophy), I will begin by posing several questions. First, was this a compelling women's health issue? At first glance, the answer seems to be yes. After all, it is important for women to have access to the means required to regulate the number of children they have. And if this access is important, then should not women—especially poor women—have access to free birth control through their employer-provided health insurance programs?

But then why all the lawsuits on the part of religious institutions? Was this just an instance of unthinking brainwashing trumping common sense? Did the Roman Catholic Church's participation in these lawsuits amount to a form of subterfuge, waving the flag of religious freedom as cover for a more pernicious agenda: one in which men misuse their hierarchical positions as bishops to control, manipulate, and

---

and are already amply supplied with free or low-cost contraception. It is also true because women have a true variety of reasons for not using contraception that the law cannot mitigate or satisfy simply by attempting to increase access to contraception by making it 'free.'"

72. A nation-state is "sovereign" when "it demonstrates the ability to be independent from the protection of another state, to treat its citizens decently, and to foster a vibrant civil society: sovereignty as responsibility." Elshtain, *Sovereignty: God, State, and Self: The Gifford Lectures*, 228.

73. Elshtain, *Augustine and the Limits of Politics*, 27.

74. Elshtain, *Augustine and the Limits of Politics*, 94.

75. Elshtain, *Sovereignty: God, State, and the Self*, 240.

ultimately dominate women and their bodies? According to Maureen Dowd of the *New York Times*, and many others, the answer is "yes."

In my estimation however, the answer is "no." A close examination of Catholic Church teaching on contraception and related women's health issues reveals that the Church's position is based on reasoned argument stemming from a set of rational presuppositions about the nature of human beings and what constitutes human fulfillment. The overall framework is both logical and coherent, and it is one with which reasonable people, including non-Catholics, potentially could agree. At least four points are salient in this regard. First, sexual intercourse is theorized under the heading of love, and love is understood not as mere sentiment, of a transient nature—as in "I love you tonight, but tomorrow, next week, next year . . . who knows?"—but as the lifelong commitment to the good of the other and to mutual growth in holiness. Marriage is thus a necessary, though not sufficient, condition for sex to be fully loving.

Second, within this context, the Church absolutely is in favor of responsible parenthood; it teaches that married couples can limit the number of children for a broad range of reasons: including their psychological and physical health, the condition of their marriage, the overall good of their family, and their social and economic circumstances.[76] Our Church takes issue only with the *means* used to attain this good end. Whereas contraception subverts the person's natural power of fertility, by artificially rendering it impotent, natural family planning works with the natural cycles of fertility which the Church affirms as more conducive to human fulfillment. For example, by refusing to contracept, the couple preserves the sacred meaning of sex as both unitive and procreative, and the ideal of sex as a privileged opportunity for total self-gift—a complete gift of both body and soul—in which nothing whatsoever is intentionally withheld from one's spouse, not even one's fertility.

NFP also promotes the equal dignity of men and women, because both partners must abstain together rather than one spouse bearing the burden of contraception alone (typically the woman). In the case of hormonal contraception, that burden includes an increased risk of stroke, an increased risk of breast cancer, and a diminished sex drive. Another benefit: the abstinence portion of NFP (typically one week per month) helps couples to develop the virtue of chastity, which improves the quality of their subsequent sex acts. By helping them to acquire self-mastery, NFP empowers couples to treat each other in a way that is intentional and deeply personal rather than as animals driven by mere instinct, or worse as mere objects for one's self-gratification.

Importantly, the science of natural family planning has greatly advanced since the 1960s, when the rhythm method (also known as Vatican roulette) was the form of periodic abstinence practiced. Thanks to cutting-edge research, modern methods

---

76. See John Paul II, *Man and Woman He Created Them: A Theology of the Body* (2006, 125:3) and *Familiaris Consortio* (1981.30); Paul VI, *Humanae Vitae* (1968, nos. 10, 16); Second Vatican Council, *Gaudium et Spes: Pastoral Constitution on the Church in the Modern World* (1965.50); and Pius XII, *Address to the Seventh International Congress of Hematology in Rome* (1958) and *Letter to Italian Catholic Midwives* (1951).

of NFP (such as those taught at the Saint Paul VI Institute for the Study of Human Reproduction in Creighton, Nebraska and the Institute for Natural Family Planning at Marquette University) have a 98–99 percent effectiveness rate when used correctly, which is similar to both the birth control pill and condoms.[77] Consequently, a couple who chooses to practice NFP, rather than contracepting, does not necessarily forfeit anything in terms of practical effectiveness.

Third, the Church maintains that all human beings possess dignity, not just some human beings. Because human life begins at fertilization, and continues to develop after implantation, contraceptives that harm fertilized ova function as abortifacients, and thus are deemed particularly morally objectionable. For Catholic employers, subsidizing health insurance that funds abortifacients constitutes moral cooperation with evil; it is tantamount to giving someone money that might be used to get an abortion. Because children—even those still in the womb—are worthy of protection, abortion is considered a form of murder, and requiring people to cooperate financially in the murder of children is no small thing.

Fourth, the Church's opposition to contraception does not automatically translate into a lack of support for women's health. Birth control pills are morally permissible for therapeutic reasons, such as the need to regulate one's cycle or to treat endometriosis. Moreover, this permission is not new; it was codified in paragraph 15 of the Catholic Church's 1968 document *Humanae Vitae*. It also is deemed morally permissible, utilizing the principle of double effect, to remove a cancerous uterus while a woman is pregnant, or a fallopian tube in the case of an ectopic pregnancy, even though the death of the fetus occurs indirectly as a result. In addition, paragraph 36 of the U.S. Catholic Bishops' ERDs (*Ethical and Religious Directives for Catholic Health Care Services*) explicitly permits Catholic hospitals to treat rape victims with medications that would prevent pregnancy, as long as they can be reasonably certain that the patient is not already pregnant.[78]

The upshot of all of this is that it is possible *both* to protect women's health *and* to prevent unplanned pregnancies without a thoroughgoing commitment to free

---

77. For a scholarly study on the Marquette method (demonstrating 97–98 percent effectiveness when used correctly), see Fehring, Schneider, and Barron, "Efficacy of the Marquette Method of Natural Family Planning," 348–54. For a similar study on the Creighton method (demonstrating 99.6 percent effectiveness when used correctly), see Fehring, Lawrence, and Philpot, "Use Effectiveness of the Creighton Model Ovulation Method of Natural Family Planning," 303–9.

78. "Compassionate and understanding care should be given to a person who is the victim of sexual assault. Health care providers should cooperate with law enforcement officials and offer the person psychological and spiritual support as well as accurate medical information. A female who has been raped should be able to defend herself against a potential conception from the sexual assault. If, after appropriate testing, there is no evidence that conception has occurred already, she may be treated with medications that would prevent ovulation, sperm capacitation, or fertilization. It is not permissible, however, to initiate or to recommend treatments that have as their purpose or direct effect the removal, destruction, or interference with the implantation of a fertilized ovum" (USCCB, *Ethical and Religious Directives for Catholic Health Care Services*.36).

contraception, abortifacients, and sterilization even for non-therapeutic reasons. Consequently, the religious institutions who sued the federal government cannot be written off as having acted on the basis of *mere* religious reasons not amenable to rational discourse, which is why, thankfully, the new HHS guidelines are broad enough to accommodate some moral objections of a non-religious nature.

So where does this recent battle leave us? In my estimation, one overarching question remains: Who gets to decide what counts as a compelling public health or safety issue, compelling enough to restrict free exercise claims? Does the government need to make a rational argument to defend its positions? Are these arguments amenable to public debate? Do all three branches of government need to concur? Should religious organizations have a chance to make their case as well? Can the government always be trusted to act in the public good, regardless of whether there are Democrats or Republicans (or some combination of both) in power? Or does it depend on who speaks for the government at any given time?

I do not have an answer to the question of who gets to decide, but I worry about the lack of public debate. If an individual has a serious conscience-based disagreement with his or her church, or synagogue, or mosque, then he or she has the freedom to leave either the denomination or the religion. However, if an individual has a serious conscience-based disagreement with his or her government, then he or she does not possess the same freedom. Coercing individuals to act against their consciences, by requiring them to pay for ethically objectionable services—even indirectly—is harmful not only to those individuals, but arguably to the public good generally. One harm lies in the fact that when religions are forced indirectly to retreat from the public square, then non-believers who benefited from their schools, hospitals, and social service work will forfeit important goods.

But arguably, there is something even larger at stake here. By providing such a narrow exemption for religious employers, a "liberal" government ironically found itself in the position of acting in a decidedly "illiberal" fashion: violating the right to religious freedom by forcing non-exempt religious employers to act against their consciences. Prudentially, this was a big problem, because it placed government on a dangerous path: that of *establishing* a secular religion.

A state-established secular religion would be problematic for the same reasons that a state-established theistic religion is problematic. It sets up a society for conflict in the long run. For as history has taught us, when citizens in a pluralistic society are forced by their government to act against their most deeply held ethical commitments, violence tends to ensue. One of the most important rationales for disestablishment of state religion is to ensure peace.

Here I draw on the work of the twentieth-century Jesuit theologian and political philosopher, Fr. John Courtney Murray, who helped to draft *Dignitatis Humanae*. In his 1960 book, *We Hold These Truths: Catholic Reflections on the American Proposition*, Murray included a chapter titled, "Civil Unity and Religious Integrity:

The Articles of Peace." There he argued as follows: How are we to understand civil unity? As a unity of different communities, divided among themselves, and linked by public consensus. Civil society builds unity through dialogue and discussion, not through suppression and coercion. In Murray's words, "the pluralism remains as real as the unity."[79] He explains,

> The United States is a good place to live in; many have found it even a sort of secular sanctuary. But it is not a church, whether high, low, or broad. It is simply a civil community, whose unity is purely political, consisting in "agreement on the good of man at the level of performance without the necessity of agreement on ultimates." As regards important points of ultimate religious belief, the United States is pluralist.[80]

Given this pluralism, the two articles of the first amendment function as "articles of peace."[81] By permitting sufficient space for the free exercise of religion, the values and beliefs that divide us need not bring us to the brink of civil war.

According to Murray, this is the precise context that the American founders had in mind. They "were not radical theorists intent on constructing a society in accord with the *a priori* demands of a doctrinaire blueprint" but rather keen observers of "what was actually 'given' in history." Like all good lawmakers, they sought to preserve public peace under a set of particular conditions. They recognized that "social peace . . . is the highest integrating element of the common good" and that this peace can only be ensured "by equal justice in dealing with possibly conflicting groups."[82] They made the prudential judgment that privileging one worldview at the expense of others would be a form of injustice that would naturally inspire conflict among those who disagree.

Are the social conditions today as ripe for conflict as they were in 1789? Would a government-imposed secular religion, even in incipient form, sow the seeds of rebellion? The cautious response can only be "yes," for human nature has not dramatically changed in the past 230 years. As Elshtain asserts, we are fallen creatures who live out our human existence "in the *saeculum*, in the time between creation and the eschaton" and as such are not always pacific in our dealings with others.[83] She cites various "signs of the times" that seem to bear out Dietrich Bonhoeffer's vision of a social milieu in which "the beasts were always straining at their leashes, rattling their chains, and awaiting release upon a complacent and uncomprehending and perhaps even occasionally joyous world. And we are the beasts."[84]

79. Murray, *We Hold These Truths*, 45.

80. Murray, *We Hold These Truths*, 54. His quotation adopts a phrase from the 1945 *Harvard Report on General Education in a Free Society*.

81. Murray, *We Hold These Truths*, 56.

82. Murray, *We Hold These Truths*, 57–58.

83. Elshtain, *Who Are We?* 35.

84. Elshtain, *Who Are We?* 34.

In this context, even a seemingly innocuous government mandate, stemming from a genuinely good intention (to better the lives of women), ironically can end up stirring discord and social unrest. Forcing a comprehensive vision of how women's health ought to be construed on social groups who possess an alternate vision constitutes a small but nonetheless perilous step toward state establishment of a secular religion. Government reliance on coercion, rather than persuasion—even if done for a good reason—could very well threaten to unravel the delicate threads of our fragile civic order.

Elshtain proposes an alternative solution, one in which we work out such differences from the bottom-up rather than the top-down.

> The dialectic of normative commitments . . . should be . . . primarily a dialectic of citizens, variously located, through a culture of democratic argument: citizens engaging one another and sorting things out, as often they will, in a rather untidy, rough and ready way. . . . For it is likely to be true that an issue of religious and political importance that could be worked out informally becomes far more intractable if one group or another brings a test case seeking a controlling precedent. In such a circumstance, the battle lines harden; the dialectic is frozen before it even begins to unfold. . . . The best way to work this out is on the level of public deliberation and contestation rather than on the level of preemptive adjudication. Let a thousand arguments, dialogues, and debates bloom! The legal cases should be many fewer.[85]

And to that we can surely add: the occasions for civil unrest would be fewer as well.

In conclusion, perhaps by adopting this dual strategy—(1) recapitulating our theological defense of religious freedom, accompanied by a political argument that specifies the ongoing importance of religious freedom to democracy; and (2) defending our theological rationale for any controversial issues that arise through reasoned argument that is accessible to the general morality—Catholics can more effectively live out their gospel mission to be in the world but not of it. Furthermore, by so doing, we can work hand in hand with our Jewish brothers and sisters to preserve a public arena in which both our religious communities can flourish.

Bibliography

Alvaré, Helen. "Free Exercise/Non-Establishment Law and its Implications for the Church." Albert Cardinal Meyer Lecture Series, University of St. Mary of the Lake/Mundelein Seminary, March 19, 2019. https://usml.edu/event/the-albert-meyer-lecture-series-with-helen-alvare-esq/.

———. "No Compelling Interest: The 'Birth Control' Mandate and Religious Freedom." *Villanova Law Review* 58.3 (2013) 379–436.

---

85. Elshtain, "Freedom of Religion and the Rule of Law: A Response to Chief Justice McLachlin," 39–40.

Aquinas, Thomas. *Summa Theologiae*. Translated by Fathers of the English Dominican Province. Westminster, MD: Christian Classics, 1981.

Elshtain, Jean Bethke. *Augustine and the Limits of Politics*. Notre Dame, IN: University of Notre Dame Press, 1995.

———. "Freedom of Religion and the Rule of Law: A Response to Chief Justice McLachlin." In *Recognizing Religion in a Secular Society: Essays in Pluralism, Religion, and Public Policy*, edited by Douglas Farrow, 39–40. Montreal, Canada: McGill-Queen's University Press, 2004.

———. *Sovereignty: God, State, and Self: The Gifford Lectures*. New York: Basic, 2008.

———. *Who Are We? Critical Reflections and Hopeful Possibilities*. Grand Rapids: Eerdmans, 2000.

Fehring, Richard, Donna Lawrence, and Connie Philpot. "Use Effectiveness of the Creighton Model Ovulation Method of Natural Family Planning." *Journal of Obstetric, Gynecologic, and Neonatal Nursing* 23.4 (1994) 303–9.

Fehring, Richard, Mary Schneider, and Mary Lee Barron. "Efficacy of the Marquette Method of Natural Family Planning." *American Journal of Maternal Child Nursing* 33.6 (2008) 348–54.

HHS Press Office. "Trump Administration Issues Final Rules Protecting Conscience Rights in Health Insurance." HHS.gov. November 7, 2018. https://www.hhs.gov/about/news/2018/11/07/trump-administration-issues-final-rules-protecting-conscience-rights-in-health-insurance.html.

John Paul II. "Familiaris Consortio." *Libreria Editrice Vaticana*. November 22, 1981. http://www.vatican.va/content/john-paul-ii/en/apost_exhortations/documents/hf_jp-ii_exh_19811122_familiaris-consortio.html.

———. *Man and Woman He Created Them: A Theology of the Body*. Translated by Michael Waldstein. Boston: Pauline, 2006.

Murray, John Courtney. *We Hold These Truths: Catholic Reflections on the American Proposition*. New York: Sheed and Ward, 1960.

Novak, David. *Covenantal Rights: A Study in Jewish Political Theory*. Princeton: Princeton University Press, 2000.

———. *The Image of the Non-Jew in Judaism: The Idea of Noahide Law*. Littman Library of Jewish Civilization. Liverpool: Liverpool University Press, 2011.

———. *In Defense of Religious Liberty*. Wilmington, DE: ISI Books, 2009.

———. "Is Natural Law a Border Concept between Judaism and Christianity?" *Journal of Religious Ethics* 32.2 (2004) 237–54.

———. *Jewish Justice: The Contested Limits of Nature, Law, and Covenant*. Waco, TX: Baylor University Press, 2017.

———. "Natural Law and Judaism." In Anver M. Emon, Matthew Levering, and David Novak, *Natural Law: A Jewish, Christian, and Islamic Trialogue*. Oxford University Press, 2014.

———. *Natural Law in Judaism*. Cambridge: Cambridge University Press, 1998.

———. *Talking with Christians: Musings of a Jewish Theologian*. Grand Rapids: Eerdmans, 2005.

Paul VI. "Humanae Vitae." *Libreria Editrice Vaticana*. July 25, 1968. http://www.vatican.va/content/paul-vi/en/encyclicals/documents/hf_p-vi_enc_25071968_humanae-vitae.html.

Pius XII. "Address to the Participants of the Seventh International Congress of Hematology." *Libreria Editrice Vaticana.* September 12, 1958. https://www.vatican.va/content/pius-xii/fr/speeches/1958/documents/hf_p-xii_spe_19580912_ematologia.html.

———. *Letter to Italian Catholic Midwives.* October 29, 1951. https://www.vatican.va/content/pius-xii/es/speeches/1951/documents/hf_p-xii_spe_19511029_ostetriche.html.

Rashkover, Randi, and Martin Kavka, eds. *Tradition in the Public Square: A David Novak Reader.* Grand Rapids: Eerdmans, 2008.

Second Vatican Council. "Gaudium et Spes: Pastoral Constitution on the Church in the Modern World." *Libreria Editrice Vaticana.* December 7, 1965. http://www.vatican.va/archive/hist_councils/ii_vatican_council/documents/vat-ii_const_19651207_gaudium-et-spes_en.html.

United States Conference of Catholic Bishops (USCCB). *Ethical and Religious Directives for Catholic Health Care Services.* 5th ed. Washington, DC: United States Conference of Catholic Bishops, 2009.

Response to

Melanie Susan Barrett's "David Novak and Jewish Natural Law"

DAVID NOVAK

MY GRATITUDE GOES TO Melanie Susan Barrett for her careful and sympathetic reading of my theology, and I'm happy that some of it has been helpful to her in forging the task of both Christians and Jews to be "in the world but not of it." The "world" here is the secular political and cultural domain, where no warrant for any public policy can be drawn from any tradition grounded in divine revelation. Thus in Western democracies, no public policy warrant can be drawn from Judaism or Christianity per se. Most Jews and Christians can accept that in good faith, thereby avoiding three extreme positions, all of which Barrett is well aware, and against which she argues skillfully. Let me now show how much I have learned from her.

The first extreme position to be avoided is being *in the world as well as of it*. That is the position taken by many liberal Jews and Christians, who will their Judaism or Christianity to be confined to a "private" closet, thereby ceding any role in public policy making to "secularists," being those who regard their secularist ideology (especially when they are in positions of power) to be ultimately authoritative. These secularists have become "increasingly hostile to religion," because they cannot tolerate any competing authority in what they take to be "their" world.

The second extreme position to be avoided is being *neither in the world nor of it*. That is the extreme position taken by some Jews and some Christians. Among Christians one thinks of the Amish; among Jews one thinks of the Hasidim. This position has been called "sectarian." Its first problem is theological. Jews and Christians affirm that God has declared all that He has made is "good" (Gen 1:31). Doesn't that call into serious question, though, the sectarian abandonment of much of the world that is outside the confines of their religious communities? Sectarianism is also politically problematic insofar as it plays right into the hands of the very secularists who would drive all faithful Jews and Christians into a private closet, where the secularists hope these religious people will eventually wither away due to their losing more and more public oxygen. Like it or not, however, even sectarians are members of a secular society and cannot help being affected by its public policies. So, it is politically prudent that they be "in the world," if for no other reason than being proactive politically and even culturally, they are in a better position to affect pro-religious public policies more in general, and in a better position to defend themselves and others like them from anti-religious public policies.

The third extreme position to be avoided is termed "imperialist." One might say that for its proponents, Christians and Jews are to be *in the world so that the world be under their rule*. This position is problematic theologically, because, short of a religious *coup d'état*, its implementation would still require a secular polity to enforce public policies warranted by divine revelation. This position is also politically problematic insofar as it is essentially undemocratic, privileging citizens of one religion over citizens of other religions or those having no religion at all. Surely, even any hint of this position would play right into the hands of secularists who often declare that any public policy proposed or even endorsed by Christians or Jews (and now by Muslims too), however philosophical it might appear, is still directly derived from theological, revelation-based premises nonetheless. Undoubtedly aware of this secularist reductionism, as a Catholic thinker, Barrett is wise to not argue for the pre-Vatican II position that the Church has moral authority even in secular societies.

Barrett adopts my criteria for a Jewish public philosophy, understanding that they provide a valid *modus operandi* for Catholics as well. As we shall see, employing them helps all of us avoid the extreme positions just mentioned above, which are so problematic. These criteria are that any public policy proposed should be (1) theologically grounded; (2) useful to the community of its proponents; (3) in general morally effective. All of the three extreme positions cited above fall short according to some or all of these criteria.

The first position, i.e., the liberal one, seems to fall short according to all three criteria. (1) Even when some liberals claim their public policy advocacy is "religiously inspired," they are usually at a loss to explain exactly where in their tradition there is any definite warrant for public practices like abortion or euthanasia, which they argue for based on reasons any secularist could employ more easily and more genuinely. (2) Usually claiming to have left their allegiance to the interest of any specific traditional community out of their employment of "public reason," their advocacy of the morality of their own cultural and economic class makes their claims of being "universalistic" or "global" quite hollow nevertheless. (3) A public policy can only be generally effective if it is argued for philosophically, not just ideologically. However, most liberals are as suspicious of classical philosophy as they are of classical theology (with its talk of a direct God-human relationship). Now classical philosophy has an idea of human nature that is both rational and political. Since any such idea of human nature (let alone cosmic nature) is metaphysical, a viewpoint that goes against the modern liberal notion that humans make their own condition autonomously, liberals usually argue for their "progressive" public policies on what they think human reality ought to be ideally (i.e., the projection of their ideology) rather than on what it actually is. Instead of employing rational arguments against their non-liberal opponents, too many liberals dogmatically dismiss them as being too "retrograde" to be engaged rationally.

The second position, i.e., the sectarian one, is strongest according to the first criterion. (1) There is plenty in both the Christian and Jewish traditions that engenders suspicion of any political regime whose warrant is not received directly from divine revelation. But the fact that "render unto Caesar what is Caesar's" is not only a Christian notion, but also has a parallel in the Jewish tradition (viz., the law of a legitimate polity is morally binding on Jews living there), makes sectarian rejections of their opponents within their own communities as heretics or quasi-heretics highly objectionable. (2) Often sectarian arguments, made in the interest of their own community, do not consider whether what they are advocating can be shown to be in the general interest of their secular society too. Due to this kind of political myopia, sectarians often alienate other members of their democratic society, whose support (or at least not their opposition) they need to be politically effective. Too many Christians, and even some Jews, although not themselves officially "sectarian," still adopt this sectarian approach, thus turning themselves into one more "special interest group" of whom more and more citizens of democracies are becoming increasingly suspicious. (3) Since most sectarians, like secularists (ironically) eschew any philosophically formulated idea of universal human nature whereby they might persuade those outside their tradition, they thereby eschew any authentically philosophical argumentation for their public policies. And that is the case even though their own traditions have ample resources for such public philosophical argumentation.

The third position, i.e., the imperialist (or "triumphalist") one, has Christian and Jewish proponents. (1) There are sources in both the Christian tradition and the Jewish tradition teaching that possessing divine revelation therefore gives the community governed by that revelation and its accompanying tradition the right to impose what it regards as binding on all human beings on whomever it has political power over. However, neither Christianity nor Judaism has such political power over anybody in the world today. As such, this position is questionable both theologically and politically. Theologically, it seems to equate earthly power with the Kingdom of God. Politically, it turns everybody outside the confines of one's own community, and who are unwilling to live in such a subordinate role, into enemies. (2) This is hardly useful to the survival and the best interest of traditional religious communities in democratic societies. (3) Due to the use of arguments from authority, which are philosophically repugnant, proponents of this kind of imperialism alienate all rational people, even those within their own communities. And even when these religious imperialists try to make arguments that sound rational, they make them so badly that they come across as disingenuous rationalizations or shallow apologetics for public policies that could be much better argued for by those who reject this irrational imperialist mindset.

Barrett makes convincing arguments for why her Catholic approach to public policy questions accords with all three criteria discussed above. (1) It is certainly well grounded in the Catholic tradition (which, being scripturally rooted, has much in common with the Jewish tradition). (2) It is in the best interest of the Catholic community to promote the duty to "be fruitful and multiply" (Gen. 9:7) since the community is certainly enhanced by fecund families. (3) However, although I understand Barrett's Catholic argument against artificial birth control, it is not easy to argue for it as a rationally evident (*ratio quoad nos*) natural law precept. Many natural law proponents (even a number of Catholics) see this prohibition as more theological than philosophical, i.e., something the Church can require of the faithful only. That is why I think Barrett would be better advised to have chosen the prohibition of abortion as her prime case. In a moral climate where rights-talk is ubiquitous, it is easier to argue that nobody has the right to kill (except in self-defense) than anybody has the right to kill their offspring or somebody else's offspring (even if done with the consent of the parents).

In this well-argued essay, by adopting and adapting my approach to questions of public policy in democratic societies, Melanie Barrett has helped me understand it better. I do hope that by learning from a thinker of her caliber, my approach might actually be improved, thus making it more theologically cogent, more useful politically, and more rationally persuasive.

Chapter 2

A Christian Account of Why David Novak Is Right about the Same-God Question

FRANCIS J. BECKWITH

> Ring them bells Sweet Martha for the poor man's son
> Ring them bells so the world will know that God is one
> Oh the shepherd is asleep
> Where the willows weep
> And the mountains are filled with lost sheep
>
> —BOB DYLAN (A.K.A. ROBERT ZIMMERMAN) (1989)[1]

DO JEWS AND CHRISTIANS worship the same God? Over the years, David Novak has addressed this question from a Jewish perspective in various venues,[2] most prominently on September 10, 2000 in a full-page advertisement in the *New York Times*. Drafted by Novak and three other scholars, and signed by over 150 rabbis, the document, "*Dabru Emet* (Speak the Truth) A Jewish statement on Christians and Christianity,"[3] affirmed, among other things, that "Jews and Christians worship the same God."[4] The document offers this explanation: "Before the rise of Christianity, Jews were the only worshippers of the God of Israel. But Christians also worship the God of Abraham, Isaac, and Jacob, Creator of heaven and earth. While Christian worship is not a viable religious choice for Jews, as Jewish theologians we rejoice that, through Christianity, hundreds of millions of people have entered into relationship with the God of Israel."[5]

---

1. Dylan, "Ring Them Bells."

2. See, e.g., Novak, "Because of What God Has Done," 22–23; Novak, "Supersessionism Hard and Soft," 27–31; Novak, "The Jewish Mission," 39–43; Novak, "Les Juifs et les chretiens reverent-ils le meme Dieu?" 95–132.

3. It was republished, with only a partial list of signatories, in the periodical, *First Things*, November 2000, 39–41.

4. Brownfeld, "Jews Are Called Upon to Reassess Their Views of Christianity."

5. "*Dabru Emet*," *First Things*, 40.

In a 2003 article published in the French language, Novak suggests that Christians who reject the same God thesis have appropriated reasoning similar to that which gave rise to the Marcionite heresy, the view embraced by followers of the second-century Christian, Marcion.[6] The Marcionites "rejected the writings of the Old Testament and taught that Christ was not the Son of the God of the Jews, but the Son of the good God, who was different from the God of the Ancient Covenant."[7] Although, as Novak rightly notes, "nowadays many Christians totally repudiate Marcionist-type Gnosticism,"[8] there are many learned Christians—especially among Evangelical Protestants—who nevertheless reject the idea that Christians and Jews worship the same God. Their reasoning, though not technically Marcionite insofar as distinguishing an Old Testament "God" from a New Testament "God," relies on Marcionite reflexes when its champions argue that the God of post-Christian Judaism is not the God of Christianity. In this chapter, I argue that this view is mistaken, that Christians ought to believe that they worship the same God as Jews worship. Since the case I make requires (or so I will argue) that the Christian must also believe that she worships the same God as Muslims worship, I mention all three faith traditions. I should note, however, that I am writing only to persuade my fellow Christians. I am not addressing my remarks to Jews and Muslims. For that reason, much of what follows appeals to authorities and arguments that I believe Christians should find compelling.

Christians and the Same God Question

Wheaton College is an Evangelical school in suburban Chicago, founded in the nineteenth century by Protestant Christian abolitionists. In December 2015 the institution became embroiled in a very public controversy. It had put on administrative leave Larycia Hawkins, one of its political science professors, who had written these words on her Facebook wall: "I stand in *religious solidarity* with Muslims because they, like me, a Christian, are people of the book. And as Pope Francis stated last week, we worship the same God."[9] According to the school, Hawkins's statement was inconsistent with the set of theological beliefs that all of Wheaton's faculty members are contractually required to affirm. These beliefs include the doctrines of the Trinity and the incarnation, both of which are denied by Islam, and both of which are essential to Christianity. So, the administration reasoned, if Professor Hawkins says that Muslims and Christians worship the same God, then it must be the case that she is either denying (explicitly or implicitly) the veracity of beliefs essential to the Christian faith or she does not understand the school's doctrinal positions well

---

6. Novak, "Les Juifs et les chretiens reverent-ils le meme Dieu?" 105.

7. Arendzen, "Marcionites."

8. Novak, "Les Juifs et les chretiens reverent-ils le meme Dieu?" 105 (my translation). (Original: "de nos jours, de nombreux Chrétiens répudient profondément le gnosticisme de type marcioniste.")

9. See Graham, "The Professor Wore a Hijab in Solidarity—Then Lost Her Job."

enough to assent to them in good conscience.[10] Either way, she is not theologically fit to remain on the faculty at Wheaton.

Although I took the side of Professor Hawkins,[11] and still believe that her position is the correct one,[12] answering "yes" to the question of whether Muslims and Christians (and Jews) worship the same God need not entail a sappy-squishy-Kumbaya-around-the-campfire interreligious ecumenism, which I suspect is what Wheaton feared would be the inevitable long-term result of not disciplining Professor Hawkins when there still remained a critical mass at the college who harbored real doctrinal convictions. Wheaton was not yet prepared to install Professor Hawkins as the John Lennon Chair in Nothing to Kill or Die For and No Religion Too.

Similar concerns seem to motivate some Christian writers who argue that Jews and Christians do not worship the same God. For example, Evangelical philosopher and literary scholar, Lydia McGrew, argues that "in one sense Christians and modern religious Jews worship the same God; in another sense they don't. Old Testament Jews, of course, didn't reject the Trinity and the incarnation, since those doctrines hadn't been revealed. If one emphatically rejects these truths about God, however, and explicitly worships God as non-triune and non-incarnate, then this makes a pretty good case that, in one sense, such a person does not worship the same God whom Christians worship."[13] This leads McGrew to the seemingly odd conclusion that modern Christians worship the God of the ancient Jews, but modern Jews don't.[14] Another Evangelical philosopher, Jerry Walls, holds a similar view.[15] Relying on a theory of reference defended by philosopher Gareth Evans,[16] Walls argues that the distinctly Christian doctrines of divine tri-unity and the incarnation are so central to our idea of the Christian God that to claim that one is worshipping the one true God minus those doctrines is no different than claiming that the term "Saint Nick" refers to both the historical Saint Nicholas and the fictional Santa Claus. Just

---

10. That encapsulates the reasoning implied by several pointed questions addressed to Professor Larycia Hawkins by then-Wheaton provost, Stanton L. Jones, in a December 15, 2015 memo (on file with author).

11. Beckwith, "Do Muslims and Christians Worship the Same God?"; and Beckwith, "Why Muslims and Christians Worship the Same God."

12. See, e.g., Beckwith, "All Worship the Same God: Referring to the Same God"; and Beckwith, *Never Doubt Thomas*, chapter 3.

13. McGrew, "The 'Same God' Debate Is Too Important to Leave to Philosophers."

14. McGrew writes: "In another sense, however, Christians can say to modern religious Jews: [']The true God who called your forefathers out of the land of Egypt, who gave the law at Sinai, who chose you as his beloved, chosen people, really is the one who sent Yeshua the Messiah to die for our sins. We worship the God who really did found Judaism thousands of years ago, who really did give the Torah. And we are here to tell you more about him.[']" McGrew, "The 'Same God' Debate."

15. Walls, "None Worship the Same God: Different Conceptions View."

16. Walls champions Evans's view as it is presented by Tomas Bogardus and Mallorie Urban in their article, "How to Tell Whether Christians and Muslims Worship the Same God." Bogardus and Urban cite two works by Gareth Evans: "The Causal Theory of Names"; and *The Varieties of Reference*.

as the fictionalizing of the historical Saint Nicholas over time resulted in a reference shift—what we refer to as "Santa Claus" is not the real figure from which the fictional one emerged—the acceptance by Christians of both the New Testament and creedal revelatory claims about God's tri-unity and incarnation means that when Christians refer to God they are not referring to the figure to which Muslims and Jews refer when they claim to be worshipping God.

Although I think that Wheaton College and Professors McGrew and Walls answer the same God question in the wrong way, their concerns about the theological integrity of their faith tradition should not be gainsaid, just as it should not be for non-Christians like Novak who give an opposite answer to the same God question while rightfully guarding what they believe are theological truths that cannot be compromised without courting apostasy.[17] For this reason, in what follows, my affirmative answer to the same God question tries to avoid two extremes: the sort of reasoning that gave rise to the Marcionite heresy and the relativist reflexes that underwrite the hope of some for a woke confessional church.

Sense and Reference

One way to show it is *at least possible* that the Christian, Jewish, and Muslim faiths refer to the same God, despite their differences, is to make a distinction between sense and reference. Consider these examples.

Imagine two fraternal twins, Tony and Tessy. They are separated at birth. Tony continues to live with their mother, Ruby, while Tessy is adopted by their uncle, Joe. The reason for this arrangement is that their father, Simon, abandons them in their infancy. When they reach the age of fifteen, Tony and Tessy are told that they are not really cousins, but brother and sister. Unsurprisingly, each wants to know more about their father, Simon. Joe, Simon's brother, tells Tessy that her father was a wonderful man, but that he had to move to a faraway country and change identities because he was a CIA agent who could not remain with them without endangering his family. Ruby, on the other hand, tells Tony that his father was a risk taker who changed his name and abandoned them for a life of international travel in order to rid himself of the burden of caring for a wife and children. Tessy concludes that her father was a hero, while Tony concludes that his father was a cad. Tony and Tessy know they are referring to the same person, even though they have different senses about him. St. Thomas Aquinas seems to imply this sense/reference distinction when he writes that "to know that someone is approaching is not the same as to know that Peter

---

17. "Aucun tribunal juif ne pourrait accepter qu'un chrétien demande de se convertir au judaïsme [giyyour] sans qu'il renie le Christ. De même, la conversion d'un Juif au christianisme est plus que de l'hérésie ; c'est de l'apostasie [shemad]." Novak, "Les Juifs et les chretiens reverent-ils le meme Dieu?" 127. Translation: "No Jewish tribunal could accept a Christian who requests to convert to Judaism ... without denying Christ. Likewise, the conversion of a Jew to Christianity is more than heresy; it is apostasy. . . ." (my translation).

is approaching, even though it is Peter who is approaching."[18] In other words, two people, like Tony and Tessy, can have the same reference—"that man who is approaching" (or "that man is my father")—though one may have the sense that it is Peter (or a hero) while the other may have the sense that it is Judas (or a cad).

Pat takes a constitutional every morning. When he looks up in the sky on a clear day he never fails to see *the morning star*. Pat's wife, Liz, takes her constitutional every evening. When she looks up in the sky on a clear day she never fails to see *the evening star*. At dinner they sometimes discuss their astronomical observations, with both believing that the morning star and the evening star are two different objects with two different sets of properties (much like their dogs, Blackie and Rebel). It turns out, however, the morning star and the evening star are not two different stars, but one planet, Venus. Pat and Liz not only have different senses of the same thing, but unlike Tony and Tessy, they do not know that they are referring to the same thing.

The comic book character Superman is the alter ego of *The Daily Planet* reporter Clark Kent. Superman, whose given name is Kal-El, is not a human being. He is a child of the planet Krypton, sent to earth by his parents, moments before the planet's destruction. Superman's girlfriend is Lois Lane. Clark's girlfriend is Lana Lang. Lois believes her boyfriend is a non-human with superpowers, while Lana believes her boyfriend is an ordinary human being. When talking to others about Superman and Clark, Lois and Lana think they are referring to two different beings, when in fact they are referring to the same being, Kal-El.

Tom is a big fan of YouTube boxing videos. Over the past couple of years he has become enamored with the 1960s fighter, Cassius Clay. In the midst of telling you about Clay's May 1965 first round knockout of Sonny Liston, Tom asks, "Whatever happened to Clay?" For some reason, Tom does not realize that Clay changed his name to Muhammed Ali and continued to fight until 1981. Until you tell him the truth, Tom will continue to believe that Clay and Ali are two different fighters.

We can see in each of these cases the distinction between sense and reference. In the first, Tony and Tessy have different senses about what they know is the same thing, their father Simon. In the other cases, the senses are so disparate that the parties involved—Pat, Liz, Lois, Lana, Tom—come to believe that they are talking about two different things—morning star/evening star, Superman/Clark, Clay/Ali—rather than one thing. For our present purposes, the point of these illustrations is simply to show that it is possible that contrary senses of the same thing can still have the same reference, even when those who harbor these senses do not know (or believe) they are referring to the same thing. However, the reason why we can see this is because we *know* that the morning and evening stars are the planet Venus, that Superman and Clark are Kal-El, and that Muhammed Ali is Cassius Clay's Muslim name. With the same God question it's a bit more tricky, since we can't secure the reference to God *in the same way* we can secure the references to Venus, Kal-El, and The Greatest. This

---

18. Aquinas, *Summa Theologica* I, q. 2, a. 1, ad. 1. (*ST*, hereafter.)

is because God—as understood by Christians, Muslims, and Jews—is not a creature *in the* universe, but the one and only being with underived existence on which the universe depends and who discloses himself in a variety of different ways, such as mystical experience, general revelation, and Sacred Scripture. In what follows is a way to secure this reference to God while at the same time accounting for disagreements between Christians, Muslims, and Jews about that God.

Securing the Reference to God

Ahmed, Benjamin, Cecilia, and the Preambles of Faith

In Fall 2018 Ahmed, Benjamin, and Cecilia were freshmen at the University of Nevada, Las Vegas (UNLV), where they were all enrolled in Dr. Gray Matter's Philosophy of Atheism course. Each arrived on campus as a religious believer: Ahmed was Muslim, Benjamin was Jewish, and Cecilia was Christian. But after taking Dr. Matter's class they became atheists. In Spring 2019, another UNLV philosopher, Dr. Sophia Mind, caught wind of this. Convinced that Ahmed, Benjamin, and Cecilia had not carefully thought through their conversions to unbelief, Dr. Mind invites each of them to take from her during the upcoming summer session a special independent study course on the rationality of belief in God. In the course, Dr. Mind exposes the three students to a rigorous examination of the arguments for God's existence in the works of the Muslim philosopher Avicenna (980–1037),[19] the Jewish philosopher Moses Maimonides (1135–1204),[20] and the Christian philosopher St. Thomas Aquinas (1225–74).[21] After completing the course, each student comes to Dr. Mind individually to confess that he or she now believes in God. Ahmed admits he found Maimonides's argument convincing. Benjamin explains why he was persuaded by Avicenna's case. And Cecilia concedes that she was moved to belief by Aquinas's reasoning. What Dr. Mind finds fascinating is that each of them believes virtually the same things about the nature of God: He is *the one, uncaused, perfect, unchanging, self-subsistent, eternal Creator and Sustainer of all that which receives its being from another*. (To clarify, any being "which receives its being from another," like you, me, the toaster, or the planet Venus, only exists because another existing thing[s] caused it to be and/or keeps it in existence.) At this point, none of the former atheists identifies with his or her prior faith, but simply believes, as a consequence of rational argument, that God exists. You can say that Ahmed, Benjamin, and Cecilia are now *mere theists*. You can also say, on Aquinas's understanding of faith and reason, that they

---

19. Avicenna, *The Metaphysics of the Healing*.
20. Moses Maimonides, *The Guide for the Perplexed*.
21. Aquinas, *On Being and Essence*.

now know one of the *preambles of faith*, those beliefs that "are a necessary presupposition to matters of faith" that one *may know* by means of reason.[22]

Ahmed, Benjamin, and Cecilia go on to tell Dr. Mind that there can in principle be only one God. For if there were "two Gods," they would have to differ in some way, and if two beings of the same kind (or genus) differ in some way, one must have what the other lacks and vice versa, and there must be a cause to account for that difference. But this cannot be true of God, who is unchanging, perfect, uncaused, and the source of all contingent being. For this reason, God is not one in the sense that He is one of a kind, like the last Dodo Bird was one of a kind. Rather, He is one in the sense that He is that which is metaphysically ultimate and has underived existence, the Creator and Source of all kinds that by their nature require a cause to account for their existence. Because, as Novak points out, "[i]n the primordial sense, the logic of strict monotheism requires that God be apprehended as the One who is uniquely 'without limit'";[23] to think otherwise would be to acquiesce to the logic of polytheism, "where each god's power is limited by the power of some other god with whom he or she has to exist."[24]

What's more, because God has underived existence, it means that it is God's nature to exist. But this is not true of any creatures, since they are brought into and kept in existence by things external to their being. Thus, if it were not God's nature to exist, then He too would require an external cause to account for His existence. But this would mean, as Aquinas notes, that God would be "a being by participation,"[25] and thus would not be that which is metaphysically ultimate and has underived existence. "He will not therefore be the first being—which is absurd. Therefore God is His own existence."[26]

At this point it seems uncontroversial to say that the former Muslim, Ahmed, the former Jew, Benjamin, and the former Christian, Cecilia, all ex-atheists, are now theists who *believe in the same God*. To employ concepts we learned in section II, Ahmed, Benjamin, and Cecilia are using the term "God" with the same reference and in the same sense.

But Ahmed, Benjamin, and Cecilia are not satisfied by the philosophical sterility of *mere theism*. Even though they are convinced that God exists, they long for spiritual depth and meaning in their lives. For this reason, each begins a yearlong intensive examination of the three great Abrahamic faiths, carefully studying their scriptural, historical, apologetical, and ethical claims as well as observing their various liturgical and devotional practices. At the end of the year, Ahmed, the former

---

22. *ST* I-II, q. 1, a. 5, ad. 3. Here is the quotation from Aquinas in its context: "Things which can be proved by demonstration are reckoned among the articles of faith, not because they are believed simply by all, but because they are a necessary presupposition to matters of faith, so that those who do not know them by demonstration must know them first of all by faith" (*ST* I-II, q. 1, a. 5, ad. 3).

23. Novak, *Covenantal Rights*, 38.

24. Novak, *Covenantal Rights*, 38.

25. *ST* I, q. 3, a. 4, *resp.*

26. *ST* I, q. 3, a. 4, *resp.*

Muslim, becomes a Christian, Benjamin, the former Jew, becomes a Muslim, and Cecilia, the former Christian, becomes a Jew. Together they visit Dr. Mind to tell her of their newfound faiths. Curious about their conversions, Dr. Mind asks them: "Do you each still believe that God is the one, uncaused, perfect, unchanging, self-subsistent, eternal Creator and Sustainer of all that which receives its being from another?" In almost perfect unison, they answer, yes. [27] "So," Dr. Mind continues, "you continue to believe that God is *He who is metaphysically ultimate and has underived existence*." The three UNLV students nod their heads. "But," Dr. Mind asks, "surely, given your new beliefs, you do have different ideas about God and His actions in history, don't you?" Again, they answer, yes. Ahmed explains that as a Christian he now believes that God has specially revealed through the New Testament and Church tradition that God is a Trinity and that Jesus is the Son of God. Benjamin candidly admits his disagreement with Ahmed, for as a Muslim he accepts the authority of the Qur'an, which affirms: "[God] begetteth not nor was begotten" and "It befitteth not (the Majesty of) Allah that He should take unto Himself a son."[28] Cecilia says that as a Jew she is now required to reject the authority of both the Christian and Islamic sources of revelation, though she agrees with the Muslim Benjamin that beliefs in the Trinity and Jesus's divine sonship are mistaken. Dr. Mind interrupts, "Is it then fair to say that each of you now believes that you know more about God than when you were mere theists?" They answer, yes. When she then asks them, "But do you know less?" they reply with an emphatic NO. To use the language of Aquinas, when the three UNLV students were mere theists they held to one of the preambles of faith—"the existence of God and other like truths about God"[29]—and thus they all believed in the same God: the one, uncaused, perfect, unchanging, self-subsistent, eternal Creator and Sustainer of all that which receives its being from another. But when they converted to Christianity, Islam, and Judaism respectively, Ahmed, Benjamin, and Cecilia did not abandon that understanding of the true and living God. They merely assented to more beliefs about God and salvation history that were not contrary to what they had believed as mere theists. So, it seems that the Christian Ahmed, the Muslim Benjamin, and the Jewish Cecilia, when speaking of God, are referring to the same God, even though they have different senses about God.

---

27. "Hear, O Israel: the Lord our God, the Lord is one" (Deut 6:4; JPS); "I believe in one God, the Father almighty, maker of heaven and earth, of all things visible and invisible" (United States Conference of Catholic Bishops, "What We Believe,"); "He is God: there is no god other than Him. It is He who knows what is hidden as well as what is in the open, He is the Lord of Mercy, the Giver of Mercy. He is God: there is no god other than Him, the Controller, the Holy One, Source of Peace, Granter of Security, Guardian over all, the Almighty, the Compeller, the Truly Great; God is far above anything they consider to be His partner. He is God: the Creator, the Originator, the Shaper. The best names belong to Him. Everything in the heavens and earth glorifies Him: He is the Almighty, the Wise" (Qur'an Al-Hashr 59:22–24).

28. Qur'an 112:3; 19:35, as quoted in *The Meaning of the Glorious Koran*, 454, 223.

29. *ST* I, q. 2, a. 2, ad 1.

The Project of Contemporary Christian Apologetics

Since the mid-twentieth century, there has been a renaissance of Christian apologetics, mostly, though not exclusively, among Protestants who identify as Evangelical.[30] (Ironically, C. S. Lewis, a traditional Anglican, is the writer often credited as being the most influential figure in launching this renaissance.) As far as the same God question goes, the most dominant methodology found in this apologetic literature should lead one to an affirmative answer. To see why, let us consider the works of several leading Christian apologists.

In his book, *Reasonable Faith*, Evangelical philosopher William Lane Craig makes a case for the truth of Christian theism. After addressing the relationship between faith and reason and then arguing for the absurdity of life without God, in the next two chapters he defends the rationality of belief in God. One of the arguments he offers is the *kalām* cosmological argument,[31] whose proponents include the Muslim philosopher Al-Ghazali (1058–1111).[32] Craig concludes that the argument shows that "a personal Creator of the universe exists, who is uncaused, beginningless, changeless, immaterial, timeless, spaceless, and unimaginably powerful. This, as Thomas Aquinas was wont to remark, is what everybody means by 'God.'"[33] Following his two chapters on God's existence Craig then moves on to defend the possibility of both historical knowledge and miraculous events as well as the reality of both Jesus's self-understanding as divine and the historicity of his resurrection.

Now suppose we had a time machine and we could transport Ghazali to the year 2019, give him an Arabic translation of *Reasonable Faith*, and ask him to read it. It is not difficult to imagine after reading Craig's book he would tell us that he is delighted that Craig has published a powerful rendition of his *kalām* argument. But, as a good Muslim, Ghazali would likely go on to say something like the following: "Although I agree with Craig that my argument establishes that 'a personal Creator of the universe exists, who is uncaused, beginningless, changeless, immaterial, timeless, spaceless, and unimaginably powerful,' I think that Craig is mistaken about Jesus's divinity and resurrection." Consequently, it cannot be the case that Ghazali and Craig—and by default Muslims, Christians, and Jews—are *not* referring to the same God, though each believes different things about that one God and his revelation in history. (Ironically, Craig does not once in his book offer a defense of God's tri-unity, even though the book's subtitle is *Christian Truth and Apologetics*).

Craig's apologetic procedure is fairly typical among Christian thinkers. In Mere Christianity Lewis first introduces the reader to the concept of the one true God by way of the moral law, distinguishing that concept from the God of pantheism and

---

30. See Dulles, *A History of Apologetics*, 325–67; Dulles, "The Rebirth of Apologetics."
31. Craig, *Reasonable Faith*, 111–56.
32. See Craig, *The* Kalām *Cosmological Argument*, 42–49.
33. Craig, *Reasonable Faith*, 154.

calling it the view "held by Jews, Mohammedans and Christians."[34] Lewis identifies this God as the one who "made the world—that space and time, heat and cold, and all the colours and tastes, and all the animals and vegetables, are things that God 'made up out of His head' as a man makes up a story." [35] It is only later in *Mere Christianity* that Lewis explains to the reader the idea of Jesus as divine and the doctrine of the Trinity.[36] J. P. Moreland, in his *Scaling the Secular City*, spends considerable space defending the existence of God before moving on to distinctly Christian concerns, including the historicity of the New Testament and the resurrection of Jesus.[37] At the end of his chapter on cosmological arguments for God's existence, Moreland concludes that "it is most reasonable to believe that the universe had a beginning which was caused by a timeless, immutable agent[,] . . . that the world had its beginning by the act of a person."[38] And like Craig, Moreland does not offer a defense of the Trinity. One finds similar treatments in the works of Stuart C. Hackett (*The Reconstruction of the Christian Revelation Claim*) and Norman L. Geisler (*Christian Apologetics*). Prior to offering direct defenses of Christian claims about Christ and Scripture, Hackett and Geisler each establishes the existence of God. Hackett defines "God as an absolutely necessary Being, characterized by personal intelligent will, and constituting essential or absolute Goodness—a Being, furthermore, whose relation to the contingent world order . . . is that of creative Causality, sustaining Ground, and providential Direction, while at the same time this Being transcends in existence and nature that world order of which it is thus the ultimate foundation."[39] Geisler, an Evangelical Thomist, maintains that if Aquinas's principle of existential causality is sound, then there must exist an Uncaused Cause who is "Infinite, Unchanging, All-Powerful, All-Knowing, and All-Perfect."[40] The great Reformed Christian philosopher, Alvin Plantinga (*Warranted Christian Belief*), though not including natural theology as part of his case for Christian belief as one finds in thinkers like Craig, Lewis, Moreland, Hackett, and Geisler, nevertheless argues, following John Calvin, that God has implanted in human beings a *sensus divinitatis*, "a disposition or set of dispositions to form theistic beliefs in various circumstances, in response to the sorts of conditions or stimuli that trigger the working of this sense of divinity."[41] So, for example, "you see the blazing glory of the heavens from a mountainside at 13,000 feet; you think about those unimaginable distances; you find yourself filled with awe and wonder, and you form the belief that God must be

---

34. Lewis, *Mere Christianity*, 24.

35. Lewis, *Mere Christianity*, 26.

36. Lewis, *Mere Christianity*, 32–37, 84–97. Lewis does mention in the preface the Christian belief "there is one God and that Jesus Christ is His only Son," but he does so just to introduce the reader to the book.

37. Moreland, *Scaling the Secular City*, 15–132.

38. Moreland, *Scaling the Secular City*, 132.

39. Hackett, *The Reconstruction of the Christian Revelation Claim*, 87.

40. Geisler, *Christian Apologetics*, 247 (italics removed).

41. Plantinga, *Warranted Christian Belief*, 173.

great to have created this magnificent heavenly host."[42] This God, according to Plantinga, is "the all-powerful, all-knowing creator of the universe . . . with properties of being infinite, transcendent, and ultimate."[43] Plantinga calls this the "theistic component" of Christian belief, distinguishing it from "the uniquely Christian component," which includes such doctrines as Jesus's resurrection and his divine sonship.[44]

If the arguments for God's existence offered by Craig, Lewis, Moreland, Hackett, and Geisler could be accepted by a devout Jew or Muslim, and if Plantinga is right that God has implanted in human beings a *sensus divinitatis* that under the appropriate conditions triggers belief in the same God that may be arrived at by the arguments of natural theology, then it seems that Christians, Jews, and Muslims worship the same God, even if they disagree over what Plantinga calls the "unique Christian component." Thus, by first securing the reference to God, the Christian apologist establishes that Christians, Jews, and Muslims share the same understanding of what constitutes a divine nature, despite the fact that their beliefs diverge as a result of what each group accepts (or rejects) as specially revealed truths about God found in its inspired scripture (or the other groups' inspired scripture).

Moses, Paul, and Athanasius

Christianity, Judaism, and Islam believe that Moses encountered God in the burning bush on Mt. Horeb.[45] The book of Exodus records their exchange: "Then Moses said to God, 'If I come to the people of Israel and say to them, "The God of your fathers has sent me to you," and they ask me, "What is his name?" what shall I say to them?' God said to Moses, 'I am who I am.' And he said, 'Say this to the people of Israel, "I am has sent me to you"'" (Exod 3:13–14). Christians, following Maimonides,[46] have traditionally interpreted God's name—"I am who I am"—as a description of His ontological status:[47] He is the fullness of being, the self-existent One, the metaphysically ultimate and underived Source of everything that receives its being from another.[48] As Aquinas notes: "God is the first being, with nothing prior to Him. His essence is, therefore, His being. This sublime truth Moses was taught by our Lord. When Moses asked our Lord: 'If the children of Israel say to me: what is His name? What shall I say to them?' The Lord replied: 'I AM WHO AM [. . . .]' By this our Lord showed that His own proper

---

42. Plantinga, *Warranted Christian Belief*, 173.
43. Plantinga, *Warranted Christian Belief*, 4.
44. Plantinga, *Warranted Christian Belief*, vii.
45. For the Qur'an's account of Moses at the burning bush, see Qur'an, Ta-Ha 20.
46. Maimonides, *The Guide for the Perplexed*, I, 63.
47. See, e.g., St. Jerome, "Letter 15" (ca. 376); St. Augustine, *On the Trinity* (400–428) 5.2; and Aquinas, *Summa Contra Gentiles* 1.22.10.
48. See Levering, *Scripture and Metaphysics*, chapter 2; and Pelikan, *The Emergence of the Catholic Tradition (100–600)*, 54; Gilson, *The Christian Philosophy of St. Thomas Aquinas*, 94.

name is HE WHO IS. Now, names have been devised to signify the natures or essences of things. It remains, then, that the divine being is God's essence or nature."[49]

In John 8:58, as Christians have traditionally read this passage,[50] Jesus reveals himself as the self-existent one in the burning bush who conversed with Moses: "Jesus said to them, 'Very truly, I tell you, before Abraham was, *I am*'" (emphasis added). But, of course, God did not disclose to Moses that He was Father, Son, and Holy Spirit, for this would have to wait until the writing and dissemination of the New Testament and the establishment of an ecclesiastical council, the Council of Constantinople (AD 381),[51] that would issue an authoritative pronouncement on the matter. (It goes without saying that Judaism rejects trinitarian theology as revealed truth.) This is why it would seem strange to claim that because Moses (or Abraham, Isaac, or Jacob) did not affirm that the self-existent One includes the eternally begotten Son (along with the Holy Spirit) that the great patriarchs worshipped a different God than Christians worship.

Consider now St. Paul's famous sermon that he preached on the Areopagus in Athens to a crowd of pagan listeners:

> Athenians, I see how extremely religious you are in every way. For as I went through the city and looked carefully at the objects of your worship, I found among them an altar with the inscription, "To an unknown god." What therefore you worship as unknown, this I proclaim to you. The God who made the world and everything in it, he who is Lord of heaven and earth, does not live in shrines made by human hands, nor is he served by human hands, as though he needed anything, since he himself gives to all mortals life and breath and all things. From one ancestor he made all nations to inhabit the whole earth, and he allotted the times of their existence and the boundaries of the places where they would live, so that they would search for God and perhaps grope for him and find him—though indeed he is not far from each one of us. For "In him we live and move and have our being"; as even some of your own poets have said, "For we too are his offspring." (Acts 17:22b–28)

But St. Paul's sermon does not end there. He goes on to explain to his audience the relationship between this "unknown God" and what He will reveal, and has revealed, in history through the person of Jesus of Nazareth: "[God] has fixed a day on which he will have the world judged in righteousness by a man [Jesus Christ] whom he has appointed, and of this he has given assurance to all by raising him from the dead" (Acts 17:31). Notice what St. Paul is doing here. He first secures the correct reference to God—"The God who made the world and everything in it . . . [, he in whom] we live and move and have our being"—and then presents to his Athenian audience a

---

49. Aquinas, *Summa Contra Gentiles* 1.22.9–10.
50. Levering, *Scripture and Metaphysics*, 40–41, 63–64.
51. "What We Believe." See generally Ayres, *Nicaea and Its Legacy*.

very brief summary of the gospel message. Contrast this with what is recorded in the earlier portions of Acts 17 (vv. 1–9), in which we are told about a journey made by St. Paul and Silas to Thessalonica. While there they visited a Jewish synagogue where St. Paul argued for a suffering and resurrected Messiah who he identifies as Jesus. Not surprisingly, this presentation was not warmly received by most of the congregants. Nevertheless, unless he supposed that both he and his Jewish listeners were referring to the same God, it does not make any sense for St. Paul to have argued that Jesus was the true Messiah sent by God. We cannot, for example, coherently argue over whether Madison Hemings is really the son of Thomas Jefferson unless we suppose that we are referring to the same Thomas Jefferson.

In Acts 17 we see how St. Paul engages two different groups, pagans and Jews. With the latter, the right reference to God is secured in the very preaching of the gospel, since St. Paul is making the case that Jesus of Nazareth is the Messiah promised by the God of Abraham, Isaac, Jacob, and Moses. With the pagans, on the other hand, St. Paul procures a different strategy. He first secures the right reference to God—"[He in whom] we live and move and have our being"—*and then* moves on to introduce his Athenian listeners to the Christian message. In both venues, the many who walked away without accepting the Christian message did not fail to "change Gods." Rather, what they failed to do was to embrace St. Paul's claim that the one and only true and living God specially revealed himself in history in the person of Jesus.

It was not until the fourth century at the First Council of Nicaea (AD 325) that the Christian church issued an official account of what it means to say that Jesus is the Son of God. At the time, the Church included two warring factions. One group sided with Arius of Alexandria (256–336),[52] who took the position that the incarnate Son of God had not always existed, was a creation of the Father, and thus was *not* "God of God, Light of Light, True God from True God."[53] The other faction was led by Athanasius of Alexandria (296–373). He defended the view that Jesus as the Son of God is in fact fully God, the pre-incarnate Word revealed by St. John at the beginning of his Gospel (John 1:1).[54] So, the dispute that was resolved at Nicaea was between those who with Arius held that the Son of God was made, not begotten, of a different substance than the Father, and those who with Athanasius held that the Son of God was "begotten, not made, consubstantial with the Father."[55] Although the council declared Arianism a heresy, there was no doubt that both factions were referring to the same one and only true and living God—that which is metaphysically ultimate and has underived existence—with their dispute being over the question of whether *that* God has an eternally begotten Son that is of the same substance. Consequently, what divided Arius and Athanasius is not unlike what divides Christians from Jews and

---

52. Kelly, *Early Christian Doctrines*, 226–31.
53. United States Conference of Catholic Bishops, "What We Believe."
54. Athanasius, *De Synodis*.
55. United States Conference of Catholic Bishops, "What We Believe."

Muslims: the identity of Jesus of Nazareth and his relationship to the divine nature. But if Arius and Athanasius worshipped the same God, despite their disagreement, then it stands to reason that Christians, Jews, and Muslims worship the same God, even though they differ on the nature of God's internal life.

Conclusion: Answering McGrew and Walls

In light of what we covered in sections II and III, we can now respond to McGrew and Walls.

McGrew raises the question: Why should the idea of God as Creator—which Christians have in common with Muslims and Jews—take precedence over distinctly Christian beliefs about God, such as the Trinity, the incarnation, and so forth?[56]

There is a kernel of truth in McGrew's question. She correctly implies that what separates Christianity from both Judaism and Islam is its understanding of God's internal life (whether or not God is Triune) and the extent to which he has revealed himself in human history (whether or not Jesus is God Incarnate). However, on the question at issue here—whether or not Christians, Jews, and Muslims worship the same God—the Christian distinctives do *not* take precedence over what constitutes a divine nature. To understand why, we will have to enlist the help of Tony and Tessy, the fraternal twins we met when we discussed sense and reference.

After graduating from high school, Tony and Tessy attend UNLV, where they take a course taught by Dr. Mind, the same philosophy professor who helped Ahmed, Benjamin, and Cecilia return to belief in God. Tony and Tessy, like their three peers, become convinced of God's existence after reading Aquinas, Avicenna, and Maimonides. Several months later, Tony goes on to become a Catholic, and thus is required to assent to what the Church teaches, including its beliefs on the Trinity and the deity of Christ. Tessy, on the other hand, becomes a Latter-day Saint (LDS), and confesses to have faith in all that the LDS Church teaches, including its beliefs on the Trinity[57] and Christ's deity.[58] Although Tony and Tessy seem to believe the same

---

56. McGrew phrases her query exclusively in terms of Islam, though given what she says about modern Judaism, it is fair to extend it to include both faiths: "Islam says more than that God doesn't happen to be triune or that God didn't in fact come down as man. Islam insists God cannot be triune or incarnate. It denies Jesus could be the Son of God, much less God himself. Why is the fact that Allah (as conceived in Islam) is the Creator more important to the question at hand than the fact that he cannot be triune or incarnate?" (McGrew, "The 'Same God' Debate").

57. "The Trinity of traditional Christianity is referred to as the Godhead by members of the Church of Jesus Christ of Latter-Day Saints (Mormon). Like other Christians, Latter-Day Saints believe in the Father, the Son and the Holy Spirit (or Holy Ghost)" (The Church of Jesus Christ of Latter-Day Saints, "Godhead").

58. "The incarnation is the foundational Christian teaching that Jesus Christ, who was God (Jehovah) in the premortal existence, 'was made flesh, and dwelt among us' (John 1:14).... The Great Jehovah, the Creator of all things (Mosiah 3:8; 5:15), the Eternal Father of heaven and earth (Mosiah 15:4), took upon himself the tabernacle of a mortal body" (Skinner, "The Incarnation/Incarnate God," 319).

distinctly Christian doctrines, they no longer believe in the same God, since Tessy, by embracing LDS doctrine *denies* that God is the one, uncaused, perfect, unchanging, self-subsistent, eternal Creator and Sustainer of all that which receives its being from another. According to the LDS Church, "Church teachings about the Godhead differ from those of traditional Christianity. For example, while some believe the three members of the Trinity are of one substance, Latter-Day Saints believe they are three physically separate beings, but fully one in love, purpose and will."[59] This is why the Catholic Church accepts the validity of Protestant baptisms if the correct formula is used ("I baptize you in the name of the Father, and of the Son, and of the Holy Spirit"), while rejecting LDS baptisms, even though the LDS affirm the Trinity and seemingly use the same formula. As noted in a summary of a 2001 decision issued by the Catholic Church's Congregation for the Doctrine of the Faith: "There is not a true invocation of the Trinity because the Father, the Son, and the Holy Spirit, according to the *Church of Jesus Christ of Latter-Day Saints,* are not the three persons in which subsists the one Godhead, but three gods who form one divinity. One is different from the other, even though they exist in perfect harmony.... The very word divinity has only a functional, not a substantial content, because the divinity originates when the three gods decided to unite and form the divinity to bring about human salvation.... This divinity and man share the same nature and they are substantially equal."[60] What this means is that getting the doctrine of the Trinity right requires the correct understanding of the divine nature: he who is metaphysically ultimate and has underived existence. Because, under Christianity, Judaism, and Islam, there can in-principle be only one such being, one can have the correct reference to God while getting some things about him wrong. This is, after all, one of the many lessons of Eve's encounter with the serpent in the Garden of Eden. Although they both had the right reference to God, Eve came to accept a false belief about him (Gen 3:4–5). So, to answer McGrew's question, getting the divine nature right is in fact more important, even though it does not prevent one from holding what others may think are wrong beliefs about God. Perhaps this is why in Acts 17, St. Paul first secures the right reference to God before telling his audience about Jesus.

Our answer to McGrew also answers Walls's claim that the Christian understanding of God constitutes a reference shift from the Jewish understanding. For unlike Walls's Saint Nicholas/Santa Claus illustration, in which the radical disparity between the two figures undermines the same reference, in the case of Judaism and Christianity (as well as Islam) the same reference to God is established because there is agreement on what constitutes a divine nature *per se*: God is the one, uncaused, perfect, unchanging, self-subsistent, eternal Creator and Sustainer of all that which receives its being from another. To claim, for example, that God is a Trinity

---

59. The Church of Jesus Christ of Latter-Day Saints, "Godhead."

60. Ladaria, "The Question of the Validity of Baptism Conferred in The Church of Jesus Christ of Latter-Day Saints," 4.

as the Council of Constantinople understood the term, requires that one first know what a divine nature is. After all, the council was trying to figure out the best way to explain how he who is metaphysically ultimate and has derived existence, the one and only true and living God worshipped by Abraham, Isaac, Jacob, and Moses, could be one substance and three persons. If that is the problem that the council was addressing—as it indeed seems to be—then Christians and Jews (along with Muslims) worship the same God, even though they hold contrary understandings of that God and what they take to be revealed truth.

Bibliography

Aquinas, Thomas. *On Being and Essence*. Translated by Armand Maurer. 2nd rev. ed. Toronto: Pontifical Institute of Mediaeval Studies, 1968.
———. *Summa Contra Gentiles: Book One: God*. Translated by Anton C. Pegis, F.R.S.C. Notre Dame, IN: University of Notre Dame Press, 1975.
———. *Summa Theologica*. Translated by Fr. Laurence Shapcote, O.P. Edited by John Mortensen and Enrique Alarcón. Lander, WY: The Aquinas Institute for the Study of Sacred Doctrine, 2012.
Arendzen, J. "Marcionites." In *The Catholic Encyclopedia*. New York: Robert Appleton Company, 1910. Retrieved March 25, 2019 from *New Advent*. http://www.newadvent.org/cathen/09645c.htm.
Athanasius. *De Synodis*. Translated by John Henry Newman and Archibald Robertson. In *Nicene and Post-Nicene Fathers, Second Series*, vol. 4, edited by Philip Schaff and Henry Wace. Buffalo, N.Y.: Christian Literature Publishing Co., 1892. Revised and edited for New Advent by Kevin Knight, http://www.newadvent.org/fathers/2817.htm.
Augustine. *On the Trinity* (400–428) 5.2. Translated by Arthur West Haddan. In *Nicene and Post-Nicene Fathers* (NPNF), vol. 6., http://www.newadvent.org/fathers/130105.htm.
Avicenna. *The Metaphysics of the Healing*. Translated by Michael E. Marmura. Provo, Utah: Brigham Young University Press, 2005.
Ayres, Lewis. *Nicaea and Its Legacy: An Approach to Fourth Century Trinitarian Theology*. New York: Oxford University Press, 2004.
Beckwith, Francis J. "All Worship the Same God: Referring to the Same God." In *Do Christians, Muslims, and Jews Worship the Same God? Four Views*, edited by Ronnie Campbell and Christopher Gnanakan, 65–86. Grand Rapids: Zondervan Academic, 2019.
———. "Do Muslims and Christians Worship the Same God?" *The Catholic Thing*, December 17, 2015. https://www.thecatholicthing.org/2015/12/17/do-muslims-and-christians-worship-the-same-god/.
———. *Never Doubt Thomas: The Catholic Aquinas as Evangelical and Protestant*. Waco, TX: Baylor University Press, 2019.
———. "Why Muslims and Christians Worship the Same God." *The Catholic Thing*, January 7, 2016. https://www.thecatholicthing.org/2016/01/07/why-muslims-and-christians-worship-the-same-god/.
Bogardus, Tomas, and Mallorie Urban. "How to Tell Whether Christians and Muslims Worship the Same God." *Faith and Philosophy* 34.2 (2017) 176–200.

Brownfeld, Allan. "Jews Are Called Upon to Reassess Their Views of Christianity, Recognizing We Worship The Same God." American Council for Judaism. September–October 2000. http://www.acjna.org/acjna/articles_detail.aspx?id=18.

The Church of Jesus Christ of Latter-Day Saints. "Godhead." Available at https://newsroom.churchofjesuschrist.org/article/godhead.

Craig, William Lane. *The Kalām Cosmological Argument*. New York: Macmillan, 1979.

———. *Reasonable Faith: Christian Truth and Apologetics*. 3rd ed. Wheaton, IL: Crossway, 2008.

"Dabru Emet: A Jewish Statement on Christians and Christianity." *First Things*, November 2000, https://www.firstthings.com/article/2000/11/dabru-emet-a-jewish-statement-on-christians-and-christianity.

Dulles, Avery Cardinal, S. J. *A History of Apologetics*. 2nd ed. San Francisco: Ignatius, 2005.

———. "The Rebirth of Apologetics." *First Things* 143, May 2004, 18–23.

Dylan, Bob. "Ring Them Bells." On the album *Oh Mercy*. New York: Columbia Records, 1989.

Evans, Gareth. "The Causal Theory of Names." *Proceedings of the Aristotelian Society, Supplementary Volumes* 47 (1973) 187–208.

———. *The Varieties of Reference*. New York: Oxford University Press, 1982.

Geisler, Norman L. *Christian Apologetics*. Grand Rapids: Baker Book House, 1976.

Gilson, Étienne. *The Christian Philosophy of St. Thomas Aquinas*. Translated by L. K. Shook. Notre Dame, IN: University of Notre Dame Press, 1994.

Graham, Ruth. "The Professor Wore a Hijab in Solidarity—Then Lost Her Job." *The New York Times Magazine*. October 13, 2016. https://www.nytimes.com/2016/10/16/magazine/the-professor-wore-a-hijab-in-solidarity-then-lost-her-job.html.

Hackett, Stuart C. *The Reconstruction of the Christian Revelation Claim: A Philosophical and Critical Apologetic*. Grand Rapids: Baker Book House, 1984.

Hawkins, Larycia. Unpublished Memo Addressed to Wheaton College Provost Stanton L. Jones. December 15, 2015.

Jerome. "Letter 15" (ca. 376). In *Letters of St. Jerome*, translated by W. H. Fremantle, G. Lewis and W. G. Martley. In *Nicene and Post-Nicene Fathers, Second Series* (*NPNF*), vol. 6, edited by Philip Schaff and Henry Wace. Buffalo, NY: Christian Literature Publishing Co., 1893. Rev. and ed. for New Advent by Kevin Knight, http://www.newadvent.org/fathers/3001015.htm.

Kelly, J. N. D. *Early Christian Doctrines*. 5th ed. San Francisco: HarperCollins, 1978.

Ladaria, Luis. "The Question of the Validity of Baptism Conferred in The Church of Jesus Christ of Latter-Day Saints." *L'Osservatore Romano* (August 2001) 4. Available at https://www.vatican.va/roman_curia/congregations/cfaith/documents/rc_con_cfaith_doc_20010605_battesimo_mormoni-ladaria_en.html.

Levering, Matthew. *Scripture and Metaphysics: Aquinas and the Renewal of Trinitarian Theology*. Oxford: Blackwell, 2004.

Lewis, C. S. *Mere Christianity*. 1952. Reprint, Toronto: Samizdat, 2014.

Maimonides, Moses. *The Guide for the Perplexed*. Translated by Michael Friedländer. 2nd ed. London: Routledge Kegan Paul, 1904.

McGrew, Lydia. "The 'Same God' Debate Is Too Important to Leave to Philosophers." The Gospel Coalition. January 16, 2016. https://www.thegospelcoalition.org/article/the-same-god-debate-is-too-important-to-leave-to-philosophers/.

Moreland, J. P. *Scaling the Secular City: A Defense of Christianity*. Grand Rapids: Baker, 1987.

Novak, David. "Because of What God Has Done." *First Things*, December 2011, 22–23.

———. *Covenantal Rights: A Study in Jewish Political Theory*. Princeton, NJ: Princeton University Press, 2000.

———. "The Jewish Mission: On Whether Jews Can or Should Proselytize." *First Things*, November 2012, 39–43.

———. "Les Juifs et les chretiens reverent-ils le meme Dieu?" ["Do Jews and Christians Worship the Same God?"]. In *Le christianisme au miroir du judaisme,* edited by Shmuel Trigano, 95–132. Paris: In Press Editions, 2003.

———. "Supersessionism Hard and Soft." *First Things*, February 2019, 27–31.

Pelikan, Jaroslav. *The Emergence of the Catholic Tradition (100–600)*. Vol. 1 of *The Christian Tradition: A History of the Development of Doctrine*. Chicago: University of Chicago Press, 1971.

Plantinga, Alvin. *Warranted Christian Belief*. New York: Oxford University Press, 2000.

The Meaning of the Glorious Koran: An Explanatory Translation by Muhammad Marmaduke Pickthall. New York: New American Library, 1988.

The Qur'an. Translated by M. A. S. Abdel Haleem. Oxford: Oxford University Press, 2008.

Skinner, Andrew C. "Incarnation/Incarnate God." In *LDS Beliefs: A Doctrinal Reference,* edited by Robert L Millet, Camille Fronk Olson, Andrew C. Skinner, and Brent L. Top. Salt Lake City: Deseret, 2011.

United States Conference of Catholic Bishops. "What We Believe." http://www.usccb.org/beliefs-and-teachings/what-we-believe/.

Walls, Jerry L. "None Worship the Same God: Different Conceptions View." In *Do Christians, Muslims, and Jews Worship the Same God? Four Views*, edited by Ronnie Campbell and Christopher Gnanakan, 161–83. Grand Rapids: Zondervan Academic, 2019.

Response to

Francis J. Beckwith's "A Christian Account of Why David Novak Is Right about the Same God Question"

DAVID NOVAK

I AM GRATEFUL TO Francis Beckwith for his Catholic defense of my Jewish insistence that Jews and Christians worship the same God. Let me begin by elaborating on Beckwith's defense by showing how the view that Jews and Christians do *not* worship the same God, against which he argues so well, destroys any theologically valid Jewish-Christian relationship. I shall then try to show the difference between Beckwith's and my arguments for the same God thesis. Let me say at the outset that our agreement is much greater than our difference. So, let me begin by supplementing Beckwith's argument against those who see the "Christian" God to be different from and superior to the "Jewish" God (which could be called "neo-Marcionism").

If Judaism and Christianity each taught a "henotheism," i.e., the view that each religion has its one and only (*henos* in Greek) god, there then would be no quarrel with anybody who says, "you have your one and only god, and we have our one and only god," hence our respective religions are incommensurable. In this view, each religion lives on its henotheistic turf, surrounded by a polytheistic world, i.e., a world containing multiple gods. When each religion and its god remain within their own turf, not interacting with any other religion and its god, we then have a truly pluralistic world. The philosophy best suited to this world is relativism. If, however, each religion sees its god as participating in a higher, all-encompassing universe (what Aristotle called *physis* or "Nature"), we then have what might be called a "trans-theistic" world. That is, there is *the* Absolute to which (or to whom) all lesser beings, whether human or gods (*theoi* in Greek) are subordinate. Here we have one supreme, universal God or Divinity (*to theion* in Greek) over and above the lesser gods functioning in a pantheon. Some have called this Absolute "the God beyond (*transire* in Latin) all gods."

Being *monotheistic* religions, Judaism and Christianity (and Islam) cannot regard their God as anyone less than the one and only (*monos* in Greek) God of the whole universe. Hence, local henotheism and universal trans-theism are out. Henotheism is out because of its lack of ontological universality. Trans-theism is out because it denies the absoluteness of the God about whom the Scripture shared by Jews and Christians says "I am God, there is nothing beyond (*ein od*)" (Isaiah 45:22). The Lord God of Israel will not allow Himself to be part of a pantheon, even as its first member. Moreover, since all the gods worshiped by "gentiles," even if assumed to be real and even assumed to be immaterial, are still but creatures, they are all unworthy of worship *ipso facto*. Those who do worship them are "idolaters," performing what the ancient Rabbis called "strange" (or "alienated/alienating") worship (*avodah zarah* in Hebrew). In pre-Christian times, when Jews were the only monotheists, everybody else was considered to be an idolater. Moreover, since only the Jews received a revelation from the Creator-God identifying Himself as such ("Hear O' Israel the LORD our God is the only God [*ehad*]"; Deut 6:4), only they were required to be monotheists in practice, which is why in Scripture the gentiles or "pagans" are never condemned for their polytheistic (even henotheistic) practices.

Christians, and Muslims, having received revelation, are good monotheists, but everybody else (i.e., everybody else who worships anything else) is an idolater. Nevertheless, if one assumes that proper worship of the one true Creator-God also requires the acceptance of everything one's own community (Jewish, Christian, or Muslim) teaches about the character of this one and only universal God, then it would seem that anybody who doesn't subscribe in full to that community's teaching is also an idolater. That person is worshiping something other than the one true God in all His fullness. It is either all or nothing here. Also, such persons are deluded idolaters, believing they are worshiping the one true God, when in fact they are worshiping a phantom. It thus follows that Christians who hold this view have to regard Jews and Muslims, neither of whom accepts an incarnate God or a triune God, as being such deluded idolaters. And, since Jews and Muslims have long been exposed to Christian evangelism, they are not only deluded idolaters, but they are willingly obstinate idolaters, refusing to acknowledge what they cannot claim ignorance of. Finally, it would seem, Jews are the worst offenders since we were the first ones to be given the Christian gospel by no one less than its Jewish subject, Jesus.

Lest this triumphalism be seen as an exclusively Christian outlook, there have always been Jewish triumphalists, claiming that Christians worship "another god" (see Exod 20:3), because they consider it a falsehood to assert that the one transcendent God is either incarnate or triune or both. So, it might be said that for Christian triumphalists, Jews do not say enough about God, while for Jewish triumphalists, Christians say too much about God. Each of these triumphalists, both Christian and Jewish, are what I have called in an article cited by Beckwith "hard supersessionists."[1] Moreover, since Jews and Christians were once members of the same covenantal community, their respective triumphalists seem to hold that the other is a deviant.

1. Novak, "Supersessionism Hard and Soft."

It is Christian triumphalism or hard supersessionism that Beckwith as a Christian argues against. Indeed, it would have been ridiculous to have invited a Christian triumphalist or hard supersessionist to contribute to a volume of irenic engagement of the thought of a Jewish theologian like me. Any such invitation could have only led to the type of disputations that most Christian theologians and certainly most Jewish theologians want to leave in the irretrievable past. Nevertheless, while such interreligious disputation is to be avoided for the sake of a valid interreligious relationship between Christians and Jews, Beckwith has admirably engaged in an inner-religious, inner Christian, disputation with Christian theologians like Lydia McGrew and Jerry Walls. I might add that I have had to engage in similar inner-religious disputations with some of my fellow Jews, dealing with similar issues.

Those of us, whether Jewish or Christian, who do not want to go this triumphalist and supersessionist route, regard the Christian or Jewish "other" as different from all "others" in not being a worshiper of another god. As such, we have to employ the kind of logic Beckwith skillfully uses in his essay. Rather than the *all-or-nothing* logic of the triumphalists and supersessionists, we seem to employ *general-specific* logic. So, if I understand Beckwith correctly, he employs this kind of logic while doing what has long been called "natural theology." In this kind of theology, it is assumed that there are certain general truths about God that are available that any person can discover about God through ratiocination. In the famous definition of Anselm of Canterbury, as interpreted by Thomas Aquinas, one can discover rationally "that which nothing greater can be thought of" (*aliquid quo maius cogitari possit*). Subsequent to that general rational discovery, through what Calvin called "special revelation," Christians are given truths about God's being triune and becoming incarnate in the body of a Jew, Jesus of Nazareth.

In the development of this *general-specific* logic by Christians, it is often assumed that the Jews have not gone far enough in their knowledge of God, by remaining at the level of general rather than specific knowledge. In other words, Jews haven't progressed far enough. However, in the development of this logic by Jews, it is argued that Christians have made specific claims about God that contradict the original, rational knowledge of God. As such, Christians have regressed. Nevertheless, there is still enough of the original, rational knowledge of God for Jews and Christians to still retain a modicum of respect for and toleration for the theological integrity of the other. This modicum of respect and toleration enables Jews and Christians to argue against triumphalist *all-or-nothing* advocates in their respective communities.

On the question of natural theology, I respectfully differ with Francis Beckwith. Let it also be said that our difference is not a Jewish-Christian difference. There have been Jewish thinkers who adhere to natural theology; and there have been Christian thinkers who have been opposed to it (the best example being Karl Barth, whose influence of my thinking is gratefully acknowledged).

I cannot agree with Beckwith's employing Aquinas's notion about the rational *"preambles of faith*, those beliefs that 'are a necessary presupposition to matters of faith' that one *may know* by means of reason."[2] Aquinas's position is similar to that of the Muslim theologian Avicenna and the Jewish theologian Maimonides. However, this is not a description of the God *only* Jews and Christians (and Muslims too) could worship. It is a description of the God *any* rational person could worship, i.e., if that person accepts the philosophical validity of natural theology's God-talk. Thus, eighteenth-century theists (like Unitarians) could worship this God without regarding it as necessary or even preferable to then move on to the Jewish or Christian specifications of the nature or character of this universal God. It is possible for *any* rational person to worship this God. So, even if Jews and Christians (and Muslims) could worship this "theistic" God, they could only do so *generically*, but without any connection to their *specific* traditions at all. So, when this "preamble" becomes more than just a precondition for Jewish or Christian *special* theology, but instead becomes a sufficient substitution for them, then Jews *qua Jews* and Christians *qua Christians* are not really worshiping *their* same God after all. That is because in this kind of theistic worship, neither Jews nor Christians can invoke "the Lord God of Israel." Following Pascal, we could say that they are worshiping the "God of the philosophers," not the "God of Abraham, Isaac, and Jacob." And since the God of the philosophers is not the Creator God (*ex nihilo*), this God is not the God of the Muslims either.

In fact, this kind of non-Jewish, non-Christian, "nonsectarianism" became the stuff of what Spinoza (who opted out of Judaism) and Rousseau (who opted out of Christianity) advocated as a sufficient religion for the post-Jewish and post-Christian secular societies they hoped would emerge in their respective countries. Conversely, for Aquinas and his Muslim and Jewish predecessors, the type of secular society this kind of theism requires in order to be a praxis and not just a theory was non-existent. Everybody had to live in a Christian or Islamic or Jewish community. There was no secular societal option then. Back then, "philosophical," ahistorical religion couldn't be publicly practiced, but only privately contemplated. Like language, which is essential to worship (as Wittgenstein pointed out, a "private" language is an oxymoron), private (often clandestine) prayer or meditation does not really qualify to be called a "religion," i.e., a public service (*avodah* in Hebrew; *leitourgia* in Greek). Therefore, natural theology poses no practical challenge to revelation-based Judaism or Christianity like the challenge civil religion has posed since the Enlightenment. That is why post-Enlightenment Jewish and Christian theologians should be wary of employing natural theology. For in the mediaeval setting, natural theology could only provide a theoretical or hypothetical preamble to real, practical Judaism or Christianity. But in early modernity it did offer a real, practical alternative. Nevertheless, today that challenging alternative seems to be gone. Therefore, there are now good reasons for Jewish and Christian theologians to avoid natural theology altogether.

2. p. 73, citing *ST* I-II, q. 1, a. 5 ad 3; emphasis in original.

There are now two main reasons why natural theology should not be employed to provide true commonality for Jews and Christians who want to cogently affirm we both worship the same God.

Philosophically, natural theology has been problematic ever since Kant convinced many of us that natural theology's metaphysic of nature presupposes a hierarchal natural world with God at its apex. But this is a view of the natural world that has not been entertained scientifically ever since the scientific revolutions of Copernicus, Galileo, and Newton (let alone those of Einstein and Bohr). Theologically, it seems the unchanging impassive God posited by natural theology cannot be identified with the Lord God of Israel, the God who responds to His creatures, thereby changing from what He *was before* their previous situation, to what He *is at* their current situation, and to what He *will be in* their future situation. Moreover, whereas for the philosophers, change would be a sign of God's imperfection; for Jewish and Christian theologians, change is a sign of God's freedom to be whatever God wants to be (Exod 3:14; 33:19). Yet by not changing into something else (Mal 3:6), God always retains His perpetual identity. "I am the first and I am the last, aside from Me no one is God" (Isa 44:6).

Therefore, it seems best to say that both Jews and Christians worship the same God who, most superlatively, revealed Godself at Sinai. This prime revelation (*Uroffenbarung* in German) has been supplemented sometimes by Jewish *and* Christian theology similarly, sometimes by Jewish *or* Christian theology dissimilarly. And both have done so towards an eschatological horizon in an as yet unredeemed world. So, when neither theology attempts to replace Sinaitic revelation (the gnostic temptation), nor displace the cognate community from the covenant with the Lord God of Israel (the supersessionist temptation), then it can be honestly said it is surely this same God they are both serving in good faith, sometimes together and sometimes apart, but never alone, i.e., never exclusively at the expense of the other. This is what Francis Beckwith, David Novak, and the other authors in this volume are doing, and should be doing during the time God has given us on earth.

Chapter 3

In the Beginning

The Primordial Character of the Problem of Suicide in David Novak's Scholarship

JOHN BERKMAN[1]

> My brethren are distant from me,
> and my friends are wholly estranged
> My kinfolk have abandoned me,
> and my fellows have forgotten me.
>
> —JOB 19:13–14[2]

IN HIS LIFE AND in his academic career, the question and reality of suicide have been of immense importance for David Novak. As an academic question, the issue has been with David from the start. It was the topic of his doctoral dissertation, a philosophical analysis of the morality of suicide in Plato, Aquinas, and Kant. But that was by no means the entire dissertation. David's study of the question of suicide was not limited to the philosophical arguments but also examined the social scientific literature on suicide. He found the latter to provide key insights regarding the etiology of suicide, which in turn suggested more effective means to keep some persons from committing suicide. David concluded that a study of suicide discussing only the moral arguments would fail as a substantive contribution to overcoming the problem of suicide as it exists in contemporary society.

Although that initial work on suicide focused on suicide from the perspective of classic philosophy and contemporary social scientific literature, David's reflections on suicide have since broadened. His more recent work includes more explicitly theological perspectives on suicide. He also calls for a rethinking of the legal status of suicide in contemporary society, a call that could and should be heard by a

---

1. I am grateful for correspondence with Laurie Zoloth, who has saved me from some grievous errors regarding Jewish ethics. Of course, all the remaining deficiencies are my own.

2. This quote from Job is on the dedicatory page of Novak, *Suicide and Morality*.

variety of American states.[3] However, in David's adopted country of Canada, his call will necessarily fall on deaf ears, since Canada has excitedly embraced physicians killing their patients.[4]

In addition, and perhaps most importantly, the question of suicide has been of profound existential significance to David. David's interest in suicide preceded even the writing of his dissertation. In fact, the existential reality and significance of suicide for David seems to have been an impetus for David to choose the topic of suicide for his doctoral dissertation. When David began his doctoral program in philosophy at Georgetown University in 1966, he also started working as a rabbi and chaplain at St. Elizabeths Hospital in Washington DC. St. Elizabeths is perhaps the most famous medical facility for those with mental illnesses in the United States of America. Three of its most high-profile residents have included the assassin and would-be assassins of Presidents Andrew Jackson, James Garfield, and Ronald Reagan.

David's work at St. Elizabeths brought him into contact with a number of suicidal patients, many of whom became friends. As he recounts in *Suicide and Morality*, four patients whom he came to know ended their lives during his time working at St Elizabeths. In David's estimation, these individuals committed suicide because they saw themselves as alone and abandoned.[5] David feared that he too might possibly have abandoned those people. As I shall argue, this notion of "abandonment" is central for David's analysis of the contemporary problem of suicide. As for David, his prayer is that when he is ultimately judged, he will not be found to have abandoned these four people.

It was during those years of the late 1960s, when David was simultaneously working at St. Elizabeths as a chaplain, and doing his doctoral coursework in philosophy at Georgetown University, that David came to see a massive disconnect between the thinking about suicide in philosophy in comparison to the social sciences. On the one hand, the philosophers were able to make concrete judgments about suicide

---

3. In David's view, the ideologically committed liberal state can provide no justification for making suicide illegal, and the logical eventuality is that such a state will legalize assisted suicide and euthanasia.

4. By speaking of "physicians killing their patients," I am not engaging in provocative hyperbole but am being overly benevolent. I am merely employing the traditional definition of "murder," namely the killing of innocent persons, which seems to have recently gone out of fashion. By "innocent," I am again using the standard meaning, that of a person who has done nothing to deserve being killed. Canada has now given its explicit blessing for an employee of the state to euthanize (murder) people, and some provinces have contemplated mandating murder by their physicians if they wish to keep their medical licenses. Since "euthanasia" and "killing" (much less "murder") are such unpleasant terms, Canada has resorted to using the acronym "MAID," that is, medical assistance in dying. When the state decides people should be killed, it is no surprise that they would want an acronym that makes direct killing sound like garden-variety palliative care. The corruption of the Canadian judiciary is shown in its creating an acronym where every word is a falsehood. Euthanizing persons is not a medical treatment; euthanizing persons is not merely "*Assisting In*" their death; while we all have to *Die*, which of us want to be killed?

5. Novak, *Suicide and Morality*, x.

based on moral principles. However, they were mostly oblivious to the existential and psychological realities that actually led individuals to contemplate, and sometimes commit, suicide. On the other hand, when he engaged in conversations with researchers and clinicians at St. Elizabeths, he found that they had great expertise in explaining the social contexts and psychological pathologies that led individuals to consider suicide. However, these clinicians, at least at a conscious level, either did not want to, or were unable to, reflect on the moral aspect of suicide with any sophistication and/or seriousness. What these clinicians typically failed to recognize was that they too had moral convictions about suicide, i.e., in seeking to help patients overcome their desire for suicide. Like much of contemporary society, they typically resisted seeing suicide as a moral question at all. This problematic disconnect can even be seen in the title of David's *Suicide and Morality*.

This disconnect would inspire David's dissertation. On the one hand, David sought to understand and articulate the arguments of philosophers such as Plato, Aquinas, and Kant, all of whom understood that killing oneself was immoral. On the other hand, he wanted to make these arguments relevant for those seeking social scientific understandings of suicide.

How did this disconnect between the moral use and non-moral use of "suicide" arise? "Suicide" is a relative newcomer to the English language.[6] It only "arrived" as a term with widespread usage in English with its inclusion in 1759 in Dr. Johnson's highly influential English dictionary.[7] Dr. Johnson defined suicide as "self-murder" and this was typical of dictionary entries on "suicide" up through the nineteenth century. "Suicide" was understood as a shorthand for "self-murder" or "wrongful self-killing."

It was part of the social scientist Emile Durkheim's project in *On Suicide* (1897) to detach any inherent moral judgment from the notion of "suicide." Durkheim's project has only been partly successful. While dictionary definitions of "suicide" no longer include any inherent moral judgment, in general society still presumes the term "suicide" to have negative connotations. Whether it is seen as shameful, or morally wrong, or

---

6. The term "suicide" was coined by Thomas Browne, which he used once in his *Religio Medici* (1643). It appears in the context of Browne mocking some preachers, who from the pulpit "allow a man to be his owne assassine, and so highly extoll the end and suicide of Cato; this is indeed not to fear death, but to bee afraid of life" (see Barraclough and Shepard, "A Necessary Neologism: The Origin and Uses of 'Suicide,'" 115). The first defense of the morality of self-killing, John Donne's posthumous *Biathanatos* (1646), speaks not of "suicide," but "self-homicide," "self killed," and "homicide of himself" (Barraclough and Shepard, "A Necessary Neologism: The Origin and Uses of 'Suicide,'" 117). Remarkably, in his poetic work, even Donne refers to the act of killing oneself as "self-murder."

7. Barraclough and Shepard argue that only with Dr. Johnson's 1758 dictionary does "suicide" arrive as a word in the English language, and Johnson too defines it as "self-murder" (Barraclough and Shepard, "A Necessary Neologism," 117). In the century from Browne coining the term until Johnson's dictionary, the term "suicide" was not widely used. When it did appear, it tended to be used by those who believed killing oneself could be morally acceptable, presumably because the term seemed less loaded than the alternatives—"self-murder," "self-destruction," etc. Nevertheless, when "suicide" was included in dictionaries and lexicons of that era (although most did not), it was invariably defined as "self-murder."

simply painful for family and friends to have to acknowledge, the term is often avoided. We see this, for example, in obituaries.[8] Or consider, for example, those particularly tragic cases where someone (particularly a young person) has inexplicably killed himself.[9] It is common for family and friends to request that "suicide" not be mentioned at the funeral or otherwise as a description of the cause of death. Presumably this is because in the midst of their terrible pain and grief, they consider "suicide" to be a source of shame or moral judgment on their loved one they are grieving.

Although the use of the term "suicide" no longer necessarily presumes a negative moral judgment, it continues to imply an intentional action, one that is freely chosen. All contemporary dictionaries continue to define "suicide" as an act requiring intentionality and/or choice. At the very least, dictionaries want us to be clear why "suicide" is not to be used for the person who falls off a bridge but is used for someone who throws himself off a bridge.

However, contemporary usage of "suicide" is not restricted to, say, acts that are completely freely chosen. In recent decades, many (particularly western) societies have increasingly come to see that many if not most suicides, while intentional, lack full human freedom, and thus mitigating or even eliminating moral culpability on the part of the person who kills himself.[10] In his more recent work, which I discuss below, David argues that all suicides are not freely chosen.

Among suicides to which we attach a lack of full human freedom, there are variants. Those suicides which seem completely inexplicable are particularly tragic, especially when the person is young. Other suicides are by those who may suffer for a very long time from depression, who in their more balanced moments have no desire whatsoever to kill themselves but recognize the possibility of a desire to do so that they will not be able to overcome. Still others make a lot of sense, as in the recent case of Jeffrey Epstein, who likely had had no desire whatsoever to commit suicide until his crimes were revealed and he became the latest "poster-boy" for what is wrong with America. Perhaps facing unbearable shame (and perhaps guilt) and a life behind bars, he presumably decided that he did not have the courage nor desire to face that future. And then there are still other suicides which appear to be chosen with as much freedom as is possible to ascribe to a person, as in the situation with euthanasia in Canada, where an individual has to deliberately request and choose it, and then wait

---

8. This was at least true of the ethos of traditional print media. With the rise of crassly commercialized click-bait internet news, more delicate information such as the fact of a suicide is now more likely to be communicated.

9. NB: I will use a masculine pronoun to refer to the person who commits suicide, not to ignore or deny that women also commit suicide, but for fluidity of style and as an acknowledgment and reminder that men kill themselves far more often than do women.

10. For example, some who struggle with bipolar disorder or other forms of depression seem to be compelled to kill themselves, no matter how hard and how long they struggle against it. A particularly public case is of the Catholic theologian Stephen Webb who contributed an article to *First Things* entitled "God of the Depressed," published only two weeks before he committed suicide.

at least a week (at least in theory), before being able to have a doctor kill them. This is not strictly suicide, although it is not that different if the physician acts as merely a technician following the orders from the one wishing his own death. There are of course innumerable other variants, to which it seems reasonable to ascribe a kind of sliding scale of responsibility or culpability.

Recently, especially by those who experience an inexplicable—and thus particularly tragic—suicide among their loved ones, there is further sentiment expressed. It is that to even consider a suicide as possibly immoral or even as a freely chosen act is "callous" and "offensive." Furthermore, it "stigmatizes" those who might consider suicide, which in turn makes it more likely that such persons will commit suicide.[11] With respect to the claim about "stigma," which in public debates has functioned at times as a way to shut down serious moral dialogue, the evidence is not there to support the claim. In fact, the overall evidence appears to point to the opposite conclusion.

While it is extremely important to understand the particularly tragic cases where it seems clear that the person who kills himself was not acting by a free and deliberated choice, this paper will bracket them, as they require a far more extensive and detailed treatment than is possible in this paper. Instead, this paper focuses on the many cases of suicide that are deliberated and freely chosen. These are cases of suicide where there are clear and intelligible motives for a person to kill himself or herself, and the act is done on the basis of those intelligible motives.[12] There are innumerable examples of those who kill themselves to provide for loved ones through an insurance policy, those who kill themselves after engaging in a mass shooting or murdering an alienated spouse or girlfriend, those who kill themselves because they are "tired of life," some who kill themselves out of a sense of shame, honor, or embarrassment, those engaged in "suicide bombings," etc. It is likely that such a case was among those with which David was engaged at St. Elizabeths, and it is these kinds of (relatively) freely chosen suicides with which this paper is concerned.

In *Suicide and Morality*—his initial intellectual creation—David wrestled with a particularly puzzling and troubling moral question and brought insight and thus life to it. I call it his first "L'Chaim," one formative for his career since the beginning.[13] David has worked resolutely to integrate different kinds of intellectual reflection together in order to have a fuller understanding of abundant and virtuous human life. In doing so, David has been particularly adept in helping all of us reflect on moral questions in a more holistic manner.

11. The rise of appeals to "stigma" to shut down considerations of morality is troubling, especially when "stigma" is used in vague ways, and there is inadequate empirical basis for such claims. For an important counter-argument, see Phillips, "The Dangerous Shifting Cultural Narratives around Suicide."

12. To say that there are "clear and intelligible" motives does not mean that there are correct ones. Of course, to maintain that an action is rational is not to say that it is morally acceptable, but merely that it liable to moral evaluation.

13. For a brilliant reflection on "L'Chaim," see Kass, "L'Chaim and Its Limits."

David has maintained this emphasis of "choosing life" throughout his career. One way he has argued this is to show that a Judeo-Christian ethic has a more inclusive and more adequate anthropology than the secular alternatives, alternatives that typically proclaim a reductive rationalistic and/or libertarian view of the human person. As David's puts it, while rationality and freedom are certainly "desirable human attributes . . . humanness cannot be reduced to them alone."[14] The "mantra" of the nominalist anthropologies characteristic of contemporary liberal societies are "reason" and "freedom." In some contexts, human beings lacking or devoid of these characteristics are benignly tolerated or even embraced, but in other contexts they are deliberately marginalized or denied their human dignity altogether, losing their status as "persons." Since the natural-law-based anthropology of the Judeo-Christian tradition is obviously more inclusive than its secular alternatives, it should appeal to the "main moral concerns of secular society today; greater inclusiveness in the human community with greater rights protection for it."[15]

Furthermore, David argues that the pursuit of justice in contemporary society should look to the greatest inspiration possible for it. And that surely includes maximal protection of all human beings. Justice must always address itself to what David calls the "perpetual moral choice of the world," that is, to choose between life and death. David's call, as always, is that Jews and Christians "must encourage the world to choose life and respect it in all its dimensions."[16]

As the purpose of this volume is to engage David's work from a variety of Catholic perspectives, I will discuss ways in which David's work is important for Catholic scholars who consider the question of suicide. Since David addresses many aspects of the question of suicide, I will have to be very selective in my discussion. I will limit myself to three important elements of David's work on the question of suicide.

The first aspect is David's natural law arguments regarding suicide. The second aspect discusses David's analysis of the nature and function of rights language in contemporary liberalism. As we shall see, David presents a very interesting argument that the doctrine of "privacy" has come to be the form that autonomy takes in contemporary debates.[17] In both of these aspects of David's work, we see aspects of his moral, political, and legal approaches to suicide.[18] For Catholic thinkers, I believe

14. Novak, "The Moral Crisis of the West: The Judeo-Christian Response," 20.

15. Novak, "Moral Crisis of the West," 21.

16. Novak, "Moral Crisis of the West," 21.

17. See especially, Novak, *The Sanctity of Human Life*, 14 and onward. This critique also appears in his 1997 article which appeared in *First Things*.

18. For example, David's view that suicide should be legally prohibited, but that it should not be prosecuted. In the last few decades a number of (but by no means all or even the majority of) typically Western countries did away with their criminal sanctions regarding self-killing. Others maintained the prohibition of suicide on the books, but made it clear that that crime would not be prosecuted. It seems to me that there were and are many good reasons for countries to have decided not to prosecute those who committed or attempted suicide. For one thing, over the last decades there was an increased appreciation of the number of non-voluntary suicide attempts. Second, many countries thought that

David's argument regarding "privacy" is particularly important, not only because of its inherent interest, but also because it has not been integrated into Catholic moral thought, whether on suicide specifically or Catholic bioethical literature more generally.[19] The third aspect I will evaluate is the evolution of David's thought on suicide, namely his coming to follow two tenets of the currently dominant view in Jewish ethics regarding suicide, namely that *a) suicide is never a free and deliberate choice and/or b) the Jewish community can never* post facto *judge that a suicide was freely and deliberately chosen.* I will suggest that these perspectives are highly attuned to pastoral concerns. I have full sympathy with these pastoral concerns and believe the Catholic tradition also currently emphasizes a pastoral approach to the question. However, here I believe we see the developing—at least in a small way—in the Jewish tradition a divergence from Catholic theological teaching. Thus, it functions as a challenge to the Catholic tradition of thought on suicide, and in this last section I engage in debate the two tenets of current Jewish thought regarding suicide.

David Novak and the Morality of Suicide

Historically, for both Christianity and Judaism, killing oneself was a grave moral wrong.[20] This does not necessarily mean that Christians and Jews have had identical views with regard to killing oneself.[21] There may be minor discrepancies whether (for example) in certain cases one who intentionally kills himself or herself can properly be called a martyr.[22] However, in comparison to modern moralities that deify autonomy or privacy,

---

there was no particular benefit to keeping criminal sanctions against suicide, and so repealed or stayed enforcement of such laws.

19. Novak's critique of the political uses of "privacy" could be helpfully incorporated into Catholic teaching on the common good, and thus inform Catholic perspectives on biomedical, sexual, and social teaching.

20. Gratian's twelfth-century authoritative work in canon law places killing oneself as well as the killing of others under the fifth commandment, "Thou Shalt not Kill." It was thus considered self-murder. However, a sharp distinction was made between killing oneself accidentally versus killing oneself intentionally. So, whereas falling off a bridge was not a sin and not sanctioned by canon law, throwing oneself off a bridge was a mortal sin. With regards to attempted suicide, since for Jesus the desire or attempt to kill oneself involved the same wrong intention as actually killing oneself, attempting suicide was sanctioned in canon law by a period of penance. See Schrage, "Suicide in Canon Law," 59–61.

21. Judaism is more prone to exceptions to the prohibition of suicide. As Reines puts it "while the Rabbis in general condemned suicide, an exception was made in situations in which the threat of death was used to force a Jew to betray his faith, to commit another grave sin (such as adultery), or to affect his action in time of war. The Bible (I Samuel 17:23; I Kings 16:18) reports case of suicide committed during political rebellion when the individuals concerned have reason to fear that they would be executed when their plans collapsed" (Reines, "Jewish Attitude toward Suicide," 165–66).

22. According to David, Judaism is willing to apply the term "martyr" (and thus presumably justify the act of self-killing) to some Jews who directly take their own lives (e.g., Masada). David argues that for the Jewish tradition "the only exception to [the divine prohibition of suicide] would be martyrdom, and the Jewish tradition has tried to make as sharp a difference as possible between suicide and martyrdom" (*The Sanctity of Human Life*, 114). This perspective is also shared by the Catholic

Christians and Jews have stood as one on this question. Both understand that our lives (including our bodies) do not belong to us but to God.[23] Therefore, killing oneself (like killing innocent others) is an attack on what belongs to God and to the divine prerogative. Our lives are a divine gift to which the appropriate response of gratitude to God precludes the rejection of this gift as pronounced by killing oneself.

In David's early work on the morality of suicide, David's natural law views on suicide are very similar to those of the Catholic tradition. For David as well as for the Catholic tradition, the wrongfulness of self-killing, like that of killing others, is known not only by revelation but also by the Noahide Law, that is, by the natural moral law which can be known by all persons apart from revelation. This being the case, it can be legitimate for a society to prohibit it under civil law. David thinks that suicide should indeed be prohibited (or remain prohibited) by law.[24] At the same time, David argues that this law should entail no penalty or sanction, neither for those who attempt or commit suicide, nor for his or her heirs.[25]

David presents both philosophical and theological reasons for concluding that suicide is wrong. I will present what I take to be four arguments shared by David and the Catholic moral tradition, three of which are more philosophical, and one more theological.

The first and most fundamental natural law argument for the wrongfulness of self-killing is its self-evidence. By "self-evident" I mean that if my interlocutor does not accept that freely killing an innocent person is wrong, then without further contextualization as to why my interlocutor might be so obtuse, is there really any

---

tradition. Even St. Augustine, perhaps the most vehement opponent of suicide in the Catholic theological tradition, notes that with regard to the case of women (e.g., St. Pelagia) who took their own lives to avoid being raped, Augustine says that "on who accepts the prohibition against suicide may kill himself when commanded by one whose orders must not be slighted; only let him take care that there is no uncertainty about the divine command" (Augustine, *City of God*, Book I, ch. 26, p. 37). In this, Augustine was following similar statements of Jerome, Chrysostom, and Ambrose.

23. Representative of the Jewish tradition is that "the life of man is not his possession, but the possession of the Holy One, Blessed be He. When there is conflict between the words of the Master (God) and the disciple (man), one follows the words of the Master" (Mackler, *Introduction to Jewish and Catholic Bioethics*, 66). Mackler is quoting from Waldenberg, *Ramat Rahel*, 5:38–39. Representative of the Catholic tradition is that "Everyone is responsible for his life before God who has given it to him. It is God who remains the sovereign Master of life. We are obliged to accept life gratefully and preserve it for his honor and the salvation of our souls. We are stewards, not owners, of the life God has entrusted to us. It is not ours to dispose of" (*Catechism of the Catholic Church*.2280).

24. Novak notes that changed secular attitudes toward suicides have had a great influence on secular systems of law, which has led to the decriminalization of suicide in many jurisdictions. Central to this transformation in social psychology and law has been a mistaken notion of autonomy (Novak, *The Sanctity of Human Life*, 115–16).

25. The view that suicide should be criminalized is very old, while the move to remove any penalties associated with suicide is relatively recent. Even more recent is the move by some legal jurisdictions to remove suicide from the criminal code entirely. Interestingly, I believe this has been done by relatively few jurisdictions, although I do not have the relevant statistics.

further moral argument which one could offer to convince such a person that killing innocent persons was always wrong?

A second natural law argument is based on Aquinas's account of the natural inclinations human beings share with other animals. According to Aquinas, three most basic inclinations, which Aquinas also calls "instincts," are: to protect one's life; to protect one's bodily integrity; and to protect the basic goods or property necessary for the sustenance of one's life. Thomas considers their relative priority abundantly obvious: "Who wouldn't give up their property to save a limb, or their eyesight? And who would not give up a limb or eyesight to save their life?"[26] Thus, Aquinas concludes that the preservation of one's life is the most basic human inclination and instinct.

As he notes in *Suicide and Morality*, David considers Aquinas's claim about the objectivity of the natural inclinations in human beings extraordinarily fruitful, for three reasons. First, of the various natural law arguments against suicide, it requires the fewest and least controversial presuppositions. Second, the natural inclinations involve the intentional and teleological pursuit of objects that are truly good. As such, they engage the world rather than simply the individual's perceptions. Third, Aquinas's account of the natural inclinations fits very well with (at least what was at that time) the leading work in psychoanalysis and suicidological social science research.

For this most basic natural inclination to preserve your life to operate appropriately and thus successfully in your life, it must be right ordered (i.e., ordered by appropriate virtues). This process of rightly ordering your natural inclinations (including the preservation of your life) must commence in childhood and adolescence. The likelihood of this happening depends in large part on the right-ordering in your parents of the second most basic natural inclination, the inclination of parents to raise and educate their offspring well.[27] If your parents have sufficient virtue to train you as a child to

---

26. Aquinas, *De Perfectione*, chapter 14. Here Aquinas is discussing "natural instinct" in human beings: "Second, the way in which we are commanded to love our neighbor, namely *as ourselves*, proves that our charity ought to be rightly ordered and sincere. For true and rightly ordered love prefers the greater to the lesser good. Now it is clear that of all human good the welfare of the soul is the greatest; next in degree comes physical well-being; and external goods occupy the last place. It is natural to man to observe this order in his preference. For who would not rather lose bodily eyesight than the use of reason? Who would not part with all his property in order to save his life? *Skin for skin, and all that a man has he will give for his life* (Job 2:4)."

27. The most famous account of the natural inclinations is found in Aquinas's *Summa Theologiae* (I-II, q. 94, a. 2). I have italicized the three basic natural inclinations which belong to the natural law: "According to the order of natural inclinations, is the order of the precepts of the natural law. Because in man there is first of all an inclination to good in accordance with the nature which he has in common with all substances: inasmuch as every substance seeks the preservation of its own being, according to its nature: and by reason of this inclination, whatever is a means of *preserving human life, and of warding off its obstacles,* belongs to the natural law. Secondly, there is in man an inclination to things that pertain to him more specially, according to that nature which he has in common with other animals: and in virtue of this inclination, those things are said to belong to the natural law, 'which nature has taught to all animals,' such as *sexual intercourse, education of offspring* and so forth. Thirdly, there is in man an inclination to good, according to the nature of his reason, which nature is proper to him: thus man has a natural inclination to *know the truth about God,* and

rightly order your natural inclinations (i.e., develop virtues), these virtues become in you a kind of second nature. As a child, you are truly blessed if you are brought up by virtuous parents who show you love and care and concern. The virtuous parent necessarily demonstrates the great good of your human life, typically without any direct reference to it. Virtuous parents constantly work to keep you from hurting yourself; they teach you to look both ways before crossing streets, and in innumerable other ways inculcate you into a community which says that human life is a great and precious good. Furthermore, they will emphasize not only that your life is precious, but also those of your friends, neighbors, and even strangers if their lives are endangered. When you are taught that human life (whether yours or another person's) is to be safeguarded, this is not a mere theoretical principle (like "all swans are white"). Rather, you are being morally formed to make wise judgments about how to safeguard human life, you are being trained how to morally specify and exercise a now deeply ingrained conviction. You are being formed not only to see the basic good of safeguarding life, but to actively pursue that good, both in oneself and others.

A third natural law argument concerning suicide is oriented very differently, not appealing inherently to the dictates of human reason or human nature, but to the wisdom of various religious and cultural traditions. For most cultures in history, and for what David calls the "classical philosophical tradition," freely killing oneself was understood as morally wrong.[28] The near-universal convergence across a variety of wisdom traditions on the morality of self-killing is another kind of natural law reasoning.[29] This historical wisdom also points to reasons *why* suicide has been considered morally wrong. Most cultures have seen self-killing as the killing of an innocent person, and hence a species of murder. Hence, as noted above, the dominance for well over a millennium of "self-murder" as the appropriate description of the act of killing oneself both in civil and ecclesiastical laws, as well as in society more generally.[30] Unlike English, which in the eighteenth century begin to substitute

---

to live in society: and in this respect, whatever pertains to this inclination belongs to the natural law; for instance, to shun ignorance, to avoid offending those among whom one has to live, and other such things regarding the above inclination."

28. Schrage argues that contrary to the traditional viewpoint, the Romans had no generalized prohibition of suicide. This may be the influence of Stoicism, as the "wise Stoic has the opportunity to consider all the relevant aspects and to decide to leave this earthly life. This rationally chosen free death is his natural right" (see Schrage, "Suicide in Canon Law," 58). Augustine's sharp response to the views of the Stoics can be found in *The City of God*, Book XIX, chapter 4. Augustine's views would be highly influential for Christianity. For example, Gratian's work in canon law quotes from Augustine when characterizing canon law regarding self-killing.

29. This more historical approach to the natural law is emphasized in the book *In Search of a Universal Ethic*, written by the International Theological Commission of the Catholic Church and available on the website of the Vatican. David Novak contributes to a collection of essays on this document. See his essay "Some Questions on the International Theological Commission Document on Natural Law."

30. In *Sanctity of Human Life*, David argues extensively against closely associating "suicide" with "homicide" in terms of a proper reading of Scripture or Jewish law. However, from my admittedly

"suicide" for "self-murder" or "self-destruction," other cultures and languages have retained the traditional term, e.g., Yiddish and German have retained *zelbstmord* (Yiddish) or *selbstmord* (German).

A fourth argument against suicide that supports these natural law arguments is found in Jewish and Christian teaching on the two greatest commandments—love of God and neighbor.[31] More specifically, it is an argument inherent in the teaching on love of neighbor. The command to love one's neighbor presumes appropriate love of self.[32] More specifically, the command that I love my neighbor presumes that I have a rightly ordered love of self—the presumption is embodied in the very grammar of this command. If my love of self is disordered, so will be my love of neighbor. Thus, a failure to love oneself (of which suicide is a paradigmatic expression) is thus contrary both to the natural law of justice and to the divine law of charity. Here, on the one hand, we see that a natural law prohibition of self-killing is in no way dependent on any divinely revealed moral norm. On the other hand, the recognition that suicide is incompatible with divine law may give one additional confidence regarding one's grasp of the natural law with regards to killing oneself.

The Suicide-Logic of Characteristically Liberal Societies

Let us begin by considering the attitudes of Canadian society concerning suicide. While opinion polls are often assumed to be the best (or even only) way to ascertain the attitudes of a society, that seems to me to be mistaken, at least for attitudes regarding serious moral questions. Such polls typically make such issues abstract, but people are more likely to give their most serious and heartfelt moral response when the question is put in a context. But when a serious moral question is put in a context, the polls typically follow a prominent news story featuring a divisive issue, and that particular drama is likely to generate reactive and skewed responses.

An alternative means of discovering societal attitudes is to look for them in deeply embedded practices of a society, practices that have arisen from shared moral assumptions. Typically, deeply held societal attitudes are not questioned or even noticed. An example of a shared assumption in my home Province of Ontario, Canada is its commitment to its social safety net and to healthcare, to which it devotes well over half of its financial resources. Within that healthcare system, it has and continues to assume that suicide is a very bad thing. We as a society should commit significant resources trying to prevent it. For example, almost any mental health questionnaire

---

limited reading of historical sources, his view seems to be a minority position.

31. Some natural law thinkers argue that the Ten Commandments are comprised of two tablets, where the first tablet pertains to the love of God and is required by divine law, and the second tablet concerns love of neighbor and is required by natural law. Whether such claims constitute either good exegesis or good theology is beyond the scope of this paper.

32. According to Aquinas, the natural law of justice is perfected by the divine law of charity, which calls me to love my neighbor as myself. See *Summa Theologiae* II-II, q. 25, a. 4.

includes questions about a) whether one has, or has previously had, any thoughts of committing suicide; and b) whether one has made or imagined plans to commit suicide. A positive answer to either of these two questions is considered a very bad sign in terms of the person's mental health and well-being. Furthermore, as a society we set up "helplines" to aid and counsel those contemplating suicide. Canadian academics and concerned individuals write books and articles on characteristics of suicidal people, again in an effort to discover warning signs and try to prevent suicides. And as David has pointed out, therapists working with suicidal persons have a moral obligation to try to prevent suicide, which reflects a moral judgment on the therapist's part, even if it goes unrecognized. These examples, and many others that could be noted, reflect a general societal view that suicide is an evil, something to be prevented if at all possible. This view, as discussed in the previous section, has been the practically universal wisdom of Western societies for over a thousand years. They have been privileged to share in the extensive philosophical and theological reasoning of the intellectual traditions of Judaism and Christianity.

In his work, David questions whether an increasingly dominant mode of moral and political discourse in Canadian and American society—the logic of modern liberalism—provides any adequate or coherent basis for rejecting suicide that reflects the still dominant Canadian ethos concerning most suicides. Or is modern liberalism at best parasitic on the moral convictions of this alternative tradition when it comes to the question of suicide?[33]

In modern liberalism, moral and legal discourse is dominated by "rights talk." The dominance of modern liberalism in Canada is succinctly summed up in Canada's 1982 *Charter of Rights and Freedoms*.[34] There is not even a need to argue for the primacy of individual "rights" and "freedoms;" it is simply a given.

In this framework, the questions concerning suicide are practically pre-ordained. Is suicide (or should it be) a right and/or basic freedom for Canadians? The answer is also pre-ordained, at least if liberalism remains dominant for enough time. Since the dominant assumption in Canadian politics and law is that all right-thinking Canadians will work to continually increase rights and freedoms, there will necessarily be constant pressure to do so with regard to suicide. What typically holds up such changes in law is a sense that it is opposed to public opinion, so rights advocates work at transforming (or manipulating) public opinion sufficiently to allow a new right to be added. This then binds the rest of society to accept it.

David has questioned modern liberalism's capacity to have a morally substantive view regarding suicide, in part because the current dominance of rights talk in

---

33. David believes that modern liberalism has no adequate basis for rejecting suicide (Novak, *Sanctity of Human Life*, 152).

34. The *Charter of Rights and Freedoms* is the first (and foundational) part of the 1982 Canadian Constitution. It is so prominent that it is typically referred to as "The Charter." With its foundation on inalienable rights, it joins the United States in basing its society on a philosophical mistake.

Canadian society shows the priority of the legal to the moral—a still regnant version of legal positivism. After all, a significant aspect of rights in contemporary liberalism is the right to do morally wrong things.[35] Unless of course, one's view of morality has become so attenuated that once something is legal, it simply must also be morally acceptable. And sadly, this is by no means an uncommon viewpoint in liberal societies such as Canada. What modern liberalism fails to see is that once one's mindset presumes that passing laws is what matters, and moral questions are to be considered private, then one gets backlashes where reactionary populist governments are similarly emboldened to impose laws independently of substantive moral considerations.[36]

The priority of the legal to the moral does not mean that liberal societies are devoid of moral or philosophical appeals concerning human nature as the basis for making "rights" the dominant legal and moral category. Rather, it is that the picture of human nature proffered by liberalism is terribly reductionistic. Typically, the underlying philosophical justification is understood to be an appeal to "autonomy." However, there is more than one account of autonomy.[37] As David reminds us, Kant's original doctrine of "autonomy" focused far more on societal duties than on rights. Contemporary appeals to autonomy focus almost exclusively on rights and freedoms. And appeal to rights and freedom have legalized not only suicide, but also euthanasia, which ironically cannot be autonomous.

David's analysis and critique of the claimed "right" to suicide is more sophisticated than the necessarily simple account I have been able to present. He has recognized that the right to suicide is typically justified not merely or even primarily from a generic appeal to autonomy, but from a specific understanding of autonomy, one which appeals to the recently created doctrine of privacy.[38] David asks:

> Is killing myself, in fact, the greatest exercise of my right to privacy? Conversely, is my right to kill myself, within my larger right to privacy, something society (through the institution of state officials) should revoke by invading my privacy, as it were, when I have abused that right by harming myself, and most likely harming the people who are nearest and dearest to me? . . . Is my

---

35. Governments with more substantive views of the good may still allow wrong behavior, if a prudential decision is made that in a particular cultural context to attempt to prohibit the activity would lead to even worse activities. But such governments would generally not speak of individuals having the right to do so.

36. In the recent Canadian context, this can be seen in Quebec with its ban on displaying any religious symbol on one's person if one is employed by the government. In Ontario, this can be seen in the Ontario government's appeal to the "notwithstanding" clause to squash any appeals to its decision to slash the number of aldermen on the Toronto City Council. Novak asks, is "independence as liberty only the property of those who have the power to defend themselves? If that is the case, then even for radical liberals the social contract has been irrevocably broken" (Novak, "Suicide is Not a Private Choice," 31).

37. For an account of the development of the doctrine of autonomy, which culminated with Kant, see Schneewind, *The Invention of Autonomy*.

38. Novak, *The Sanctity of Human Life*, 148–49. See also Novak, "Suicide is Not a Private Choice," 31.

right to privacy virtually absolute, or is it much more conditional, contingent upon the approval of the society in which I am so dependent for my life and well-being in this world?[39]

David goes on to argue that in a very short period of time, modern liberalism has come to see the right to privacy as the foundation of *all* moral rights and duties.

David explains in a highly cogent and convincing manner that the rise and increasing dominance of the privacy-focused version of autonomy is an even more reductive—and ultimately destructive—account of the human self. The development of the doctrine of autonomy from Kant's "duties"-focused autonomy to contractarianism's "rights"-focused notion of autonomy had produced a solipsistic view of the self. The more recent doctrine of "privacy" leads to a narcissistic view of the self. It is narcissistic because it demands the respect of others in all one's deeds and attitudes. At the same time, this doctrine of privacy views the nature of the individual as essentially solitary. The individual is true to his fundamental nature when alone. The doctrine of privacy also appeals to the American myth of self-sufficiency, a myth that conveniently ignores the sacrifices of one's biological and societal forebears that created and developed the society which now provides the leisure-class the time to fantasize the fiction of the "self-made man."

Thus, according to David, when the "true believer" in privacy and self-sufficiency as the defining characteristics of the individual engages in any work in the public sphere, this work will have a distinct character. Though such a person's labors may appear oriented to a public good, his or her labors are performed merely as a necessary evil for the benefit of the solitary self. Public service must be instrumental, oriented to the individual's "private" good. The true believer in the "private" person is inherently selfish. If they actually act according to this doctrine of privacy, they will neither give, nor can expect, any trust or loyalty from others. A "private person" is not and cannot be a part of any true or authentic community.

Here we see a dual notion of "private" that David emphasizes. While we now see "private" as simply pertaining to the individual, "*privatio*" means a privation, a fundamental lack. Historically, the "private" realm of human existence and activity was that deprived of any importance. It was that realm of activity too trivial for society to bother to supervise it.[40]

According to David, the state of the person committed to this doctrine of privacy is the state of death. While we typically think of "death" as the state of non-being, we cannot make any existential sense of such a notion—we have no idea what might constitute that. David's view is that death is best understood as ultimate loneliness and abandonment. As he memorable puts it, "Death is our own ultimate loneliness,

---

39. Novak, *Sanctity of Human Life*, 144.
40. Novak, *Sanctity of Human Life*, 14.

our anticipation of being abandoned to our ultimate privacy.[41] David notes, in quoting the epigraph of this essay, that for Job, estrangement from kin and friends was the meaning of death.

Sad, the truly private person cannot even authentically employ the notion of "abandonment," since there is never authentic or necessary community to begin with. Thus, it is by no means a stretch to think that there is a connection between the rise of influence of this modern doctrine of privacy—and the resulting loneliness that is a significant factor in suicide. There is certainly a correlation between societies which embrace this doctrine of privacy—and the loneliness it inherently entails—with an increased prevalence of suicide.

From his earliest work, drawing on the social scientific literature, David has recognized the connection between strong community ties and a lower incidence of suicide. He thus contrasts the privacy doctrine of modern liberalism with societies that live presuming that humans are truly social beings. David tells the story of a Hutterite community, whose people seem to have a genetic predisposition to bipolar disorder. David relates that the Hutterites, when they see that one of their community members is showing signs of the depression associated with bipolar disorder, are never left alone. As a result, there is a surprisingly low incidence of suicide among the Hutterites.[42]

In terms of the importance of David's work for Catholic ethics, his analysis and critique of the rise of the modern doctrine of privacy is one I do not find in the Catholic tradition—or at least the bioethical literature of the tradition. David's understanding of this impediment to the realization of the Catholic commitment to an authentic pursuit of the common good is one that the Catholic tradition would do well to integrate it into its social, biomedical, and sexual teaching.

Are There Actually Suicides and Can We Judge Them? A Jewish-Catholic Conversation

David's work on suicide clearly underwent a development between *Suicide and Morality* (1976) and *The Sanctity of Human Life* (2007). Certainly it did so in emphasis, and also, it seems to me, in substance. In the more recent book, David emphasizes his agreement with what he refers to as the current consensus in Jewish ethics. Besides agreeing that a freely and deliberately chosen suicide is morally wrong, the current consensus in Jewish ethics with regards to suicide consists of two controversial tenets.

Tenet #1: Post facto, a suicide must always be seen as a psychotic or delusional act.

Tenet #2: The Jewish community is never competent to judge morally whether a person has killed himself in his right mind.

---

41. Novak, *Sanctity of Human Life*, 157.
42. See Novak, *Sanctity of Human Life*, 157–58.

In this final section, I do three things. First, I will summarize five major points of agreement between the Jewish and Catholic traditions regarding suicide. Second, I will analyze the two controversial tenets, questioning their coherence and their compatibility with each other. Third, I will examine the relationship between moral and pastoral perspectives in the two traditions. Fourth, I will consider an apparent divergence between the two traditions. However, it is essential, regardless of the significance of an "intra-mural debate," to locate any disagreement within the context of widespread agreement between Jewish and Catholic ethics on the question of suicide. I limit myself to five key points of agreement between the two traditions.

Five Points of Agreement

First, Jews and Christians agree that one can freely choose to kill oneself. In *Suicide and Morality*, David argues that the "classical tradition" of philosophy, which for David encompasses Plato, Aristotle, Augustine, Maimonides, Aquinas, and Kant, agrees that killing oneself can be a rationally chosen action. More importantly, both Jewish and Christian traditions find a scriptural basis for this view, and it is affirmed by authoritative voices in their respective traditions. Furthermore, it would seem that logic requires both traditions to affirm this. Evaluating suicide morally presupposes a freely chosen action, and thus it is subject to moral evaluation.[43]

Second, Jewish and Christian traditions recognize that to freely kill oneself is morally wrong. The wrongfulness of killing oneself is knowable according to Noahide law (i.e., the natural law), i.e., known apart from the authority of Jewish or Christian Scripture. At the same time, both traditions recognize that although killing oneself is contrary to the natural law, some philosophical traditions defend the practice as morally acceptable or even laudatory in some circumstances. Thus, for example, Augustine and Moses Mendelssohn argue against Stoicism's defense of the practice.[44]

Third, while the Jewish and Christian traditions recognize and affirm natural law arguments against killing oneself, their foremost authority for the prohibition of killing oneself is the authority of Scripture, followed by other authorities in their respective traditions. Up through the nineteenth century, both traditions, as well as Western societies more generally, regularly referred to killing oneself as "self-murder."[45]

43. If suicide could not involve a free or deliberate choice, why would any of these philosophers raise moral objections to it? It would be like arguing that it would be wrong for a person to order his heart to stop, or that it would be wrong to decide to stop defecating. It is absurd to morally evaluate matters that are *per se* not under human control.

44. Augustine, *City of God*, Book XIX, chapter 4; Moses Mendelssohn, *Gesammelte Schriften* (1843), 156 and onward. The reference to Mendelssohn is found in Reines, "Jewish Attitude toward Suicide," 163. David also believes that Rabbi Eleazar argues against a Stoic or Stoic-like viewpoint (Novak, *The Sanctity of Human Life*, 135).

45. For a variety of Jewish authorities that saw killing oneself as "self-murder," and which resulted on restrictions with regard to a Jewish burial, see Mackler, *Jewish and Catholic Bioethics*, 65. The primary text appealed to in the Jewish tradition for the wrongfulness of suicide is Genesis: "I will

Fourth, both the Catholic and Jewish traditions have come to the conclusion that *at least* many suicides are not freely chosen.[46] This is evident in the burial practices in both Judaism and Catholicism. Whereas at one time those who had committed suicide would not receive a full Jewish or Catholic funeral and burial, now, overwhelmingly, Jews and Christians who commit suicide receive them. According to David, this is now a given in the Jewish tradition, and some in the Catholic tradition effectively agree.[47]

Fifth, neither the Jewish or Catholic traditions still believe that a freely chosen suicide necessarily precludes salvation. Both traditions leave the ultimate judgment regarding one who has committed suicide to the mercy of God. According to *The Catechism of the Catholic Church*, "We should not despair of the eternal salvation of persons who have taken their own lives. By ways known to him alone, God can provide the opportunity for salutary repentance. The Church prays for persons who have taken their own lives."[48]

Analyzing Two Controversial Tenets

The first controversial tenet is that no suicide is rationally chosen, at least considered after the fact.[49] David explains the claim by saying that in all cases of suicide, the person who kills himself is not in his right mind, but is "psychotic" or "delusional."[50] He states, "All suicides are now regarded, after the fact, as having been psychotic behavior."[51] To

---

certainly demand an account for your life-blood" (Genesis 9:5). Similarly, the Catholic tradition, in putting suicide under the commandment not to kill, is linking suicide to the prohibition of murder. An example of this Catholic view can be found in the current *Catechism of the Catholic Church*. David argues that suicide does not and cannot come under the fifth commandment because in the commandment to kill is a transitive verb and is thus limited to killing others. While David seems to be correct that the fifth commandment has not been the primary scriptural basis for Judaism's rejection of suicide, I have not found evidence in the Jewish tradition to support David's reasoning as to the reason why.

46. Here I emphasize "at least" because a point of disagreement will be whether all suicides, *post facto*, should be understood as not freely chosen.

47. Now, if a priest speaks of "suicide" in a funeral homily, his bishop may revoke his right to conduct funerals. See "Priest Pulled from Funerals after Repeatedly Citing Teenager's Suicide in 'Pastoral Disaster.'"

48. *Catechism of the Catholic Church*.2283.

49. Novak, *The Sanctity of Human Life*, 113.

50. Novak, *The Sanctity of Human Life*, 113, 114, 131, 136.

51. Novak, *The Sanctity of Human Life*, 114. Here, David refers to all non-rational (and thus non-culpable) self-killing as "psychotic." At first glance, this seems to be an overly narrow limitation of the conditions under which a person may be non-culpable for killing themselves. For psychotic disorders are only one kind of (serious) mental illness. "Psychotic disorders are severe mental disorders that cause abnormal thinking and perceptions. People with psychoses lose touch with reality. Two of the main symptoms are delusions and hallucinations. Delusions are false beliefs, such as thinking that someone is plotting against you or that the TV is sending you secret messages. Hallucinations are false perceptions, such as hearing, seeing, or feeling something that is not there. Schizophrenia is one

understand the exact nature of this claim, let us recall the two basic requirements for any free and deliberate action. The first requirement is that you know what you are doing (e.g., you cannot commit suicide while sleeping). The second is that you freely will to commit suicide, that is, have control over your actions. I take it that David is claiming that all persons who kill themselves fail the first requirements. All who commit suicide have lost any fundamental grip on reality; they have unwillingly been gripped by a delusional *persona*. A paradigmatic example would be the person who, having taken a psychedelic drug, believes he can fly, and so leaps off a tall building.

The difficulty with the "delusional" explanation of any, much less all, suicides, is that it proves too much. We are no longer even discussing suicide, properly understood. The action of the person convinced by a delusion that he can fly cannot properly be described as a "not-freely chosen" suicide. Rather, the deluded person does not commit suicide, period. The deluded person not only does not intend to kill himself, he is not even aware that his action is dangerous. While under the delusion of an ability to fly, leaping off the building involves no intent whatsoever to kill oneself.[52] In such cases, the death is an accident, analogous to someone being hit by a car while walking down the street, or dying in a skiing accident, or slipping and falling off a bridge. The very notion of suicide—e.g., throwing oneself off the bridge—requires some expectation of bringing about one's own death.

So, what is the difference between a freely chosen and not-freely chosen suicide? A distinction must be made between the nature of an act and the culpability of an action. To be classed a suicide, one must in some basic sense know that one is attempting to commit suicide. The nature of such an act is, objectively speaking, wrong. However, in various circumstances, one's subjective culpability in so acting may be reduced or even eliminated. That is what is typically meant by a "not-freely chosen" suicide.

From other comments David makes about suicide, he does not seem to be entirely convinced about the first tenet. He completes the above quoted sentence acknowledging that a freely chosen suicide would be objectively wrong, that killing oneself is not

> . . . permitted *ab initio* to anyone who is capable of making an intelligent moral choice and who, as such, is not psychotic by definition.[53]

---

type of psychotic disorder. People with bipolar disorder may also have psychotic symptoms. Other problems that can cause psychosis include alcohol and some drugs, brain tumors, brain infections, and stroke" [The Medline (the US national library of medicine) website]. However, it is certainly possible that David would want to argue that for a person who commits suicide to be deemed as not having acted culpably, the person must be deemed to have been suffering from this extremely serious condition (i.e., psychosis).

52. One might prefer the following analogy: an adolescent, wanting to go swimming, mistakenly thinks that jumping into the water from a high bridge is as safe as jumping from a very low bridge. It is a foolish mistake, a tragic mistake, but it is no suicide.

53. Novak, *The Sanctity of Human Life*, 114.

David is clearly correct that anyone capable of making a moral choice is not psychotic. However, if he is committed to the view that all suicides are psychotic/delusional, then this qualification is irrelevant, since no one ever kills themselves in their right mind.

But David recognizes the power of the traditional prohibition of suicide among observant Jews and Catholics. There is no doubt that the traditional understanding that to commit suicide could endanger their salvation was a major impediment to such persons killing themselves. We see this today in the much lower rates of suicide in societies that strongly disapprove of it.

However, if one accepts the first tenet, then the observant Jew or Christian can be reassured that regardless of whether suicide is seriously morally wrong, he could commit suicide with the reassurance that *post facto* it would be determined necessarily that he was not responsible for it.[54] The first tenet allows contemporary Jewish ethics to maintain *in theory* the traditional prohibition of suicide, but *in practice*, no one is ever able to commit it.

The second tenet bypasses the question of the state of mind of the person who kills himself. It focuses on the Jewish community's inability to ever make a moral *judgment* regarding the person who has killed himself.[55]

> Whether the suicide was really beyond the control of the now-deceased person who killed himself or herself, however, is left to the judgment of God in and for the world-to-come.[56]

Here David appears to hedge his bets. Now he acknowledges that some suicides can be judged morally. But only God can pass such judgments. There is some historical precedent for this view in Jewish ethics. Some commentators note that at times the Jewish tradition required an unusually high burden of proof to judge that a suicide had taken place.[57] Be that as it may, the degree of proof required by Jewish religious

---

54. Or as I have argued above, that according to the logic of the first tenet, one cannot actually commit "suicide."

55. I specify the Jewish community because for both arguments, David cites the Babylonian Talmud as the source of authority for his claim. Here David does not indicate whether his arguments can also be known by the natural law and thus are relevant to all persons.

56. Novak, *The Sanctity of Human Life*, 113.

57. According to Reines, medieval Rabbinic authorities had "stringent qualifying requirements [which] made it difficult for a case to be classified legally as suicide. Thus, a death could be ruled suicide only when the individual had explicitly declared his intent to commit suicide, and there were eye witnesses to the act. But if the individual was found hanging on a tree, for example, it was ruled that death may have been accidental" (see Reines, "Jewish Attitude toward Suicide," 169–70).

In addition, David notes that in the Jewish tradition, one cannot be convicted of a capital crime solely by self-incrimination, i.e., confessing to the crime, but can only be convicted on the basis of two witnesses. Novak argues that the traditional justification for this requirement was based on the tradition's prohibition of suicide. The Jewish tradition is aware that many who are suicidal do not wish to take full agency in bringing about their own death and thus will, for example, confront police in order to be killed, or may falsely confess to a heinous crime so that he may be executed for the crime. Here we see the Jewish tradition's general abhorrence to killing oneself.

authorities clearly varied in different times and places. But there does not seem to be any historical precedent for this second tenet, which takes judicial humility to an extreme on the question of suicide. David acknowledges this judicial humility is atypical in Jewish law, and thus he develops an intricate argument regarding the uniqueness of the "reflexive" action involved in suicide.

Initially, it would appear that the first tenet (all suicides are psychotic/delusional) drives the second (suicides cannot be *judged* by mortals). However, I am convinced that the argument proceeds in the opposite direction. The refusal to ever *judge* a suicide as "a contemplated, deliberate choice" encourages the decision to consider *post factum* that all suicides are beyond the individual's control. This is evident in David's most extended explanation of the relationship between divine and human judgment when it comes to cases of suicide:

> One's responsibility for a suicide committed in this world will be judged by God in the world to come; with regard to the judgment for any questionable act committed in this world, God alone knows the heart and its true motives and will surely judge whether the successful suicide was compelled by forces beyond one's control to stop them or not. (In this world, however, we judge all suicides after the fact as having been compelled by forces beyond the person's control, and that judgment should include persons who seemingly commit suicide as a result of contemplated, deliberate choice.)[58]

Here David makes it clear that *not* all suicides are *necessarily* beyond the person's control. In fact, here David acknowledges that in some cases it appears clear that the person killed himself with a contemplated and deliberate choice. But this is overridden by a general principle of incompetence to judge any suicide as within the person's control, at least after the fact of the suicide.

Thus, is unclear why David accepts the first tenet. It seems unnecessary and gratuitous for the overall argument. While the first tenet takes the form of an empirical claim, David does not treat it that way, never offering any medical or psychological evidence. This leads me to conclude that David's commitment to this viewpoint is independent of empirical evidence.[59]

There is also the paradoxical claim that it is only *after the fact* that a suicide should be regarded as necessarily delusional. Viewed prospectively, David maintains that killing oneself can and should be morally proscribed. There does seem to be an important reason why David must maintain this distinction. David believes that not only should suicide be prohibited morally, he also thinks it should be proscribed by civil law. I am very sympathetic to this latter view, and I am sympathetic for all the reasons discussed above in terms of both the philosophical and theological reasons

58. Novak, *The Sanctity of Human Life*, 133–34.

59. If David were trying to make an empirical claim, what evidence could possibly be presented to establish its truth? The sciences are ultimately incompetent to make fundamental claims about free will. On this point, see Alasdair MacIntyre, "What the Natural Sciences Do Not Explain."

discussed in the first section regarding the wrongfulness of suicide. I am also in full agreement with David that although suicide should be legally proscribed, no civil punishment or sanction should be attached to such a law.

How can this proscription be justified? For good or ill, many in contemporary Canadian society take the law as a pseudo-guide for their morality. As David points out, it is a fact of social psychology that we are all influenced (to varying degrees) in our moral viewpoints by our society (as evidenced by the jump in moral approval of suicide after the change of the law in Canada). Cathleen Kaveny argues that the law is a moral teacher.[60] Legally proscribing activities or disincentivizing them in other ways, if done wisely and proportionately, has a salutary effect on the practices in a society. Thus, there are some good reasons for societies who do not wish to prosecute suicides or attempted suicides to leave the law on the books, as an indication that suicide is not going to be seen as a morally good and/or praiseworthy practice in Canadian society.

The Primacy of the Pastoral

I believe that the most sense can be made of David's complex viewpoint if one sees both of his arguments as undergirded by a pastoral imperative, namely, that all Jews who kill themselves still receive Jewish funeral and burial rites. While his discussion of suicide in *The Sanctity of Human Life* does not discuss Jewish burial practices, I see that as a key unstated context for his discussion. This seems to be another reason for David's emphasis that only retrospectively can one conclude that no suicide was freely chosen. For after the fact of a suicide, the pastoral perspective comes to the fore. Prior to the fact, in exhorting Jews not to commit suicide, the moral perspective predominates.

As I indicated earlier, I am highly sympathetic with David's perspective that Jews who kill themselves be given the benefit of the doubt with regard to their non-culpability and be given a Jewish burial. Contemporary Catholicism has very similar sympathies. Currently, its dominant pastoral practice, at least in the West, is similar to that of Judaism. The Church presumes that *prima facie*, the person who kills himself was not acting freely. Thus, typically the person receives a Catholic funeral and burial. However, Catholic practice cannot be, or at least should not be, identical to that which David defends. The primary objection must be to the dominant Jewish viewpoint that *all persons* who kill themselves are psychotic.

But there remains a serious concern with this pastoral perspective. For, as noted earlier, if one either refuses to ever ascribe agency to the one who commits suicide, or refuses to judge any suicide, that seems to me to abandon Halachic responsibility of the Jewish leader, or the teaching responsibility of the Catholic authority. For the evidence points to there being no clear line between the freely chosen and not-freely chosen suicide. And culpability certainly appears to be on a kind of spectrum.

---

60. See Kaveny, *Law's Virtues*.

The vast majority of those persons who contemplate suicide are highly vulnerable persons, who for the most part do not have a stable nor continuous desire to die.[61] Refusing to judge even the most obvious cases of freely chosen suicide seems to me to communicate to this highly vulnerable population that we do not consider their lives important enough to fully communicate the nature of God's call to us to embrace our lives, even in the midst of obstacles and suffering. That, it seems to me, cannot help but being a form of abandonment of such persons.

Catholic Concerns

There are a number of concerns that arise from the Catholic tradition to these two tenets, some philosophical and some theological. Philosophically, why does Jewish ethics treat suicide uniquely? Why is Jewish ethics unable to pass judgment on the one who kills himself but is able to pass judgment on the one who kills other persons?[62] In some places David seems to indicate that a suicide is the most private of all acts, but in other places he severely questions the claim that suicide can be a private act.

In addition, do David's arguments apply only to Jews, or only to persons in moral or religious traditions that consider suicide morally wrong? Would David claim that, even though Stoics justify and even laud self-killing, all Stoics who commit suicide are in a psychotic state?

Third, I noted above that the rate of suicide varies tremendously between different parts of the world. It is clear that varying cultural and moral perspectives, as well as the nature of social relationships in different societies, affects the rate of suicide. David notes this reality; as social beings Westerners are clearly influenced by our societies. As our societies increasingly accept the appropriateness of suicide as a response to life crises, so too are Jews and Christians more likely to commit suicide. However, David's acceptance of the first tenet would appear to deny the relevance of this trend, unless these changing mores in Western societies regarding suicide are somehow the cause of increased psychotic or delusional states of mind.

Finally, the Catholic tradition must have serious theological concerns with the two tenets. First of all, it has been the constant teaching of the Catholic tradition (and for that matter the Jewish tradition) that suicide can—at least in some circumstances—be a freely chosen action—and at least in some circumstances can be judged to have been so. This has also been the nearly universal view in Western societies for most of the last two thousand years. This fundamental point remains

---

61. More generally, most persons do not have stable convictions about their end-of-life decisions in the period leading up to their death. This fact alone is a challenge to typical assumptions about the reality of the liberal doctrine of human autonomy. It is an aspiration for many in a liberal society, but it is in reality illusory.

62. "Legally, the greatest different between suicide and homicide is that whereas we now judge all suicides to be accidental, we still judge homicides to have been premeditated (*zadon*), careless (*shegagah*), or accidental (*ones*)" (Novak, *The Sanctity of Human Life*, 113).

true, even though over the last century evidence from the social sciences have shown that the matter of suicide is more complex than previously acknowledged, and that many suicides are not freely chosen. This is why the Catholic and Jewish traditions have emphasized the distinction between the objective nature of the act, versus the degree of culpability that should be assigned to it.[63]

My pastoral concerns stated above may also be thought of in terms of Catholic teaching on the sin of scandal. In the New Testament, scandal (*skandalon*) comes from the notion of causing someone to stumble. In Catholic moral theology, scandal refers to the sin of leading another person into sin. With regard to Catholic burial, the logic is as follows: if a proper church burial is given to those whose final decision is what is obviously a freely and deliberately chosen mortal sin, does the Church, given that Catholic burial is to be given only to persons who die in communion with the Church, not in practice deny that a freely and deliberately chosen suicide is a sin? And if so, is that not likely to lead others to think that killing themselves is a legitimate way to end their lives? While the way I have just put the matter does not have the kind of nuance that ideally would be added, it does convey the basic and very real problem of scandal involved in refusing to ever judge suicide as a seriously wrong action. A recent *New York Times* article indicates that this is in fact a societal trend in the US, that suicide is simply seen as an alternative and perfectly legitimate "end of life" option.

David argues that Jews who commit suicide have no negative impact on other Jews, since suicide is not considered permitted to any Jew who can make a free moral choice. But since he also defines suicide as something only done by the psychotic, could not Jews in their right mind choose to commit suicide, knowing that retrospectively they will have been considered to be psychotic and thus not held responsible for their action?

Furthermore, if all suicides are in the end to be considered psychotic or delusional, it is not clear how David can argue that suicide should be prohibited by law. He asks whether we could "justify a legal prohibition of suicide to save suicidal persons from their own self-destructive designs."[64] If all suicides are irrational, then there is no basis for a *legal* prohibition of suicide. Those considered psychotic who are "a danger to themselves" are restrained by a medical order, not a legal order. A legal order presumes the possible voluntariness of a suicide.

Conclusion

While I have expressed some significant disagreements with David in the final section of the paper, everything I have argued in this paper is part of an expression of the highest

---

63. As Mackler notes, in the Jewish tradition there is now a strong presumption that the person was not "in full control of his or her actions—so guilt is mitigated subjectively, even though the deed is objectively wrong" (Mackler, *Introduction to Jewish and Catholic Bioethics*, 66).

64. Novak, *Sanctity*, 148–49.

admiration for David's work. I am incredibly grateful for his deep and sophisticated call for us to choose life at all times. That is, for us to choose what are truly good and holy lives, lives which embrace our families and all those we have the opportunity to come to know. For such a life is what leads us to true happiness, which ultimately is fully resting in God. Meanwhile, as Jews and Christians seek to advance in convivial friendship, it is essential that we understand each other's traditions as well as possible. I do not pretend to have a full understanding of David's complex and often brilliant arguments. But my goal will have succeeded if my essay provokes further dialogue that helps understand one another better, and in so doing, better love one another as God's children. This in itself may serve as a joint witness to God's Law and God's Love.

Bibliography

Aquinas, Thomas. *De Perfectione*. Translated as *The Religious State: The Episcopate and the Priestly Office*. St. Louis, MO: B. Herder, 1903.

Aquinas, Thomas. *Summa theologiae*. Translated by Fathers of the English Dominican Province. Westminster, MD: Christian Classics, 1981.

Augustine. *City of God*. Translated by Henry Bettenson. London: Penguin, 1984.

Barraclough, Brian, and Daphne Shepard. "A Necessary Neologism: The Origin and Uses of Suicide." *Life-Threatening Behavior* 24 (1994) 113–26.

Catechism of the Catholic Church. 2nd ed. Vatican City: Libreria Editrice Vaticana, 1997.

International Theological Commission. *In Search of a Universal Ethic: A New Look at the Natural Law*. 2009. http://www.vatican.va/roman_curia/congregations/cfaith/cti_documents/rc_con_cfaith_doc_20090520_legge-naturale_en.html.

Kass, Leon. "L'Chaim and Its Limits: Why Not Immortality?" *First Things*, May 2001. https://www.firstthings.com/article/2001/05/lchaim-and-its-limits-why-not-immortality.

Kaveny, Cathleen. *Law's Virtues*. Washington, DC: Georgetown University Press, 2012.

MacIntyre, Alasdair. "What the Natural Sciences Do Not Explain." Notre Dame Center for Ethics and Culture. August 22, 2014. https://www.youtube.com/watch?v=MZ_rHV2KTPY.

Mackler, Aaron. *Introduction to Jewish and Catholic Bioethics: A Comparative Analysis*. Washington, DC: Georgetown University Press, 2003.

Novak, David. "The Moral Crisis of the West: The Judeo-Christian Response." *Scottish Journal of Theology* 53 (2000) 1–21.

———. *The Sanctity of Human Life*. Washington, DC: Georgetown University Press, 2007.

———. "Some Questions on the International Theological Commission Document on Natural Law." In *Searching for a Universal Ethic: Multidisciplinary, Ecumenical, and Interfaith Responses to the Catholic Natural Law Tradition*, edited by John Berkman and William Mattison, 136–45. Grand Rapids, Eerdmans, 2015.

———. *Suicide and Morality*. New York: Scholars Studies, 1975.

———. "Suicide is Not a Private Choice." *First Things* 75 (1997) 31–34.

Phillips, Julie. "The Dangerous Shifting Cultural Narratives around Suicide." *Washington Post*, March 21, 2019. https://www.washingtonpost.com/outlook/the-dangerous-shifting-cultural-narratives-around-suicide/2019/03/21/7277946e-4bf5-11e9-93d0-64dbcf38ba41_story.html.

"Psychotic Disorders." MedlinePlus. https://medlineplus.gov/psychoticdisorders.html.

Reines, Chaim. "Jewish Attitude toward Suicide." *Judaism: A Quarterly Journal* 10.2 (1961) 160–70.

Schneewind, J.B. *The Invention of Autonomy*. Baltimore: Johns Hopkins Press, 1999.

Schrage, Eltjo. "Suicide in Canon Law." *Journal of Legal History* 21.1 (2007) 59–61.

Waldenberg, Eliezer Yehudah. *Ramat Rahel* 29. In *Tzitz Eliezer*, 5:38–39. Jerusalem: n.p., 1985.

Webb, Stephen. "God of the Depressed." *First Things*, February 19, 2016. https://www.firstthings.com/web-exclusives/2016/02/god-of-the-depressed.

Zaveri, Mihir and Jacey Fortin. "Priest Pulled from Funerals after Repeatedly Citing Teenager's Suicide in 'Pastoral Disaster.'" *The New York Times*, December 17, 2018. https://www.nytimes.com/2018/12/16/us/maison-hullibarger-suicide-funeral.html.

Response to

John Berkman's "In the Beginning: The Primordial Character of the Problem of Suicide in David Novak's Scholarship"

David Novak

I AM GRATEFUL TO John Berkman for his very careful reading of most of my writings on the moral problem of suicide and for expressing the usefulness of my various reflections as a Jewish theologian in his work as a Catholic moral theologian dealing with this problem. Nevertheless, John is honest enough with me (which is the sign of a true friend) to question some of my specific points in dealing with this problem, about which we have so much general and even specific agreement. As John puts it, "Christians and Jews have had [not necessarily] identical views with regard to killing oneself."[1] So, let me try to now clarify my position on three of these specific questions, all of which involve the problem of self-reference, a problem that the very *sui* in *sui-cide* (literally, "*self*-murder") immediately raises for any reflection on the act it names. In so doing, I hope to now do more than just repeat, more than just paraphrase, my earlier statements that John has so assiduously studied. Rather, I hope John's questioning of some of these earlier statements forces me to think up at least some new thoughts on this important moral/theological problem.

In his first question, John writes, "David argues extensively against closely associating 'suicide' with 'homicide' in terms of a proper reading of historical sources. . . . However, from my admittedly limited reading of historical sources [I assume he means 'historical *Jewish* sources'], his view seems to be a minority position."[2] Here, John is at disadvantage due to the fact that my first book, *Law and Theology in Judaism* (New York, 1974), in which there is a chapter titled "Suicide in Jewish Perspective" (pp. 80–93), does deal with the Jewish sources, and in a way that makes my interpretation of them by no means "a minority position." That book, however, has long been out of print and is not as readily available as the other works John has

1. p. 96.
2. pp. 99–100n30.

seen and used. So, let me reiterate the main source in the Talmud for the prohibition of suicide brought in that book.

The biblical proof text (indeed, there is one for virtually every rabbinical ruling) quoted there (Baba Kama 91b) states (in my translation there), "For your life-blood too I will require a reckoning" (Gen 9:5). From this reading of Genesis 9:5, Rabbi Eleazar derives the prohibition of harming oneself, of which suicide is the most extreme example. In his interpretation, Rabbi Eleazar has done two things to the scriptural text. One, he has made the first clause of this verse stand on its own, separating it from the second clause, which speaks of God's requiring a reckoning from wild beasts and from fellow humans who have committed *homicide.* Two, as the great mediaeval exegete Rashi pointed out, Rabbi Eleazar has the verse say, "*from* your life, God will require a reckoning *for* your blood [which you have shed]." Suicide is connected to homicide as regards God's condemnation of both acts, yet suicide is not subsumed under the prohibition of homicide.

As I have argued in my book, *The Sanctity of Human Life* (Washington, DC, 2007), which John cites extensively, the phenomenology of suicide is different enough from that of murder to warrant thinking about them differently. To be sure, since they are both prohibited *ab initio*, they are both considered unwarranted "bloodshed" (*shefikhut damim*); yet their legal consequences are quite different. For murder one is culpable in a human court; for suicide one is not culpable there. In the case of murder, the perpetrator of the crime and its victim are two different persons; in the case of suicide, they are one and the same person. As such, in the case of murder, we can punish the perpetrator and avenge the victim; in the case of suicide, were we to punish the perpetrator, wouldn't we be simultaneously punishing the victim? In fact, in such cases where we cannot make this essential differentiation, we should leave the judgment of the act to God, who alone can make this differentiation. Moreover, in the case of murder, we assume free choice in committing the act unless proven otherwise; in the case of suicide, we almost always assume there was no free choice in committing the act.

All that notwithstanding, why not cite the Decalogue, viz., "you shall not murder" (Exod 20:13; Deut 5:17), and subsume suicide under this general prohibition, despite the specific differences just noted? Although none of the classical sources do that (as pointed out in the excellent 1961 article, "The Jewish Attitude Toward Suicide" by C. W. Reines that Berkman cites), none of these sources to my knowledge says why. So, despite the weaknesses of any *argumentum ex silentio*, let me venture an answer. While Thomas Aquinas considers the Decalogue to be the prime declaration of universal natural law, the Jewish tradition locates it elsewhere. That is because just preceding the presentation of the Decalogue the Torah states, "Moses came down to the people [*el ha'am*], and he said to them [*aleihem*] that God spoke all the following words" (Exod 19:25–20). Both the prescriptions and the proscriptions of the Decalogue are addressed to the people Israel.

Even though several rabbinic sources say that the Torah was published so that the gentiles might learn from it, however, their actual responsibility to obey the prohibition of "shedding (innocent) human blood" (according to Rabbi Eleazar) already came from what God told Noah—the progenitor of universal humankind. Hence, Rabbi Eleazar is giving a specific scriptural source for this general Noahide prohibition. Yet the text from Genesis 9:5 does not actually prohibit this bloodshed (murder and suicide), i.e., it does not state what *shall not be done* by humans (i.e., *adam*). Instead, it states what God *will do* to those who kill the innocent, including those who kill themselves. (The text confines the prohibition of killing to killing the innocent, as the following verse 9:6 prescribes capital punishment for murderers.) But where does the actual prohibition to humans, the *you shall not*, come from?

Although one rabbinic source (Sanhedrin 56b) gives a rather forced interpretation of Genesis 2:16 that says "the LORD God commanded [*va-yitsav*] humans [*al ha'adam*, i.e., 'about shedding their blood (*dam*)']," it would seem that the fact that shedding innocent blood is culpable presupposes that its prohibition is already known. Yet if it is not stated, it must be something humans ought to know insofar as the prohibition in effect commands itself to all rational humans. As such, it is a natural law precept. That is why God judges Cain culpable for the murder of his brother Abel, even though Cain does not seem to have received any explicit prohibition from God. This is discussed in my book, *Natural Law in Judaism*.[3] Therefore, may I be so bold to say that Rabbi Eleazar makes a better natural law argument for the prohibition of bloodshed than even Aquinas does, insofar as the Torah does not have to tell humankind of this prohibition. And since the people Israel are part of humankind that already knows this prohibition, the Decalogue is not even reiterating what they know already, but making a general prohibition involving an inter-human relation into a specific prohibition involving the covenantal relationship between God and His people Israel.

The main theoretical problem with the prohibition of suicide is that it involves self-reference. "Kill" is a transitive verb, and the subject of a transitive verb is different from the verb's object. Who is killing whom? This is also the problem with autonomy, i.e., who *commands* (the *nomos* in "auto-nomy") whom? (Surely, it is no accident that many "autonomists" today are vociferous advocates of the "right to die.") John and I agree that there is a problem with making the subject and the object of a command the same person simultaneously. However, this same problem emerges if one advocates self-love. Following Aquinas, John states that "the command that I love my neighbor presumes that I have a rightly ordered love of self—the presumption is embodied in the very grammar of this command. If my love of self is disordered, so will be my love of neighbor."[4] Moreover, in the case of suicide, it could be said following this logic, "If I hate myself, so will I hate my neighbor." Indeed, history's most famous mass murderer,

3. David Novak, *Natural Law in Judaism* (Cambridge, 1998), 31–36.
4. p. 100.

Adolf Hitler, killed himself. The question is: Did he kill others as a retroactive suicide, or did his killing of others lead him to kill himself? To avoid the problem of self-reference, I prefer the latter opinion about Hitler.

Now Leviticus 19:18 reads: "You shall love your neighbor as yourself [*kamokha*]." Along with many in the Jewish tradition, Aquinas and John Berkman assume that this means, "you shall love your neighbor as *you love* yourself." As the Latin of the Vulgate states, *Diligens amicum tuum sicut teipsum*, thus implying *sicut teipsum diligens*. Along these lines, Aristotle says about true friends, who are themselves good persons, thus enjoying self-esteem, that "each partner both loves his own good self [*to autō agathon*] and makes an equal return in the good he wishes for his partner."[5] The problem here is logical, i.e., who loves whom? And the problem is psychological, i.e., isn't self-love narcissistic? As such, self-love doesn't lead to love of others. In fact, narcissists, believing themselves to be good and thus worthy of (in the words of W. H. Auden's poem "September 1, 1939") "being loved alone," want others to join them in loving themselves. They only want to be the loved objects of others, not loving subjects of others.

So, for that reason, it seems better to interpret "as yourself" as "as you yourself *are loved*." And by whom are you so loved? By God, as Leviticus 19:18 ends: "I am the Lord." Therefore, you are to love your fellow human as you are loved by God; indeed, that is *because* you *and* they are loved by God *together*. As such you can never regard yourself as "being loved alone," which Auden says is "the error bred in the bone of each woman and of each man." That is why nobody can regard himself or herself as either the prime subject or the prime object of love. Being loved before one can love means that nobody is the prime subject of love. Being loved along with others means that nobody is the prime object of love. No human person is either the *terminus a quo* of love or love's *terminus ad quem*. (This is similarly argued in my responses to David Elliot and Christopher Tollefsen in this volume.)

Lastly, John argues that "David is clearly correct that anyone capable of making a moral choice is not psychotic. However, if he is committed to the view that all suicides are psychotic/delusional, then this qualification is irrelevant, since no one ever kills themselves in their right mind."[6] In other words, John sees my psychosis argument as making morally culpable suicide into a null class, i.e., a class having no members. I have two answers to John's argument.

One, there is a principle in the Talmud called "innocent though prohibited" (*patur aval asur*). In such cases, there are reasons why our inability to punish a wrong act *post factum* (discussed above) does not mean that the act itself is permitted *ab initio*, although, to be sure, there are those who will presume that non-culpability presupposes permission just as culpability presupposes prohibition. Nevertheless, because we cannot determine whether a suicide was freely chosen or not, we do not

---

5. *Nicomachean Ethics*, 8.6/1157b35, translation altered. See Aristotle, *Nicomachean Ethics*, trans. Martin Oswald (Englewood Cliffs, NJ, 1962), 224.

6. p. 106.

punish a suicide posthumously. It is also a principle in the Talmud that in doubtful cases of the taking of human life, we judge leniently. And, as John recognizes, this is meant to spare the already grieving, guilt-ridden family the added grief and guilt-feeling that would be involved were the one who had committed suicide not to receive normal burial and mourning rites.

Two, when John questions the value of making the distinction between the prohibited commission of the act before the fact and the community's exoneration of the act after the fact, this teaches me to drop the "psychosis plea" in the increasing number of cases today when persons plan their own suicide while they are clearly *compos mentis*, and often with the approval of their family, their friends, and the larger society (especially now that assisted suicide is legal in Canada and other countries). For the main (in John's words) "pastoral" reason for judging a suicide to have been psychotic is to spare the dead person's family the ignominy of less than normal funeral and burial rites. However, if the family is supportive of the decision to commit suicide, then obviously they are not guilt-ridden about it (though I wonder); hence, we needn't be concerned about their right to consolation since they have in fact waived it. The issue of societally approved, even encouraged, suicide means for some of us that it is these others who deserve our condemnation, not the dead person. For despite the argument that in such cases the person who commits suicide has acted autonomously, the fact usually is that such people are acting out what they believe their "significant others" want them to do. This approval might be the best example of what Pope John Paul II called our modern secular world: "the culture of death."

In resisting this culture of death, John Berkman and I are following the scriptural commandment read in synagogues the day after I am now writing this response: "Life and death I have placed before you, the blessing and the curse; you shall then choose life" (Deut 30:19).

Chapter 4

The Divine Commandments in Moral Theology

DAVID ELLIOT

IT IS AN HONOR to offer a paper celebrating the achievement of Professor and Rabbi David Novak. Quite apart from being one of the most distinguished Jewish scholars of his generation, Novak's own work, teaching, and example awoke in me precisely those interests that led to my becoming a moral theologian. I offer this paper as a modest token of gratitude and contribution to the Jewish-Christian dialogue which Novak so superbly exemplifies.

In this paper I will discuss Novak's Jewish ethics in relation to Catholic moral theology. The obvious place to look here is natural law theory, where there have been decades of important collaboration between him and Catholic interlocutors.[1] There is much convergence between Catholic models of natural law and Novak's. On that subject, I think we are bending similar ideas in slightly different directions. Collaboration here is between two intellectual traditions in a position of some strength. But there are areas where I think much Catholic theology, in its current form, is rather weak, and that in those same areas Novak's theology, and perhaps the Jewish tradition in general, is very strong.

For instance, it is a strange fact that recent Catholic moral theology does not much employ the concept of *idolatry* and is hardly better when it comes to *covenant*. But the particular omission I want to focus on has to do with the central role that Novak ascribes to the divine *commandments*. With notable exceptions,[2] these do not play a focal or substantive role in most recent Catholic moral theology.[3] Much of the reason

---

1. Novak's lengthy contributions to this are discussed and advanced in Emon, Levering, and Novak, *Natural Law*.

2. Perhaps most notably, Pope John Paul II's encyclical *Veritatis Splendor* (esp. nos. 15–24) which strongly connects commandments with aspiration for the good and beatitude. The *Catechism of the Catholic Church* also gives sustained attention to the commandments in its moral section (see CCC nos. 1691–1877), which overall is structured around beatitude and the virtues.

3. Jean Porter addresses this lacuna in her "Divine Commands, Natural Law, and the Authority of

is historical. Post-Vatican II theology defined itself against the preceding "manualist" tradition, which theologians across a wide spectrum dismissed as legalistic. John Mahoney captures this spirit of repudiation in *The Making of Moral Theology*: "The miasma of sin which emanates from the penitential literature and from the vast majority of manuals of moral theology is not only distasteful, but profoundly disquieting."[4] As part of this repudiation, the commandments have been downplayed so as to stress a clean break from what was felt to be a prior ethic of suffocating rigidity.[5] And even when the commandments do receive some attention, it often proves conceptually opaque. For instance, theologians will readily agree that a commandment such as "love your neighbor" should be observed. But there is little reflection on how the fact of it's being commanded is a reason for action, or what this could mean.

Deflationary views of the commandments apply far beyond the academy and may be found in the Church. Pope Francis himself is often interpreted as downplaying the commandments and the moral law to a surprising extent. For many, the cumulative effect of the pope's frequent warnings against "rigorism," "throwing stones," "legalism," "doctors of the law," and so forth, is to make a serious concern for the commandments seem suspect or even pernicious. I have argued elsewhere that this is a misreading of Pope Francis, but the perception is not uncommon.[6]

Nonetheless, few would deny that the commandments must have *some* serious role if their prominence in Scripture and the life of the Church is to make sense. Moreover, our commitment to strong Jewish-Catholic relations should make us extremely wary about polemics against "legalism." Historically, this has involved mission creep of the sort that nods vaguely toward Marcionism, and it has often been implicated in noxious anti-Semitic tropes.[7]

Granted that we should not try to restore manualist excesses, what might we do, theologically speaking, to dispel the shade of Marcion and take the commandments more seriously in Catholic moral theology? There are, of course, resources in the Catholic tradition to help us get there. But I think that Novak's own theology offers unique insights that would profit the Catholic theology even at its best. Part of my interest here is that I am a Thomist who appreciates the approach of Servais Pinckaers and others who focus on virtue and beatitude while also thinking them reticent on this topic in ways that Novak helps to address. I therefore wish to look at his account and offer a Catholic and Thomistic response. My specific interest is with the meaning of the commandments for believers, and so I will assume God's justified sovereignty

---

God." See also Mattison and Cloutier, "Method in American Catholic Moral Theology after *Veritatis Splendor*."

4. Mahoney, *The Making of Moral Theology*, 28.

5. Representative is the subtitle of James F. Keenan, S.J.'s, *A History of Catholic Moral Theology in the Twentieth Century: From Confessing Sins to Liberating Consciences*.

6. I discuss this at length in my "Irregular Unions and Moral Growth in *Amoris Laetitia*."

7. Fredriksen, "Roman Christianity and the Post-Roman West."

in the present discussion. My question will not be "Why obey God?" but rather, "What does it *mean*, exactly, to obey God?"

In particular, I will address the following questions. First, just how necessary are divine law and commandments for our moral guidance given that natural law seems to convey so much of what we morally need to know? I argue that Novak and Aquinas both take a "high" view of the commandments which sees them as safeguarding even that moral terrain which is covered by natural law. Second, how are we to understand our motivations in terms of obeying divine commands? Both Novak and Aquinas answer this in terms of love of God primarily, Aquinas adds love of neighbor secondarily, and both allot an ancillary role to "fear of God." Of course, designating love as the primary motivation for keeping the commandments helps to allay anxieties about "rigidity" and legalism. By contrast, even a slight intrusion of religious fear may seem to revive manualist preoccupations, but I argue that Novak and Aquinas help us to see the topic in a nuanced way that safeguards love itself. Lastly, I examine what the relationship of the commandments is to the virtues. Given the ascendancy of virtue ethics in Catholic moral theology, the question is salient. I show that for Aquinas the commandments are not "in tension" with the virtues, but facilitate them, so that a virtue approach to ethics would profit by integrating the commandments more thoroughly.[8] More generally, I think that reading Novak alongside of Aquinas is an extremely valuable exercise for Catholic moral theologians. His focus on love for God as our primary reason for keeping the commandments helps to show that the commandments are not just externally imposed rules, but a means for grasping the moral life in terms of relationship to God.

Novak on Divine Commandments

While the topic appears elsewhere, Novak most fully develops his "phenomenology of the commandments" in his *Covenantal Rights*. There he argues that the commandments are essential human actions constitutive of the image of God. He writes: "We humans not only owe God everything for having made us, but more directly and positively we owe God everything for enabling us to know how to live according to our own nature and in consistency with the nature of the rest of creation."[9] The commandments imply that God has dignified us with the freedom of the image of God by which we may respond to his claims and which allows us to make a life together. Rather than an act of domination, commandments imply a *concession* on God's part in that "God relinquishes some of his space, as it were, to allow his human creatures a space to stand before him" freely rather than simply being determined. In a phrase that recalls Karl Barth, Novak stresses that "God is for us through his

---

8. I hasten to add that I will not be proposing a "divine command theory" of ethics, or anything like it.

9. Novak, *Covenantal Rights*, 42.

commandments" and that "we are for God through our obedience" (41).[10] This relationship is the precondition for our flourishing, and it brings about the covenantal world we share together with God.

While Novak argues that God has the right to command us before we understand what the results of this will be, he also affirms the traditional talmudic category of "reasons of the commandments (*ta 'amei ha-mitsvot*)" according to which we may seek to understand *why* something has been commanded with the confidence that there is a reason. Moreover, the reason will not be arbitrary or cruel, but for our good and the good of the world.[11] He quotes Deuteronomy: "the LORD has commanded us to practice all of these statutes . . . for our own good (*le-tov lanu*). . . . [I]t is beneficial (*u-tsedaqah*) for us that (we obey them)" (Deut 6:24–25).[12] For Novak, obedience to God is the source of human flourishing and constitutes our very identity as *imago Dei*. Hence the ultimate indignity of death is that a person is "free from the commandments."[13]

Novak says that the commandments imply God's "personal involvement" in the moral life,[14] but what does this mean from the perspective of the agent who is being commanded? To address this, Novak says we need "a phenomenology of the commandments" which will address "what it *means* to be commanded as a person."[15] This is what I want to focus on in his account.

Novak locates discussion of the commandments in his theology of creation and phenomenology of divine encounter. He stresses human finitude relative to God's power and asserts the medieval doctrine of "creation out of nothing" (*yesh m'ayin*), both as a bulwark against polytheism and surety that God is "without limit" (*Ein Sof*).[16] As creatures, our existence is entirely derivative, and our mortality is certain. Those who do not acknowledge this risk making themselves "into gods" through sinful arrogance.[17] Self-idolatry is thus the primordial temptation. "Did not the serpent tempt the first human couple with divine power?" Novak asks.[18] The first lesson of *creatio ex nihilo* is that we have "no ontological foundation upon which" to stand against God.[19]

Based on ontological distance and the pattern of biblical theophanies, Novak argues that a proper response to divine power is the "fear of God" (*yir' at elohim*).

10. Novak, *Covenantal Rights*, 41.

11. In general, the "reason" pertains to (1) God, especially that we might "fulfill his purposes for the world, the highest of which is relationship with himself," and (2) humans, particularly, that we might "fulfill human needs," appropriately understood. See Novak, *Covenantal Rights*, 67.

12. Novak, *Covenantal Rights*, 42.

13. Novak, *Covenantal Rights*, 43.

14. Novak, cited in Levering, *Jewish-Christian Dialogue and the Life of Wisdom*, 102.

15. Novak, *Covenantal Rights*, 45.

16. Novak, *Covenantal Rights*, 38.

17. Novak, *Covenantal Rights*, 36n1.

18. Novak, *Covenantal Rights*, 39.

19. Novak, *Covenantal Rights*, 39.

At this point he recalls themes from Rudolf Otto's *Idea of the Holy*, which described the divine encounter in terms of a "numinous" quality which excites awe or fear (*tremor*). Otto himself leans heavily on Scripture, where theophanies and angelic visions arouse wonder and dread. In "numinous" experiences, the divine presence comes across as supremely majestic, overpowering, unapproachable, urgent, and "wholly other." This gives rise to an awe that may be accompanied by shuddering, a sense of creaturely smallness, and a perceived unworthiness in need of "covering" before the divine presence.

Ordinary believers may not be mystics, but Novak writes that "any inkling of the presence of God, however mediated by nature or tradition"[20] imparts a certain awe or reverence which becomes a moral quality when informed by awareness of God's claims upon us. For Novak, fear of God in its moral sense is a proper response to the negative commandments, such as those forbidding murder, adultery, and theft. He writes:

> The basic human feeling that accompanies this experience of being commanded negatively is fear (*yir'ah*). The negative commandment is itself a warning (*azharah*) that dangerous disorder lies on the other side of the commandment, that is, when one attempts to overcome it (*averah*) rather than living within its limits.[21]

More than just a feeling, fear involves "the practical recognition of divine order within the world." Hence the biblical phrase "there is no fear of God in this place" (Gen 20:11) implies a context of moral chaos and self-destruction.[22] The practical role of fear (*yir'ah*) is to show "respect for the awesome limits God has set down within which humans are to freely choose to live."[23] (One might say, analogously, that the "fear of gravity" felt atop a dizzying height helps one to "respect" the law of gravity and respond well to the practical necessity of not walking off a cliff.)

At the same time, Novak's "phenomenology of the commandments" gives a far larger role to love than to fear. Following the "normative experience of the Jewish people,"[24] Novak says that "God's claim on our love is far more intense and intimate than his claim on our fear." Whereas fear corresponds to the negative commandments, the positive commandments "are to be motivated by love," or what one rabbinic source calls "service of the heart" (*avodat ha-lev*).[25]

Novak thus argues that there is hierarchy to the commandments. The positive commandments, such as honoring parents or keeping the Sabbath holy, have priority

---

20. Novak, *Covenantal Rights*, 42.
21. Novak, *Covenantal Rights*, 39.
22. Novak, *Covenantal Rights*, 47.
23. Novak, *Covenantal Rights*, 42.
24. Novak, *Covenantal Rights*, 55.
25. Novak, *Covenantal Rights*, 51.

over negative commandments, or "thou shalt nots." This raises the question of the relationship of fear to love, and notably, the question of whether love may grow to the point where fear becomes unnecessary. Novak addresses this in the context of an intra-Jewish debate between Maimonides, who thinks fear recedes as love grows, and Nahmanides, who sees the two as complimentary. Both agree as to the priority of love over fear. But Maimonides insinuates a Platonic ascent of sorts in which the immature will first observe the commandments out of fear, but will later, it is hoped, be sufficiently motivated by love of God alone.[26]

But as Novak shows, Maimonides is here an outlier in his own tradition. The more received Jewish interpretation, going back to the ancient midrashes and better adjusted to Scripture itself, is that fear and love exist in a "dialectical" relationship.[27] Fear of God is reverence for him as source of the divine order who saves us from self-destruction, and this is not only compatible with love for God and neighbor, but safeguards it. I will return to this point when discussing Aquinas's approach.

As a summary of this dialectic, Novak endorses the following passage from the thirteenth-century Jewish theologian Nahmanides, who is commenting on the positive commandment to "remember" the Sabbath day and the negative one to "guard" it:

> The truth is that the quality of "remember" is hinted at in the positive commandment (*be-mitsvat aseh*), which comes from the attribute of love and is for the sake of the attribute of mercy (*le-middat ha-rahamim*). For one who does what his master commands does so because he loves him and his master is merciful to him. But the quality of "guard" applies to the negative (*lo ta'aseh*) commandments. It is for the sake of the attribute of justice (*din*) and comes from the attribute of fear (*yir'ah*). . . . Therefore, a positive commandment is greater than a negative commandment inasmuch as love is greater than fear. For one who affirms (*hemaqayyem*) and practices what his master wills, both with his body and his property, is greater than one who simply guards himself (*me-ha-nishmar*) from doing evil in his [master's] eyes.[28]

Out of love, we "remember" to keep the positive commandments, and out of fear, we "guard" against violating the negative ones. Subjectively speaking, observing the commandments involves a characteristic state of remembering, on the one hand, and guarding, on the other, and it is primarily motivated by love.

Underlying all these points is the traditional Jewish view that "law" (*halakhah*) does not exist in a vacuum, but presupposes the "narrative" (*aggadah*) of God's intervention in the world, and from this takes its overarching meaning. In Scripture the two categories are often held together. To take just one example:

---

26. Novak, *Covenantal Rights*, 52.
27. Novak, *Covenantal Rights*, 54.
28. Novak, *Covenantal Rights*, 51.

> Thus you shall say to the house of Jacob, and tell the people of Israel: You have seen what I did to the Egyptians, and how I bore you on eagles' wings and brought you to myself. Now therefore, if you will obey my voice and keep my covenant, you shall be my own possession among all peoples. (Exod 19:3–5)

The first sentence operates as *aggadah*, narrating that God has been good to Israel, and so can be trusted as the source of its *halakhah*, to which the second sentence then adverts. Paraphrasing Kant, Novak concludes: "aggadah without halakhah is empty; halakhah without aggadah is blind."[29] There is an obvious takeaway point here for Catholic moral theologians. So long as the narrative/law relationship is kept healthy, it will push against "legalism" understood as law purely for law's sake, or rules imposed without life-giving meaning.

Aquinas on Divine Law

I want to address what Novak's account has to offer contemporary Catholic moral theology when it comes to the commandments. To take one mainstream example, I will consider broadly Thomistic theologies of the post-Vatican II period which prioritize the role of happiness or "the good life," particularly in terms of the role ascribed to the virtues.[30] Though the recent academic focus on the virtues and happiness is due to work that began in the last half of the twentieth century, the interest itself marks a historically distant homecoming. As the philosopher Julia Annas noted, "The question 'In what does my happiness consist?' is the most important one in ancient ethics."[31] (It goes without saying that the model of "happiness" in such thought bears little relation to today's popular sense of the term.) The same could be said for patristic, early, and high medieval ethics. Aquinas stands firmly within this tradition, arguing that our final end is happiness (*beatitudo*), which in turn is "activity (*operatio*) in accordance with virtue," or as we might say, the good and virtuous life as a whole.[32] Through the influence of Fr. Servais Pinckaers and assorted figures, a focus on virtue and happiness has become mainstream in Catholic moral theology and is clearly reflected in the current *Catechism of the Catholic Church*, whose moral section Pinckaers helped to draft. I was trained in this style of moral theology at the University of Notre Dame and find it compelling yet somewhat reticent about the commandments. These are by no means denied, but this approach often hurries past them to get onto happiness and the virtues, which then do the ethical heavy lifting. Yet when we look at Aquinas himself, generous space is allotted to the commandments. The point merits consideration.

29. Novak, "What is Jewish Theology?" 5.

30. The history and major figures of this movement are described in Elliot, "The Turn to Classification in Virtue Ethics," and in Cloutier and Mattison, "The Resurgence of Virtue in Recent Moral Theology."

31. Annas, *The Morality of Happiness*, 46.

32. *ST* I-II, q. 3, a. 2.

For Aquinas, what we call a divine commandment (*praeceptum* or *mandatum*) is an act of divine law issuing some form of permission, prohibition, mandate, or punishment.[33] As is well known, he believes that law is "an ordinance of reason for the common good, made by him who has care of the community, and promulgated."[34] Divine law is justified by the authority of God, and yet Aquinas insists that it is a work of practical *reason*, not an arbitrary assertion of power. This accords with what I take Novak to mean by "reasons of the commandments (*ta 'amei ha-mitsvot*). Aquinas even rejects "the Jurist's" (i.e., Ulpian's) platitude that "whatsoever pleases the sovereign has the force of law."[35]

We should obey the commandments for two reasons. The first is the "authority of the lawgiver," whose claims upon us as Creator, Legislator, Sovereign, and Benefactor are fully justified and should be met with reverence (*reverentia*). The second is "the benefit derived from the fulfilment" of the commandments, since their point is to effect good relations with God and neighbor.[36] Aquinas writes of the Decalogue:

> The Old Law contained some moral precepts; as is evident from Exodus 20:13–15: "Thou shalt not kill, Thou shalt not steal." This was reasonable: because, just as the principal intention of human law is to create friendship between man and man; so the chief intention of the Divine law is to establish man in friendship with God. Now since likeness is the reason of love, according to Sirach 13:19: "Every beast loveth its like"; there cannot possibly be any friendship of man to God, Who is supremely good, unless man become good: wherefore it is written (Leviticus 19:2; 11:45) "You shall be holy, for I am holy." But the goodness of man is virtue, which "makes its possessor good" (Ethic. ii, 6). Therefore it was necessary for the Old Law to include precepts about acts of virtue: and these are the moral precepts of the Law.[37]

Divine law and its commandments aim "to lead their subjects to their proper virtue" with a view to establishing "friendship of man to God."[38] Already we see that for Aquinas, commandments and virtues as such are not in any sort of opposition at all, but are mutually reinforcing; a point to which I will return.

The Insufficiency of Natural Law Alone

Aquinas says that we need divine law for four reasons. The first is to direct us to a supernatural end which exceeds the scope of both natural and human law. The second

---

33. Aquinas, *Summa theologiae* (hereafter *ST*) I-II, q. 92, a. 2 (unless otherwise noted, all translations come from the Fathers of the English Dominican Province: Christian Classics, 1981).
34. *ST* I-II, q. 90, a. 4.
35. *ST* I-II, q. 90, a. 1.
36. *ST* I-II, q. 99, a. 5.
37. *ST* I-II, q. 99, a. 2.
38. *ST* I-II, q. 92, a. 1.

is to provide much-needed moral certainty on essential matters where human reason is fallible. The third and fourth have to do with regulations of moral activity that are required for virtue but which human law is unequal to. Specifically, divine law is able to regulate our interior motives and actions, and it both forbids and punishes evil actions for which human law makes no provision.[39]

While this may seem to make divine law a matter of urgency, Aquinas believes that divine law and natural law overlap to a substantial extent. He identifies the natural law as "nothing other than the rational creature's participation in the eternal law" of God.[40] We experience it as an inner moral law directing us through practical reason and our natural inclinations to the proper ends of human nature.[41] As such, he interprets Romans 1:14 ("the Gentiles, who have not the Law, do by nature those things that are of the Law")[42] to mean that the moral precepts of the Decalogue coincide with those of natural law. The overall impression may be that natural law therefore covers most of the ordinary terrain of morality, with divine law adding content of purely supernatural value. It may thus seem that natural law absent divine law more or less suffices for this-worldly ethics. So common were such impressions of Aquinas not that long ago that he was often described as a "natural law thinker" full stop, as though his other moral interests were just off-hours fretwork.[43] This would put him at odds with Novak, who certainly affirms natural law but believes that it is best understood within a theological context.[44] Novak writes:

> Being commanded, however we hear that commandment, is something that enables us to do well in the world. Without that sense of being commanded, when our own practical power becomes the measure of all things, we destroy ourselves and our world. For when this happens, our reason forgets that it is but a reflection of the wisdom of God who structures the natural world, and our will forgets that it is but the reflection of God's will who brought the world into existence.[45]

Aquinas appears to part ways with Novak at this point, since the latter holds that even without knowledge of divine law, something better than the destruction of our world may be achieved. Aquinas affirms, for instance, the possibility of purely

---

39. *ST* I-II, q. 91, a. 4.

40. *ST* I-II, q. 91, a. 2.

41. The story of natural law's structure and intricacy in Aquinas has been told many times before. In general terms, natural law involves an inner nisus of physical, biological, and rational drives by which humans according to Aquinas are both propelled to their proper ends and have significant moral knowledge about what means they ought to pursue to attain those ends. For a recent state-of-field report, see chapter 1 of Hittinger, *The First Grace*.

42. *ST* I-II, q. 100, a. 1.

43. See Bourke, "Is Thomas Aquinas a Natural Law Ethicist?"

44. See Novak, *Jewish Social Ethics*.

45. Novak, *Covenantal Rights*, 42.

natural or "pagan virtue" and therefore a certain limited and imperfect natural justice and happiness.[46] Natural justice by itself may have no salvific value, but a world shaped by it would be faring well in important ways. It therefore seems that Aquinas is more optimistic than Novak about where natural law, absent divine commands, can take humanity.

This is true so far as it goes but must be carefully qualified. Aquinas believes that one of the reasons we need the divine law has to do with our consistent moral peccability. Moral corruption is not just of the appetites; it involves epistemic deformities which cloud our moral judgement.[47] He writes: "Divine law was needed in that the natural law was corrupted (*corrupta erat*) in the hearts of some men, so that they esteemed those things good which are naturally evil, and this corruption stood in need of correction."[48] In times of social corruption, or in situations of doubt and temptation, even the well-disposed may vacillate, and be confused or misled. Aquinas's view is that divine law importantly helps to confirm good people in right beliefs, and this becomes more necessary when the natural law begins "to be obscured (*obscurari*) on account of the exuberance of sin."[49] As this suggests, Aquinas is concerned with the impact of bad socialization on even good people's ability to perceive the natural law. He concludes that divine law was needed not just to restrain the wicked but to direct the good "who, through being instructed by the law, are helped to fulfill what they desire to do."[50] Commandments provide much-needed certainty, as well as both encouragement and warning. This brings Aquinas close to Nahmanides's point about both "remembering" and "guarding."

Put just this way, it sounds like the role of divine law is as a kind of "tutor" in the natural law, as though God were merely handing out grades and corrections to students in natural law's classroom. But while divine law does correct our natural moral errors, Aquinas's scope for divine law is far more ambitious. This is in part owing to original sin, a subject which increasingly preoccupied Aquinas's later work.[51]

To see this we must look at Aquinas's own excursion into *aggadah* or narrative. Unlike Augustine, Aquinas does not often produce moral genealogies, but he does ponder the timing of divine legislation. In particular, he asks why God waited

46. Aquinas distinguishes between "acquired" or natural virtue and "infused" or supernatural virtue. The former are obtained by habituation and are proportionate to our connatural good, whereas the latter are gratuitously "poured" (*infundit*) into us by grace and are proportionate to the supernatural end. This is not to be mistaken for a "two-tiered" approach, though a full treatment is beyond my present scope. See my *Hope and Christian Ethics*, 54–69. For a recent discussion of the many recent debates surrounding the acquired and infused virtues, see Goris and Schoot, eds., *The Virtuous Life: Thomas Aquinas on the Theological Nature of Moral Virtues*, especially 47–72, 117–30.

47. *ST* I-II, q. 94, a. 4.

48. *ST* I-II, q. 94, a. 5.

49. *ST* I-II, q. 98, a. 6.

50. *ST* I-II, q. 98, a. 6.

51. Aquinas's extremely long and late work on evil (*Questiones disputatae De malo*) is indicative. See the discussion by Torrell in *Saint Thomas Aquinas*, vol. 1: *The Person and His Work*, 202–7.

thousands of years to issue a divine law that would help stop the moral bleeding of humanity that began with the Fall. Given humanity's plight, why put off divine instruction until the time of Moses?

Aquinas could have told a story implying that natural law and acquired virtue more or less sufficed during this period, insinuating that our plight was not *that* bad. Yet he does the exact opposite. The passage is worth quoting at length:

> It was fitting that the Law should be given at such a time as would be appropriate for the overcoming of man's pride (*superbia*). For man (after the Fall) was proud of two things, namely, of knowledge and of power. He was proud of his knowledge, as though his natural reason could suffice him for salvation: and accordingly, in order that his pride might be overcome in this matter, man was left to the guidance of his reason without the help of a written law: and man was able to learn from experience that his reason was deficient, since about the time of Abraham man had fallen headlong into idolatry and the most shameful vices. Wherefore, after those times, it was necessary for a written law to be given as a remedy for human ignorance: because "by the Law is the knowledge of sin" (Romans 3:20). And after man had been instructed by the Law, his pride was convinced of his weakness.[52]

It is important to stress that the goal of this long and painful process was "the overcoming of man's pride." Without this, Aquinas assumes, divine law would be scornfully dismissed by most and do them no good. Aquinas's *aggadah* depicts fallen humanity somewhat as the arrogant adolescent who needs to "hit bottom" before he will accept parental help. Recalling Novak's point about destroying ourselves, Aquinas says that it was "most fitting" (*convenientissime*) for God to delay giving the law until "the time of Moses," because the delay itself, which left us with only natural law to guide us, would result in a catastrophic moral failure that would humble our pride and make us divinely teachable again. The so-called "period of natural law" was a success pedagogically precisely by being a failure performatively.

In a very late text Aquinas adds: "Though God gave man this law of nature in creation, the Devil has sown in man another law on top of it, that of concupiscence." The result is that "man needed to be brought back to the works of virtue and drawn away from vice, and for that the law of Scripture (*lex Scripturae*) was necessary." Surprisingly, Aquinas even goes so far as to say that "the law of nature was destroyed (*destructa erat*) by the law of concupiscence."[53] By this he does not mean that natural law ceased to exist after the Fall, but that its moral efficacy, taken by itself, was severely undermined.

This is not to denigrate natural law, which remains good and continues to direct us to our proper ends. Aquinas construes it as our "participation in the eternal law of

---

52. *ST* I-II, q. 98, a. 6.

53. Thomas Aquinas, *Collationes in decem preceptum, prooemium*, available in Latin and English at https://isidore.co/aquinas/TenCommandments.htm.

God,"[54] and without it our very nature, and any grasp we might have on morality, would be destroyed. Yet he thinks that humanity weighed down by concupiscence, deprived of original justice, and untutored in divine law is prone to go astray even in natural matters when we lack divine instruction and the power of grace.[55] This may seem puzzling, since Aquinas affirms the possibility of "virtuous pagans," if by that we mean agents who lack divine law and habitual grace but possess the acquired or natural virtues.[56] But while such virtues enable agents to keep much of the natural law, Aquinas is not very optimistic about the odds of that happening with any regularity.[57] Even at the natural level, the divine law and commandments are for him a matter of urgent necessity.

Aquinas on Love's Primacy in the Commandments

Supposing divine law and the commandments to be as important as Aquinas makes out, we still need an explanation of what is morally distinctive about being commanded by God as distinct from guided by him in some other way. What does the consideration *I am being commanded* add which other reasons for being virtuous lack? Unless we grasp this, commandments will appear awkward or unintelligible.

The most obvious thing commandments add is binding power. "*Lex*," Aquinas suggests, is "derived from *ligare*, because it binds (*obligat*) one to act."[58] Whereas exhortations and advice (*monitio*) to virtuous conduct may be disregarded, the binding power of law makes it a "more efficacious inducement to virtue."[59] "Law," Aquinas states, "makes use of the fear of punishment in order to ensure obedience."[60]

At the same time, Aquinas agrees with Nahmanides and Novak that God's commandments primarily regard love. This is unsurprising given that love of God and neighbor are the two greatest commandments. Aquinas specifies how these commandments are fulfilled in both positive and negative ways. Positively, loving God with all of one's heart, soul, mind, and strength is fulfilled by intending God for his own sake and habitually in our actions ("heart"), zealously seeking that his will be done ("soul"), submitting

54. *ST* I-II, q. 91, a. 2.

55. *ST* II-II q. 109, a. 8.

56. See, for instance, I-II q. 65, a. 2, and *De Regno*, lib. 1 cap. 8, available at https://www.corpusthomisticum.org/orp.html. The debates on how to interpret Aquinas's claim are vast and intriguing, but not my topic here.

57. Virtuous action is in keeping with natural law (*ST* I-II, q. 94, a. 3). But whereas intermittent acts contrary to virtue will not cause those with the acquired virtues to lose them, those who violate the natural law cannot be said to "fulfill the commandments of the law" (*impere mandata legis*), and Aquinas thinks that all those who lack grace will fail in this respect, on pain of Pelagianism (I-II, q. 109, a. 4; *In II Rom.*, lectio 3). Note that by "law" [*lex*] Aquinas has in mind here the Torah or "Old Law" (*lex vetus*), as he calls it. But since he believes the moral precepts of the Old Law are included in natural law (I-II, q. 100, a. 1), his point here equally applies to it.

58. *ST* I-II, q. 90, a. 1.

59. *ST* I-II, q. 90, a. 3.

60. *ST* I-II, q. 92.2.

our intellect to God ("mind"), and serving him with all of our powers ("strength").[61] Loving our neighbor in turn is fulfilled by willing and seeking his good for God's sake, through actions such as the corporal and spiritual almsdeeds. These include everything from feeding the hungry and visiting the sick to consoling the sorrowful and forgiving injuries.[62] As this suggests, almost every human interaction can be an occasion of charity understood as commandment-observance.

Aquinas agrees with Novak that positive commandments are prior to the negative. "All the precepts of the Decalogue," he writes, "are directed to the love of God and of our neighbor."[63] He even sees the relation as one of logical entailment, where negative commandments stand to the positive "as conclusions to general principles."[64] In fact, all divine commandments are "virtually contained" (*virtute continentur*) in the two great positive commandments to love God and neighbor.[65] This is more easily seen in positive commandments, such as keeping the Sabbath or honoring one's parents. But it can also be seen in negative commandments. We love God by refusing subtle forms of idolatry which threaten that love. Similarly, we love our neighbors by refusing to injure them when we otherwise might, such as through violence, sexual misconduct, or false speech. By not taking advantage of them, we safeguard our neighbors' goods from our selfishness through regularly mortifying our own concupiscence. Doing this consistently "demands much labor," as Aquinas laconically notes, and to undertake this for our neighbors' sake is to love them.[66] Hence Aquinas argues quite consistently that "because love is the end of all the virtues: the end of the commandment is love."[67] The commandments, therefore, are premier means to the end of love.

An Ancillary Role for the "Gift of Fear"?

The commandments may primarily regard love, but Aquinas does not hesitate to affirm the scriptural and traditional view that they secondarily regard fear. The commandments

---

61. This is not to say that we are obligated to consciously refer all our capacities to God at every moment, which Aquinas thinks only beatified souls may do. He distinguishes between intending God "habitually," through virtuous habits; "actually," as with prayer or contemplation; and "implicitly," as in fasting or celibacy. In all of our actions in these various respects, people may "direct themselves to God as their end," so that God "remains implicitly in all those things they do for his sake. That is why there can be merit in all that we do, if we have charity" (see *Quaestio disputata De caritate*, q. 2 a. 11 ad 2; English translation taken from *Disputed Questions on Virtue*).

62. *ST* II-II, q. 32, a. 2.

63. *ST* II-II, q. 44, a. 1, ad. 3.

64. *ST* I-II, q. 100, a. 3.

65. *ST* II-II, q. 44, a. 2.
 That is, they are contained in them "not actually or formally, but equivalently and implicitly." See Wuellner, *A Dictionary of Scholastic Philosophy*, 131.

66. Aquinas, *Collationes in decem preceptum*, 12.

67. *ST* II-II q. 44, a. 1, citing 1 Timothy 1:5.

are acts of divine law[68] and to disobey them is sin (*culpa*) understood as a "transgression of the Divine law, and a disobedience to the commandments of heaven."[69] As I have noted, Aquinas believes that to dissuade from sin "law makes use of the fear of punishment in order to ensure obedience."[70] He cites Isaiah: "If you be willing, and will hearken to Me, you shall eat the good things of the land. But if you will not, and will provoke Me to wrath: the sword shall devour you" (Isa 1:19–20).[71]

Of course, religious fear strikes many as archaic, monstrous, and unsuited to the lived experience of charity. It may recall everything dreaded from the manualist era and pre-conciliar piety, such as "obsession with the law"[72] and the shopworn theme of "Catholic guilt." Yet it would be anachronistic to project these anxieties onto Aquinas's account. While he views its role as secondary, he takes the "fear of the Lord" seriously as a recurrent biblical theme and one of the seven traditional "gifts of the Holy Spirit" from Isaiah 11. Properly understood, such fear cannot be reduced to groveling, and it does not render our love for God schizophrenic. How is this so?

Aquinas distinguishes a variety of fears to clarify which he associates with fear of God. All fear is a dread of losing what one loves: "fear is born of love, since a man fears the loss of what he loves."[73] When the beloved is not infallibly and permanently possessed, fear in some form is a proper effect of love itself.

Aquinas therefore distinguishes kinds of fear according to the kinds of love to which they correspond. Servile fear (*timor servilis*) dreads punishment and therefore is based on self-love (though Aquinas does not believe that makes it vicious).[74] Filial fear (*timor filialis*) dreads separation from God and so is a fear based on love of God. Initial fear (*timor initialis*) is proper to spiritual beginners and mingles these two.[75] Depending on the agent's level of charity, all three may play a valued role. Yet Aquinas believes the ideal expression of the gift is filial fear, whose object is not punishment, but separation.

---

68. *ST* I-II, q. 100, a. 2.

69. *ST* I-II, q. 100, a. 2.

70. *ST* I-II, q. 92, a. 2.
A standard objection to this is that agents who obey laws or commandments through fear of punishment do so for servile rather than moral motives and so are not being made virtuous at all. While this can be true, Aquinas believes that we may begin from mixed motives and graduate onto better ones through being habituated into moral conduct over time and increasingly coming to appreciate its purpose and benefits. He writes: "from becoming accustomed to avoid evil and fulfill what is good, through fear of punishment, one is sometimes led on to do so likewise, with delight and of one's own accord. Accordingly, law, even by punishing, leads men on to being good" (I-II, q. 92, a. 2, ad 4). See Keys, *Aquinas, Aristotle, and the Promise of the Common Good*, 203–15; and Mattison, "Aquinas, Custom, and the Coexistence of Infused and Acquired Cardinal Virtues."

71. *ST* I-II, q. 99, a. 6.

72. Mahoney, *The Making of Moral Theology*, 35.

73. *ST* II-II, q. 19, a. 3.

74. For a discussion of self-love appropriately understood, see my *Hope and Christian Ethics*, 72–85.

75. *ST* II-II, q. 19, a. 4.

Given its object, such fear is perfectly compatible with (indeed, is a consequence of) the love by which we cling to God. It is expressed by keeping the commandments and thereby recoiling from the sins that might separate us from God while entrusting ourselves to God for the grace needed to do just that. To use Novak's term, fear has a "dialectical" relationship with love. Regarding this theme, Novak writes:

> The positive commandments save the fear of God from turning into hatred of the repressive God of the negative commandments, and the negative commandments save the love of God from being our own motivation *to approach a passive God whichever way we like*.[76]

In Thomistic terms, approaching "a passive God whichever way we like" is the sin of presumption, which roughly is the policy of disregarding the commandments in the expectation of "glory without merits, and forgiveness without repentance."[77] The presumption is that God is so merciful that observance of the commandments is not necessary, that only extravagant wickedness could imperil salvation. The sociologist Christian Smith has recently argued that something like this is the majority religious view of America's youth, including Catholics. "Moralistic therapeutic deism," as he calls this outlook, is fundamentally "about providing therapeutic benefits to its adherent." It involves "belief in a God who created the world . . . but not one who is particularly involved in one's affairs—especially affairs in which one would prefer not to have God involved." A hallmark of this view is that "one does not really need to keep commandments, especially commandments one would prefer not to keep."[78]

Could it be that such widespread complacency about the commandments is a rather predictable result of not "standing before [God] in awe," as Novak puts it? If so, then something important has been missing from much recent Christian thought and practice. The Jewish theology that Novak articulates can help us here. Although Novak writes that "our terror of God's power is mostly sublimated into our reverence for God's wisdom," Novak adds that "It should reappear only when we are tempted to stand up against God in contempt rather than standing before him in awe."[79]

Along these lines, Catholics may want to ponder retrieving what our tradition calls the "gift of fear," one of the seven gifts of the Holy Spirit.[80] Historically, various practices have helped to cultivate this as respect and awe for God and the commandments. Apart from scriptural reading and the homiletic tradition, these include a focus on set liturgical days and seasons, such as Advent, Ash Wednesday, and Lent generally; practices such as examination of conscience, sacramental confession, fasting, pilgrimages, and retreats; "spiritual exercises" like those of St. Ignatius, various

---

76. Novak, *Covenantal Rights*, 55 (emphasis mine).
77. *ST* II-II, q. 21, a. 1.
78. Smith, *Soul Searching*, 163–64, 171.
79. Novak, *Covenantal Rights*, 46.
80. I put in a good word for the gift of fear in my *Hope and Christian Ethics*, 131–38.

meditations on time, divine judgment, one's mortality, and so forth.[81] Religious fear has notoriously been misused at times, and we should not want to revive crude excesses. But the Thomistic model does not in any way recommend this. Rather, Aquinas construes fear as a safeguard from the presumption which corrupts love itself. As we see in other kinds of relationships,[82] a certain kind of fear is not a threat to love, but exists in its service.

Relating the Virtues to the Commandments

I have discussed the primary roles of love of God and neighbor in the commandments, and the tertiary role of fear. It remains to address the relation between commandments and virtues so as to relate this discussion to the resurgence of virtue in moral theology. As I have already noted, Aquinas believes that keeping the commandments "demands much labor."[83] This phrase raises the old question of how *burdensome* the commandments might be and therefore touches on anxieties about legalism. This anxiety is especially acute if we consider the "interiorization" of the commandments required by the Sermon on the Mount.[84] In it Christ describes anger and insults as in some sense forms of "murder," lustful glances as forms of "adultery," and so forth, widening the application of the commandments (Matt 5:22 and 28, respectively). To avoid infractions in such extended senses seems to require a program of determinedly ascetic self-policing, and this can make the law seem far more burdensome.

In relation to this, Aquinas asks how the law's seeming burdensomeness fits with Christ's statement: "My yoke is sweet and My burden light."[85] The virtue perspective makes a tremendous difference at this point. Aquinas writes that keeping the commandments (*mandata*) is:

> very difficult to a man without virtue: thus even the Philosopher states (*Ethic* v, 9) that it is easy to do what a righteous man does; but that to do it in the same way, that is, with pleasure and promptitude (*delectabiliter et prompte*), is difficult to a man who is not righteous.[86]

Grudging or half-hearted obedience will not seriously cultivate the virtues needed to keep the commandments *delectabiliter et prompte*.[87] To those who obey with what

---

81. Elliot, *Hope and Christian Ethics*, 133.

82. For example, a husband may rightly "fear" to commit adultery against his wife, not in the sense that he fears he *will* do so, but in the sense that he dreads and shuns the very thought or occasion for doing so.

83. Aquinas, *Collationes in decem preceptum*, 12.

84. See Pinckaers, "The Place of Philosophy in Moral Theology," 68–72.

85. *ST* I-II q. 107, a. 4.

86. *ST* I-II q. 107, a. 4.

87. *ST* II-II q. 24, a. 6.

Dante called *lento amore* ("sluggish love"),[88] the psalmist's claim that the precepts of the Lord are "sweeter than honey and the honeycomb" (Ps 19:10) must sound like a cruel joke. Aquinas thinks that doing the minimum required to avoid sin *makes* the commandments more burdensome. Far better, he believes, to obey with fervent love for God ("charity is represented by fire," he reminds us).[89] This is because commandment-observance done with fervent charity and the power of grace helps to build up the virtues opposed to those tendencies which tempt us to transgression.[90] While the road may be long and hard, gradually the commandments then become easier to keep, and even a source of delight.[91] Aquinas therefore makes sense of Scripture's injunction to "Serve the LORD with gladness" (Ps 99:2) in light of the virtues, since these as good habits impart facility in good moral conduct, allowing us to keep the commands with characteristic delight and promptness.[92]

Yet the delight (*delectatio*) had in keeping the commandments is not just due to the fact that this entails doing virtuous things, and the virtuous do so with characteristic facility. That broadly Aristotelian point is true but also fails to capture an equally important Augustinian point. Specifically, it leaves out the delight in commandment observance proper to its *interpersonal* aspect in relation to the divine beloved. Aquinas raises this point when discussing the Scripture passage: "His commandments are not heavy" (1 John 5:3). He twice quotes Augustine to the effect that the commandments "are not heavy to the man who loves; whereas they are a burden to him that loves not," and: "love makes light and nothing of things that seem arduous and beyond our power."[93] The idea is that to obey God precisely out of love for him is to seek to please the highest and most deserving object of one's love, and this is a source of delight (the point is compatible with believing that obedience may be difficult in other respects).[94]

So, the commandments may be a source of delight in two ways. First, in that we do them out of love for God, so that by our obedience we draw close to and seek to please him as divine friend and beloved. Second, they may be a source of delight for those who have the virtues co-extensive with the actions the commandments stipulate, and such

---

88. Dante Alighieri, *Purgatorio*, canto xvii, l. 131.

89. *ST* II-II q. 82, a. 2.

90. See, for instance, *ST* II-II q. 24, a. 4–6.
For an important discussion see Sherwin, "Infused Virtue and the Effects of Acquired Vice." For the role of merit and grace in the increase of charity, see Wawrkyow, "Grace."

91. *ST* I-II, q. 32, a. 5; *De virtutibus*, q. 1 a. 10 ad 15.

92. *ST* I-II q. 100, a. 9, ad. 3.
This will not always be the case. The virtuous do not escape moral struggle, though all things being equal, the tasks of virtue are far less of a struggle for them than for the continent and incontinent. See, for instance, *ST* I-II, q. 91, a. 6.

93. *ST* I-II q. 107, a. 4.

94. See *ST* I-II q. 100, a. 9, ad. 3.

agents experience characteristic facility in enacting God's commands. Commandment observance and the exercise of the virtues should therefore overlap at all points.[95]

"Static Fact" and "Interpersonal Relationship"

I have tried here to draw on Novak's insights to retrieve aspects of the Catholic and Thomistic tradition which have been recently neglected. Of course, Novak's account cannot be fully imported into Catholic theology, because at a certain point it would cease to be Catholic theology. Besides this, there are notable philosophical differences between Novak and a Thomistic virtue perspective. Approaches to Aquinas which look to his eudaimonistic and virtue-heavy interests are philosophically far closer to Aristotle than to Kant. Biblically, they are closer in tone to "wisdom literature" than to legal discussions in Deuteronomy. In both respects they differ from Novak's emphases. So what can a Catholic and Thomistic approach take from him? Most basically: the reminder to consistently frame moral action in interpersonal terms indexed to God's covenant and commandments on top of more general descriptions focused on virtues and the final end. In a very illuminating passage Novak notes that commandments as such do not just convey the content of norms, but alter their very form. He writes:

> Even if we are able to discern the specific reasons for each and every one of the commandments, that would in no way detract from the overall revealed *Gestalt* of the commandments as *Torah*. That *Gestalt* is that each of the commandments bespeaks God's own personal involvement in the life of the elected community in the world.[96]

The most crucial way in which this is true is that the commandments frame ethics as a matter of "interpersonal relationship" rather than "static fact."[97] Rather than letting ethics drift off into purely human considerations, the commandments keep ethics focused on God's personal involvement in the moral life. This is the practical consequence of Novak's primary focus on love in relation to positive commandments and his secondary focus on fear in relation to negative commandments.

---

95. Of course, the other virtues have an essential role. Understood as imposing an obligation, observing the commandments is an act of justice. Insofar as anger, lust, or avarice tempt us to break the commandments, observing them engages the virtue of temperance (and so forth with assorted commandments and virtues). Nevertheless, Aquinas believes that "The precepts of the decalogue pertain to charity as their end, according to 1 Timothy 1:5, 'The end of the commandment is charity'" (*ST* II-II q. 122, a.1). The commandments are for the sake of charity, and to the extent other virtues are engaged to keep the commandments, they are directed or "commanded" by charity to its own end. This explains how refraining from theft or insults, though it might rely on "elicited" acts of temperance, is ultimately done for God's sake, and therefore is in its most important sense an act of charity (*ST* I-II q. 6, a. 4; *ST* I-II q. 18, a. 7). Aquinas cites the New Testament to this effect: "It is written (Colossians 3:14) 'Above all things have charity, which is the bond of perfection' (*vinculum perfectionis*) because it binds, as it were, all the other virtues together in perfect unity" (*ST* II-II q. 184, a. 1).

96. Novak, *Natural Law in Judaism*, 90.

97. Novak, *Covenantal Rights*, 35.

At this juncture, at least, Aquinas is very close to Novak. For Aquinas, the "new covenant" (*novum testamentum*) is essentially "the grace itself of the Holy Spirit, which is given to those who believe in Christ."[98] The moral acts of the infused or grace-informed virtues which characterize the Christian covenant are here cast in interpersonal human-divine terms. Aquinas writes: "[it is] essential to charity that man should so love God as to wish to submit to Him in all things, and always to follow the rule of His commandments; since whatever is contrary to His commandments is manifestly contrary to charity."[99] This is a highly interpersonal view of commandments, charity, and by extension the infused virtues which charity informs. But my impression is that Catholic and Thomistic moral theologians, perhaps under the influence of their Aristotelian cousins, sometimes leave this interpersonal quality in soft focus.[100] It is perhaps a question of optics, but we do well to remember that for Aquinas something like an "act of charity" (or any other infused virtue, by extension) is equally describable as an act of "keeping the commandments" in direct relation to the God with whom we are in covenant. The latter point throws into bold relief that moral action is related to God and therefore to salvation history, in which God's actions on behalf of his people are recorded. One benefit of this is to make clear that "law" (*halakhah*) depends for its intelligibility on "narrative" (*aggadah*). This in turn touches on Catholic anxieties related to the legacy of pre-Vatican II manualism. For instance, at one point in his account Novak issues a cautionary note about the negative commandments or "thou shalt nots." These, he says:

> ... demarcate the area within which valid human relationships may take place. However, no one could possibly live at this level alone. Without positive content within these limits, they would ultimately negate any human capacity for concrete action. They would block human existence at every turn. It could even lead one to hate God.[101]

Someone who avoids poison may yet starve, and Novak's point is that the negative commandments may keep us from harm, but they do not feed us. I suspect that we may trace to this pattern much Catholic discontent with moral theologies that narrowly focused on lists of prohibitions at the expense of positive content.[102] By contrast, Aquinas holds that love of God and neighbor give the commandments their basic intelligibility. The overall quality of the commandments is thus supremely positive. Even the "fear

---

98. *ST* I-II, q. 106, a. 1.

99. *ST* II-II, q. 24, a. 12.

100. This is counterbalanced by the fact that work on the theological virtues, for instance, implies God's involvement by definition.

101. Novak, *Covenantal Rights*, 50.

102. For a discussion of this history, see Mahoney, *The Making of Moral Theology*, 27–36; Keenan, *A History of Catholic Moral Theology in the Twentieth Century*, 9–34; Servais Pinckaers, *Sources of Christian Ethics*, 254–279.

of the LORD" is construed in such terms: as preserving charity from the presumption which threatens to corrupt love of God with casual disregard.

To close, I wish to return to Novak's claim, citing the Talmud, that "Greater is one who acts because of being commanded than one who acts without being commanded." This is best understood not as law for law's sake, but as doing what is necessary for the relationship's sake. Novak cites a passage from Nahmanides which captures this quality: "For one who does what his master commands does so because he loves him and his master is merciful to him."[103] In this respect, observing the commandments because they are commanded ideally refers to "loving God for his own sake." Echoing Novak's point about love, Aquinas holds that doing something for God's sake out of obedience to him expresses the highest form of love or charity. This is because it gives one's very will to God, which is greater even than giving one's body in martyrdom.[104] Even when we do appreciate the "reason of a commandment," and might have done what it enjoins anyway, we give our will to God in love by doing it precisely *as* an intentional act of obedience.[105] In Thomistic terms, obeying the commandments, insofar as we do so considered precisely as God's commandments, instances the highest form of love in that it makes a gift of one's will and therefore one's very self to God. So disobedience is, among other things, a refusal to love.

A serious interest in the commandments need not invite lazy caricatures about legalism, and Jewish-Christian dialogue is perhaps the most fitting context to recall this point. Besides the focus on love or charity, I have tried to show that the commandments are facilitated by the virtues and not in some sort of tension with them. Moral theology which adopts a virtue approach should therefore, I suggest, give a generous role to the commandments rather than keeping them at a distance. Such considerations may help us to get beyond the downplaying of the commandments that is inevitable if we treat them as though they were the special preserve of the manualists. Novak is surely right that the commandments should be viewed positively, and this is one way, within the Catholic tradition, to build a bridge to that approach.

Bibliography

Annas, Julia. *The Morality of Happiness*. New York: Oxford University Press, 1995.
Aquinas, Thomas. *Summa theologica*. Translated by Fathers of the English Dominican Province. Westminster, MD: Christian Classics, 1981.
———. *Disputed Questions on Virtue*. Translated by Jeffrey Hause and Claudia Eisen Murphy. Cambridge, UK: Cambridge University Press, 2012.
———. *Collationes in decem praecepta*. https://www.corpusthomisticum.org/iopera.html.
———. *De regno ad regem Cypri*. https://www.corpusthomisticum.org/iopera.html.
———. *In Epistolam ad Romanos*. https://www.corpusthomisticum.org/iopera.html.

---

103. Novak, *Covenantal Rights*, 51.
104. *ST* II-II, q. 124, a. 3.
105. *ST* II-II, q. 104, a. 3.

———. *Quaestiones disputatae De Malo.* https://www.corpusthomisticum.org/iopera.html.

———. *Quaestiones disputatae De virtutibus.* https://www.corpusthomisticum.org/iopera.html.

———. *Summa theologiae.* https://www.corpusthomisticum.org/iopera.html.

Bourke, Vernon J. "Is Thomas Aquinas a Natural Law Ethicist?" *The Monist* 58.1 (1974) 52–66.

Catechism of the Catholic Church. 2nd ed. Vatican City: Libreria Editrice Vaticana, 1997.

Cloutier, David M., and William C. Mattison. "The Resurgence of Virtue in Recent Moral Theology." *Journal of Moral Theology* 3 (2013) 228–59.

Elliot, David. *Hope and Christian Ethics.* Cambridge: Cambridge University Press, 2017.

———. "Irregular Unions and Moral Growth in *Amoris Laetitia*." *Journal of Moral Theology* 8. Special Issue 2 (2019) 31–59.

———. "The Turn to Classification in Virtue Ethics: A Review Essay." *Studies in Christian Ethics* 29.4 (2016) 477–88.

Emon, Anver M., Matthew Levering, and David Novak. *Natural Law: A Jewish, Christian, and Muslim Trialogue.* Oxford, New York: Oxford University Press, 2014.

Fredriksen, Paula. "Roman Christianity and the Post-Roman West: The Social Correlates of the Contra Iudaeos Tradition." In *Jews, Christians, and the Roman Empire: The Poetics of Power in Late Antiquity*, edited by Natalie B. Dohrmann and Annette Yoshiko Reed, 249–66. University of Pennsylvania Press, 2013.

Goris, Harm, and Henk Schoot. *The Virtuous Life: Thomas Aquinas on the Theological Nature of Moral Virtues.* Leuven: Peeters, 2017.

Hittinger, Russell. *The First Grace: Rediscovering the Natural Law in a Post-Christian World.* Wilmington, DE: ISI, 2003.

John Paul II. "Veritatis Splendor." *Libreria Editrice Vaticana.* August 6, 1993. http://www.vatican.va/content/john-paul-ii/en/encyclicals/documents/hf_jp-ii_enc_06081993_veritatis-splendor.html.

Keenan, James F. *A History of Catholic Moral Theology in the Twentieth Century: From Confessing Sins to Liberating Consciences.* London: Continuum, 2010.

Keys, Mary M. *Aquinas, Aristotle, and the Promise of the Common Good.* Cambridge: Cambridge University Press, 2008.

Levering, Matthew. *Jewish-Christian Dialogue and the Life of Wisdom: Engagements with the Theology of David Novak.* London: A&C Black, 2011.

Mahoney, John. *The Making of Moral Theology: A Study of the Roman Catholic Tradition.* Oxford: Clarendon, 1989.

Mattison, William. "Aquinas, Custom, and the Coexistence of Infused and Acquired Cardinal Virtues." *Journal of Moral Theology* 8.2 (2019) 1–24.

Mattison, William, and David Cloutier. "Method in American Catholic Moral Theology after *Veritatis Splendor*." *Journal of Moral Theology* 1.1 (2013) 170–80.

Novak, David. *Covenantal Rights: A Study in Jewish Political Theory.* Princeton: Princeton University Press, 2009.

———. *Jewish Social Ethics.* Oxford: Oxford University Press, 1992.

———. "What Is Jewish Theology?" In *The Cambridge Companion to Jewish Theology*, edited by Stephen Kepnes. Cambridge: Cambridge University Press, forthcoming.

Pinckaers, Servais. "The Place of Philosophy in Moral Theology." In *The Pinckaers Reader: Renewing Thomistic Moral Theology*, edited by John Berkman and Craig Steven Titus, 64–72. Washington, DC: Catholic University of America Press, 2005.

———. *Sources of Christian Ethics*. Translated by Mary Thomas Noble. Washington, DC: Catholic University of America Press, 1995.

Porter, Jean. "Divine Commands, Natural Law, and the Authority of God." *Journal of the Society of Christian Ethics* 34.1 (2014) 3–20.

Sherwin, Michael. "Infused Virtue and the Effects of Acquired Vice: A Test Case for the Thomistic Theory of Infused Cardinal Virtues." *The Thomist* 73.1 (2009) 29–52.

Smith, Christian. *Soul Searching: The Religious and Spiritual Lives of American Teenagers*. Oxford: Oxford University Press, 2005.

Otto, Rudolf. *The Idea of the Holy*. 2nd ed. Translated by John W. Harvey. Oxford: Oxford University Press, 1958.

Torrell, Jean-Pierre. *Saint Thomas Aquinas*. Vol. 1: *The Person and His Work*. Rev. ed. Translated by Robert Royal. Washington, DC: Catholic University of America Press, 2005.

Wawrkyow, Joseph. "Grace." In *The Theology of Thomas Aquinas*, edited by Rik Van Nieuwenhove and Joseph Wawrykow, 193–209. Notre Dame, IN: University of Notre Dame Press, 2005.

Wuellner, Bernard J. *A Dictionary of Scholastic Philosophy*. 2nd ed. Milwaukee: Bruce, 1966.

Response to

David Elliot's "The Divine Commandments in Moral Theology"

David Novak

I AM GRATEFUL TO my former student David Elliot for his most careful and most generous reading of my moral theology, skillfully and sympathetically employing it in his own work as a constructive Catholic moral theologian. (When David was finishing his undergraduate work at the University of Toronto, and was considering continuing doing graduate work with me, I advised him to do his graduate work with scholars of his own Catholic tradition. This paper of his confirms my hope at the time that this route would be best for him and best for his own Catholic community.) In responding to David's paper, I want to deal with one key point: the relation of natural law to divine law. On this point, I have not so much an essential difference with David as I differ somewhat with his Thomistic constitution of the relation of naturally known law and divinely revealed law.

Inasmuch as David is such a committed Thomist, no doubt he fully agrees with Aquinas. Like him David "is more optimistic than Novak about where natural law, absent divine commands, can take humanity."[1] Despite my many agreements with Aquinas on natural law and on the divine commandments, which David shows so well, the difference between us is (in my opinion) due to the fact that Aquinas's notion of natural law is more maximal than mine, or mine is more minimal than his. The best way to see this difference is to see our differing views on the fundamental commandment pertaining to the interhuman relationship: "You shall love your neighbor as yourself" (Lev 19:18). The fundamental role this commandment plays in God's law is emphasized by both Jesus (Matt 22:37–39) and Rabbi Akibah (*Palestinian Talmud*: Nedarim 9.3/41c). (This is similarly argued in my responses to John Berkman and Christopher Tollefsen in this volume.)

Aquinas quotes 1 Timothy 1:5 that "the end of the precepts is love" (in the Vulgate: *Finis autem praecepti charitas*), himself saying, "the acts of the other virtues are ordained

---

1. p. 129.

to charity, which is the end of the commandment."[2] Just above this, Aquinas says that "as an act by itself... it falls under the precept of the law which specifically prescribes it,... *Thou shalt love thy neighbor*." Here Aquinas is dealing with the teleology (in the Greek New Testament, the term used is *to telos*) of the "Old Law," i.e., the commandments (*mitsvot* in Hebrew) of the Hebrew Scriptures, especially those of the Pentateuch, which Jews call the "Mosaic Torah" (*torat mosheh* as in Mal 3:22).

Now Aquinas does not mean that the act of love is its own end (like those who are "in love with love"). Love does not command itself; it requires both a subject and an object. Rather, it seems Aquinas means that all the commandments enable humans to love God. God is the ultimate object of all creaturely love. Humans, i.e., the "neighbor," are to be loved as the "image of God" (which is the view of Rabbi Akibah's interlocutor, Ben Azzai in the Talmud text previously cited). That is why both for the Rabbis and for Jesus, the commandment of neighbor-love is secondary to the primary commandment to love God.[3] Indeed, were one to love one's neighbor in God's stead, that would constitute something like the prohibition of idolatry. ("The concept of idolatry" is something David thinks "recent Catholic moral theology does not put to serious ethical work.")[4] On the other hand, if one were to only love God in one's neighbor's stead, that might constitute a sin of omission, viz., a refusal to love those whom God Himself loves. Indeed, before one can love God, one must acknowledge those whom God loves, who are more than oneself alone. Thus God is not only the object of all true love—the ultimate *beloved*—but God is even more the original subject of love. God is the original *lover*, the *terminus a quo*, of all true love.

Both the commandment to love God and the commandment to love one's neighbor are positive commandments. Indeed, as David insightfully notes,[5] love of God is what essentially characterizes all the *positive* commandments of the Torah, which is a point I have learned from the great mediaeval theologian and exegete, Nahmanides (d. 1270). Thus, truly loving acts involve teleological intention: *who* loves intends *whom* is loved. That person is the *telos* or *terminus ad quem* of the act of love, the attractive object to whom one directs one's desire. As such, one *desires* to be intimately related to the direct object of one's desire. Therefore, all love is erotic (*eros* being essentially different from lust, what Aquinas calls *cupiditas*.) That is love's essential teleology. (Interestingly enough, in the Talmud [Kiddushin 41a] "neighbor love" also applies to the mandate to love one's legitimate spouse, both emotionally and carnally.) Moreover, to be *the* attractive object of human desire, God must first reveal Himself to humans before they can realize that He is truly the object of their desire. In fact, humans only become aware of their desire after its divine Object has already revealed Himself to them.

2. *ST* I-II, q. 100, a. 10.
3. See *ST* II-II, q. 26, a. 2.
4. p. 120.
5. p. 125.

On the other hand, *negative* commandments do not intend a definite object. Rather, by keeping a negative commandment, one avoids the object of his or her illicit desire. So, for example, when I am commanded "you shall not commit adultery" (Exod 20:13; Deut 5:17), I must resist being tempted to carnally love somebody I am not allowed to love this way. When I recoil from following my illicit desire, this "drawing back" from action into inaction (the meaning of the Latin *recessio*) is what "fear" (*yir'ah* in Hebrew) is. When my drawing back is because of my experience of God's prohibition, of God's saying "No" to me, then this fear is truly the "fear of God" (*yir'at elohim* as in Gen 20:11). This fear of God is most wholesome for human flourishing when one fears offending the God whom one loves ultimately, if not always immediately. David states this beautifully: "[T]he negative commandments may keep us from harm, but they do not feed us."[6] In fact, the Hebrew verb for "guard" is *shamor*, so when it introduces a commandment, the Rabbis take that commandment to be a negative commandment. In other words, the Rabbis teach that the Torah is telling one to "guard or restrain yourself from doing what is forbidden to you" (Berakhot 23a; Zevahim 106a). That is also why the negative Noahide commandments cannot be seen as a sufficient body of law or "code." Instead, they are presupposed by any morally acceptable body of positive law. In scholastic terms, these negative commandments function as a *conditio sine qua non*, not as the *conditio per quam* of the bodies of law (even revealed law) which they *inform* rather than substantiate. Appending the definite article "the" to natural law, i.e., *the* natural law, is to my way of thinking a misnomer.

I have long argued that the Noahide commandments (*mitsvot bnai noah*) are the Jewish version of natural law. All of these commandments are negative commandments (*mitsvot lo ta'aseh*), except the positive commandment for any human society to enforce or react to the violation of these negative commandments or prohibitions (*isurim* in Hebrew). They can best be summarized in what the ancient sage Hillel the Elder said to a gentile who wanted such a summary of the Torah that applies to him. Hillel stated it negatively: "Do not do to somebody else what you wouldn't want done to you" (Shabbat 31a). Now some have seen Hillel's dictum being the negative inverse of the positive commandment to "love your neighbor as yourself" (i.e., as you yourself want to be loved). That is, they are taken to be two sides of the same coin. However, the great Jewish philosopher Franz Rosenzweig (d. 1929) saw Hillel's dictum as being moral minimalism, which could be known without revelation (i.e., as natural law). Conversely, the commandment of neighbor love, being theological maximalism, requires revelation. And, for Rosenzweig, revelation is essentially God's revealing God's love for humans directly to humans. That revelation of God's original love is historical, not natural. It is an event (*Ereignis* in German). The normative import of this event is the commandment of neighbor love. (Among Christian theologians, I agree with

---

6. p. 138.

Karl Barth, contra Augustine and Aquinas, that there is no natural love of God. David notes my affinity to Barth.)

Following this we could say that we can have some natural knowledge of what God would *not* want to be done in His world which, if done without social restraint, would be a world that no human would want to live in. This is the natural fear of God (see Gen 20:11; Exod 1:17, 21). However, what God wants to *be done* in His world, especially what God wants for His positive relationship with His people, that needs to be heard directly from God Himself. Moreover, only a loving God whose love has been experienced by humans, only this God could command us to love Him and our neighbors. To cite an analogy, only loving parents, whose love has been experienced by their children, can cogently expect love from their children, and also cogently command their children to love one another. This love must be positively revealed; it is not automatic. Unlike the proscription of murder, which our political nature can tell us of, the positive prescription of love is not natural. That is why in the Jewish tradition, many of the negative commandments apply to both Jews and gentiles, whereas almost all of the positive commandments only apply to Jews as the recipients of Sinaitic revelation. As David has pointed out,[7] positive commandments frequently outweigh negative commandments in cases of conflict between the two. Furthermore, there are more positive commandments (365) than negative commandments (248) in the Mosaic Torah, i.e., according to the Talmud (Makkot 23b).

My more minimal notion of natural law is very much influenced by the fifteenth-century Spanish-Jewish theologian Joseph Albo. He was the chief Jewish theologian in the last of the mediaeval disputations between Catholic and Jewish theologians. The Catholic theologians there were Dominicans, Thomas Aquinas's order. Because of that, Albo was very familiar with Thomistic theology. Moreover, as a Jewish theologian, Albo was very much concerned with the whole question of law, with which Aquinas too was so concerned. It is now good to see that this exchange between Catholic David Elliot and Jewish David Novak on this question is a dialogue rather than a disputation. Sometimes, things do change for the better.

---

7. pp. 123–24.

Chapter 5

Natural Law: Having It Both Ways

TOM ANGIER

Introduction

LET ME BEGIN WITH two anecdotes:

1. At the 2017 meeting of the Joint Session of the Aristotelian Society (the UK equivalent of the American Philosophical Association), I got talking to a philosopher over drinks at the bar. Having let slip that I was "religious"—and therefore probably a unique specimen in that context—the conversation turned, somehow, to marriage and the family. Where did I stand on same-sex marriage? With some trepidation, I answered that, if we no longer see fit to restrict marriage by sex, I saw no reason—on liberal grounds, that is—to restrict it by number. The philosopher looked at me, quizzically, paused for about fifteen seconds, and then said: "I think I agree. There are no grounds to restrict it by number. So I suppose I have no objections to polygamy." (This was a male philosopher.)

2. My second anecdote derives from my years as a PhD student at the University of Toronto, where I was privileged to take David's course on natural law. A fellow graduate informed me that she had been engaged to be married, but because she was "practically minded," she had asked her fiancé for a pre-nuptial agreement (or "pre-nup"). With some strain in her voice, she proceeded to tell me that the negotiations between her and her fiancé's respective lawyers had become so acrimonious that they decided to call off the engagement. They never got married.

What can we learn from these two incidents? The philosopher at the Joint Session made a discovery that, on (pretty brief) reflection, he didn't believe what he had, up to that point, taken himself to believe. His doxastic condition was, in other words, far less transparent than he had assumed. And that it was did not take much effort to demonstrate. By contrast, my fellow graduate, although she was reflectively aware of her beliefs, had not reckoned with their *consequences*. The supposedly "practical" beliefs she had about marriage turned out, in fact, to be radically impractical. Indeed, her conception of the practical had made impossible the kind of trust on which actual practice, and certainly the practice of marriage, is predicated.

What is the upshot of these modest vignettes? I think they point to far wider cultural tendencies than their limited contexts might suggest. First, the majority of our opinion-formers, although not actively dedicated to dismantling our inherited culture, tend to be unaware of its presuppositions and structuring rationales. It follows that when their inherited beliefs are challenged, they discover that those beliefs were, to borrow Cardinal Newman's distinction, never *real* beliefs in the first place, but only *notional* ones. They had never genuinely believed them in the first place. And second, even where our *bien pensants* do come to reflective awareness about their beliefs in the moral-cultural sphere, they tend not to have a grasp of their practical (and especially long-term) implications. So while they are, in general, cognitively innocent, in the sense of guiltless, they are innocent also in the sense of insufficiently informed. And the consequences of their innocence for the rest of us are far from . . . innocent. What, then, as intellectuals—though not as part of the intelligentsia—can we do about this?

David Novak on Natural Law

It seems to me that in such a situation of cultural uninformedness (in the ordinary but also Aristotelian sense) and pervasive lack of prudence (in the ordinary but also Aristotelian sense), we need to draw on all the intellectual and practical resources available to us. We need to quarry robust philosophical arguments to support a realistic, i.e., less naïve and sentimental philosophical anthropology, one that can both uphold an essentialist view of marriage and resist its seductive alternatives. But we also need to quarry theological arguments, for those already committed to theistic premises, yet who are tempted to construe them in ways more accommodating to a fundamental revision in the understanding of marriage. (I take marriage as merely a salient current example.) Such an approach can yield, at the very least, consistency between a philosophical approach and various theological approaches, and at most, will generate significant overlap between the two (both at the level of premises and of conclusions). Either way, philosophers and theologians are best advised to work *in tandem*, I would argue, rather than viewing each other as rivals. And this for two main reasons, one logical and the other pragmatic. First, if our positions are well-founded, they will be at least mutually consistent and at most mutually reinforcing. Secondly, we have enough rivals already, without espying them within our own camp. If ever there was a time to pull together, it is the present.[1]

Now it should be clear that, notwithstanding my great appreciation of David's work, and everything I've learned from it, we do differ on a crucial point—namely, the

---

1. As David notes, "Jews and Christians are strangers in the modern world," in particular to the "secular ethos of the West" ("Defending Niebuhr from Hauerwas," 282; cf. Novak, "Is Natural Law a Border Concept between Judaism and Christianity?" 252).

merits of the traditional Catholic approach to natural law, which, I take it, approximates what I have called the "philosophical approach." This approach, he maintains, is both ill-founded (on grounds I'll outline) and unlikely to persuade those whom we need to persuade. Only what he calls "theologically formulated"[2] or "theistically cogent" natural law theory is both well-founded and likely to persuade. At the very least, "theistically cogent natural law theory can be shown," he holds, "to be more cogent than its ancient Greek or modern (especially Kantian) rivals."[3] It follows that what we should be doing is building an "overlapping consensus" between different theological traditions, by showing how "the logic involved in [one's] constitution of a universal horizon is similar in principle to what is being done by thinkers working in other historical traditions."[4] This both fits our multicultural and pluralistic context, David writes, while not giving up hope for what he calls "intercultural" effectiveness.[5] A key example here is different religious traditions' agreement on the notion that humans are created *b'tselem elohim*, "in the image of God," and this as a foundation for human rights. As David puts matters, "we have better reasons than they [viz. the secularists] have for doing what we both think ought to be done in the world."[6] While, as a theist, I am sympathetic to the claim that theistically informed reasons of this kind are, in certain respects, "better" than their non-theistic counterparts, I think it is vital not to infer that non-theistic reasons are not reasons at all. They are reasons, albeit ones lacking the depth and resonance of their theistic counterparts. But this lack is precisely an *advantage* when it comes to persuading those who inhabit non-theistic religious traditions, and certainly when it comes to persuading those who inhabit no religious tradition at all. Furthermore, and even more vitally, it does not follow from this that theistic and non-theistic reasons are in any sense "rivals," which somehow challenge or displace one another.[7] Far from it: in my view, non-theistic reasoning provides essential philosophical ballast for conclusions that can be reached from different, yet non-rival theological premises. Why, then, is David convinced that there is not just difference here, but also rivalry? I think he has three main arguments, which I shall call the argument from the history of ideas, the argument from metaphysics, and the argument from the nature of law. In each case, he maintains that a traditional philosophical

2. Emon, Levering, and Novak, *Natural Law*, 6.
3. Emon, Levering, and Novak, *Natural Law*, 7–8.
4. Emon, Levering, and Novak, *Natural Law*, 29.
   In at least one place, David rejects an "overlapping consensus" between secularists and theists, on the grounds that it can be only "accidental," rather than "essential" (in the sense of emerging from a shared view of human nature) (see "Is Natural Law a Border Concept," 249, 251). I am more sanguine than he is on this score, since I think that secularists and theists can come to agreement on core facts about human nature, which are also evaluative facts.
5. Emon, Levering, and Novak, *Natural Law*, 30.
6. Emon, Levering, and Novak, *Natural Law*, 38.
7. At *Covenantal Rights*, 17n67, David writes that Greek and biblical views of natural law are "ultimately antithetical"; at *Covenantal Rights*, 25, he holds that "Jerusalem makes its own alternative claims, claims that I am convinced are . . . superior."

approach to natural law fails, or at least rests on very dubious assumptions. But in each case, I will contend that the arguments he offers fall short and that the philosophical approach remains a valuable, indeed an essential complement to the one offered by philosophical theologians such as himself. In short, in this domain we need a both/and strategy, rather than an either/or one, and only on this basis can we hope for a natural law stance that is both well-founded and persuasive.

The Argument from the History of Ideas

David's first locus of argument is indebted to Helmut Koester, who wrote a paper in 1968 entitled "ΝΟΜΟΣ ΦΥΣΕΩΣ: The Concept of Natural Law in Greek Thought."[8] Koester's argument is complex but his conclusion relatively straightforward: namely, that the notion of natural law is hardly present in ancient Greek thought, and that its true origin is Philo of Alexandria. As Koester puts it, Philo is the "crucial and most important contributor to the development of the theory of natural law," indeed that "most probably, Philo was its creator."[9] Koester grants that although Philo's "doctrine," as he calls it, influenced the early Greek Church, it was not important for the later, mediaeval Latin Church, which drew rather on the Roman notion of a *lex naturalis*, a term found extensively in Cicero. Nonetheless, the lesson Koester draws is that the contribution of ancient Greek thought as such to the natural law tradition—whether it be Platonic, Aristotelian or Stoic—is exiguous. And David builds on this claim to argue that if the most exalted philosophers of antiquity had no interest in and ascribed no role to a ΝΟΜΟΣ ΦΥΣΕΩΣ, then it is perverse to think of natural law as a *bona fide* philosophical (or purely philosophical) concept in the first place. Instead, it is a concept that comes into its own only once biblical monotheism is taken seriously by philosophers—first with Philo, then with the advent of Christian philosophy. Without such fructification by monotheism, and its core commitment to a divine lawgiver, "natural law" appears as a merely vestigial notion within the history of ideas.

Let us look a bit more closely at Koester's argument. He points out that the pre-Socratic philosophers do not use the term "law of nature" or "natural law" at all, referring rather to divine law or unwritten law.[10] The sophists, for their part, view the spheres of nature and law as antithetical, the first being a realm of physical or biological necessity (or at least regularity), the second being a realm of mere human convention.[11] While Plato begins to challenge this antithesis, law is still something for him that originates in *logos* (reason) or *nous* (intellect), i.e., faculties confined to *human* nature.[12] Admit-

---

8. In Neusner, *Religions in Antiquity*. For appreciative references to this paper in David's work, see, e.g., *Natural Law in Judaism*, 119n105; *Covenantal Rights*, 17n67; *Natural Law*, 5n10.
9. Koester, "ΝΟΜΟΣ ΦΥΣΕΩΣ: The Concept of Natural Law in Greek Thought," 540.
10. Koester, "ΝΟΜΟΣ ΦΥΣΕΩΣ: The Concept of Natural Law in Greek Thought," 522.
11. Koester, "ΝΟΜΟΣ ΦΥΣΕΩΣ: The Concept of Natural Law in Greek Thought," 524.
12. Koester, "ΝΟΜΟΣ ΦΥΣΕΩΣ: The Concept of Natural Law in Greek Thought," 526.

tedly, Aristotle speaks of "nature" *simpliciter*, invoking the idea that certain modes of disposition and action are *kata phusin*, according to nature, or *para phusin*, against nature.[13] But he, like Plato, hardly refers to a law or laws of nature, and holds that no one is virtuous by nature, but only once they are directed by *logos*. It follows, according to Koester, that although nature endows us with reason, it is not nature as such that is the source of law.[14] And even when it comes to the Stoics, who are usually viewed as the originators of natural law thought, Koester is skeptical. Nature and law remain antithetical for them, he maintains, the only reconciliation being between reason and law, which are now, as he puts it, "positively correlated."[15] Where the Stoics appeal to nature in moral contexts, this is not to nature *simpliciter*, but rather to human nature in particular, which is, of course, rational.[16] As Koester summarizes matters, the term "natural law" is "almost totally absent" from the Greek Stoics;[17] instead, we find coinages like *logos orthos* (right reason) or *nomos koinos* (common law). Only with Cicero, i.e., with Roman philosophy, do we find the liberal use of *lex naturalis*, a usage which, according to Koester, translates not *nomos phuseôs* but rather *logos phuseôs* (there being no "*ratio naturae*" in Latin Stoic sources).[18]

What are we to make of this argument? Koester is right that the sophistic antithesis between nature and law proved difficult to dislodge, showing up even among some of the Greek Stoics. But nature and law remained antithetical only insofar as law was understood as positive, human-made law, rather than the normative background against which such law was to be judged adequate or inadequate in the first place. In the latter sense, nature embodies a *form* of law, indeed a superordinate and overriding form of it. This is plain especially in the fragments of the sophist Antiphon. In fragments 44a–c, he presents nature, *phusis*, as a normative source that can precisely challenge the claims of human law or convention, *nomos*.[19] And there is more explicit evidence of this in the Platonic dialogues. In the *Gorgias*, notably, Callicles berates legally imposed norms in the name of what is "natural." Take, for example, his reproaches against Socrates: "I believe that nature itself reveals that it's a just thing for the better man and the more capable man to have a greater share than the worse man and the less capable man" (483d); "this is what's just by nature . . . [that] cattle and all the other possessions of those who are worse and inferior belong to the one who's better and superior" (484c). Indeed, Callicles refers explicitly in this

---

13. Koester, "ΝΟΜΟΣ ΦΥΣΕΩΣ: The Concept of Natural Law in Greek Thought," 523.
14. Koester, "ΝΟΜΟΣ ΦΥΣΕΩΣ: The Concept of Natural Law in Greek Thought," 527.
15. Koester, "ΝΟΜΟΣ ΦΥΣΕΩΣ: The Concept of Natural Law in Greek Thought," 527.
16. Koester, "ΝΟΜΟΣ ΦΥΣΕΩΣ: The Concept of Natural Law in Greek Thought," 528.
17. Koester, "ΝΟΜΟΣ ΦΥΣΕΩΣ: The Concept of Natural Law in Greek Thought," 529.
18. Koester, "ΝΟΜΟΣ ΦΥΣΕΩΣ: The Concept of Natural Law in Greek Thought," 529, 540. Koester acknowledges two occurrences of *nomos phuseôs* in Epictetus, but judges that these are "trivial" in content (530).
19. See Pendrick, *Antiphon the Sophist: The Fragments*, 59–61, 159–89. Cf. MacIntyre, *Whose Justice? Which Rationality?* 146.

context to a "law of nature," a *nomos phuseôs*: "I believe that these men [Xerxes and his father] do these things [viz., engage in military campaigns] in accordance with the nature of what's just—yes, by Zeus, in accordance with the law of nature, and presumably not with the one we institute" (483e).

By the time we come to the Stoics, law *qua* the instantiation of divinely or rationally sponsored norms no longer stands opposed to nature at all. And this highlights the weakness of Koester's focus on natural law *terminology* in Greek philosophy. From the absence of certain terms, we cannot infer the absence of the correlative *concepts*.[20] Take the example of Aristotle. While Aristotle rarely refers to a natural law or laws as such,[21] he does understand the virtues and virtuous norms of behavior as reflecting the human *ergon* or function.[22] This is grounded, in turn, in the life-form of a particular animal species. And there is no sign that he reduces this animal life-form to the exercise of a hypostasized reason, as if he were an ancient version of Kant. Rather, reason gains its substantive content from the natural, embodied teleology proper to the human species.[23] Likewise, although Aristotle holds we are not naturally virtuous, in the sense of innately or *automatically* virtuous, he argues that we are naturally virtuous in the sense of being made to "receive" the virtues in and through the process of habituation. In this sense, we are ordered to a "second nature," which inclines us to both right affect and right conduct. From this it is hardly a long journey, I take it, to the kind of natural law thinking we find in Cicero, for the conceptual repertoire requisite for Cicero's *lex naturalis* is already widely present within Aristotle's texts. And if this is true for Aristotle, it is so *a fortiori* for the Greek Stoics, whose *nomoi* are clearly coordinate with both reason and nature.

So, if my argument is sound, we should not make too much of the fact that the Greek philosophers rarely refer explicitly to a law or laws of nature. The absence of these terms in their texts does not mean they lacked the correlative concepts. But even if—to be maximally concessive—they *did* lack such concepts, it does not follow that their successors were or are similarly lacking. Indeed, I will now argue that

---

20. David uses the same argument to justify incorporating the concept of "rights" into the Jewish tradition, even though the term is not found in traditional Jewish sources. See *Covenantal Rights*, 34.

21. Where he does invoke a natural law, however, it is in a full-blooded and unequivocal way. N.B. *Rhetoric* I.13: "Universal law is the law of nature. For there really is, as everyone to some extent divines, a natural justice and injustice that is common to all, even to those who have no association or covenant with each other" (1373b6–9). At this juncture, Aristotle refers to Sophocles's Antigone, who claims that her burial of her brother Polyneices "was a just act in spite of the [positive legal] prohibition: she means it was just by nature" (1373b10–11).

22. See *Nicomachean Ethics* [*NE*] I.7.

23. Granted, insofar as Aristotle believes that contemplative reason [*theôria*] constitutes primary *eudaimonia* or fulfilment, he does see reason as distinct from the operation of the "practical" or character virtues [*ēthikai aretai*]. It is the latter that register the human good as fully embodied and grounded in natural *telē*; by contrast, contemplative virtue assimilates the human good to the disembodied, divine good.

such conceptual impoverishment is exactly what contemporary, neo-Aristotelian philosophers have been ensuring against.

The Argument from Metaphysics

David's second argument against the traditional, philosophical conception of natural law is that it is metaphysically ill-founded, or at least rests on foundations that are metaphysically too controversial to generate widespread consensus. As he puts things in *Covenantal Rights*, it "depends on the ontological assumption of universal teleology, and that is quite impossible to rationally ascertain without reverting to a by now irretrievable scientific cosmology."[24] Or as he holds further on, "without a teleological natural science, there is no basis for assuming that the human ends proposed by Plato and Aristotle are not in truth human projects."[25] Similar claims are made throughout his work.[26] The idea here is that after Darwin, we can no longer appeal to a natural scientific order that instantiates distinct species-ends, because the theory of evolution has demonstrated that such ends are not *in* nature, but reduce to projections *onto* nature. Where natural teleology appears to exist, it can be explained, or explained away, as a form of functioning that increases reproductive fitness relative to a particular environment. This kind of view has had some notable supporters, for instance, Bernard Williams, who espouses a similarly anti-Aristotelian view,[27] and Alasdair MacIntyre, who, in *After Virtue*, maintains that Aristotle's "metaphysical biology" is no longer tenable, and that if we wish to argue for a form of moral teleology we will have to reconstruct it on the basis of social practices and the traditions that inform them.[28] Whereas Williams thus thinks modernity leaves no room for a teleological understanding of human life, MacIntyre is more sanguine—but both philosophers are equally convinced that Aristotelian natural teleology is defunct and cannot be resurrected.

Although in such a limited space I cannot address the manifold issues raised by David's, Williams's and MacIntyre's views, I think some circumstantial points are worth highlighting. First, their rejection of Aristotelian teleology, and natural teleological views more generally, is less argued than asserted, as if the advent of Darwinian evolutionary biology were itself sufficient argument. But not only is this weak—since it is not clear that the development of species from other species or

---

24. Novak, *Covenantal Rights*, 21.
25. Novak, *Covenantal Rights*, 22n100.
26. See (e.g.) Novak, *Jewish Social Ethics*, 73, 78; Novak, *Natural Law in Judaism*, 26, 136–37, 189; Novak, "Is Natural Law a Border Concept," 244; Novak, "The Universality of Jewish Ethics: A Rejoinder to Secularist Critics," 200n10; Novak, "Some Questions for the International Theological Commission Document on Natural Law," 136–45, 140, 142; Novak, *Natural Law*, 29.
27. See *Ethics and the Limits of Philosophy*, especially chapter 3, "Foundations: Well-Being."
28. See *After Virtue: A Study in Moral Theory*, chapter 12, "Aristotle's Account of the Virtues."

the process of "natural selection" preclude the existence of distinct ends indexed to different species—the demise of natural teleology has been called into question by MacIntyre's later work. As he puts matters, "I . . . came to recognise . . . that my conception of human beings as virtuous or vicious needed not only a metaphysical but also a biological grounding. . . . This I provided . . . in *Dependent Rational Animals* [1999], where I argued that the moral significance of the animality of human beings, of rational animals, can only be understood if our kinship to some species of not yet rational animals . . . is recognized."[29] And later on, in *Ethics in the Conflicts of Modernity* (2016), MacIntyre further retracts his dismissal of natural teleology, endorsing the view that there are a set of goods that condition any well-lived human life, where these goods are substantially conditioned, in turn, by our biological nature.[30] So at the very least, this suggests that evolutionary biology *per se* does not preclude the kind of moral teleology to which traditional natural law has been committed. True, such teleology does not rest on claims about Platonic Forms or a Prime Mover, but there is no reason to suppose that *these* are essential to any *bona fide* teleological schema. Indeed, since the millennium there has arisen a highly sophisticated research program arguing for a neo-Aristotelian natural teleology grounded in a neo-Aristotelian scientific essentialism, which incorporates the data of evolutionary biology.[31] The two simply need not exclude each other.

Why so? Here I will give a summary outline of the neo-Aristotelian teleology and essentialism which have been gaining ground over the last two decades. First, Aristotle's teleological conception of nature has been resurrected and revised by scholars advocating what they call *dispositional essentialism*. Echoing Aristotle's notions of potentiality and actuality, they argue that both agents and objects have determinate "powers," which are directed intrinsically toward certain characteristic manifestations.[32] This intrinsic directedness can be intentional, as it is in conscious agents, but it need not be: take the example of an acorn, which is directed intrinsically toward growth into an oak tree (given the right conditions). This type of power exhibits "physical" or "natural" intentionality, in the sense of a directedness which obtains in the absence of any mentality. And in this way, "power ontology" in effect recapitulates Aristotle's natural teleology and the final causality that underpins it.[33] Secondly, neo-

29. MacIntyre, *After Virtue*, 3rd ed., xi.

30. See MacIntyre, *Ethics in the Conflicts of Modernity*, § 4.11.

31. See Ellis, *Scientific Essentialism*; Koons, Simpson, and Teh, *Neo-Aristotelian Perspectives on Contemporary Science*; Novotny and Novak, *Neo-Aristotelian Perspectives in Metaphysics*; Oderberg, *Real Essentialism*.

32. See Feser, *Scholastic Metaphysics*; Feser, *Aristotle's Revenge*; Heil, *From an Ontological Point of View*; Molnar, *Powers: A Study in Metaphysics*; Place, "Dispositions as Intentional States."

33. This recapitulation impugns the idea that material and efficient causality exhaust the causality present in nature. Furthermore, it points the way to a final causality or end-directedness in human life that incorporates—but also transcends—conscious intentionality. For an application of dispositional essentialism to the human, ethical sphere, see, e.g., Mumford, Anjum, and Lie, "Dispositions and Ethics."

Aristotelian analytic metaphysicians have been rehabilitating the notion of species essences, which evolutionary biology had purportedly consigned to history.[34] Key here is the idea that species essences are no mere metaphysical posits, but are grounded in features of the world which are scientifically respectable and verifiable. For example, they may be identical to "clusters of covarying traits."[35] And if species essences are construed in such a way, they will be perfectly compatible with the scientific finding that species both come into being and go extinct. For this type of change requires that species taxa—far from being mere theoretical stipulations or artefacts of classificatory fiat—find their objective correlates in nature.[36]

Now clearly, if David, Williams, and the early MacIntyre are nevertheless right, and natural science somehow demonstrates the bankruptcy of natural teleology and species essentialism, we need an alternative grounding for the moral consensus which traditional, philosophical natural law seeks. Here it seems to me there are basically two alternatives. First, we can go down the road of David's "overlapping consensus" between traditions, which, in the case of Judaism and Christianity, will appeal ultimately to claims about God's will, humans being created in the image of God, the divine *mitzvot*, etc. While I am not opposed to this *per se*, and indeed think it a valuable route to take in many respects, its disadvantage is that it will persuade only those already persuaded of its biblical and monotheistic premises. Furthermore, there are several religious traditions that are not monotheistic in form (such as Buddhism and Hinduism), so even within the religious sphere overlap will be impossible to achieve. The second alternative is to appeal to history, and in particular to the experience of historical communities, whether these are theistic in culture or not. This has the advantage that, as David puts it, natural law theory is not erected on a "view from nowhere,"[37] or constructed *sub specie aeternitatis*,[38] i.e., without recourse to the rich inheritance of any actual culture. The disadvantage here, however, is the likelihood of relativism, something the early MacIntyre found difficult to avoid, and which David himself acknowledges. For him, history without any transcendent moorings is always liable to mistake the transient and inessential features of human valuing for the permanent and essential. So, in sum, if we give up on natural teleology, we seem faced with a destructive dilemma: either we achieve a powerful—yet demonstrably limited—"overlapping consensus" between those already committed to certain monotheistic axioms, or we struggle to resist historicist relativism. Either way, we forfeit the increasingly robust philosophical resources of natural teleology, which appeal across

---

34. See Austin, "Aristotelian Essentialism: Essence in an Age of Evolution"; Boulter, *Metaphysics from a Biological Point of View*; Devitt, "Resurrecting Biological Essentialism"; Dumsday, "A New Argument for Intrinsic Biological Essentialism."

35. See Okasha, "Darwinian Metaphysics: Species and the Question of Essentialism."

36. See Boulter, *Metaphysics*, 108–9.

37. Novak, *Natural Law in Judaism*, 140.

38. Novak, *Natural Law in Judaism*, 138.

The Argument from the Nature of Law

The third and final argument I want to tackle identifies a supposed inadequacy in the traditional, philosophical construal of "law." According to David, natural law thought is not found among the ancient Greeks, and this is because the only adequate ground for positing a law of nature (in the moral sense) is that nature is created, i.e., the product of a divine lawgiver. As he expresses things in *Natural Law*, "Natural Law Requires a Cosmic Lawgiver."[40] For what reason? At this point, several arguments come into play. One is abductive in form, that is, an inference to the best explanation. As David writes, "the assumption of the divine cosmic lawgiver best explains why [the] ever-present necessity [of law in human life] is truly universal."[41] A second argument is that absolute, exceptionless moral laws can find no adequate grounding apart from divine commands, because natural norms always admit of exceptions. Where they are grounded in human flourishing, for instance, there is never irrefragable reason for upholding a natural moral norm which, in *this* or *that* case, will undermine human flourishing. A further argument is that where laws rest on rights, a right constitutes an entitlement, and hence requires a person or persons to grant or authorise that entitlement. In the case of natural law, such entitlements can derive only from the author of nature, viz., God.[42] And finally, David argues that "Any order less intelligent than our own is more often than not something to be manipulated *by* us, not something for us to respect and aspire *to*. The only order having an inherent normative pull is one that is more intelligent than our own."[43] It follows that we have to look beyond the natural order itself in order to identify the ultimate and genuine source of normativity. On all these grounds, David concludes that Aquinas is correct to hold that natural law, *qua* law, requires "promulgation,"[44] and that it amounts essentially to a set of divine commands.[45]

---

39. David argues, further, that natural teleology tends to incorporate yet mask various local, cultural commitments, and thus serves as a vehicle of cultural "imperialism" (see, e.g., *Natural Law in Judaism*, 138, 179, 188–90; *Natural Law*, 28–29). But if the neo-Aristotelian project I outlined above is metaphysically robust, this worry is unfounded. Indeed, I suggest that developing natural law on the basis of one's own cultural resources (albeit with the aim of elaborating their "universal horizon," Novak, *Natural Law in Judaism*, 189) is *more* likely to devolve into a form of cultural imperialism.

40. Novak, *Natural Law*, 20.

41. Novak, *Natural Law*, 19.

42. See, e.g., Novak, *Covenantal Rights*, 13; Novak, *Natural Law*, 21–22.

43. Novak, *Natural Law in Judaism*, 137.

44. See Novak, *Natural Law in Judaism*, 23n1.

45. See Novak, "The Universality of Jewish Ethics," 200n10; Novak, *Natural Law*, 8, 9n20, 37.

Once again, it is difficult to grapple with these arguments in full, especially since they do not exhaust the arguments David provides. But I will offer the following thoughts. To begin with, there is no inconsistency in holding both that the natural order is divinely created, and that one need not acknowledge or recognize this in order to discern (at least some of the) norms governing that order. Indeed, I take it that this is precisely Aquinas's view of the natural law: we can discern it, that is, without prior assent to any theological claims or hypotheses. So, I depart from David's position not insofar as he affirms the *ontological*, but only the *epistemic* dependence of natural law on God. With that said, what of his positive arguments? The claim that the "ever-present necessity" of law in human life is best explained by a divine lawgiver can surely be challenged. Is it not better explained by the various natural, exigent needs of human beings, whose well-being depends intimately and crucially on honouring and fulfilling those needs? For instance, wife and children and subsequent generations are hurt profoundly by a husband's adultery, and this (partly) explains the prohibition of adultery. This impinges, in turn, on the view that natural teleology is insufficient to ground such norms. For if we appeal to God's commands *instead*, and insist that they render such prohibitions properly intelligible and justifiable, the obvious response is: but isn't it rather the overriding *good* that hangs on observing such commands that does so? Here David enters detailed considerations about why, *contra* much moral philosophical opinion, the right precedes the good, and hence that God's commands do not await the kind of axiological explication and justification which I understand natural law as providing.[46] But suffice it to say that I don't fully grasp either these considerations or their force,[47] and that, philosophically, I still believe that any command stands in need of moral justification—justification that is in key part naturalistic—and that, theologically, David's position thus remains

---

46. See Novak, *Covenantal Rights*, 16–20.

47. E.g., David holds that goods "are the measure of how adequate to the nature of both the claimant and the respondent, *between* whom the claim operates, that claim really is. Hence these claims/rights are the true criteria of justice" (*Covenantal Rights*, 16). If "criteria" here indicates that rights claims are a *mark* of justice, this inference seems unexceptionable. But such claims are not self-validating, in the sense of demonstrating why they are justified in the first place. This, I take it, is the role of goods. Further on, David argues that the "good to be done for someone is for the sake of the one who holds the right, who makes the claim. The justice of the claim is what makes the content of the claim good. Hence right precedes good in the sense that persons are prior to their acts and to the things their acts involve" (*Covenantal Rights*, 17). The first sentence here seems cogent, but the second is pivotal without being perspicuous. Perhaps the justice of a claim—e.g., "I have a right to compensation for the harm you caused"—renders its content good, in the sense that its content is to be affirmed. But we can still ask why such a claim is just to begin with, i.e., why compensation is owed. The fact that persons are prior to their acts (in some sense) does not clearly provide such an explanation. By contrast, its being good for them does so. At *Covenantal Rights*, 18n74, David refers to Jewish sources which maintain that good is "primarily aesthetic" in meaning, and it may be that this view informs his wider denial that good is "morally fundamental." But the view in question is highly controversial and requires more substantiation. (For an account that seems to ascribe a less subsidiary role to goods, see *Jewish Social Ethics*, 14–17.)

systematically vulnerable to the *Euthyphro* dilemma. At least, I want to hear how it can avoid such systematic vulnerability.

As to the argument that rights are entitlements which require a person or persons to authorize them, this may be true of positive legal rights, but it is not clear why it must hold of rights that govern and indeed can trump legal rights, viz., the rights that inform natural legal norms. After all, not all declarations of human rights infer from the existence of such rights to the existence of a divine authorizer—as if such rights remain empty and unaccountable until such an authorizer can be found. Rather, they assume the intelligibility and justification of those rights can be grasped *independently* of any such authorizer. Lastly, the argument that the only order that has normative "pull" or authority over us is one that transcends the natural order is also questionable. It assumes or suggests that the natural conditions to which we are subject can be subjected, *in toto*, to our will, and hence that, far from finding ourselves subordinate to those conditions and the norms that inform them, we are in fact superordinate to both. The only order to which we are ineluctably subordinate is hence located wholly beyond the natural order, out of reach, as it were, of our superintending grasp. But this picture of our powers, both practical and moral, looks oddly and unaccountably Promethean. Granted, we may *try* to attain absolute control over the conditions of life, and assert, hubristically, that this somehow warrants our independence of the norms that inform them. But such Prometheanism seems illusory. For as soon as we have emancipated ourselves from one set of natural conditions, we find ourselves subjected to another, and there is anyway no warrant for inferring from such a change to our having authority over norms in the first place. The natural order may, admittedly, and in large part, not be minded or intelligent, but there is no reason to think that only minded or intelligent things condition our well-being.

Conclusion

I have argued, then, that although "theologically formulated" natural law theory is a welcome weapon in our armory, it is not sufficient either as a means of defense or for achieving victory. It will not persuade the unbelieving or the theologically illiterate, and furthermore, it itself stands in need of philosophical resources that are not of its own making. Of course, if, as David's work contends, these resources are fundamentally flawed, and incapable of repair, my case would be unsustainable—but I have argued that this is not so. Far from it: the argument from the history of ideas, the argument from metaphysics, and the argument from the nature of law do not show that traditional, philosophical natural law thinking is ailing or moribund. Rather, it is robust and bursting with health. Given this, therefore, we should do everything in our power to bolster and make use of it. Our strategy should, in other words, and as I said at the start, be both/and, rather than either/or—for we can have natural law both ways.

Bibliography

Austin, Christopher. "Aristotelian Essentialism: Essence in an Age of Evolution." *Synthese* 194.7 (2017) 2539–56.

Boulter, Stephen. *Metaphysics from a Biological Point of View*. Basingstoke, UK: Palgrave Macmillan, 2013.

Devitt, Michael. "Resurrecting Biological Essentialism." *Philosophy of Science* 75 (2008) 344–82.

Dumsday, Travis. "A New Argument for Intrinsic Biological Essentialism." *The Philosophical Quarterly* 62 (2012) 486–504.

Ellis, Brian. *Scientific Essentialism*. Cambridge: Cambridge University Press, 2001.

Emon, Anver, Matthew Levering, and David Novak. *Natural Law: A Jewish, Christian, and Muslim Trialogue*. Oxford: Oxford University Press, 2014.

Feser, Edward. *Aristotle's Revenge: The Metaphysical Foundations of Physical and Biological Science*. Heusenstamm, Germany: Editiones Scholasticae, 2019.

———. *Scholastic Metaphysics: A Contemporary Introduction*. Heusenstamm, Germany: Editiones Scholasticae 2014.

Heil, John. *From an Ontological Point of View*. Oxford: Clarendon, 2003.

Koons, Robert C., William M. R. Simpson, and Nicholas J. Teh. *Neo-Aristotelian Perspectives on Contemporary Science*. London: Routledge, 2018.

MacIntyre, Alasdair. *After Virtue: A Study in Moral Theory*. 3rd ed. Notre Dame, IN: University of Notre Dame Press, 2007.

———. *Ethics in the Conflicts of Modernity: An Essay on Desire, Practical Reasoning, and Narrative*. Cambridge: Cambridge University Press, 2016.

———. *Whose Justice? Which Rationality?* London: Duckworth, 1988.

Molnar, George. *Powers: A Study in Metaphysics*. Oxford: Oxford University Press, 2003.

Mumford, Stephen, Rani Lill Anjum and Svein Anders Noer Lie. "Dispositions and Ethics." In *Powers and Capacities in Philosophy: The New Aristotelianism*, edited by Ruth Groff and John Greco, 231–47. London: Routledge, 2013.

Neusner, Jacob, ed. *Religions in Antiquity: Essays in Memory of Erwin Ramsdell Goodenough*. Leiden: Brill, 1968.

Novak, David. *Covenantal Rights: A Study in Jewish Political Theory*. Princeton, NJ: Princeton University Press 2000.

———. "Defending Niebuhr from Hauerwas." *Journal of Religious Ethics* 40.2 (2012) 281–95.

———. "Is Natural Law a Border Concept between Judaism and Christianity?" *Journal of Religious Ethics* 32.2 (June 2004) 237–54.

———. *Jewish Social Ethics*. Oxford: Oxford University Press, 1992.

———. *Natural Law in Judaism*. Cambridge: Cambridge University Press, 1998.

———. "Some Questions for the International Theological Commission Document on Natural Law." In *Searching for a Universal Ethic: Multidisciplinary, Ecumenical, and Interfaith Responses to the Catholic Natural Law Tradition*, edited by J. Berkman and W. C. Mattison III, 136–45. Grand Rapids: Eerdmans, 2014.

———. "The Universality of Jewish Ethics: A Rejoinder to Secularist Critics." *Journal of Religious Ethics* 36.2 (2008) 181–211.

Novotný, Daniel, and Lukáš Novák. *Neo-Aristotelian Perspectives in Metaphysics*. London: Routledge, 2014.

Oderberg, David. *Real Essentialism*. London: Routledge, 2007.

Okasha, Samir. "Darwinian Metaphysics: Species and the Question of Essentialism." *Synthese* 131 (2002) 191–213.

Pendrick, Gerard J. *Antiphon the Sophist: The Fragments*. Cambridge Classical Texts and Commentaries 39. Cambridge: Cambridge University Press, 2002.

Place, U. T. "Dispositions as Intentional States." In *Dispositions: A Debate*, edited by D. M. Armstrong, C. B. Martin, and U. T. Place, 19–32. London: Routledge, 1996.

Williams, Bernard. *Ethics and the Limits of Philosophy*. London: Fontana, 1985.

Response to

Tom Angier's "Natural Law: Having It Both Ways"

David Novak

I AM GRATEFUL TO my former student Tom Angier for his critique of what he considers to be my overly theological natural law theory. This does not mean that Tom, as a self-declared "theist," is opposed to my or anybody's theology or to its relevance and even importance for a fully developed natural law theory. Rather, Tom and I seem to differ as to what philosophy can or cannot do for a theory of natural law. Our differences might well be termed "intramural."

Both of us would agree that a natural law theory that could only persuade theologically committed theists of its truth doesn't have to present itself as "natural" law at all. In fact, it is ill advised to even try to do so. A direct divine command theory can avoid the question of *nature* in "natural" law altogether by sticking to what Calvin called "special revelation," which is the proper subject matter of dogmatic theology. To persuade non-theists (whether atheists or agnostics) of the truth of a natural law theory, and even theists who think that knowledge of created nature is not confined to theology, a natural law theory needs philosophy, whose proper subject matter is nature.[1] Moreover, since the vast majority of those involved today in what might be called "academic culture," who would be those most likely to have any interest in a theory of "natural" anything, are non-theists, for whom any theologically based theory would be of no interest (but only of historical curiosity). So, what role would Tom have theology (i.e., revelation-based theology) play in his modern natural law theory, other than subsequent confirmation (logically if not chronologically) of what philosophy can already argue independently? It is hoped this will come out in his own work now in progress.

---

1. This point is developed in my new book, based on my 2017 Gifford Lectures, *Athens and Jerusalem: God, Humans, and Nature* (Toronto: University of Toronto Press, 2019).

Let me now deal with what are Tom's two main objections to what he considers to be my essentially theological view of natural law. These two objections are very much interrelated.

Tom writes, "I depart from David's position not insofar as he affirms the *ontological*, but only the *epistemic* dependence of natural law on God."[2] By "ontological" dependence I assume he means that natural law, being part of *created* nature, like any *ens creatum*, requires God as its Creator. On the other hand, by "epistemic" dependence I assume he means that we do not need to *know* natural law as what has been *given* by God (even indirectly as in Calvin's "general revelation"). Natural law is epistemically independent (although not quite "autonomous" in the Kantian sense). Interestingly enough, Maimonides seems to have made the same point when he indicated that the blessing said before the performance of a commandment (*mitsvah*), praising God as "the One who commands us," is not said before performing a commandment pertaining to interhuman relations, the vast majority of which, being rationally evident (what Aquinas calls *ratio quoad nos*), qualify as natural law precepts (*Mishneh Torah*: blessings, 11.2). It is not that Maimonides denies that God is the ontological *source* of all the commandments, whether they pertain to divine-human relations or to interhuman relations; rather, he could be interpreted to be saying that God as the source of the *ethical* commandments pertaining to interhuman relations need only be generally assumed, instead of having to be specifically acknowledged as the divine Commander or Lawgiver each and every time such a commandment is performed.

In a lecture delivered at Princeton University in May 2019 (just about six weeks after the first version of Tom's paper was delivered at a conference about my thought held at Mundelein Seminary), I tried to argue that natural law, in my view, is not derived *from* theological premises, but rather theology gives natural law a more satisfactory ontological status than does philosophy. Let me quote a key passage in that lecture.

> [N]atural law precepts are not conclusions deduced from theological premises. Rather, natural law is aided by theology insofar as theology shows natural law its origin (its *archē*) and its ultimate end (its *telos*); but it does not show natural law's intelligibility (its *logos*) nor its practicality (its *ēthos*). Even though we do not deduce from our theologically formulated doctrines (*Torah* in Hebrew) what is to be done in secular space ... these larger doctrines strengthen and deepen our practical judgments ... by *informing* our moral acts, by ultimately placing them in the reality of the created, purposeful cosmos, thus giving them their greater dimension.

In other words, I think theology does the ontological "heavy lifting" best, while Tom thinks philosophy does it best. Our disagreement centers around teleology, which we both think needs ontological grounding. Unlike John Finnis, Robert

---

2. p. 156.

George, and other advocates of the "new natural law," Tom and I both think that practical reason alone cannot supply the teleology a fully adequate natural law theory surely needs. Only ontology (or "metaphysics") can do that. So, let me now argue why philosophy cannot do the ontological heavy lifting regarding teleology Tom thinks it can do. Interestingly enough, philosopher Elizabeth Anscombe (herself a devout Catholic), at the outset of her famous essay "Modern Moral Philosophy," in arguing for the philosophical validity of a more virtue-based ethic rather than a more law-based ethic, proclaims that those committed to the latter (as she certainly was in her personal religiously constituted life) are best advised to go to "the Torah" as the source of the "Hebrew-Christian ethic."

Tom correctly quotes key lines in my 2000 book *Covenantal Rights* about teleology, viz., that it "depends on the ontological assumption of universal teleology, and that it is now quite impossible to rationally ascertain without reverting to a by now irretrievable scientific cosmology";[3] also that "without a teleological natural science, there is no basis for assuming that the human ends proposed by Plato and Aristotle are not in truth human projects."[4] According to these quotes, Tom honors me by putting me in the company of Bernard Williams and (whom he calls) the "earlier" Alasdair MacIntyre, as I have explicitly followed the lead of Ernst Cassirer, Leo Strauss, and Jürgen Habermas on this point. However, Tom then goes on to claim that "[t]he idea here is that after Darwin, we can no longer appeal to a natural scientific order [what Aristotle called *taxis*] that instantiates distinct species-ends, because the theory of evolution has demonstrated that such ends are not *in* nature, but reduce to projections *onto* nature."

Nevertheless, Tom's pinning my argument against Aristotelian teleology on the assumption that Darwin's biological theory of evolution is altogether true (which I didn't say anywhere in *Covenantal Rights*), and then showing how its anti-teleology has been challenged by some contemporary scientific theorists, begs the question. For even if this newer more teleological scientific theory is true, it does not do for natural law what Aristotle's scientific teleology did for natural law. (I made this point in response to a question asked by philosopher Robert Koons at the Princeton lecture, whom Tom refers to in his paper.) Why? It is because the only teleology that has normative significance for Aristotle is the teleology he discerns in astrophysics or cosmology. (Aristotelian teleology is discussed at length in chapter 5 of my *Athens and Jerusalem*.) Why? It is because, for Aristotle (following Plato and other earlier Greek thinkers), the heavenly bodies are higher, cosmic, godly (*theoi*) intelligences who can be imitated by lower earthly intelligences like humans (*anthropoi*).

The biological teleology beneath humans, however, has no such normative significance for them. Its only significance for human ethics is that it provides a certain unintelligent potential that humans can intelligently actualize by the coordination of

---

3. p. 152.
4. p. 152.

(or at least not contradicting) their purposeful actions with the higher, more intelligent, cosmic teleology. In what A. O. Lovejoy called "the great chain of being," human action comes in somewhere at midpoint (what Eric Voegelin called "metaxy") between earth and heaven. In fact, the difference between a law based ethic and a virtue based ethic (a là Aristotle) is that the former is concerned with moral norms as commandments *from* God, while the latter is concerned with excellent human characteristics (*aretai*) ultimately functioning as imitations *of* what God does for and by Godself as the End of all ends (who is the *ultima ratio* of all intelligent action), but not what God does *for* God's human creatures *by* commanding them how to live in the world. Therefore, despite the growing attraction of neo-Aristotelian teleology for biological theorists (like what Tom calls "the later work" of Alasdair MacIntyre), it does not do the ontological heavy lifting that natural law requires. As I pointed out in my Princeton lecture, "[o]nly a revelation-based theology can speak of a purposeful cosmos in which our little island of natural law rationality is a participant, not the one exception. Theology can thus help us deal with the fear that our commitment to natural law is to some sort of fluke in an otherwise impersonal universe." And in what might be called the Jewish "summa theologica," i.e., the Talmud, God's purposes for God's world are often inferred from the commandments revealed in Scripture (what the Rabbis call *ta'amei ha-mitsvot*), based on the scriptural narratives (*aggadah*) that describe and transmit God's purposeful activity in relation to God's human creatures, especially the people Israel as God's covenant partners, who are the direct recipients of the divine commandments. This theology supplies the ontological *archē* or source, and the ontological *telos* or end, for any truthful human participation in God's cosmos. "I am He; I am the first and I am the last" (Isa 48:12).

I think Tom claims too much from philosophy for natural law theory. I hope I do not claim too much from theology. Perhaps, by lessening our respective claims, our respective positions on natural law might come closer together than they are now already.

Chapter 6

David and Goliath

DOUGLAS FARROW

The Philistines stood on the mountain on the one side, and Israel stood on the mountain on the other side, with a valley between them. And there came out from the camp of the Philistines a champion named Goliath, of Gath, whose height was six cubits and a span. He had a helmet of bronze on his head, and he was armed with a coat of mail, and the weight of the coat was five thousand shekels of bronze. And he had greaves of bronze upon his legs, and a javelin of bronze slung between his shoulders. And the shaft of his spear was like a weaver's beam, and his spear's head weighed six hundred shekels of iron; and his shield-bearer went before him. He stood and shouted to the ranks of Israel, "Why have you come out to draw up for battle? ... Then [David] took his staff in his hand, and chose five smooth stones from the brook, and put them in his shepherd's bag or wallet; his sling was in his hand, and he drew near to the Philistine. (1 Sam 17:3–8, 40 *RSVCE*)

THIS TEXT FROM 1 Samuel 17 puts me in mind of the context in which I met David Novak. It was the autumn of 2002, and the occasion was a conference I was co-chairing at McGill, called Pluralism, Religion and Public Policy. Drawn up on one side was our then Chief Justice, Beverley MacLachlin, and on the other, Jean Bethke Elshtain. William Galston and Richard John Neuhaus were there, also facing opposite directions, the former speaking on "Religion and Liberal Society," the latter giving a rousing rendition of his "Liberal Democracy and Acts of Faith" essay. Charles Taylor was there, perhaps facing both directions; and H. T. Engelhart Jr., not exactly on anyone's side either, since no one was altogether on his side, as Treebeard would say. And then there was David,[1] a Jewish counterweight to Prince Hassan of Jordan, albeit without the armed bodyguards and with philosophical rather than political muscle. Not long off the boat from London, England at that time, and only beginning to engage the North American scene, I made many new friends and some sparring partners among these fine folk, but

---

1. For the obvious reason, I shall take the liberty of using Rabbi Novak's first name freely in the present piece.

it was Fr. Richard and Rabbi David who took me into their company, the *First Things* company, and helped me learn to fight the good fight.

David and I shared the Canadian context, of course, in which we faced our northern Goliath in the form of an increasingly militant "liberal" government and court, both operating with what David identifies as a secularist and individualist form of social contract theory and having at their disposal the requisite means to make the theory bite, namely, the new *Canadian Charter of Rights and Freedoms*, then a mere twenty years old. One year later the Ontario Court of Appeal delivered its *Halpern* decision, which brought same-sex marriage to Canada, where (through a process that occupied the following two years) it became the law of the land in 2005.[2] The dominoes were beginning to fall, and not only in Canada. The international cabal of lawyers and activists who were orchestrating the fall met in Yogyakarta in 2006 to spell out the principles of the legal and public policy revolution that would entrench worldwide the sexual revolution of the West, which was also a theological and political revolution, in hopes of carrying it forward into territory only the likes of Shulamith Firestone had envisioned. There were to be no holds barred in wrestling sexual difference to the ground and removing all traces of the morals and mores based upon it. Or rather there were to be no holds barred on their side. On the other side (anyone who doubts that there are distinct sides and that this is a fight to the finish has his head in the sand) many holds were to be barred, beginning with our linguistic grasp of reality. Ordinary gendered pronouns, for example, were to be forbidden, which triggered a now famous fight at the University of Toronto led by the redoubtable Jordan Peterson.

Before these and other such developments took place, whether to the north, south, west or east, David understood that it was necessary to attack this Goliath, this deracinating giant whose spear is more than capable of lifting those it strikes clean off the ground on which they thought they stood. At the time we met, David was working on his book *The Jewish Social Contract*, extending the line of thought pursued earlier in *Covenantal Rights*. He produced for our 2002 conference an essay distilling some of that which appears as chapter 4 in *Recognizing Religion in a Secular Society*, the book that emerged a couple of years later. His essay is entitled "Human Dignity and the Social Contract,"[3] from which, in light of the aforementioned books, I mean to draw five smooth stones useful for carrying on the fight, which thus far has gone about as badly as possible, leading to much glee on the side of the Philistines.

When I have presented these smooth stones, I will attempt two things. First, I will point to the unprotected spot at which they must be aimed. Second, I will remark on the fact that it was but a single stone that slew Goliath.

---

2. See Cere and Farrow, eds., *Divorcing Marriage*.
3. In Farrow, ed., *Recognizing Religion in a Secular Society*, 51–68 (chapter 4).

Five Smooth Stones

First Stone. I begin with David's claim that "most modern arguments for democracy, based as they have been on foundationally secularist premises, have not been formulated with much perspicacity, either theological or philosophical."[4]

This assumes, or at least concedes for the sake of the argument, that democracy is a good thing and at present the best thing. The question is how democracy ought to work, for plainly it is not working at all well now and, arguably, is in imminent danger of collapse through corruption and by way of major breaches in the social contract.

So, what are these secularist premises? We will speak here of just two. First, that individual autonomy is the main building block of democracy and that the social contract is constructed by way of individual consent. David challenges this individualism: "Persons are social beings by nature, not by mutual agreement. There cannot be contracting human persons who are not *already* socialized."[5] Second, that society at large is more fundamental than the communities in which individuals are and have already been socialized. This too is challenged: "When one begins with society, there is no real place for community, [whereas] when one begins with community there is the potential to make a real place for society."[6]

Now, one reason that secularists have difficulty with the prior socialization of persons is that it seems to compromise individual consent through predispositions that may be at odds with one another and may also favor voting blocs that are not themselves the product of public debate. Unfortunately, they overlook what ought never to be overlooked, namely, a basic fact of life. Politically active citizens, like politically passive citizens, are not unformed social or political matter but rather preformed social and political matter.

As David rightly says, pressing home this point: "A real point of departure is preferable to a hypothetical one for any theory. But secularist social contract theory cannot claim historical priority, let alone ontological priority. It is rooted neither in history nor in nature, but only in human imagination."[7] Perhaps we should allow, however, that secularists do not overlook it. Rather they see the prior socialization of persons as a kind of original sin. Yet, try as they may, they cannot offer any redemption from this original sin other than deracination. Which brings me to claim number two.

Second Stone. Most modern arguments for democracy, says David, "have been recipes for the public disappearance of traditional communities."[8] Let me repeat

---

4. Novak, "Human Dignity and the Social Contract," 53.

5. Novak, "Human Dignity and the Social Contract," 58. As he indicates at n.11, he borrows the phrase "social beings by nature" from Aristotle (*Politics* 1.1/1251b1ff.), but is not going to agree either with Aristotle (cf. *Nicomachean Ethics* 8.9/1162a15–20) or with Plato (*Republic* 485Eff.) on the priority of the polis or the republic over the family.

6. Novak, "Human Dignity and the Social Contract," 64.

7. Novak, "Human Dignity and the Social Contract," 64.

8. Novak, "Human Dignity and the Social Contract," 54.

that. *Most modern arguments for democracy have been recipes for the disappearance of traditional communities.* We might observe that this is not just true of modern arguments, nor of arguments for democracy. He himself mentions Plato's *Republic* in a footnote. In the modern sphere of socialism and communism, Stalin and Mao and Xi come quickly to mind. Tyrannies of all times and places have developed such recipes. War itself is such a recipe. Pogroms likewise, be they the work of mobs or of bureaucrats. What sort of company is this, then, into which Novak thus places modern arguments for democracy?

David Novak is no enemy of democracy itself, but before he fights with the Goliath of tyrannical democracy—the giant De Tocqueville saw looming on the horizon a long time ago—he fights with the lion and the bear of modern democratic and social contract theorists, with the men whose ideas are popular on the front lines of the Philistines.

Regrettably, these men are not all gentiles. There are fellow Jews among them. Take Joseph Raz, for example, whose perfectionist liberalism has a utopian feel to it. Both Canada and America, as I point out in *Theological Negotiations*, have begun fulfilling Raz's prophecy—or was it a prescription?—in *The Morality of Freedom* about the disappearance even of the natural family as that ur-community in which tradition first operates. The autonomy-based democracy Raz envisions is busy deracinating the family:

> More recent changes are uncertain and incomplete. Some tendencies, e.g. to communal families, or open marriages, may wither away. Others, e.g. homosexual families, may be here to stay. It is too early to have a clear view of the consequences of these developments. But one thing can be said with certainty. They will not be confined to adding new options to the familiar heterosexual monogamous family. They will change the character of that family. If these changes take root in our culture then the familiar marriage relations will disappear. They will not disappear suddenly. Rather they will be transformed into a somewhat different social form, which responds to the fact that it is one of several forms of bonding, and that bonding itself is much more easily and commonly dissoluble. All these factors are already working their way into the constitutive conventions which determine what is appropriate and expected within a conventional marriage and transforming its significance.[9]

David Novak makes no reference to Raz in the material we are treating. But he does say that the main question here is "whether civil society can radically redefine the family as its own institution,"[10] which it must do if it is to make good on its own claim to be everyone's *primary* community—if society, in other words, is to precede community rather than community preceding and grounding society.

---

9. Raz, *The Morality of Freedom*, 393; see further Farrow, *Theological Negotiations*, 181 and onward.
10. Novak, "Human Dignity and the Social Contract," 60.

The answer to this question was tested in Canada by *Halpern* and two similar cases (*Halpern* was first past the post, so to say, though not the first launched), and the answer that was given by the courts confirmed what David worried about in that McGill essay. "Very few people," he observed, "would really want their children to be wards, *de facto* if not yet *de jure*, of the institution of contractual society, the state. Yet that is the most obvious result of looking at the liberty of the family as something to be overcome in the institution of society."[11]

Wards of the state? Precisely, as I went on myself to argue in *Nation of Bastards*: wards now both *de iure* and *de facto*. For same-sex marriage is all about putting homosexual unions on the same legal footing as heterosexual unions, or rather about replacing the latter on that footing. Which cannot be done without making marriage itself an institution that excludes procreation from its purview—no more "Be fruitful and multiply"—and without making the connection between parents and children strictly a legal fiction. At a single blow the natural family unit, understood as the possessor of pre-political rights, is done away with and the legal family unit takes its place, a unit the state can modify at will.[12]

Moreover, if marriage is not procreative, it is not educative either. The state now controls what even our youngest children are taught about sex and religion and other fundamentals of tradition. The state now interferes in homes as it never did before. The state now teaches children even in kindergarten that there is no such thing as male and female; that perversity is merely diversity; that sex itself is an arbitrary cultural convention which they are free to challenge without interference from their parents. (In British Columbia, for example, the lower court has recently forbidden a parent to withdraw his daughter from puberty-blocking hormone treatments and even to refer to her as female.)[13] And all this in the name of democracy, democracy dismembered by that "javelin of bronze" slung over the shoulders of our judiciary, the javelin it has affectionately dubbed *Dignity and Autonomy!*

All this has come to America as well. Where it has not come, it is coming. And David was among the few who saw it coming, among the still fewer who some time ago began attacking it at its philosophical and theological roots—in David's case, with the weapons to be found in holy writ and in the rabbinical traditions. For he knew that both the family and the synagogue or religious community were simultaneously under attack, that traditional cultures as such were under attack. He knew that these cultures, even where they deserve to survive, cannot survive without a renewed and deepened self-understanding, a self-understanding capable of public articulation and defense. "Without a traditional culture that is not only defensible theologically and philosophically but defensible in public, individual members of these cultures do not have enough

---

11. Novak, "Human Dignity and the Social Contract," 61.
12. See further *Nation of Bastards: Essays on the End of Marriage*, 49 and onward.
13. See Farrow, "The New Family Violence."

cultural capital to maintain their traditional identity even in private. For them, a democratic commitment turns out to be the sale of their very souls."[14]

This defense cannot be made, he insists, without enquiry into the foundations of democracy and of the social contract. "Minorities need to think out a democratic theory by themselves, especially a democratic social contract theory, inasmuch as social contract theory seems to be the best explanation of a rights-based democratic order."[15] They need, especially if they are Jewish or Christian, to think out "rights" and "dignity" from a covenant-based perspective. For just as community precedes, both historically and ontologically, civil society, and civil society precedes the state that ought to be no more than "a body in its service" (to import the anthropological language of Augustine), so the covenant precedes the contract. The social contract must be shown to be no more than a political and legal arrangement in service of the covenant.

Unfortunately, in Latin *foedus* does double duty for covenant and contract, and this (as my late teacher, J. B. Torrance, used to stress) did no end of harm in the Calvinist sphere that was so influential in the modern development of political philosophy. It tended to the sublimation of sound theology to political ends, sometimes very questionable political ends, such as those of Apartheid in South Africa. But our situation is rapidly deteriorating into something just as bad, albeit in the guise of anti-Apartheid regimes. In the former context, Torrance tried to bring to bear the resources of Christian covenantal thinking. In our present context, David Novak has brought to bear all the riches of Jewish covenantal thinking, and we are deeply indebted to him for doing so. I will say more about this in relation to the fourth stone drawn from this stream and found in his pouch.

Third Stone. Third is the claim that "the hallmark of a democratic social order is the continuing limitation of its governing range."[16] This, in our context, must be deemed a battle-cry. For the hallmark of *non*-covenantally based democratic theory is its relentless attempt to limit the impact and governing range, not of civil society or even of the state, but of the natural family and of the religious community. David counters by insisting that "membership in these traditional communities is *outside* the range of civil society because of their historical precedence, and it is *above* the range of civil society because of the ontological status the relationship of these communities with God gives them."[17] He makes good on that in *The Jewish Social Contract* and in *Covenantal Rights*, much as Oliver O'Donovan tries to make good on it, from a Christian perspective, in *The Desire of the Nations* and in *The Ways of Judgment*.[18] "Only a

---

14. Novak, "Human Dignity and the Social Contract," 54.
15. Novak, "Human Dignity and the Social Contract," 53.
16. Novak, "Human Dignity and the Social Contract," 56.
17. Novak, "Human Dignity and the Social Contract," 57, emphasis added.
18. It is a pity that their time in Toronto did not overlap, for it is at this intersection especially that there is great promise for strengthening the Jewish/Christian intellectual coalition. (This is of course the intersection occupied by the Institute on Religion and Public Life, in which Novak plays a pivotal role.)

civil society that is largely made up of such religious people," writes David, "is in any position to respect the universal transcendence of such communal origins and such communal destinies," meaning the transcendence of *ad hoc* political instruments such as democracy, the purpose of which ought to be no more than to make a secular space for the cooperation of these more primordial communities. For "only religious people in a democratic society have sufficient reasons for the limitation of the normative reach of that society"[19] and of what I call "the savior state."[20]

Fourth Stone. The fourth, rather startling, claim follows: "One can only accept a human-made normative order when it attempts to imitate a normative order that is *not* of human making, even though it substantiates human being."[21] Why? Because human freedom is grounded in the freedom of God our Creator, who brings us into being *ex nihilo*, creating a shared space in which we as human agents may cooperate with him. It is in this "may cooperate" that our own freedom consists and in actually cooperating that the *imago Dei* consists.

Irenaeus of Lyons, the first great expositor of *creatio ex nihilo*, argues similarly in *Adversus haereses*. In making it his business to address Marcionite and Gnostic repudiations of Israel, of Torah, and of the God of Israel—that is, in trying to show that Christianity was not in any way a religion that rejected either the present creation or the laws that govern it—he contends that Jesus did not abolish the law of Moses but rather fulfilled it in such a way as to deepen and widen its scope and power by imbuing the covenant people with a new spirit of liberty based on affection and gratitude.[22] Lest it be thought that this was somehow a matter of religion only, however, he added that those precepts that were natural to all people were likewise prised open and ennobled by a more generous recognition of the goods they serve.[23] Everything, as Augustine also argues, "rings with newness" while remaining just what it is in God's creative design and purpose.[24]

Now David does not need Irenaeus to say such things, nor do I need here to debate with David whether Irenaeus, and Christianity generally, makes more or less sense of the claim in hand than does the rabbinical tradition. I can simply agree with him that, in biblical terms, "there is always some sort of covenant (*berit*) operating between the community and God, and simultaneously among the members of the community itself." That "unlike a contract, this covenant is not initiated by the mutual agreement of equals,

19. Novak, "Human Dignity and the Social Contract," 63.

20. Cf. Farrow, "The Audacity of the State."

21. Novak, "Human Dignity and the Social Contract," 68.

22. This, he claimed, was the spirit and the substance of the Eucharist, considered in its human dimension.

23. "Those laws that are natural, and liberal, and common to all, he has enlarged and expanded, generously and ungrudgingly granting to men, through adoption, to know God [as] Father, and to love him whole-heartedly, and to follow his word unswervingly, abstaining not only from evil deeds but even from the desire of them" (*Haer.* 4.16.5, translation mine).

24. See Augustine, *De Civitate Dei*, 16.26.

and unlike a contract [it] is interminable." Hence that "the community is there before any of its members are born or reborn into it" and can "survive the loss of any of its members." That it nonetheless "requires the free acceptance of communal authority in order for the covenant to work" and that "free acceptance, rather than an egalitarian agreement," is the dimension of covenant reality that enables the concept of a social contract to emerge; that "it is the possibility of mutual trust, freely given and freely accepted, that causes a contract to be initiated and sustained in a promise." And further—here is the payload—that "only when this non-coercive, intelligent and benevolent heteronomy is acknowledged" can we speak of political autonomy.[25]

All this requires a radically different view of secular space than what is proffered by most secularists, just as it requires a radically different view of autonomy than what is proffered either by Kant, on the one hand—Kant the cornshucker, as I think of him, because he already regards particular traditions as the disposable husk on the kernel of universal reason[26]—or by Mill and Raz, on the other, whose idea of autonomy strays to the voluntarist side of the nominalist tradition, from which they all come and which they are all bound and determined to see triumph over the Jewish and Catholic and, as Mill likes to say, "Calvinist" traditions.[27] It makes possible a different view of democracy than has been emerging in recent generations and is already collapsing into irreconcilable party conflict. The view that holds heteronomy and autonomy in dialectical tension, that holds the universal and the particular in dialectical tension—thinking its way to the universal from the particular and back again without either Kantian or Hegelian corn-shucking, and without the visceral hatred of everything traditional, especially the family, that has come to characterize post-modernity—also makes possible a recovery of the sense of home and homelands that today is threatened by the deracinating forces of globalism: a sense that is hospitable not reactionary, open to the other rather than merely or dangerously populist.[28]

What kind of space is it in which democracy should operate? Secular space. And what is that? Not itself a secular culture but a space that allows cultures, especially religious cultures, to thrive. "The generation of secular space is the result of an inter-cultural agreement to create a realm distinct from the sacred space of any primal community, one in which many cultures can take part, but clearly without the creation of some new secular culture to replace the older cultures of the contracting

---

25. Novak, "Human Dignity and the Social Contract," 67 and onward. These ideas are all developed in Novak, *The Jewish Social Contract*; cf. Novak, *The Election of Israel*, 163 and onward.

26. See *Religion within the Limits of Reason Alone*. Novak, on my view, is much too sanguine about Kant, or so I judge from his Gifford lectures.

27. We are all "Calvinists" to Mill!

28. Cf. Farrow, "'The Lady Left for Dragon's Meat.'"

parties."²⁹ So, then, it is a multicultural space "where no one culture is civilly, politically or legally privileged over any other culture."³⁰

I wonder, though, whether this stone is properly smoothed or fully polished so that it will fly straight. What does such a space look like and how is it maintained? Is it purely procedural? If so, are procedures themselves neutral about cultures or are they bearers of culture? How does justice operate in this sphere? How is it conceived? Are we somehow to rescue Rawls's idea of "justice as fairness"? How will that turn out, if not as it already seems to have turned out? Namely, as a stripping from law and public policy of all those things that seem evidently to be religiously or culturally derived; as a general prejudice against whatever constrains individual liberty, hence as a favoring of license over liberty; as a misconstrual of liberty as "freedom from" rather than "freedom for," since it is impossible to identity "freedom for" in a neutral secular sphere, to give it positive content without favoring any particular culture. How will this secular space, in which democracy must work and justice must also be done, *not* become an anti-culture, one that does not try to substantiate human being but rather insists that for public purposes the human being can and must substantiate itself, and can do so at will, *de novo* if not *ex nihilo*?

I fear that this stone in particular might miss its mark. The next and last stone is the most provocative of all to modern or postmodern man, the most dangerous to modern states, and I would like to make it a little more dangerous or subversive still.

Fifth Stone. This is the claim that "no one can stand up against God successfully." It appears as the opening gambit of *Covenantal Rights,* and it is David's direct reply to Goliath. Methodologically it is borne out by refusing Saul's armor (armor that in our David's case he is in fact quite able to wear) and by insisting instead on the priority of exegesis and theology over the tools and weapons of political science.

David begins with the one God, the Father almighty, Creator of heaven and earth and of all things visible and invisible. He begins with man as male and female made in the image of God, with that still-mortal man who is invited into the image by sharing with his God the creaturely time and space in which God has made room for him. What follows in *Covenantal Rights* is a wonderful example of how thinking that is unafraid to glory in the wealth of Scripture and tradition may and does proceed.

Man is not merely invited into fellowship with God and so into genuine human flourishing. Man is also the object of divine commands, commands that have both his *esse* and his *bene esse* in view. "Being commanded," writes David, "however we hear that commandment, is something that enables us to do well in the world. Without that sense of being commanded, when our own practical power becomes the measure of all things, we destroy ourselves and our world. For when this happens, our reason forgets that it is but a reflection of the wisdom of God who structures

---

29. Novak, "Human Dignity and the Social Contract," 55 and onward.
30. Novak, "Human Dignity and the Social Contract," 62 and onward.

the natural world, and our will forgets that it is but the reflection of God's will who brought the world into existence."[31]

Where is this more obvious than in the sphere of positive law, by means of which man himself becomes a lawgiver, organizing the boundaries of his own communal existence, and to that extent demarcating the space in which his life together takes place? I agree with David that Jews and Christians should encourage public prayer as a sign of man's dependence on the Creator and divine Lawgiver. But here I have to say that I am not as sanguine as David about a secular or public space that attempts some kind of neutrality towards religion. Certainly it cannot be allowed that this space is a space where humans may act as if God were not. That is to set man above God. God no doubt permits this, for a time, just as he permitted the golden bull to be erected or the *baalim* or Jupiter to be worshiped. But "it must be reiterated whenever humans act as if they were equal, let alone superior, to God, [that] God is not yet exercising his right."[32] Which he will do in due course. It's called judgment, the Day of the Lord.

"A right is not only a power; it is a politically structured claim that calls for duty on the part of someone else."[33] We are that someone else. Not just practicing Jews and Christians, but all people. For that reason, the promotion of atheism was understood to be a public crime, until relatively recently; and the deicide of which Nietzsche spoke, the deicide of the moderns, he knew to be the reversal of lawfulness and lawlessness, hence in principle the revaluation of all values.

My own view of modern political philosophy, from at least Lessing onwards, is that it is militantly supersessionist, structurally anti-Semitic, opposed to the particular, ultimately opposed to the very notion of heteronomy. It cannot tolerate the fact that man is not merely invited into fellowship with God and so into genuine human flourishing but is also the object of divine commands. What it lacks in consequence is any way to construe the relation between reason and will that is still connected to the way things actually are in God's world. As David says, "basic opposition to law itself—antinomianism—takes the form of resentment at being limited by anyone else. Philosophically, this resentment takes the form of the will resenting the necessity of its being limited by reason, that is, its having to justify itself rationally by continual reference to enclosing nature."[34]

Just so! Law itself is becoming increasingly irrational, and so also tyrannical, in a relentless drive to make a safe space for resentment, not only of God, but of the creaturely forms that God has built into creation itself. And this resentment does not stop short of a conspiracy to violate even "a child's natural right" to its own father and mother, or at least to some father and mother. Such moral violations "should goad people like myself," remarks David elsewhere, "to work for legal change in the

31. Novak, *Covenantal Rights*, 42.
32. Novak, *Covenantal Rights*, 39.
33. Novak, *Covenantal Rights*, 39.
34. Novak, *Covenantal Rights*, 45.

whole area of family relations, including change of laws that permit an unborn child to be deprived of his or her right to life, which is the basis of all other rights, like the right of a living human being to have parents who are responsible for his or her upbringing."[35] And of course it has so goaded. Yet on this front the battle is all but lost, unfortunately, and not only on this front.

As Augustine famously concludes in *The City of God*, "a people is the union of a multitude of rational creatures, associated through consensual sharing of the things it loves; certainly then, to see what is the quality of any 'people', these are the things that must be considered—the things it loves."[36] We do not love justice, I fear, though we talk endlessly about justice. If justice really is among the things we love, if we mean to be lawful rather than lawless, to be virtuous rather than vicious, then we must hold *as the first point of justice* the obligation to render thanks to the true God, Creator of all. For "true justice is found where the one supreme God rules an obedient city . . . and where in consequence the soul rules the body . . . and reason rules the vices in lawful order." In other words, where God and neighbor are not properly loved, true justice cannot exist.[37] Where God is not yet acknowledged or thanked, true justice has not even begun.

Collectively we need not render thanks in a specifically Jewish or a specifically Christian way in order to re-embark on the road to justice, but we can and must choose whether we will acknowledge the one God worshiped by Jews and Christians or substitute something or someone in place of that God. In which case, we will be trying to stand up against God, which we will do to our own ruin. For no one *can* successfully stand against God.

The Stone of Consequence

> When the Philistine looked, and saw David, he disdained him; for he was but a youth, ruddy and comely in appearance. And the Philistine said to David, "Am I a dog, that you come to me with sticks?" And the Philistine cursed David by his gods. The Philistine said to David, "Come to me, and I will give your flesh to the birds of the air and to the beasts of the field." Then David said to the Philistine, "You come to me with a sword and with a spear and with a javelin; but I come to you in the name of the LORD of hosts, the God of the armies of Israel, whom you have defied. This day the LORD will deliver you into my hand, and I will strike you down, and cut off your head; and I will give the dead bodies of the host of the Philistines this day to the birds of the air and to the wild beasts of the earth; that all the earth may know that there is a God in Israel, and that all this

---

35. "Why We Should Oppose Same-Sex Marriage."
36. *Civ.* 19.24 (translation mine).
37. *Civ.* 19.23 (trans. William Babcock). Justice is only present where we "give full thanks to God for the benefits we receive" and where God comes into view as our supreme good (19:27).

assembly may know that the LORD saves not with sword and spear; for the battle is the LORD's and he will give you into our hand." (1 Sam 17:42–47 *RSVCE*)

Now, our David, however comely in appearance, is no longer but a youth; if he were, we would not be producing this volume in his honor. But let there be no counsel of despair such as the biblical David had to contend with. Our David also, in his way, has been showing us how to come out against the giant with the right weapons—weapons derived from knowledge of God and his salvation, and of the divine order for creation through which human beings, in being saved, will be substantiated. May his disciples flourish and his tribe increase, in the synagogues and churches, in the academies and public life. May they be just as fearless, and still more fearless.

Let them also grasp, if they hope to be fearless, the existential import of the point Professor Anderson has made, viz., that the truth of Genesis, the truth about creation, is established by way of the truth of the exodus; or, in Christian terms, by the truth of the new exodus, the truth of the resurrection of the dead. Faith in these truths is what will move them to bold action.

It is no counsel of despair to say that it is past time to call people back to a general morality and to natural law. We must continue to do that, of course. But we must also invite them to lift up their hearts to the Lord while they still have opportunity. We must remind them that it is only right and just that they do so, and that there are consequences for not doing so.

Goliath is bellowing out his curses against God, when he is not busy trying to carve out a space in which it is not and cannot be admitted that the God of Israel even exists. The unprotected spot, as the story tells us, where the stone from the sling can strike its fatal blow, is on the giant's forehead, right between his eyes. That, I propose, is the spot we must aim for. We must not be afraid to speak biblically and theologically and, as David constantly reminds us, to speak with a thick cultural accent out of our actual biblical and theological traditions—intelligibly, not unintelligibly, making plain to the Philistines our meaning—and to act accordingly. For God will bring down this giant, as he brought down all that went before him.

No one can stand successfully against God! Not even the Goliath of godless democracy, whose evils (as David reminds us, passing on Rabbi Heschel's advice) we must strive to conquer one by one, until the One comes who will conquer all evil. That one is the stone of real consequence, the messianic stone, the stone cut without hands and drawn by God from the pouch of the covenant—the stone for the sake of which the covenant itself exists, the stone by which God will exercise his right.[38] "Give me a man, that we may fight together," says Goliath. And God obliges. He obliges with the Son of Man, who approaches the Ancient of Days in fulfilment of the duties of man and is given dominion and power to exercise the rights of God, to

---

38. Cf. Daniel 3 and 7.

rule over a kingdom that shall never pass away. None who has faith in that man need suppose his own pouch empty.

Bibliography

Augustine. *The City of God (De Civitate Dei). Books 1–10.* Translated by William S. Babcock. Hyde Park, NY: New City, 2013.

Cere, Daniel, and Douglas Farrow, eds. *Divorcing Marriage.* Montreal: McGill-Queens, 2004.

Farrow, Douglas. "The Audacity of the State." *Touchstone: A Journal of Mere Christianity* 23.1 (2010) 28–35.

———. "'The Lady Left for Dragon's Meat': Comments on the Paris Statement." *Communio* 45.1 (2018) 197–20.

———. *Nation of Bastards: Essays on the End of Marriage.* Toronto: BPS, 2007.

———. "The New Family Violence." *First Things* (Web Exclusives). May 8, 2019. https://www.firstthings.com/web-exclusives/2019/05/the-new-family-violence.

———. *Theological Negotiations.* Grand Rapids: Baker Academic, 2018.

Novak, David. *Covenantal Rights: A Study in Jewish Political Theory.* Princeton: Princeton University Press, 2000.

———. *The Election of Israel: The Idea of the Chosen People.* Cambridge: Cambridge University Press, 1995.

———. "Human Dignity and the Social Contract." In *Recognizing Religion in a Secular Society: Essays in Pluralism, Religion, and Public Policy*, edited by Douglas Farrow, 51–68. Montreal, Canada: McGill-Queen's University Press, 2004.

———. *The Jewish Social Contract: An Essay in Political Theology.* Princeton, NJ: Princeton University Press, 2005.

———. "Why We Should Oppose Same-Sex Marriage." The Public Discourse. June 19, 2009. https://www.thepublicdiscourse.com/2009/06/259/.

Raz, Joseph. *The Morality of Freedom.* Oxford: Clarendon, 1986.

Response to
Douglas Farrow's "David and Goliath"

David Novak

I AM GRATEFUL TO my friend and colleague Douglas Farrow for his most generous, sympathetic treatment of my theological-political theory. Douglas has informed the readers of this volume of the occasion when our common theological-political concerns brought us together for the first time. The 2002 McGill conference Douglas remembers so well was titled "Pluralism, Religion, and Public Policy." There the battle lines were clearly drawn; and Douglas and I knew which side each of us and now both of us were on, and who was there with us. What made this conference so significant was the fact that the issues we were dealing with are perennial issues of politics in the deepest sense, namely, issues concerning our interhuman relations, divine-human relations, and their inner connection. None of these issues can ever be ignored by any serious political theory or praxis.

These battle lines go back to the archetypal modern Jewish heretic, the seventeenth-century philosopher Baruch Spinoza. Up until Spinoza's time, it was assumed by both Jews and Christians that public morality needs to be ultimately validated by a traditional religion. Spinoza, however, inverted that validation by arguing that traditional religions have to be immediately validated by public morality. Since public morality was now to be in the hands of a basically secular state, the only thing the state wants from any traditional religion is for it to give some sort of ecclesial endorsement of state policy. That, then, leads to the type of "civil religion" suggested in the eighteenth century by the erstwhile Christian Jean-Jacques Rousseau, the orthopraxis Jew Moses Mendelssohn, and the still officially Christian Immanuel Kant. Up until the twentieth century, however, a secular state still needed this kind of ecclesial endorsement, or at least it needed to silence any ecclesial opposition to its public policies, if for no other reason than still the vast majority of its citizens still had some sort of loyalty to their traditional religions. That is clearly not the case today.

One could see the battle to overcome Spinoza's inversion beginning with the iconoclastic nineteenth-century Danish Lutheran thinker Søren Kierkegaard, and going into the twentieth century with the Swiss-Reformed theologian Karl Barth, and the German-Jewish philosopher Franz Rosenzweig. Nevertheless, by anticipation, we see the opposition to the subordination of religion to state policy already in the sixteenth century, when Thomas More put his life on the line by telling his sovereign, King Henry VIII, "I am the King's good servant, but God's first." Those following Spinoza (many of whom unknowingly) might well have said, though, "We and God are the King's good servants." Indeed, something like that was said 2,000 years earlier to the prophet Amos by the priest Amaziah: "Do not continue to prophecy at Beth-El, for it is the King's sanctuary [*miqdash melekh*]; it is the royal house" (Amos 7:13). The true prophets of Israel were willing to be the king's servants, but only in those areas where the king's policies do not go against the law of God.

Very much standing on the shoulders of these giants at the McGill conference were the late Lutheran social theorist and political activist, Jean Bethke Elshtain, and the late Catholic social theorist and political activist, Father Richard John Neuhaus. And standing with them were Douglas, newly arrived at McGill, and myself, newly arrived at the University of Toronto. Here is where we all had to engage such heavy weights as the political philosopher William Galston and the Canadian Chief Justice Beverley MacLachlin. What we were arguing then concerned the very essence of democracy: what a democracy can require of its citizens, and what its citizens can require of it.

Douglas is right when, in analyzing the paper I delivered at that conference, he deems that my paper "assumes . . . that democracy is a good thing" and that "David Novak is no enemy of democracy itself."[1] In fact, this assumption seems to have been held by all the participants in the conference; at least nobody I recall questioned it. Yet, Douglas seems to question that assumption, wondering whether my multicultural constitution of democracy, i.e., what I think democracy ought to be and can be, "will fly straight," asking, "What does such a space look like and how is it maintained? Is it purely procedural? If so, are procedures themselves neutral about cultures or are they bearers of culture?"[2] Furthermore, Douglas states that "it is impossible to identify 'freedom for' in a neutral secular space, to give it positive content without favouring any particular culture;" therefore, as he boldly puts it, "I am not as sanguine as David about a secular or public space that attempts some kind of neutrality towards religion."[3] Finally, he concludes that "it is past time to call people back to a general morality and to natural law. . . . We must not be afraid to speak biblically and theologically . . . to speak with a thick cultural accent out of our actual biblical and theological traditions."[4]

Let me now try to briefly address Douglas's very incisive questioning of my position, which he has so carefully and collegially studied.

1. pp. 166–67.
2. p. 172.
3. p. 173.
4. p. 175.

At the aforementioned McGill conference, one could say that Galston, MacLachlin *et alia* were on the "left side" of the theological-political divide, and Elshtain, Neuhaus, Farrow, Novak *et alia* were on the "right side" of this divide. (Jean Elshtain and Richard John Neuhaus, alas, are no longer with us in this world, so that leaves Farrow and Novak to continue in their stead.) Nevertheless, it is important to bear in mind who were not present at that great debate, viz., those farther to the left than Galston and MacLachlin, and those farther to the right than Douglas and me. Farther to the left are those socialists who would make state ideology the official religion of the polity, not even tolerating the public practice of any traditional religion at all. (We see this already in the official *laïcité* of the province of Québec, where Douglas lives and works.) Farther to the right are those who advocate some kind of "theocracy." In its current connotation, this means there is only *one* official religion (or State Church), and the clergy of that one official religion are the final arbiters of public policy (as in Iran). And (as in Iran or Saudi Arabia), those who do not adhere to the one and only official religion are, at best, tolerated as second- or third-class citizens (*dhimmi* is the Arabic term); at worst, they are "aliens." This is what we call "theocracy," which is actually "clerisy."

Now, what prevents Douglas and me from adopting the "theocratic" position? I submit that what prevents us from that move is our respective adherence to natural law. Natural law mediates between our existential commitment to biblical revelation (albeit sometimes but not always interpreted differently by our respective theological traditions) and our political commitment to democracy, even if democracy is (as Winston Churchill once said) the worst political system, i.e., unless you look at the alternatives.

Natural law performs that mediation by showing that it is possible for adherents of a revelation-based religion like Judaism or Christianity (or Islam) to be proactive citizens of a multicultural, democratic society in good faith. For proponents of natural law, our respective religions do not claim to be God's kingdom on earth and, as such, we believe ourselves authorized by our religious traditions not to force our religion on anybody having a different religion, or even no religion. Instead, natural law provides a criterion for living in peace with justice even with those who do not share our ultimate commitments. Natural law provides the minimal criterion for living in the present between the time of revelation past and the time of redemption future. The only ones who do not seem to be able to enter natural law type discourse are socialists on the far left, believing a state under their control will be salvific. Also, we cannot talk natural law with theocrats to the far right of us, who believe that redemption is already in their hands, and all they need now is the political power to finally implement it. (As a friend of mine said about a prominent Jewish theocrat in our own community, "thank God he doesn't have an army!") I would call this position "monoculturalism."

I do agree with Douglas's pessimism about the persuasive ability of natural law type discourse in our current society, where the centres of political power are not only secular (as they should be), but are militantly secularist, thus disallowing any adherence to a law not of human making (and unmaking), which is the essential characteristic of both minimalist natural law and maximalist revealed law. Therefore, our natural adherence has to be more defensive than persuasive. That is, basing ourselves on the inherent rationality of natural law, we can show the irrationality of the positions of its opponents. Moreover, we have to constantly rethink natural law and translate it into contemporary idioms, instead of simply falling back on authoritative traditional texts. Finally, it is our faith in the same God who is Creator, Lawgiver, and Redeemer that sustains us, and saves us here and now from the imperialist temptation of trying to conquer the world or the despairing temptation to abandon the world by fleeing to sectarian hiding places.

Chapter 7

The Pedagogy of *Dabru Emet*

How a Catholic Professor Teaches a Jewish Document to Multireligious Students

Rita George-Tvrtković

For the past decade, I have taught a theology course called "Catholic Perspectives on Interreligious Dialogue" at Benedictine University, a Catholic institution in suburban Chicago. To ensure that students learn that every religion's approaches to dialogue are complex and variegated, I have them read diverse Muslim perspectives when learning about Islam, diverse Jewish perspectives when learning about Judaism, etc.[1] In the case of Judaism, one document is especially useful for helping us to consider what multiple Jewish scholars have to say about the Christian-Jewish relationship. That document is *Dabru Emet: A Jewish Statement on Christians and Christianity*, published in 2000 and authored by four Jewish scholars, including David Novak.

While my interreligious dialogue course has a triple Catholic frame (the professor, the university, and the approach to the subject), in practice the learning context is not quite as Catholic: Benedictine University's student body is less than 50 percent Catholic (self-reported), with over 25 percent Muslims, 5 percent Hindus, plus significant numbers of Sikhs, Jains, Syro-Malabar Catholics, Protestants, and "nones."[2] We have very few Jewish students. Nevertheless, Christian-Jewish dialogue remains central to my syllabus because of Christianity's unique relationship with

---

1. In this practice, I am following the advice given by Swidler in his now classic "Dialogue Decalogue: Ground Rules for Interreligious Dialogue," in which Commandment 5 states: "Each participant must define himself. Only the Jew, for example, can define what it means to be a Jew. . . . Conversely, the one interpreted must be able to recognize herself in the interpretation."

2. The "nones" are the religiously unaffiliated, or those who check the "none" box in surveys of religious identity. It is a growing demographic in the United States and globally. According to a 2012 Pew Charitable Trust study, the religiously unaffiliated make up 16.3 percent of the global population, the third largest group after Christians and Muslims, respectively. See https://www.pewforum.org/2012/12/18/global-religious-landscape-exec/. For a primer on teaching theology in Catholic universities with growing numbers of nones, see Fletcher, "Among the Nones: Questing for God in the Twenty-First Century Classroom."

Judaism. In fact, it is irrelevant whether or not there are *any* Jews in the class or at the university; the theology of this special relationship must always be highlighted, and in my course I spend more time on Christian-Jewish dialogue than any other. This emphasis is especially necessary on our campus, because unfortunately we have had some incidences of antisemitism.

My own pedagogical context as outlined above will thus serve as the backdrop for this chapter's discussion of *Dabru Emet* ("speak the truth"), which I consider a vital pedagogical tool for imparting both the *content* and *method* of Christian-Jewish dialogue. A Catholic professor teaching about interfaith issues in a religiously diverse classroom is greatly assisted by this multi-authored, practical Jewish document which is the fruit of experience. This chapter will consider two areas of content (monotheism and reciprocity) and one aspect of method (polyvalence) that *Dabru Emet* is particularly adept at highlighting in an undergraduate course.

Monotheism

When students read *Dabru Emet*'s very first bullet point (it has eight such points), "Jews and Christians worship the same God," many are surprised. They wonder why the authors need to state the obvious. For they are used to hearing Judaism, Christianity, and Islam classified together as the three Western, monotheistic faiths (a.k.a., the "Abrahamic faiths").[3] Some students are also familiar with the older term "Judeo-Christian," a hyphenated form which seems to imply an especially close relationship between these two religions (and thus recently this term has been used to make a distinction between Jews and Christians on the one hand, and Muslims on the other).[4] Yet by beginning *Dabru Emet* with the explicit declaration that Jews and Christians worship the same one God, the authors reveal this question to be a live one for some in the Jewish community. In so doing, *Dabru Emet* begins right from the start not with a similarity, but with a disagreement that most students never considered before, having assumed that monotheism is one of the few topics about which Jews and Christians can easily agree.

Some of my students are aware of a related question, "Do Christians and Muslims worship the same God?" which has been asked increasingly since 9/11, mainly by evangelical Christians, but also by some Muslims and Jews, and even by politicians and the

---

3. Use of this term can be traced to the mid-twentieth century writings of the French Orientalist Louis Massignon (d. 1962), who was the professor of several *periti* at the Second Vatican Council, including Archbishop Joseph Descuffi and Georges Anawati, O.P., the latter of whom helped wrote *Nostra Aetate*'s section three on Islam. See Massignon, "Trois Prières de Abraham." Some scholars have taken issue with the term "Abrahamic faiths." See for example Levenson, *Inheriting Abraham*.

4. The term "Judeo-Christian" has been revived of late by American politicians such as Donald Trump, who wish to remove Islam from the Western monotheistic religion trifecta; see Haynes, "Donald Trump, Judeo-Christian Values, and the Clash of Civilizations." Some scholars questioning this term include Fischer, "Is there a Judeo-Christian Tradition? A European Perspective."

popular press.[5] In 2003, a comment by President George W. Bush stating that Christians and Muslims worship the same God provoked vehement disagreement from evangelical leaders like Ted Haggard, then head of the National Association of Evangelicals.[6] In response to the growing debate, *The Christian Century* published a series of articles entitled "Do Christians and Muslims Worship the Same God?" featuring editorials by a variety of scholars including the Jewish Jon Levenson, the Muslim Umar F. Abd-Allah, the Christian S. Wesley Ariarajah, and others.[7] Since then, several books and articles with similar titles have appeared, both academic and popular.[8] And after a 2015–16 controversy in which a tenured political science professor at Wheaton College, an elite evangelical Christian institution in suburban Chicago, was put on administrative leave after stating on Facebook that Christians and Muslims worship the same God (and quoting Pope Francis to support her claim), the question has reemerged as a live topic among a broader range of Christian theologians, Catholics included.[9]

But the current debate about the same God is mostly a Christian-Muslim one. Few seem to be asking whether Christians and *Jews* worship the same God. Indeed, the *Christian Century* article about one God written by the Jewish scholar Jon Levenson attempts to adjudicate the question for Christians and Muslims, not Jews.[10] The same holds true for Catholics. For example, documents from Vatican II dealing with other religions, including *Nostra Aetate* and *Lumen Gentium*, do not explicitly say that Christians and Jews share the same one God, because it is simply assumed that they do. In contrast, these same documents explicitly affirm Islam's monotheism. For example, *Lumen Gentium* states: "the plan of salvation also includes those who acknowledge the Creator. In the first place amongst these there are the Muslims, who, professing to hold

---

5. Historically, this was a non-question for medieval Latin and Arabophone Christians. They assumed that Christians and Muslims worshiped the same God and argued instead about other issues, such as the revelatory status of the Qur'an and Jesus's identity as son of God or prophet.

6. "The Christian God encourages freedom, love, forgiveness, prosperity and health. The Muslim god appears to value the opposite. The personalities of each god are evident in the cultures, civilizations and dispositions of the peoples that serve them. Muhammad's central message was submission; Jesus' central message was love. They seem to be very different personalities" (Haggard as quoted by Waldman in "Commandment the First." The author notes that he is writing in response to Bush's statement a few weeks earlier and gives Haggard's response.)

7. The *Christian Century* series ran from April through August of 2004.

8. Recent publications on this topic include Neusner, Levine, Chilton, and Cornell, *Do Jews, Christians, and Muslims Worship the Same God?*; Volf, ed., *Do We Worship the Same God?*; the document jointly written by international Muslim scholars, *A Common Word between Us and You* (2007); Volf, *Allah: A Christian Response*; and chapter 4 (pp. 160–211) of D'Costa's *Vatican II*, entitled "The Council and the Muslims: Worshipping the Same God?" Also within the past five years, several non-academic books on this same topic have been published by non-mainstream presses.

9. The professor, Larycia Hawkins, is a Christian who donned a hijab during Advent 2015 to show what she calls "embodied solidarity" with Muslims at a time of increasing political rhetoric against Muslims and threats of a "Muslim ban." Hawkins, the first tenured African-American female professor at Wheaton College, has since left and is now a professor at the University of Virginia.

10. Levenson, "Do Christians and Muslims Worship the Same God?"

the faith of Abraham, along with us adore the one and merciful God."[11] At that time, the Catholic Church needed to say that Islam is "in the first place" among religions because they acknowledge the same one God, while Jews are placed in a separate category altogether—they are the first among all religions and "on account of their fathers . . . most dear to God," according to *Lumen Gentium* 16. The implicit assumption here is that the God who holds Jews dear *is* the same one God. Likewise, compare this explicit affirmation of Muslim monotheism in *Nostra Aetate* 3 ("The church regards with esteem the Muslims, they adore the one God . . .") with what *Nostra Aetate* 4 says about Jews ("The Church . . . received the revelation of the Old Testament through the people with whom God in His inexpressible mercy concluded the Ancient Covenant" and also "God holds the Jews most dear for the sake of their Fathers; He does not repent of the gifts He makes or of the calls He issues—such is the witness of the Apostle" [Rom 11:28–29]). The fact that Christians and Jews share the same God is never explicitly stated in any of these documents; the fact is simply assumed.

But with *Dabru Emet*, students are able to see the *asymmetry* in the monotheism question: for their part, Christians take for granted that Jews and Christians worship the same God (and I would add, most of my Muslim, Hindu, and "none" students take this for granted too), but Jews do not. Furthermore, my students begin to see the complexity of Jewish views on the subject when they read *Dabru Emet* in concert with other articles on the same issue, for example, David Berger's "Some Reservations on a Jewish Statement about Christians and Christianity," the first part of which is an explicit response to *Dabru Emet* point 1.[12] Berger reads the monotheism question in light of the traditional Jewish notion of *avodah zarah* (which he translates as "foreign worship"). He notes that historically, Jews have disagreed about whether Christians are guilty of foreign worship either via means of worship or object of worship. Therefore, Berger warns, answering the question of whether Jews and Christians worship the same God is not as clear-cut as *Dabru Emet* seems to suggest.

In response to Berger's point (about Jews questioning the object of Christian worship), some of my students have perceptively pointed out that to ask this question in the first place could be seen as problematic, for it seems to contain an implicit polytheism: if Jews, Christians, and Muslims do not worship the same god, what other god exists that they would be worshiping? Our in-class discussion of *Dabru Emet*'s point 1 is often useful because it helps students to see the *intra*-religious and multilateral dimensions of any interreligious question. The one God issue cannot just be tackled in isolated bilateral dialogues (meaning Christian-Jewish on the one hand, or Christian-Muslim on the other). Rather, Jewish-Christian dialogues about

---

11. *Lumen Gentium*.16. Cf. *Nostra Aetate*.3: "The Church regards with esteem also the Muslims. They adore the one God, living and subsisting in Himself; merciful and all-powerful, the Creator of heaven and earth."

12. Lecture given by David Berger at the inaugural meeting of the Council of Centers on Jewish-Christian Relations (CCJR) in Baltimore on October 28, 2002. "Some Reservations" was later published in Berger, *Persecution, Polemic, and Dialogue*.

monotheism are enriched when similar topics from Christian-Muslim and intra-Jewish dialogues are brought in. For example, as a scholar of medieval Christian-Muslim relations, I read this line from *Dabru Emet* ("While Christian worship is not a viable religious choice for Jews, as Jewish theologians we rejoice that, through Christianity, hundreds of millions of people have entered into relationship with the God of Israel") and am reminded of medieval Latin Christian polemicists writing against Islam, who similarly praise Muhammad (albeit begrudgingly) for bringing monotheism to the formerly polytheistic Arabs. Despite what medieval Latins saw as Islam's other doctrinal errors, they could still recognize the religion as staunchly monotheistic, which allowed them to categorize Islam as a step up from paganism. Western Christian theologians including Peter the Venerable, Petrus Alfonsi, John of Damascus, and William of Tripoli all give Muhammad some credit for getting Arabs to accept monotheism; implicit in this approval is the recognition that Islam professes the *correct* monotheism, thus worshipping the same one God that Christians do.[13] Some Eastern Christian Arabophone theologians even went as far as to affirm Muhammad's *localized* (but not universal) prophethood precisely because he was successful in bringing monotheism to the Arabs.[14]

When *Dabru Emet*'s statement on monotheism is read in concert with the Christian-Muslim dialogue on monotheism, a parallel can be detected between the skepticism Judaism has about Christian monotheism and the skepticism Christianity has about Islamic monotheism. When medieval Christians reflected on Islamic monotheism, and when *Dabru Emet*'s Jewish scholars reflected on Christian monotheism, in both cases it seems that the older religion acknowledges some limited legitimacy in a later religion, even while it also tries to highlight the later religion's deficiencies (e.g., premodern Christians acknowledged Muslim monotheism but often classified Islam as a heresy due to its Christology).

Dabru Emet's point 1 forces my students to begin their study of Christian-Jewish dialogue by reconsidering what they take for granted about even the most basic theological issues, such as monotheism. It also helps them to recognize multiple

---

13. Many medieval Latin and Arabophone Christian polemicists note that the Arabs had been polytheists during the *jahiliyya* (the "time of ignorance," or pre-Islamic Arabia) and grudgingly give the prophet a measure of credit for introducing monotheism. For example, William of Tripoli (fl. 1270s) notes that Muhammad "invited the idolaters to follow one God." See William's *Notitia de Machometo* (Latin and German) in *Wilhelm von Tripolis: Notitia de Machometo; De statu Sarracenorum*, ed. and trans. Peter Engels; English translation here is mine. Peter the Venerable (d. 1156) says that the prophet "left idolatry completely and also persuaded whomever he could that it must be abandoned, and taught that one God was to be worshipped" (English translation of Peter's *Summa totius haeresis sarracenorum* by Irven Resnick in Peter the Venerable, *Writings against the Saracens*).

14. For example, the *Risala ila al-Muslimin* of Bishop Paul of Antioch (twelfth century) includes the following affirmation of Muhammad's localized prophethood: "We know that he was not sent to us, but to the Arabs of the *Jahiliyya* of whom he said that there had come to them no warner before him. We know that he did not obligate us to follow him because there had come to us before him prophets who had preached and warned us in our own languages" (as quoted in Michel, *A Muslim Theologian's Response to Christianity*, 88).

areas of asymmetry in the Christian-Jewish dialogue and identify parallels between the questions that Christian-Muslim and Jewish-Muslim dialogues are asking separately, but should be asking together.

Reciprocity

The second content area that *Dabru Emet* helps students to consider is reciprocity, a dialogical ideal which implies equality among interlocutors, and mutuality in terms of actions towards one another and the way in which conversation topics are selected and discussed.[15] The syllabus has us read *Dabru Emet* just a few days after *Nostra Aetate*, and this juxtaposition begs comparison between the two documents. In fact, some of my students call *Dabru Emet* the "Jewish *Nostra Aetate*." They are usually able to identify the most obvious parallels: both are formal religious statements with multiple authors that appear to be written primarily for an *intra*-religious audience, to teach them about an *inter*-religious relationship. (Novak indicates, however, that *Dabru Emet*'s intended primary audience was actually Christians, and he later wrote an article to encourage Jews to read it.)[16] Another similarity between the two documents is that both were written as much, if not more, for the average believer than for experts—this is clear especially in the case of *Dabru Emet*, which was published as a full-page advertisement in the Sunday edition of *The New York Times* (September 10, 2000). And both documents tend to stress points of theological agreement rather than differences, which are not ignored but are definitely played down. Without ground-breaking official Christian documents like the Catholic Church's *Nostra Aetate* in 1965 and the (largely) Protestant *Ten Points of Seelisburg* in 1947,[17] and the resulting changes in attitudes about Jews and Judaism among Christians in the decades that followed, it is likely that *Dabru Emet* would never have been written in 2000. Indeed, in its introduction, *Dabru Emet* explicitly refers to these Christian documents as the primary motivator for its writing: "An increasing number of official Church bodies, both Roman Catholic and Protestant, have made public statements of their remorse about Christian mistreatment of Jews and Judaism. These statements have declared, furthermore, that Christian teaching and preaching can and must be reformed. . . . We believe these changes merit a thoughtful Jewish response . . . we believe it is time for Jews to learn about the efforts of Christians to honor Judaism. We believe it is time for Jews to reflect on what Judaism may now say about Christianity."

Given all this, should *Dabru Emet* be characterized as a form of Jewish reciprocity in response to Christian overtures? Even the timing of the document's release suggests

---

15. Reciprocity is mentioned twice in Leonard Swidler's Dialogue Decalogue: Commandment 2 "Dialogue must be a two-sided project" and 7 "Dialogue can only take place between equals."

16. Novak, "Why the Jews Need *Dabru Emet*."

17. See Sherman, "Protestant Parallels to Nostra Aetate." Note also the parallels between *Dabru Emet*'s structure (eight points) and Seelisberg's (ten points).

reciprocity: its publication date of September 10, 2000 came directly on the heels of the Vatican's August 6, 2000 promulgation of *Dominus Iesus*, a document which clarified some aspects of Catholic doctrine on interreligious dialogue (naturally, both documents were in preparation a long time before publication). And indeed, Novak himself seems to confirm reciprocity as an overall goal of *Dabru Emet*, because one of his later reflections on the document includes this statement: "Jews need to develop a Jewish theology of Christianity/religions . . . how can we ask Christians to respect us Jews if we don't show how we Jews respect Christianity?"[18]

But is reciprocity a good idea? And if it is, is it even possible to achieve? Scholars of interreligious dialogue such as Oddbjørn Leirvik have identified a tension between reciprocity and asymmetry in dialogue, both in theory and praxis, while Ruth Illman has questioned reciprocity's necessity and achievability due to power inequalities: "Is reciprocity a necessary condition for dialogue or does it represent naïve ignorance of the power relations that always set the ground for concrete and contextualised dialogues?"[19] An early Jewish response to Christians who were asking Jews to reciprocate in dialogue came from Joseph Soloveitchik, who argued that the "standardization of practices, equalization of dogmatic certitudes, and waiving of eschatological claims spell the end of the vibrant and great faith experience of any religious community."[20] More recently, Jon Levenson has been skeptical of reciprocity in general, and *Dabru Emet*'s brand of reciprocity in particular, criticizing the document as a form of negotiation, not dialogue.[21] In David Berger's response to *Dabru Emet*, in which he outlines some of his reservations, he argues that reciprocity is "the most dangerous problem generated by interfaith dialogue," adding, "For Jews, the dynamic of interfaith dialogue has produced pressure from within or from without to see Jesus as a prophet, or even as a Messiah for non-Jews; to see the incarnation as a theologically acceptable, even if erroneous belief; to downplay the problem of 'foreign worship' (*avodah zarah*)."[22]

Similar reciprocity pressures exist in Christian-Muslim dialogue. Since Islam acknowledges Jesus as a prophet, Muslims frequently ask Christians why they do not reciprocate by recognizing Muhammad as a prophet, or at least why they do not seriously entertain the possibility. But given the long history of Christian polemicists

18. Novak, "Why the Jews Need *Dabru Emet*," 135.

19. See Leirvik, "Philosophies of Interreligious Dialogue," especially p. 19, where he contrasts Buber's reciprocity with Levinas's asymmetry. See also Illman, "Reciprocity and Power in Philosophies of Dialogue The Burning of a Buddhist Temple in Finland," especially 59–60, where she continues the above quote about "contextualized dialogues": "Does reciprocity imply similarity and acceptance, or can it be reframed as a notion acknowledging difference and asymmetry while still creating a shared space of interpersonal understanding? . . . Such questions cannot be answered by a simple yes or no. As a commitment to justice and integrity, reciprocity may be an indispensible dimension of any dialogue situation. As a demand for agreement, uniformity, and spiritual unity, however, reciprocity can be dismissed on a number of compelling grounds."

20. See Soloveitchik, "Confrontation," 19.

21. Levenson, "The Agenda of *Dabru Emet*."

22. Berger, "Some Reservations," 392.

arguing that Muhammad was a pseudoprophet or worse, the way most modern Christian theologians have responded to this request for reciprocity is simply to ignore the question. For example, *Nostra Aetate* is completely silent on the topic of Muhammad's prophethood. In the latter half of the twentieth century, only a very few Christian theologians had broached the topic, most notably two Anglicans, David Kerr and Kenneth Cragg, in the 1980s.[23] More recently, the Catholic theologian Anna Moreland has written a constructive theology using the Thomistic criteria of prophethood to reexamine Muhammad's status as a prophet.[24] Moreland's project should probably be characterized as a form of comparative theology rather than reciprocity, because she explores the possibility of Muhammad's prophethood—a seemingly shared concept—using Christian, not Islamic, criteria.[25] A comparative theological study of a concept might prove to be more asymmetrical than reciprocal.

In the name of reciprocity, Christians have sometimes also felt pressure to focus on monotheism (and downplay the Muslim rejection of the Trinity) or embrace the Islamic idea of *ahl al kitab* (people of the book) to prove a mutual acceptance of each other's scriptures. But in the case of scripture, reciprocity may be deceptive, because most Christians do not recognize the revelatory status of the Qur'an, while Muslims believe that the Christian *injil* mentioned in the Qur'an (a word often translated as "gospel") is different from the Gospels Christians possess today. Rather, Muslims believe that the *injil* the Qur'an is referring to is the book Jesus (`Isa) brought when he came, which has since been corrupted by Christians over time, such that the scriptures Christians possess today are not the same. Thus, a seeming reciprocity about scripture actually obscures important questions such as: in what sense do Muslims acknowledge the sacred text Christians *actually* have (the Bible) versus the one Muslims believe they *used to have* (*injil*)? And how does this discrepancy between the *injil* and the Gospels affect the application of the Islamic category of *ahl al kitab* to Christians?

Likewise, some participants in Jewish-Christian dialogue are concerned about the pressures inherent in reciprocity. As noted above, David Berger believes that the very existence of *Dabru Emet* proves reciprocity to be its basic assumption, an assumption of which he disapproves. But is he right, does reciprocity really stand at *Dabru Emet*'s foundation? After all, the document itself explicitly rejects forced mutual affirmation in point 6: "Neither Jew nor Christian should be pressed into affirming

---

23. See Kerr, "The Prophet Muhammad in Christian Theological Perspective," and Cragg, *Muhammad and the Christian*.

24. Moreland, *Muhammad Reconsidered*.

25. Moreland's study could be seen as one half of a comparative theology of prophethood. To complete the comparison would require a discussion of the Muslim theology of prophethood, which she does not (however, Cragg does in *Muhammad and the Christian*). Comparative theology has been defined as "acts of faith seeking understanding which are rooted in a particular faith tradition but which, from that foundation, venture into learning from one or more other faith traditions. This learning is sought for the sake of fresh theological insights that are indebted to the newly encountered tradition as well as the home tradition" (see Clooney, *Comparative Theology*, 10).

the teaching of the other community." Furthermore, in a different article, Novak assures his readers that *Dabru Emet* is not merely a Jewish response to Christians, but a Jewish initiative.[26] In this he seems to be moving beyond reciprocity. Yet in other writings, Novak might appear to be an advocate for reciprocity. For example, in the book *Christianity in Jewish Terms*, which presents an extended scholarly dialogue on *Dabru Emet* and related topics, Novak's chapter on the commandments includes this statement: "the task for Jews who wish to appreciate Christianity authentically is to understand how Christian lawfulness is consistent with, but not subordinate to, Jewish lawfulness."[27] Is Novak asking for reciprocity from Jews here? And yet, just a few lines earlier, it seems that he doesn't expect the same from Christians, saying that Christians are free to "see the Jewish following of commandments as a lesser but legitimate form of piety." This latter idea ("lesser but legitimate") is reminiscent of the Catholic theologian Jacques Dupuis's idea of mutual asymmetrical complementarity, in which the home tradition claims the fullness of truth but can still be open to recognizing some edifying aspects in other religions. The concept is fundamentally asymmetrical, not reciprocal.[28] This is illustrated in the "lesser but legitimate" comment from Novak above, where Christians are asked to acknowledge Jewish lawfulness in some way, but are allowed to consider their version superior. But instead of telling Jews they should see Christian lawfulness as "consistent with, but not subordinate to, Jewish lawfulness," why wouldn't Novak ask Jews to see Christian lawfulness as lesser but still containing some legitimacy? *That* would be true reciprocity: to allow both religions to judge the other based on its own internal criteria. Paradoxically, this form of reciprocity is fundamentally asymmetrical on both sides.

But reciprocity suggests equal concern on both sides, and my students can clearly see that the Jewish document *Dabru Emet* raises some issues that are markedly different from those outlined in the Catholic document *Nostra Aetate*: for example, the State of Israel (point 3), plus concerns about assimilation, intermarriage, and conversion (point 7). Some of these differences have to do with the fact that *Nostra Aetate* was written in 1965, nearly four decades before *Dabru Emet*, and thus the escalation of the Arab-Israeli conflict (e.g., Six Day War of 1967, the Intifada of the 1980s, etc.) hadn't yet happened, nor had the dramatic rise of Christian-Jewish intermarriage in the 1970s and 80s.[29] But even given the time differential, it is instructive to read *Nostra*

---

26. Novak, "Why the Jews Need *Dabru Emet*," 135.

27. Novak, "Mitsva," 117.

28. Jacques Dupuis describes "mutual asymmetrical complementarity" as follows: "Whereas other religious traditions can find in the Christ event their fullest meaning . . . the reverse is not true. . . . God's self-manifestation and self-giving in Jesus Christ are not in need of a true completion by other traditions, even though they are interrelated . . . and can be enriched by mutually interacting with other religious traditions" (in *Christianity and the Religions*, 257).

29. For a study of interfaith marriage between American Jews and Christians, see Mehta, *Beyond Chrismukkah*.

Aetate and *Dabru Emet* together so that students can see that for some dialogue topics, Jews and Christians express asymmetrical, not reciprocal, concern.

Polyvalence

This last section considers not the *content* but the *method* of interreligious dialogue taught by *Dabru Emet*. One insight about method that students gain when reading this document is that even a seemingly bilateral dialogue like the Christian-Jewish begs the involvement of many other dialogues happening at the same time, in different directions: the "combined power" of these multidirectional dialogues is what I will call polyvalence. The directions of dialogue to be highlighted in this section are: intra-religious, inter-bilateral, and insider-outsider.

First, the introduction to *Dabru Emet* explicitly acknowledges the intrareligious diversity of its authors: "Speaking only for ourselves—an interdenominational group of Jewish scholars—we believe it is time for Jews to learn about the efforts of Christians to honor Judaism." What began as an intrareligious dialogue between four Jewish scholars became an ongoing conversation among many more Jews that took place before, during, and after its writing. The initial intrareligious discussions animating the text took place not only among its four authors, but also between the authors and other preliminary Jewish consultors. The publication of *Dabru Emet* led to the next round of intrareligious dialogue between Jews who endorsed the document and Jews who did not. Some of the Jews who declined to endorse went on to write their own documents. For example, in 2015, the International Group of Orthodox Jews published the statement "To Do the Will of Our Father in Heaven," which is critical of *Dabru Emet*'s content, but mimics its structure: it too has bullet points (but seven, not eight) and signatories.[30]

Second, in-class discussions of the issues raised by *Dabru Emet* show once again that bilateral dialogues are best not conducted in a vacuum. Rather, it is helpful when they are informed by other bilateral dialogues. For example, as noted in section one above, Christian-Jewish discussions about monotheism have been enriched by Christian-Muslims discussions about the same. Other topics raised by *Dabru Emet* which could benefit from bringing Christian-Muslim, Jewish-Muslim, theist-atheist, and other bilateral dialogues into the conversation include covenant, prophethood, scriptural exegesis, redemption, and forgiveness.

Furthermore, the success of bilateral dialogues between Christians and Jews after the writing and reception of *Dabru Emet* and *Nostra Aetate* have inspired people of other

---

30. 2015 Orthodox Rabbinic Statement on Christianity, "To Do the Will of Our Father in Heaven: Toward a Partnership between Jews and Christians." Its central question is not about worship of the one God, but whether is it permissible for Jews to cooperate with Christians in *Tikkam Olam*, repair of the world: "We seek to do the will of our Father in Heaven by accepting the hand offered to us by our Christian brothers and sisters. Jews and Christians must work together as partners to address the moral challenges of our era."

religions to write similar authoritative documents on the topic of interfaith relations. For example, in 2007, a group of international Muslim scholars wrote *A Common Word between Us and You*; the document begins with a statement of similarities between Christians and Muslims based on their respective scriptures, and was originally published with 138 Muslim endorsements, similar to *Dabru Emet*'s list of signatories. But instead of taking out an ad in a major newspaper, the Muslim scholars posted their document on an interactive website created especially for this purpose, which has allowed for an ongoing dialogue and the continual addition of new signatories and endorsements.[31] Even though *A Common Word* comments on a bilateral Christian-Muslim relationship, the website includes sections for Jewish and other endorsements. Thus, while using different media, the aim of *Dabru Emet* and *A Common Word* is the same: to get a broader public (not only experts) engaged in dialogue and to continue the conversation long after the document's original publication date.

Third, in-class discussions of *Dabru Emet* also elicit comments from individuals observing Christian-Jewish dialogue from the outside; in fact, the majority of my students are outsiders, not insiders, to this dialogue. In class, I ask my students to add their own perspectives on the issues raised by *Dabru Emet*; some of my students are Christians, but the "nones," Sikhs, Hindus, and Muslims also provide unique insights into the Christian-Jewish dialogue that enrich our conversation. For example, discussion of bullet point 5 On Nazism and its relationship to the theology of contempt has led to conversations about the difference between anti-Judaism and antisemitism, and the difference between Christian, Muslim, and secular antisemitisms.[32] Insider-outsider discussions can help students see the "big picture" on any given issue, which they might miss if they spend too much time focusing on a particular topic solely using an insider's lens.

Polyvalence occurs not only in terms of dialogue partners but also in terms of topics. For example, when evangelical Christians discuss the one God question, this can sometimes be a proxy for an intra-evangelical dialogue about a more general concern with religious pluralism.[33] One must be aware of all these polyvalent layers of dialogue: between different partners (intra-religious, inter-bilateral, insider-outsider), and also between topics.

---

31. The *A Common Word* website can be found here: https://www.acommonword.com/

32. For more on Islamic anti-Semitism, see Schroeter, "Islamic Anti-Semitism in Historical Discourse," and Bauer, "Beyond the Fourth Wave: Contemporary Anti-Semitism and Radical Islam." Bauer argues that in the 1950s, the Egyptian Sayyid Qutb influenced the creation both of radical Islam and Islamic anti-Semitism by mixing traditional Qur'anic anti-Judaism with Nazi anti-Semitism.

33. On the one God question as a proxy for the religious pluralism question among evangelicals, see Cimino, "No God in Common."

Conclusion

It is clear from the chapters published in this festschrift that David Novak is a talented philosopher and theologian. Let us add pedagogue to that list. Collaborating in the writing and broad dissemination of a document like *Dabru Emet* shows him to be a public teacher of both the theory and praxis of dialogue. But his teaching role didn't end with *Dabru Emet*; rather, it just began. For Novak has maintained his pedagogy of dialogue by writing follow-up works that invite even more people to engage with issues only hinted at in *Dabru Emet*, for example the already-mentioned book *Christianity in Jewish Terms*. The pedagogy of both the book and the document is found precisely in their *form*. Both are dialogical in their very structure: *Dabru Emet* was written by four interdenominational Jewish authors and signed by even more interdenominational Jewish leaders, while the book is organized by chapters, each having a single topic and three interlocutors, two Jewish and one Christian. These interactive formats make both the book and the document especially useful in the classroom.

Furthermore, many of the authors of *Dabru Emet*, including David Novak, not only theorize about dialogue but also model it personally through their ongoing involvement in real-life interreligious dialogues. For example, Peter Ochs is one of the founders of the Scriptural Reasoning Network (which fosters Christian-Jewish-Muslim dialogues centered on their respective scriptures), while Michael Signer, as the first Jewish professor in the Theology Department at the University of Notre Dame, taught generations of Christian theologians and led scores of Christian-Jewish student groups to Europe to study the Shoah and its impact on interfaith relations.[34] The rules of dialogue are best written and taught by those who have done it themselves.

Dabru Emet is not only the product of dialogue, but is in itself an expression of the current state of dialogue, and the means for future dialogue. As such, it is a dynamic pedagogical tool. In great part because of *Dabru Emet*, Christian-Jewish conversations in 2021 are richer and more polyvalent than David Novak and his colleagues could ever have imagined when they endeavored to "speak the truth" about Christians and Christianity in September of 2000. Thank you, David Novak, for inviting my students and me to enter into the conversation.

Bibliography

Bauer, Yehuda. "Beyond the Fourth Wave: Contemporary Anti-Semitism and Radical Islam." *Judaism*, January 2006, 55–62.

Berger, David. "Dabru Emet: Some Reservations about a Jewish Statement on Christians and Christianity." Lecture, Inaugural Meeting of the Council of Centers on Jewish-Christian Relations (CCJR), Baltimore, MD, October 28, 2002.

---

34. For more on Ochs's Scriptural Reasoning, see Ochs, "Philosophical Warrants for Scriptural Reasoning." For more on Signer's scholarship and dialogue work, see the introduction to Harkins, *Transforming Relations*.

———. *Persecution, Polemic, and Dialogue: Essays in Jewish-Christian Relations*. Boston: Academic Studies Press, 2010.

Cimino, Richard. "No God in Common: American Evangelical Discourse on Islam after 9/11." *Review of Religious Research* 47.2 (2005) 162–74.

Clooney, Francis X. *Comparative Theology: Deep Learning across Religious Borders*. Oxford: Wiley-Blackwell, 2010.

Cragg, Kenneth. *Muhammad and the Christian*. Maryknoll, NY: Orbis, 1984.

D'Costa, Gavin. *Vatican II: Catholic Doctrines on Jews and Muslims*. Oxford: Oxford University Press, 2014.

Dupuis, Jacques. *Christianity and the Religions: From Confrontation to Dialogue*. Maryknoll, NY: Orbis, 2002.

Fischer, Lars. "Is There a Judeo-Christian Tradition? A European Perspective." *Journal of Jewish Studies* 68.2 (2007) 413–17.

Fletcher, Jeanine Hill. "Among the Nones: Questing for God in the Twenty-First Century Classroom." In *Comparative Theology in the Millennial Classroom*, edited by Mara Brecht and Reid B. Locklin, 141–52. London: Routledge, 2016.

"The Global Religious Landscape." Pew Research Center. December 18, 2012. https://www.pewforum.org/2012/12/18/global-religious-landscape-exec/.

Harkins, Franklin T., ed. *Transforming Relations: Essays on Jews and Christians throughout History in Honor of Michael Signer*. Notre Dame, IN: University of Notre Dame Press, 2010.

Haynes, Jeffrey. "Donald Trump, Judeo-Christian Values, and the Clash of Civilizations." *The Review of Faith and International Affairs* 15.3 (2017) 66–75.

Illman, Ruth. "Reciprocity and Power in Philosophies of Dialogue The Burning of a Buddhist Temple in Finland." *Studies in Interreligious Dialogue* 21.1 (2011) 46–63.

Kerr, David. "The Prophet Muhammad in Christian Theological Perspective." *International Bulletin of Missionary Research* 8.3 (1984) 112–16.

Leirvik, Oddbjørn. "Philosophies of Interreligious Dialogue: Practice in Search of Theory." *Approaching Religion* 1 (May 2011) 16–24.

Levenson, Jon. "The Agenda of *Dabru Emet*." *Review of Rabbinic Judaism* 7 (2004) 1–27.

———. "Do Christians and Muslims Worship the Same God?" *Christian Century*, April 20, 2004, 32–33.

———. *Inheriting Abraham: The Legacy of the Patriarch in Judaism, Christianity, and Islam*. Princeton: Princeton University Press, 2012.

Massignon, Louis. "Trois Prières de Abraham." In *Testimonies and Reflections: Essays of Louis Massignon*, edited by Herbert Mason, 3–20. Notre Dame, IN: University of Notre Dame Press, 1989.

Mehta, Samira K. *Beyond Chrismukkah: The Christian-Jewish Interfaith Family in the United States*. Chapel Hill, NC: University of North Carolina Press, 2018.

Michel, Thomas. *A Muslim Theologian's Response to Christianity*. Delmar, NY: Caravan Books, 1985.

Moreland, Anna. *Muhammad Reconsidered: A Christian Perspective on Islamic Prophecy*. Notre Dame, IN: University of Notre Dame Press, 2020.

Neusner, Jacob, Baruch Levine, Bruce D. Chilton, and Vincent Cornell. *Do Jews, Christians, and Muslims Worship the Same God?* Nashville: Abingdon, 2012.

Novak, David. "Mitsva." In *Christianity in Jewish Terms,* edited by Tikva Frymer-Kensky, David Novak, Peter Ochs, David Sandmel, and Michael Signer, 115–26. Boulder, CO: Westview, 2000.

———. "Why the Jews Need *Dabru Emet.*" *Dialogue and Universalism* 4 (May 2002) 133–44.

Ochs, Peter. "Philosophical Warrants for Scriptural Reasoning." In *The Promise of Scriptural Reasoning,* edited by David Ford and C.C. Pecknold, 121–38. Oxford: Blackwell, 2006.

Orthodox Rabbinic Statement on Christianity. "To Do the Will of Our Father in Heaven: Toward a Partnership between Jews and Christians." The Center for Jewish–Christian Understanding & Cooperation. 2015. https://www.cjcuc.org/2015/12/03/orthodox-rabbinic-statement-on-christianity/

Peter the Venerable. *Summa totius haeresis Saracenorum.* In *Peter the Venerable: Writings Against the Saracens,* 34–50. The Fathers of the Church: Mediaeval Continuation, vol. 14. Translated by Irven Resnick. Washington, DC: Catholic University of America Press, 2016.

The Royal Aal al-Bayt Institute for Islamic Thought. "A Common Word between Us and You." 2007. https://www.acommonword.com/the-acw-document/.

Schroeter, Daniel. "Islamic Anti-Semitism in Historical Discourse." *American Historical Review* 123.4 (2018) 1172–189.

Sherman, Franklin. "Protestant Parallels to Nostra Aetate." *Studies in Christian-Jewish Relations* 10.2 (2015) 1–13.

Soloveitchik, Joseph. "Confrontation." *Tradition: A Journal of Orthodox Jewish Thought* 6.2 (1964) 5–29.

Swidler, Leonard. "Dialogue Decalogue: Ground Rules for Interreligious Dialogue." *Journal of Ecumenical Studies* 20.4 (1983) 1–4.

Volf, Miroslav. *Allah: A Christian Response.* New York: HarperCollins, 2011.

———, ed. *Do We Worship the Same God? Jews, Christians, and Muslims in Dialogue.* Grand Rapids: Eerdmans, 2012.

Waldman, Steven. "Commandment the First: Do Muslims and Christians Worship the Same God?" *Slate,* December 17, 2003. https://slate.com/human-interest/2003/12/do-muslims-and-christians-share-a-god.html.

William of Tripoli. *Notitia de Machometo.* In *Wilhelm von Tripolis: Notitia de Machometo; De statu Sarracenorum,* edited and translated by Peter Engels. Würzburg: Echter, 1992.

Response to

Rita George-Tvrtković's "The Pedagogy of *Dabru Emet:* How a Catholic Professor Teaches a Jewish Document to Multireligious Students"

DAVID NOVAK

I AM GRATEFUL TO Rita George-Tvrtković for her most thoughtful reflection on *Dabru Emet: A Jewish Statement on Christians and Christianity*, the 2000 document of which I am one of the four authors (and also the author of the original working paper that led to it). Her critical reading of *Dabru Emet*, plus her engagement with some of my subsequent writings about its claims, causes me to try to answer some of her queries about the document itself and, also, try to answer some of her queries about the controversy it stirred up in the Jewish community. Here let me try to analyze why there was opposition to *Dabru Emet* in the Jewish community and how these objections can be answered. It is hoped that my answer to the main objection of our opponents will help George-Tvrtković and her students appreciate *Dabru Emet* more by having answers to the charge that it distorts the Jewish tradition, especially its first point, viz., "Jews and Christians Worship the Same God."

George-Tvrtković reports that many of her students, both Christians and non-Christians, were "surprised" by this point. "Most students never considered [this] before, having assumed that monotheism is one of the few topics about which Jews and Christians can easily agree."[1] Moreover, "the fact that Christians and Jews share the same God . . . is simply assumed."[2] What George-Tvrtković and her students learned is that this statement, like all the statements in *Dabru Emet*, is controversial. In fact, it is more controversial for Jews than it is for Christians. This shows the asymmetry in the Jewish-Christian relationship that George-Tvrtković clearly notes throughout her paper.

1. p. 182.
2. p. 184.

The reason this proposition is less controversial for Christians than it is for Jews is because of the Marcion heresy, which is the first heresy the Church had to condemn. For if Marcion's claim is valid, i.e., that Christians worship a different God from the God of the Jews (who is the Lord God of Israel), then all the claims of Jesus and his disciples are thereby belied. So, the perennial Marcion temptation that has always attracted some Christians throughout the ages is easily refuted (though less easily eliminated). Even Christian "hard supersessionists," i.e., those Christians who claim Christianity has replaced Judaism (and, therefore, Christians have replaced Jews in the covenant between God and Israel), even they have to admit that there was something real and holy there to be replaced. Even hard supersessionists cannot deny Christianity's Jewish origins. So, no matter how *de novo* Christians might regard Christianity to be, none but an explicit Marcionite can claim Christianity was brought into the world by a new god *ex nihilo*.

Conversely, it is much easier for Jews not to acknowledge that Christians worship the Lord God of Israel. That is, unless Jews acknowledge Christianity to be Judaism's "fulfillment." However, such acknowledgement by Jews who have converted to Christianity, even if they have retained some Jewish religious practices, constitutes for most traditional Jews apostasy. So, two questions now arise. One, if Jews hold that Christians do not worship the same God as do the Jews, how are Jews to regard Christian claims that they do? Two, if Jews hold that Christians do worship the same God as do the Jews, how are Jews to differentiate ourselves from Christianity nonetheless? In other words, is Christianity the antithesis of Judaism, or is Christianity derivative of Judaism?

For Jews who do not hold that Christians worship the same God as do the Jews, how should Christian worship or "religion" be judged? George-Tvrtković sees the clearest proponent of that negative Jewish view of Christianity to be the Orthodox Jewish historian David Berger.[3] She writes, "Berger reads the monotheism question in light of the traditional Jewish notion of *avodah zarah* (which he translates as "foreign worship"). He notes that historically, Jews have disagreed about whether Christians are guilty of foreign worship, either via means of worship or object of worship."[4] It is quite clear that David Berger thinks Christianity is *avodah zarah*, and he is hardly alone in that opinion. (In fact, he has told me and others so in conversation.) Obviously, George-Tvrtković and her students do not agree with Berger *et alia*. Neither do I. So, let me now try to counter Berger's charge and, it is hoped, give George-Tvrtković and her students better reasons for agreeing with *Dabru Emet*'s first claim, i.e., that "Jews and Christians worship the same God." This requires us to better define *avodah zarah*.

The term *avodah zarah* sometimes covers both the "means of worship" and the "object of worship." More accurately, though, *avodat elilim*, i.e., "worship of other gods" denotes the wrong object of worship, however its method of worship corresponds to

3. pp. 183–84n12.
4. pp. 183–84.

the right worship of the right God. *Avodah zarah*, however, more accurately denotes the wrong worship of the right God. Now, to be sure, there were Jewish theologians who, when seeing something like Christian veneration of icons, believed that Christians were worshiping the "other gods" (*elohim aherim*) whom Scripture (Exod 20:3–5) had proscribed for any worshiper of the LORD God of Israel (see 2 Kgs 5:18). (Christian iconoclasts, too, believed such *veneratio* bordered on actual worship of them, i.e., it was in fact *adoratio*, like *avodah* in Hebrew.) Nevertheless, some Christian theologians compared the veneration of icons to be like the Cherubim in the Jerusalem Temple (see Exod 25:18–22), which were certainly not the objects of worship.

So, if it be granted that Christians are to be believed that they do worship the same God as do the Jews, then the question devolves on the different or "strange" (*zarah*) worship of this same God. Clearly, Christian worship (with or without icons or images) is proscribed to Jews, because all Christian worship is conducted *though* Jesus as the Messiah, i.e., the *Christ*. But Jews do not accept Jesus as the Messiah. Therefore, Jews do not believe we need Jesus's mediation in our covenantal relationship with God. That Christian mediation, then, is clearly "strange worship" *for us*. However, this is not *strange worship* for the millions and millions of gentiles for whom there is no other relationship with the Lord God of Israel except through Jesus as the Christ.

Now if Christians are taken to be "idolaters" in practice, i.e., "devotees of strange worship" (*ovdei avodah zarah*), then one has to conclude that even their different Christian worship of the right God should be forbidden even to them. In other words, if any worship of the right God other than traditional Jewish worship of the right God is wrong, then those Jews who advocate that position should either proclaim to Christians that they are idolaters and will suffer the consequences of their great sin, or those Jews who hold this position should actively proselytize these erring Christians and thus save their souls from damnation. (Jews have long been subjected to Christian zealots who have spoken similarly to us.) However, it should be noted that David Berger is a prominent disciple of the great Jewish theologian Joseph B. Soloveitchik, who was opposed to the efforts of my late revered teacher Abraham Joshua Heschel that led to *Nostra Aetate* and its more favorable view of Jews and Judaism. (For my critique of Soloveitchik's opposition to theological Jewish-Christian dialogue and interaction, see my 1989 book *Jewish-Christian Dialogue: A Jewish Justification*.) Unlike Berger's opposition, Soloveitchik's opposition was not theological. Rather, its argument was more political, viz., that Jews and Christians should not interfere in each other's communal affairs but that they should only interact in secular space, where their incommensurate theologies are irrelevant, and even dangerous to be invoked. Nevertheless, since Berger is neither condemning Christians nor proselytizing them, I suspect that his invocation of the idea of *avodah zarah* is, in fact, consistent with his teacher's approach. After all, Jews have been able to deal with gentile "idolaters," i.e., as long as their morality is similar enough to Jewish morality to make for some common political stances. In other words, both Soloveitchik and Berger want to avoid the theology altogether.

Nevertheless, this approach is quite naïve. For secularists would like to so privatize (which is the first step to eventual elimination) both Jewish and Christian "theopolitics" altogether. But if that is the case, both Jews and Christians lose, because we are both at risk at the hands of militant secularists who seem to be gaining more and more power in an already secularized society. So, for that reason alone, it is best to affirm that Jews and Christians do worship the same God—necessarily differently in this world—this same God whose Torah for interhuman relations is remarkably similar for both Jews and Christians. In short, there is a "Judaeo-Christian ethic," even though there isn't nor should there be a "Judaeo-Christian religion." And, even if not deduced from theology, that ethic is informed by theology through and through. As such, Jews shouldn't even imply that Christianity is *avodah zarah* for Christians, any more than Christians should tell Jews that Judaism is *avodah zarah* for us.

I do hope my answer to David Berger *et alia* helps Rita George-Tvrtković and her students know that not all Jewish theologians brand them as idolaters and that this answer will enable them to continue in the Jewish-Christian dialogue in good faith.

Chapter 8

Pope Pius IX and the Mortara Case

A Catholic Critique

Matthew Levering

Introduction

The Anglican theologian Ephraim Radner, David's colleague at the University of Toronto, has remarked that in the past half century the Church (by which he means Christians across a wide array of traditions) has "for the first time in her history, begun to face the greatest failure of her navigation of collective identity—that is, her relationship to the Jews."[1] The horror of the Holocaust produced the Church's painfully overdue re-assessment.[2] In a process that is still ongoing, the Catholic Church has had to face and seek to understand theologically its terrible "complicity and cultural nurturing of anti-Semitism, often fueled through aspects of anti-Jewish theology."[3]

The present essay is not about the relationship of the Catholic Church to the anti-Catholic Nazi regime that perpetrated the Holocaust, a theme that has been well canvassed from various perspectives. Instead, I investigate another aspect of the Church's relationship to the Jewish people, which has recently become again a point of controversy: Blessed Pope Pius IX's decision in 1858 to send papal police to remove Edgardo Mortara from his loving Jewish family, due to the claim that the boy had been secretly baptized as an ill infant by his Catholic nanny.[4] In his role as the ruler of the

---

1. Radner, *Church*, 9.

2. See D'Costa, *Vatican II: Catholic Doctrines on Jews and Muslims*, 114. He cites Connelly, *From Enemy to Brother*, 11–93, as well as Bauman, *Modernity and the Holocaust*. See also Isaac, *The Teaching of Contempt*; Bea, *The Church and the Jewish People*.

3. D'Costa, *Vatican II*, 114. I hold that the prevalent Catholic attitudes are best described as "anti-Jewish" rather than "anti-Semitic" (in order to distinguish them from the Nazi's explicitly racial animus), but these "anti-Jewish" attitudes, as D'Costa notes, clearly influenced and provided part of the seedbed for Nazi racial anti-Semitism (which grew in part out of the racial notions of Enlightenment modernity, racial notions present already in Kant and especially Hegel).

4. I have chosen the term "remove" or (elsewhere) "forcibly remove," because of the involvement of the Papal States' police (whereas "kidnapping" or "abduction" connote a non-legal forcible removal,

Papal States, Pope Pius IX never returned the boy to his family. Instead, Edgardo lived in the Vatican and received an education that taught him the tenets of the Catholic faith and led him, by God's grace, to become a Catholic priest.[5] The Jewish historian Bertram Wallace Korn has shown that at the time, many of Pope Pius IX's Catholic defenders—and it is important to note that Pope Pius IX had many Catholic critics— "regarded all those who questioned the wisdom of the Pope or the righteousness of canon law as anti-Christians, infidels, and worse."[6] Many of Pope Pius IX's Catholics critics, by contrast, were deeply mortified and sought urgently to persuade him to release the boy back to his parents. In the end, his decision was widely unpopular and served as one of the reasons for the loss of the Papal States in 1870.

This controversy has gained a new life due to the research of the Jewish historian David Kertzer and the plans for developing his book, *The Kidnapping of Edgardo Mortara*, into a Hollywood film. In response, some Catholics in Europe and the United States have proclaimed their support for Pius IX's action. Most notably, the Catholic journalist Vittorio Messori, best known for the excellent interview-books that he published with Joseph Ratzinger (*The Ratzinger Report*) and Pope John Paul II (*Crossing the Threshold of Hope*), has stated that as soon as the infant Edgardo was baptized by the servant girl Anna Morisi, there was no other possible choice but to remove Edgardo from his Jewish family and educate him as a Christian, "at least until the age of majority," when he could "choose between persevering in the gospel faith" or "returning to the synagogue."[7] According to Messori, who recently pub-

---

not by police acting in accordance with a governmental process but by rogue agents). I am not implying, however, that the forcible removal was, in the eyes of God, anything but a kidnapping.

5. In a series of recent books, the Jewish historian David Kertzer has demonstrated the anti-Jewish attitudes and embarrassing political misdeeds of numerous leaders of the nineteenth-century Church. Kertzer's (understandable) animosity toward the Catholic Church is evident, but his historical work—while narrowly focused—is well informed. See Kertzer, *The Popes Against the Jews*. See also Kertzer, *The Kidnapping of Edgardo Mortara*; Kertzer, *The Pope and Mussolini*; Kertzer, *The Pope Who Would Be King*. From a Catholic perspective, Justus George Lawler has unsuccessfully attempted to discredit Kertzer's *The Popes Against the Jews*, to which Lawler devotes a book-length response (though the book briefly addresses some other topics as well). See Lawler, *Were the Popes Against the Jews?* For his part, Vittorio Messori, "The Mortara Case," in *Kidnapped by the Vatican?* makes repeated efforts to discredit Kertzer's *The Kidnapping of Edgardo Mortara*.

6. Korn, *The American Reaction to The Mortara Case: 1858–1859*, 19.

7. Vittorio Messori, "The Mortara Case," 4. Writing some years prior to the recent support given by Messori and some other Catholics to Pope Pius's decision, the atheist-evangelist Richard Dawkins employed the Mortara case as evidence that Christians, and other religious people, should not be allowed to educate children in their faith. Dawkins comments, "Edgardo's story was by no means unusual in Italy at the time, and the reason for these priestly abductions was always the same. In every case, the child had been secretly baptized at some earlier date, usually by a Catholic nursemaid, and the Inquisition later came to hear of the baptism. It was a central part of the Roman Catholic belief-system that, once a child had been baptized, however informally and clandestinely, that child was irrevocably transformed into a Christian. In their mental world, to allow a 'Christian child' to stay with his Jewish parents was not an option, and they maintained this bizarre and cruel stance steadfastly, and with the utmost sincerity, in the face of worldwide outrage. That widespread outrage, by the way, was dismissed by the Catholic newspaper *Civiltà Cattolica* as due to the international

lished Italian and English editions of Mortara's previously unpublished memoirs, "the Church has no choice (not even today, as we will see), if she is not to disown her entire sacramental theology."[8]

In what follows, I inquire into whether Pope Pius IX's action toward the boy Edgardo Mortara should be defended by Catholics or should be part of the broader post-Holocaust reassessment of the Church's relationship to the Jewish people. My first section, indebted to the Catholic theologian Matthew Tapie, contextualizes Pius IX's action within some aspects of the history of Catholic treatment of the Jewish people. Second, I examine the claims of natural law and justice in light of Thomas Aquinas's condemnation of the forced baptism of Jewish children. Third, I offer six reasons from a Catholic perspective for condemning Pope Pius IX's action as objectively unjust, imprudent, and unacceptable.[9]

---

power of rich Jews—sounds familiar, doesn't it? . . . Yet all the indications are that Catholic apologists, from the Pope down, sincerely believed that what they were doing was right: absolutely right morally, and right for the welfare of the child. Such is the power of (mainstream, 'moderate') religion to warp judgment and pervert ordinary human decency. The newspaper *Il Cattolico* was frankly bewildered at the widespread failure to see what a magnanimous favour the Church had done to Edgardo Mortara when it rescued him from his Jewish family" (Dawkins, *The God Delusion*, 311, 313).

8. Messori, "The Mortara Case," 4. Messori adds later in his essay, "Even though the Vatican is once again a state, a Mortara case, though possible in theory, will no longer be possible in practice. No papal gendarmerie today will take a child away from his family in order to give him a Catholic education until he reaches majority. I am the first to rejoice that tragedies like this, which confront parents with heartrending alternatives, are unthinkable. But at the same time it should be noted that even the postconciliar Church has not denied but has confirmed the theological principles from which Pius IX inferred consequences that enraged so many enemies against him. There is in the faith a strict logic, in which each truth presupposes another and leads to still another. We cannot and should not be nostalgic for the type of temporal power that Pius IX defended, being unable to do otherwise; but Catholics ought to want the principles to be safeguarded" (Messori, "The Mortara Case," 42). The question is what are the "principles" and what does "safeguarding" them mean with respect to what a pope (who had the power to choose) should do today if another such case appears.

9. In his memoirs as edited and translated by Messori, Father Mortara disagrees. He notes first of all, "The Mortaras profess the Jewish religion, which is contradictory and surpassed by history. Consequently, the parental authority of Signor and Signora Mortara is diminished, disabled, and is not in full possession of its rights, nor does it know its duties" (Mortara, *The Mortara Child and Pius IX*, in *Kidnapped by the Vatican?* 159). Second, Mortara sets the scene: "God guides and impels the hand of that girl, places her at the foot of the Cross of the divine Redeemer, from whose pierced Heart flows and separates a drop of His adorable blood. Mixed with the baptismal water, this drop regenerates, purifies, and sanctifies that soul, which men do not appreciate because they do not know it; but God loves, predestines, and protects it because it cost all the blood of God. What rights can be asserted by the parents of the child who has been abandoned by men and welcomed by God? Who interfered here; who profaned the sacred power of liberty; who did violence to the will of that child? All the 'blame', if 'blame' there be, belongs to God. There is no doubt that God's rights are superior to those of parental authority, which in this case happens to be completely destitute even of merely apparent rights" (Mortara, *The Mortara Child and Pius IX*, in *Kidnapped by the Vatican?* 160). As a third step, he appeals to the civil laws as well: "We repeat: the civil laws in a Christian state are explicit in this case. The Mortara child must be separated from his parents. Of course, if the gentler, more conciliatory measures do not obtain the hoped-for result, and if the moral perversion of the child is evident and inevitable, the laws justify, command, and prescribe sequestration. And this is exactly what Pius IX did. He neither stole nor kidnapped a child from his parents, as the anti-Catholic press repeated tirelessly. After resorting

The Jewish People and Forced Baptism

As Tapie has observed, under the Catholic Code of Canon Law, a child can receive a valid baptism even when the baptism is performed against the wishes of the parents.[10] In addition, in Pius IX's day, "the civil law of the Papal States require[d] that legitimately baptized children receive a Catholic education."[11] This was the linchpin of the Vatican's decision to send papal police to remove Edgardo Mortara from his loving family, so as to be able to educate him as a Catholic.

Lest there be misunderstanding with regard to the motivations or perspective of Pope Pius IX, let me briefly sketch some historical background regarding the baptism of Jews in Catholic lands and in the Papal States. Over the centuries, some Catholic rulers issued "ultimatum[s] that Jews of the kingdom either convert or be expelled from the country."[12] Influential Catholic bishops responded sharply against such practices. At the Fourth Council of Toledo in 633, for example, St. Isidore of Seville delivered a sharp rebuke to King "Sisebut's campaign of forced baptism," insisting in Canon 57 that no one should be forced to believe in Christ by threats and punitive measures.[13] However, canon 57 also required that "those who had been baptized by force must remain Christian," and Canon 60 adds the point that "forcibly baptized children . . . must receive a Christian education" and must therefore be removed from their (Jewish) families.[14]

At the same time, "forcible conversion of Jews was condemned repeatedly by numerous popes, as indicated by the well-known letter of Gregory IV (r. 827–844)."[15] Once forcibly baptized, the Jews were under compulsion to live as Catholics. Yet even this issue remained somewhat open. Tapie notes that "some popes allowed Jewish converts to return to their religion. Pope Alexander II (1061–73) permitted all Jews baptized by force during the First Crusade of 1096 to return to practicing Judaism."[16] By the late twelfth century, furthermore, canonists had begun to distinguish between

---

to all possible methods of persuasion and conciliation, after proposing gentle paternal measures to the parents . . . Pius IX proceeded to separate the child. He was then seven years old and had attained the use of reason" (Mortara, *The Mortara Child and Pius IX*, in *Kidnapped by the Vatican?* 162).

10. See Tapie, "*Spiritualis Uterus*," 290, referencing the 1983 *Codex iuris canonici*, canon 868. In this canon, the Church teaches that for baptism to be licit, "the parents or at least one of them or the person who legitimately takes their place must consent" and "there must be a founded hope that the infant will be brought up in the Catholic religion," but nonetheless "an infant of Catholic parents or even of non-Catholic parents is baptized licitly in danger of death even against the will of the parents" (*Code of Canon Law: Latin-English Edition*, 285–86).

11. Tapie, "*Spiritualis Uterus*," 290.

12. Tapie, "*Spiritualis Uterus*," 295, drawing here upon Roth, *Jews, Visigoths, and Muslims in Medieval Spain*; as well as upon Linder, *The Jews in the Legal Sources of the Early Middle Ages*, and the essays (including work on forced conversion) in Tolan et al. (ed.), *Jews in Early Christian Law*.

13. Tapie, "*Spiritualis Uterus*," 295.

14. Tapie, "*Spiritualis Uterus*," 296.

15. Tapie, "*Spiritualis Uterus*," 297.

16. Tapie, "*Spiritualis Uterus*," 298, citing Flannery, *The Anguish of the Jews*, 76.

absolute and conditional coercion. In the former case, no consent whatsoever is given by the recipient of baptism; in the latter case, under threat of violence or other harm, the recipient gives consent. For thirteenth-century canonists, the latter case—despite occurring under severe duress—constitutes a valid baptism, even if the canonists also held that it is a sin to administer forced baptism. Having affirmed the validity (even if not the licitness) of forced baptisms except in cases where the recipients actively and steadfastly refused to go along with it, canonists engaged in a further debate in the thirteenth century regarding "whether to baptize Jewish children against the will of their parents."[17] I discuss that debate further on.

In the eighteenth century, Tapie observes, Pope Benedict XIV reiterated the Church's teaching that Jewish children should not be baptized without their parents' consent, something that apparently was happening relatively frequently in Rome.[18] But Benedict XIV made exception for two cases: when a Christian finds a Jewish child in danger of death, and when a Jewish child is found alone outset the Jewish ghetto (and thus has been, supposedly, "abandoned" by his or her parents). On the basis of these exceptions, Benedict XIV set forth additional exceptions, by a process of logical extension. Tapie explains: "Jewish children could be baptized in the following circumstances: if the Jewish parents were absent, and their guardians consented; if the Jewish father commanded it, even if the mother were unwilling; or if a Jewish convert to Christianity made 'offering' of a Jewish family member to the Church."[19] These exceptions were made on the canonical principle of acting in favor of the faith, much as in the case of Pauline privilege. It became standard practice in the Papal States that if such a baptism was known to have occurred, "the police removed the Jewish child from the parents' home and sent it to the House of the Catechumens."[20] Normally, these children were related to a recent male Jewish convert to Catholicism.

Jews, Justice, and Natural Law: Thomas Aquinas's Perspective

Let me now turned to the thirteenth-century debate over forced baptism, focusing on Thomas Aquinas's perspective. In his reflections on the virtue of faith, Aquinas identifies a case of grave injustice when he states, as two *objections* to his own view, that

17. Tapie, "*Spiritualis Uterus*," 301, indebted to Pakter, *Medieval Canon Law and the Jews*.

18. Kleinberg, "Depriving Parents of the Consolation of Children"; Ravid, "The Forced Baptism of Jewish Minors in Early Modern Venice." Both of these are cited in Tapie, "*Spiritualis Uterus*," 294.

19. Tapie, "*Spiritualis Uterus*," 302, indebted to Pakter and Kleinberg, as well as to Caffiero, *Forced Baptisms*. For Pope Benedict XIV's teachings on this matter, see his *Lettera a Monsignor Archivescovo di Tarso Vicegerente sopra il Battesimo degli Ebrei o infanti o adulti* (February 28, 1747) and his *Lettera della Santità di Nostro Signore Benedetto Papa XIV a Monsignor Pier Girolamo Guglielmi Assessore del Sant'Officio sopra l'Offerta fatta dall'Avia Neofita di alcuni suoi Nipoti infanti Ebrei alla Fede Christiana* (December 15, 1751), translations of his Papal Bulls (published on the same dates) *Postremo mense* and *Probe te meminisse*. See also Pennington, "The Law's Violence against Medieval and Early Modern Jews," 40–43.

20. Tapie, "*Spiritualis Uterus*," 303–4.

"kings and princes have the power to do what they will with Jewish children" and that "it is not unjust if Jewish children be taken away from their parents, and consecrated to God in baptism."[21] In his response, Aquinas argues first that the Church already would have sanctioned this practice if it were "at all reasonable," whereas in fact the Church has never sanctioned it.[22] Aquinas goes on to explain that "it is against natural justice. For a child is by nature part of its father: thus, at first, it is not distinct from its parents as to its body, so long as it is enfolded within its mother's womb; and later on after birth, and before it has the use of its free-will, it is enfolded in the care of its parents, which is like a spiritual womb."[23] Before children have the use of reason and can freely make

21. Aquinas, *Summa theologiae* II-II, q. 10, a. 12, obj. 3 and 4. I have standardized some capitalizations.

22. II-II, q. 10, a. 12. The *sed contra* of this article reads in full, "Injustice should be done to no man. Now it would be an injustice to Jews if their children were to be baptized against their will, since they would lose the rights of parental authority over their children as soon as these were Christians. Therefore these should not be baptized against their parents' will." Tapie raises the question of whether Aquinas here means to imply that the illicit baptisms would be *valid* and therefore the children would be taken from their Jewish parents (who "would lose the rights of parental authority") and be raised by the Church as Catholics. This is what Pope Pius IX and the Vatican understood Aquinas to be saying. Drawing upon Stahl's *The Mortara Affair, 1858*, Tapie observes: "Soon after Edgardo was abducted, the Mortara family, with the assistance of the Jewish community of Rome, submitted a formal document (referred to as *Pro-memoria* and *Syllabus*) that argued that the child must be returned because the Church, according to Aquinas, prohibits baptizing children of unbelievers without the consent of their parents. . . . Yet the Vatican's refutation also appealed to Aquinas's teaching in order to defend the decision to separate Edgardo from his parents. The Vatican agreed with part of the Mortara's argument. The church has always been against forced conversions. But the papal counsel argued that even an unlawful baptism is valid, and cites Aquinas as authority for this position" (Tapie, "Spiritualis Uterus," 291). In Tapie's view, this is a misunderstanding of Aquinas's position: Tapie thinks that Aquinas actually held that such forced baptisms are not only illicit but also invalid. Tapie emphasizes that for Aquinas, "the acceptance of the faith on the part of the recipient [of baptism] is a matter of the will," and this free act "is an essential part of a valid baptism" (Tapie, "Spiritualis Uterus," 313, referring to such passages as *ST* II-II, q. 10, a. 8, ad 3 and *ST* III, q. 68, a. 7). Tapie argues, "Aquinas's view of the role of the human will in salvation undermines the accepted view among canonists that 'conditional coercion' of unbelievers is a valid baptism. Aquinas's view of faith and baptism makes clear that if there is no consenting will, there is no baptism" (Tapie, "Spiritualis Uterus," 314). In support of this position, he cites Weed, "Aquinas on the Forced Conversion of the Jews"; Weed, "Faith, Salvation, and the Sacraments in Aquinas." A forced baptism of a Jewish child is invalid for Aquinas, Tapie concludes, because a legitimate stand-in for the child (the parents or their legitimate representative) does not will it. For my part, I doubt whether this is an accurate interpretation of Aquinas. I also think more standing should be given to the practice of the Church as found in the contemporary Code of Canon Law.

23. *ST* II-II, q. 10, a. 12. For discussion see Moschella, *To Whom Do Children Belong?* 28 and elsewhere. Regarding Aristotle and Aquinas, Moschella states, "Although they do refer to children as in some sense 'a part' of their parents, their own metaphysics would forbid taking that literally. Their claim is most plausibly interpreted to mean that children are a part of their parents not in the strict metaphysical or biological sense, but in the sense that they are a part of the natural community which is based on and extends from their parents' conjugal union (at least in the focal case, which for Aquinas and Aristotle would also be normative). Aquinas' metaphor of the family as a 'spiritual womb' seems to suggest as much. Given Aristotle and Aquinas' understanding of marriage as a conjugal union inherently aimed at procreation and childrearing (though choice-worthy in itself and not merely instrumental to procreation), their view that children are 'part' of their parents should therefore be understood to mean that children are part, not of each spouse individually, but of the conjugal union

their own choices, the parents justly have care of the child, including care of the child's spiritual welfare. Aquinas concludes that because "according to the natural law, a son, before coming to the use of reason, is under his father's care," it follows that "it would be contrary to natural justice, if a child, before coming to the use of reason, were to be taken away from its parents' custody, or anything done to it against its parents' wish."[24] He reiterates this point even more strongly when he says that "no one ought to break the order of the natural law, whereby a child is in the custody of its father, in order to rescue it from the danger of everlasting death."[25]

In response to the objection that because every child belongs to God it is appropriate to seize Jewish children and baptize them, Aquinas answers along the same lines, asserting the dignity of the natural order and the fact that the supernatural order does not achieve its ends by violating the natural law: "Man is directed to God by his reason, whereby he can know Him. Hence a child before coming to the use of reason, in the natural order of things, is directed to God by its parents' reason, under whose care it lies by nature: and it is for them to dispose of the child in all matters relating to God."[26] He makes the same point in his discussion of the sacrament of baptism. Prior to attaining to the use of reason and freely choosing a religious faith, the child "is ordained to God, by a natural order, through the reason of its parents, under whose care it naturally lies."[27] He argues that baptizing a Jewish (or other non-Christian) child against the will of the parents has the same standing as baptizing an adult against his or her will. Namely, it is a sin against justice. He repeats his insistence that no one should "infringe the order of the natural law, in virtue of which a child is under the care of its father, in order to rescue it from the danger of eternal death."[28]

Aquinas also cautions prudentially against overturning the natural order of the parents' care for their children. As he says, one reason not to infringe the order of nature is that such an action will often backfire. This is because the order of nature is generally strong, with the result that children forcibly baptized are "liable to lapse into unbelief, by reason of their natural affection for their parents."[29] Aquinas suggests here that the Church's longstanding "custom" of not forcibly baptizing Jewish children has its roots in a firm respect for the natural order.[30]

---

that gives rise to those children. . . . It is also plausible to interpret Aquinas and Aristotle's reference to children as 'part' of their parents to emphasize the permanent and identity-constituting link that children have with their parents (qua joint biological cause of the children's existence and identity)" (Moschella, *To Whom Do Children Belong?* 28).

24. *ST* II-II, q. 10, a. 12.
25. *ST* II-II, q. 10, a. 12, ad 2.
26. *ST* II-II, q. 10, a. 12, ad 4.
27. *ST* III, q. 68, a. 10, ad 3.
28. *ST* III, q. 68, a. 10, ad 1.
29. *ST* III, q. 68, a. 10.
30. *ST* III, q. 68, a. 10. Aquinas's use of the term "custom" here is important; see his remark in I-II, q. 97, a. 3 that "when a thing is done again and again, it seems to proceed from a deliberate judgment

In his discussion of justice, Aquinas gives us further insight into his perspective. Indebted to Aristotle, Aquinas defines justice as "a habit whereby a man renders to each one his due by a constant and perpetual will."[31] But what if charity toward a person requires doing something that otherwise might seem unjust (as in the case of baptizing a Jewish infant against his or her parents' will)? Should not justice be defined as Augustine does, namely, by affirming that "justice is love serving God alone"?[32] Aquinas replies that the relationship of charity and justice does not involve a conflict, but nonetheless justice is best defined in terms of the natural order, taken up and fulfilled in charity. Aquinas explains, "Just as love of God includes love of our neighbor . . . so too the service of God includes rendering to each one his due."[33]

In this way, Aquinas makes clear that in a family, it is just that the parents raise their child in their religion, at least until the child reaches the age of reason and is able to decide on his or her own. The charitable person owes it to the parents of the child to ensure that they receive what is due to them in justice, namely, the raising of their child in their religion. The order of charity and the order of the natural law are not in conflict, but should work together in harmony.[34]

The Edgardo Mortara Case

I now turn to the Mortara case itself. The boy's forcible removal was put into motion when a papal investigation determined that Edgardo, while an infant suffering from an illness, had been secretly baptized by his Catholic nanny in the Papal States.[35] The Pope

---

of reason. Accordingly, custom has the force of a law, abolishes law, and is the interpreter of law."

31. *ST* II-II, q. 58, a. 1. I have removed the italics. See also Franks, "Aristotelian Doctrines in Aquinas's Treatment of Justice," 139–66.

32. *ST* II-II, q. 58, a. 1, obj. 6.

33. *ST* II-II, q. 58, a. 1, ad 6.

34. For discussion of how Aquinas and John Duns Scotus understand biblical cases where God appears to have worked outside the natural law, see my "God and Natural Law."

35. Edgardo Mortara would turn seven on August 27, 1858. Oddly, Father Mortara, in his *The Mortara Child and Pius IX*, claims (speaking of himself at the time of his removal from his parents) "He was then seven years old and had attained the use of reason" (162). In favor of Pius IX's action, see also Roy Schoeman's preface to *Kidnapped by the Vatican?* vii–xi. Schoeman, who is a convert to Catholicism from Judaism, contends, "The Mortara case arose in the center of this 'perfect storm' of social and political turmoil. In addition to the Risorgimento in Italy, revolts against the confessional state were occurring or were soon to occur throughout Europe, as the 'shackles' of Christendom were thrown off in favor of materialistic secularism in France, England, Spain, and Germany—and, of course, in Holy Mother Russia. Into that battle waded, unknowingly, an innocent six-year-old boy, a Catholic nursemaid, and a pope of uncompromising integrity and courage. The result was the Mortara affair. Pope Pius IX stood as a bulwark against this secularizing trend that was transforming Italy and all Europe. The Mortara case provided an ideal opportunity for his opponents to attack him personally, as well as the authority of the Church and the very idea of a confessional state. For one's view of the morality of his actions depends on one's acceptance, or rejection, of the truths of the Catholic faith. In the light of the faith, what the pope did can be seen as not only legally justified but also morally justified; in the darkness of a total rejection of the faith, it appears unconscionable" (Schoeman,

commanded that his police take the boy because in the Papal States, the parents of a baptized child were legally bound to raise and educate the child in the Catholic faith—as parents of baptized children still today are canonically bound to do.[36] Edgardo's parents, being Jews, could not do this. Therefore, the priest-inquisitor who investigated the case, and eventually the Pope himself, deemed that the Church (or the Papal States) must take the child from his parents and raise the child.

Contemporary Catholics who have praised Pope Pius IX's action, including Vittorio Messori and Romanus Cessario, consider that what is at stake is the supernatural character impressed by the sacrament of baptism and the corresponding duties associated with baptism. I concur that Catholics must cherish and defend the supernatural greatness of the sacraments, against the supposition that the sacraments are quaint rituals or that there is no such thing as graced transformation. Expositing the meaning of baptism, Colman O'Neill aptly speaks of "the active intervention of the heavenly Christ in the ceremony of baptism," an intervention that, through the sacred sign, causes an enduring ontological relationship of the baptized person to Christ—no matter whether, in the exercise of his or her freedom, the person goes on to act in such a way as to "correspond to this sacramental incorporation into Christ."[37] The power of baptism is such that in this sacrament the risen Christ "sends the Spirit to transform the whole person of the believer" and "incorporates the believer into his sacramental body."[38] Roger Nutt remarks in the same vein, "The teaching of the Magisterium insists that the sacraments have an intrinsic causal power and that contact with the sacraments is operative in the outpouring of grace on the soul. . . . Grace is conferred in the sacraments, as long as the rite is properly celebrated."[39] In my view, O'Neill and Nutt—neither of whom has the Mortara case in mind,

---

in *Kidnapped by the Vatican?* ix). In brief popular-audience pieces, Catholics such as Holly Taylor Coolman, Robert Miller, and Nathaniel Peters have recently mounted arguments for repudiating Pius IX's action. See also Chaput, "The Mortara Affair, Redux." These essays respond to Romanus Cessario, O.P.'s deeply regrettable "Non Possumus," a book review of the English translation of *Kidnapped by the Vatican?* in *First Things*.

36. Indeed, the sacrament of baptism also involves this requirement. In asking for (or in emergencies administering) the sacrament of baptism to children below the age of reason, the parents do so in the faith of the Church and with promises that bind them to raise the child in the faith.

37. O'Neill, *Sacramental Realism*, 125, 135.

38. O'Neill, *Sacramental Realism*, 136. O'Neill rightly critiques human-centered (rather than God-centered) theologies of the sacraments: see O'Neill, *Sacramental Realism*, 140–42. He remarks, "When it comes to speaking about divine intervention in the sacraments, the fundamental question is not one of the phenomenology of symbolism. Such an approach, because of the categories it employs and the point of view it adopts, systematically excludes, as a matter of method, any consideration, either for or against, of the action of God. It may consider the believer's conviction that, as a member of a community, he experiences God's saving help; but this is not at all the same thing as making statements about God which can be shown to be meaningful and are affirmed as true" (O'Neill, *Sacramental Realism*, 141–42). The key, O'Neill observes, is "God's objective way of acting in the world," or what O'Neill also calls sacramental "realism" (O'Neill, *Sacramental Realism*, 142).

39. Nutt, *General Principles of Sacramental Theology*, 110. See also Lynch, *The Cleansing of the Heart*.

because they are simply stating Catholic doctrine—are correct. But this does not mean that Pope Pius IX's action was correct. I will here briefly offer six considerations, each of which could be significantly expanded.

(1) Natural law and natural justice were violated by Pope Pius IX's action. In his discussion of charity in the *Summa theologiae*, Aquinas holds that "the aspect under which our neighbor is to be loved, is God, since what we ought to love in our neighbor is that he may be in God."[40] But to do an injustice to a person, even with the goal of ordering him toward God, is in Aquinas's view a sin. As Novak observes in his *Natural Law in Judaism*, often justice is the most that we can expect, but "in the covenant, justice is only the minimum. The covenant transcends nature, but as something more not less than it."[41]

Yet what about the canonical expectation that once a child has been baptized (even against the will of his parents), the Church must ensure that the child is raised and educated in the Catholic faith, as legally required in the Papal States? Can this justify doing a natural injustice to the parents—and to the child who has a natural right to be raised by his parents—in the name of supernatural charity toward the child? Assuming that the infant Edgardo *was* secretly baptized by the servant Anna Morisi (and this assumption has been challenged on good grounds, as we will see), this was a secret baptism of an infant without the consent of his parents. Even if one insists (mistakenly in my view) that supernatural charity may require doing a natural injustice to the parents and to the child, there are pertinent distinctions to be made with regard to the sacramental order. A secret baptism against the will of an infant's parents needs to be distinguished from a normal baptism with respect to the expectations regarding education in the faith. In the case of a secret baptism of an infant against the will of the parents, it does not make sense to argue that just because a good in the supernatural order has been bestowed, there must then follow a severe injustice in the natural order toward the parents who are the natural caretakers of the child as well as toward the child who has a natural right in justice to be raised by his parents. The supernatural order can recognize diverse circumstances and can adjust the requirements of charity toward the boy accordingly.

Here we need to attend to the fact that Catholics would be utterly appalled if our children were forcibly removed by State power from our homes, in order to be educated in the faith of a confessional non-Catholic State or by an atheistic State that deemed the inculcation of Christian beliefs to be tantamount to child abuse. As the

---

40. *ST* II-II, q. 25, a. 1.

41. Novak, *Natural Law in Judaism*, 47. For further reflection on natural law, see the essays that David Novak and I wrote for our co-authored book with Anver M. Emon, in Emon, Levering, and Novak, *Natural Law: A Jewish, Christian, and Islamic Trialogue*. See also Novak, *Covenantal Rights*; and my *Biblical Natural Law: A Theocentric and Teleological Approach*. For further exposition, reflecting our somewhat different approaches but also our agreement regarding the basic precepts of natural law, see Novak, "Natural Law and Divine Command: Some Thoughts on *Veritatis Splendor*"; and my *Jewish-Christian Dialogue and the Life of Wisdom*, chapter 4: "Natural Law and Noahide Law."

Apostle Paul says, Christian "love does no wrong to a neighbor" (Rom 13:10). Forcibly taking away a child from his loving parents, unless necessary due to insanity or physical abuse on the part of the parents, commits a grievous wrong against the neighbor (both the parents and the child). Even for those who insist that Pope Pius's action was required in charity toward the boy Edgardo once he had been baptized, there still needs to be a reckoning with the circumstances of this baptism. Given the secrecy of the baptism of the infant Edgardo and the fact that the baptism occurred (*if* it even did occur) against the parents' will, charity and justice toward all involved will not insist upon the normal requirements that pertain with respect to freely baptized Catholics. As I explain further below, there are other ways to move forward charitably, in prayer, that do not involve separating a young boy from his loving parents—an act that was gravely unjust to the parents and to the boy who had a right to be raised by his parents.[42]

(2) To violate the order of the natural law in this manner, even if sincerely for the purpose of obeying the supernatural order of charity vis-à-vis the boy, causes scandal and undermines the public credibility of both the natural and the supernatural order, and therefore is deeply imprudent. Aquinas recognizes that forcible baptism of Jewish children "would be detrimental to the faith" because, under normal circumstances, the parents would later be able to demonstrate to the children (once they had reached the age of reason) that an injustice had been done in the name of the Catholic faith. He notes that this would be likely to discredit the Catholic faith in the eyes of children who naturally love their parents, unless this natural love had been stamped out in the interim.[43] Furthermore, today—and in 1858—affirming that a secret baptism of an infant against the will of his parents mandates the forcible removal of the boy from his family discredits one of the Church's greatest sacraments.

(3) Defenders of the forcible removal of the boy Edgardo affirm that this action was necessary in order to ensure that Edgardo was educated in the Catholic faith.[44] But this excuse for violating the natural justice (and charity) due to Edgardo's parents does not hold up under theological scrutiny. Aquinas teaches, "The physician of souls,

---

42. Cessario argues, "No one who considers the Mortara affair can fail to be moved by its natural dimensions. It is a grievous thing to sever familial bonds. But the honor we give to mother and father will be imperfect if we do not render a higher honor to God above. Christ's authority perfects all natural institutions—the family as well as the state. This is why he said that he came bearing a sword that would sunder father and son. One's judgment of Pius will depend on one's acceptance of Christ's claim" ("Non Possumus," 58). For Cessario, it was an act of charity (and justice) toward the boy Edgardo, once he had (supposedly) been baptized secretly, to ensure that he be educated as a Christian—and the enactment of this charity (and justice) sadly required separating him from his loving Jewish parents.

43. *ST* II-II, q. 10, a. 12.

44. Edgardo Mortara himself, of course, held this position. Attention needs to be paid here to a phenomenon described by Jonathan Sacks, who points out that Jews, including Jews who convert to Christianity, have been among the prominent advocates of persecution of Jews: see Sacks, *Covenant and Conversation*, 216–17.

i.e., Christ, works in two ways. First, inwardly, by himself: and thus he prepares man's will so that it works good and hates evil."[45] This interior mission of the incarnate Word takes place whenever and to whomever Christ wills. Assuming Edgardo was validly baptized, the interior missions of the Son and Spirit could have operated within him and borne fruit efficaciously after he had reached the age of reason.[46] Those who claim that he would otherwise likely never have enjoyed the supernatural grace of his baptism neglect the fact that not only could God have continued to work interiorly in Edgardo, but also God could have used many external instruments to awaken the *adult* Edgardo to the supernatural grace of his baptism.[47]

(4) Some Catholics have contended that because Pope Pius IX has been declared "Blessed," his prudential decision in this case should be accepted as an exercise of virtuous prudence, given that Pius IX repeatedly reaffirmed what he did to Edgardo Mortara and his family, and given that his beatification "preclude[s] the view that Pius IX was an unrepentant sinner committed to violations of the natural law."[48] But even saints can adhere to grievous prudential error, for example by misunderstanding the elements of a case due to unconscious cultural prejudices.[49] John A. McHugh and Charles J. Callan point out that even virtuous prudence can determine upon an erroneous course

---

45. *ST* III, q. 68, a. 4, ad 2; cf. *ST* I, q. 43, a. 5.

46. Cessario comments in defending Pope Pius IX's action: "Allow me to recall that, according to Catholic teaching, the character of baptism does not work like magic. The new life that Catholics believe baptism brings requires instruction in the faith of the Catholic Church. Such instruction precedes baptism for adults. On the other hand, baptized children require rearing in the faith just as any child requires instruction in order to develop his or her human capacities" ("Romanus Cessario, O.P., replies," 4). Of course this is so, but the question is whether there is an alternative to removing a child, (supposedly) baptized as an infant without his parents' knowledge, from his loving parents.

47. See also Aquinas, *De veritate*, q. 14, a. 11, ad 1. For diverse perspectives, see Garrigou-Lagrange, *De revelatione per ecclesiam proposita*, 500–502 ("On those who are invincibly ignorant of the preaching of the Catholic faith"); Nicolas, *Synthèse dogmatique*, 706–18.

48. Cessario, "Romanus Cessario, O.P., replies," 4. Messori makes a similar point more than once. He remarks, "Much more of a pastor than a politician, much more candid than astute, this pontiff was incapable of falsehood. He was a priest who made painful, rigorous examinations of conscience, trusting in the mercy of Christ, whose vicar he was, and at the same time afraid of not living up to the gospel, knowing that he was supposed to be the greatest witness to it. Nevertheless, this sincere, scrupulous man, although beset by the storm that was raging halfway around the world, never had any hesitation, and years later he coolheadedly confirmed it on a public, solemn occasion: 'What we did for that boy, We had the right and the duty to do. And if the opportunity presented itself, We would do it again.' The Church has proclaimed this pope Blessed, declaring his heroic virtues and proposing him therefore to the faithful as a role model and an intercessor. The tranquility of this pope's conscience says something, does it not, to Catholics at least?" (Messori, "The Mortara Case," 32). Messori is mistaken to suggest that Catholics need to defend all the prudential decisions made and defended by sainted popes. Cessario recognizes that "a beatification does not endorse every political decision of the blessed" ("Romanus Cessario, O.P., replies," 4), but Cessario suggests that the fact that Pius IX repeatedly confirmed this decision means it should be embraced.

49. See Sherwin, *On Love and Virtue*, 176; *ST* II-II, q. 47, a. 14, ad 1.

of action.⁵⁰ The idea that no one declared "Blessed" could have persisted in a serious prudential error is not credible, either theologically or historically.

Moreover, according to David Kertzer, there was plausible evidence given to Pope Pius IX that indicated that Anna Morisi did not tell the truth about what she claimed to have done. Edgardo's parents stated that she was never alone with the baby Edgardo. The Mortara's family doctor, Pasquale Saragoni, "testified that at the time that Anna Morisi said she performed the baptism of the sick child, she herself was very ill and confined to bed."⁵¹ Maria Capelli, a Catholic, supported Saragoni's testimony secondhand by reporting what her mother, a daytime servant of the Mortaras, had told her. Another Catholic servant, Ippolita Zacchini, also confirmed Saragoni's account; as did both her daughter, Marianna Zacchini, and the seamstress Giuseppina Borghi who lived in the floor below the Mortara family. Anna Morisi claimed that she had asked a local grocer, Cesare Lepori, how to baptize a child, but Lepori denied that he had spoken to Anna or that he even knew the procedure for baptizing. Furthermore, many testified that Anna Morisi was—to say the least—not trustworthy in her overall behavior.⁵² The point is that not only could Pope Pius IX (as "Blessed") have erred prudentially, but also much of the evidence that was known to Pius IX undermined the credibility of Anna Morisi's claim.

(5) The *signification* of the sacrament of baptism, insofar as it is associated with the forcible removal of a Jewish child from his parents, is undermined. Christians affirm that "all of us who have been baptized into Christ Jesus were baptized into his death" (Rom 6:3). Paul states, "For as many of you as were baptized into Christ have put on Christ" (Gal 3:27). Given that baptism is an efficacious sign of our sharing in Christ's death and our configuration to Christ, the action of forcibly removing a child secretly

---

50. See McHugh and Callan, *Moral Theology*, vol. 2, 21, 28. See also the perspective of Alphonsus de Liguori as summarized by Raphael Gallagher, C.Ss.R.: "Honest error of conscience does not constitute sin for Alphonsus. . . . [R]ight reason often fails because of a variety of circumstances and human conditions" (Gallagher, "Where Moral Theology Begins: '*Aditus ad Universam Moralem Theologiam*,'" 25). See also Maritain, *Distinguish to Unite, or, The Degrees of Knowledge*, Appendix VII: "Speculative" and "Practical," 481–89, especially 488; as well as the discussion of the errors committed by even saintly Church leaders in exercising their functions in the Church, in Nicolas, *Synthèse dogmatique*, 700–704; and Maritain, *On the Church of Christ*, 135–242.

51. Kertzer, *The Kidnapping of Edgardo Mortara*, 97.

52. Father Mortara, in his *The Mortara Child and Pius IX*, erroneously presents Morisi as a devout Catholic, well instructed in her faith and knowledgeable in the mode of baptism, and he also insists that he (as an infant) was indeed on the point of death: "The child Edgardo was seriously ill; the doctors had lost all hope of saving him. His parents, confronted with all the most unequivocal signs of a fatal end of the incident, abandoned themselves to a desperate sorrow. The child was on the point of taking his last breath; only a few moments more and he would be in Eternity. . . . In such a terrible predicament, the Morisi woman, who had been appropriately instructed, knew her catechism well and the manner and form for administering the Sacrament of Baptism to a dying person. She took a glass of water, dipped her hand into it, and baptized the child. . . . [S]hortly afterward, the child miraculously recovered and was completely restored to health" (153–54).

baptized by a servant functions inevitably as a counter-sign, expressive not of union with the crucified Christ but of overweening worldly power.

(6) Kertzer has demonstrated that many positive details put forward by the Catholic press of the day were fabrications intended to paint the Church in a better light.[53] He has also demonstrated that the recent Italian edition of Edgardo Mortara's memoirs, along with the recent English edition, has been heavily doctored by Vittorio Messori in order to make the Church look better.[54] Cessario remarks: "If Catholics are to respond effectively to David Kertzer's allegations in *The Kidnapping of Edgardo Mortara* . . . they might strengthen their grasp on certain facets of the question. . . . One involves the facts of the case: Evaluation of Pope Pius IX's actions . . . should be based

---

53. For example, Kertzer notes, "The part of the memoir that the conservative Catholic media is most loudly trumpeting today is Edgardo's description of how, after learning of the baptism but before Edgardo was taken away, Pius IX repeatedly tried to arrange some kind of compromise with his parents. In Edgardo's original account, the pope proposed sending him to a Catholic boarding school in Bologna, for, 'That way, his parents would be able to visit him whenever they wanted.' The Inquisitor, Edgardo writes, repeatedly went to the Mortara home to convince his parents to accept the pope's thoughtful plan. . . . Yet this account is pure invention—and not by Messori, but by Edgardo himself. The Inquisitor went on trial in 1860 on charges of kidnapping the boy; trial transcripts offering hundreds of pages of first-hand accounts—from the boy's parents, the police, and the Inquisitor—all make clear that the Inquisitor never spoke with the Mortaras before the papal police took Edgardo away. The appearance of the police that night in June 1858 came as a complete shock to the Mortaras. The only offer that Church authorities ever made came *after* the boy was already securely in Rome in the House of the Catechumens, the Church institution dedicated to converting the Jews. Edgardo's parents were then told that if they themselves were to enter the House of Catechumens along with the rest of their children, and accept baptism, they would once again be able to live together as a family—a Christian family" (Kertzer, "The Doctored 'Memoir' of a Jewish Boy Kidnapped by the Vatican"). For further details about Edgardo's kidnapping and its immediate aftermath, see Kertzer's *The Kidnapping of Edgardo Mortara*, especially 3–73, 83–117.

54. Kertzer points out, "The actual document Edgardo wrote differs in many passages from what Vittorio Messori . . . has published. Messori's work represents the first translation of Edgardo's memoir—originally written in Spanish—first into Italian, then into English. . . . I personally compared the Italian and English versions of the Edgardo Mortara memoir published by Messori with the original, which I too located at the Canons Regular archive and digitized. In Messori's version of the memoir, the reader is treated to a heartwarming story of a six-year-old child who is overjoyed to be taken from his parents so that he can become a Catholic. . . . But this is not the narrative Edgardo actually wrote. The happy version instead emerges from numerous changes to the original, including the addition and deletion of entire paragraphs—changes that are common to both published versions of the Edgardo Mortara memoir in Italian and English. A case in point is the addition of a 300-word paragraph, presented seamlessly with the rest of the text. It offers a justification for Pius IX's action in ordering Edgardo's removal from his family, and also describes the touching scene of the Inquisitor, Father Feletti, the man responsible for ordering the boy taken, going to see little Edgardo. 'In Rome, with great pleasure and tears in his eyes,' Messori's version of the memoir reads, 'Father Feletti hugged the Mortara child, for whose eternal salvation he had suffered so much, and he always had a special affection for him. Father Mortara will always hold very dear the memory of this respectable friar, who was one of those who more closely intervened in the spiritual regeneration and rehabilitation of his soul.' Neither this scene, nor the rest of the paragraph in which it appears, are to be found in Edgardo's original memoir" (Kertzer, "The Doctored 'Memoir' of a Jewish Boy Kidnapped by the Vatican"). Kertzer goes on to show that Messori softened the anti-Semitic remarks that Mortara makes in the memoir, language that leaves "the impression that Church mentors may have filled a Jewish child's mind with anti-Semitic ideas" (Kertzer, "The Doctored 'Memoir' of a Jewish Boy Kidnapped by the Vatican").

on the most accurate detailing of the facts that political, legal, and religious history can provide."[55] Surely this is so, but Cessario is naming his own deficiency. Cessario does not recognize the doctored state of the memoirs, and he demonstrates almost no knowledge of the ambiguities of the case—including the many reasons for doubting Anna Morisi's story—or of the relevant historical studies.

Cessario also takes at face value, without researching further, the following point: "the chief rabbi of Rome, Sabatino Scazzocchio, wrote a private letter praising 'the benign and charitable nature' of Pius while lamenting the interference of the secular press. When Rome's Jews were invited to join Garibaldi's campaign against Pope Pius, they declined."[56] Cessario implies that this means that the Roman Jews appreciated Pope Pius's motivations. Even the slightest study of the actual situation in Rome and the tenuous situation of the Jews there, as well as their utter outrage over Pius's actions, makes clear how farfetched Cessario's interpretation is. In addition, Cessario approvingly quotes Edgardo Mortara's praise of Pius IX, where Mortara describes the Jewish (and non-Jewish) critics of Pius IX as low-life calumniators and Christ-killers: "There will come a day, yes, and it is not far away, in which, once they have stopped listening to the calumnies and the '*Crucifige*' (shouts of 'Crucify!') of the dregs of humanity, posterity will accept the poor arguments of the Mortara child."[57] This is an example of nineteenth-century Catholic anti-Semitism pure and simple.[58]

55. Cessario, "Romanus Cessario, O.P., replies," 4–5.

56. Cessario, "Non Possumus," 58.

57. Mortara, *The Mortara Child and Pius IX*, 175, cited in Cessario, "Non Possumus," 58. Shortly earlier, Mortara states similarly: "Ah! Amid your cackling, in the middle of the whirlpool of your hatreds and resentments, over the thick cloud and the dense fogs of your ignorance and pride, high above the movement of the base, treacherous passions that the infernal Serpent awakens and provokes in your ignoble hearts, arises, ascends and towers, like a new Moses on Sinai, at the summit of the Vatican, the great admirable, immortal Pontiff of the Immaculate and of the *Syllabus*. The flash of his glance, together with the thunder of his sublime '*Non possumus*', silences your 'Tolle, tolle, crucifige eum' (Away with him, away with him, crucify him) (Jn 19:15) and leaves Pius IX on a throne that is still great, still noble, and unvanquished.... The accusers of Pius IX, like those of Jesus, of whom he is the visible vicar, are squashed under the weight of their inconsistent, ridiculous calumnies" (Mortara, *The Mortara Child and Pius IX*, 174).

58. Cessario concludes "Romanus Cessario, O.P., replies" with the following words: "My review of a book that reports the story of a man who died in 1940 does not in any way purport to compromise what, in 1965, Blessed Paul VI set down in *Nostra Aetate*, especially no. 4: 'In her rejection of every persecution against any man, the Church, mindful of the patrimony she shares with the Jews and moved not by political reasons but by the Gospel's spiritual love, decries hatred, persecutions, displays of anti-Semitism, directed against Jews at any time and by anyone'" (5). The problem is that his quotation from the last page of Mortara's memoirs—a perfect example of nineteenth-century Catholic anti-Semitism—is quoted as though there were no problem with its sentiments. See also the response to Cessario by Kertzer, "The Enduring Controversy over the Mortara Case." Kertzer fills in further historical details about Father Mortara's life and ministry, with assistance from Pizzorusso, "Il caso Mortara: due libri e un documento Americano"; and Mancini, "Pier Gaetano Feletti e l'affare Mortara." It is clear that Father Mortara continued to seek relationships with his parents and to think of himself as well disposed toward Judaism, despite also condemning it in strong terms. Describing an interview given by Father Mortara to the *Catholic Standard* in Philadelphia in 1898, in which Mortara recalls the

The historian John Y. B. Hood has commented on the issue of forced baptism: "Aquinas stands his ground: The parent-child bond is inviolable, even if the consequences include allowing the child to suffer eternal alienation from God. . . . No doubt his position reflects his deep commitment to natural law and his absolutist insistence that no consequence, however heinous, can justify a morally wrong act."[59] Hood adds that Blessed John Duns Scotus "also believed in natural law, and he simply invoked hierarchy to conclude that Jewish children should be baptized: God's *dominium* supersedes all others, including that of parents."[60] For Scotus, the supernatural order can and does override and negate the natural law. Scotus considers that an unjust action can rightly be done in the name of Christ's charity.

I hope that Aquinas would have repudiated Pope Pius IX's action, and I am sure that he would have repudiated Scotus's reasoning. The sacrament of baptism does not need to be defended in this injurious way; nor does Christ's charity need to be associated with such a grave natural injustice. God can and does work in other, more appropriate ways, as for example through the interior missions of the Son and Spirit. The testimony that tells against Morisi's claim should also be given weight. The reality of persecution of the Jewish people in the Papal States needs attention as well.

The Church owes the Jewish community and the descendants of the Mortara family (assuming that there were survivors after the Shoah) a deep apology, including for teaching the boy Edgardo that the Jews are degraded "Christ-killers." The fact that such an action was done to Jews, whom the *Catechism of the Catholic Church* calls "the people of 'elder brethren' in the faith of Abraham,"[61] underscores the shame and disrepute of the act. The forcible removal of the boy Edgardo from his loving family was unjust, imprudent, and a grave abuse of Pope Pius IX's power.

Conclusion

Unfortunately, some Catholics have made papal abuses of power into an excuse for denigrating the Catholic Church's priesthood and sacramental doctrine. For example,

---

events of 1858, Kertzer notes: "much of Mortara's account of what had happened to him is pure fiction. . . . We know much of this thanks to several hundred pages of testimony about these events taken in early 1860 as part of the trial of the Inquisitor on charges of kidnapping Edgardo. In those records, we find lengthy testimony given by almost all of the principals involved in the taking of Edgardo from his family, including his father, his mother, the policeman who removed him from his parents, and indeed of the Inquisitor himself. In fact, this is a historical case where we have an excellent documentary record of what happened, available for anyone to consult in the state archives of Bologna. We also have many hundreds of contemporaneous documents on the case to be found both in the Vatican Secret Archives and in the historical archives of the Jewish community of Rome" ("The Enduring Controversy over the Mortara Case," 7).

59. Hood, *Aquinas and the Jews*, 92.

60. Hood, *Aquinas and the Jews*, 92. See also Turner, "Jewish Witness, Forced Conversion and Island Living."

61. *Catechism of the Catholic Church*, 63.

the Mortara incident has a significant place in Garry Wills's polemical *Papal Sin*, whose purpose is to undermine the authority of the Petrine office in the promulgation of Catholic doctrine.[62] Likewise, in his chapter on "Priestly Imperialism" in *Why Priests? A Failed Tradition*, Wills argues that most sacraments are about "the priestly controlling of life."[63] Toward the end of his *Constantine's Sword: The Church and the Jews*, the Catholic author James Carroll proposes a solution to the terrible wrongs committed by Catholics against the Jewish people over the centuries: "The Church's own experience—in particular, of its grievous sin in relation to the Jews—proves how desperately in need of democratic reform the Church is. . . . Vatican III must restore the broken authority of the Church by locating authority in the place where it belongs, which is with the people through whom the Spirit breathes."[64] On this view, if Catholic laypeople had been in charge, such abuses of power against the Jewish people would not have occurred. This blaming of priestly power is absurd, given the level of anti-Judaism that characterized the broad Catholic populace at the time and that unfortunately did not need stimulation from prelates.

What is needed instead is a deeper sense of the fact that God has willed to mediate his revelation through the instrumentality of sinful human beings. Jesus chose to communicate his life, death, and resurrection—his living presence—to us through the mediation of the apostles, all of whom were sinners. In the Gospel of Luke, Peter falls down "at Jesus' knees, saying, 'Depart from me, for I am a sinful man, O Lord'" (Luke 5:8). Paul accuses both Barnabas and Peter of acting with "insincerity" in their relationships with gentiles (Gal 2:13). The disciples characteristically debated with each other about who among them "was the greatest" (Mark 9:34). The followers of Jesus have always been sinners.

There is no need, then, to adopt a simple-minded "anti-Roman attitude" that blames the bishop of Rome for all the Church's (or world's) woes.[65] As Hans Urs von Balthasar aptly remarks, "there is—and always has been among Catholics—a healthy popular sentiment that is faithful to Rome without being blind to the faults and human failings of the curia and even of the pope."[66] May this healthy sentiment, both in its fidelity and in its realism, long continue.

---

62. See Wills, *Papal Sin: Structures of Deceit*. On the reaction provoked by scurrilous arguments, see Joseph Ratzinger, "The Church's Guilt: Presentation of the Document *Remembrance and Reconciliation* from the International Theological Commission," 280–81.

63. Wills, *Why Priests? A Failed Tradition*, 236.

64. Carroll, *Constantine's Sword*, 598. See also the documentation in Nicholls, *Christian Antisemitism*, including his chilling comparison of patristic and medieval canonical laws against Jews with Nazi laws against Jews on 204–6. For further documentation see Marcus, *The Jews in the Medieval World*.

65. von Balthasar, *The Office of Peter and the Structure of the Church*, 29.

66. von Balthasar, *The Office of Peter and the Structure of the Church*, 29.

Bibliography

Aquinas, Thomas. *Summa Theologiae*. Fathers of the English Dominican Province. Westminster, MD: Christian Classics, 1981.

Balthasar, Hans Urs von. *The Office of Peter and the Structure of the Church*. Translated by Andrée Emery. San Francisco: Ignatius, 1986.

Bauman, Zygmunt. *Modernity and the Holocaust*. Cambridge: Polity, 1991.

Bea, Augustin. *The Church and the Jewish People: A Commentary on the Second Vatican Council's Declaration on the Relation of the Church to Non-Christian Religions*. Translated by Philip Lovetz. London: Geoffrey Chapman, 1966.

Benedict XIV, Pope. *Lettera a Monsignor Archivescovo di Tarso Vicegerente sopra il Battesimo degli Ebrei o infanti o adulti* (February 28, 1747).

———. *Lettera della Santità di Nostro Signore Benedetto Papa XIV a Monsignor Pier Girolamo Guglielmi Assessore del Sant'Officio sopra l'Offerta fatta dall'Avia Neofita di alcuni suoi Nipoti infanti Ebrei alla Fede Christiana* (December 15, 1751), translations of his Papal Bulls (published on the same dates) *Postremo mense* and *Probe te meminisse*.

Caffiero, Marina. *Forced Baptisms: Histories of Jews, Christians, and Converts in Papal Rome*. Translated by Lydia G. Cochrane. Berkeley, CA, 2012.

Carroll, James. *Constantine's Sword: The Church and the Jews: A History*. Boston: Houghton Mifflin, 2001.

Catechism of the Catholic Church. 2nd ed. Vatican City: Libreria Editrice Vaticana, 1997.

Cessario, Romanus. "Non Possumus," a book review of the English translation of *Kidnapped by the Vatican?* In *First Things* 280, February 2018, 55–58.

———. "Romanus Cessario, O.P., replies." *First Things* 282, April 2018, 4–5.

Chaput, Charles J. "The Mortara Affair, Redux." *Jewish Review of Books*, January 2018. https://jewishreviewofbooks.com/articles/2979/mortara-affair-redux/.

Franks, Christopher A. "Aristotelian Doctrines in Aquinas's Treatment of Justice." In *Aristotle in Aquinas's Theology*, edited by Gilles Emery and Matthew Levering, 139–66. Oxford: Oxford University Press, 2015.

Code of Canon Law: Latin-English Edition. Translated by Canon Law Society of America. Washington, DC: Canon Law Society of America, 1999.

Codex iuris canonici. Vatican City: Libreria Vaticana Editrice, 1983.

Connelly, John. *From Enemy to Brother: The Revolution in Catholic Teaching on the Jews, 1933–1965*. Cambridge: Harvard University Press, 2012.

D'Costa, Gavin. *Vatican II: Catholic Doctrines on Jews and Muslims*. Oxford: Oxford University Press, 2014.

Dawkins, Richard. *The God Delusion*. Boston: Houghtin Mifflin, 2006.

Emon, Anver, Matthew Levering, and David Novak. *Natural Law: A Jewish, Christian, and Muslim Trialogue*. Oxford: Oxford University Press, 2014.

Flannery, Edward. *The Anguish of the Jews: Twenty-Three Centuries of Antisemitism*. 2nd ed. NJ: A Stimulus Book, 2004.

Gallagher, Raphael. "Where Moral Theology Begins: 'Aditus ad Universam Moralem Theologiam.'" In *Contemplating the Future of Moral Theology: Essays in Honor of Brian V. Johnstone, C.Ss.R.*, edited by Robert C. Koerpel and Vimal Tirimanna, 21–37. Eugene, OR: Pickwick, 2017.

Garrigou-Lagrange, Reginald. *De revelatione per ecclesiam proposita*. 5th ed. Rome: Desclée, 1950.

Hood, John Y. B. *Aquinas and the Jews*. Philadelphia: University of Pennsylvania Press, 1995.

Isaac, Jules. *The Teaching of Contempt: Christian Roots of anti-Semitism*. Translated by Helen Weaver. New York: Holt, Rinehart and Winston, 1964.

Kertzer, David I. "The Doctored 'Memoir' of a Jewish Boy Kidnapped by the Vatican." *The Atlantic*. April 15, 2018. https://www.theatlantic.com/international/archive/2018/04/edgardo-mortara-doctored-memoir/554948.

———. "The Enduring Controversy over the Mortara Case." *Studies in Christian-Jewish Relations* 14 (2019) 1–10.

———. *The Kidnapping of Edgardo Mortara*. New York: Knopf, 1997.

———. *The Popes Against the Jews: The Vatican's Role in the Rise of Modern Anti-Semitism*. New York: Knopf, 2001.

———. *The Pope and Mussolini: The Secret History of Pius XI and the Rise of Fascism in Europe*. New York: Random House, 2014.

———. *The Pope Who Would Be King: The Exile of Pius IX and the Emergence of Modern Europe*. New York: Random House, 2018.

Kleinberg, Aviad M. "Depriving Parents of the Consolation of Children: Two Legal *Consilia* on the Baptism of Jewish Children." In *De Sion exibit lex et verbum domini de Hierusalem: Essays on Medieval Law, Liturgy and Literature in Honour of Amnon Linder*, edited by Y. Hen, 129–44. Turnhout: Brepols, 2001.

Korn, Bertram Wallace. *The American Reaction to The Mortara Case: 1858–1859*. Cincinnati, OH: The American Jewish Archives, 1957.

Lawler, Justus George. *Were the Popes Against the Jews? Tracking the Myths, Confronting the Ideologues*. Grand Rapids: Eerdmans, 2012.

Levering, Matthew. *Biblical Natural Law: A Theocentric and Teleological Approach*. Oxford: Oxford University Press, 2008.

———. "God and Natural Law: Reflections on Genesis 22." *Modern Theology* 24 (2008) 151–77.

———. *Jewish-Christian Dialogue and the Life of Wisdom: Engagements with the Theology of David Novak*. London: Continuum, 2010.

Linder, Amnon. *The Jews in the Legal Sources of the Early Middle Ages*. Detroit, MI: Wayne State University Press, 1997.

Lynch, Reginald M. *The Cleansing of the Heart: The Sacraments as Instrumental Causes in the Thomistic Tradition*. Washington, DC: Catholic University of America Press, 2017.

Mancini, Massimo. "Pier Gaetano Feletti e l'affare Mortara." In *Dominikaner und Junen*, edited by Eias H. Füllenback and Gianfranco Miletto, 421–37. Berlin: De Grutyer, 2015.

Marcus, Jacob. *The Jews in the Medieval World: A Sourcebook, 315–1791*. New York: Jewish Publication Society, 1938.

Maritain, Jacques. *Distinguish to Unite, or, The Degrees of Knowledge*. Translated from the 4th French ed. by Gerald B. Phelan, rev. ed. Notre Dame, IN: University of Notre Dame Press, 1995.

———. *On the Church of Christ: The Person of the Church and Her Personnel*. Translated by Joseph W. Evans. Notre Dame, IN: University of Notre Dame, 1973.

McHugh, John A., and Charles J. Callan. *Moral Theology: A Complete Course Based on St. Thomas Aquinas and the Best Modern Authorities*. Revised and enlarged by Edward P. Farrell, O.P., vol. 2, edited by Paul A. Böer. N.p.: Veritatis Splendor, 2014 [originally published 1929].

Messori, Vittorio. "The Mortara Case." In *Kidnapped by the Vatican? The Unpublished Memoirs of Edgardo Mortara*, edited by Vittorio Messori, 1–67. San Francisco: Ignatius, 2017.

Mortara, Pio Maria. "The Mortara Child and Pius IX." In *Kidnapped by the Vatican? The Unpublished Memoirs of Edgardo Mortara*, edited by Vittorio Messori, 77–175. San Francisco: Ignatius, 2017.

Moschella, Melissa. *To Whom Do Children Belong? Parental Rights, Civic Education, and Children's Autonomy*. Cambridge: Cambridge University Press, 2016.

Nicholls, William. *Christian Antisemitism: A History of Hate*. Northvale, NJ: Aronson, 1993.

Nicolas, Jean-Hervé. *Synthèse dogmatique. De la Trinité à la Trinité*. Paris: Beauchesne, 1985.

Novak, David. *Covenantal Rights*. Princeton: Princeton University Press, 2000.

———. "Natural Law and Divine Command: Some Thoughts on *Veritatis Splendor*." In *John Paul II and the Jewish People: A Jewish-Christian Dialogue*, edited by David G. Dalin and Matthew Levering, 61–79. Lanham, MD: Rowman & Littlefield, 2008.

———. *Natural Law in Judaism*. Cambridge: Cambridge University Press, 1998.

Nutt, Roger W. *General Principles of Sacramental Theology*. Washington, DC: Catholic University of America Press, 2017.

O'Neill, Colman E. *Sacramental Realism: A General Theory of the Sacraments*. Edited by Romanus Cessario. Chicago: Midwest Theological Forum, 1998.

Pakter, Walter. *Medieval Canon Law and the Jews*. Ebelsbach, Germany: Gremer, 1988.

Pennington, Kenneth. "The Law's Violence against Medieval and Early Modern Jews." *Rivista internazionale di diritto comune* 23 (2012) 23–44.

Pizzorusso, Giovanni. "Il caso Mortara: due libri e un documento Americano." *Il Veltro* 42 (1998) 134–41.

Radner, Ephraim. *Church*. Eugene, OR: Cascade, 2017.

Ratzinger, Joseph. "The Church's Guilt: Presentation of the Document *Remembrance and Reconciliation* from the International Theological Commission." In Joseph Ratzinger, *Pilgrim Fellowship of Faith: The Church as Communion*, translated by Henry Taylor, 274–83. San Francisco: Ignatius, 2005.

Ravid, Benjamin C. I. "The Forced Baptism of Jewish Minors in Early Modern Venice." *Italia: Studi e ricerche sulla cultura e sula letteratura degli ebrei d'Italia* 13–15 (2001) 259–301.

Roth, Norman. *Jews, Visigoths, and Muslims in Medieval Spain*. Leiden: Brill, 1994.

Sacks, Jonathan. *Covenant and Conversation: A Weekly Reading of the Jewish Bible. Leviticus: The Book of Holiness*. New Milford, CT: Maggid, 2015.

Schoeman, Roy. "Foreword." In *Kidnapped by the Vatican? The Unpublished Memoirs of Edgardo Mortara*, edited by Vittorio Messori, vii–xi. San Francisco: Ignatius, 2017.

Sherwin, Michael S. *On Love and Virtue: Theological Essays*. Renewal Within Tradition. Steubenville, OH: Emmaus Academic, 2018.

Stahl, Sharon. *The Mortara Affair, 1858: Reflections of the Struggle to Maintain the Temporal Power of the Papacy*. PhD diss., Saint Louis University, 1987.

Tapie, Matthew A. "*Spiritualis Uterus*: The Question of Forced Baptism and Thomas Aquinas's Defense of Jewish Parental Rights." *Bulletin of Medieval Canon Law* 35 (2018) 289–329.

Tolan, John et al., eds. *Jews in Early Christian Law: Byzantium and the Latin West, 6th–11th Centuries*. Turnhout: Brepols, 2014.

Turner, Nancy L. "Jewish Witness, Forced Conversion and Island Living: John Duns Scotus on Jews and Judaism." In *Christian Attitudes towards the Jews in the Midde Ages: A Casebook*, edited by Michael Frassetto, 183–209. London: Routledge, 2007.

Weed, Jennifer Hart. "Aquinas on the Forced Conversion of the Jews." In *Jews in Medieval Christendom: "Slay Them Not,"* edited by Kristine T. Utterback and Merrall L. Price, 129–46. Leiden: Brill, 2013.

———. "Faith, Salvation, and the Sacraments in Aquinas: A Puzzle Concerning Forced Baptisms." *Philosophy, Culture, and Traditions* 10 (2014) 95–110.

Wills, Garry. *Papal Sin: Structures of Deceit.* New York: Doubleday, 2000.

———. *Why Priests? A Failed Tradition.* New York: Penguin, 2013.

Response to

Matthew Levering's "Pope Pius IX and the Mortara Case: A Catholic Critique"

DAVID NOVAK

I AM GRATEFUL TO Matthew Levering, my close colleague and even closer friend, for his passionate and thoughtful critique of the famous (or infamous) case of the secret baptism of Edgardo Mortara and his subsequent "kidnapping" (in the moral though not in the legal sense) from his Jewish parents by Pope Pius IX. Matthew's critique is occasioned by factors that are connected to me and my work. Let me now respond to Matthew's paper in three ways: (1) by locating the immediate context of Matthew's critique of the Mortara affair and its contemporary defenders; (2) by showing how one's stand on the theoretical issue involved here puts me in the company of some very distinguished Catholic theologians in the distant past and the more recent past; (3) by remembering how a mediaeval Jewish theologian-jurist dealt with a somewhat similar case, and then suggesting how a Catholic theologian today might learn from this by analogy.

The Mortara case has been the subject of continuing controversy ever since it occurred almost 160 years ago. There have been those who have defended the act of Pius IX, and there have been those who have condemned it. Obviously, Jews have been in the forefront of the condemnation, but there have been significant Catholic opponents of the act of Pius IX too, most recently Matthew Levering himself. And he has done so as a deeply committed Catholic theologian, with an impressive command of both primary and secondary sources.

Now the most recent occasion of the ever recurring controversy is the review in *First Things* (February 2018) of the English translation of Edgardo Mortara's memoirs, *Kidnapped by the Vatican?* by the American Dominican theologian, Father Romanus Cessario. In that review, Cessario defends the secret baptism of Edgardo and the decision of Pius IX to permanently remove him from the home and parental authority of his Jewish parents.

RESPONSE TO LEVERING'S "POPE PIUS IX AND THE MORTARA CASE"

As soon as this review appeared, to put it bluntly, "all hell broke loose." As a member of the executive board of *First Things*, I at once prepared a memorandum calling for an emergency meeting of the board to confront the editor-in-chief Dr. Russell Reno, in order to demand an apology for ever having published this review in the first place, and for this apology to appear prominently in the journal. The rather tepid response provided by Reno basically apologized for having offended many readers of *First Things* by publishing Cessario's review, rather than actually repudiating its thesis that justifies the action of the Pope. In preparing this memorandum, the first person consulted was the Catholic theologian I feel closest to, Matthew Levering. Not at all surprisingly, Matthew was as outraged by Cessario's review as was I. In fact, he seemed to be more outraged by it. Why?

Well, in his paper here, arguing how the action of Pius IX is totally contrary to natural law (especially as formulated by Cessario's greatest Dominican confrère Thomas Aquinas), Matthew writes: "To violate the order of the natural law in this manner ... causes scandal and undermines the credibility of both the natural and the supernatural order, and ... discredits one of the Church's greatest sacraments."[1] Furthermore, this *apologia* couldn't have come at a worse time for the Catholic Church. For when the whole role of parents' authority in raising and educating their children according to their own communal traditions is under attack from militant secularists, part of their overall attack on the moral priority of the natural family to the state, Cessario is in effect arguing that when the state was controlled by the Pope (as was Bologna, the home city of the Mortara family), his civil authority (along with his ecclesial authority) trumped the natural familial authority of Edgardo's Jewish parents. In a *tu quoque* retort, Matthew writes: "Catholics would be utterly appalled if our children were forcibly removed by the state power from our homes, in order to be educated in the faith of the confessional state."[2]

We Jews call such unjust public actions, even when they are within the letter of the Law, *hillul ha-shem*, i.e., "profanation of the divine Name," because they so violate the spirit of God's Law. "Profaining God's Name" means besmirching God's reputation as the Giver of what is to be taken as "God's perfect Law (*Torah*)," especially when done by those charged with authoritatively teaching God's Law and exemplifying its loftiest teachings. The thirteenth-century theologian Moses Nahmanides castigates those who "offensively act within the Torah's legal domain." Such authorities cause decent people, whether Jewish or gentile, to look upon the Torah with disgust, as it is often difficult to separate the Torah's message from its messengers.

When such injustices have taken place, Jewish theologians have searched for resources *within* the Jewish tradition itself in order to rectify them, plus trying to close such "loopholes" in the Law, so that these notorious past injustices will not become precedents for similar actions in the present and in the future. On the other hand, those

1. p. 209.
2. p. 208.

Jewish theologians who have actually defended such injustices and those who have committed them, are as much of an embarrassment to us Jews as Romanus Cessario (and his defenders) has been to Matthew Levering and many other Catholics. Indeed, Matthew and some other Catholic theologians and historians have been searching the Catholic tradition similarly to the way we Jewish theologians and historians have been searching our own Jewish tradition. Of course, it would be inappropriate of me as a Jewish theologian to even suggest this parallel research to Catholic theologians, i.e., were it not for the fact that we have those among us who seem to believe that the higher Law of God annuls the lower natural law rather than presupposing it. However, whether that research will be conducted according to Matthew Tapie's more radical criteria, or whether it will be conducted according to Matthew Levering's more conservative criteria, is not for me as a non-Catholic friend to weigh in on either side of this very specific inner-Catholic difference of opinion.

In his paper, Matthew puts my theory of the relation of natural law and divine law (i.e., law *revealed* by God supernaturally, which is distinct from law *discovered* naturally) in the company of the theories of no less than Thomas Aquinas and the twentieth-century theologian Hans Urs von Balthasar. So, what is it we all have in common? Well, it seems to me that this commonality is expressed in a key Talmudic principle: "There is nothing permitted to the Jews that is prohibited to gentiles" (Sanhedrin 59a). Now what is "prohibited to gentiles" are the Noahide prohibitions of such violent acts as murder, incest, and robbery. (Kidnapping falls under the prohibition of robbery.) In my view (arguable to be sure), the Noahide commandments are the Jewish version of natural law. Indeed, Noahide law functions as the *conditio sine qua non* of divine law, the "Mosaic Torah." As such, divine law must only never contradict natural law, i.e., it must not "permit" the Jews to do what has been "prohibited" to the gentiles. Thus, natural law is the "bottom line" that divine law presupposes and builds upon but which divine law does not overcome or ever abolish. Divine law, though, only applying to the community elected by God (i.e., Israel or the Jewish people), is the *conditio per quam* of natural/Noahide law. The higher law provides the highest end or *telos* (i.e, the *ultima ratio*) of the lower law as Maimonides taught (employing the same Aristotelian teleology as did Aquinas).

Nevertheless, natural law alone cannot provide its subjects with their true human fulfillment, not even in this world. That only comes from divine law, and its messianic consummation in the world-beyond (*olam ha-ba*), which must be brought via revelation to the human subjects of natural law. They can never attain it by their own wisdom or by their own virtue. Also, one is not necessarily led from natural law to divine law as one is led from the premise of an argument to its necessary conclusion. Natural law does not entail divine law; instead, natural law always *accompanies* divine law and its traditional interpretation and its practical application, remaining ever intact. It is something like a Kantian *a priori* that always accompanies (*begleitet*) what is given to us in experience *a posteriori*. No *a priori*, however, produces the content of experience;

that must be given as a *datum*. This reasoning (*mutatis mutandis*) is common to Judaism, Christianity, and Islam (the three monotheistic revealed religions) as shown in the 2014 book, *Natural Law: A Jewish, Christian, and Isalmic Trialogue*, which Matthew and I coauthored with our distinguished Muslim colleague Anver Emon. That reasoning (having both theological and philosophical validity) seems to have been ignored by Pope Pius IX, Edgardo Mortara himself (who became a Catholic priest and an anti-Jewish polemicist), and most recently by Romanus Cessario.

Finally, let us now look at how one great mediaeval Jewish theologian-jurist dealt with a similar injustice as that committed by Pius IX in the Mortara case, viz., a case where something done with the letter of the law greatly violated the spirit of the law. Moreover, let me show how this theologian-jurist not only bemoaned this injustice but how he effectively penalized it.

According to the letter of Jewish law (*halakhah*), polygamy is permitted. A Jewish man may marry more than one woman. Nevertheless, around the year 1,000, the Franco-German theologian-jurist Rabbenu Gershom outlawed polygamy. But how could he do that? How could he rescind something the Torah clearly entitled Jews to do? (See, e.g., Deut 21:15–17.) In fact, didn't the patriarchs Abraham and Jacob marry more than one woman? Didn't almost all the kings of Judah and Israel marry more than one woman (in addition to having numerous legitimate concubines)? However, as far as we know, Rabbenu Gershom did not declare polygamous marriages null and void (which he could have done with legal validity). What he did was to excommunicate any Jewish man who contracted more than one marriage for himself. This decree is known as the *herem* or "ban of Rabbenu Gershom." The exact wording of Rabbenu Gershom's ban has not been preserved, and even if it had been, such bans frequently do not inform us of what are the real reasons for their enactment. (Some have speculated, though, that Rabbenu Gershom may have been responding to the contemporary ban on polygamy in Christendom where his community dwelled and, perhaps, he even agreed with its prescription of monogamy as morally and theologically superior.)

As with excommunication in the Catholic tradition, no *herem* can actually expel any Jewish violator of it from "the congregation of Israel," i.e., it cannot turn a Jew into a gentile. As such, Rabbenu Greshom's ban did not expel polygamists from the Jewish people (at least in this world). Indeed, he could not do that since birth or conversion (i.e., *anagenēsis* or "rebirth") into the Jewish people—like baptism—is indelible (Yevamot 24a and 48b). It cannot be erased by humans and, according to the Talmud, even God has promised not to do that to any sinner, at least not in this world (Sanhedrin 44a). No human authority, no matter how exalted and well meaning, can undo what God has done by electing the Jewish people, both collectively and individually, forever (see Isa 54:9–10). In fact, Rabbenu Gershom included polygamists in a ban that usually applied only to apostates. Yet even apostates are not declared to be gentiles, even though the Rabbis believed they would be expelled from what could be called "eschatological

Israel" (i.e., at "the end of days" or the *eschaton*), when most of the Rabbis thought the "righteous gentiles" would be included with "righteous Israel."

What the ban or excommunication does is to remove the excommunicated person from the communal privileges of the covenanted people, such as active participation in synagogue rites, burial in a consecrated Jewish cemetery, or being publicly mourned (i.e., if the excommunicated person has not publicly repented of his or her sin punishable by excommunication). In other words, *communion* with the covenanted community is suspended. Nevertheless, when the excommunicated sinner repents of his or her sin, the community is obligated to take him or her back into the fold immediately, usually after a purification rite has been performed. But if they do not repent before they die, they do not die in what might be called a "state of grace."

In legal terms, what is a valid act *post factum* is still prohibited and penalized for what was done *ab initio* nonetheless. So, now let me suggest what Catholic theologians and canonists might learn from Rabbenu Gershom's prohibition of polygamy and his penalization of polygamists.

Despite the fact that Matthew Levering disagrees with Matthew Tapie's assertion that the baptism of Edgardo Mortara could have been annulled *ipso facto* due to the irregularities in the way it was conducted, he nevertheless agrees with Tapie that this does not justify the act of Edgardo's Catholic nanny, Anna Morisi, in baptizing him without the consent of his Jewish parents who, in fact, would have vigorously opposed it initially as they did retroactively. What Anna Morisi did was in violation of natural law, which she being illiterate, certainly did not know. What Pius IX did, however, was done with full knowledge that he was violating natural law, specifically, the natural rights of Edgardo Mortara's parents to raise their child Jewishly. The Pope was violating the explicit teaching of St. Thomas Aquinas, long called *Doctor Angelicus*.

Therefore, let me suggest that Catholic canonists penalize those performing the baptism of children without the consent (and probable opposition) of their parents. Also, let those who authorize such baptisms, despite the theological validity of the sacramental act itself, themselves be penalized. Perhaps that penalization might only be moral opprobrium, without actual legal consequences. Nevertheless, this could go a long way in discouraging certain fanatics from either using such action as a precedent for present and future action, or from honouring unjust conduct in the past that should be condemned in the present.

As Matthew has honored me by associating me with Thomas Aquinas, let me honor him by associating him with Rabbenu Gershom.

Chapter 9

Giving Justice More Than Its Due[1]

Daniel Philpott

I WISH TO PAY tribute to the extraordinary corpus of writings composed by Rabbi David Novak by offering an argument that intersects with two of his books, one that he subtitles, *A Study in Jewish Political Theory*, and the other that he subtitles, *An Essay in Political Theology*.[2] My argument is one of Christian political theory, and even more so of political theology, for, much like Rabbi Novak's work, it draws from the Bible and from a religious tradition that flows out of the Bible in order to engage the problems of modern political orders. It engages a concept that thinkers as diverse as John Rawls and Thomas Aquinas have thought to be the first virtue of political orders, namely justice. In constitutional liberal democracies around the world today, and in the liberal tradition of thought, justice exalts and pivots around rights. Rights, in turn, are entailed in and owe much to a conception of justice that originated in Roman law and was given great prominence in the Western tradition of thought by Thomas Aquinas: justice defined as the firm and constant will to render another his due.[3] Rights are not the only enduring idea to come from justice as due. Retribution, giving a criminal his due, as well as equality, equity, fairness, respect, and liberty are all entailed in this justice and all have a central place in modern liberal institutions and thought.

Justice as due retains prominence in Christianity as well. The *Catechism of the Catholic Church* defined justice in this way as recently as 1994.[4] Although Rabbi No-

---

1. This essay is adapted, with permission, from Daniel Philpott, "There is a Wideness in God's Justice," *Nova et Vetera*, Vol. 18, No. 4, Fall 2020, pp. 1147–1179.

2. Novak, *The Jewish Social Contract*; and *Covenantal Rights*.

3. The definition is attributed to Ulpian, the second- and third-century Roman jurist, whose writings were compiled by Justinian in his *Digest*, completed in the sixth century. Other medieval Christian scholars, of course, may have preceded Thomas in using this definition. See Wolterstorff, *Justice: Rights and Wrongs*, 22. Aquinas presents the definition in *Summa Theologica* II-II, q. 58, a. 1, co. The version of the *Summa* used in this essay is Aquinas, *Summa Theologica*, trans. Fathers of the English Dominican Province.

4. *Catechism of the Catholic Church*, 1807.

vak does not highlight this definition in his own Jewish thought, he strongly stresses rights and also endorses retribution and other notions entailed in due.

A Christian or a Jew, however, would be justified in suspecting that something is missing in this classic definition of justice, especially insofar as she roots her thinking in both religions' most important source, the Bible. The teaching about justice found there cannot easily be confined to the justice of due and its component concepts. The justice found in the Bible, insofar as one can summarize it, can be called the justice of right relationship, and its hallmarks are its comprehensiveness and its holism. I will argue that it contains rights, retribution, and their siblings, but that it also contains qualities of flourishing and relationship that exceed these components of justice as due. As a result, biblical justice does not admit of dichotomies that the justice of due yields and that typify modern liberalism. Justice as due, in its modern forms, includes rights but excludes virtues like generosity, solidarity, mercy, care, and compassion; contrasts retribution sharply with mercy; focuses on exterior action, not interior motives; and claims to be public while other virtues are private. Biblical justice, by contrast, is wider and encompasses more.

What implications might biblical justice hold for public life? I explore this question briefly at the end of the paper. Here my aim is to describe the Bible's justice of right relationship and to argue that it includes but exceeds the core commitments of justice as due. I pursue this argument in two parallel parts, corresponding to two valences of justice, what I refer to as primary justice, denoting a condition or state of affairs, and rectifying justice, pertaining to past wrongdoing—a distinction I borrow from philosopher Nicholas Wolterstorff.[5] Let us begin with primary justice.

Justice as a State of Right Relationship

Biblical Justice

What most distinguishes biblical justice from the justice of rendering what is due, I argue, is its comprehensive quality. Manifested as primary justice, biblical justice is a holistic state or condition in which people are acting rightly towards one another and towards God.

The argument for this understanding of justice in the Bible begins with the words in Scripture that translate to justice. In the Old Testament, the most common of these words, and the ones that denote the widest range of conduct, are Hebrew terms with the root, *sdq*-, which appear 523 times.[6] Of these, it is *sedeq* and *sedeqah*, masculine and feminine variants of the same term, that translate to justice most often.[7] Appearing across the Old Testament in manifold contexts, these terms pos-

---

5. Wolterstorff, *Justice*, ix–x.
6. Scullion, "Righteousness (OT)," in *The Anchor Bible Dictionary*, 725.
7. Scholars disagree about whether the masculine and feminine forms carry different meanings.

sess a wide semantic range yet share an overarching meaning, which is fidelity to the demands of right relationship in all spheres of life.[8] *Sedeq* and *sedeqah* characterize God's fidelity to his promises to the Israelites and to all of humanity as well as the right conduct of humans in a wide variety of relationships, including between parents and children, merchants and buyers, judges and disputants, kings and subjects, priests and worshippers, people and God, and members of the Jewish community and the widows, orphans, poor, and sojourners among them.[9] Renowned Bible scholar Gerhard von Rad observes that "[t]here is absolutely no concept in the Old Testament with so central a significance for all the relationships of human life as that of *sdqh* . . . . [I]t embraces the whole of Israelite life."[10]

The other major term in the Old Testament that often translates to justice is *mishpat*, which commonly refers to the standards of justice in courtroom procedures but also carries a much wider set of meanings and sometimes denotes right conduct in all spheres, much as *sedeq* and *sedeqah* do.[11] Frequently, *sedeq*/*sedeqah* and *mishpat* appear as a hendiadys, a type of couplet, in which the two words together denote right conduct in the social and political order, often involving a king, as in Isaiah 16:5, "A throne shall be set up in mercy and on it shall sit in fidelity [in David's tent]/ A judge upholding right (*mishpat*) and prompt to do justice (*sedeq*)."[12]

As this last verse shows, it is not only *mishpat*, but also other words such as *hesed* (steadfast love, loyalty), *shalom* (peace), *emet* (truth, fidelity), *tesua* and *yesua* (salvation, saving action), and *rahamin* (mercy) that often parallel, and serve to complement and shape the meaning of, *sedeq* and *sedeqah*.[13] It is primarily *sedeq*, *sedeqah*, and sometimes *mishpat*, though, that mean right conduct in a universal

---

G.A.F. Knight argues that they do, with *sedeqah* referring to something that humans do and *sedeq* referring to the actions of God, in "Is 'Righteous' Right?" 10. Other scholars hold that there is little difference between the terms. Scullion holds this view and offers examples of scholars on both sides of the debate in "Righteousness (OT)," 725. Other *sdq*- words are also important and related to the present argument, for instance, *saddiq*, which means a righteous or just person, and appears often in Psalms and Proverbs.

8. This definition is close to that of Donahue, "Biblical Perspectives on Justice," 69. The case for an overarching meaning of justice is also found in Knierim, *The Task of Old Testament Theology*, 88; Scullion, "Righteousness (OT)," 735; and Koch, "*sdq*," in *Theological Lexicon of the Old Testament*, 1055.

9. See Achtemeier, "Righteousness in the OT," 80–82; and Donahue, "Biblical Perspectives on Justice," 69.

10. von Rad, *Old Testament Theology*, 370, 373.

11. Johnson, "Mishpat," in *Theological Dictionary of the Old Testament*, 89; Scullion, "Righteousness (OT)," 725–26, 735–36.

12. Brackets in original, Hebrew words added. On this hendiadys and its connotations, see Scullion, "Righteousness (OT)," 727–28; and Weinfeld, *Social Justice in Ancient Israel*. Bible quotations in this essay are taken from the New American Bible translation in *The Catholic Study Bible* (Oxford: Oxford University Press, 1990).

13. Scullion, "Righteousness (OT)," 734; Knierim, *The Task of Old Testament Theology*, 86–87.

and comprehensive sense: all of God's ways, and all human conduct performed in fidelity to God's ways.[14]

In the New Testament, the Greek words that translate into justice are ones that share the *dik-* root (*dikaios, dikaioo, dikaiousune,* and *dike*), which appear 302 times. The authors of the Septuagint, the third-century BCE Greek translation of the Old Testament, translated *sedeq* and *mishpat* through *dik-* terms, most prominently *dikaiousune*, which appears ninety-two times and more than any other *dik-* term.[15] *Dik-* words import the meaning of comprehensive right relationship from the Hebrew terms and carry this meaning into the New Testament. *Dikaiousune* appears seven times in the Gospel of Matthew, for instance, where it means acting rightly towards other persons and God in a general sense.[16] It is also prominent in the First Letter of John, where it means the entire set of God's commandments.

To translate these Hebrew and Greek terms into English, scholars have settled mainly on words from two families, one, derived from Latin roots, consisting of *just-* terms (just, justice, justify, justification), the other, stemming from Anglo-Saxon origins, consisting of *right-* terms (right, righteous, righteousness).[17] In each of these families, justice and righteousness are the nouns that express a broad state of relationship and are thus the key terms for the argument at hand. Translators turn to both families of words not only frequently but also fluidly. The words that translate into justice in one version of the Bible will often translate into righteousness in another version. The upshot of their intimately close semantic relationship is that the Bible's justice is virtually synonymous with righteousness and that both mean comprehensive right relationship.[18]

A look at one English translation of the Bible confirms this meaning of justice.[19] Justice describes the character and desires of God, as in Psalm 11:7: "The LORD is just (*sedeqah*) and loves just deeds (*sedeqah*)."[20] Many other verses in the Old Testament aver that the LORD is just, loves justice, rules the world with justice, and is known through his justice.[21] Rabbi Abraham Joshua Heschel writes that justice is "God's stake in history."[22] Several verses in the New Testament likewise describe Jesus as righteous,

---

14. Knierim stresses this universality strongly in *The Task of Old Testament Theology*, 15–16, 86–87.

15. Reumann, "Righteousness (NT)," in *The Anchor Bible Dictionary*, 747.

16. Nardoni, *Rise Up, O Judge*, 217.

17. On these families of English words, see Reumann, "Righteousness (NT)," 746; and Marshall, *Beyond Retribution*, 35–37; Donahue, "The Bible and Catholic Social Teaching," 13–15.

18. Scholars who argue for this interchangeability include Dunn, *The Theology of Paul the Apostle*, 341; Marshall, *Beyond Retribution*, 35–37; Nardoni, *Rise Up, O Judge*, 217, 267; Mattison, *The Sermon on the Mount and Moral Theology*, 32; Haughey, "Jesus as the Justice of God."

19. Again, I use the New American Bible.

20. *ST* I, q. 21, a. 1. Aquinas identifies the Psalm as 10.

21. Deut 32:4; 2 Chr 12:6; Job 34:17; Pss 9:9, 17; 33:5; 50:6; 71:16, 19, 24; 92:16; 116:5; Isa 5:16; 56:1; 61:8; Jer 23:6; 33:16; Rom 3:21; 2 Cor 5:21; 2 Thess 1:6; Rev 15:3.

22. Heschel, *The Prophets*, 198.

or just (*dikaios*), while the Apostle Paul in his First Letter to the Corinthians identifies Jesus with righteousness (denoted by *dikaiousune*, thus meaning also justice) "Christ Jesus . . . became for us . . . righteousness . . . ."[23]

Justice is also the term for the totality of ways in which God desires for people to act in their relationships with one another and towards Him. This is clear in Deuteronomy 16:20: "Justice (*sedeq*) and justice (*sedeq*) alone shall be your aim, that you may have life and possess the land which the LORD, your God, is giving you." In the language of numerous Old Testament verses, justice is walking in the ways or the paths of the LORD, for instance, Proverbs 8:20, "[o]n the way of duty I walk, along the paths of justice."[24] In the Gospel of Matthew, Jesus similarly teaches that justice (often translated righteousness) is that for which the blessed hunger and thirst, for which people are persecuted, which characterizes those who keeps God's commandments, which leads to the kingdom of heaven, and which his followers ought to seek first.[25] Again and again, the Bible speaks of justice as the entirety of the ways in which God's followers are to interact with one another and to form community in fidelity to God. No terms apart from justice and righteousness connote the same entirety.

God promulgates this justice through his covenants, especially those—such as the ones revealed to Moses—through which he communicates commands and promises blessings to those who follow them and curses to those who break them.[26] God's laws, though, are not arbitrary or to be followed merely in response to extrinsic rewards or punishments but rather are the pathway to flourishing, happiness, and holiness. Among the many verses that make this point is Deuteronomy 6:24–25: "Therefore, the LORD commanded us to observe all these statutes in fear of the LORD, our God, that we may always have as prosperous and happy a life as we have today."[27]

For whom does God establish his justice? It was the people of Israel to whom God communicated his justice at Sinai, with all of its precepts, codes, and injunctions, and whom Isaiah names in the verse, "[t]he LORD is exalted, enthroned on high: he fills Zion with right and justice."[28] Other verses, though, especially in the Psalms, speak of judgment or justice with respect to "all living creatures," "all peoples," and "all the nations," indicating all of humanity.[29] Jesus then pronounced justice (or righteousness) as the way of the Kingdom of God, into which he invited all

---

23. Acts 3:14; 7:52; 22:14; 1 Pet 3:18; 1 Cor 1:30; 1 John 2:1; Hoang and Johnson, *The Justice Calling*, 3.

24. See also Gen 18:19; Deut 19:9; 2 Sam 22:33; Pss 5:8; 19:10; 37:34; 81:3; 119:3, 75, 121; 128:1; Mica 4:2; 6:8; Zech 3:7.

25. Matt 5:6, 10, 19–20; 6:33. Nardoni writes that justice in the Gospel of Matthew is "a person's action in obedience to God's will concerning his relationship to others" in Nardoni, *Rise Up, O Judge*, 234.

26. Deut 30; Ps 34:18–20; Wis 3:10, 18; Ps 89:15; Isa 9:6; 16:5; Jer 10:23.

27. Deut 16:20; 30:16; Pss 19:8–12; 33; 35:28; 37:17, 29; 89:16; 106:3; Isa 32:16–17; Hos 2:21.

28. Isa 33:5.

29. Pss 36: 7; 50:6; 97:6; 82:8.

of humanity.³⁰ Wide, too, then—and increasingly wider—is the collection of people invited to participate in God's justice.

Granting the Bible Its Due

Is the holistic justice of the Bible compatible with the justice of rendering another his due? What exactly is the justice of due? It is a justice that features rights, I argue. To make the case that rights is a central meaning of due, I turn to the writings of Thomas Aquinas, who, more than anyone else, propounded and propelled justice as due into historical prominence. Although scholars dispute whether the writings of Aquinas contain rights—the modern subjective kind—I am persuaded that the concept is to be found in the *Summa Theologica*, indeed at the heart of Aquinas's definition of justice, which he presents in Question 58 of the *Secunda Secundae*.³¹ Towards the end of Aquinas's definition are found the words, *ius suum unicuique*, which are often translated to English as "to each his due," but are equally translatable as "to each his right," or "to each what is his by right."³² Just earlier in the same article, he explains, "[h]ence the act of justice in relation to its proper matter and object is indicated by the words, *rendering to each one his right* since, as Isidore says (*Etym. x*), *a man is said to be just because he respects the rights* (jus) *of others*"; and, at the end of the previous article, he writes, "[i]t belongs to justice to render each one his right."³³ In Aquinas's extended discussion of justice, the word *ius* (sometimes written as *jus*), translates directly to "rights" as well as to "law," and by law it means a norm requiring a rendering of what is due or owed.³⁴ *Ius* is synonymous with *suum*, which means "his," as well as a third term that Aquinas often employs, *debitum*, or "debt," which also implies something due or owed.³⁵ In all of these meanings, justice involves actions that render a person what is his, belongs to him, or is owed to him.³⁶ This is

---

30. Matt 5:19–20.

31. *ST* II-II, q. 58, a. 1, co. The interpreters whom I follow most closely on this question include Finnis, *Natural Law and Natural Rights*, 198–230; Finnis, *Aquinas: Moral, Political, and Legal Theory*, 133–38; Porter, *Justice as a Virtue*, 131–46; and Williams, *Who Is My Neighbor? Personalism and The Foundations of Human Rights*, 256–300. Other scholars, however, dispute the presence of (subjective) rights in Aquinas. See, for instance, an exchange involving Brian Tierney, Michael P. Zuckert, Douglas Kries, and John Finnis, "Natural Law and Natural Rights: Old Problems and Recent Approaches," *The Review of Politics* 64, no. 3 (2002): 389–420. Tierney, Zuckert, and Kries (representing Ernest Fortin) take a skeptical view.

32. *ST* II-II, a. 58, a. 1, co. Here I am indebted to the explanation of Williams, *Who Is My Neighbor?* 272.

33. *ST* II-II, q. 58, a. 1, co (italics in the original); *ST* II-II, q. 57, a. 4, ad 1.

34. Finnis, *Aquinas*, 133–35.

35. On this point, see Williams, *Who Is My Neighbor?* 264–65.

36. For the rest of this paragraph, for simplicity's sake, I use the term person, but groups can also claim rights from the beneficiary standpoint or fulfill rights from the standpoint of a performer of an obligation. Sovereign states, for instance, have a right against aggression and a duty not to commit aggression upon other states.

the essence of a right, in which an obligation is viewed from the standpoint of its beneficiary, who may assert rightfully that other people refrain from treating him in certain ways (such as lying, killing, stealing, torturing, or defaming, as in a negative right) or that they provide him with certain goods (such as subsistence, safe working conditions, or the deliverables in a contract, as in a positive right).[37] If the performers of the obligation fail to refrain from the proscribed action or to provide the good in question, then they will have wronged the beneficiary.[38]

Is the justice of due present in the Bible? In some respects, yes. Rights receive mention in several places.[39] These explicit references are sporadic, none is systematic, and, while some of them exude universality, none teaches directly or thoroughly that rights are intrinsic to justice.

A more indirect yet potentially fruitful argument for rights in Scripture is that rights are entailed in natural law, the moral precepts that are known through reason. Voices over the course of the Christian tradition have held that natural law can be found in the Bible, citing Paul's teaching in Romans that the gentiles have the law "written in their hearts" even though God did not reveal it to them, as well as other passages that point to a natural law.[40] A smaller number of voices, many of them scholars influenced by Aquinas, have held, too, that people possess natural rights by virtue of natural duties, for instance, a right to life is a consequence of the proscription of murder.[41] Here again, I only adumbrate arguments—here, about the place of natural rights in natural law—about matters that are and have been disputed in the Christian tradition, doing so with the purpose of showing how the justice of due, understood in terms of rights, need not be at odds with biblical morality.

---

37. Stressing the importance of the standpoint of the beneficiary is Finnis in *Natural Law and Natural Right*, 205. I also concur with Finnis, who follows Wesley Hohfeld, in the view that rights may take the form of claims (negative and positive); liberties; powers; and immunities. In addition, some rights are natural (human) rights, while others are positive, meaning that they are posited by authorities such as legislatures and, except in the case of international law, that they only pertain to a bounded group of people. Thus, the set of beneficiaries and the people who owe them something will be different depending on the right.

38. Bolstering the argument for rights in Aquinas are several places in his writings in which he refers to a right in a specific context, for instance, the right of the poor to take from the rich in cases where they are desperate; the rights of parents to decide whether their children will be baptized; the rights of those accused of crimes; the right of self-defense; the right of entering on one's inherited estate; the right to receive eucharistic communion; the right to receive tithes; and other rights. For a discussion and identification, see Porter, *Justice as a Virtue*, 140–146; Finnis, *Aquinas*, 133–34n.10; and Hering, "De Iure Subjective Sumpto apud S. Thomam."

39. Prov 31:5; Job 36:6; 1 Cor 9:12. For other examples, see Exod 21:8, 10; Lev 25:29, 48; Deut 24:17; Prov 29:7; Isa 5:23; 10:2; Lam 3:35; 1 Cor 9:15, 18.

40. Rom 2:14–15. See Levering, *Biblical Natural Law*, 56–68.

41 See, for instance, Finnis, *Aquinas*, 135–40; Williams, *Who Is My Neighbor?* 292–99; and Maritain, *Man and the State*, 95–97.

Granting the Bible More Than Its Due

But if justice in the Bible includes what is due, it is not exhausted by it. The justice of right relationship also includes duties that do not fulfill what is due, are owed, or correspond to a right. These duties fit the description of what Immanuel Kant called wide (or imperfect) duties, ones that require the promotion of an end but do not specify (or prohibit) the actions that this promotion involves, in contrast with narrow (or perfect) duties, which prohibit either performing or omitting certain actions. Wide duties are open-ended, leaving their performer discretion as to when, where, to what degree, or toward whom they are performed.[42] Wide duties vary in width. The Bible's injunction to love one's neighbor is quite open-ended, including not only negative prohibitions against lying, stealing, and the other misdeeds, but also a duty of beneficence that does not specify who one's neighbor is and how one's neighbor is to be served. Other duties are somewhat less wide, such as the biblical teaching to serve the poor, which narrows somewhat the set of people to be served, yet remains considerably open-ended.

Wide duties do not easily admit of corresponding rights. Let us say that Miriam has an obligation to serve the poor, that is, to discharge a portion of her time and money to assist the poor in addition to her other duties in life. She confronts the reality that her town alone—let alone the entire globe—contains far more poor people than she alone could possibly befriend. Does she volunteer at a homeless shelter? Tutor children? Give to a charity that promotes economic development in Bangalore, India? Her capacities are adequate only to a tiny portion of the world's needs. It would be strange to say that any one person—say a poor person in Bangalore—has a right to Miriam's resources, implying that Miriam would be committing a wrong if she did not help this particular person. She has a duty to serve the poor, but which poor is at her discretion.

The justice of right relationship does not deny that the poor have rights—to subsistence, basic forms of care, housing, and safe working conditions, for instance.[43] Still less does it deny that all persons have rights—natural rights, human rights—which arise from their dignity. The justice of right relationship, though, is not confined to rights. Miriam and the society of which she is a part are obliged to promote the cause of the poor beyond what the poor claim a right to.

---

42. Kant, *The Metaphysics of Morals*, 194; for a good explanation of Kant's distinction, see Donagan, *The Theory of Morality*, 154.

43. It may also be the case that there are situations in which the poor, or, more broadly, those in need, have rights to care from other individuals. One might argue that if an individual person comes into close proximity to another person in great distress, then the distressed person has a right to the able person's care. For instance, a capable swimmer may pass by a lake where a person is drowning and be obligated to rescue him. These situations demand more treatment than I can give here. My broader argument is that a poor person in general does not have the right to any other particular individual's assistance. Any particular individual's duties towards the poor are in good part open-ended, that is, unspecified by the rights of the poor alone.

Duties of justice correspond with rights most plausibly when the duties are specified in their actions and their criteria for fulfillment. Most negative human rights (immunities) meet these criteria. The right not to be murdered, tortured, or have one's property stolen is honored when people refrain from murder, torture, and stealing. Many positive rights (entitlements) pass muster, too, most clearly those that are specified by a contract—a creditor's right to be paid as promised, for instance—but also certain human rights like subsistence and safe working conditions.[44] As duties grow wider, however, it becomes less plausible to associate them with a right. What would it mean that everyone has a right to the love of one's neighbor? The justice of right relationship, then, contains duties that correspond with rights—and with what is owed or due—but also duties that do not because they are wide, or open-ended.

The same is true of biblical justice, which is not limited to rights but also entails wide duties to promote the well-being of others. Much of the Bible's teachings on justice are directed towards the poor, condemning abuses and deprivations in language that involve or may imply rights, but also calling for a positive alleviation of their plight, an open-ended duty.[45] Deuteronomy 15:7 teaches, "[i]f one of your kinsmen in any community is in need in the land which the Lord, your God, is giving you, you shall not harden your heart nor close your hand to him in his need." Nardoni comments that in Deuteronomy, relationships between rich and poor are determined "not just on the basis of principles of commutative and distributive justice, but primarily on the basis of a beneficent justice, suffused with a compassionate love in imitation of the love of God towards Israel."[46] When Jesus tells his disciples in Matthew 25 that when they see the hungry, the thirsty, the naked, the ill, and the imprisoned, they are seeing him, he is commanding a wide commitment to the poor, one that has no strict boundaries.[47]

Some of the Bible's commandments to assist the poor appear to fly in the face of rights. To honor the Jubilee Year, that is, to free one's slaves and cancel debts, is to forego one's rights, as does following the injunction to continue to loan to the poor as the Jubilee Year approaches and repayment becomes unlikely.[48] The injunction that farmers leave gleanings in their fields for the poor at the time of harvest appears to be a commandment of generosity. In several places, the Bible commands the Israelites to protect and assist the vulnerable among them on the grounds that

---

44. This is not to deny that virtually any right requires some degree of specification. The right not to be tortured, for instance, raises the question of what constitutes torture, one that was hotly disputed in the United States in the 2000s in the context of combatting terrorism. Many positive rights—to subsistence and to health care, for instance—require a specification of what kind and how much.

45. On this point, see Deede and Hoang *The Justice Calling*, 92.

46. Nardoni, *Rise Up, O Judge*, 84–85.

47. Other verses that stress a generalized commitment to the poor include, among others, Deut 10:18–19; 15:7–11; Pss 9b:12–18; 72:4, 12; 82; 103:6; Prov 31:9; Isa 1:17; 11:4; Jer 22:16.

48. Deut 15:1–4, 9–11.

they ought to show gratitude that God delivered them from vulnerability, not on the grounds that the vulnerable have rights.[49]

The Book of Sirach explicitly teaches that almsgiving is an act of righteousness (and thus justice). Commenting on this teaching, Bible scholar Gary A. Anderson explains that almsgiving is a mode of laying up treasures in heaven. Jesus then discusses almsgiving as a "righteous deed" in the Sermon on the Mount and promises heavenly reward for it, at least when it is performed without fanfare. Jesus does not specify, though, the poor people toward whom one should direct alms or how much one ought to give them, and he indicates no limits to the treasure that can be stored up in heaven.[50] Almsgiving is a duty of justice, but a wide one.

Above, I argued that the righteousness and justice of the Bible enfold other virtues that direct people towards others. Some of these are wide. One of them is mercy, which Aquinas defines as "heartfelt sympathy for another's distress, impelling us to succor him if we can." A merciful action is driven by this sympathy and alleviates distress caused either by sin or by unmerited suffering.[51] The latter sort is most relevant to primary justice. The Bible calls for mercy, as in Micah, where mercy is associated with justice: "[D]o the right (*mishpat*) and . . . love goodness [or mercy], and . . . walk humbly with your God," and as in the Gospel of Luke, where Jesus commands, "[b]e merciful, just as [also] your Father is merciful."[52] Other virtues enumerated in the Bible like compassion and generosity are similarly wide. So, too, is solidarity, which has emerged as an explicit virtue more recently in the Christian tradition and means identification with the suffering of every other person, much as Jesus taught in the parables of the Good Samaritan and of the Rich Man and Lazarus.[53]

Justice as the Restoration of Right Relationship

The argument with respect to rectifying justice runs parallel to that for primary justice: the justice of right relationship, whose main source is the Bible, includes but exceeds the justice of rendering another his due. In rectifying justice, the most plausible meaning of due is retribution, the infliction of hardship upon a perpetrator as a payment for his crime in accordance with the rule of law and standards of proportionality. A perpetrator receives his due or pays his debt, thus receiving retribution.

With respect to rectifying justice, the justice of right relationship is also comprehensive, involving a holistic restoration of right relationship. It can involve retributive punishment but also grants people what they do not deserve. Rectifying

49. See, for example, Deut 10:18–19.

50. Anderson, *Charity: The Place of the Poor in the Biblical Tradition*, 132; Matt 6:1.

51. *ST* II-II, q. 30, a. 1.

52. Mic 6:8. In other versions of this verse, right is translated as justice (or act justly) and goodness is translated as mercy. Luke 6:36.

53. See John Paul II, *Solicitudino Rei Socialis,* 1987; Grisez, *Living a Christian Life,* 342.

justice converges with mercy insofar as mercy addresses what has been ruptured by wrongdoing, not just misfortune. In Pope John Paul II's encyclical of 1980, *Dives in Misericordia* (paragraph 6), he defines mercy consistently with Aquinas's definition yet accents this virtue's holistic, restorative character: "mercy is manifested in its true and proper aspect when it restores to value, promotes and draws good from all the forms of evil existing in the world and in man." If mercy characterizes action that wills to restore all that evil has sundered, then it is much the same as the justice that restores right relationship.

This justice is also manifested through forgiveness, which instantiates mercy. Forgiveness in the Bible is not merely the relinquishment of wrath, anger, or resentment, but it also seeks the restoration of relationship. God forgives the people of Israel in order to restore his covenant with them in the Old Testament and forgives all of humanity in a New Covenant so it may live in friendship with God in the New Testament. The forgiveness that the Bible teaches people to practice towards one another is also directed towards the restoration of right relationship. In the story of the Prodigal Son, for instance, the father forgives the dissolute son in order to receive him back into the family. Forgiveness, like mercy, is not owed to the perpetrator of a wrong, yet manifests justice.[54]

In both the Old and the New Testament can be seen a justice that includes but also is wider than retribution and that involves a holistic restoration of right relationship.

God's Saving Justice in The Old Testament

Aquinas uses the term original justice to describe what he calls the primitive state, or the Garden of Eden.[55] He describes it as perfect rectitude and right order; it is the justice of right relationship. Then came sin, which violates the justice of right relationship, whose norms are not extrinsic to, but rather furthering of, flourishing and fullness of being. The Bible then proceeds to recount a long series of descents into sin and acts of restoration on the part of God. God renews the world after the great flood in Genesis; delivers the Israelites from Pharaoh (whose sin he punishes); forgives the Israelites after they build a golden calf; liberates Israel from exile in Babylon; and definitively redeems humanity through Jesus Christ. Several times, in the wake of

---

54. Here, I partially disagree with Grisez, whom I follow in holding that forgiveness manifests mercy, which is the justice of God's kingdom. Thus, it appears that Grisez holds that forgiveness manifests God's justice, and here again, I follow him. But Grisez then argues that the duty of forgiveness, arising from the mercy that God has shown humanity, implies that sinners have a right to be forgiven by fellow sinners. I would argue, by contrast, that while Christians have a duty to forgive, sinners do not have a corresponding right to be forgiven. Rather, just as Christians have been forgiven by God without their deserving it, so, too, they ought to forgive those who wrong them without their deserving it. This is the message of the parable of the unforgiving servant in Matt 18:23–35, I believe. See Grisez, *Living a Christian Life*, 362–67.

55. *ST* I-II, q. 82, a. 1, ad 1; *ST* I-II, q. 85, a. 1, co.

sin, God establishes covenants, as he did with Noah, Abraham, and Moses and the Israelites, and as Jesus Christ did with all of humanity.

The Bible frequently uses the language of justice to describe God's act of restoration. Psalm 103:6–7, for instance, describes God's "mighty deeds" of deliverance for Moses and Israel in the language of justice and righteousness. Justice meaning deliverance is most pronounced in Second Isaiah, which addresses the people of Israel during their exile in Babylon and promises return. Referring to a messianic figure, Isaiah announces, "Here is my servant whom I uphold, my chosen one with whom I am pleased, upon whom I have put my spirit; he shall bring forth justice (*mishpat*) to the nations," and a few verses later, "I, the LORD, have called you for the victory of justice (*sedeq*)."[56] Several times, God's justice is equated with salvation, as in Isaiah 45:21: "There is no just (*sedeq*) and saving God but me."[57] As Pope St. John Paul II wrote in *Dives in Misericordia*, "to the psalmists and prophets . . . the very term justice ended up by meaning the salvation accomplished by the Lord and His mercy."[58]

Justice is not only the action through which God restores his people but also the condition to which God restores his people. God would make Jerusalem, "the city of righteousness, the faithful city."[59] The restored people is also characterized by peace, calm, security, prosperity, and the rectification of the plight of the poor: land is restored, debts are canceled, wrongs are redressed, orphans and widows are protected and provided for, the lame walk, and the blind receive sight.[60]

The scriptures in Isaiah and other books of the Bible speak of God's saving justice as faithfulness to his covenant but not as something that God owes Israel. God's decisions to restore Israel are ones of love, mercy, and *hesed*, or faithfulness to his covenant.

And what of retribution? There is plenty of punishment in the Old Testament. Sometimes sinners are punished intrinsically, by suffering the consequences of their sin, and sometimes extrinsically, through being punished by another party, usually the political authorities, God, or some agent of punishment that God has deployed such as a conquering nation. Retribution reflects the extrinsic logic, for to say that punishment is due implies that one party applies it to another, the one to whom it is due.

In the Old Testament, retribution resides in covenants in which God couples commandments with blessings for obedience and curses for disobedience—most prominently, the covenant given at Sinai. When the Israelites and others sin, curses come. Isaiah 60:18 puts it starkly—"[The LORD] repays his enemies their deserts, and

---

56. Isa 42:1; 42:6–7. Other verses speaking of God's restorative action as justice include Deut 32:4–14; Judg 5:11; Ps 40: 10–11; Isa 11:4–5; 45:8, 13, 19, 21, 25; Isa 54:14.

57. See also Isa 46:12–13; 51:5, 8, and 56:1.

58. *Dives in Misericordia*, 4.

59. Isa 1:26–27.

60. Isa 40:17–20.

requites his foes with wrath" and many other verses indicate or describe retribution.[61] The *lex talionis*—an eye for an eye, etc.—also expresses the idea of punishment as repayment.[62] Sometimes God destroys people and entire groups of people for their sin.[63] He inflicts punishment through natural phenomena—frogs, boils, gnats, flies, earthquakes, famine, and the like.[64] Many times, retribution is associated with the language of justice and judgment.[65]

Retribution, though, is only a portion of the Bible's rectifying justice. Equally noteworthy as the episodes of requiting are those in which God does not mete out the punishment that sinners deserve. God foregoes punishment; promises it and then withdraws; applies punishment partially and then ceases; withholds punishment when his people repent, as with the city of Nineveh;[66] and relents in response to pleas for mercy, as God did for Moses after the Israelites worshipped a golden calf.[67] Psalm 103:8–10 expresses this restraint most directly: "Merciful and gracious is the LORD, slow to anger, abounding in kindness. God does not always rebuke, nurses no lasting anger, [has] not dealt with us as our sins merit, nor requited us as our deeds deserve." The Bible describes other restorative measures, too, including Israel's return from exile and a renewal of the land itself. Kings, too, perform a restorative justice, as Bible scholar Moshe Weinfeld comments: "[f]orgiveness and amnesty on the part of the ruler is called *doing righteousness and justice*."[68] Finally, retribution is challenged not merely by the waiving of deserved punishment but also from the other direction through harsh punishment that confounds retributivism's prized principle of proportionality, as when God orders Saul to destroy the Amelekites, including "men and women, children and infants."[69]

While retribution is only a portion of the Bible's wide rectifying justice, it fits the character of justice as the restoration of right relationship. Retributive punishment involves a payment but not one that is abstracted from God's renewal of his covenant. Deuteronomy repeats the phrase, "[s]o you shall purge the evil from your midst," indicating that punishment has a purifying aim.[70] This, of course, does not imply the compatibility of the Bible's full range of penalties, including the prescription of

---

61. Ps 9:8, 11; 34; 37:9; 58:12; 62:12; Job 34:11; Prov 10:16; 24:12; Eccl 12:14; Isa 3:10–11; 59:18; Jer 17:10; 25:14; 32:19; Lam 3:64; Hos 4:9.

62. Exod 21:24; Lev 24:19–22; Deut 19:21.

63. See, for instance, Deut 7:4; 9:8; 19; 25; Num 16:21; Ezek 22:31; 43:8.

64. For the plagues (frogs, etc.), see Exod 7–11; for earthquakes, see Isa 29:26 and Amos 8:8; for famine, see Ezek 5:12, 16. I have benefitted in this paragraph from the interpretation of Marshall, *Beyond Retribution*, 121–22.

65. See, for instance, Ps 34.

66. John 3:19.

67. Deut 32:14.

68. Weinfeld, *Social Justice in Ancient Israel*, 11, italics in original.

69. 1 Sam 15:3.

70. Deut 13:6; 17:7, 12; 19:19; 21:21; 22:21, 22, 24; 24:7.

the death penalty for a wide variety of sins, with contemporary Christian ethics. The point is rather that biblical retributive punishment has a restorative purpose, in contrast to the retributivism of Immanuel Kant, who, zealously distinguishing his ethics of duty from any form of eudaimonism, insisted that punishment take place for principle alone apart from any consequences for the well-being of the perpetrator or others affected by the crime.[71] In the Old Testament, retributive punishment is one of several measures involved in the justice through which God purifies and restores the people and communities he has created, most of all the people of Israel. No coherent theory describes these measures except that all aim to restore right relationship and perform God's faithfulness to his covenant.

God's Saving Justice in the New Testament

Bible scholar N. T. Wright argues that Jesus's death and resurrection are the climax of Israel's story of God's saving justice.[72] Jesus proclaims his mission of saving justice in the Gospel of Matthew, where he directly identifies himself with the servant of Isaiah who "brings justice to victory."[73] Similarly, Jesus's words to John the Baptist that he would "fulfill all righteousness (*dikaiousune*)," signal not only his clarification and deepening of God's law but also his forthcoming saving action.[74] Likewise, when Paul writes in First Corinthians that Jesus became righteousness, he places this quality in a series with sanctification and redemption, signifying that righteousness is saving justice.[75] Then, the First Letter of John holds that "[i]f we acknowledge our sins, he is faithful and just and will forgive our sins and cleanse us from every wrongdoing," where the word just (*dikaios*) implies the saving actions of forgiveness and renewal.[76] Finally, Paul uses *dikaiousune* in his letter to the Romans, when he writes "for in [the gospel] is revealed the righteousness (*dikaiousune*) of God,"[77] and, similarly, when he expounds:

> But now the righteousness (*dikaiousune*) of God has been manifested apart from the law, though testified to by the law and the prophets, the righteousness (*dikaiousune*) of God through faith in Jesus Christ for all who believe. For there is no distinction; all have sinned and are deprived of the glory of

71. Kant, *The Metaphysics of Morals*, 140, 141, 168.

72. See, among Wright's many works, *Evil and the Justice of God*, 75–100.

73. Matt 12:20. The reference in Isaiah is 42:6, "I, the LORD, have called you for the victory of justice," where the word for justice is *sedeq*. Matthew renders justice as *krisis*, rather than *dikaiousune*, in presenting Jesus's quote of Isaiah. *Krisis* means judgment, though a judgment is always in accord with justice.

74. Matt 3:15. Nardoni comments that the verse refers back to messianic verses, Ps 2:7 and Isa 42:1, in *Rise Up, O Judge*, 231. See also Reumann, "Righteousness (NT)," 755.

75. 1 Cor 1:30.

76. 1 John 1:9.

77. Rom 1:17.

God. They are justified (*dikaioo*) freely by his grace through the redemption in Christ Jesus, whom God set forth as an expiation, through faith, by his blood, to prove his righteousness (*dikaiousune*) because of the forgiveness of sins previously committed, through the forbearance of God—to prove his righteousness (*dikaiousune*) in the present time, that he might be righteous (*dikaios*) and justify the one who has faith in Jesus.[78]

Righteousness here, is the saving action of Jesus Christ—and so, then, is justice.[79]

How does Jesus Christ perform this saving justice, the justice that restores right relationship? There is both a negative and a positive dimension to the action, both expressed in an important verse in First Corinthians that describes Christ's reconciliation of humanity to himself: "For our sake [God] make him to be sin who did not know sin, so that we might become the righteousness (*dikaiousune*) of God."[80]

First, the negative side of Christ's justice is that he forgives sin and takes it away from humanity through his sacrifice on the cross. "This is my blood of the new covenant, which will be shed on behalf of many for the forgiveness of sins," he tells his disciples at the last supper.[81] His sacrifice is also conveyed by John the Baptist, who describes him as the "Lamb of God, who takes away the sins of the world."[82]

The positive side of Christ's justice is his actual restoration of justice in people who follow him: "that we might become the righteousness of God." Through the cross and resurrection, Christ not only takes away sin but also, in triumphing over death and being restored to fullness of life by the Father, invites people to join in this restoration and thereby become just themselves—a "new creation," as Paul puts it in Second Corinthians.[83]

The positive, restorative, work of justice is consummated at the Last Judgment. "[W]e await new heavens and a new earth in which righteousness (*dikaiousune*) dwells," says the Second Letter of Peter (3:13), indicating, first, that it is *dikaiousune*—righteousness, or justice—that will prevail, and second, that the heavens and the earth will be made new in an actual restoration. The *Catechism of the Catholic Church* echoes that "[t]he Last Judgment will reveal that God's justice triumphs over all the injustices committed by his creatures."[84]

The saving character of justice and its positive and negative sides come together in justification, Paul's most important concept for describing what Christ accomplished through his death and resurrection. Taking issue with Wright's view that justification

---

78. Rom 3:21–26.

79. Nardoni argues just this in *Rise Up, O Judge*, 281; as do Dunn and Suggate in *The Justice of God: A Fresh Look at the Old Doctrine of Justification by Faith*, 35.

80. 1 Cor 5:21.

81. Matt 26:28.

82. John 1:29.

83. 2 Cor 5:17.

84. *Catechism of the Catholic Church*, 1040.

is God's bestowal of "not guilty" status upon the sinner according to Paul's metaphor of the courtroom, Bible scholar Thomas Stegman argues that justification includes not only acquittal but also a bestowal of grace that transforms the sinner interiorly—the historic position of the Catholic Church.[85] In several passages in Paul's letters, he holds that Christ's passion and justification bestow transforming grace.[86] In justification, then, God restores right relationship not only by coming to look upon the sinner as one no longer guilty but also in regenerating the sinner—both the negative and positive movements of saving justice.

Justification, the justice that saves and that restores right relationship, is shaped by the divine charity that initiates the salvation that takes place through the incarnation, cross, and resurrection. It is also equivalent to mercy, the quality of actions that will to restore. In the Gospels, Jesus foretells the mercy that he will accomplish in his passion, for instance, in the story of the prodigal son, while other books of the New Testament also describe his passion in terms of mercy.[87]

Saving justice is a gift, not something owed. Paul stresses in his Letter to the Romans that Christ died for us "while we were still sinners," not after first demanding that humans pay up for their sins, that sinners "are justified freely by his grace," and that Jesus Christ is a "gracious gift."[88] The *Catechism* likewise speaks of "God's gratuitous justice."[89] Out of love, the Father sends the Son to bring about justice to which humanity did not have a right, was not owed, and was not due.

Does this mean that due has no place in God's saving justice? Let us turn again to Thomas Aquinas, who helps us to see that retribution has a part, but is not the whole, of this justice.

Thomas Aquinas and the Place of Due in Rectifying Justice

Aquinas accepts the major features of saving justice in the Bible. This is clear in all that he says about God's justification of humanity through Christ: that justification is itself an act of justice;[90] that it involves not only a remission of sin but also an infu-

---

85. Stegman, "Paul's Use of Dikaio-Terminology: Moving Beyond N. T. Wright's Forensic Interpretation." N.T. Wright expresses his view in *Justification: God's Plan and Paul's Vision*.

86. In addition to 2 Cor 5:14–21, Stegman focuses on 2 Cor 1:18–22; Gal 2:15–21; Phil 3:7–11; Rom 1:17; 3:21–26; 5:1–11, 15–21; 6:10–19; 8:28–30; 12:1—15:13.

87. See, for instance, Rom 11:30–32; 15:6; Eph 2:4–7; Titus 3:5; 1 Pet 2:10; 1:3–5; Jude 1:21.

88. Rom 3:24; 4:4, 16; 5:8, 15, 17.

89. *Catechism of the Catholic Church*, 2009.

90. *ST* I, q. 21, a. 4, a. 1.; *ST* II-II, q. 58, a. 2., co, *ST* III, q. 1, a. 2, co.

sion of grace;[91] that this grace makes the sinner just, both in his actions and in his soul;[92] and that this justice is a gift.[93]

Is there any sense in which Aquinas views the justice by which God saved humanity as involving due—retribution, payment, something owed? Yes, there is. A century-and-a-half before Aquinas wrote the *Summa Theologica*, Anselm of Canterbury wrote *Cur Deus Homo?* in order to explain the incarnation, including the reasons for Christ's death. Anselm reasons that humanity incurred debt for its sin that it could not repay. God, who wished to be faithful to what he had created, sent his Son to redeem (a word connoting payment) humanity through a sacrifice that would be pleasing to God. God's act involved both justice insofar as it repaid what was owed and mercy insofar as God, rather than humanity, paid the debt, Anselm argues.

In the Third Part of the *Summa*, Aquinas takes up Anselm's argument and makes the case that payment of debt is an important part of how Christ's passion is to be understood. He argues that humanity's sin has incurred debt, which holds humanity in bondage, and that this is a matter of justice. Christ's sacrifice redeemed humanity from this debt, and this was an act of justice.[94] Aquinas's use of the language of debt, price, payment, and redemption find support in certain passages in the New Testament.[95]

Still, while Aquinas indisputably employs the logic of justice as due with respect to rectifying justice, in certain ways his argument does not follow the logic of retribution. Contrary to Anselm, Aquinas holds that God would not have acted unjustly had God chosen instead to save humanity without a rendering of satisfaction. God could have accomplished salvation otherwise. Unlike a human judge, who cannot rightly waive what one person owes another, God would have wronged no-one in forgiving humanity without demanding payment, much like a person who waives a wrong committed only against himself.[96] Aquinas, then, retains the notion that humanity owed a debt—the logic of due—but he does not invoke a requirement that the debt be paid or that a penalty be incurred, as a retributivist does. God could have waived the debt justly. Even still, he proceeds to argue that Christ's sacrifice was nonetheless a fitting way to restore humanity—not necessary, yet most suitable for a range of reasons.

---

91. *ST* I, q. 21, a. 4, a. 1.; *ST* I-II, q. 100, a. 12, co.

92. *ST* II-II, q. 58, a. 2, ad 1; *ST* I-II, q. 113. a. 1, co. See Levering, *Christ's Fulfillment of Torah and Temple*, 120.

93. *ST* III, q. 46, a. 1, ad 3.

94. *ST* III, q. 48, a. 4, co, and a. 5, co; *ST* III, q. 49., a. 1, co; *ST* III, q. 50, a. 1, co.

95. Several verses speak of Christ as ransoming humanity from its sins. It is an ambiguous metaphor since it is not clear to whom the ransom is being paid. Still, it implies a payment. See Mark 10:45; Matt 20:28; Mark 10:45; Gal 3:13; 4:5; 1 Tim 2:6; 1 Pet 1:18; 2 Pet 2:1. An example of a passage where Aquinas uses the word ransom can be found at *ST* III, q. 48, a. 4. In two other places, the Scriptures speak of Christ's sacrifice as a price paid: 1 Cor 6:20; 1 Cor 7:23.

96. *ST* III, q. 46, a. 2, ad 3.

Aquinas makes another argument, this one in agreement with Anselm, that does not square neatly with retribution, which is that "[b]y suffering out of love and obedience, Christ gave more to God than was required to compensate for the offense of the whole human race." Because Christ's passion was "superabundant," it exceeded what was due.[97]

Departing from retribution still more is the vicariousness of Christ's sacrifice. Retributivists insist that a penalty be paid by the one who committed the wrong, a principle that retributivists tout for protecting the innocent as well as directing justice to the guilty. But Christ, an innocent man, paid humanity's debt in its stead. Anselm calls this mercy, but it also confounds justice, understood as rendering a wrongdoer her due. Pope Benedict XVI made the point in his Lenten Message of 2010:

> [W]hat kind of justice is this where the just man dies for the guilty and the guilty receives in return the blessing due to the just one? Would this not mean that each one receives the contrary of his "due"? In reality, here we discover divine justice, which is so profoundly different from its human counterpart.

In Christ's divine justice, he did not give wrongdoers their due but rather forgave them.

Finally, Christ's rendering of satisfaction for debt through his sacrifice is only one of several ways that Aquinas cites in which Christ's passion was fitting. The New Testament contains a host of terms and metaphors to explain how the cross and resurrection achieved salvation, and theologians have proffered manifold theories in the centuries since. Anselm's theory of satisfaction was one of these theories, but only one. Prior to him, virtually no Christian thinker had given satisfaction of debt such a central place. Another medieval scholar, Peter Abelard, reacted against what he saw as the harsh transactional character of Anselm's account and emphasized instead Christ's loving initiative and the charity that it inspires in those who would follow him. Aquinas weaves both accounts into his own, stressing not only satisfaction but also Christ's example of virtue, which inspires charity, excites hope of rising from the dead, and delivers humanity from fear of death. Recall as well Aquinas's strong affirmation that Christ's cross and resurrection yield grace that transforms those who place faith in him.[98] Not at all is his view one of mere mercantile exchange. The payment of what is due is a part, but only a part, of Aquinas's account of God's saving action, which is in turn, the justice of restoring right relationship that the Bible describes. In Aquinas, as in the Bible, saving justice is wider than the justice that renders what is due.

---

97. *ST* III, q. 48, a. 2, co.

98. *ST* III, q. 53, a. 1, co. For an interpretation of Aquinas that stresses both satisfaction and restoration, see Cessario, *The Godly Image*, 148–49.

Connections and Implications

My argument is simple, despite its complex parts: The justice of right relationship, found primarily in the Bible, includes but exceeds the justice of rendering another her due. With respect to primary justice, the justice of right relationship includes rights but also wide duties. With respect to rectifying justice, the justice of right relationship includes retribution but also other forms of restoring right relationship.

The argument intersects with the work of Rabbi Novak in several ways and thus carries potential for dialogue between Christian and Jews. Much like Novak's political theology, it aims to retrieve a way of thinking about social and political life from the Bible and bring it into conversation with contemporary politics and political thought. The Bible is not the whole of either the Jewish or the Christian tradition but is its most important source and part of it is shared entirely by the two traditions. The concept of justice as right relationship, I contend, can be grounded in both the Old Testament, or Hebrew Bible, as well as the New Testament, and thus might elicit the assent of Christians and Jews.

These scriptural roots are important, for Novak maintains that a Christian or Jew ought to participate in modern democracy not from "nowhere" or from a standpoint of putative neutrality, as Enlightenment thinkers would have it, but rather out of fidelity to God's covenants. Novak's political thought is a model of this approach. To be sure, he is committed to participate in—and enter a social contract with—modern liberal democracy. By historical standards, Jews have fared well under such regimes of equal citizenship, he points out. Yet they participate in these regimes out of fidelity to God's covenant and look to this covenant to ground their contributions to public life. Indeed, Novak argues that if law and government are not grounded in the sacred realm, they are prone to become unlimited and tyrannical.[99]

Novak brings these same commitments to rights, which he believes are a critically important feature of modern political orders. He rejects the narrative, propounded by political philosophers of several stripes, that rights emerged only when religion was sidelined from political discourse by Enlightenment thinkers. Not only do rights have earlier, and religious, roots, but they are also grounded far more strongly in God's covenants than they are in a social contract, notions of moral creativity, or personal autonomy. Here again, Jews not only benefit from rights in modern democracies but they also offer rights a grounding that secular outlooks cannot provide.[100]

While I am in deep sympathy—and indebted to—Rabbi Novak's political theology, my argument about justice differs from his views in certain particulars. I have argued that biblical justice consists of duties that correspond with rights as well as those that do not, whereas I understand Novak to argue in *Covenantal Rights* that justice consists entirely of rights claims and their corresponding duties. In the same book, Novak argues

---

99. *Jewish Social Contract*, 9; *Covenantal Rights*, 28–30.
100. *Covenantal Rights*, x, 10–12, 24–32.

that "every duty has a correlative right, just as every right has a correlative duty," while my view is that some duties do not correlate with rights, just as some aspects of justice towards past wrongs do not correlate with retribution.[101] The justice of right relationship, rooted in the Bible, I argue, is wider than the justice of due.

That this justice is wider does not mean that it is better. Its width is exactly what worries many of today's defenders of due, especially in the liberal tradition. The full normative argument for this justice is beyond the reach of this essay. It is an argument that is worth pursuing, though, for the meaning of justice carries implications for public life.[102]

In broad outline, the argument for biblical justice would contend that such justice overcomes some of the dichotomies associated with the justice of rendering due, especially in its modern liberal incarnation, mentioned in the introduction to this essay.

Against the claim that justice is limited to rights, retribution, and principles linked closely with rights like equality, equity, fairness, and liberty, biblical justice includes wide duties associated with mercy, care, compassion, and the common good. Biblical justice finds an ally in contemporary care feminist theorists who call for a justice that extends beyond rights and includes wide duties to care for the vulnerable.[103]

Against the claim that justice is concerned only with right external action, biblical justice includes right motives and interior virtue. The Scriptures refer to certain persons as "just" or "righteous" to indicate that their heart and their soul are rightly directed to God and to others.

Against the claim that justice is public while other virtues associated with wide duties are apposite only for personal life or civil society, biblical justice encompasses the whole of human interactions and admits of no sharp division between those aspects that are appropriate for politics and those that are not.

Against the claim that peace is a cessation of hostilities and that justice is a separate development, biblical justice understands peace, which the Bible renders most familiarly as *shalom*, as a condition of holistic right relationship, little different from the justice of right relationship conveyed by *sedeq*. A collection of contemporary Christian ethicists place this conception of peace—which one of them has termed "justpeace"—at the center of their thinking about social ethics.[104]

Against the claim that mercy is separate from justice, stands in tension with justice, and means clemency, as when a judge foregoes or reduces punishment, biblical justice envisions mercy as something far wider—the will to restore all that is

---

101. *Covenantal Rights*, 10, 16.

102. For an exploration of biblical justice conceived as "civic righteousness," see Carlson, "Rights versus Right Order."

103. For a Catholic expression of this view, see Schiltz, "West, MacIntyre, and Wojtyla."

104. See, for instance, Lederach and Appleby, "Strategic Peacebuilding: An Overview"; Grisez, *Living a Christian Life*, 371.

broken—and converging with the justice that restores right relationship. Forgiveness, an expression of mercy, and reconciliation join in this same justice. Political orders who have confronted the past evils of genocide, civil war, and dictatorship in the past generation—South Africa, Germany, Chile, and many others—have frequently hosted a debate between advocates for the restoration of right-based liberal democracy and judicial punishment for war criminals on one hand, and voices, many of them from Christian churches, proposing reconciliation, mercy and forgiveness, on the other. A similarly conceived "restorative justice" has been applied to criminal justice in western countries. While biblical justice does not necessarily reject rights and criminal punishment, it enfolds other measures that make it more holistic.[105]

Thus adumbrated, this defense of biblical justice might be developed elsewhere. Critics will demand a clarification of the meaning of this justice for institutions and policy, its compatibility with the limited government of constitutional liberal democracy, and the respective roles of religion and state. For Christians and Jews who believe that the Bible communicates "divinely revealed realities," as the Second Vatican Council document *Dei Verbum* puts it, the pursuit of this defense must not be shunned.

Bibliography

Achtemeier, Elizabeth. "Righteousness in the OT." In *The Interpreter's Dictionary of the Bible*, vol. 4, edited by G. A. Buttrick, 80–82. Nashville: Abingdon, 1962.

Anderson, Gary A. *Charity: The Place of the Poor in the Biblical Tradition*. New Haven, CT: Yale University Press, 2013.

Aquinas, Thomas. *Summa Theologica*. Translated by Fathers of the English Dominican Province. 5 vols. Notre Dame, IN: Ave Maria, 1948.

Carlson, John D. "Rights versus Right Order: Two Theological Traditions of Justice and Their Implications for Christian Ethics and Pluralistic Politics." *Journal of the Society of Christian Ethics* 36 (2016) 79–100.

Catechism of the Catholic Church. 2nd ed. Vatican City: Libreria Editrice Vaticana, 1997.

Cessario, Romanus. *The Godly Image: Christ and Salvation in Catholic Thought from St. Anslem to Aquinas*. Petersham, MA: St. Bede's, 1989.

Donagan, Alan. *The Theory of Morality*. Chicago: The University of Chicago Press, 1977.

Donahue, John R. "The Bible and Catholic Social Teaching: Will This Engagement Lead to Marriage?" In *Modern Catholic Social Teaching: Commentaries and Interpretations*, edited by Kenneth F. Himes, 9–40. Washington, DC: Georgetown University Press, 2005.

———. "Biblical Perspectives on Justice." In *The Faith That Does Justice: Examining the Christian Sources for Social Change*, edited by John C. Haughey, 68–112. Eugene, OR: Wipf & Stock, 1977.

Dunn, James D. G. *The Theology of Paul the Apostle*. Grand Rapids: Eerdmans, 1998.

Dunn, James D. G., and Alan M. Suggate. *The Justice of God: A Fresh Look at the Old Doctrine of Justification by Faith*. Grand Rapids: Eerdmans, 1993.

Finnis, John. *Aquinas: Moral, Political, and Legal Theory*. Oxford: Oxford University Press, 1980.

---

105. I explore this contrast in Philpott, *Just and Unjust Peace*, 207–50.

———. *Natural Law and Natural Rights*. Oxford: Oxford University Press, 1980.

Grisez, Germain. *The Way of the Lord Jesus*, vol. 2: *Living a Christian Life*. Quincy, IL: Franciscan, 1993.

Haughey, John C. "Jesus as the Justice of God." In *The Faith That Does Justice: Examining the Christian Sources for Social Change*, edited by John C. Haughey, 276–88. Eugene, OR: Wipf and Stock, 1977.

Hering, H. "De Iure Subjective Sumpto apud S. Thomam." *Angelicum* 16 (1939) 295–97.

Heschel, Abraham Joshua. *The Prophets*. New York: Harper and Row, 1962.

Hoang, Bethany Hanke, and Kristen Deede Johnson. *The Justice Calling: Where Passion Meets Perseverance*. Grand Rapids: Brazos, 2016.

John Paul II. "Dives in Misericordia." *Libreria Editrice Vaticana*. November 30, 1980. http://www.vatican.va/content/john-paul-ii/en/encyclicals/documents/hf_jp-ii_enc_30111980_dives-in-misericordia.html.

———. "Solicitudino Rei Socialis." *Libreria Editrice Vaticana*. December 30, 1987. http://www.vatican.va/content/john-paul-ii/en/encyclicals/documents/hf_jp-ii_enc_30121987_sollicitudo-rei-socialis.html.

Johnson, Barbara. "Mishpat." In *Theological Dictionary of the Old Testament*, edited by G. Johannes Botterweck, Helmer Ringgren, and Heinz-Josef Fabry, translated by David E. Green, IX. Grand Rapids: Eerdmans, 1998.

Kant, Immanuel. *The Metaphysics of Morals*. Translated by Mary Gregor. Cambridge: Cambridge University Press, 1991.

Koch, Klaus. "*sdq*." In *Theological Lexicon of the Old Testament*, vol. 2, edited by Ernst Jenni and Claus Westermann, translated by Mark E. Biddle, 1046–62. Peabody, MA: Hendrickson, 1997.

Knierim, Rolf. *The Task of Old Testament Theology: Method and Cases*. Grand Rapids: Eerdmans, 1995.

Knight, George Angus Fulton. "Is 'Righteous' Right?" *Scottish Journal of Theology* 41.1 (1988) 1–10.

Lederach, John Paul, and R. Scott Appleby. "Strategic Peacebuilding: An Overview." In *Strategies of Peace: Transforming Conflict in a Violent World*, edited by Daniel Philpott and Gerard F. Powers, 19–44. Oxford: Oxford University Press, 2010.

Levering, Matthew. *Biblical Natural Law: A Theocentric and Teleological Approach*. Oxford: Oxford University Press, 2008.

———. *Christ's Fulfillment of Torah and Temple*. Notre Dame, IN: University of Notre Dame Press, 2002.

Maritain, Jacques. *Man and the State*. Washington, DC: Catholic University of America Press, 1951.

Marshall, Christopher D. *Beyond Retribution: A New Testament Vision for Justice, Crime, and Punishment*. Grand Rapids: Eerdmans, 2001.

Mattison, William C. *The Sermon on the Mount and Moral Theology: A Virtue Perspective*. Cambridge: Cambridge University Press, 2017.

Nardoni, Enrique. *Rise Up, O Judge: A Study of Justice in the Biblical World*. Translated by Seán Charles Martin. Grand Rapids: Baker Academic, 2004.

Novak, David. *Covenantal Rights: A Study in Jewish Political Theory*. Princeton: Princeton University Press, 2000.

———. *The Jewish Social Contract, An Essay in Political Theology*. Princeton: Princeton University Press, 2005.

Philpott, Daniel. *Just and Unjust Peace*. New York: Oxford University Press, 2012.
Porter, Jean. *Justice as a Virtue: A Thomistic Perspective*. Grand Rapids: Eerdmans, 2016.
Reumann, John. "Righteousness (NT)." In *The Anchor Bible Dictionary*, vol. 5, edited by David Noel Freedman, 745–73. New York: Doubleday, 1992.
Schiltz, Elizabeth R. "West, MacIntyre, and Wojtyla: Pope John Paul II's Contribution to the Development of a Dependency-Based Theory of Justice." *Journal of Catholic Legal Studies* 45 (2006) 369–414.
Scullion, J. J. "Righteousness (OT)." In *The Anchor Bible Dictionary*, vol. 5, edited by David Noel Freedman, 724–36. New York: Doubleday, 1992.
Stegman, Thomas D. "Paul's Use of *Dikaio-* Terminology: Moving Beyond N. T. Wright's Forensic Interpretation." *Theological Studies* 72 (2011) 496–524.
Tierney, Brian, with responses by Michael P. Zuckert, Douglas Kries, and John Finnis. "Natural Law and Natural Rights: Old Problems and Recent Approaches." *The Review of Politics* 64 (2002) 389–420.
von Rad, Gerhard. *Old Testament Theology*. Vol. 1, translated by D. M. G. Stalker. Peabody, MA: Prince, 1962.
Weinfeld, Moshe. *Social Justice in Ancient Israel and in the Ancient Near East*. Minneapolis, MN: Fortress, 1995.
Williams, Thomas D. *Who Is My Neighbor? Personalism and the Foundations of Human Rights*. Washington, DC: Catholic University of America Press, 1995.
Wolterstorff, Nicholas. *Justice: Rights and Wrongs*. Princeton: Princeton University Press, 2008.
Wright, N. T. *Evil and the Justice of God*. Downers Grove, IL: IVP, 2006.
———. *Justification: God's Plan and Paul's Vision*. Downers Grove, IL: IVP Academic, 2009.

Response to

Daniel Philpott's "Giving Justice More Than Its Due"

David Novak

I AM GRATEFUL TO Daniel Philpott for his recognition that the biblical roots of my political theory give it a commonality with the political theory of Thomas Aquinas, which is also rooted in the Bible. In this way, Daniel has shown how Hebraic notions of justice exceed in scope and depth the notions of justice presented by Plato, Aristotle, and the Stoics. As such, western political theory should be more beholden to Jerusalem than it is to Athens or to Rome, let alone to Königsberg (a là Kant) or to Harvard (a là Rawls). Therefore, at a time when the question of justice is being debated with special vigor, and when western justice is under severe attack both from within and without, Jews and Christians need to enter the debates from our common biblically based notions of justice. On that point, Daniel and I are in total agreement.

While our general agreement far surpasses any specific disagreements we might have, our specific disagreements should not be ignored for the sake of some superficial agreement simply based on the fact that biblically based morality, whether enunciated by Christians or by Jews, is under attack by militant secularists who think all rights and duties are humanly invented, and just as easily un-invented by humans. Since our reflections on our common morality, which center around our common notions of justice, are the stuff of political polemics *ad extra*, we still need to constantly think and rethink these common notions of justice *ad intra*. We need more than our having a common enemy. Thinking and discoursing among ourselves, it is inevitable that certain specific disagreements will emerge.

In the case of the specific disagreement between Daniel and me, however, that disagreement is not religious in the sense that Daniel is a Catholic and I am a Jew. As we examine Daniel's specific disagreement with me argued in his paper, it should be noted that there are Jews who would agree with Daniel's position more than they do with mine; and there are Catholics who would agree with my position more than they do with Daniel's. Moreover, if Daniel's and my interaction in this volume is truly dialogical, it is hoped that both of us will learn enough from each other so that we might overcome our specific difference of opinion about rights and duties and gain more philosophic commonality, or at least we might formulate our respective opinions better after having better listened to each other.

Our specific disagreement concerns the relation of rights and duties in a biblically based morality.

Daniel cites a key proposition in my 2000 book, *Covenantal Rights*, viz., "every duty has a correlative right, just as every right has a correlative duty." He then states, "while I am in deep sympathy—and indebted to—Rabbi Novak's political theology, my argument about justice differs . . . my view is that some duties do not correlate with rights."[1] Also, on the same page of *Covenantal Rights* quoted by Daniel, I say that "rights are not only correlative with duties, they actually generate them." Conversely, earlier in his paper, Daniel agrees with Thomists (like John Finnis, Thomas Williams, and Jacques Maritain) who hold "that people possess natural rights by virtue of natural duties, for instance, a right to life is a consequence of the proscription of murder."[2] (Writing on Jewish law in the 1980s, I held this same view. By the late 1990s, however, my view changed.) So, our difference is whether rights engender duties or whether duties engender rights.

Let me now more carefully clarify what I mean by a "right" and by a "duty." Also, who is a rights-holder and who is a duty-holder?

A right is a justified claim of one person upon another person. A negative or minimal right is my claim upon you not to prevent me from pursuing some good I want for myself (*bonum sibi*). A positive or maximal right is my claim upon you to aid me in pursuing some good I want for myself. However, rights-holders are not only individual persons pursuing their own individual goods; a community also has a claim on individual persons within its domain or on other communities outside its domain not to prevent them from pursuing their own communal good (*bonum commune*) or to aid them in that pursuit. In turn, individual persons can make similar claims on their community; and one's own community can make a claim on another community and vice-versa.

However, what *justifies* a right/claim so that one is duty bound to respond to it by doing what its holder wants done for them, or by not doing what its holder does not want done for them? Conversely, when a right/claim is *unjustified*, one is then often duty bound to prevent it from being done and always duty bound not to aid its being done. What *justifies* the opposite duties as the appropriate responses to *unjustifiable* claims?

All rights are given by God who, as Creator *ex nihilo*, is the original rights-holder, making all claims but never to be claimed, i.e., never being beholden to any creature (who is everybody and which is everything that is not-God). As such, God entitles,

1. p. 243.
2. p. 231.

but is not Himself entitled. God's rights alone are original; the rights of creatures are all derivative. Human creatures, enjoying a unique relationship with God (as *imago Dei*), are entitled to make claims upon each other in God's name. When claims are justifiable, those being claimed should know *ipso facto* that they are duty-bound to respond to them appropriately. What justifies a right/claim is whether it could be ultimately considered to be what God wants to be done in His world. What makes a right/claim unjustifiable is that it could not be considered to be what God wants to be done in His world. But how do we know what God wants done or not done in His world?

The Bible states, "For thus says the LORD Creator of the heavens, who is the God who formed the earth, who made it and established it: Not as chaos [*tohu*] did He create it, but He formed it for dwelling [*la-shevet*]; I am the LORD and no one else" (Isa 45:18). Now would a wise Creator want His unique creatures murdering, raping, and robbing (i.e., violating) one another in His world that He declared to be "very good" (Gen 1:31)? Let it be recalled that in the creation narrative in Genesis 1, God declared each part of the overall creation as "good" (*tov*), meaning that each part of creation is to function well for itself and well for the overall whole of "all that God made." This is God's creation of a purposeful cosmos, in which as the ancient Rabbis put it, humans are God's "partners" (albeit unequal, junior partners), who are thus uniquely responsible for positively developing the world and protecting it from negative forces (see Gen 2:15). That responsibility begins in the conduct of the world of humans as "communal beings" (*politikon zōon*) in Aristotle's words. As such, basic human rights are reasonable claims in and of themselves. They are, as Thomas Jefferson put it, "self-evident." As an ancient Rabbi put it, "what you wouldn't want done to yourself, do not do to anybody else" (Shabbat 31a). A theology of creation gives these rights a sufficient ontological grounding. Its moral force, though, comes from practical reason.

If these rights are self-evidently reasonable, whose holders do not claim from others what they cannot be reasonably expected to do, then their dutiful responses should be equally self-evident. Thus, when the ancient Rabbis imagined that Abel pleaded with Cain not to violate his right to live, Cain should have already known that he was duty bound to respect that reasonable claim. When he violated that right by not doing his duty to restrain his murderous violence, God holds him responsible. And God holds Cain responsible *because* He is the same God who entitled Abel—and every human being created in His image—to live and not be murdered in his world, which is a world where "true justice effects peace (*shalom*)" (Isa 32:17). But when was Cain commanded the duty "you shall not murder" (Exod 20:13)? How could he be held responsible for not performing a duty that he (or anybody else) had not been commanded? Is it reasonable to punish somebody for a crime not already prohibited (*nulla poena sine lege*)?

The answer seems to be that Abel's created human right not to be murdered itself de facto *engendered* Cain's human duty to respect that self-evident or *prima facie* right. But if so, why did the Torah have to explicitly command the duty not to murder?

That might well go back to our childhood experience of the correlation of rights and duties. As children we experience being duty-bound before we learn how to exercise our own rights/claims. Our parents are the rights-holders; we are the duty-holders. When we subsequently experience these parental claims as reasonable (i.e., consistent and benevolent), we then learn by their example how to make our own rights/claims on others. In order to make reasonable claims, we first have to experience being reasonably claimed. And when we subsequently learn that our parents' rights are entitlements from God, we then learn that they have no right to require us to do things that go against God's original rights, one of which is God's entitling authority to create rights for His human creatures. Rights are the *reasons* for their correlative duties. Rights *justify* duties, i.e., they are what make duties reasonable. Duties are to be carried out for the sake of the rights that engendered them. (This is called in the Jewish tradition *ta'amei ha-mitsvot*, "the reasons of the commandments.") Natural law consists of the *legislated* duties or precepts that are the appropriate responses to the natural, self-evident (in Aquinas's terms, *ratio quoad nos*) rights of other humans. God is the ultimate legislator of natural law.

Nevertheless, since we humans are so frequently tempted to violate the rights of others, we need to be *directly* commanded by the God who has given these human rights, to respect them, rather than letting us *indirectly* infer that the ultimate source of that right and its correlative duty is the Creator-God. That is why the Decalogue (with a commandment like "you shall not murder") is more than natural law. As such it requires special revelation. As the ancient Rabbis frequently put it, "the Torah has to speak to sinful, fallible humans." Also, "some things that have been written down in the Torah, would have been known by human reason even if they hadn't been written down there" (Yoma 67b). In other words, optimally we should be able to infer the duty from the right, i.e., understanding the reason before the actual command for it. Realistically, though, we often need to hear the command first and, it is hoped, we will then understand the *right* reason for it. In effect, then, God has to make a person's right/claim when that person is incapable of doing so or when they cannot persuade other persons to respect it *per se*.

Therefore, I think phenomenologically speaking, Daniel is correct in taking duties to be prior to rights. Ontologically speaking, I think I am correct in taking rights to be prior to duties. Nevertheless, this difference between us is theoretical. At the much more important practical level, Daniel and I seem to be in virtually total agreement. That general agreement is what makes our dialogue possible and sustainable. Our specific differences are what make our dialogue interesting and never to be fully resolved in this yet-to-be fully redeemed world.

Chapter 10

Reason's Revelation and Revelation's Reason

Reading Apuleius's *De Deo Socratis* and Augustine's *De Civitate Dei* through the Lens of Novak's *Athens and Jerusalem*

Thomas Slabon

David Novak's *Athens and Jerusalem* (*A&J*) derives its title and point of departure from Tertullian's infamous challenge:

> What then belongs to Athens and Jerusalem? What belongs to the academy and the church? What belongs to heretics and Christians? Our teaching comes from the Porch of Solomon, who himself taught that the Lord should be sought in simplicity of heart. Let those who produce a Stoic or Platonic or dialectical Christianity look after themselves! We have no need of curiosity after Jesus Christ, nor of inquiry after the Gospel. When we believe, we desire to believe nothing further, for we believe this first—that we need to believe nothing further.[1]

The *Tertullian Dichotomy*,[2] as I will refer to it, separates the grounds and forms of intellectual inquiry in two: Athens and the academy stand in for the classical philosophers' project of rational inquiry, and Jerusalem and the church for the theological elaboration of revealed truth found in the writings of the Evangelists and early Church Fathers.[3] Clearly, Tertullian intends for the response to his dichotomy to be *nihil—*

---

1. Tertullian, *De Praescriptione Haereticorum*, VII.9–13. Unless otherwise noted, all translations are my own.

2. Recent scholarship has problematized the reading of the dichotomy developed below (see, for instance, Osborn, *Tertullian, First Theologian of the West*, 27–47, who argues that Tertullian is in fact only advancing a "pretended ban on philosophy" (39)), but for the purposes of this paper I will proceed, like Novak, on the traditional understanding of Tertullian's argument.

3. To which Novak, in his own work, attaches the Jewish rabbinical tradition. Novak also views the conflict between Athens and Jerusalem as continuing throughout the history of philosophy (*Athens and Jerusalem*, 43–44). Though I will use "Athens" and "Jerusalem" interchangeably with "philosophy" and "theology," in this paper I will be focusing on the conflict's development within the context of classical Greco-Roman philosophy and Christian responses thereto.

that there is nothing shared between Athens and Jerusalem. This *nothing* should not be taken, however, to indicate mere disinterest or disengagement between the two divisions, such that philosophy has its proper domain of inquiry, and revelation its own, and never the twain shall meet. Rather, as Novak understands the challenge, Tertullian's dichotomy describes an existential, zero-sum confrontation between philosophy and theology.[4] In this way, there is nothing shared between Athens and Jerusalem, not in the sense that the overlapping set between their two domains of inquiry is empty, but rather that the two sides lay claim to the exact same domain, while also being unwilling to cede any element of this domain to the opposing party. Ironically, Athens and Jerusalem have nothing in common because they have *everything* in common—both lay claim to the truth in its entirety, and the mutually exclusive nature of their claims means that nothing Athens holds as a true element of its domain can also be an element of Jerusalem's domain.[5]

This paper begins by retracing Novak's radical response to Tertullian's dichotomy: the relationship between Athens and Jerusalem is not to be understood as a conflict between reason and revelation but rather between two (sometimes competing) revelations about which philosophy and theology reason.[6] In the first section, I attempt to justify Novak's reading of the dichotomy as existential and mutually exclusive. Next, I discuss why Novak thinks that his understanding of philosophy and theology as reasoning about distinct revelations better characterizes the relationship between Athens and Jerusalem than the Tertullian dichotomy, showing how philosophy depends on "theological" revelation and theology makes use of "philosophical" reason. I then discuss Novak's completion thesis—that Athens is unable to complete the intellectual projects it sets itself by means of its own resources and thus always stands in need of Jerusalem's revelation.

In the second half of the paper, I argue that the blueprint Novak gives us for Athens and Jerusalem's relationship can be fruitfully applied to the study of the Christian reception of Greco-Roman philosophy in antiquity. Novak's own work in *Athens and Jerusalem* focuses exclusively on Jewish engagement with philosophy throughout

---

4. Here, as elsewhere, Novak's reading is inspired by Strauss's work (see especially Strauss, "Jerusalem and Athens: Some Preliminary Reflections," 149; Strauss, "The Mutual Influence of Theology and Philosophy," 114)—the central importance of which for Novak's overall project should become clear in what follows.

5. Tertullian's anticipated response to his *quid ergo?* then, is not *nihil simpliciter*, but rather *omnia, et igitur nihil*.

6. Novak's recent Gifford lectures are his most thoroughgoing articulation of this response, but we find it first discussed in his reflections on the philosophy of one of his own teachers, Leo Strauss, decades earlier ("Philosophy and the Possibility of Revelation" in *Leo Strauss and Judaism*). Novak's philosophy of revelation, it is important to note from the outset, has evolved over the course of decades, is located in several different works, and is in constant dialogue with a myriad of different sources. My task in the first part of this paper is to unify and develop Novak's reflections, and then to defend the theory that emerges against a number of possible objections, in the process making use of a number of conceptual resources provided by sources like Strauss, Maimonides, and Tertullian.

history since, as Novak affirms, Judaism "is the only place in the world from which I can see other places in the world with my own eyes."[7] I demonstrate the importance of Novak's theory for better understanding Christian authors by way of a case study of Augustine's reception of Apuleius's *De Deo Socratis* (*DDS*) in his *De Civitate Dei contra paganos* (*DCD*). I begin by summarizing Apuleius's text, showing how Novak's understanding of philosophy's relationship to revelation accurately tracks Apuleius's interaction with Plato and contemporaneous religious belief. Then, I show how Augustine's engagement with Apuleius has been misunderstood by modern commentators and how Novak's work allows us to clarify these misunderstandings. In *De Civitate Dei* VIII and IX, Augustine embraces the completion thesis, arguing that Apuleius's philosophical project can only be successfully fulfilled through Christian revelation. Understood in this way, we can see Augustine relating to Apuleius not (or not only) as the hostile subject of a polemical refutation but also as a fellow sojourner in need of the correction and completion made possible by Christianity. Novak's theory thus allows us to better make sense of Augustine's aims and strategies when engaging with Apuleius, in turn suggesting that the blueprint drafted in *Athens and Jerusalem* might be successfully applied to other Christian engagements with philosophy throughout Western intellectual history.

A Tale of Two Revelations: The Tertullian Dichotomy

The reading of the Tertullian dichotomy outlined in the opening paragraph immediately raises two questions: why does the confrontation between Athens and Jerusalem carry *existential* weight, and why should we think of the conflict as a *mutually exclusive* dichotomy? In other words, why could we not view this conflict in a deflationary light, as a mere question of scholarly interest, or as a conflict wherein a compromise (some sort of sharing of the intellectual playing-field, perhaps) might be possible?

First, the conflict must have existential import because both philosophy and theology are life-ordering commitments—to engage in one or the other is not merely to, for instance, assent to one set of propositions in contrast to another (regardless of how (in)compatible these two sets of beliefs may be) but to *commit* oneself to reason or revelation. This commitment is to a distinct method of inquiry, to the propositional truths that issue from this method, and above all to a *modus vivendi* derived from this method and these truths.[8] To accept the central truth-claims of philosophy or theology without changing one's life to conform to those truths would be either hypocritical or incoherent.

---

7. Novak, *Athens and Jerusalem*, 42.

8. It is important, however, to speak of a singular *commitment*—as the method, way of life, and propositional truths we call "philosophy" or "theology" are all intricately bound up in each other. For a magisterial discussion of how the methods and truth-claims of philosophy are interwoven as a way of life within the context of classical philosophy, cf. Hadot, *Philosophy as a Way of Life*.

As to the mutually exclusive nature of the dichotomy, Novak might argue as follows. Philosophy takes universally accessible facts as the "raw material" of its inquiry and has as its aim universal truth—that is, truth with a public "criterion of verifiability" which is, at least in principle, universally accessible to human beings[9]—that can undergo rational interrogation and offer arguments in favor of their endorsement. Scientific truth represents the paradigm of this sort of truth: at the heart of the scientific method is the need for experimental results to be (in principle) repeatable by and therefore accessible to any observer, and the conclusions drawn from these results must be defended through rational argumentation. Conversely, theology proceeds on the basis of unique and singular events that are, by their very nature, not universally accessible.[10] Furthermore, because of the overwhelming nature of theophany, any attempt to reason about or express this revelation will inevitably fall short—revelation can never be shared in such a way that the truth contained in the initial moment of revelation would become fully accessible to an audience.

Finally, theological truth cannot submit to rational critique without losing its authority, because engaging in the process of rational interrogation and justification threatens to reduce revelation to the predictable and repeatable domain of empirico-scientific experience.[11] Miracles, for instance, can be reduced to remarkable-but-not-impossible exceptions to scientific laws of nature, which themselves (in a Humean light) only express regularities in the natural world without ever claiming to be exceptionless. However, understanding a miracle as *merely* an exception to characterizations of natural regularities causes us to, so to speak, miss the point of the revelation—we fail to understand the miracle as happening at a particular time and place, and to a particular community, as part of God's providential plan for God's creation.[12] The reason for the *who* and *when* and *where* of revelation cannot be arrived at or defended using the same criteria of publicity as philosophical truth. Rational inquiry allows us to understand a miracle as an exception to a regular pattern that admits of exceptions but cannot lead us to the *why* that explains this exception.

One might object, however, that this argument fails to rule out the possibility of compromise. The initial, miraculous *datum* of revelation might be inaccessible to philosophical inquiry—but what about other domains of knowledge, like natural science or ethics? Surely, we might think, *these* fields of inquiry fall under the purview of philosophy and are beholden to philosophy's standard of universal accessibility. If this is the case, shouldn't Athens and Jerusalem be sharing the domain of truth, cultivating their distinct fields of inquiry side by side?

Here, Tertullian's arguments help fill in Novak's line of thought. Recall Tertullian's initial challenge to the possibility of a synthesis of Athens and Jerusalem, quoted above.

9. Novak, *Athens and Jerusalem*, 11.
10. What Fackenheim calls "root experiences" (*God's Presence in History*, 8–14).
11. Novak, *Athens and Jerusalem*, 32, 34.
12. Novak, *Athens and Jerusalem*, 67.

There, he claimed that Christians have no need for curiosity (*curiositas*) or inquiry (*inquisitio*) after the revelation of the Gospels, and stronger still, that the first article of belief for Christians is that there is nothing we must believe beyond this revelation.[13] For Tertullian, this revelation finds its full expression in the Rule of Faith (*regula fidei*), whose articulation in the *De Praescriptione Haereticorum* is very similar to the later Apostle's Creed (XIII). Once one has discovered and embraced this *regula*, there is nothing more that one *needs* to know. Although Tertullian sometimes writes as if there is nothing else to inquire about or believe beyond the *regula* (IX.4), his actual position seems to be that there is nothing else *of existential value* to inquire about or believe. Once one has arrived at the revealed truths of the Christian faith, one can engage in philosophical inquiry to one's heart's content, but only as a sort of idle preoccupation. Athens can continue to toil quietly in its own corner, so long as it does not disturb one's certainty in Jerusalem's revealed truths—and if ever Athens's toil should threaten this certainty, the work of philosophy must be abandoned without hesitation. Better to remain ignorant, Tertullian tells us, than to lose one's faith.[14]

So, Tertullian and Novak might reply to the suggestion of compromise that there is indeed a domain of philosophical truth, and the theologian can philosophize in her spare time—but to engage in philosophical inquiry *as a philosopher* would require an existential commitment to philosophy. One would have to believe that there are things one *must* know beyond revelation, things without the knowledge of which life would be incomplete.[15] Proper philosophical inquiry requires commitment to a truth beyond revealed truth, or a truth that *completes* revealed truth, and thus requires one to admit the *inadequacy* of revealed truth. Sure, there might be domains of truth beyond the domain of revealed truth, but these are not the domain over which Athens and Jerusalem are ultimately contending.

The Tertullian dichotomy thus posits a mutually exclusive decision of existential importance: *either* one accepts the method and truth criteria of philosophic rationality, *or* one embraces a way of life grounded in an a- (though, the theologian would claim, not ir-)rational particular moment of epiphany. The two cities are, on this line of thought, irreconcilable. To embrace the theological way of life of Jerusalem is, necessarily, to reject philosophical Athens—without any opportunity for compromise or truth shared between the two sides.

Novak's radical solution to the foregoing problem—and the orienting project of *Athens and Jerusalem*—is to reject Tertullian's dichotomy as an inadequate characterization of the confrontation of theology and philosophy. For Novak, the tension between Athens and Jerusalem is not a conflict between unrevealed reason and arational revelation, but between two distinct revelations about which philosophical

---

13. Tertullian, *De Praescriptione Haereticorum*, VII.12–13.
14. Tertullian, *De Praescriptione Haereticorum*, XIV.1–2.
15. Tertullian, *De Praescriptione Haereticorum*, XI.2.

and theological communities individually reason.[16] Taking his inspiration from Socrates's reliance on revelation in the form of both his *daimonion* and the Delphic oracle, Novak argues:

> Both philosophy and theology involve a total existential response to a revelation a philosopher or a theologian has received, either directly (via prophecy) or indirectly (via tradition). Such a receptive response is an act of faith, which is required of both theologians and philosophers. Both philosophy and theology engage content by means of the method each brings to what it has received unambiguously and unconditionally, i.e., what it has received faithfully.[17]

If this is correct, we can resolve the dichotomy by affirming that Athens and Jerusalem "still occupy the same discursive world";[18] that is to say, they are both engaged in the search for the same truth by way of the same method. Philosophy and theology will differ with respect to *which* revelation they explore through rational inquiry, but their methods and the end of their inquiry will be shared—creating the possibility of a shared domain of truth between the two cities.

In order to evaluate whether Novak's account better characterizes the relationship between Athens and Jerusalem than the traditional interpretation of Tertullian's dichotomy, we will need to first understand philosophy's faith and theology's response, and then investigate whether this account accurately tracks how theologians and philosophers have thought of their own projects and their interactions with each other. To this end, in the following two sections I will sketch how Novak thinks of the various forms of reason's revelation and revelation's reason before turning to consider how Novak's account might be applied to the engagement of Christian philosophers with their pagan antecedents.

Reason's Revelation

What is the "Hellenic revelation"[19] of the philosophers? In *Athens and Jerusalem*, Novak focuses on two distinct theoretical commitments that constitute (at least in part) reason's revelation within the context of classical Greek philosophy: 1) to the philosopher's god, both as (i) the origin of philosophical activity and (ii) the teleological end of the philosopher's system; and 2) to nature as a *datum*, that is to say, to (i) there being a world "out there" that can be experienced and known, and to (ii) our intellect being adequate to the task of knowing this world. As we shall see, it will also be helpful to add to this list Strauss's idea of the philosopher's aphilosophic commitment 3) to methodological

---

16. Novak, *Athens and Jerusalem*, 27, 39 and elsewhere.
17. Novak, *Athens and Jerusalem*, 13–14.
18. Novak, *Athens and Jerusalem*, 42.
19. Novak, *Athens and Jerusalem*, 104.

principles that cannot undergo the rational interrogation these principles require. Let us consider each of these commitments in turn.

First, the philosophers of classical Athens—and those of most other periods of Western philosophy—are committed to the existence of a divine figure or set of figures,[20] and this commitment plays an essential structuring role for their philosophical activity. Plato's depiction of Socrates, for instance,[21] consistently emphasizes his reliance on revelation to justify and direct his engagement with philosophy. This is most clearly the case, of course, in the famous story of the oracle from Delphi that prompts Socrates—or so he tells us[22]—to first engage in the elenchtic interrogation of his fellow citizens. Novak repeatedly points to Socrates's divine justification for *elenchus* as his foundational evidence of philosophy's revelation,[23] but it is far from the only example in the Platonic corpus of Socrates justifying his activity and way of life by appeal to divine revelation.

Let us briefly consider a few other examples of divine revelation guiding Socrates's actions in the Platonic corpus. First, in the *Phaedrus*, Socrates's divine sign (his *daimonion*) prevents him from leaving the spot where he has been conversing with Phaedrus until he remedies the offense he has caused to Eros in his first speech, leading him to deliver his Palinode.[24] Second, when asked at the beginning of the *Phaedo* why he has spent his last days in prison composing music and poetry, Socrates tells his friends that he has been repeatedly visited by a dream saying: "Socrates, make and practise *mousikē*."[25] Socrates had hitherto understood the dream as commanding him

---

20. Unfortunately, I do not have the space here to enter into a detailed discussion of the singular or plural nature of the divine in Aristotle and Plato, nor of the relationship between the various objects of their philosophical discussions and the traditional pantheon of their cultural context. I will often use singular terms to refer to the divine figures in Plato and Aristotle (but, should the reader prefer, the singular can be read as a plural without any significant change in my discussion) and will return below to the question of the nature of the divine in Plato.

21. Which I take to be the deliberate construction, by Plato, of a paradigm for philosophical activity. The task of creating an archetype for philosophy out of the life of Socrates was also pursued in the contemporaneous works of other members of the so-called "Socratic Circle" and taken up in later Stoic discussions of the life of the sage or *sophos*.

22. We must wonder, however, what prompted Chaerephon to first ask the oracle whether anyone was wiser than Socrates, if not because Socrates had already gained a reputation for wisdom by philosophizing—and how Socrates's account of the origins of his philosophical activity interacts with his earlier engagement with natural philosophy as he describes in his own "intellectual autobiography" in the *Phaedo* (95e7–99d2).

23. See Novak, *Athens and Jerusalem*, 13 and 116.

24. Plato, *Phaedrus*, 242b8–243d7.

25. Plato, *Phaedrus*, 60e6-7. It is important to remember that the Greeks often conceived of dreams not as visions or other facsimiles of conscious experience, but as distinct *figures* who appear and communicate messages to the dreamer (see, for instance, *Iliad* II.6–35, where Zeus sends a dream to Agammenon, telling the dream what to say, and the dream is said to stand at the head of the hero's bed). When Socrates tells his companions what the dream said, then, we should have in mind such a direct message from a divine dream-figure. On this and other aspects of divinely inspired dreams in the Greek imaginary, see Dodds, *The Greeks and the Irrational*, chap. IV. Here, I leave *mousikē*

to practise philosophy, since he regarded philosophy as the highest form of *mousikē*,[26] but decided to practice a more conventional form of *mousikē* so that he might, to borrow a colloquial expression, "cover all his bases" before his death. Third, at the start of the *Crito*, Socrates relates how he was visited by a dream-figure, beautiful and robed in white, who told him: "Socrates, may you come to fertile Phthia on the third day."[27] Socrates interprets the dream to be telling him that he will die on the third day (counting inclusively) from his dream, and that, presumably, his soul will move on to a fertile dwelling like the Isles of the Blessed.[28] Finally, midway through the *Phaedo*, Socrates explains his readiness to continue his philosophical investigation concerning the immortality of the soul despite the fact that he will soon be forced to commit suicide (and should his belief in the soul's immortality be disproven, would presumably go to his death hopelessly distraught), by way of a prophetic art (*mantikē*) he shares with swans, who are Apollo's servants. Swans, Socrates claims, sing most beautifully just before their death, because they have been given insight into the joy that awaits them after death—and Socrates, sharing this revealed insight, can confidently continue to discuss the immortality of the soul in the face of his impending death.[29]

In the above examples, the divine plays a number of important roles for Socrates: it prompts Socrates to philosophize *ab initio*, provides normative guidance as to what Socrates should and shouldn't do when philosophizing, confirms his decisions by providing assurance that they will turn out for the best, and so forth. To these functional roles of the philosopher's god, Novak also emphasizes the divine's role as *telos*. God is, in Novak's reading of Plato and Aristotle, the structuring end or *Summum Bonum* of the natural world, towards which the entirety of nature is ordered in an interdependent teleological hierarchy.[30] God is also the completion or perfection of morality—interhuman justice is, at best, an approximation of or analogy for the perfect justice of the divinity, a perfection that the philosopher strives to identify herself with as much as possible by way of her philosophical activity.[31] God is therefore the *telos* of philosophy as a whole, both as the ultimate object of knowledge for philosophical inquiry and the highest good that the philosopher aims to attain.

So, god serves as the beginning and the end of the Greek philosophical project, providing both the normative injunction that motivates philosophical activity[32] and

---

untranslated, as no English term can properly capture the range of meanings contained in the Greek term, which covers everything from instrumental music to lyric poetry to theatrical performances.

26. "ὡς φιλοσοφίας μὲν οὔσης μεγίστης μουσικῆς" (Plato, *Phaedo* 61a3–4).

27. Plato, *Crito*, 44a10–b3.

28. I trust that the invocation of "fertile" (ἐρίβωλον) Phthia would immediately have reminded Plato's readers of the Isles.

29. Plato, *Phaedo*, 84d8–85b9.

30. Novak, *Athens and Jerusalem*, 54–55.

31. Novak, *Athens and Jerusalem*, 87, 118.

32. Among the Greek philosophers Novak considers, this divine origin is only made explicit in the case of Socrates, but I suspect Novak thinks that, as with Judeo-Christian revelation, we should regard

the *telos* of natural and moral philosophy as a whole, while also playing an essential role in guiding and sustaining the philosopher in the midst of her inquiry. One might object, however, that philosophers in the ancient world sometimes denied either the existence of god or the fact that the divine has any direct causal involvement with the world—a denial that has become all the more common among contemporary philosophers. This suggests that the philosopher's commitment to god is, at best, a contingent form of philosophic revelation, rather than a necessary *conditio sine qua non* of philosophy. Philosophers who make use of a divine figure in their inquiry may be committed to a form of philosophical revelation, but this is not enough to show that philosophy is *necessarily* committed to such a revelation.

Still in search of such a necessary commitment, let us consider Novak's second suggestion, namely, that philosophy is committed to nature as a *datum*. This commitment takes two forms: the philosopher is committed to the existence of a mind-independent external world that is "given" insofar as it is experienced and to the rational comprehensibility of this world given to her in experience. Novak speaks of this commitment as a form of philosophical *faith*. Faith, as Novak understands it, is an unreasoned commitment that both precedes and is presupposed by whatever beliefs we may form—and just as the theologian's faith in God's existence and loving nature comes before any rational arguments about God, any belief we form about the world always presupposes a commitment to that world's existence and intelligibility.[33] This faith commitment is expressed in the Scholastic definition of truth as *adaequatio intellectus ad rem* (which Novak translates as "truth is the intellect adjusting itself to its greater object") as the very notion of truth already presupposes a commitment to an object (*rem*) given to it as an object of intellectual inquiry.[34]

But even here, one can adduce numerous instances of philosophers who reject the world as a *datum*, or at least reject the possibility of *knowing* this *datum*. Various strands of ancient skepticism seem to lack this commitment, for instance, and Descartes's methodological skepticism has at its heart a refusal to take the external world as an unargued-for or arational faith commitment. Novak thus seems to have again pointed to a contingent form of philosophic revelation—a commitment that most philosophers share most of the time but not a commitment that is essential to the practice of philosophy *tout court*.

At this point, we seem to have arrived at something of an impasse. Novak's claim is not merely that philosophy is committed *for the most part* to its own revelation but rather that such a commitment is the essential and unavoidable ground of philosophy.

---

the original normative injunction to philosophize that was revealed to Socrates as transmitted to those who follow after him in the philosophical tradition, just as the Law continues to have normative force for those who follow after Moses. Plato's magnetic chain of inspiration in the *Ion* (533c9–535a2) gives us a model for this sort of transmission of revelation: insofar as subsequent philosophers take their philosophical inspiration from Socrates, the beginning of their philosophical activity is still divine.

33. Novak, *Athens and Jerusalem*, 16–17, 29–30.
34. Novak, *Athens and Jerusalem*, 12.

So far, we have yet to find any such universal commitment—but here, I think, Strauss is able to lend his student a helping hand.

Strauss argues that as soon as philosophy acknowledges the *possibility* of a way of life the commitment to which is derived from revelation, the philosopher's decision to commit herself to philosophy must inevitably rest on an "unevident decision," that is to say, on an "act of will" that cannot itself be rationally justified.[35] Theology and philosophy, as we have already seen, both ask for commitment to (at least apparently) irreconcilable ways of life. When presented with this mutually exclusive decision, how can I know that philosophy presents the correct way of life and therefore that revelation does not? In order to *know* that revelation is not the correct commitment, Strauss argues, I would need to know that the ground which justifies revelation's way of life—miracles, and in particular, the miracle of theophany—is impossible. And how could I know that miracles are impossible? I would either need to know (i) that God does not exist, or (ii) that the possibility of miracles would be incompatible with God's existence. In order to know either (i) or (ii), however, I would need to possess what Strauss calls a "completed metaphysic," that is, an understanding of the natural world that leaves no gaps in which God or the possibility of miracles might hide.[36] Given that such a completed metaphysic isn't available to finite human beings (or, at the very least, has never yet been achieved by anyone facing the decision between Athens and Jerusalem), those who choose the philosophical way of life must commit to philosophy without *knowing* that this commitment is correct. The choice of philosophy, ironically, ends up being an act of faith rather than an act on the basis of knowledge that has withstood philosophical interrogation. Every philosopher philosophizes on the basis of a faith commitment that cannot itself be entirely rationally justified—and this is, for Strauss, a sort of revelation.

In response, one might object that Strauss has failed to correctly characterize the sort of methodological commitment Athens demands of its citizens: a philosophical way of life, we might think, does not require that we *only* act on the basis of knowledge, but that we act on the basis of knowledge whenever possible, and on the basis of our most trustworthy beliefs when such knowledge is unavailable. Even if Strauss were to grant this qualification, however, he can still reply that the philosophical commitment to act on the basis of whichever beliefs have proven most robust under rational interrogation—whether those beliefs qualify as knowledge or merely as reliable beliefs—still constitutes a commitment that cannot itself be reasoned about. Again, our objector might argue that this commitment can be reasoned about and point us to a wealth of contemporary literature on the question of why we should be rational. And Strauss, again, can reply that the need to ask why we should be rational, and the (eminently rational) methods we bring to bear in trying to answer this question, must go unquestioned. Ultimately, Strauss would contend, we must reach a point in our investigation

---

35. Strauss, *Spinoza's Critique of Religion*, 29.
36. Strauss, "The Mutual Influence of Theology and Philosophy," 113.

where our spade is turned and we can dig no further.³⁷ Philosophy's inquiry proceeds from a set of questions or methodological assumptions whose foundation and structuring role in the activity of philosophy goes unquestioned.³⁸

Philosophy therefore inevitably begins with a leap of faith, in Strauss's analysis, insofar as it begins with a commitment to thoroughgoing rational interrogation that cannot withstand the very sort of rational interrogation it is committed to. Strauss's arguments thus add to Novak's original list a basic *datum* of reason to which every philosopher must be committed, and this *datum*, ironically enough, is the basic commitment that originally gave rise to Athens's side of Tertullian's dichotomy through the life of Socrates. Even if we try to weaken the force of this initial commitment so as not to give rise to the apparent paradox Strauss points us towards, it seems we will always arrive at a set of bedrock assumptions that must be taken as a philosophical given for our inquiry.

Revelations' Reason

In the preceding section, we discussed three different forms of reason's revelation: the philosopher's god, the *datum* of an experienceable and intelligible world, and the commitment to philosophical inquiry itself, or at least some part of the grounds therefor. Now, I want to consider the other side of the dichotomy—what roles does reason play in theology's response to revelation? Novak suggests three interrelated ways in which theology makes use of reason in its response to revelation: 1) through exegesis and hermeneutics, when theology seeks to interpret the *datum* of revelation; 2) by clearing away impediments to the reception of revelation; and 3) by enabling humans to worship the subject of revelation, God, through rational contemplation.

To begin with, reason allows theologians to "make sense" of the content of revelation, serving as a sort of bridge between an individual's initial and miraculous encounter with the divine and the entire community of human beings with whom God enters into relationship through revelation. For Novak, this sort of hermeneutical mediation has two forms. First, reason provides theologians with *conditiones sine quibus non* for the interpretation of revelation, setting out minimal criteria for possible

---

37. Cf. Wittgenstein, *Philosophical Investigations*, §217.

38. Our earlier discussion of god as the origin of philosophy in the case of Plato's Socrates helps make this unquestioned basis explicit. Socrates justifies his philosophical activity by way of the Delphic oracle and various other divine messages, but the normative force of these messages is not interrogated. Although Socrates investigates the oracle related by Chaerephon in order to understand what it means, he never questions the fact that he should act in accordance with it—once he understands it. One of the great puzzles for contemporary commentators has thus been why Socrates, for whom the unexamined life is not worth living, fails to examine the divine motivation for his way of life (see, for instance, McPherran, *The Religion of Socrates*; Vlastos, "Socratic Piety"; Smith and Woodruff, *Reason and Religion in Socratic Philosophy*). Within the framework I have been sketching, however, Socrates's failure to interrogate the divine ground of his philosophical vocation is merely an exceptionally clear instance of the justificatory structure shared by all philosophical activity.

theological interpretations. Reason's limiting function is demonstrated, for instance, by the Talmudic principle that nothing forbidden to human beings in general can be permitted for Jews in particular (B. Sanhedrin 59a). Novak has argued that this principle requires that any revealed moral principle is beholden to the limitations imposed by natural law.[39] Moral principles arrived at by philosophical inquiry in no way exhaust the demands (understood by way of revelation) that God makes of humanity, but such rationally justified principles cannot be *superseded* by revealed commandments: as Novak emphasizes, "there is much more to revelation than morality, but not anything less."[40] Second, reason provides linguistic and conceptual resources by which those who have encountered the divine and their religious descendants can attempt to give finite propositional content to the infinite and non-propositional *datum* of the moment of revelation. Theologians must *make sense* of revelation, and this interpretive process is inherently rational in nature.

However, we must be careful not to understand this interpretive process as a response to an already-complete *datum*, seeing revelation as a *fait accompli* and theology's exegesis a mere parergon of revelation. To do so would be fall into what Heschel called the trap of theological dogmatism or objectivism, reducing the dynamic richness of revelation to a static and unchanging (and hence "objective") *datum*.[41] Instead, Novak argues with Heschel, we must recognize the role of prophets—and theologians more generally—in *constituting* revelation: "revelation goes *through* the prophet and is actively mediated *by* him . . . in other words, the prophet structures the content of revelation so that it can be transmitted to the world."[42] Properly understood, the *datum* of revelation is always something *datum nobis*. The fact that the *datum* is communicated to us in a publicly accessible manner, using language and concepts shared in common by the theologian's audience, shows that revelation has already entered into the domain of philosophy.[43] It is for this reason, ultimately, that Novak (inspired by Maimonides) argues that "all philosophers are not prophets, but all prophets are first philosophers."[44] To interpret revelation—and every communication of revelation is always already an interpretation of revelation—is unavoidably to *philosophize* about revelation.[45]

---

39. See Novak, *The Image of the Non-Jew in Judaism*.

40. Novak, "Possibility of Revelation" 18. See also Novak, "Theology and Philosophy: An Exchange with Robert Jenson."

41. Heschel, *Die Prophetie*, 2–3.

42. Novak, "Heschel's Phenomenology of Revelation," 41.

43. Recall how, earlier, the domain of philosophy was identified with universally accessible facts.

44. "Possibility of Revelation" 18. cf. Novak, *Athens and Jerusalem*, 28; Strauss *Philosophy and Law* III.104–6; Maimonides *Mishna Torah—Book of Foundations* 7.1, 7.5; *Guide for the Perplexed* II.36.

45. It is important to note that we already saw this reasoning out of the meaning of revelation also taking place in the context of philosophical revelation—Socrates must make sense of the Delphic oracle, or Asclepius's injunction at the beginning of the *Phaedo* to engage in *mousikē*.

Second, Jerusalem makes use of reason to clear away obstacles to the reception of revelation, a role that Novak associates with the Heideggerian concept of "letting be" (*seinlassen*) and terms reason's "critical function."[46] We might think of this clearing away of obstacles in several ways. Reason can expose the conceptual inconsistencies of other theological systems, a process which Novak associates with the negation of idolatry in the *Tanach*, and in which we will see Augustine readily engaged in the following sections. The *conditiones sine quibus non* of morality, which we already saw constraining the theologian's interpretive possibilities, also serve to clear away the obstacles of superstition and fanaticism. The interpretive constraints imposed by philosophically justified moral precepts should prevent theology's descent into the blind and unreflective endorsement of false interpretations of revelation—or, at the very least, interpretations that must be false on moral grounds.[47] Finally, reason is needed in order to properly appreciate the *miraculous* character of revelation. Neither philosophy nor theology alone can properly situate a miracle against the backdrop of the natural world. As we saw earlier, only theology is able to explain why a miraculous exception to the laws of nature takes place in a particular context for a particular people as foretold by a particular prophetic figure.[48] At the same time, however, only philosophy can arrive at the understanding of laws of nature that is needed to recognize an exception to natural regularities *as an exception*—thus making possible our engagement with revelation as miraculous in the first place.

Third, reasoning about the natural world allows us to enter into relationship with the God who created it—reason can thus also function as a form of worship of the revealed God, worship that is only possible once the subject of revelation is revealed to us. Once we have come to recognize that the regularities of the laws of nature were created by a loving God for our sake,[49] the rational contemplation of this natural order through scientific inquiry takes on a reverential character. To learn about the natural world now is to learn about God's love for us as expressed through God's creation, and learning about God's love inevitably requires our thankful acknowledgement (*hoda'ah* in Hebrew) for this love.[50]

---

46. Novak, *Athens and Jerusalem*, 31

We might also connect this critical function with Heidegger's notion of clearing (*Lichtung*)—in Heideggerian terminology, reason's critical function would create a clearing-space within which we let the beings of revelation be.

47. Novak, "Theology and Philosophy" 245–46; Novak, "Possibility of Revelation," 17.

48. Novak, *Athens and Jerusalem*, II.24–27.

49. This recognition being encapsulated for Novak (Novak, *Athens and Jerusalem*, 90) in the Rabbinic dictum: "every human ought to say: for my sake is the world created" (M. Sanhedrin 4.5).

50. Novak, *Athens and Jerusalem*, 95–96.

Theology and Philosophy: The Completion Thesis

Having now established that philosophy is committed to various forms of revelation and that theology is necessarily in need of reason, we might appear to have come to something of a deadlock in the conflict between Athens and Jerusalem. We have seen how both cities have their own revelation about which they reason, but we seem no closer to resolving the mutually exclusive nature of the Tertullian dichotomy. The standard interpretation of the dichotomy mischaracterized the struggle by claiming that the conflict was between philosophy's reason on one side and theology's revelation on the other, but one might object that we have not made much progress if we have only succeeded in arriving at an equally insuperable divide between philosophy's rationally unfolded revelation on one side and theology's rationally unfolded revelation on the other.

However, such a deflationary reading of the foregoing arguments misses the radical opportunity offered by coming to think of philosophy and theology as both reasoning about their own revelations. Athens and Jerusalem are now speaking the same language within the same conceptual domain. Philosophy and theology can no longer be seen as laying claim to the same domain of truth by way of incommensurable forms of evidence and standards of justification but as laying claim to the same domain by way of the same evidence and standards.

Novak's line of thought, therefore, has laid the groundwork necessary to now argue that theology *completes* the project of philosophy—that theology, by adding its own insights to the conceptual resources provided by philosophy, is better able to accomplish philosophy's own project than philosophy itself. This *completion thesis* has both a descriptive and normative dimension. Descriptively, it holds that theologians throughout Western intellectual history have conceived of their own work as completing the projects begun by their philosophical antecedents. Normatively, it contends that philosophy could not effect this completion by itself: philosophy is in need of theology to accomplish the goals it has set itself and is (whether individual philosophers recognize it or not) teleologically oriented to the same ends as theology.[51]

In *Athens and Jerusalem*, we find Novak arguing for this completion thesis in two ways. The latter half of the book serves as an inductive argument for the descriptive dimension of the thesis, showing how various Jewish theologians (in particular, Philo, Maimonides, Hermann Cohen, and Novak himself) have used the philosophical resources of their predecessors to develop theological systems that they see as, at least in part, the natural perfection of the projects those predecessors began. Second, Novak suggests several arguments that might be used to establish the normative dimension of the thesis.[52] For instance, one can reason as follows:

---

51. As Novak puts it: "theology presupposes philosophy, and philosophy intends theology" ("Possibility of Revelation," 19); cf. Novak, *Athens and Jerusalem*, 111.

52. It is important to note that many of these arguments are aimed at establishing theology's

if the God of Judeo-Christian revelation is indeed the Creator of the world, and if the world cannot be fully understood without understanding its relation to its Creator, and if this Creator cannot be understood except by way of theology's revelation, then it will be impossible for philosophy to understand the world independent of theology. Strauss also gestures towards an argument for the completion thesis in his interpretation of Maimonides, grounded in a distinction between the way things are known through revelation and the way they are known through rational inquiry. According to Strauss's reading of Maimonides, the prophet knows things *immediately* through revelation, whereas the philosopher only knows things by way of conclusions arrived at diachronically through the conjunction of premises, and so the prophet can know things that the philosopher cannot.[53]

In what follows, however, I want to put aside the normative dimension of the completion thesis. Whether or not we accept the thesis as a necessary feature of the relationship between philosophy and theology, I think it is a profoundly useful hermeneutic lens through which to read the interaction between philosophers and theologians throughout history. Above, I have attempted to lay out Novak's blueprint for the meeting of Athens and Jerusalem: independently, philosophy and theology receive their own revelations (understood both as commitments to a methodology and way of life and as commitments to certain propositional truths) about which they reason; then, once theology and philosophy engage with each other, theology alone is able to complete the projects that philosophy began because of the superiority of theology's revelation. In *Athens and Jerusalem*, Novak shows how productive this blueprint can be for reading the history of Jewish philosophy, demonstrating that figures like Philo respond to the challenge of philosophy by arguing that philosophy (i) is engaged in the same projects as theology and (ii) is in need of theology in order to successfully fulfill those projects. Now, I hope to show that Novak's framework can prove equally fruitful when applied to Christian philosophers.

I will do so, following Novak's own way of proceeding, by focusing on a particular case study from the history of philosophy: Augustine's engagement with Apuleius's *De Deo Socratis* (*DDS*) in Books VIII and IX of his *De Civitate Dei* (*DCD*). Given limitations of time and space, I must put aside the broader issue of Augustine's relationship to Platonism in general and the still-broader question of how Christian thinkers in antiquity appropriated and responded to their pagan philosophical heritage. Nevertheless, as we shall see, a careful reading of Augustine's engagement with

---

superior, rather than *exclusive*, ability to accomplish the ends of philosophy—for instance, Philo's arguments that theology is better able to integrate the practical and theoretical ends of human life than philosophy (Novak, *Athens and Jerusalem*, 109–11), because the object of theology's study (God) perfectly unifies the practical (insofar as God is the Creator of the universe) and the theoretical (insofar as God knows this created universe perfectly). Ultimately, however, Novak also wants to assert theology's *exclusive* ability to complete philosophy's projects.

53. Strauss, *Philosophy and Law*, 106. Strauss, as far as I can tell, does not develop this thought any further, and it is unclear what sorts of things he thinks can *only* be known immediately.

Apuleius shows him relating to his philosophical antecedent just as Novak sketches, recognizing philosophy's own revelation while also demonstrating that only theology's revelation can adequately reveal the way the world truly is. In this way, our case study suggests that the structure of the relationship between Athens and Jerusalem that Novak points us towards can be applied to patristic thinkers (and, I would suggest, to Christian intellectuals throughout history) just as productively as to their fellow Jewish citizens of Jerusalem.

The rest of this paper thus proceeds in two parts. I begin by briefly summarizing Apuleius's work, paying particular attention to how Apuleius's arguments adhere to the blueprint laid out in the foregoing sections in their own right. Then, I argue that Augustine deliberately and explicitly engages with the *DDS* as setting out a sort of revelation—albeit an *inadequate* revelation—about which Apuleius is subsequently reasoning and which aims at the same end as Judeo-Christian revelation. I advance this claim by focusing on four key themes in *DCD* VIII and IX: (i) Augustine's insistence that the Platonists are his philosophical brethren; (ii) his demonstration of the inadequacy of philosophical revelation by way of philosophy's own intellectual resources; (iii) the way in which the Platonists' non-Christian, incomplete revelation leads them astray; and (iv) the way Christian revelation completes the metaphysical structure of mediation that Augustine finds in Apuleius's work.

The Problem of Mediation: Apuleius's *De Deo Socratis*

As indicated by its title, Apuleius's *De Deo Socratis* presents itself as a discussion of Socrates's divine sign or *daimonion*.[54] This divine force (or *potestas*, as Apuleius describes it)[55] intervenes in Socrates's life at various points throughout the Platonic dialogues, as was already discussed above, in order to prevent Socrates from doing

---

54. For an excellent introduction to and translation of the work, see Harrison, *Apuleius: A Latin Sophist*, 137–73; "De Deo Socratis." Jones, *Apuleius: Apologia, Florida, De Deo Socratis* offers the most recent English translation. Moreschini, ed., *Apulei Platonici Madaurensis Opera quae supersunt* is the most commonly consulted modern critical edition of the text. For detailed readings of Apuleius's arguments in their own right, see Baltes, Lakmann, Dillon, Donini, Häfner, and Karfíková, eds., *Apuleius: De Deo Socratis*; Beaujeu, *Apulée: Opuscules philosophiques (Du Dieu de Socrate, Platon et sa doctrine, Du Monde) et Fragments*, 183–247; Moreschini, *Apuleius and the Metamorphoses of Platonism*; Moreschini, "La Polemica Di Agostino Contro La Demonologia Di Apuleio." Importantly, what is transmitted to us as the *DDS* may not be a complete text—for a discussion of the connection of the "false premise" to the rest of the speech, and the question of whether an introductory and/or concluding section has been lost in transmission, see Harrison *Sophist* 141–44. For the purpose of this paper, I will treat the text as it is transmitted to us (and, so far as I can tell, as it was transmitted to Augustine) as complete.

55. Apuleius, *DDS*, 132. Page numbers for the *DDS* follow von Oudendorp's 1823 edition. Here and throughout, I do not differentiate between "Apuleius" and the speaker of the *DDS*, nor does Augustine at any point in the *DCD*. Should anyone insist that such a distinction must be maintained, and that the views expressed by the speaker of the *DDS* cannot be identified with Apuleius, then the arguments below should be applied *mutatis mutandis* to the philosophical perspective the speaker articulates.

things that would be harmful to him. The *daimonion* was already cause for confusion and interpretive disagreement among Plato's philosophical progeny in antiquity. We repeatedly find Platonists asking (i) what *is* this *daimonion*, (ii) what *place* do such forces have in the natural world in general, and (iii) what *role* does it play in Socrates's life in particular?[56] Of course, these questions remain relevant for modern commentators on Plato—in antiquity, however, attempts to respond to these questions led to the articulation of a philosophical *demonology* or *Geisterlehre*, of which Apuleius's *DDS* is a key surviving example.[57] So, although the *DDS* is explicitly about Socrates's *daimonion*, much of the work is devoted to the development of a general system of demonology, which Apuleius then employs to explain the particular divine force operative in Socrates's life.

The *DDS* can be divided into four general sections,[58] roughly corresponding to the questions posed in the preceding paragraph. First (answering question (ii) above), Apuleius outlines the elements of the general structure of the universe relevant to his investigation; namely, the nature of the gods and human beings, and the need for a mediating force between the divine and mortals.[59] Second (question (i)), he discusses the precise nature of the class of divine forces known as *daemones*,[60] of which Socrates's *daimonion* is a member.[61] Third (iii), Apuleius gives an interpretation of the role of Socrates's divine sign on the basis of a careful exegesis of Plato's text.[62] Finally, as a sort of *coda* to the

---

56. Apuleius is not the first to raise these questions—we find prior discussion in several of Plutarch's works (chiefly his *De genio Socratis*) and a contemporaneous treatment in Maximus of Tyre's eight and ninth *Orations*. The influence of Plutarch and Maximus on Apuleius is another question we must put aside (though see Timotin, *La démonologie platonicienne*, 202 n.125 and Harrison, *Sophist*, 138 for discussions on the topic). For an overview of the history of Platonic demonology and our extant sources, however, see Timotin.

57. For contemporary contributions to the discussion of Socrates's divine sign, see the articles in Smith and Woodruff, *Reason and Religion in Socratic Philosophy*; Destrée and Smith, eds., *Socrates' Divine Sign: Religion, Practice, and Value in Socratic Philosophy*; McPherran, *The Religion of Socrates*. The focus of modern and classical discussions of the *daimonion* are, however, importantly different: whereas the ancients were concerned first and foremost with the identity and nature of the divine sign itself, contemporary commentators are more interested in understanding the relationship between the *daimonion* and other Socratico-Platonic claims (for instance, how Socrates can unreflectively endorse the dictates of his divine sign while also endorsing other positions—like the seemingly universal need for the elenchtic interrogation of our beliefs—that seem to contradict the way he relates to his *daimonion*).

58. Cf. Harrison, *Sophist*, 144; "De Deo Socratis," 192.

59. Apuleius, *DDS*, 114–132.

60. I generally favor translating the Greek daimōn as "angel" rather than "demon," because I think the modern, popular conception of angels better tracks the role of these ancient divine figures (think, for instance, of how much Socrates's *daimonion* acts like a "guardian angel"). However, given the importance of Augustine's distinction between angels and demons in his response to Apuleius, and in order to avoid prejudicing the reader in her interpretation of Apuleius's text, I will leave the word untranslated throughout.

61. Apuleius, *DDS*, 132–56.

62. Apuleius, *DDS*, 157–67.

work, Apuleius uses the *exemplum* of Socrates's divinely inspired life as a springboard for a general protreptic exhortation to the philosophical way of life.[63]

In the first section of the *DDS*, Apuleius lays out a number of properties of living beings in the cosmos that will be necessary for the forthcoming discussion. Living beings, Apuleius tells us Plato believed, are divided into three parts: the immortal gods are the "highest" part, perishable beings like humans the "lowest," and *daemones* constitute an intermediary division between the two. Some of the gods are known to humans by sight (that is, the sun/moon/stars), and others by means of rational reflection (like the traditional gods of the Greco-Roman pantheon). Apuleius offers some brief insight into the character of these gods—they are, he tells us, souls unsullied by bodies or any other attachment to the material world, eternal, dependent on nothing outside of themselves to attain their ends, and so forth—before claiming that the nature of the highest of these gods is ultimately inexpressible. He thus turns to discuss the lowest rung of his *scala naturae*, human beings and other animals. Humans are embodied souls that, though rational, have become depraved (*depravaverint*) and bestial (*efferarint*), which threatens to create an insuperable gap between immortals and mortals.[64] This is because celestial gods could not interact with human beings without being polluted by them, or, at the very least, without diminishing the heights of their divine happiness. Nevertheless, Apuleius claims, humans require access to the divine in order to live the sort of life appropriate to them as human beings.[65]

The need to bridge this divide between gods and mortals leads Apuleius to shift his focus to "certain intermediate divine powers (*quaedam divinae mediae potestates*),"[66]

63. Apuleius, *DDS*, 167–78.
Understood in this way, the structure of the *DDS* should not make us think that Apuleius's discussion of Socrates's *daimonion* is something of an afterthought, or merely a rhetorical excuse for Apuleius to discuss what he is really interested in, that is, the nature of demons in general. Instead, the interpretation of Socrates's *daimonion* can be seen as the natural end-point of the work, with the preceding discussion laying the necessary general groundwork for Apuleius to present his interpretation of Socrates's particular example.

64. Apuleius, *DDS*, 125.

65. Apuleius's reasoning here (*DDS* 127–32) raises a number of problems. As I see it, the two most pressing are:

1) Why would *any* interaction with humans whatsoever sully the divine? In response, I suggest that Apuleius might be reasoning as follows: the gods must be as perfect/happy/independent as possible; if interactions with human beings rendered the gods more perfect/happy, then the gods would need to interact with humans to be as perfect/happy as possible; this would, however, make the gods less independent or autonomous than they could otherwise be; otherwise, if interacting with humans has no impact on the perfection or happiness of the gods, then they have no reason to interact with humans; therefore, the gods do interact with mortals. This response, however, is purely speculative.

2) Apuleius argues that humans need to interact with the divine in order to be able to swear oaths by the gods. But why is this such a pressing concern—indeed, the only concern Apuleius raises? Again, in response, I suggest that the swearing of oaths is intended to serve as a sort of rhetorical metaphor for the human need for the divine in order to live together socially and act correctly as moral beings. The swearing of oaths would thus serve as an analogue for promise-keeping more generally, and promise-keeping in turn as essentially connected to correct moral action in general.

66. Apuleius, *DDS*, 132.

that is, *daemones*. *Daemones* are defined as "living beings in kind, rational creatures in mind, susceptible to emotion in spirit, in body composed of air (*aer*), everlasting in time."[67] These beings serve as intermediaries, carrying prayers upwards from humans to the gods, and aid downwards from the gods to humans, with this aid taking the form of dreams, (in)auspicious omens, and other similar events with which it would not be fitting for the gods themselves to be involved. They also reside within the air,[68] the element lying between the aether (the domain of the celestial gods) and the earth, where mortal beings live. Why the air? Apuleius gives two reasons: first, air constitutes an intermediate physical location among the elements, which matches the intermediary nature of the *daemones*; second, given a Platonic principle of plenitude (even more than nature, the Platonists of antiquity abhor an ontological vacuum), air requires its own natural inhabitants in keeping with the other elements, and the *daemones* fill what would otherwise constitute a sort of ontological void.

The functional and material intermediary status of the *daemones* also manifests itself in other characteristics. Most importantly, they are immortal like the gods but susceptible to emotions like human beings. The gods are unable to feel emotions, as this would be a mark of imperfection—mutability (emotional or otherwise) always being a change from a less perfect state to a more perfect state.[69] Emotional susceptibility is thus necessary for *daemones* to fulfill their intermediary role, as it makes them capable of responding to the prayers of mortals. The gods, in contrast, are entirely unmoved by our prayers, as being moved would require them to be capable of feeling emotions. Apuleius also uses this susceptibility to explain the diversity of religious practices in the world.

---

67. Quippe, ut fine comprehendam, daemones sunt genere animalia, ingenio rationabilia, animo passiva, corpore aeria, tempore aeterna (Apuleius, *DDS*, 148).

68. A claim already advanced in the pseudo-Platonic *Epinomis* (981c–985b), and picked up, *inter alios*, by Philo (*De Gigantibus* 7–9) in his description of angels. Apuleius's demonology, it is important to remember, is not developed solely out of an initial Socratico-Platonic revelation but forms part of an ongoing tradition of interpretation (for a detailed analysis of how the *DDS* fits into the historical development of Platonic demonology, see Habermehl, "Quaedam divinae mediae potestates").

69. Again, Apuleius's claim seems problematic: why think that *every* change must be from better to worse or the inverse, excluding the possibility of "neutral" changes? One might think, for instance, that changing from enjoying listening to Beethoven's 14th string quartet to enjoying listening to his 15th is not a change from better to worse or the opposite, but a shift between indiscernible goods. Even if we admitted the possible of such neutral changes, however, Apuleius might still respond as follows: if every intentional action is essentially teleological, and if the gods (being perfectly unconstrained in deciding upon and attaining their ends) always act intentionally, then to change from feeling one emotion to another (that is, to stop performing one action and begin another) would require a change of ends, which would require the gods to have a *reason* to change their end. Were this the case, then either the two ends would be indiscernible (which would fail to give the gods a reason to change their end), or their present end would be worse than some other possible end (which would be absurd since, the gods being perfectly unconstrained, we could not explain why they had not set the better end for themselves *ab initio*), or their present end would be better (in which case, again, they would have no reason to change). However, this response is entirely speculative and raises a number of further questions itself that I cannot pursue here.

Because of their mutability, different *daemones* can respond to differing rites in different ways, with each spirit favoring distinct ceremonies.

Over the course of the second section of the *DDS*, Apuleius introduces a number of more specific distinctions within the class *daemones*. First, *daemones* are divided between those that have never been embodied and those that have taken on human form. Unembodied *daemones* are further subdivided into forces with designated spheres of authority (like the *daemon* responsible for erotic love and the one responsible for sleep) and those that act as guardians for human beings. Embodied *daemones* (that is, human souls) form a lower class than those spirits that have never been embodied. When still embodied, a member of the lower sub-division of *daemones* is identified as a *genius*, a concept Apuleius borrows from popular Roman religion, and with a *lemur* after death.[70] Furthermore, after death, these once-embodied *lemures* are separated into four further sub-divisions: *larvae*, *daemones* who punish the morally wicked while they live; *manes*, neutral figures about which Apuleius has little to say; the *lares familiares*, the souls of good humans who become household "gods" and the guardians of their families; and the heroes, good souls who are worshipped as divinities after their death.[71]

Once Apuleius has established the relevant metaphysical structure of the world (showing the general need for mediation) and the basic properties/roles of *daemones* (showing the general nature of the mediators), he is ready to discuss Socrates's *daimonion* in particular. Socrates's divine sign, as already discussed above, intervened throughout his life to protect him from performing harmful actions, and a number of these divine interventions are recorded by Plato.[72] Apuleius identifies the *daimonion* with a member of the class of non-embodied guardian *daemones* he described in the second section of the *DDS*. Importantly, the force is said to intervene "*whenever the functions of wisdom were cut off* and [Socrates] stood in need not of advice but of foresight, so that whenever he faltered with uncertainty, at that moment he might stand firm with divine insight."[73] This interpretation is grounded

---

70. For a detailed reading of how Apuleius uses and transforms Roman religious concepts in the *DDS*, see Habermehl 129–34.

71. Commentators have frequently noted the difficulties created by these sub-divisions (Hijmans, "Apuleius: Philosophus Platonicus," 443; Habermehl, "Quaedam divinae mediae potestates," 127). For instance, it might seem as if the only distinction between the *lares* and the higher guardian *daemones* is the fact that the *lares* were once embodied—but if this is the only distinction, why are the guardian *daemones* still described as higher beings even *after* the *lares* are no longer embodied? More generally, the distinction between *genius/lemur* and human beings is complicated: why is it that a human soul *qua genius* is considered a member of the class of *daemones*, but a human being *tout court* is not? For the purposes of this paper, however, I can only note such puzzles before putting them aside.

72. The reliability of Plato's reports of Socrates's life, and the possibility of retrieving the "historical" Socrates from beneath his Platonic guise, point, of course, towards a host of hoary interpretive questions. What is important for us here, however, is that both Apuleius and Augustine understand Plato as accurately reporting actual historical occurrences in Socrates's life.

73. Sicubi tamen interceptis sapientiae officiis non consilio sed praesagio indigebat, ut ubi dubitatione clauderet, ibi divinatione consisteret (*DDS* 157–58), emphasis mine, reading *interceptis* with Harrison ("De Deo Socratis" 209n.53) in place of the transmitted *interfectis*.

in a careful exegesis of Plato's report of Socrates's words, in a manner remarkably similar to the sort of close reading common to Judeo-Christian biblical exegesis. Apuleius is careful to point out that Socrates says he heard not "*a voice*" but "*a certain voice*," which he takes as evidence that Socrates's experiences cannot be reduced (in a skeptical or deflationary spirit) to mere kledomancy or excessive superstition on Socrates's part. Apuleius applies this same model of the relationship between wisdom and prophecy to various examples from Homer: whereas "wise" men are called for to adjudicate disputes or to sneak into an enemy camp, when the Greek army confronts a situation like that at Aulis where they are in need of "advice alien to the resources of wisdom (*aliena sapientiae officiis consultation*),"[74] as Socrates was in the moments when his *daimonion* would intervene, they must turn to a prophet. Finally, in the closing section of the DDS, this exegesis of Platonic revelation has a practical protreptic upshot. Carefully attending to Socrates's life should compel us to devote ourselves to the same way of life, that is, the care of our soul and the cultivation of the virtues through the practice of philosophy.

Before turning to Augustine's response, it should already be apparent that Apuleius's speech, read in its own right, exemplifies many of the key claims we saw Novak making earlier about the ways in which philosophy is grounded in its own distinct revelation. Most obviously, Apuleius is philosophizing about the divine, seeing no clear boundary between the domain of philosophical inquiry and that of religion.[75] But Apuleius's conformance to Novak's theory runs much deeper than this. First, as the closing section of the *DDS* shows, Apuleius thinks of philosophy not only as the search for true propositional knowledge about the world but as a *way of life*. Merely gaining a correct theoretical understanding of the nature of *daemones*, and of Socrates's *daimonion* in particular, does not mark the end of his philosophical inquiry—this theoretical knowledge must lead his audience to change their lives. At the same time, Apuleius arrives at this correct theoretical understanding through the interpretation of various forms of revealed *data*:

1. Socrates's direct experience of the divine (recall, in particular, the way his demonology is grounded in the precise wording of Socrates's description of his experience of the divine);
2. Plato's own inspired writings (indeed, Apuleius presents himself as a sort of interpreter or *mediator* between his audience and Plato, who himself has an almost divine status);[76]

---

74. Apuleius, *DDS*, 162.

75. Cf. Habermehl 134n.69: "For Apuleius, philosophy and religion were twin efforts toward the same goal." Strikingly, in his *Apologia* (41.3), Apuleius will go so far as to describe the philosopher as a "priest of all the gods" (*omnium deum sacerdotem*).

76. See, for instance, Apuleius, *DDS*, 155: "you all, who are hearing this divine idea of Plato with myself as interpreter (*me interprete*)." Fletcher, *Apuleius' Platonism: The Impersonation of Philosophy*, 157–59 makes much of this interpretive dynamic, suggesting that Apuleius seeks to blend his role as

3. The popular beliefs and concepts of those in the same religious tradition as Apuleius and his audience (as seen, for instance, in his reinterpretation of traditional Roman spirits as representing various classes of *daemones*); as well as

4. The religious experiences of other communities (such as the distinct rites and mythology found among the Egyptians).

Apuleius seeks to fit diverse "pieces" of revelation together (from Plato and Socrates to the Roman religious tradition to Egyptian mythology to Homer and Virgil), which may initially seem to conflict with each other, into a cohesive and universalizing narrative about the structure of the world. This is, of course, just the sort of interpretive work Novak has led us to expect to see philosophy performing vis-à-vis revelation.

Finally, Apuleius's discussion of the *daimonion* seems to articulate a form of the completion thesis in response to Socratic revelation, since philosophers like Socrates find themselves in need of revelation once they have exhausted the resources provided by philosophical wisdom. This is not, we must remember, *precisely* Novak's version of the thesis. After all, Apuleius never claims that revelation completes philosophy's *own* projects in a way that philosophy cannot but only that revelation enables the completion of projects that fall outside the bounds of wisdom. However, these projects (like the cultivation of virtue) are intimately connected with—perhaps even identical to—the project of philosophy as Apuleius conceives of it. Thus, although Apuleius never explicitly says that philosophy stands in need of the revelation provided by *daemones* in order to complete its own projects, he seems remarkably close to making this claim.

Angels and Demons: Augustine's *De Civitate Dei* VIII/IX

Above, I have tried to show how Novak allows us to read Apuleius's discourse as fitting into a general *schema* of philosophical discourse repeated throughout the history of Western philosophy. I now want to suggest that Augustine's engagement with Apuleius's demonology in books VIII and IX of his *De Civitate Dei* also conforms to Novak's blueprint and that this blueprint can help us better appreciate Augustine's general aims when responding to Apuleius. Indeed, when we read Augustine through the lens Novak has provided us with, we can see how *DCD* VIII and IX are intended to show that philosophy is dependent on revelation, that the Platonico-Socratic revelation Apuleius relies on is inadequate for the task Apuleius sets himself, and that Apuleius's project, though originating out of philosophical revelation, can only be fully completed by Christian revelation.[77]

---

interpreter of Plato (which functionally mirrors the mediatory nature of the *daemones* under discussion) with an *identification* of his voice with Plato's and, in turn, of Plato with the highest god of Apuleius's *scala naturae*. Plato is thus a unique revelation at least on par with—if not transcending—the original Socratic revelation he also reports.

77. Inevitably, we must confront the question of *why* Augustine chose to engage with Apuleius's *DDS* in particular, given the abundance of other instances of Platonic demonology he would have

Reading Augustine by way of Novak thus allows us to avoid misunderstanding what Augustine is up to in this part of the *DCD*, as—or so I intend to argue—many commentators have in the past. Contemporary commentators on *DCD VIII* and *IX* tend to focus on the *polemical* nature of Augustine's engagement with Apuleius, often reading Augustine as engaged in "une argumentation tendancieuse et disqualifiante qui déstructure le discours d'Apulée et en dénature la doctrine."[78] The goal of this hostile rebuttal of Augustine's position, in the eyes of readers like Saudelli and Fick, is to destabilize the pagan worldview of Apuleius's followers by creating a sort of "choc psychologique" once they recognize the absurd conclusions that follow from their commitment to the existence of *daemones* of the sort described in the *DDS*.[79] Augustine's critique of Apuleius, then, reduces to a sort of propaedeutic path-clearing, eliminating the false pagan system in order to replace it wholesale with a Christian alternative—as Fick writes, "pour instaurer la nouvelle spiritualité, il faut anéantir l'ancienne."[80]

---

been exposed to. There are at least six possible responses to this question, all but the first of which, I think, had some role to play in Augustine's choice of text:

1) Hermann ("Le Procès d'Apulée fut-il un procès de Christianisme?"; "Le Dieu-roi d'Apulée") suggested that Apuleius was a Christian and that his prosecution on the charge of practicing magic was in fact an oblique way of prosecuting him for his Christianity—if Augustine knew this, then he might have chosen the *DDS* because of Apuleius's connection to the Christian community. Such a claim, however, is wildly speculative. Hermann has (it seems to me) only the most tenuous of evidence for such a sweeping claim.

2) Augustine writes that Apuleius was said to have performed miracles equal to or even greater than those of Christ (cf. *Epistulae* 136; 137; 138)—refuting Apuleius's theory thus also allowed Augustine to deflate the image of a pagan miracle-worker (Moreschini, *Metamorphoses* 351–52; Saudelli, "«Dieu» ou «démon» de Socrate? Augustin contre Apulée," 88).

3) Apuleius was from North Africa, like Augustine, and so his work was particularly prominent in the intellectual circles within which Augustine participated at the time (cf. Hunink, "'Apuleius, qui nobis Afris Afer est notior': Augustine's Polemic against Apuleius in De Civitate Dei").

4) Apuleius's focus on the need for *mediation* between the gods and human beings presented Augustine with an ideal counterpoint concerning a topic he already intended to discuss at this point in his *DCD*, while also providing him with an opportunity to demonstrate (as I will argue in what follows) the close affinities between Apuleius's Platonism and Augustine's Christianity.

5) Apuleius's text might have been viewed as the most developed example of Platonic demonology accessible in Latin (or, perhaps, *simpliciter*) in Augustine's time, so that when deciding how to best present the complex relationship between pagan and Christian accounts of divine mediation, Augustine merely chose the best account available to him (cf. Saudelli 72: Apuleius's work "peut être considérée comme le traité démonologique le plus approfondi, le plus systématique, et le plus élégant de l'Antiquité.")

6) The *DDS*, while being an important example of Platonic demonology, was also reflective of popular Roman religious beliefs and practices at the time, allowing Augustine to respond to both intellectual and "folk" conceptions of *daemones* at the same time (cf. Moreschini, "Polemica" 587–88 on Apuleius's intention to address a general Roman audience with his work).

78. Saudelli, "«Dieu» ou «démon» de Socrate?" 88.

79. Fick, "Saint Augustin pourfendeur des démons païens," 197–98.

80. Fick, "Saint Augustin pourfendeur des démons païens," 192–93. So also Bernard, "Zur Dämonologie des Apuleius von Madura," 373: "Diese durchdachte Dämonologie hat Augustinus offenbar als für das Christentum gefährlich angesehen und sie darum unter Einsatz aller (auch der polemischen) Mittel der Rhetorik zu widerlegen gesucht."

Conversely, Moreschini contends that Augustine's arguments cannot be aimed at converting Platonists or pagans in general to Christianity, as these arguments are only successful if one is already committed to many of the main premises of Christianity.[81] Fick, in a similar vein, also claims that Augustine's polemic is riddled with sophisms and bad arguments, which she suggests Augustine employs deliberately in order to create the desired psychological shock by way of a presentation "de manière plus ou moins caricaturale" of Apuleius's position, followed by a series of rhetorically persuasive but ultimately fallacious arguments.[82]

None of these readings, however, allow us to make sense of the ensemble of Augustine's response to Apuleius. It seems clear that Augustine intends the work as a serious refutation of the errors in Apuleius's reasoning on Apuleius's own terms—and, *pace* Fick, if we are able to provide an interpretation of this part of the *DCD* that allows us to avoid attributing a series of deliberately false (or at least grossly misleading) arguments to him, we should. Moreover, any purely polemical reading of Augustine's response will fail to account for just how much of Apuleius's demonology Augustine appropriates during the course of the two books under discussion. Pépin, for instance, rightly draws our attention to several ways in which Augustine's angelology and demonology borrow from Apuleius, seeing this appropriation as the other side of Augustine's negative polemic.[83] It would be exceedingly odd for Augustine to deliberately borrow a number of important concepts and arguments from a philosophical system that he is trying to discredit and upend.

Much like Pépin, Moreschini has suggested that Augustine's engagement with Apuleius is an example "di quel rapporto contrastante di ostilità e di recezione, che è stato tipico del cristianesimo nei confronti della cultura pagana."[84] Reading Augustine's response to the *DDS* as oscillating between hostility and appropriation leads both Moreschini and Karfíková to argue that his incorporation of Apuleius's ideas within his own account of *daemones* and angels is neither accidental nor arbitrary but rather a deliberate attempt to show how his Christianity is an heir to the Platonic tradition, better preserving Plato's own insights than later Platonic demonology.[85]

81. Moreschini, "Polemica," 589; 596.
82. Fick, "Saint Augustin pourfendeur des démons païens," 198–201.
83. Pépin, "La doctrine platonicienne des anges et des démons."
84. Moreschini, "Polemica," 583.
85. Karfíková, "Augustins Polemik gegen Apuleius," 189; Moreschini, *Metamorphoses*, 354, 362. Fick also, at times, endorses this interpretation ("Augustin se présente, lui, comme le champion de l'orthodoxie platonicienne," 195), though I find it difficult to understand how, in her view, Augustine aims both to present himself as a champion of Platonic orthodoxy *and* to destroy the very roots of the pagan worldview. Finally, Saudelli ("«Dieu» ou «démon» de Socrate?" 88) also claims that Augustine seeks to show that Apuleius has betrayed his Platonic roots by failing to preserve Socrates's monotheistic theology. The attribution of a pre-Christian monotheism to Socrates is, of course, a highly contentious claim. However, what is important here is that Saudelli sees Augustine's response to Apuleius as (at least in part) presenting himself as a better Platonist than the Platonists. Her interpretation thus faces the same challenge as Fick's—how can Augustine be both a champion of Platonism *and* a destroyer of the pagan worldview, of which Platonism must be seen as an integral part?

We thus see two key lines of interpretation developing in the contemporary scholarship. First, there are those who read Augustine's response as purely polemical, but they fail to account for his appropriation and redeployment of many of the key elements of Apuleius's demonology. Others read Augustine as engaged in a dynamic relationship that moves repeatedly between polemical hostility and appropriation for Augustine's own theological purposes, with some commentators also seeing this dynamic relationship as indicative of Augustine's desire to present himself as a better Platonist than the Platonists—that is to say, as a philosopher more faithful to Plato's original insight than his philosophical successors.

This dynamic interpretation still fails, however, to properly account for the positive stance Augustine adopts towards his Platonic brethren and mischaracterizes Augustine's relationship to Plato and his school. As we shall see in what follows, Augustine ultimately relates to Platonists like Apuleius as fellow sojourners, rather than as competitors, but also as travellers who are incapable of completing the journey they have embarked on by way of their own resources. Augustine's response to Apuleius, then, is not a question of being more faithful to Plato but rather of fulfilling the project that both Plato (and his followers) and Christian theologians have already engaged it. Augustine has no interest in being a good Platonist—but he is concerned with successfully completing the project Plato, *inter alios*, was engaged in and in ensuring his audience understands that Plato could not have completed that project himself. Understood correctly, Augustine's stance towards Apuleius is thus not one of hostility so much as *correction*, and not of appropriation so much as *completion*.

I imagine the focus of contemporary commentators on the polemical and hostile character of Augustine's response, which often prevents them from seeing the underlying connections that unify Apuleius and Augustine's projects together, results from the same imagined incompatibility of Athens and Jerusalem that earlier motivated Tertullian's dichotomy—and I think we can arrive at a correct understanding of Augustine's project by reading DCD VIII and IX in the light of Novak's arguments against the traditional interpretation of Tertullian's dichotomy and for the completion thesis we discussed above. In particular, I want to draw attention to four key elements in Augustine's discourse: first, the way in which Augustine relates to Platonists as his brethren because of their shared access, at least in part, to the same revelation; second, how Augustine uses the conceptual resources of philosophy to show Apuleius and his audience that they have arrived at the wrong conclusions by their own lights; third, the role of false moments of revelation in leading the Platonists to incorrect conclusions; and finally, the way Augustine argues that Christian revelation alone is capable of completing the Platonists' project. These elements mirror key elements of Novak's theory—we see Augustine arguing that the philosophers have their own revelation about which they have (incorrectly) reasoned and that only the revelation of the theologians is capable of adequately responding to the projects philosophy has set itself. Let us briefly consider them in order.

Augustine repeatedly tells us in the opening chapters of *DCD* VIII that he "prefers (*anteponimus*)" the Platonists to the other philosophical schools[86] and that he acknowledges them as his philosophical "neighbours (*nobis propinquiores*)."[87] This is because none of the other philosophical schools, in Augustine's eyes, have come as close as the Platonists to the truths of Christianity.[88] The Platonists accept a number of true propositions concerning the divine—they recognize the existence of a transcendent Creator God[89] who is "the cause of being, the order (*ratio*) of thinking, the guide (*ordo*) of living."[90] God is thus understood by the Platonists, I take it, as the efficient and final cause of the natural world, intimately implicated in our rational activity, and the ethical standard against which we measure ourselves. Of course, I do not have the space here to properly investigate what Augustine means when he claims, for instance, that both Platonists and Christians find in God the "*ratio intellegendi*." What is important for the questions at hand is that Augustine identifies several critical areas of overlap between Platonists and Christians, and this overlap leads him to accept the Platonists as partners in his inquiry. But whence, one might ask, does this overlapping consensus originate? That is to ask: how is it the case that the Platonists have arrived at so many correct beliefs about the nature of the divine?

Augustine's response is that God must have revealed these truths to the Platonists through Plato, like God revealed them to the Jews through the prophets.[91] But one might still wonder how this could be the case. Plato offers us, after all, no record of an epiphany of the sort that an Old Testament prophet would receive. One possibility Augustine considers is that Plato might have become acquainted with Judeo-Christian revelation by way of the prophets, either directly[92] or indirectly.[93] The other possibility is that God revealed these truths directly to Plato, just as revelation was given to the

---

86. Augustine, *DCD*, VIII.7.322.3, 9.334.17–18, 10.335.31. All references to the *DCD* are to the 1877 edition of Dombart's Teubner text.

87. Augustine, *DCD*, VIII.9.334.18.

88. Augustine, *DCD*, VIII.5. See also *De vera religione* VII.

89. Augustine, *DCD*, VIII.1.

90. Augustine, *DCD*, VIII.4.326.19–20. Cf. VIII.5.328.6–8 (*Platonicis philosophis . . . qui verum Deum et rerum auctorem et veritatis inlustratorem et beatitudinis largitorem esse dixerunt*) and VIII.10.335.27–31 (*nobis consentiunt de uno Deo huius universitatis auctore, qui non solum super omnia corpora est incorporeus, verum etiam super omnes animas incorruptibilis, principium nostrum, lumen nostrum, bonum nostrum*).

91. Augustine, *DCD*, VIII.6. On the extent to which Augustine conceives of the Platonists as having access to Christian revelation, see also Madec, "«Si Plato viveret . . .» (Augustin, De Vera Religione, 3.3)."

92 Augustine discusses a popular belief that Plato might have met the prophet Jeremiah, but dismisses the idea as historically impossible.

93. Augustine, *DCD*, VIII.11. That is, by way of a Greek translation of the Jewish Scriptures, or some sort of Greek-speaking interpreter of the Scriptures. Remarkably, Augustine also thinks it possible that some elements of Plato's cosmology in the *Timaeus* might show signs of inspiration from the Old Testament, in particular from the creation narrative in *Genesis*.

prophets.[94] In either case, Augustine clearly believes that the Platonic philosophers are reasoning about revelation—indeed, the *same* revelation (at least in part) as Christian theologians—just as Novak has led us to expect.

Christus Mediator Bonus: *Completing the Platonic Project*

Ultimately, for Augustine, the philosophy of the Platonists is itself grounded in revelation, a revelation that is from *the same God* and reveals *the same truths* as Christian revelation. The Platonists have been led astray, however, by (i) reasoning incorrectly about the revelation they have been given, and (ii) assenting to false revelations, that is, accepting things as revelation that do not come from God.[95] Augustine elaborates each of these failings with different lines of argument.

First, Augustine uses the resources of philosophy to show that philosophy is wrong by its own standards, because the philosophers have reasoned wrongly about their revelation. To do so, Augustine employs all of the philosophical resources Apuleius himself employs in *DDS*. Consider, to be begin with, Augustine and Apuleius's use of rhetoric. Apuleius's treatise is a striking demonstration of his oratorical and philosophical abilities—envisioned as a public speech, Apuleius deploys an array of literary devices and rhetorical tropes in the service of convincing his audience of his philosophical position. Augustine does the same in *DCD* VIII and IX.[96] For instance, we find the elaborate employment of wordplay throughout text,[97] as well as the repeated use of literary devices like anaphora.[98] Of course, Augustine's rhetorical training and literary skill meant that he used such tools in all of his writings, but as Hagendahl notes in his discussion of VIII.20.355.26–351.10,[99] we find in the two books of the *DCD* passages

---

94. Augustine, *DCD*, VIII.12. Augustine also believes that other philosophers—such as those in Egypt or Persia—could also have access to such revelation, and he claims that he focuses on the Platonists because he is most familiar with their writings (VIII.10).

95. Interestingly, Augustine grounds this reading of Platonic revelation on Christian revelation, in particular, on *Romans* I.18–23, where the author of the epistle writes that God revealed truths about the divine to those who claimed to be wise, but they nonetheless came to worship images of humans and animals rather than God (VIII.10).

96. For a discussion of the various ways in which Augustine's discussion mimics Apuleius's at the level of literary devices etc., see Hagendahl, *Augustine and the Latin Classics*, 680–89. Hunink is perhaps too extreme when he writes that some of Augustine's discussion "may seem a school exercise in rhetoric rather than a theological discussion" (92), but the emphasis he places on the *rhetorical* form of much of the two books is very much on the mark.

97. E.g., the gods are "*eudaemones, non sunt eudaemones daemones*" (Augustine, *DCD*, IX.13.385.29–30).

98. Cf. in particular the anaphoric opposition of *cum daemones* and *nobis vera religio praecipit* at Augustine, *DCD*, VIII.17.347.7–18 (Fick, "Saint Augustin pourfendeur des démons païens," 202).

99. *Praeclara sanctitatas Dei, qui*
non miscetur homini supplicanti,
et miscetur daemoni arroganti;
non miscetur homini paenitenti,

"distinguished by a profusion of scornful irony and rhetorical devices that surpasses everything to be found even in his writings."[100] In the very *form* of Augustine's writing, then, we already see him demonstrating how he, although a theologian, is nonetheless capable of surpassing the philosopher in the practice of philosophy, which includes the use of rhetorical forms of persuasion.

Next, we see Augustine engaged in careful exegesis, paying as close attention to the *precise* wording of Apuleius's text as Apuleius paid to Socrates's words at the *DDS* 165. For example, Augustine argues that Apuleius titled his work *De Deo Socratis* rather than *De Daemone Socratis* because he himself was ashamed of Socrates associating with a *daemon*, given the malignant nature of these spirits, and so tried to hide Socrates's association with a *daemon* from his audience at the outset of his work.[101] Importantly, Augustine is at pains to emphasize the careful attention that is evident in Apuleius's work[102] and that Apuleius requires of his readers.[103] Here, again, we see Augustine demonstrating his ability to philosophize even better than the philosophers—in the very same chapter that he praises Apuleius's careful attention in differentiating between gods and *daemones*, most markedly, Augustine demonstrates his own ability to proceed *diligenti disputatione* in critiquing Apuleius's choice of title.

Finally, Augustine engages in the same logical development of and extrapolation from various elements of the Platonic revelation as Apuleius. He derives contradictions (or, at least, unacceptable conclusions) from several of the properties Apuleius and Plato ascribe to the *daemones*, as well as from several other of Plato's philosophical commitments, just as Apuleius motivates the *DDS* from the very first lines by presenting his project as expanding upon insights established by Plato. For instance, Augustine poses a trilemma based on Plato's own banishment of theatre

---

et miscetur daemoni decipienti
non miscetur homini confugienti ad divinitatem,
et miscetur daemoni fingenti divinitatem;
non miscetur homini petenti indulgentiam,
et miscetur daemoni suadenti nequitiam;
non miscetur homini per philosophicos libros poetas de bene instituta civitate pellenti,
et miscetur daemoni a principibus et pontificibus civitatis per scaenicos ludos poetarum ludibria requirenti;
non miscetur homini deorum criminal fingere prohibenti,
et miscetur daemoni se falsis deorum criminibus obiectanti.

100. Hagendahl, *Augustine and the Latin Classics*, 684.

101. Augustine, *DCD*, VIII.14.

There are other reasons for thinking Apuleius's title is as it is (see Beaujeu, 201–3), but this does not change the fact that Augustine is here employing precisely the same argumentative strategy as Apuleius.

102. Apuleius's distinction between *daemones* and gods, Augustine tells us, is "most clear (*apertissime*) and most thorough (*copiosissime*)" and he "discusses Plato's thought with attentive argument (*diligenti disputatione*)" (*DCD*, VIII.14.342-4-6).

103. The point of his arguments only being made clear "to *discerning* readers (*significavit tamen prudentibus*)" (Augustine, *DCD*, IX.9.379.23, emphasis mine).

(and therefore the *daemones* associated with tragedy) from his *Republic*: either Apuleius was wrong and Socrates's spirit was not a *daemon*; or, Plato contradicted himself by first honoring the *daemones* in the form of Socrates's *daimonion* and then, later, removing their festivals from his ideal state; or, Socrates is not to be congratulated on the friendship of a *daemon*.[104] Note the way in which Augustine's argument proceeds. Beginning from Apuleius's *data* (among which number Plato's teachings, including the critique of theatre in the *Republic*, as well as popular religious beliefs, including the belief that divinities are directly implicated in theatre productions), he reasons to an exhaustive trichotomy, none of whose branches is a palatable conclusion for Apuleius.[105] This form of argument appears over and over again in *DCD* VIII and IX. To consider another key example, we find Augustine arguing that if mediation is needed in order to preserve the *goodness* of the gods, then the fact that the *daemones* are susceptible to the emotions (and so, to one extent or another, morally imperfect, because sometimes carried away by movements of the soul other than those of reason) should cause interaction with them to sully the perfect goodness of the gods just as much as interaction with humans.[106] Again, Augustine begins from Apuleius's own initial premises (the goodness of the gods being a central belief for the Platonists),[107] and reasons in the same logical manner as Apuleius, but in order to reach conclusions that would be entirely unacceptable to him.

This argument in particular inevitably calls into question the central claim of the *DDS*: why should we think that the *daemones* are superior to humans, and occupy an intermediary position relative to the gods, if they appear to be at least as imperfect as we are? Indeed, Augustine challenges, if the *daemones* are changeable (which, as we saw above, is necessary for them to be intermediaries), then surely they experience negative emotions—but then, will they not be worse off than morally outstanding human beings?[108] Augustine seems to be led to this conclusion in the following manner. He first establishes that passions are "a change in the soul contrary to reason (*motus animi contra rationem*)"[109] and furthermore, that the gods are happy because they are free from the perturbations of the passions. If the *daemones* experience these perturbations, he then argues, they must also experience unhappiness. To reach this conclusion, I think

104. Augustine, *DCD*, VIII.14.

105. Various commentators have taken issue with this line of argument (cf., e.g., Fick, "Saint Augustin pourfendeur des démons païens," 198), as it is unclear why Augustine thinks he is entitled to associate the theatre directly with *daemones*, given that Apuleius does not discuss the theatre in the *DDS*. But this criticism misses the way in which Augustine views Apuleius as beholden to his own tradition of revelation. I suspect that, in Augustine's mind, Apuleius is required to account both for what Plato says and for the popular religious beliefs that are central to the development of his demonology—much like Augustine, *qua* theologian, is required to account for both biblical revelation and the traditions of the Church.

106. Augustine, *DCD*, VIII.20.

107. Augustine, *DCD*, VIII.13.

108. Augustine, *DCD*, IX.3.

109. Augustine, *DCD*, VIII.17.346.22.

Augustine reasons as follows: perfect happiness is when the soul is either unchanging (like the gods) or changes entirely in accordance with reason (like perfect human beings); hence, any change counter to reason will cause unhappiness; the *daemones* experience psychic changes counter to reason; so, the *daemones* experience unhappiness. Furthermore, Apuleius has to accept that the *daemones* feel these passions—he is "compelled to admit"[110] these facts because they follow from his definition of *daemones*, which is itself merely the philosophical elaboration of a set of revealed Platonic *data*.[111] From this, Augustine concludes that the *daemones* cannot be superior to humans (as they must be if intermediate between humans and the divine) because of their happiness since their essential liability to the passions leaves them worse off than the perfectly happy life that the saints can hope for.[112]

If this is right, then the *daemones* also cannot be superior to human beings by virtue of their eternality, because, as Augustine asserts, the eternal existence of *daemones* merely condemns them to "either an unhappy eternity or eternal unhappiness (*vel misera aeternitas vel aeterna miseria*),"[113] whereas humans can at least hope to achieve eternal happiness through the cultivation of virtue and the practice of philosophy.[114]

110. Augustine, *DCD*, VIII.17.347.9.

111. We can thus defend Augustine against the charge that, given that Apuleius claims there are *good daemones* who function as a sort of guardian or conscience for human beings, his arguments fail to properly account for what Apuleius actually says (Hunink, "Apuleius, qui nobis Afris Afer est notior," 93–95). If the *daemones* are essentially affected by emotions, and emotions necessarily move us to act contrary to reason, then either: (i) these *daemones* will be, at best, imperfect guardians liable to moments of emotional irrationality; or (ii) these guardian *daemones* must not be capable of being moved against reason by way of their emotions . . . but then they will fail to satisfy the definition of *daemones* Apuleius provides (as Moreschini, despite his own concerns about the Augustine's arguments, saw clearly ("Polemica," 592)). I trust that a similarly charitable reading of Augustine would also help defuse Fick's list of objections and alleged sophisms (198–201), though I do not have the space to engage in a point-by-point response here.

112. Augustine, *DCD*, VIII.15, VIII.16, IX.3. One might wonder whether Augustine is entitled to attribute these claims to Apuleius. Why should we think, after all, this is how Apuleius conceives of emotions, or of the emotional state of *daemones*, or of the potential happiness of human beings? However, all of these claims seem to follow quickly from Apuleius's other commitments. The fact that emotions incline a soul to act contrary to reason is an important, if complicated, theme in Plato's moral psychology. Furthermore, as I have tried to show above, the susceptibility of the *daemones* to emotions is required by the intermediary status Apuleius attributes to them, and the potential perfection of human beings, while never explicitly stated in the *DDS*, seems to be alluded to at several points (particularly in Apuleius's descriptions of the virtues of Socrates and Odysseus), and was an important part of Middle Platonic and Stoic conceptions of the ideal human being or sage.

113. Augustine, *DCD*, IX.13.385.2–3.

114. Karfíková thus misses Augustine's point when she asks why he does not consider the possibility that the *daemones* might be sometimes happy and sometimes unhappy ("Augustins Polemik gegen Apuleius," 178). The question here is rather, I think, what state the *best* of the *daemones* are capable of achieving, relative to the best of human beings. Humans are capable of attaining perfect happiness (that is, they are capable, with God's grace, of always acting in accordance with reason, since the perturbations of the *passiones* are not *essentially* part of what it is to be human), whereas *daemones*, because these psychic perturbations are an essential part of what it is to be a *daemon*, cannot achieve this perfect happiness, and thus are consigned to eternal unhappiness—though not necessarily eternal unhappiness without any happiness whatsoever mixed in.

Finally, we might think that the *daemones* are superior to humans because of the superiority of the elemental material from which they are composed. However, Augustine argues, this material difference shouldn't be sufficient for the *daemones* to be essentially superior, because we spurn other humans who are, for instance, physically fit but morally base.[115] Note how, like a dialectician in a philosophical debate (or Socrates engaged in *elenchus*) Augustine traps Apuleius. Although we *shouldn't* think that a material difference is sufficient to make *daemones* better than humans, it is the only property available to Apuleius on the basis of his definition, such that Apuleius must admit, or so Augustine claims, that the *daemones* "are hung up and tied together (*ligati atque suspensi*) with the happy gods by their body, that of a slave, and with miserable human beings by their soul, that of a master."[116]

We thus see Augustine employing various philosophical tools to demonstrate that the conclusions Apuleius reaches in *DDS* are unacceptable to the philosopher. This must be at least in part because Apuleius and his imagined audience have imperfectly practiced philosophy—Augustine thus asserts his philosophical superiority to the philosophers by leading them to recognize their errors by means of their own tools. At the same time, Augustine asserts that the Platonists have reached these false conclusions about the nature of *daemones* because they have been led astray by false revelation. Many people, Augustine tells us, have been tricked by the *daemones* through various manifestations of their power into thinking that they are gods. Others, again by way of various deceptions wrought by the *daemones*, have come to think they have a privileged role as intermediaries between humans and the divine. Finally, others have come to believe that telling the general populace about the true nature of these figures would scandalize the masses.[117] The *daemones*, which Augustine, in the light of what he understands to be true Christian revelation, identifies with the demons mentioned in the Bible, also have a direct interest in deceiving humans in order to divert them from the truth.[118] Hermes Trismegistus is employed as a helpful case study for how false revelation leads the Platonists astray, despite having access to some elements of true revelation received (in)directly from God. Hermes says true things about God, inspired by true revelation, but false revelation from the *daemones* leads him to defend these evil spirits in his writing.[119]

The fact that Apuleius arrives at false conclusions about the *daemones* while having access to true revealed *data* by way of Plato can thus be attributed both to errors in reasoning and to an intermixing of false or improperly understood revelation with the true revelation the Platonists share with the Christians. We thus see Augustine, over the course of *DCD* VIII and IX, seeking to *correct and complete*

115. Augustine, *DCD*, VIII.15.
116. Augustine, *DCD*, IX.9.381.11–13.
117. Augustine, *DCD*, VIII.22.
118. Augustine, *DCD*, IX.18.
119. Augustine, *DCD*, VIII.23–4.

Apuleius's interpretation of Platonic revelation. This completion is made possible, as will soon be apparent, because Augustine has access to the truth of Christian revelation *as a whole*, whereas philosophers like Apuleius—and even Plato—can only ever have access to some *part* of this truth.

Apuleius was correct in asserting that we need *some sort of mediator*—this insight, drawn from the perfect goodness and transcendence of the divine, forms part of the shared revelation that both Christians and Platonists have received. Apuleius has even come so far as to correctly identify intermediate non-human elements of the universe. After all, the *daemones* that Apuleius points to, and which Augustine further subdivides into demons and angels, are indeed intermediate between God and humans in terms of their metaphysical properties, having neither the perfection of God nor the precise form of imperfection that humans possess, being mortal and unhappy, but capable of perfect eternal happiness.[120] However, although Apuleius has correctly identified the metaphysical structure of the universe which makes mediation between man and God necessary, he has failed to recognize the particular(s) that complete this structure—he has seen the need for a mediator, and pointed to certain intermediate figures, but has failed to identify just who this *good* mediator is.[121] To do so correctly, Christian revelation is needed.

Suddenly, in Augustine's account, Christ—the true mediator—appears.[122] The very form of Augustine's presentation of the incarnation of the Word appears in the text as a sort of *revelation*—after not mentioning Jesus by name for a book and a half, Christ is named and discussed in IX.15. I take this to be a deliberate construction on Augustine's part, allowing the form of his discussion (Christ appearing as the true mediator in a sort of epiphany after not being named throughout the preceding arguments, but being repeatedly pointed to by the lines of reasoning Augustine advances) to mirror its content. We must turn to Christian revelation, the central premise of which being the incarnation, in order to properly complete the structure of mediation both Augustine and Apuleius have sketched. Indeed, Augustine argues that this Christian mediator is better able to satisfy the requirements Apuleius places on his mediating figures than the *daemones* Apuleius himself turns to, because the unique nature of Christ (being both fully human and fully divine) allows him to share perfectly in both divine happiness and human misery. In contrast, the *daemones* are only able to have a

---

120. Augustine, *DCD*, IX.15.

121. It might be helpful, at this point, to introduce a distinction between something being *intermediate* (that is, possessing some of the properties of two distinct classes of entities "between" which, metaphysically speaking, it stands) and something being a *mediator* (that is, helping to communicate between these two classes in order to bridge the gap between them). Augustine and Apuleius both aim to identify intermediate mediators, but Apuleius only succeeds in picking out intermediate entities.

122. The precise nature of human-divine mediation is, I take it, one of the central concerns motivating Augustine's discussion of Apuleius *et al.* (a fact that Jean-Claude Guy, *Unité et structure logique de la «Cité de Dieu» de saint Augustin*, 62 and Saudelli ("«Dieu» ou «démon» de Socrate?" 81–86) are both admirably aware of in their discussions).

partial share in the forms of both human and divine life—their essential susceptibility to the passions leaves them unable to fully participate in God's perfect happiness, as we have already seen, while their eternality and material form nevertheless renders them in some ways more than human.[123]

Christian revelation, giving complete access to the way the universe truly is, thus allows us to envision a more perfect mediator than the incomplete revelation of the Platonists enabled them to imagine. Christ, fully human and fully divine, intervenes not merely to bring prayers from humans to the gods and aid from the gods to humans, like the *daemones*, but helps lead humans "from mortal misery to blessed immortality."[124] Furthermore, given that the end of human beings is unity with the divine, the *singularity* of Christ relative to the multiplicity of *daemones* also makes him a more perfect mediator—the singularity of the Christian mediator mirrors the singular goal towards which this mediator guides us, a sort of symmetry that seems foreclosed to Apuleius and his fellow Platonists because of their need to account for the polytheistic nature of their revelation and popular religious beliefs.[125] Christian revelation therefore perfects and completes the Platonic project, showing how the structure of human-divine mediation elaborated by Athens is best filled by a figure we can come to know only through the revelation of Jerusalem.

Conclusion

In Augustine's response to Apuleius, we find Novak's general blueprint for Jerusalem's relationship with Athens reproduced once again. Augustine recognizes that the Platonists have their own revelation about which they have reasoned—part of this revelation is shared with Christian revelation, which makes possible the sort of fraternal or neighborly dialogue Augustine is engaged in, while part of it constitutes their own, distinct, and ultimately false revelation. Augustine also engages with Apuleius in just the way the completion thesis has led us to expect. At every turn, he seeks to demonstrate his own (and, by extrapolation, the theologian in general's) ability to reason better than the philosophers—because, as Novak has shown us, the tools of reason fall just as much under the purview of Athens as Jerusalem—as well as to show the philosophers' need for Christian revelation in order to complete the project they have undertaken. Apuleius, left to his own revelation, has arrived at an incorrect

---

123. Karfíková ("Augustins Polemik gegen Apuleius," 186) emphasizes this perfect sharing in both the divine and the human, suggesting that this marks a *shift* in the nature of mediation from Apuleius (for whom mediation is merely to be in an intermediate physical location) to Augustine (for whom mediation requires full participation in both of the mediated parties). But this is not a shift so much as a *completion* or perfection of Apuleius's project: Augustine's Christ provides so much more perfect of a model of mediation than Apuleius had envisioned, constrained as he was by various false premises about the nature of *daemones* that he had to incorporate into his account.

124. Augustine, *DCD*, IX.15.387.10–11.

125. Augustine, *DCD*, IX.15. See also Karfíková, "Augustins Polemik gegen Apuleius," 183.

understanding of the nature of divine mediation in the universe. To arrive at a correct understanding, he is in need of Christian revelation, as the structure of divine mediation he discusses can only be perfectly fulfilled by Christ.

Novak has thus allowed us to see the centrality of revelation to both Apuleius and Augustine's projects and to properly understand Augustine's relationship to his Platonic antecedent, seeing him not (or at least, not only) as the target of polemical refutation, but also as a fellow sojourner, led astray by false revelation and standing in need of correction. This suggests, in conjunction with Novak's own reading of Jewish thinkers, that Novak's theory can be applied with equally fruitful results to other examples of Judeo-Christian theologians engaging with non-Judeo-Christian philosophy throughout history. In turn, I think that Novak's theory can help religious philosophers like myself better make sense of the "live options"[126] of philosophy and theology and the apparently dichotomous choice we are incessantly asked to make between them—and this should come as no surprise. Novak is, after all, as much a rabbi as a philosopher, and his reflections—no matter how theoretical—are always grounded in practical, frequently pastoral, concerns.

Having spent much time interpreting texts, both those of Novak and of classical philosophy, I want to close by briefly recalling a reflection of one of Novak's own most important teachers on the role of teachers and texts in the lives of their students. Abraham Joshua Heschel once wrote: "It is the personality of the teacher which is the text that the pupils read; the text that they will never forget."[127] Novak's careful reading of texts, his unwillingness to allow Athens and Jerusalem to be quarantined one from the other, the central importance he places on the history of philosophy for helping us to wrestle with the problems confronting contemporary philosophers and theologians, his daring attempts to marshal the entirety of the Western tradition behind his project, and the creativity and insight of the conclusions he brings his readers to, all while remaining grounded in and ever mindful of the unique perspective of his own faith—all of these are elements of Novak's personality by which I have been inspired, from which I have learned much, and which have created a "text" I trust I will never forget. I can only hope that some small part of this intellectual personality, which Novak has always shared so generously with me, might also be found in my own work.

Bibliography

Apuleius. "De Deo Socratis." In *Apuleius: Rhetorical Works*, edited by Stephen Harrison, 185–216. Oxford: Oxford University Press, 2001.

Baltes, Matthias, Marie-Luise Lakmann, John M. Dillon, Pierluigi Donini, Ralph Häfner, and Lenka Karfíková, eds. *Apuleius: De deo Socratis. Über den Gott des Sokrates. Eingeleitet,*

---

126. Novak, *Athens and Jerusalem*, 10.
127. Heschel, "The Spirit of Jewish Education," 19.

übersetzt und mit interpretierenden Essays versehen. Darmstadt: Wissenschaftliche Buchgesellschaft, 2004.

Beaujeu, Jean. *Apulée: Opuscules Philosophiques (Du Dieu de Socrate, Platon et Sa Doctrine, Du Monde) et Fragments*. Paris: Les Belles Lettres, 1973.

Bernard, Wolfgang. "Zur Dämonologie Des Apuleius von Madura." *Rheinisches Museum für Philologie* 3.4 (1994) 358–73.

Destrée, Pierre, and Nicholas D. Smith, eds. *Socrates' Divine Sign: Religion, Practice, and Value in Socratic Philosophy*. Kelowna, BC: Academic Printing and Publishing, 2005.

Dodds, Eric R. *The Greeks and the Irrational*. Sather Classical Lectures 25. Berkeley: University of California Press, 1951.

Fackenheim, Emil L. *God's Presence in History: Jewish Affirmations and Philosophical Reflections*. New York: HarperCollins, 1970.

Fick, Nicole. "Saint Augustin pourfendeur des démons païens, ou la critique de la démonologie d'Apulée, De Civit. Dei, VIII, 14–22." In *Discours religieux dans l'antiquité: Actes du colloque de Besançon, 27–28 Janvier 1995*, 189–206. Besançon: Université de Franche-Comté, 1995.

Fletcher, Richard. *Apuleius' Platonism: The Impersonation of Philosophy*. Cambridge: Cambridge University Press, 2014.

Guy, Jean-Claude. *Unité et structure logique de la «Cité de Dieu» de Saint Augustin*. Paris: Études Augustiniennes, 1961.

Habermehl, Peter. "Quaedam Divinae Mediae Potestates: Demonology in Apuleius' De Deo Socratis." In *Groningen Colloquia on the Novel VII*, edited by Heinz Hofmann and Maaike Zimmerman, 117–42. Groningen: Egbert Foster, 1996.

Hadot, Pierre. *Philosophy as a Way of Life: Spiritual Exercises from Socrates to Foucault*. Oxford: Blackwell, 1995.

Hagendahl, Harold. *Augustine and the Latin Classics*. Gothenburg: Elander, 1967.

Harrison, Stephen. *Apuleius: A Latin Sophist*. Oxford: Oxford University Press, 2000.

Hermann, L. "Le Dieu-roi d'Apulée." *Latomus* 18 (1959) 110–16.

———. "Le procès d'Apulée fut-il un procès de christianisme?" *Revue de l'université libre de Bruxelles* 4.2 (1951) 339–50.

Heschel, Abraham Joshua. *Die Prophetie*. Krakow: Polska Akademja Umiejetnosci, 1936.

———. "The Spirit of Jewish Education." *Jewish Education* 24.2 (1953) 9–62.

Hijmans, B.L. "Apuleius: Philosophus Platonicus." *Ausftieg und Niedergang der Römischen Welt II* 36.1 (1987) 395–475.

Hunink, Vincent. "'Apuleius, qui nobis Afris Afer est notior': Augustine's Polemic against Apuleius in De Civitate Dei." *Scholia: Studies in Classical Antiquity* 12 (2003) 82–88.

Jones, Christopher P. *Apuleius: Apologia, Florida, De Deo Socratis*. Loeb Classical Library. Cambridge: Harvard University Press, 2017.

Karfiková, Lenka. "Augustins Polemik Gegen Apuleius." In *Apuleius: De deo Socratis. Über den Gott des Sokrates. Eingeleitet, übersetzt und mit interpretierenden Essays versehen*, edited by Matthias Baltes et al., 162–89. Darmstadt: Wissenschaftliche Buchgesellschaft, 2004.

Madec, Goulven. "«Si Plato viveret...» (Augustin, De vera religione, 3.3)." In *Néoplatonisme: Mélanges Offerts à Jean Trouillard*, 231–48. Fontenay-aux-Roses: École normale supérieure, 1981.

McPherran, Mark. *The Religion of Socrates*. University Park, PA: Pennsylvania State University Press, 1996.

Moreschini, Claudio, ed. *Apulei Platonici Madaurensis Opera quae supersunt*. Leipzig: Teubner, 1991.

———. *Apuleius and the Metamorphoses of Platonism*. Turnhout: Brepols, 2015.

———. "La polemica di Agostino contro la demonologia di Apuleio." *Annali Della Scuola Normale Superiore Di Pisa. Classe Di Lettere e Filosofia* 2.2 (1972) 583–96.

Saudelli, Lucia. "«Dieu» ou «démon» de Socrate? Augustin contre Apulée." *Revue d'études augustiniennes et patristiques* 60 (2014) 67–90.

Novak, David. *Athens and Jerusalem: God, Humans, and Nature*. Toronto: University of Toronto Press, 2019.

———. "Heschel's Phenomenology of Revelation." In *Abraham Joshua Heschel: Philosophy, Theology, and Interreligious Dialogue*, edited by S. Krajewski and A. Lipszyc, 38–48. Wiesbaden: Harrassowtiz Verlag, 2009.

———. *The Image of the Non-Jew in Judaism: The Idea of Noahide Law*. 2nd ed. Liverpool: Liverpool University Press, 2011.

———. "Philosophy and the Possibility of Revelation: A Theological Response to the Challenge of Leo Strauss." In *Leo Strauss and Judaism: Jerusalem and Athens Critically Revisited*, edited by David Novak, 173–92. Lanham, MD: Rowman and Littlefield, 1996.

———. "Theology and Philosophy: An Exchange with Robert Jenson." In David Novak, *Talking with Christians: Musings of a Jewish Theologian*, 229–46. Grand Rapids, Michigan: Eerdmans, 2005.

Osborn, Eric. *Tertullian, First Theologian of the West*. Cambridge: Cambridge University Press, 1997.

Pépin, Jean. "La Doctrine Platonicienne Des Anges et Des Démons." In Pépin, *«Ex Platonicorum Persona»: Études sur les lectures philosophiques de Saint Augustin*, 29–37. Amsterdam: Hakkert, 1977.

Smith, Nicholas D., and Paul B. Woodruff. *Reason and Religion in Socratic Philosophy*. Oxford: Oxford University Press, 2000.

Strauss, Leo. "Jerusalem and Athens: Some Preliminary Reflections." In Leo Strauss, *Studies in Platonic Political Philosophy*, edited by Thomas Pangel, 147–73. Chicago: University of Chicago Press, 1983.

———. "The Mutual Influence of Theology and Philosophy." *Independent Journal of Philosophy* 3 (1979) 111–18.

———. *Philosophy and Law: Contributions to the Understanding of Maimonides and His Predecessors*. Translated by Eve Adler. Albany, NY: State University of New York Press: 1995.

———. *Spinoza's Critique of Religion*. Edited by E. M. Sinclair. New York: Schocken, 1965.

Tertullian. *De Praescriptione Haereticorum*. Edited by François Refoulé. Sources Chrétiennes 46. Paris: Éditions du Cerf, 1957.

Timotin, Andrei. *La démonologie platonicienne: Histoire de la notion de daimôn de Platon aux derniers néoplatoniciens*. Leiden: Brill, 2012.

Vlastos, Gregory. *Socrates: Ironist and Moral Philosopher*. Ithaca, NY: Cornell University Press, 1991.

Wittgenstein, Ludwig. *Philosophical Investigations*. Edited by P. M. S. Hacker and Joachim Schulte, translated by G. E. M. Anscombe, P. M. S. Hacker, and Joachim Schulte. 4th ed. Hoboken, NJ: Wiley-Blackwell, 2009.

Response to

Thomas Slabon's "Reason's Revelation and Revelation's Reason: Reading Apuleius's *De Deo Socratis* and Augustine's *De Civitate Dei* through the Lens of Novak's *Athens and Jerusalem*"

DAVID NOVAK

I AM GRATEFUL TO Thomas Slabon for his reception of my work, especially my new book, *Athens and Jerusalem: God, Humans, and Nature*, of which he is one of the first readers. In fact, Thomas has appreciated its main thesis about the necessary relation of philosophy (a là Athens) and theology (a là Jerusalem) to the point of skillfully employing it in his own personal project of carefully preparing himself to become a constructive philosopher. This is very much evidenced in his brilliant paper for this volume. If I have been of any help to him through my written work, and through our many memorable conversations about the most profound philosophical and theological questions, that is most gratifying. As one of the ancient Rabbis said, "I have learned the most from my students" (Taanit 7a). Thomas has consistently been what another ancient Rabbi called a "student/colleague" (*talmid-ḥaver*).

Let me now show how critically (in the sense of "critique," not "criticism") Thomas has read *Athens and Jerusalem*, by his selection of one of my main theses about the relation of Jewish theology and philosophy and then his application of it to his interpretation of the relation of Christian theology and philosophy. My own critical response to his critical reading of my book will be to show that the thesis he has chosen to analyze and employ for his own project may not be my own position, though it does correspond to the position of at least one of the great Jewish philosophical theologians dealt with in the book. Thomas has every right as a critical, selective reader to take from any book whatever he wants to take from it. An honest author should accept that and learn from it gladly and appreciatively.

What Thomas finds of greatest value in the book is what he calls "the completion thesis." He writes that "theology *completes* the project of philosophy . . . by adding its own insights to the conceptual resources provided by philosophy [and] is better able to accomplish philosophy's own project than philosophy itself.... [P]hilosophy could not effect this completion by itself... [because it is] teleologically oriented to the same ends as theology."[1] This is the relation of theology and philosophy that Thomas prefers. He thus transposes it to the relation of the Christian theology of Augustine and the pagan philosophy of Apuleius. He states that "when we read Augustine through the lens Novak has provided us with, we can see... that the Platonico-Socratic revelation Apuleius relies on is inadequate for the task Apuleius set himself, and that Apuleius' project... can only be fully completed by Christian revelation."[2] Thomas further asserts that "Augustine... [is] seeking to *correct and complete* Apuleius' interpretation of Platonic revelation... because Augustine has access to the truth of Christian revelation *as a whole*, whereas philosophers like Apuleius—and even Plato—can only ever have access to some *part* of this truth."[3] This is the correlation of reason (as philosophy) and revelation (as theology) that Thomas has chosen to identify with critically.

Thomas's own critical choice is better appreciated when contrasted with two other options in the correlation of philosophy and theology. The first option is one that both Thomas and I would reject. The second option is one that I prefer, and which, though he might not reject it *tout court*, is not his preference nonetheless.

The option that Thomas and I would both reject is the one that holds that reason can only be a consequent of revelation and that revelation itself has no antecedents, no *a priori*. That is, the content of revelation is something that God has hurled down from heaven to human recipients on earth, for which these humans have no prior preparation, and which they can only accept or refuse to accept totally. Their acceptance, then, can only be a Kierkegaardian "leap of faith." However, as the ancient Rabbis frequently put it, "the Torah speaks in human language." That alone makes the Torah intelligible to humans on earth, requiring theoretical interpretation and practical application in the most intelligent human language possible. The most intelligent or rational language seems to be philosophy (although some have found the language of literature more useful). Yet, philosophy as intelligent human language always follows revelation. As such, its role is hermeneutical (*midrash* is the Hebrew term). In relation to revelation it always functions *a posteriori*. In this view, philosophy is very much theology's "handmaiden" (*ancilla theologiae*). Now Thomas and I would reject this view insofar as it gives philosophy a role that most philosophers wouldn't accept for their *critical* enterprise. It turns philosophy into something like the police, merely obediently enforcing rules simply because they have been ordered to do so.

The option that Thomas clearly prefers is the one he calls "teleological." The term itself is Aristotelian, though Thomas uses it in dealing with Augustine, for whom Plato (and his epigones) is the philosopher whom he has engaged with the most and whom he wants to employ the most in his own theological project. (The differences between

1. p. 266.
2. p. 273.
3. p. 283.

Plato's teleology and Aristotle's are dealt with in chapters 4 and 5 of *Athens and Jerusalem*.) Thomas seems to be an Augustinian theologically and a Platonist philosophically. Now if the *telos* or "completion" of philosophy is theology *qua* revelation or epiphany, then philosophy *qua* reason is theology's necessary antecedent. Philosophy is theology's *archē* or "beginning" (*Ursprung* is the German term for it).

Thomas's painstaking treatment of Augustine's encounter with the thought of the Platonist Apuleius is quite similar to the way Philo of Alexandria, the first Jewish philosopher-theologian, engaged the philosophy of Plato primarily, which is the subject of chapter 4 of my book. What Philo tried to show is that scriptural "theology" (mostly the Pentateuch in the Septuagint's translation), taking theology to be God's *logos* revealed to Moses, can give us more knowledge of God than philosophy alone can give us. But, since philosophy and theology have the same end-goal or *telos*, and since philosophy is more accessible, theologians cannot do an "end-run" around it, but they must work through it. Only then can they go beyond it. This is very much the method of "dialectics" Plato developed, especially in the *Republic*. As such, theologians (who in Philo's time were all Jews) can thus say to philosophers (some of whom were Jews from birth, most of whom were pagans from birth) "we can do everything you can do and better. We can attain what you hope to attain, but being bereft of revelation, you cannot do by yourselves."

Furthermore, once theologians have experienced what Moses experienced (albeit never as fully), they can then use the methods of philosophy to interpret and apply what they have obtained from revelation. The method most suited to the often mytho-poetic language of Scripture is allegory, where the historical events represented in Scripture are taken to be symbols pointing to the timeless ideas that Platonic philosophers are always looking for to contemplate. That is philosophy's hermeneutical function which has considerable precedent in Plato's allegorical interpretation of the stories told by Homer and Hesiod (and others). For Philo, though, the stories told in Scripture have so much more philosophical meaning than do those told by Homer and Hesiod, being about much more impressive characters than the Greek gods and heroes, even though the methods used to interpret the Greek "mythologists" by the Greek philosophers are much the same as Philo's scriptural hermeneutics. In fact, some of the Greek Church Fathers learned much from Philo, both concerning revelation's philosophical consequents as well as its philosophical antecedents. In Augustine, we see this influence (albeit less direct) on the premier Latin Father.

For Thomas, this is clearly a live option for a contemporary religious philosopher, who he is preparing himself to become. The advantage of doing this a là Plato rather than a là Aristotle is that one doesn't have to build this theological completion of philosophy's project on a very problematic teleological natural science, as Aristotelians have to do (Thomas Aquinas being a notable exception, however). This is a problem for such modern Aristotelians as Elizabeth Anscombe and Alasdair MacIntyre. Thomas seems to be in the company of such distinguished Augustinians as Jean-Luc Marion. Indeed, an ancient Rabbi told his chief disciple to "suspend yourself from a big tree."

While Thomas and I agree that philosophy has both an antecedent and a consequent in relation to theology, my correlation of philosophy and theology is different. As Thomas's correlation owes the most to Plato, mine owes the most to Kant. Whereas for Plato and Augustine *et alia*, philosophers and theologians are both looking for God, and many practitioners of both disciplines assume that it is the same God they are both looking for, this is not the case with Kant *et alia*. Already in the *Critique of Pure Reason*, Kant tried to show that philosophy cannot reach God as the *ens realissimum*; in fact, such a philosophical search is utterly futile. And, the God he proposes to be reachable in the *Critique of Practical Reason* is not *ens realissimum* (or "whom nothing greater can be thought"), not the Absolute, and thus not the God who revealed Himself in Scripture.

So, what do philosophy and theology have in common anymore? How can they interact when it seems they have totally different agendas? For me, philosophy functions as theology's necessary antecedent much like a Kantian *a priori*. That is, when philosophy does not attempt to supplant theology, it functions for theology very much like a *via negativa*. By not attempting to give a totalizing explanation of all reality, philosophy prepares the world for revelation by showing that revelation is not impossible in the world it has constituted, that this world is not impermeable to revelation. Thomas is right when he notices that I explicitly employ Heidegger's notion of *seinlassen* to deal with what is the *conditio sine qua non* of revelation, but not its *conditio per quam*. In other words, philosophy prepares (*Vorbedingung* is the German term) the world for revelation, but revelation is neither its source nor its goal. (This is dealt with at length in chapter 5 of *Athens and Jerusalem*.) The world philosophy constitutes is neither the anarchic world of infinite possibilities (as in much post-modernism) nor the tightly causal world of total necessity (as in much early modernism).

Finally, philosophy as theology's consequent functions as critique in the true sense, viz., arguing against any superstitious or pseudo-scientific interpretations of scriptural revelation in theory, and arguing against any fanatical or authoritarian interpretations of Scripture in practice. That is how philosophy functions *a posteriori*. As such, when properly employed by theologians, philosophy enables revelation to speak in human language most intelligently, in keeping with Moses's admonition that the Torah be "your wisdom and your understanding in the eyes of the nations of the world" (Deut 4:6).

Thomas's and my difference in our respective employments of philosophy for theology is truly Socratic in the sense that Socrates always hoped that in his interlocutions with others, truth not yet known would somehow emerge, and so enlighten anew both interlocutors.

Chapter 11

David Novak, Natural Law, and the Sanctity of Human Life

CHRISTOPHER TOLLEFSEN

Introduction

CHAPTER 1 OF RABBI David Novak's *The Sanctity of Human Life* is concerned with the ethics of human embryonic stem cell research. In one particularly rich discussion, Novak's point of departure is a text of Genesis 9:6: "Whosoever sheds human blood by humans shall his blood be shed."

Novak points out, rightly, it seems to me, that this text, by indicating a punishment for killing, presupposes that murder is impermissible, that it has been, in his words, "prohibited," without that prohibition being a matter of God's direct communication to early human beings for, "after all, the Torah as the Law has not yet been revealed."[1] Rather, he says, it "seems to be that Cain and Abel were both expected to be aware of the fact that they had been created in the image of God. As such, an assault on the image is an assault on the One whose image has been assaulted."[2] This raises an obvious problem: how were Cain and Abel to make good on that expectation, that is, how was this awareness mediated, if not through divine communication?

Novak's answer is interesting and suggestive. "The very presence of one human being to another, even when hidden from immediate view, makes a normative claim upon any other human being who has the power to either harm or help.... Our first experience of any other human person is that that person's very presence demands that we notice him or her—minimally by not harming the person, maximally by helping the person."[3]

Present or implied within these claims are the three central issues I wish to address in this paper. First, there is an issue of *scope*: how is the normative demand made by those in relation to whom I stand in a face to face encounter extended to others, "even

---

1. Novak, *The Sanctity of Human Life*, 38.
2. Novak, *The Sanctity of Human Life*, 36.
3. Novak, *The Sanctity of Human Life*, 38.

when (those others are) hidden from immediate view"? For embryos and fetuses are so hidden: we do not seem to stand in a face to face encounter with them. How do they come to be included in the Noahide, i.e., natural law, protections? Or is their protection only a matter, as is often thought, of revealed positive law—and their killing objected to only as a matter of "Christian (or Jewish, or . . .) religious beliefs"?

Second, there is an issue of *exception*: how is the normative demand, once it is extended to the hidden, and thereby to all, human beings, revoked, or rescinded, in the case of some? Novak believes, as do most Christians, that it is permissible, for example, to intend the death of some human beings, such as those who are attacking or those convicted of a capital crime. And indeed, the scriptural passage from which our reflections here are taking shape, Genesis 9:6, is used precisely to bolster that supposition by many.

Third, there is an issue of *transcendence:* how are we to understand the relationship between the norm against killing, made phenomenologically prominent in the face to face encounter of human person with human person, and understood as a claim about the image of God present *in* the person, and the idea of God as the Lord and Giver of Life whose dominion over human life is not to be usurped? Both the idea of the image of God and the idea of God as Lord and Giver of Life could be expressed using the language of human life's "sanctity." But while these two aspects of the sanctity of human life seem related, it is not immediately obvious how so: one aspect (the "image") is typically rooted in the ontological features of the human person, while the other (the "Lord" and "Giver" aspect) concerns a relationship between such persons and their Lord and Creator.

Each section of this paper addresses one of these topics, taking Novak's discussions in *The Sanctity of Human Life* and elsewhere as their point of departure. But while his approach, obviously, draws upon his particularly Jewish understanding of both the natural and the revealed law, my own approach to them will be framed by the Catholic natural law tradition within which I work.[4] I can do justice neither to the points of convergence nor the points of divergence, but I will draw attention to some of each.

The Scope of the Sanctity of Human Life

The very name, "sanctity of *human* life" indicates the projected scope of the norm that derives from and articulates that sanctity: the norm should cover all human life in some sense, with the question of exceptions to be worked out later. The core idea, put in terms of Catholic ("new") natural law thought, is this: life is a basic aspect of my

---

4. In particular, it will be shaped by the recent interpretation of that tradition initiated by Novak's PhD dissertation director Germain Grisez and furthered by Grisez's student, and later colleague of Novak's, Joseph Boyle.

well-being, a basic good, and it is not to be attacked in another who is relevantly like me; his life, like mine, is thus inviolable, sacred.[5]

What is the sense of "relevantly like me"? A natural starting point is "relevantly like me in ways that I can discern, so to speak, face to face." For I can in some sense *see* that this one, the one to whom I now stand in a face to face relationship, is relevantly like me and thus makes this special claim upon me. Indeed, the role of the face to face encounter in coming to see the other as relevantly like me runs through all the basic goods, not just the good of human life. Cain and Abel, for example, grew up in a family together; worked the fields together; got sick and well together; played together; surely took aesthetic delight in God's creation together. In other words, they shared in the pursuit of basic human goods together and they could recognize that shared pursuit in their face to face encounters.

This provides a key to the necessary insight. For recognition that I and some other being are capable of engaging in a shared pursuit or enjoyment of a common good or goods is a recognition that I and that other being share a nature: we are the same kind of being, both being fulfilled by the same objects of the same activities, that are actualizations of the same potentialities, and hence of the same natures. Such an awareness is surely first born of face to face encounters with, e.g., parents, siblings, and other family members, the children of other parents, neighbors, and so on.

Novak denies that nonpersons make such claims upon us: "the presence of nonpersons makes no immediate claim upon us—that is, their '*is*-ness' or being does not itself present an *ought* or a claim."[6] This too admits of a natural law understanding: my relations to all the nonhuman animals, for example, of which I am aware, never has the intensity of a face to face encounter with another mature human person, for it never involves the shared pursuit or enjoyment of a common good. No dog or ape is a friend to me in anything like the focal sense of that term; no dog or ape gazes with me in wonder at a beautiful work of art, or pursues excellence in skilled performance for its own sake with me, even if I toss a stick or a bone, and my dog chases it down and brings it back and drops it at my feet. The dog and I do not share a horizon of basic goods and thus stand in no genuine communion with one another. Thus, as Novak writes, "a respect for the nonhuman world is best justified when we become aware of how God has given us that world to care for it and for ourselves in it and over it."[7]

The phenomenology of the non-human animal is not even like that of the human infant, despite claims of some that a two-year old dog, for example, is as intelligent as a six-month-old human. Such claims could never be made by anyone attentive to the lives of six-month-olds. Very soon, in the face to face encounter

---

5. This "basic goods" understanding of natural law is articulated in a number of places. See, for example, Finnis, *Natural Law and Natural Rights*, chapter 4; and Grisez, Boyle, and Finnis, "Practical Principles, Moral Truth and Ultimate Ends."

6. Novak, *The Sanctity of Human Life*, 38.

7. Novak, *The Sanctity of Human Life*, 38.

even with a newborn, one meets with intelligence which manifestly is already opening to an ever-expanding horizon of possibility framed by basic goods: to a life of exploration, to smiles, play, attentiveness, and sympathy. A sensitive reader of human expressions can see in the face of a six-month old the precursors to that child's life at six, sixteen, and even perhaps sixty.[8]

But still, a problem arises: how do we move beyond the face to face to the universality of the sanctity of human life ethos? The key is in the grasp that the ultimate "likeness" that underwrites a shared and common good, and hence communion, with those in regards to whom I stand in an immediate relationship is still nevertheless in some measure a "hidden" likeness, the likeness of a common nature. To see this, consider the pervasiveness of discrimination against other human persons on the basis of skin color or ethnicity. One might think that this is explainable, even in face to face encounters, by the fact of visible difference. Yet the visible difference between a light-skinned black person and a dark-skinned white person might well be less than the visible difference between members of the same biological family.

So the judgment that the family member is "relevantly like me" cannot be an immediate judgment like: I see a red cup in front of me, or, on looking outside, I see that it is raining. Rather, going back to my claim about Cain and Abel, it is a judgment that, in virtue of our capacity for shared and common goods, we are relevantly like each other. And this is a judgment that we share a common nature, a set of potentialities that make those shared goods possible. This judgment is implicitly present, I am arguing, even in cases of the most extreme visible likeness between persons who find themselves in a face to face encounter where the presence of shared goods is most obvious. And it is this judgment that is in danger of being corrupted by the influence of our unreasoned passions, encultured prejudices, and self-interested desires.

For those passions, prejudices, and desires prevent us from pressing our judgment to its logical implication, that "relevantly like me" must include *every human being*, every being that shares with me this nature that underwrites my capacity to pursue and be benefitted by basic human goods. Under the influence of such passions, prejudices, and desires, I can see even a person who is extraordinarily like me in a visible sense to be unworthy of my "notice"—and therefore toward whom I need not act "minimally by not harming the person, maximally by helping the person." Thus, Cain's decision to kill his brother Abel. And, on the other hand, thinking clearly, allowing reason to be unfettered by the unreasoned elements of our character, allows us to extend the identification of a being as "relevantly like me" even to those who bear no visible similarity to me whatsoever: the human zygote, the human embryo, the human fetus, human beings all.

---

8. For an example of the importance of the face to face encounter from the standpoint of an infant, and its importance to the infant in socializing into the lifeworld of human goods, consider the still face experiment ("Still Face Experiment: Dr. Edward Tronick").

Let me make four final points about this judgment before moving on to my second topic. First, the extension of the scope of normative "notice" from those recognized in the face to face encounter to the broader expanse of humanity involves what I would characterize as "philosophy," or at least pre-philosophy: it requires some element of intellectual detachment and abstraction, albeit an element that is already implicitly present in the pre-philosophical recognition of any other human being as "relevantly like me."

Second, the extension of that judgment all the way out to include human zygotes and fetuses is one that requires not just philosophy but science. Is the human conceptus at its earliest stages a human being? That is the central question in determining whether the conceptus should be morally noticed, and, as Novak says, that is a "scientific question." That question can be answered mistakenly by those who misunderstand or ignore the science, and I would argue that such misunderstanding and ignoring are themselves now, in our current state of scientific knowledge, very often the product of the unreasoned influence of our prejudices, passions, and desires: in particular, too much personal and cultural investment in the obvious, and *a priori*, permissibility of abortion makes it almost impossible for some to read the science, or read it clearly.[9]

Third, there are interesting and difficult questions about the relationship between this Catholic natural law understanding of the face to face encounter and its relation to the foundational norm of the sanctity of human life and the approach of Novak and his Jewish philosophical antecedents such as Buber and Levinas. In *Natural Law in Judaism*, Novak criticizes Kant's claim that the "other person who is the object of my moral action is constituted *after* I have constituted myself as a moral subject a priori."[10] Rather, he suggests, following Buber and Levinas, "I discover that the object of my moral concern presents himself or herself to me *before* I have constituted myself as a moral subject."[11]

I agree with Novak's rejection of the view he describes here as Kantian. But I find myself uncertain in my assessment of his positive view. On the one hand, I do not think it can be the case that the other presents himself in a way that can be recognized *apart from* or *prior to* my own awareness of human goods as horizons of possibility for me. Yet some and perhaps all of my practical awareness of human goods requires the presence of others: I cannot have the idea of friendship, obviously, much less a practical awareness of its goodness, without an engagement with some other person or persons. More than this, the still face experiment (see footnote 8) suggests that some form of sociality is the portal through which our understanding of all human goods, and of ourselves as agents oriented towards those goods, is

---

9. With Robert P. George, I review the relevant science in *Embryo: A Defense of Human Life*.
10. Novak, *Natural Law in Judaism*, 166.
11. Novak, *Natural Law in Judaism*, 166.

mediated. If this is what Novak (or Buber, or Levinas) means, then there is not much of a gap between his view and mine.[12]

Fourth, the judgment that the common nature underlying shared goods underwrites the need for moral notice, by contrast with our awareness of the nature of other beings with whom we do not share goods is, it seems to me, a judgment that what is shared is a rational nature. And I would gloss that theologically as indicating that human beings are made in the image of God. Yet Novak has expressed concern that such an understanding of the "image of God" language is too "ontological" and insufficiently points to the transcendent. I'll try to address this concern, though briefly, in my final section.

Exceptions

The second main question within the sanctity of life ethic concerns the issue of exceptions to the norms against harming and killing human beings that emerge from that ethic. The question of exception is most obviously raised by the issue of conflict: when I am attacked by you, does the sanctity of my life give me some permission to make use of force in a way that otherwise the sanctity of your life would prohibit? But it is also raised in other cases, such as the question of whether pain-relieving but death-hastening drugs may be provided to those suffering at the end of life, and the question of punishment. There are, I think, three answers that have some credence in the natural law tradition and which we can see to some extent or other in Novak's work.

First, there is the thought that in some cases, an agent *forfeits* his right to life. Novak writes: "we would say in a case of self-defense, where the only way to save the life of the would-be victim is to kill the attacker, that the attacker has forfeited his or her right to life in favor of the right to life of his or her would-be victim because the only way to prevent the attacker's unjustified intent to kill from being exercised is to kill the attacker first."[13] This formulation strikes me as Kantian; the well-known variant of St. Thomas holds that the sinner "descends to the level of a beast," thus losing his immunity from being killed.[14]

Second, there is the route of double effect: in at least some cases, an effect that would be impermissible to intend is permissible to bring about if it is not intended but allowed only as a side effect.[15] Novak references this approach as well, in the context of end of life care and, for example, a request for morphine that might shorten a patient's life while also relieving pain.[16]

12. As Thomas Slabon suggested to me in conversation.
13. Novak, *The Sanctity of Human Life*, 11.
14. See St. Thomas Aquinas's discussion of capital punishment, in his *Summa Theologica* (hereafter, *ST*) II-II, q. 64, a. 2.
15. This also is discussed by St. Thomas in *ST* II-II, q. 64, a. 7.
16. Novak, *The Sanctity of Human Life*, 129.

Third is the view that God, who alone has the right to take life, delegates to some that right. This view seems congenial to an author such as Novak who both holds that capital punishment is permissible and that "God alone has the right to take back the breath of any human creature because God alone directly gave it or placed it in the human body," a position for which Novak says there is "solid scriptural support."[17] This marks, for Novak, a limit on political authority, as he explains in his discussion of Rabbi Hanina ben Teradyon's martyrdom:

> ... someone who has political power or authority over some other human or humans has no right to destroy or command others to destroy that human life, even if that "other" is the victim himself or herself. Any human placed under their power is only given to their charge for care. Only the Giver of the gift can take back what he has given; the recipient of the gift, whose charge is to care for it, is not allowed to hand back or cause the gift to be handed back to the Giver.[18]

Such a position perhaps does not require, but it strongly suggests that if capital punishment is permissible, then it proceeds uprightly only with the permission or perhaps command of the Giver of Life.

We should note that properly understood, the general norm against killing could only be one prohibiting *intentional* killing: a widespread norm against killing as such, whether as intended, or as a side effect, would not just admit of exceptions—it would be impossible to follow. So, let the starting point for reflection be this: there is a general norm against intentional killing, according to which death is neither to be chosen as a means or pursued as an end. Are there, however, exceptions to that norm?

Only the first and perhaps the third lines of thought above answer this question affirmatively. For the principle of double effect gives voice precisely to the norm against intentional killing, while recognizing that some consequences that it would be impermissible to intend may be permissible if they are outside the intention. But the first line of thought suggests that the immunity to intentional killing may be lost; and the third suggests that the Giver of Life may Himself intend death, and thus may also, given His rightful authority, give to others a share in that authority, or shield them from ultimate responsibility, in such a way as to make it permissible for them to punish capitally.

In a number of places, I have expressed my doubts about the soundness of the first and the third arguments, and I will only briefly here articulate my concerns and the extent to which such concerns might resonate in the Jewish natural law tradition.

St. Thomas's defense of capital punishment is well known and notably different from his justification of killing in self-defense, which is at its core a double effect argument. Thomas writes:

---

17. Novak, *The Sanctity of Human Life*, 124.
18. Novak, *The Sanctity of Human Life*, 124–25.

> By sinning man departs from the order of reason, and consequently falls away from the dignity of his manhood, in so far as he is naturally free, and exists for himself, and he falls into the slavish state of the beasts, by being disposed of according as he is useful to others.[19]

Clearly, if taken literally, this claim would justify intentional killing.

I believe that Aquinas's view lacks coherence: if "dignity" claims are intended to summarily capture certain truths about what it means to have a particular sort of nature, then one can lose one's dignity, if one initially has it, only by losing that nature. But losing one's nature just is ceasing to exist as the sort of thing one must be if one is to exist at all: it is to go out of existence altogether. This thought is impossible to sustain of a criminal who is the abiding subject of the drama of crime, investigation, apprehension, trial, conviction, and punishment, as even Aquinas's language, which refers to "he" throughout, makes clear.

Novak makes a similar point, in an essay on the death penalty, while discussing the views of Rabbi Akivah, who held that

> The essence of humanness is that humans are created in the "image of God" (*tselem Elohim*), which seems to mean that there is a sacred dimension to human life itself: human beings are the objects of particular divine concern or providence. So, even though the victim of homicide is designated by Scripture to be made "in the image of God" (Gen. 9:6), and that is the reason his murderer is to be executed, the murderer too is no less made in the image of God. As such, even the execution of the murderer, to use the words of Rabbi Akivah in another context, is "as if one diminished (*k'ilu me'et*) the divine likeness."[20]

Novak in fact strengthens this consideration with a further Kantian argument against capital punishment for the sake of deterrence and a traditional Jewish claim about the evidentiary needs required to prosecute a capital case. The end result is a strong case against the death penalty and an acknowledgement that in a society governed by Jewish law, the permissibility of the death penalty would in certain respects be largely symbolic.

I think the import of Rabbi Akivah's claims is even stronger: on their face they suggest that the death penalty, as an act of intentional killing, cannot possibly be justified along the lines of Aquinas's argument. As John Paul II said, in lines that resonate strongly with Rabbi Akivah's, "Not even a murderer loses his personal dignity, and God himself pledges to guarantee this."[21]

Why, in face of such considerations, is it nevertheless simply not an option for Jewish thinkers to hold that the death penalty is intrinsically immoral? The answer is simple: "because of the primacy of Scripture . . . no one could advocate on

---

19. Aquinas, *ST* II-II, Q. 64, a. 2.
20. Novak, "Can Capital Punishment Ever Be Justified in the Jewish Tradition?" 36.
21. Pope John Paul II, Encyclical Letter *Evangelium Vitae*.9.

traditional Jewish grounds that the death penalty, especially for the crime of homicide, be abolished."[22]

Novak expands on this thought in that same essay in a way that is central for bringing out a potential difference between Catholic and Jewish thought at this point, though many Catholics will disagree. Novak writes,

> In the context of dealing with ordinary homicide, no traditional Jewish thinker could be opposed to capital punishment in principle, since it is clearly mandated by Scripture. To all humankind Scripture mandates, "Whosoever sheds human blood, by humans shall his blood be shed" (Gen. 9:6). To Israel (that is, what came to be solely identified as the Jewish people) Scripture mandates . . ."[23]

And then Novak itemizes a number of passages that he takes to be speaking specifically to the Jewish people, not to "all humankind" such as Exodus 21:12 and Leviticus 24:21–22.

So: only one passage is identified by Novak in the Jewish Scriptures as speaking to all humankind on the subject of capital punishment, the well-known Genesis 9:6, from which comes the title of Edward Feser's and Joseph Bissette's recent book, *By Man Shall His Blood Be Shed: A Catholic Defense of Capital Punishment*.

I began this paper by noting that chapter 1 of *The Sanctity of Human Life* begins with a discussion of this passage, and I'll now return to that discussion. Feser and Bessette think the passage is obvious in its normative implications: the passage shows clearly the moral permissibility of capital punishment; they would endorse the quotation above in which Novak says that "Scripture mandates" the death penalty. But Novak's reading in *The Sanctity of Human Life* is somewhat more nuanced and should lead us to reconsider whether this text can be used to make pronouncements anywhere near as definitive and Feser and Bessette think.

In *Sanctity*, Novak notes that "the punishment set down for such killing is not a direct prescription. 'By humans shall his blood be shed' is written in the less direct third person form (which is to be done) rather than the more direct second-person form (what you should do)."[24] Perhaps we can go farther: the less direct third person form does not even seem to be the is-to-be of practical reason but seems rather to admit of a predictive understanding—this is what will happen. But such a description or prediction need not be understood as a mandate.

Novak notes the fact that the Noahide precepts are generally somewhat indirectly known; later, he gives the example of how the precept concerning sexual morality is known from reflection on Joseph's response to the seductions of Potiphar's wife and the language of Genesis, that "a man shall cling to his wife." So it seems not

---

22. Novak, "Can Capital Punishment Ever Be Justified in the Jewish Tradition," 40.
23. Novak, "Can Capital Punishment Ever Be Justified in the Jewish Tradition," 35.
24. Novak, *The Sanctity of Human Life*, 38–39.

to be the case that one must or even can read straightforwardly from Genesis 9:6 a mandate for capital punishment.

Moreover, while Novak might well be right that no traditional Jewish thinker could be opposed to capital punishment in principle, he nevertheless shows that there are tensions within that tradition, for the tradition contains an inertial trend away from the application of the death penalty and also contains the very idea which recent Catholic thought utilizes in defense of abolition, that the murderer is no less made in the image of God than anyone else. Thinking from the standpoint of the Jewish natural law tradition, Rabbi Novak can lead the Christian and specifically Catholic thinker to the idea that there is room for development here, and I'll try to extend that development further in the next, concluding, section of this paper.

Giver and Lord of Life

The starting point for this section will be a discussion that takes place in the third chapter of *The Sanctity of Human Life*, in which Novak discusses physician assisted suicide. He relates the story, already mentioned, of Rabbi Hanina ben Taradyon, burned at the stake by the Romans, who was entreated by his followers to open his mouth so as to die more quickly. Rabbi Hanina took the opportunity to give one last lesson: "It is better that the One who takes it [my life] be the One who gave it."[25]

Novak writes, "Perhaps the key to understanding Rabbi Hanina's dictum is to explain what one means when one says that God gives life. To say that this means that our lives are not our possessions to destroy at will but that our lives belong to God as their creator is to beg the question."[26] That is, we cannot simply gloss the claim with the moral we hope to draw from it. On the other hand, says Novak, "Rabbi Hanina also could have said that no creature is to destroy any human created in the image of God, and that concept would have been a good reason for not following his disciples' directive to him."[27] But, writes Novak, "Rabbi Hannina was making a different (though not contradictory) point to his disciples," a point he (Novak) then goes on to articulate in the following way:

> What do we mean when we say that God gives human life? To whom does God give human life? First, our lives are given to us in the sense that we are to preserve them and care for them. Accordingly, no one is allowed to destroy himself or herself. . . . There is solid scriptural support for the position that God alone has the right to take back the breath of any of his human creatures because God directly gave it or placed it in the human body. We could also say that God gives our lives to persons who are charged to care for them. These persons are not authorized to harm or destroy what has been given or

25. Novak, *The Sanctity of Human Life*, 123.
26. Novak, *The Sanctity of Human Life*, 123.
27. Novak, *The Sanctity of Human Life*, 123.

entrusted into their care. Thus, Rabbi Hanina's life is given to the Romans, who have political authority over him. Instead of properly keeping their charge over him, however, they chose to violate it by killing him.[28]

Thus, according to Rabbi Novak, the idea of God as the Giver of Life has two aspects: that our life is given to each of us to care for and that each of our lives is also given to others to care for. This gives us reason not to kill any human being, our own self or another, as killing is clearly at odds with the care of self and other that the Gift-relation requires.

Let me make two points in passing about this before I raise the main issue I wish to address. The first is that this idea of God as the Giver of Life in this context seems close to the idea of God as Lord of Life, an idea central to the work of Novak's teacher Germain Grisez, in working out the meaning of the sanctity of human life; I'll say more about this shortly. And this illustrates the second point, that this idea of God as the Giver of Life *is* an articulation of the sanctity of human life as I understand it. Sanctity of human life thus admits of a theocentric understanding.

But so, obviously, does the idea admit of an anthropocentric understanding: human beings are made in the image of God; they thereby have a special dignity that is a "good reason" for not killing them or engaging in other offenses against life. This anthropocentric pole is *also* an articulation of the sanctity of human life. And this raises the question: what is the relationship between the two poles, the theocentric articulation and the anthropocentric?

As I noted in the first section, Novak warns against one possible understanding of the relationship, viz., that there is no relationship or that any implied relationship may simply be ignored. That is, he worries that the "image of God" understanding will be seen as overly ontological, and thus a-relational, such that God will be out of the picture in consideration of human life's sanctity or inviolability. Novak worries in particular that this difficulty threatens accounts of the "image of God" if articulated in terms of human rationality and freedom. As Matthew Levering notes in his account of Novak's view, "Even if the rational and volitional powers were God-like, the lack of a need to mention God would suggest that the human person can be God-like in an autonomous fashion. Novak thus finds that those who wish to locate the image of God in a human attribute (reason and/or will) make of God merely the extrinsic cause of the attribute in which is supposed to reside the divine 'image.'"[29]

I have qualified sympathy for this worry. The qualification is this: it should not need to be immediately evident that what is recognized in the human being as generating an immunity from violence—again, and in short, a common nature fulfilled by common goods including the good of human life—is also related vertically to God in order for that recognition to be action guiding. This, it seems to me, just is a

28. Novak, *The Sanctity of Human Life*, 123, 123–24.
29. Levering, *Jewish-Christian Dialogue and the Life of Wisdom*, 69.

presupposition of calling a precept a part of the natural law: it is available to natural human (practical) reason and can direct action accordingly. I don't think that Novak wishes to deny this point, since he too thinks there can be a recognition in the natural law of the claim the other makes upon us.

But the sympathy is this: somehow present in that very recognition, and not external to it, must be the vertical, or transcendent, dimension. Here, I wish to articulate that dimension by means of an argument of Rabbi Novak's teacher, Germain Grisez.

In a 2001 article, "Natural Law, God, and Human Fulfillment," Grisez distinguished between the way in which the contingency of all things makes clear the need for an uncreated cause that is best understood as a Creator and the way in which the law—"revealed law fully and unmistakably, but even without revelation . . . the law written on every human heart"—manifests God's providence and benevolence.[30] Nothing other than a provident and benevolent God can account for the guidance of practical principles that are directed towards genuine human fulfillment. So, "as people become aware of being guided toward intelligible goods by the principles of practical reason, they also become at least dimly aware of the more-than-human source of that guidance—a source about which the guidance itself provides indications."[31] Grisez continues,

> One who follows others' guidance cooperates with them. So, awareness that the prescriptivity—which is signified by is to be—of the principles of practical reason is guidance by a more-than-human source tends to give anyone acting in accord with that guidance a sense of cooperating with that source. By the same token, following emotion against reason means failing to cooperate and disobeying the guidance received. And so, whenever one thinks that a norm depends upon the principles of practical reason, one implicitly knows not only practical reason's is to be but obligation—that is, that one is bound by that prescriptivity's source.[32]

Thus, intrinsic to the principles of practical reason, including the principle directing agents to the protection and promotion of the good of human life, are both an orientation towards transcendence—towards the creative source of those principles—and relationality, for the upshot of recognizing the transcendent orientation is awareness of the desirability and indeed obligation to cooperate with the source of those principles.

Let me extend the thought here in the direction of the two notions I am concerned with. On the one hand, recognition of the principles of the natural law, and thus, however dimly, of their source and the need for cooperation with that source, includes recognition of the good of human life and the requirement that all human

---

30. Grisez, "Natural Law, God, Religion, and Human Fulfillment," 12.
31. Grisez, "Natural Law, God, Religion, and Human Fulfillment," 13.
32. Grisez, "Natural Law, God, Religion, and Human Fulfillment," 13.

beings be protected as regards that good. The recognition of human beings as to be protected in this regard is a recognition, within the natural law, but open to further expansion and articulation, precisely of human dignity, and of human life as made in the image of God.

On the other hand, since the principle regarding the protection and promotion of human life, both in myself and in others, is available to be recognized as a matter of divine providence and benevolence, that principle, and therefore the lives it protects, are available to be recognized as, specifically, gifts of the Creator. Human life is thus a gift of the Divine Giver.

But how do we connect the two ideas up in the idea of the sanctity of life, that is, in the specific idea that intentional taking of life is wrong? For is it not the case that if something is a gift then it is alienated from the giver? Thus, Margaret Battin, citing the eighteenth-century Swedish philosophy Johann Robeck, argues that once a gift has been made, then it is the recipient's right to do with it as she pleases.[33] Were this the case, then the theocentric understanding of the sanctity of human life would not link in the desired way to the anthropocentric understanding, for from the anthropocentric standpoint, the "image of God" idea would give a reason against killing, but from the theocentric standpoint, the "gift of God" idea would not provide such as reason, specifically where suicide is concerned. Similarly, "Lord of Life" seems to grant God a potentially delegatable authority to take life. So, it also does not seem to meet up with my notion of the demands made by the image of God in regards to capital punishment.

Of some gifts it is certainly true that the recipient is now free to do with the gift what he or she wishes; hence, "if life is really a *gift* from God," then it is that "person's to do with as he or she chooses."[34] But this is not true of all gifts, and gifts which, if they are to be enjoyed as the gifts they are at all, must be enjoyed *in cooperation with* the gift giver would seem to be among the gifts of which this was not true. Such gifts may be *rejected*; but they cannot be both accepted and used freely, i.e., autonomously, since cooperation is internal to the benefit of the gift as such.

Consider, for example, a gift of tickets to my son for a concert—two tickets, given into his possession, but for our use together, to attend the concert as father and son. There are two benefits here, the concert and the relationship, and the relationship will not be realized if either the tickets are simply rejected *or* if they are taken to be used unilaterally without me. To use the tickets in this way is also a rejection of the gift as such, since the gift itself is not simply the tickets but the mutual shared use of the tickets in order to realize a relationship between father and son. This gift is entirely unlike the gift of an Amazon gift card, whereby the giver alienates the money in the act of giving and accords to the recipient the right to do with the money as he will.[35]

33. Battin, "Prohibition and Invitation."
34. Battin, "Prohibition and Invitation," 217.
35. Why deny the right claim? Because the right claim is a claim of right *to the gift* and the gift

This gives us an explanation of Novak's claim that "our lives are given to us in the sense that we are to preserve them and care for them. Accordingly, no one is allowed to destroy himself or herself."[36] Care for and preservation of the gift fosters the relationship between God and man. What of Novak's claims about persons being given stewardship of other persons? Again, in his words: "We could also say that God gives our lives to persons who are charged to care for them. These persons are not authorized to harm or destroy what has been given or entrusted into their care."[37] Well, suppose that I give the tickets to one of two sons (the elder, perhaps) so that the three of us can go together. Here, the gift is kept in stewardship for the benefit of not just one relationship but several: first, care for the gift fosters my relationship with the son who does not hold the tickets (for we will go to the concert together); second, care for the gift fosters my relationship with the son who does hold the tickets (for he is doing something for me); third, care for the gift fosters the relationship of the son who holds the tickets with the son who does not (for the one son is now doing something for the other); and finally, care for the gift fosters a mutual and reciprocal relationship between all three of us (for it is in service of the *three* of us going to the concert together). For the ticket-holding son to destroy the ticket of the other son would damage all these relationships.

Now I take it that something like this relationship-web is what God desires between himself and his people in giving those people the gift of life. It is a relationship which includes not just relationships of person to person and person to God but mediated relationships of God to one person through the care shown by another. But the upshot of such a complex web of relationships which the gift of life makes possible is that God as the giver of the gift becomes implicated in this web as the only one with a "right" to end the gift relationship. Of course, it can be ended by rejection or usurpation, but neither option, given the goodness of the gift, is appropriately construed as acting within a "right."

And if this is so, then it gives us a some understanding of the notion of the Lordship of God: that notion and the notion of God as the Giver of the Gift become very close on this account. "Lord of Life," like "Giver of Life" indicates that God has authority—final, and indeed sole authority—over the taking of life. Indeed, Lord and Giver of Life indicates that God has authority—final and compete authority—over the *giving* of life, a claim essential to one line of argument made by Grisez against the liceity of contraception.[38] But of course God's authority on this account is lordship of a special sort:

---

cannot be construed as simply the material benefit of the tickets themselves. *That* is not what was given. It is different of course if I give two tickets to someone and urge them "to have a good time."

36. Novak, *The Sanctity of Human Life*, 123.

37. Novak, *The Sanctity of Human Life*, 124.

38. "The will to prevent life is likewise irreverent toward God, the Lord of life, with whom couples are called to cooperate in responsibly procreating new persons for the kingdom" (Grisez, *The Way of the Lord Jesus*, 514). See also the citations to Pope John Paul II in footnote 106 of the same quoted passage.

not tyranny, but a lordship oriented towards the common good of the community made possible by the gift that is given. I'll return to this point momentarily in conclusion. First, let me recap this discussion. I think of the sanctity of human life not as a property of human life as such but as indicating reasons for the general inviolability of human life (I gave reasons in section 2 for thinking that inviolability is exceptionless). There are two such reasons: one is that human beings are made in the image of God, an idea that I, though not Novak, believe must be understood through the prescription of the natural law indicating that human life is a good for all human beings, not to be intentionally destroyed by any human beings. But like Novak, I think that the recognition in human beings of that which protects them from destruction is vertically oriented: we can see the protecting of human life as a form of cooperation with God.

The second reason is that God has given us life as a gift for care and service; it is thus not to be ended at our will, but at His. That reason too shows the sanctity of human life. But what is the relationship? The relationship is found in the idea of the gift of life as a gift whose goodness is partly to be found in what is given and partly to be found in the cooperation between giver and recipients that the gift makes possible. But that really is just a reframing of what I said in explaining the image of God idea. The two sides of the sanctity of life—image of God and God as Giver of the gift of life—are two sides of the same idea, or the same reality, the reality of a divine being who has gratuitously created beings whose perfections include: their lives; care for the lives of others; being cared for by others; and cooperation with the giver of life in both caring and being cared for.

And, finally, therefore only God has the authority—the right, if you will—both to give life and to take it. The right with regard to the former is violated, I think, both by the use of contraception and also by the attempt literally to "make" human life using various assisted reproduction techniques. I've suggested earlier in this paper that the right in regards to the latter is violated by all intentional killing of human beings. Yet one possible exception seems required: intentional killing mandated by God, since, after all, He has the right and authority exclusively to take human life.

I've addressed this possibility elsewhere, arguing that "God does not intend death."[39] I won't recapitulate those arguments here but rather suggest that the account of this section also suggests that it is implausible that God intends the death of human beings. For God gives life as a gift, entirely gratuitously, for the good of the recipients—a gift which encompasses both the good of life itself and the good of shared (cooperative) stewardship of the good of one's own life and the lives of others.

I think if we consider the analogy I drew earlier to the case in which I give tickets to my son, it becomes very difficult to see the circumstances under which a loving father will take the tickets away. Although it is not morally compatible with the idea of a cooperative gift that the recipient destroy the gift, it also does not seem morally compatible with the idea of such a gift that the giver intend its destruction. Similarly,

39. See Tollefsen, "Does God Intend Death?"

the idea of God as Giver of the Gift of Life seems to me to be compatible only with God's permissively willing the death of those to whom he has gifted life, and never with God's intending death. But if God does not intend death, neither does he ever delegate to others the right to intend death. The theocentric axis of the sanctity of life seems to me, just like the anthropocentric axis, to put intentional killing outside the realm of what is morally permissible, and hence to reveal not only suicide but also capital punishment, as always and everywhere not to be done.

Bibliography

Battin, Margaret. "Prohibition and Invitation: The Paradox of Religious Views about Suicide." In Margaret Battin, *The Least Worst Death: Essays in Bioethics on the End of Life*, 205–53. New York: Oxford University Press, 1995.

Feser, Edward, and Joseph Bessette. *By Man Shall His Blood Be Shed: A Catholic Defense of Capital Punishment*. San Francisco: Ignatius, 2017.

Finnis, John. *Natural Law and Natural Rights*. Oxford: Oxford University Press, 1980 (2nd ed. 2011).

George, Robert P., and Christopher Tollefsen. *Embryo: A Defense of Human Life*. 2nd ed. Princeton: The Witherspoon Institute, 2011.

Grisez, Germain. "Natural Law, God, Religion, and Human Fulfillment." *The American Journal of Jurisprudence* 46 (2001) 3–36.

———. *The Way of the Lord Jesus*. Vol. 2: *Living a Christian Life*. Quincy, IL: Franciscan, 1993.

Grisez, Germain, Joseph Boyle, and John Finnis. "Practical Principles, Moral Truth and Ultimate Ends." *American Journal of Jurisprudence* 32 (1987) 99–151.

John Paul II. "Evangelium Vitae." *Libreria Editrice Vaticana*. March 25, 1995. http://www.vatican.va/content/john-paul-ii/en/encyclicals/documents/hf_jp-ii_enc_25031995_evangelium-vitae.html.

Levering, Matthew. *Jewish-Christian Dialogue and the Life of Wisdom: Engagements with the Theology of David Novak*. New York: Continuum, 2010.

Novak, David. "Can Capital Punishment Ever Be Justified in the Jewish Tradition?" In *Religion and the Death Penalty: A Call for Reckoning*, edited by Eric C. Owens, John D. Carlson, and Eric P. Elshtain, 31–47. Grand Rapids: Eerdmans, 2004.

———. *Natural Law in Judaism*. Cambridge: Cambridge University Press, 1998.

———. *The Sanctity of Human Life*. Washington, DC: Georgetown University Press, 2007.

Tollefsen, Christopher. "Does God Intend Death?" *Diametros* 38 (2013) 191–200.

University of Massachusetts Boston. "Still Face Experiment: Dr. Edward Tronick." YouTube. November 30, 2009. https://www.youtube.com/watch?v=apzXGEbZhto.

Response to

Christopher Tollefsen's "David Novak, Natural Law, and the Sanctity of Human Life"

DAVID NOVAK

I AM GRATEFUL TO Christopher Tollefsen for his insightful, sympathetic reading of my work, especially my work on natural law, both theoretical and practical.

Although agreeing with most of my natural law theory about the sanctity of human life, and agreeing with most of my practical stands on correlated human life issues, nevertheless, Chris does not agree with all of my views. In this disagreement, he invites my reasoned response. Such a response could not be made to somebody who agrees with all my views, nor could it be made to somebody who agrees with none of my views. The former doesn't really need my response; the latter doesn't really want my response. Now at the practical level, Chris doesn't think I have gone far enough in opposing capital punishment as an affront to the sanctity of all human life, regardless of how wicked any human being has acted. At the theoretical level, Chris disagrees with some major points in my natural law theory. For the purposes of this response and its necessary brevity, our practical difference over capital punishment will be bracketed, though certainly not dismissed or ignored.

Chris's difference with my natural law theory has a history that goes back to the time when he was born. Chris's late father Olaf Tollefsen and I were students of Germain Grisez at Georgetown University in the mid-1960s, working in the area of natural law theory. Olaf and our fellow student, the late Joseph Boyle (who was my University of Toronto colleague until his recent death), became Grisez's chief disciples. In fact, Olaf and Joe co-authored with Grisez a book published in 1976, *Free Choice: A Self-Referential Argument*. Although I have ever been Grisez's respectful student (always referring to him in speech and in writing as "my revered teacher" or "my revered philosophical mentor"), I couldn't call myself his disciple, never having agreed with some of the main points of his natural law theory. Grisez himself accepted my disagreement with him because I do not reject natural law *per se*. (Also, he liked my Jewish religious commitment which, by what could be called *analogia fidei*, he saw a parallel in his own

Catholic religious commitment.) I mention this because Chris has clearly succeeded his father in adopting (as far as I can see) Germain Grisez's natural law theory, no doubt though, very much rethinking it in his own way. So, my disagreement with Chris on a main point in his natural law theory goes back to my disagreement with Grisez, who could be called Chris's "philosophical grandfather."

Let us now see how Chris applies some of Grisez's ideas to his difference with me, although he agrees with Thomas Slabon, saying, "there is not much of a gap between his [i.e., Novak's] view and mine."[1] Nevertheless, there is enough of a gap for me to respond to him, and in the same collegial spirit this point was raised.

Disagreeing with me in his paper, Chris writes, "I don't think it can be the case that the other presents himself in a way that can be recognized *apart* or *prior to* my own awareness of human goods as horizons of possibility for me. Yet some and perhaps all of my practical awareness of human goods requires the presence of others."[2] He then goes on to say that there is "the common nature underlying shared goods ... [and] what is shared is a rational nature." Earlier, Chris makes the following distinction: "The 'Image' aspect is typically rooted in the ontological features of the human person, while the other ... aspect concerns a relationship between such persons and their Lord and Creator."[3] Later, Chris distinguishes between a "theocentric" moral trajectory and an "anthropocentric" one.[4]

From an anthropocentric perspective, it would seem that a human person's moral trajectory is threefold: first, the recognition of my active nature to be a rational, goods-pursuing being; two, the recognition that others share that nature along with me, and I must share it with them; three, the recognition that this goods-pursuing nature is a gift from its Source, who is the Creator-God. Germain Grisez is quoted by Chris as saying that anybody who recognizes the contingency of everything created, including human nature and the goods that created nature is to pursue, ought to have "a sense of cooperating with that source."[5] This trajectory seems to be what Chris has called "anthropocentric" as it begins with the recognition of human nature, only ending with the recognition of God as the source or first cause of that nature. This trajectory could be called "phenomenological" insofar as it corresponds to our temporal human experience of first being related to fellow humans, and thereafter being related to God.

There is, however, a theocentric trajectory, in which the relationship with God is recognized as being prior to the relationship of a human person with oneself and with other humans. This trajectory could be called "ontological." Here, too, the trajectory is threefold: one, the acceptance of God's love for me as a member of the covenanted community, as especially revealed in God's commanding us to actively respond to

1. p. 297.
2. p. 296.
3. p. 296.
4. p. 296.
5. p. 296.

His love for us; second, my recognition that my fellow covenant members are equally loved by God, so that I must share this love with them lest I err and presume it is my possession solely. Third, I have the right, even the duty, to require my neighbors to love me as I have the duty to love them.

In each of these trajectories, point one leads to point two, and point two leads to point three. While accepting the distinction between the anthropocentric/phenomenological and the theocentric/ontological ways of understanding human nature, I differ with Chris as to which way of understanding the threefold moral trajectory is to be preferred.

The difference between our respective approaches can be seen in the way we might deal differently with the neighbor-love commandment in Leviticus 19:18, viz., "You shall love your neighbor as yourself; I am the Lord." I deal with it differently than I think Grisez and Tollefsen would deal with it. By the way, our difference is not a Jewish approach versus a Catholic approach, for there are Jewish thinkers who would agree with their approach, and there are Catholic thinkers who would agree with my approach. (This is also discussed in my responses to John Berkman and David Elliot.)

Grisez and Tollefsen (if I understand them correctly) would say: First, I love myself, which is enacted in my pursuit of the goods I want for myself (often called *bonum sibi*). Second, I recognize that my neighbor is *like* me and, therefore, his or her pursuit of these goods is one I must respect as being as valid *as my own*, plus my recognition that in most cases we both need to pursue them together (often called *bonum commune*). Third, I recognize God as the Creator of the goods to be pursued and the human nature that enables humans to pursue these goods rationally. This is an anthropocentric/phenomenological approach to the neighbor-love commandment.

On the other hand, I would approach the trajectory of Leviticus 19:18 differently, i.e., from a more theocentric/ontological perspective. First, the commandment, "you shall love your neighbor" is given by God. The chapter in which it appears begins with the words, "The Lord spoke unto Moses saying . . ." (Lev 19:1), and the commandment itself concludes with the words, "I am the Lord," which could be glossed as "*because* I am the Lord." Second, "as yourself" (*kamokha*) can be interpreted as follows: "your neighbor is *like you* insofar as he or she is the recipient of the same commandment." That is because God's commandments are not addressed to each, separate, individual person; instead, they are addressed to all persons as members of the community. The chapter in which the commandment of neighbor-love appears begins with the commandment to Moses to "speak to all the assembled Israelites" (Lev 19:2). Third, I am like my neighbors in being loved by God, who obligates me to actively love them by tangibly *benefitting* them. Simultaneously, my neighbors are obligated to benefit me. (The Torah is commanding action, which is voluntary, rather than feeling, which is involuntary—a point missed by Kant in his discussion of this commandment.)

All the commandments of the Torah are active indications of God's love for His people, which this commandment prescribes to be shared among the members of the community. This love is tangible insofar as it is experienced in God's beneficent action for us, both in God's saving us from destruction and, even more so, in God's beneficent gift of good governance. As the Jewish liturgy puts it, "You God love the House of Israel your people with an everlasting love: Torah and commandments (*mitsvot*), statutes and ordinances You have taught *us*." Thus, we can love God, not only "with all your [singular] heart, with all your life, and with all your possessions" (Deut 6:5 as interpreted in *Mishnah*: Berakhot 9.5), but even more *with* our neighbors. Yet one cannot love God and do so along with one's neighbors (which we do when we worship God together) unless all of us realize that we couldn't love anyone, neither God nor fellow humans, if God hadn't loved us first. In other words, human love is always responsive; only God's love is truly initiating. Nobody can love subsequently unless they have been loved initially.

The love humans are commanded to activate in living deeds (what the rabbinic tradition calls *gemilut hasadim*) is not self-love. I find the notion of self-love problematic: *who* is loving *whom*? "Love" (*ahev* in Hebrew) is a transitive verb, whose subject must be other than its object. (I have the same problem with "autonomy:" *who* is commanding, i.e., the *nomos* in auto-nomy, *whom*?) Now the fact that God loves me like God loves my neighbor (vertically), and then God commands us both to share that love with one another (horizontally), means that God is the active Source (*meqor* in Hebrew) of all love.

Nevertheless, that divine "sourcing" of love is not the same as God's being the *First Cause* of all creation. Contrary to the position of "natural theology," which Grisez and Tollefsen as Thomists espouse, I do not think that we can infer God's causality from the world as we experience it. Also, even if we could infer God's prime causality from looking at the external world, that wouldn't lead us to infer this First Cause is the God who commands us. Wouldn't any such inference involve us in the highly questionable inference of an "ought" from an "is"? And, in fact, didn't Grisez insist, in his arguable interpretation of Aquinas's theory of practical reason that (contrary to the view of many more traditional Thomists, though) practical reason doesn't presuppose an ontological foundation? So, for Grisez, natural law doesn't need natural theology. Hence, although both are affirmed by him, the affirmation of one neither presupposes nor entails the other.

Our experience of God's love and its requirements of us, i.e., its commandments given to us directly through revelation, is not that of a cause-effect relation. Effects are not required to *cooperate with* their cause. They have no choice in the matter. Furthermore, if love is not only transitive but transactional, i.e., mutually reciprocal, both proactive and reactive, then from the perspective of God's covenantal love for and with His elected community, to speak of God as "Cause" of a love relationship is to turn what (in Martin Buber's terms) is an "I-thou" relationship into an "I-it" relation. Our being created in the image of God means that our relationship with God is not mediated by God's causal relation with the rest of creation.

The non-causal character of divine-human cooperation comes out in a profound interpretation of Genesis 1:26, viz., "Let us make (*na'aseh*) humans in our image (*be-tsalmenu*)." Who is "us"? The person many consider the greatest modern Jewish philosopher, Franz Rosenzweig (d. 1929) interpreted "us" to be God *and* humans making human existence together in *their* ongoing mutual relationship, rather than God *making* humans and humans *being made by* God. That is why, as pointed out by Rosenzweig's teacher, the Jewish philosopher Hermann Cohen (d. 1918), God does not declare the creation of humans to be good (*tov*) as is the case with the rest of creation. Whereas the rest of creation is already fully made, human existence is still *being made*, freely by both God and humans. Hence, it is not fulfilled until it ends at the future time of death. Therefore, it cannot be judged as *having been* good or bad while one is still alive.[6] Isn't this what "cooperation *with* God" truly means?

Furthermore, I submit that natural law doesn't involve the positive, cooperative God-human relationship at all (except, perhaps negatively, in the prohibition of idolatry) and that it only universally prescribes not harming other humans as we are not to be harmed by them. Positive cooperation, be it with fellow humans or with God, is largely determined by particular positive law. It is determined by particular *lex humana* as regards the relationship with fellow humans, by particular *lex divina* as regards the relationship with God. Neither particular determination is universally obligatory. They are both very much culturally conditioned.

Finally, I thank Chris for enabling me to return to a dialogue with my late revered teacher through my current dialogue with him. As I benefitted from dialogue with Germain Grisez in the past, so do I now benefit from dialogue with Christopher Tollefsen presently. *Plus ça change, plus ce la même chose.*

---

6. See Eccl 7:1; also, Aristotle, *Nicomachean Ethics*, 1.10/1100a10–1101a20.

Chapter 12

On Good Supersessionism

Jews, Christians, and the Covenant
That Binds and Divides Us

Thomas Joseph White, O.P.

In contemporary theological discourse the notion of a Christian "supersession" of the people of Israel can have several meanings. Consider some diverse senses of this term that are commonly employed and that are at times confused with one another.

Covenantal displacement (S1) The people of Israel and their descendants (hereafter the Jewish people) were once in a covenant with God of supernatural origin that has now ceased to exist after being replaced by the New Covenant in Jesus Christ. Their status as an elective people has been transferred to the Church.

Divine reprobation (S2) The Jewish people were or are (either in the past or even now) collectively responsible for the death of Christ and accordingly by divine decree are alienated from God collectively in a historically perpetual way.

The unique mediation of Christ (S3) Jesus of Nazareth is God made human and consequently the revelation of God given in Christ has an absolute and universal character such that it supersedes all previous revelation given to Israel or subsequent claims to religious truth. Furthermore, Christ is the unique mediator of salvation for all human beings, who alone offers to human beings the life of grace by which they may attain salvation.

Christological mediation theory as Judaic displacement (S4) The idea is that if one were to affirm that Christ is the unique and universal saving mediator, then this in turn would entail the above-mentioned theories of covenantal replacement and reprobation of the Jewish people. Consequently, if one holds that Christ is the Savior of the Jewish people then one must affirm both (S1) or (S2) and if one denies *either* (S1) *or* (S2) then one must in turn deny that Christ is the universal mediator of salvation, at least insofar as he is for the Jewish people. In other words, Christological universalism is seen as anti-Judaic.

Sacramental fulfillment and sublimation (S5) This is the affirmation that the ceremonial precepts of the Old Law, though of divine institution, have been abrogated by the sacraments of the New Law that in a sense fulfill but also replace the sacraments of the Old Law.

Catholic theologians who work in the service of the New Testament as interpreted in the classical tradition and in concord with the living Magisterium have tended in the light of the Second Vatican Council (*Nostra Aetate*) to argue against extreme forms of the covenantal rejection or reprobation of the Jewish people [propositions (S1) and (S2)] while affirming the final revelation and unique mediation of Christ (S3) thus denying in turn that there is a necessary mutual connection between Christological absolutism and "supersessionism" as a kind of replacement theory. That is to say they deny (S4). They have argued in differing ways about the sacraments of the New Law in relation to the Old, but typical references to Christ "fulfilling" the ceremonies of the Old Law in contemporary theology suggest some version of (S5) as a normative Catholic view.[1]

In summary then, the developed view in doctrinally informed Catholic theology is that Christ is God and man, the definitive revelation of God in human history, and the unique mediator of grace for all people, including of course the Jewish people. Even after the coming of Christ and the rise of post-biblical Judaism, the Jewish people remain mysteriously in an enduring primal covenant with God (cf. Rom 9–11). They are not collectively responsible for the death of Christ or rightly understood as a deicide people. The Old Law including its ceremonies has been definitively fulfilled by the New Law including the sacraments of the Catholic Church and its priestly order and Eucharistic sacrifice. Therefore, the Church, following the New Testament, rightly affirms that Christ is the culmination of the Abrahamic and Mosaic covenants. The Jewish people who continue to be related to God by their original covenant also do so in a numinous way through Christ. And relatedly, if non-baptized persons attain to salvation eschatologically without the sacraments of the New Law, they do so nevertheless in strict implicit dependence on the grace of Christ. All of this can be held while rightly recognizing that the Jewish people have often been gravely mistreated by Christians at various points in history, affected in part by a theological "teaching of contempt" fueled by various versions of (S1) and (S2) noted above.

The rendering provided above seeks to insulate Catholic theology from various problematic forms of "supersessionism" associated with historical anti-Judaic beliefs and prejudices. Accordingly, one speaks today of "supersessionism" in largely negative

---

1. See the normative ecclesial statements of the Second Vatican Council, *Nostra Aetate*.4; *Catechism of the Catholic Church*, nos. 839–40; and the 2015 Reflection from the Commission for Religious Relations with the Jews, "'The Gifts and the Calling of God are Irrevocable' (Rom. 11:29) A Reflection on Theological Questions Pertaining to Catholic-Jewish Relations on the Occasion of the 50th Anniversary of 'Nostra Aetate' (no. 4)." (Official translations of these documents are available at www.vatican.va.) See also the fairly representative theological views offered by Joseph Ratzinger in *Many Religions—One Covenant*.

terms as a relic of the past. In truth, however, the notion requires deeper examination and more complex consideration. After all, the notion of supersession in itself denotes historical perfection, fulfillment and succession, which are notions central to the idea of prophetic revelation in both the Old Testament and the New.

Recently, Rabbi David Novak has argued that the concept of supersession can and should be revisited by *both* Jews and Christians together as a positive concept, albeit one that they might employ in distinct but overlapping ways.[2] As Novak points out, supersessionism is an idea that first characterizes traditional Judaism. The claim by ancient Israel and by modern orthodox Jews to have received divine revelation from the Mosaic Law and the prophets is a claim to a religious novelty in history that supersedes definitively all previous religious claims. In addition, as Novak points out, this "Jewish supersessionism" continues over into Christianity as an offshoot of Judaism and therefore, in part, unites believers in the two traditions. After all, Christians claim that the Mosaic Law and the prophets provide unique, divinely inspired teaching applicable (in Christ) to all persons. Third, then, Novak argues that if Christians claim that the revelation of the New Testament supersedes that of the Old Testament in some respects (which I have noted above in (S3) and (S5)), then they should accept to live in friendly disagreement with Jews. In other words, Novak presumes that Christians should not and perhaps cannot really sustain belief (S4) noted above: the idea that one must choose between Christ's universality and the enduring reality of God's primal covenant with Israel. Rather than prolong a seemingly unresolvable dialectic between the affirmation of their Christological views and the acceptance of a place for the Jews in the divine economy, Christians can and should seek to find a way that their unique forms of "Christological supersessionism" (my (S3) and (S5)) invite them to recognize and value the enduring covenant of God with Israel.[3] Naturally, Jews and Christians will disagree then about the grounds for the covenant of Israel, in light of Christ, but they can do so in mutual friendship and respectful theological dialogue, joined by a common search for the truth.

How then might we follow up from the Christian side of the discussion of this question so as to treat seriously Novak's consideration of ancient Israelite revelation (the Torah, the Prophets, and Writings) and the covenant with the Jewish people as a form of "good supersessionism"? How might this idea affect the Church's understanding of the Jewish people and herself in relationship to the Jewish people, interpreted in light of Christ and the New Testament?

Here below I will offer a series of brief theses, elaborated in view of this question and in response to Novak's important essay. Evidently each of these claims is intended

2. Novak, "Supersessionism Hard and Soft."

3. In my rendering of this point, Christians should not affirm or defend (S4) above as a condition for finding theological significance in the continued existence of the Jewish people as a people related to God. To do so is to seek either to deny the teaching of the New Testament regarding the universal mediation of Christ or to deny the teaching of Romans 9–11 and that of *Nostra Aetate* concerning the enduring character of the covenant of Israel with God.

uniquely as an affirmation of Catholic Christian theology, while also being of potential importance to the Church's engagement and dialogue with the Jewish people.

> *Thesis 1:* Biblical supersessionism is originally a creation of the ancient Hebraic prophets. It stems from the Torah itself in its claim to be prophetic revelation and remains essential to biblical monotheism. Without it both Christianity and Judaism cease to be intelligible.

The Old Testament prophets present their teaching in oppositional form against what they take to be the previous problematic religious confusions of the human race. They claim to offer in contrast and correction a novel, privileged form of religious knowledge and worship, one that is simultaneously particular to Israel but universal in orientation. This universality is grounded most fundamentally in the distinctive biblical notion of creation. God the Creator is the unique transcendent cause of the world, distinct from the world, but not indifferent to it, who is present in all things as he who gives them their existence. What is particular to Israel, meanwhile, stems especially from the notion of covenant: That God has revealed himself to Israel personally, so that Israel might in turn relate to God in authentic knowledge and worship of God and organize its life in this light. This particularism is qualified. The election of Israel occurs against the backdrop of God's original gift of grace and personal friendship to the whole human race, in its first ancestors. These Adamic human beings however broke with or inflicted a wound to the primal covenant of God "from the beginning." The covenant of God with Noah in Genesis 9:1–17 symbolizes and foreshadows a recapitulation of that first grace and has universal import, despite its limited and imperfect character. The covenant with Abraham and Moses then does occur within the context of a larger providential design of grace and does portend an eventual universal extension of Israel's own mystery as an elect people.

By both its monotheistic notion of creation and its appeal to a unique covenant with God, the revelation given to Israel claims to supersede the past era of human ignorance regarding the gods and all mythological cosmologies. Both these ideas, which are grounded in the Torah, have evident implications even in our own historical moment. If God is both Creator of all that exists and author of a covenant with Israel, then human existence is not explained merely by reference to an impersonal horizon of matter, nor has human life arisen as a mere physical accident of chance. Created being is ultimately derived from uncreated personhood. God, who is the origin of the world, is personal—albeit in a numinous way that we denote by imperfect analogies. And he has given being to human persons made in his image. Even more significantly he has manifested himself personally by grace to the people of Israel. In this case, not only is the notion of being personalistic at its summit, but all that exists is in some way *for* persons, so that they can live in communion with God. We might say, "being is ecclesial." If this teaching of the Torah is true, then the revelatory supersessionism of the Torah is not only normative for Christians, but it is also of an acute cultural actuality in an age of materialism and misguided ideas about the human person.

> *Thesis 2:* The revelation given to the ancient Jewish people *by its very nature* is open to fulfillment in the way that the New Testament claims to fulfill the Old. Therefore, the Second Testament is not wholly distinct from or essentially extrinsic to the First.

However perfect it is in relation to the non-revealed religious traditions of humanity, ancient biblical Judaism is also characterized by three intrinsic paradoxes or tensions that leave room for, and even suggest from within, the possibility of Christianity. First, it claims to deliver a privileged knowledge of who God is, but also leaves the mystery of God's own identity shrouded in darkness, as suggested by the cloud of unknowing at Mount Sinai. In the Torah, God is known primarily through his activities of salvation effectuated on behalf of a particular people, that is to say, as the God *of Israel* who manifests himself to that people and enshrines his covenant with them in Law. Who then is God and how does his identity relate to all peoples? Second, the Torah and the prophets stipulate that this same covenant has universal horizons of import, even though its inner essence of reception and practice is reserved to those who are descendants of Abraham, who live by the Mosaic Law. How then is this revelation of universal importance? Third, in the face of evil, human suffering, and death, ancient Judaism rightly looks to God for a response and points humanity toward an eschatological era of salvation, which includes personal judgement and the universal resurrection of the dead. But that resolution of the end times has yet to unfold in any particular determinant way. Does God's promise to redeem Israel from suffering and death have implications for the whole human race, and if so, how so?

Against the backdrop of these internal tensions, the mystery of Christ provides resolution, preserving these themes of the Old Law while transposing them into a higher key. The fullness of the knowledge of God is brought to perfection in Christ because God himself has become human, revealing the very identity of God as Father, Incarnate Word, and Holy Spirit. The knowledge of who God is in himself illumines the nature of human beings made in God's image, as beings of knowledge and love, meant for a universal communion of persons in the Church. The covenant that is restricted to the practice of the Mosaic Law achieves a genuine universality in light of the death of Christ, since his atonement fulfills the Law and simultaneously opens the covenant up to the nations by the Sacrament of Baptism. Finally, the promise that God will confront evil, suffering, and death takes on a unique and unexpected form, since it is the God of Israel himself who suffers and dies as man, and who is raised from the dead, in solidarity with the human race. The eschatological salvation of the world is inaugurated in Christ by his bodily resurrection. This event becomes the key to unlocking the prophecies of the older Testament and it prepares the human race for the end times and the life to come, doing so through the ecclesial communion of sacramental life.

> *Thesis 3:* The Christian claim that the New Testament fulfills what was originally begun in biblical Judaism cannot accurately be characterized as supersessionist, if we mean by that term that Christianity replaces ancient biblical Judaism. This being said, the sacraments of the New Law do typologically fulfill and replace the ceremonial law of the Old Testament.

A covenant-replacement scheme of that kind noted above in (S1) is inconsistent with modern Catholic magisterial teaching and its interpretation of St. Paul (Rom 9–11).[4] Its affirmation if taken at a radical enough level would invalidate Christianity itself, since according to the internal logic of the New Testament, Christian revelation claims to originate organically from and to be the culmination of all previous prophetic sources of ancient Judaism. "Salvation is from the Jews" (John 4:22). In this respect, the missionary aims of traditional Catholicism, which seeks to convert all nations to the God of the Bible, are anti-supersessionist by definition (at least in the sense of (S1) above). Because the New Testament presupposes the truth of the original supersessionism of the Torah and the prophets with regard to non-revealed human religions, the Catholic Church continually seeks to bring forth faithfully the whole teaching of the Old Testament and its internal message, expanding its reach of communication to all the gentile nations. To state things succinctly: without the monotheism of ancient Israel, there can be no Trinitarian monotheism. The Trinity simply is the God of Israel made perfectly known in Christ. Likewise, without the covenant of Israel, there is no intelligibility to the incarnation and atonement. The saving mystery of redemption that takes place in Christ occurs against the backdrop of the Old Law and the judgment of humanity's fallenness and sin that it brilliantly depicts.

In the second century, Marcion sought to renounce the use and authority of the Old Testament writings within the Church. In response, authors such as Justin Martyr and Irenaeus provided interpretations of the Old Testament built on what they themselves inherited from the apostolic writings.[5] They elaborated what was, in effect, a threefold Christian distinction for interpreting Old Testament Law: as composed of moral, ceremonial, and juridical precepts. Their writings indicate that the moral

---

4. *Nostra Aetate* n.4, CCC 839. My claim should be qualified. If Christ is the unique mediator of salvation for all persons, then the covenant of God with the Jewish people represented in the Torah and the prophets has its efficacy only ever in relation to Christ. This Christological recapitulation of the covenant is not rightly characterized as a form of replacement of the Law, but as a fulfillment and transformation of it. The notion that the Jewish people who do not know Christ down through the ages are "abandoned by God" is rejected by the Magisterium as false, especially in light of Rom 9:4–5 and 11:29. That being said, it must also be stated that the failure to recognize Christ as the divine Messiah is an objective disadvantage, and the fact that this absence of knowledge is maintained by a systemic form of religious practice, however sincerely well intentioned, is in some ways non-dispositive to the plenary revelation that has come about in the New Testament.

5. See Justin Martyr, *Dialogue with Trypho*, and Irenaeus, *Against Heresies* IV, cc. 9–26.

precepts are of perpetual significance and therefore in no way superseded but rather intensified and extended within the Christian economy, particularly through the Church's use and interpretation of the Ten Commandments. The ceremonial precepts are to be read typologically as signifying Christ, the Church, and the sacraments. They are considered fulfilled and therefore, in a real sense, taken up into but also superseded by the seven sacraments of the New Law. For example, Baptism fulfills but also universalizes circumcision, just as the Eucharist fulfills but also universalizes the sacrifices of the Torah. Thus, the Christian economy is one of sacrifice and priesthood in a way that continues the dynamic of the Old Testament in a higher and more perfect key, preserving it while also replacing it so as to universalize it. Baptism and the other six sacraments are available now so as to allow a concrete medium whereby all the gentile nations may enter the covenant. The juridical precepts pertain to the customs of civic reward or punishment of a given cultural time and place. They have an enduring religious dignity but are not necessarily universal in application, since the civic ordinances of ancient Israel are not applicable in all cultures.[6] In addition, these authors also identified an anagogical sense of Scripture: As Irenaeus notes, the Old Testament signifies many truths about the eschatological life to come. Therefore, it continues to instruct the Church about what is not yet perfectly manifest.[7] In all these ways the Old Testament revelation is always a living source of revealed truth, one that continues to enlighten the human race until the end of the ages.

> *Thesis 4:* The claim that the Church "supersedes" the body of current practitioners of post-biblical Judaism is in some real sense historically incoherent, so as to be theologically unintelligible. Therefore, the counterclaim developed in response to such an idea—that the Church must abandon a theology of supersessionism regarding the Jews—is also intrinsically incoherent in key respects. This controversy therefore is artificial and should be abandoned in favor of a consideration of authentic fundamental principles.

None of what has been said thus far directly addresses the Catholic Church's view of the status of the Jewish people—those who do not identify Jesus as the Messiah—after the time of the coming of Christ. As noted above, supersessionism is sometimes defined as the view that the living Jewish people, those now practicing post-biblical Talmudic Judaism, are no longer a people related to or in covenant with God due to the reality of the New Covenant of grace and the Church. (I have characterized this view as (S1) above.) Is that the case? Before answering the question, we might problematize it. Is the claim even intelligible in doctrinally traditional Christian terms? Orthodox Judaism as it exists for the past two millennia is in many respects a post-Christian development, one that came into being in the wake of the destruction of the Temple, after the demise of Israel as an ancient nation state, as well as in reaction to the rise of

---

6. Irenaeus, *Against Heresies*, IV, cc. 15–18. See likewise Aquinas, in *Summa Theologiae* I-II, q. 104.
7. Irenaeus, *Against Heresies*, V cc. 26, 29, 34, 35.

Christianity. Consequently, this tradition cannot really be "superseded" in any unambiguous sense of the term, since it developed alongside the Church. The New Testament affirmation that Christ is the fulfillment of the Old Covenant does provide the Church with grounds for a kind of qualified supersessionism regarding the revelation and mediation of Christ and his new sacramental economy ((S3) and (S5) above). But these claims do not refer in a straightforward way to the Jewish people who come after Christ. Consequently, to speak of the Church's relationship to them in either sense of the term "supersession" is ambiguous even from the start.

Still the question remains of the Church's theological evaluation of post-biblical Judaism and its adherents, the living community of the Jewish people. Thomas Aquinas calls them, not without respect, "the synagogue" which continues to exist alongside the Church.[8] The modern Catholic Magisterium addresses this question by appeal to a set of principles derived from Scripture. As noted above, St. Paul teaches in the Epistle to the Romans that after the coming of Christ, God remains faithful to his covenant with the Jewish people, including those who do not believe in Jesus as the Messiah and Lord.[9] God does not abandon them and in fact their continued existence remains of universal religious import, since their eventual reconciliation with the Church will have eschatological significance, signaling the end-times.[10] Correspondingly, Catholic *doctores* like Aquinas underscore that the continued existence in the world of the Jewish people can be seen to constitute a perpetual sign of the reality of the ancient covenant. Their presence is even a sign of eschatological hope for the world, since God maintains the Jewish people in existence despite adversities as a sign of his promise, as well as in view of their eventual collective recognition of the mystery of Christ. This latter event will have universal soteriological implications.[11]

Thus, there are fundamental precedents in the classical tradition for what one finds in the *Second Vatican Council* on this topic. *Nostra Aetate* rightly excludes various erroneous theological opinions, rejecting the idea that the Jewish people are either a collectively reprobate or deicide people.[12] What it promotes positively

---

8. See for example, Aquinas, *Super Sent.* IV, d. 27, q. 3, a. 1, qc. 3, corp.; *Quodlibet* VII, q. 6, a. 2, corp.

9. See in this respect, Rom 11:25–33.

10. Rom 11:12: "Now if their trespass means riches for the world, and if their failure means riches for the Gentiles, how much more will their full inclusion mean!"

11. Aquinas, *In Rom.*, XI, lect. 2, 883.; lect. 4, 917–20.

12. *Nostra Aetate*, para. 4 "[N]either all Jews indiscriminately at that time, nor Jews today, can be charged with the crimes committed during his Passion. . . . [T]he Jews should not be spoken of as rejected or accursed as if this followed from holy Scripture." The *Catechism of the Catholic Church* comments (no. 597) "The historical complexity of Jesus' trial is apparent in the Gospel accounts. The personal sin of the participants (Judas, the Sanhedrin, Pilate) is known to God alone. Hence we cannot lay responsibility for the trial on the Jews in Jerusalem as a whole, despite the outcry of a manipulated crowd and the global reproaches contained in the apostles' calls to conversion after Pentecost. Jesus himself, in forgiving them on the cross, and Peter in following suit, both accept 'the ignorance' of the Jews of Jerusalem and even of their leaders. Still less can we extend responsibility to other Jews of

has clear precedent in tradition: that the Jewish people continue to be beloved by God for the sake of their ancestors and that the covenant of God with Israel remains unbroken. It is problematic to think of this teaching as being in rupture with the pre-conciliar past, whether one does so as a detractor of the Council or as its enthusiastic adherent. To have changed in some significant way after the Council, the pre-conciliar Church would have had to have been Marcionite, denying the existence of a covenant with the ancient Hebrews. The only covenant that could be abrogated, but that in fact was not, is precisely that one that is fulfilled uniquely in Christ. Consequently, it exists in perpetuity. But if that is the case, then many arguments against "supersessionism" have no grounds in Catholic theology.

> *Thesis 5:* The chief "innovation" of *Nostra Aetate* with respect to past precedent is located in the condemnation of the teaching of contempt and in its accent on the spiritual prerogatives of charity and human justice.

The teaching of *Nostra Aetate* and its subsequent "spiritual tone" (as expressed in the interpretations of John Paul II) are novel in some respects. These novelties are not doctrinal but spiritual and ethical. The first is in the condemnation of personal contempt for the Jewish people. This condemnation is meant to apply both to contempt that is theologically motivated and to modern secular anti-Semitism. The change in tone is of course a reaction to the horrible event of the Shoah, but it also constitutes a judgment on the terrible history of Christian mistreatment of the Jewish people, especially at various times and places in the high middle ages and in early modernity. Here we might add a theological observation of Christological provenance: The harassment, killing, or torture of Jews by Christians cannot contribute to advancement of Christian life. The torture, and death of one Jew alone can save us, and that event has already taken place. Further torments add nothing. Far from advancing the return of Christ, they run the risk of directly courting the anti-Christ.

The second change stemming from the Council pertains to the advancement of relations of common friendship with Jews. Behind this change of attitude is a decision that is both prudential and pastoral, rather than doctrinal as such. The prudential decision has to do with the presupposition of guilt on the part of the Jews who do not believe in Christ. If there are persons who should recognize Christ but do not, does the Church respond best by condemnation or by love? If there are persons who are invincibly ignorant, we can ask the same question. What is the theological basis to justify the practical emphasis on Christian kindness toward Jews that we find in recent pontificates? Here again it is not Neo-modernism, but something more challenging and perhaps threatening to the Church that we should refer to: the teaching of Christ himself, specifically with regard to the commandment to love others in charity. Against diverse traditions of anti-Semitic contempt, the Church insisted at Vatican II on the

---

different times and places, based merely on the crowd's cry: 'His blood be on us and on our children!' (Matt. 27:25), a formula for ratifying a judicial sentence."

spiritual reality of the love of Christ crucified, who died for Jews and gentiles alike, and whose love, according to Christianity, truly and definitively supersedes all other human priorities. "The love of Christ compels us" (2 Cor 5:14). This mandate includes the love of one's Jewish neighbor, with whom one can have genuine personal friendship even while disagreeing, and whom one can love in the grace of Christ. Ideally, and when acting in a proper mode, members of the Church and the synagogue are able to speak to one another through the course of history animated by shared eschatological expectations. The Church is led in the course of this conversation by charity: love for the truth about God, and love of one's neighbor, simultaneously.

There are also matters of justice at stake in the Church's witness to love in her engagement with the Jews. The Church traditionally insists on rightfully respecting the human conscience in matters pertaining to religion, since free consent to the truth of the Gospel is an irreducible dimension of ecclesial life. External law and mere appearances cannot supplant inward conversion of heart.[13] Just respect for the conscience of others extends to the religious freedom of one's Jewish neighbor, as is already noted clearly in the high middle ages. In a disputed question on the topic, Aquinas addresses the issue of whether Jews of his time have rights of religious freedom despite the fact that, as he notes, they are in serious religious error and the continued practice of the ceremonial precepts is, as he sees it, objectively morally deleterious.[14] He responds unambiguously that there is a right (*ius*) of religious freedom in human beings that is to be respected.[15] The principle is universal because it pertains to human nature, not uniquely to Christians. The corollary to this is Christological: Christ died for all men, and so the charity of Christ compels any true Christian to love others in their personal dignity as people whom God has chosen in Christ, whether they recognize this or not. God does not ask us to unjustly coerce consent to the gospel from those for whom Christ died. The idea of "love through forced consent" is in some sense contrary to the very notion of salvation itself, which entails love of Christ in free consent to the truth.[16]

> *Thesis Six:* Original Covenant supersessionism of the kind shared by Jews and Christians together unites them in significant ways even while providing a framework for characterizing their disagreements clearly and constructively.

Jews and Christians both appeal to the original Mosaic covenant (the "Older Covenant") as coming from God and being of universal significance for humanity. This common claim unites them because they each believe that the Torah and the prophets provide divine revelation that supersedes all preceding human religious tradition and practice. This same belief divides them because the Church claims that the

---

13. See for example Aquinas, *Summa Theologiae*, ST II-II, q. 10, a. 8–12.

14. Aquinas, *ST* I-II, q. 103, a. 4.

15. *Quodlibet* II, q. 4, a. 2, sc and co. See the study of this text by Dominic Legge in "Do Thomists Have Rights?"

16. 2 Thess 2:10: ". . . they refused to love the truth and so be saved."

revelation of Christ brings the revelation of the Torah to fulfillment, while also altering some of the conditions for participation in the covenant by virtue of its extension or opening of membership to all the nations. In our contemporary context, there are ways that the Catholic Church can profit theologically from thinking more deeply about both dimensions of its relationship to the Jewish people.

Today Jews and Christians alike face two other forms of non-biblical supersessionism. Each is opposed to the other, in a certain sense, and both are opposed to core elements of Judaism and Christianity. I am referring here on the one hand to Islam and on the other hand to post-Enlightenment secular liberalism. We might say that Islam in its understanding of Qur'anic inspiration is thematically Marcionite in a peculiar sense. It rejects the New as well as the Old Testament as problematic, partially corrupted or containing historically uncertain prophecies, and seeks to replace them with a revelation that supersedes both. On the other hand, the secular liberalism that we inherit from Kant, Hegel, and Habermas averts to a history of rational progress in which religious civilizations give way to secular constitutional democracies, animated by market exchanges and the culture of autonomous rights. For secular liberalism, the New Testament contains symbolic typologies of our new era of post-confessional democratic secular polity.

The original supersessionism of the Torah and the universalism it evokes continue in many respects to be the key source of controversy in the secular world today. Are its teachings on marriage and sexuality superseded by those of modern liberal societies? Does its teaching that one may not murder the innocent apply to unborn people or to the terminally ill? What about its teachings on the exclusive metaphysical truth of monotheism and the imperative to worship God? Catholicism inherits these teachings from the Torah but also claims to universalize them in Christ, for all the nations. Consequently, the Church is committed perpetually to the teaching inscribed in Genesis that there are only two complementary sexes, man and woman, and that sexuality has its normative moral place within the context of committed heterosexual monogamy, open to life. So too the Church inherits and universalizes that teaching of the Torah that one may not take innocent life, be it that of the newly conceived child in the womb or those who may be subject to euthanasia. Likewise, the Church perennially affirms that the worship of God is the deepest and most significant moral inclination of the human being. These teachings of the Torah are not superseded, especially for the Church, which likewise maintains that her moral vision surpasses that of the old paganism, even when it re-emerges in new forms and in formerly Christian locations. After Christianity there is not merely an anodyne world without gods but a new world of national deities, strange sacrifices, and metaphysical superstitions. It is the Torah alone, as read through the light of Christ, that can save us from the reemergence of religious confusion.

The supersessionism found in the Torah is also a lasting key to a constructive Christian engagement with the Islamic world. Islam too claims to universalize the conditions of revelation to all people, yet it does so based on a particular people and their language, that is through the medium of the sons of Ishmael and the Arabic of the Qur'an. This teaching resembles those of Christianity and Judaism but in different ways: it aspires to universality like Christianity, but is located originally in a particular language and people, like Judaism; yet it stands over against Judaism and Christianity, which are said to have falsified prophecy or rendered its truth obscure. Christians cannot address their differences with Islam realistically if they conveniently ignore the uniqueness of the Mosaic covenant and instead speak euphemistically of "three Abrahamic religions." The Church confesses unambiguously that the original chosen people are those of Isaac, in Jerusalem, not Ismael at Mecca. The fundamental question that must be engaged with clearly is which book is truly inspired and grounded in sacred history, if any. If one wishes to avoid the latitudinarianism that relativizes all substantive claims to revelatory truth, then there cannot be a plurality of contradictory revelations. It is the Church's original response to Marcion that addresses this issue most readily: the Old Covenant is the foundational revelation for all human beings. The covenant wrought in Hebraic blood is opened to all universally not through a rival book but through the crucifixion and death of the Jewish Messiah, an event that, significantly, the Qur'an denies ever happened.[17] By rejecting the mysteries of the incarnation and the Trinity, Islam retreats into a kind of tragic immanentism, one that refuses intimacy with God on God's own terms revealed in Christ, compounding this rejection with ideologically motivated doctrinal justifications. The Islamic tradition is in many ways as successful as Christianity in governing human society, but it does so at the cost of institutionalizing behaviors of the fallen human race as normative ones. It also inadvertently alienates human beings from the shared intimacy with God made possible by the revelation of Christ. In this case the universalism promised by the Qur'an is problematic for theological reasons as well as historical ones, despite the monotheistic truths about God that it rightly promotes. Christians cannot speak to the claims of Islam realistically without appeal to the Torah as true divine revelation. In its dialogue with Muslims, the Church has to refer to the original supersessionism of pre-revelatory religions by biblical prophecy, which remains normative for Christians as well as for Jews.

In addition, we might add that Christian self-evaluation of their political treatment of the Jews (as a theoretical test case of charity and justice) can help indicate how we might respond to both Islamic regimes and secular liberalism in the age of religious intolerance that seems increasingly emergent. Evidently there is a simplistic dialectic that we see developing between religious anti-liberalism and secular liberal

---

17. The denial of the historical crucifixion of Jesus of Nazareth is a core conviction of Islam, derived from the teaching of the Qur'an in contrast to the affirmations of the New Testament. Sura 4:157: "... they did not slay him; nor did they crucify him, but I appeared so unto them." The biblical traditions of Israel and the New Testament are denoted as effectively untrustworthy (whether in part or in whole remains a debated point in Islam). See, for example, Sura 2:75; 4:46; 5:13, and 7:157. Nasr (ed.), *The Study Quran*.

anti-religionism. On one side stands the Islamic political critique of the free exercise of Christian evangelization while on the other stands the secular liberal critique of that same free exercise. And the two stand opposed to one another in such a way that their response to Christianity is meant to reflect their response to the perceived threat of the other. When Muslim governments delimit Christian freedom, they do so in part as a deterrent against westernization. When liberal cultures set limits to religious self-expression for Christians, they do so in part to respond to the fear of growing Islamization. Both sides in this process sometimes act in ways that seek to thwart the life and expression of the Church.

Catholic Christians have a long history of living in the light of divine revelation while also finding ways to articulate theological and natural law foundations for the just and charitable treatment of those who do not know or recognize Christ.[18] In the history of the Church, Christians have often failed at this, sometimes in terrible ways, in their mistreatment of the Jews. When they accomplish this successfully they practically refute the false and simplistic dialectic that is increasingly prevalent outside the Church: "One must be religious or one must be tolerant." The Church's theological commitment to the truth of Christ and his unique mediation of salvation cannot be the source of a culture of political injustice or discord but should rather be the origin of a culture of charity and justice that includes in its extension those who do not recognize Christ. The Christian seeks to be faithful to the integral truth in love and to love integrally in the truth. This is the narrow way that Christ refers to in Matthew's Gospel, and it is also broad in its consequences of charity, with one's arms open to the world, because it stems from the "catholic" love of the cross.

> *Thesis Seven:* Jesus Christ himself is the unique primary origin and most fundamental ongoing cause for the enduring relationship between Christians and Jews.

Ultimately, Christians have commitments to the original supersessionism of the Old Covenant and belief in the Jewish people as a chosen people of God principally because of Jesus Christ. It is he above all who divides Christians and Jews, and also, paradoxically he who unites us. A Christ without biblical Judaism is unintelligible. But without Christ, the gentile world would not be able to receive the light of the Torah as a light for the nations. By him the gentiles are bound to the roots of the covenant, in the form of the Mosaic Law. The universal light of the Torah continues in real history to pass through the mediation of the cross and to shine forth through the sacramental life and teaching of the Church. The Church confesses that Jesus is Lord: in doing so she reverently employs the holy name of God revealed to Moses, *Hashem*, "Lord," and applies it to Christ himself. This name is of course only intelligible within the framework of the Old Testament doctrine of creation and covenant. God reveals himself to Israel as "I am He Who Is," the Creator and Savior of Israel (Exod 3:14–15). But this

---

18. See the historical study of Wilken, *Liberty in the Things of God*.

name is also only intelligible for the Church in light of the incarnation of this same God of Israel, the Word of God made flesh, manifest as the crucified and risen Lord (Phil 2:6–11). The God of Israel has saved us in this cruciform way. This is what binds the gentiles to the Jews and what divides us as well. Note that we can say "binds," and not merely "unites": the unity that exists between Christians and Jews is the unity of a divine commission, one that implies duties and responsibilities, not mere options. The cross unites gentiles and Jews in various ways, whether one believes it does so from God (as Christians must) or not (as many Jews down through history continue to wonder or suspect). The cross points toward universal reconciliation in the life to come but also in this life because of the crucified man who is a source of grace and peace. "Peace I give you. My peace I leave you" (John 14:27). The cross does promote a kind of supersession: the supersession of peace and the victory of divine love. When Christians act against this peace and charity by violating the rights and denying the covenantal dignity of the Jewish people, then Christians have in fact superseded not the Jewish people but both the Torah (Law) and the cross (charity), a supersessionism that cuts at the very core of Christian faith.

If Jesus truly is the ground that unites and divides Christians and Jews, then we may not even agree on the theological criteria according to which we "agree to disagree." But in reality, because of him, we are bound together for the duration of history. And if the Church would really be bound to the Jewish people *by the cross*, then she must be bound not by a merely external law, or even a doctrine, but in charity. Love is love of persons. If the Church is truly to be a light to the nations, she must also be a light to that nation that is Israel. This is only possible if the original people of God, the people of Abraham, are also particularly beloved of the Church and its members, in the fullness of her commitment to the truth of Christ but also in the fullness of the respect of mutual friendship, animated by a love that stems inexorably from the side of Christ.

Bibliography

Catechism of the Catholic Church. 2nd ed. Vatican City: Libreria Editrice Vaticana, 1997.
Commission for Religious Relations with the Jews. "'The Gifts and the Calling of God are Irrevocable' (Rom. 11:29): A Reflection on Theological Questions Pertaining to Catholic–Jewish Relations on the Occasion of the 50th Anniversary of 'Nostra Aetate' (NO. 4)." Vatican. 2015. https://www.vatican.va/roman_curia/pontifical_councils/chrstuni/relations-jews-docs/rc_pc_chrstuni_doc_20151210_ebraismo-nostra-aetate_en.html.
Irenaeus. *Against Heresies* IV. Translated by A. Roberts and W. Rambaut. In *Ante-Nicene Fathers*, vol. 1, edited by A. Roberts, J. Donaldson, and A. C. Coxe. Buffalo, NY: Christian Literature, 1885.
Justin Martyr. *Dialogue with Trypho.* Translated by M. Dods and G. Reith. In *Ante-Nicene Fathers*, vol. 1, edited by A. Roberts, J. Donaldson, and A. C. Coxe. Buffalo, NY: Christian Literature, 1885.

Legge, Dominic. "Do Thomists Have Rights?" *Nova et Vetera* 17.1 (2019) 127–47.

Novak, David. "Supersessionism Hard and Soft." *First Things* 290, February 2019, 27–31.

Ratzinger, Joseph. *Many Religions–One Covenant: Israel, the Church and the World*. San Francisco: Ignatius, 1999.

The Study Quran. Edited by S. H. Nasr. New York: Harper Collins, 2015.

Wilken, Robert Louis. *Liberty in the Things of God: The Christian Origins of Religious Freedom*. New Haven: Yale University Press, 2019.

Response to

Thomas Joseph White's "On Good Supersessionism: Jews, Christians, and the Covenant That Binds and Divides Us"

DAVID NOVAK

I AM GRATEFUL TO Fr. Thomas Joseph White, O.P. for his friendship and for being the type of thinker with whom the most profound dialogues can be conducted. "Those who are in awe of the LORD do speak to one another" (Mal 3:16). In fact, our dialogue began more than a decade ago at a conference at Ave Maria University in Florida on Pope John Paul II and the Jewish people, before "TJ" (as he is known to his friends) made his final vows as a priest and a Dominican friar. He has shown subsequently how great a credit he is to the Catholic Church and to the Dominican Order. More recently, I was honored to write a blurb for his excellent commentary on *Exodus*. I could do this in good faith because he and I both accept the Torah given at Sinai to be divine revelation, even though as Maimonides pointed out, Jews and Christians at times interpret the Torah differently. Until the past fifty years or so, these differences were emphasized to the virtual exclusion of our commonalities. Now, happily, these commonalities are emphasized much more, but not to the exclusion of our differences. I would like to think that TJ and I are making some contribution to this exciting dialectic of commonality and difference now being conducted by Christian and Jewish theologians. As he puts it in this paper, "we are bound together for the duration of history."[1]

Let me now deal with two connected points in TJ's essay, part of which I mostly agree with, but part of which I question.

TJ states that "the Church claims that Christ brings the revelation of the Torah to fulfillment, while also altering some of the conditions for participation in the covenant by virtue of its extension or opening of membership to all the nations."[2] Earlier in the paper he writes that "the Torah and the prophets stipulate that this same covenant has universal horizons of import, even though its inner essence of

---

1. p. 326.
2. pp. 322–23.

reception and practice is reserved to those who are descendants of Abraham, who live by the Mosaic Law. How then is this revelation of universal importance?"[3] He then goes on to say that "Christ's atonement fulfills the Law and simultaneously opens the covenant up to the nations." As such, it "continues the dynamic of the Old Testament so as to universalize it."[4]

If I understand him correctly, TJ is making two claims for Christianity. One, he is claiming that Christianity *fulfills* what is initially given in the biblical covenant between God and the people Israel. Two, he is claiming that Christianity *universalizes* what had theretofore (i.e., before the coming of Christ) only been *parochial*, only having universal potentiality. Moreover, TJ says that these two aspects of Christian revelation function *simultaneously*. That is, they not only function in tandem historically, but they also function in tandem theo-logically. I respectfully submit, though, that these two claims can be separated from each other both historically and logically and that one of them is more persuasive than the other.

The first claim about *fulfillment* is an authentic Christian claim. It is a claim that I have called "soft supersessionism" in the recent *First Things* article of mine, "Supersessionism Hard and Soft," that TJ cites with approval in this paper. Moreover, Jews can respect the logic employed in making this claim (although obviously we cannot accept its conclusion for ourselves) since we make a similar claim about our superseding what preceded us in history but without claiming to have totally replaced it so as to deny its continued legitimacy as hard supersessionists in both traditions do. However, the second claim about *universalization* is a claim that is questionable historically, and a claim that creates a theological problem for those Christians who make it.

TJ endorses my thesis about soft supersessionism, because Christians and Jews have to regard their respective traditions as having superseded each other. Each tradition has to believe that its take on the covenant between God and His people is *fuller* or more complete than that of the other tradition. If not, Christians have no good reason for not converting to Judaism, and Jews have no good reason not to convert to Christianity. However, the completion claim is comparative: *fuller than*, not *in place of* (as in hard supersessionism). Indeed, with hard supersessionism the *dia* or "between" in *dia-logue* becomes meaningless as the legitimate separate identity of one of the dialogue partners is denied; hence the dialogue becomes a monologue conducted by the stronger party politically (as it was in the mediaeval disputations Christians forced upon Jews). Yet without any supersessionism at all, the legitimate identities of both dialogue partners are denied insofar as they have no reason not to merge into some new vapid universalism, thus losing their former legitimate or normative identity altogether. Therefore, Jews and Christians can agree on the logical necessity of their respective soft supersessionist claims, though differing on the actual substance of these claims.

3. p. 317.
4. p. 319.

Nevertheless, I question TJ's claim about Christianity being more "universal" than Judaism (whether biblical or post-biblical).

First of all, the historicity of this claim is questionable. Although it could be said (arguably though) that biblical Judaism was meant for the Jewish people alone, and that gentiles who attached themselves to this singular people (see Num 23:9) could never become full members of the covenant, this has not been true of post-biblical Judaism. Let us also recall that TJ rightly recognizes that post-biblical Judaism "developed alongside the Church."[5] In other words, both Christianity and post-biblical Judaism *developed simultaneously.* As such, Christianity did not develop out of Judaism, at least not out of the Judaism of the past 2,000 years. However, is it that Christianity and Judaism *were developed* or that they *did develop*?

Now it could be said that both traditions claim to *have been developed* by God's continual, providential participation in their ongoing histories. It could also be said that a good deal of this development has been the work of human interpretation. In that case, *what* did these Jewish and Christian theologians develop? It seems they both *developed*, i.e., they both boldly interpreted and expanded the normative range of the Hebrew Bible "alongside" each other (and often against each other). So, each tradition—Christianity in the Gospels, Judaism in the "Oral Tradition" (partially written down in the Talmud)—superseded the original revelation, not by rejecting it as passé, but rather by building upon it and with it, so that it ever remains intact and present in each tradition's ongoing development. In each tradition, the Hebrew Bible has always been the constant point of legitimating reference. Indeed, the New Testament could be considered the Christian "Talmud," and the Talmud could be considered the Jewish "New Testament." That is because both works never make claims that couldn't be based on the Hebrew Bible (for Jews *Tanakh*; for Christians *Vetus Testamentum*). All this has been done without either tradition claiming it is "only biblical" (*sola scriptura*).

Furthermore, once Christians, and Jews too, recognize that there are competing developments of the original biblical revelation, this will tone down triumphalist pronouncements that "ours is the only authentic development of biblical revelation." Such pronouncements usually come hand in hand with hard supersessionism, viz., the claim that "we are right and you are wrong"; that "we have the whole truth and what you have is totally false."

Now an important part of this development was Jews fulling opening up God's covenant with Israel to gentiles. Already in the second century BCE, we see this opening-up of the covenant in the form of the proselyzing of gentiles by the Greek speaking Jews of Alexandria. This proselyzation was often argued for by the greatest theologian of Hellenistic Judaism: Philo (also discussed at greater length in my response to Thomas Slabon). And, while some of the Rabbis were ambivalent about the success of fully converting gentiles to Judaism, nevertheless, none of them could deny the principle that "a convert is born again" (a principle common to both Judaism and

---

5. p. 320.

Christianity; see Yevamot 24a and John 3:3–5). Moreover, even when active Jewish proselytization ceased due to proscriptions of it in Christendom and Islam, Jews never ceased to accept converts (often at great political risk). To be sure, there are significant differences between Jewish and Christian "universalizing," yet both traditions have both a universalizing agenda in the present, and a universalizing future horizon. In fact, there are some Jews today who would like to revive active Jewish proselyzation of gentiles (and not just the more passive reception of converts), especially gentiles adrift in the moral anarchy and spiritual chaos of much of the contemporary secular world. These modern gentile pagans (or "nones" as we say today) are as ripe for conversion to Judaism as they are ripe for conversion to Christianity.

Christians should be wary of supersessionism, employing it very sparingly, except when having to defend their "innovations" against those who would dismiss them as distortions of the original truth they claim to have superseded and who claim to have thereby superseded them. For those who *supersede* can just as easily be *superseded* by some historical newcomer. In fact, this is what Islam did to both Judaism and Christianity. Moreover, whereas Christians acknowledge the total truth of biblical revelation, only interpreting it in ways Jews cannot accept, Islamic supresessionism is more radical (as TJ points out quite accurately) by claiming that both Jewish and Christian revelations are basically flawed, with only some parts of them being authentically divine. As such, Islam did more than complete the earlier revelations, it basically reconstituted divine revelation altogether. Nevertheless, Muslims now face the same challenge from secularists as Jews and Christians have faced since the Enlightenment.

In what TJ generously calls "Novak's important essay,"[6] I tried to argue that at the final redemption, to which Jews and Christians have not yet arrived in the world (what Jews call *olam ha-ba* or "the world yet-to-come"), it is hoped that it will not be a "zero sum game," when either Christians will say to Jews or Jews will say to Christians, "We were right all along and you were wrong all along. Therefore, God makes us the winners and you the losers." That kind of triumphalism would turn a victory that is supposed to be God's alone into human imperial triumphalism. (No Christian theologian made that point better than did Karl Barth.)

Finally, Jews and Christians (and now Muslims as well) need to be on guard against the modern secularist charge against us (of which TJ is certainly well aware, in this essay and in his other writings), viz., that all religions taking their warrant from unverifiable, *particular* historical revelations cannot claim any true universality. Modern secularism claims to be true universalism (in today's language, true "globalism") by not appealing to anything so remote from ordinary human experience as the revelation of the Torah at Mount Sinai, the resurrection of Jesus Christ, or the revelation of the Qur'an to Muhammed. So, in this view, Judaism, Christianity, and Islam have all been superseded by a universalism (employing the logic of Ockham's Razor) that claims to require the acceptance of far fewer assumptions. That is our

6. p. 315.

greatest challenge today, one that can only be countered with the most sophisticated philosophical arguments in hand.

Father Thomas Joseph always stimulates me to deal with his well thought out and well researched theological positions with the gravity they deserve. He is a first-rate theologian, who honors his interlocutors by making the same intellectual demands on us that he makes on himself. For that I am most appreciative. I eagerly look forward to our interlocutions, both in print and face-to-face, to continue well into the future (*Deo volente*).

Index

Abd-Allah, Umar F., 183
Abelard, Peter, 242
abortifacients, 57–58
abortion, 8, 38–39, 43, 51, 54, 57, 64, 66, 296
Abraham, 130; covenant of, 236, 314, 316; descendants of, 317, 326, 329; faith of, 182n3, 184, 214; God of, 3–4, 11, 67, 78–79, 82, 88; and polygamy, 223
A Common Word between Us and You, 183n8, 191
Acts of the Apostles, 78–79, 81, 229n23
adultery, 43, 49, 96n21, 124, 135, 144, 156
Advent, 134, 183n9
Aggadah, 5
ahl al kitab (people of the book), 188
AIDS, 8
Akibah ben Yosef, 142–43
Albo, Joseph, 145
Alexander II, pope, 202
Al-Ghazali, 75
Ali, Muhammed, 71
Allah, 74, 80n56, 183n8
allegory, 290
almsgiving, xi, 234
Alvaré, Helen, 51–52, 54
Amelekites, 237
American Judaism, 9, 23–24, 31–32, 44, 189n29
American Philosophical Association, 146
Amish, 63
Amos, 178, 237n64
anagogical sense of scripture, 319
analogia fidei, 308
analytic philosophy, vii, 154
Anderson, Gary A., 175, 234
angels, 268n60, 270n68, 273, 275, 283
Annas, Julia, 126
Anscombe, Elizabeth, 162, 290

Anselm of Canterbury, 87, 241–42
anthropology, 95, 147
anti-catholicism, 199, 201n9, 200n5, 215
anti-christianism, 200, 321
Anti-Defamation League of B'nai B'rith, 24
anti-Judaism, ix, 20, 191, 199–200, 213–15, 223, 313–14
antinomianism, 26, 173
anti-religionism, 64, 325
anti-Semitism, 24, 121, 173, 191, 199, 212n54, 321
apologetics, Christian, 75–76
apostasy, 70, 196, 223
Apostles Creed, 256
Apuleius, xii, 252, 254, 266–76, 278–85, 288–90
Aquinas. *See* Thomas Aquinas
Arab-Israeli conflict, 189
Areopagus, viii, 78
arguments for God's existence, 72, 75–77
Ariarajah, S. Wesley, 183
Aristotelian Society, 146
Aristotle, 34, 37, 147, 312n6; on children, 204–5; and divine revelation, 258–59; on friendship, 118; on justice, 205–6, 248; and natural law, 149–51; natural science theory of, 7n20, 85, 152–54, 162–63, 289–90; and political anthropology, 166n5, 250; potency-act logic of, 4, 6; and suicide, 105; teleology of, 222; virtue ethics of, 133n70, 136–38
Arius of Alexandria, viii, 79–80
Ash Wednesday, 134
Ashkenazic Jews, 26
Athanasius, viii, 77, 79–80
Athens, xi, 9, 31, 78, 160n1, 162, 248, 252–67, 276, 284–85, 288, 290–91

Augustine, 170, 271n72; and demonology, 268n60, 272–85; and divine law, 129, 136; on the Jewish people, 12; on justice, 206; on name of God, 77n47; and natural love of God, 145; political theology of, 55, 169, 174; on reason and revelation, xii, 252, 254, 264, 266–67, 272–85, 288–91; on suicide, 97n22, 99n28, 105
authoritarianism, 48, 291
autonomy: in Kant, 46, 102–3; in modern thought, ix–x, 95–97, 111n61, 166–68, 171, 243, 311; and suicide, 117
Ave Maria University, 328
Avicenna, 72, 80, 88
avodah zarah ("strange worship"), x, 86, 88, 184, 187, 196–98
avodat elilim ("worship of other gods"), 196
Azzai, Ben, 143

Babylonian exile, 16, 235–37
Balthasar, Hans Urs von, 215, 222
baptism, 81n60, 223, 317, 319; of Edgardo Mortara, xi, 200–201, 207–12, 214, 220–21, 224; forced, 202–5
Barth, Karl, 11–12, 29, 87, 122, 145, 177, 331
Battin, Margaret, 304
Bea, Augustin, 29, 199n2
beatification, 210
beatitude, 120–21, 126
Begin, Menachem, 26
Benedict XIV, pope, 203
Benedictine University of Chicago, x, 181
Benedict Option, 27
Benedict XVI, pope, 242. *See also* Ratzinger, Joseph
Berger, David, 184, 187–88, 196–98
Bessette, Joseph, xii, 300
bestiality, 43, 49
bioethics, 38, 97n23, 105n45, 112n63
bipolar disorder, 93n10, 104, 107n51
birth control, artificial, 55, 57, 66. *See also* contraception
blasphemy, 43
Bohr, Niels, 89
Bonhoeffer, Dietrich, 59
Boyle, Joseph, 34, 293–94, 308
breast cancer, 56
British Columbia, 168
Browne, Thomas, 92
Buber, Martin, 2, 296–97
Buddhism, 154
burning bush, 77–78
Bush, George W., 183

Cain and Abel, 117, 250, 292, 294–95
Callan, Charles J., 210–11
Calvin, John, 76, 87, 160
Canada, x, 13n41, 23, 37, 39, 51, 91, 93, 100–102, 110, 119, 165, 167–68
Canadian Charter of Rights and Freedoms, 101, 165
Canon Law, Catholic Code of, 96n20, 99n28, 200, 202–4
capital punishment, xii, 9, 117, 238, 297–301, 304, 307–8
Carroll, James, 215
Cassirer, Ernst, 162
Catechism of the Catholic Church, 97n23, 106, 120n2, 126, 211n52, 214, 225, 239–40, 314n1, 320n12; *of the Council of Trent*, 17
Cato, 92n6
celibacy, 50, 132n61
Cessario, Romanus, 207, 209–10, 212–13, 220–23, 242n98
charity, virtue of, ix, 98n26, 100, 132–33, 136–39, 143, 206, 208–9, 214, 240, 242, 321–22, 324–26
chastity, virtue of, 56
Cherubim, 197
Christendom, 206n35
Christian apologetics, 65, 75–77
Christian boasting, 17
Churchill, Winston, 179
Church of Jesus Christ of Latter-Day Saints (Mormons), 80–81
Cicero, 149–51
circumcision, 13, 319
civil disobedience, 51
civil unrest, 60
civil war, 59, 245
clerisy, 179
CNN, 33
Cohen, Hermann, 4, 9, 265, 312
Columbia University, 27
communism, 26, 167
concupiscence, ix, 130–32
Congregation for the Doctrine of The Faith, 81
Constantinople, Council of, 78, 82
contraception, 305–6; Church's opposition to, 57–58; HHS mandate of, 54–56
conversion, 5–6, 13, 15–18, 70n17, 72, 74, 189, 196, 209n44, 212n53, 223, 275, 318, 320, 322, 329–31; forced, 202–3, 204n22, 214n60
Copernicus, Nicolaus, 89
Corinthians, epistles to, 3, 40, 228–29, 231n39, 238–41, 322

cosmological arguments for God's existence, 75–76
cosmology, 152, 162, 277n93
Cragg, Kenneth, 188
Craig, William Lane, 75–77
creatio ex nihilo, 88, 123, 170, 172, 196, 249
CRISPR, 38
Crusade, First (1096), 202

Dabru Emet, viii, x, 20, 67, 181–92, 195–97
daemones, 268–75, 278–84
Dante Alighieri, 136
Darwin, Charles, x, 152, 154n35, 162
Dawkins, Richard, 200–201
Day of the Lord, 173
death penalty. *See* capital punishment
Decalogue. *See* Ten Commandments
deicide, 173, 314, 320
Dei Verbum, 245
Delphic oracle, 257, 262–63
democracy, viii, x, 8, 10–11, 13n41, 41, 50, 52, 60, 63–66, 164, 166–72, 175, 178–79, 215, 225, 243, 245, 323
Democratic Party, 24, 58
demonology, 268, 270n68, 272–76, 280n105
Der Tog, 33
De Tocqueville, Alexis, 167
Deuteronomy, 74n27, 86, 116, 119, 123, 137, 144, 223, 228–29, 231n39, 233–34, 236–37, 291, 311
Dignitatis Humanae, 52–53, 58
dignity, human, ix–x, 17, 38–39, 47, 52, 56–57, 95 169, 232, 299, 302, 304, 322
Dives in Misericordia, 235–36
divine command theory, 122n8, 160–161
Dominican Order, 145, 220–21, 328
Dominus Iesus, 187
double effect, principle of, xii, 57, 297–98
Dulles, Avery, 38, 75n30
Dulles Symposia, 29
Dupré, Louis, 1
Dupuis, Jacques, 189
Durkheim, Emile, 92
Dylan, Bob, 67

Eastern Orthodox Church, 32
ectopic pregnancy, 57
ecumenism, 69
Eden, Garden of, 81, 235
egalitarianism, 45, 47, 171
Einstein, Albert, 89
Eleazar ben Hurcanus, 105n44, 116–17
Elshtain, Jean Bethke, 55, 59–60, 164, 178–79
embryo, human, 38, 292–93, 295–96

Emon, Anver, 120n1, 148, 208n41, 223
end (*telos*): of commandments, ix, 137n95, 142–43; and emotional susceptibility of *daemones*, 270n69; final, 126, 137, 153–33, 161, 222; God as, 53, 132, 163, 257, 259, 284; of natural world, 259; of philosophical inquiry, 257, 267, 290; supernatural, 127, 129n46; of virtues, 132; of "wide" duties, 232
end of days. *See* eschaton
end of life: care, 297; decisions, 111–12
endometriosis, 57
Engelhart, H. T., Jr., 164
Enlightenment, the, 88, 199n3, 243, 323, 331
epistemology: Kantian, 7n20
Epstein, Jeffrey, 93
eschatological consummation, 4–5, 8, 12–13, 15, 17, 19. *See also olam ha-ba*
eschaton, 3, 12, 18–19, 59, 224, 317–320. *See also olam ha-ba*
essentialism, neo-Aristotelian, 153–54
Eucharist, 170n22, 231n38, 314, 319
eudaimonia, 151n23
eudaimonism, 238
euthanasia, 64, 91, 93, 102, 323
Euthyphro dilemma, 157
Evangelical Christians, 24, 26, 30, 32–33, 38, 68–69, 75–76, 182–83, 191
Evangelium Vitae, 299n21
evangelization, 13, 17, 86, 325. *See also* conversion; proselytism
Evans, Gareth, 69
evolutionary biology, 152, 154n34, 162
Exodus, book of, 77, 86, 89, 116, 126, 144–45, 197, 231n39, 237, 250, 325

faith, virtue of, 203–4
Familiaris Consortio, 56n76
fasting, 132n61, 134
fear of God, ix, 122–25, 132–35, 137–39, 144–45, 229; *timor filialis/servilis*, ix, 133
Feser, Edward, xii, 153n32, 300
fetus, 57, 293, 295–96
fideism, 35–36
final causality, 153
Finnis, John, 22, 161, 230–31, 249, 294n5
Firestone, Shulamith, 165
first amendment of U.S. Constitution, 59
first cause, 309, 311
First Things, 1, 15, 27, 30, 67, 93n10, 95n17, 165, 207n35, 220–21, 329
flood, the great, 42, 235
flourishing, human, ix, xi, 49, 54, 123, 144, 155, 172–73, 226, 235

335

Forms, Platonic, 153
Forward, The, 33
Francis, pope, 68, 121, 183
Frege, Gottlob, viii
fundamentalism, 23

Galatians, Epistle to, 211, 215, 240–41
Galileo Galilei, 89
Gallagher, Raphael, 211n50
Galston, William, 164, 178–79
Gaon, Saadiah, 2, 9
Garfield, James, 91
Gaudium et Spes, 56n76
Geisler, Norman L., 76–77
Genesis, 43n15, 49, 63, 66, 81, 105–6, 116–17, 124, 144–45, 175, 229n24, 235, 250, 277n93, 292–93, 299–301, 312, 316, 323
genocide, 245
Georgetown University, vii, 2, 34, 91, 308
Gershom ben Judah, 223–24
Gersonides, 2
Gifford Lectures, The, xi, 31, 55n72, 160n1, 171n26, 253n6
globalism, 171, 331
gnosticism, 68, 89, 170
God of the philosophers, 88
Golden Calf, 16, 173, 235, 237
Goliath, 164–65, 167, 172, 175, 177
Gratian, 96n20, 99n28
Gregory IV, pope, 202
Grisez, Germain, vii, 1, 34, 22, 234–35, 244n104, 293–94, 302–3, 305, 308–12
Gurion, David Ben, 26

Habermas, Jürgen, 162, 323
Hackett, Stuart C., 76–77
Haggard, Ted, 183
halakhah, 2, 5, 8–9, 29, 125–26, 138, 223
Halevi, Judah, 9
hallucination, 24, 106n51
Halpern decision, 165, 168
Hananiah, Joshua ben, 17
Hasidim, 63
Hauerwas, Stanley, 9, 147n1
Hawkins, Larycia, 68–69, 183n9
Health and Human Services Department of the United States (HHS), 41, 53–54, 58
Hegel, G. W. F., 171, 199n3, 323
Heidegger, Martin, 264, 291
henotheism, 85–86
Henry VIII, 178
hermeneutics, 262, 266, 289–90. *See also midrash*
Hermes Trismegistus, 282
Herrmann, Wilhelm, 4n12

Heschel, Abraham Joshua, 1, 29, 34, 37–38, 175, 197, 228, 263, 285
Hesiod, 290
heteronomy, 49, 171, 173
heterosexual unions, 49–50, 167–68, 323
Hillel the Elder, 144
Himmelfarb, Milton, 31
Hinduism, 154, 181, 184, 191
Hitler, Adolf, 34, 118
Hobby Lobby, 54
Holocaust, 10–11, 20, 38–39, 44, 192, 199, 201, 214, 321
Homer, 272–73, 290
homicide: and capital punishment, 299–300; and natural law, 43; and self-defense; and suicide, 92n6, 99n30, 111n62, 115–16. *See also* murder
homoeroticism, 43, 49–50
homosexual unions, 49–50, 167–68. *See also* same-sex marriage
Hood, John Y. B., 214
hope, virtue of, 25
Horeb, Mount, 77. *See also* Sinai
Humanae Vitae, 56–57
Hutchins, Robert Maynard, 25

iconoclasm, 177, 197
idolatry, x, 11, 15–16, 18n57, 43, 55, 86, 120, 123, 130, 132, 143, 185n13, 197–98, 264, 312. *See also avodah zarah; avodat elilim*
Ignatius of Loyola, 134
Illman, Ruth, 187
imago Dei (image of God), xii, 10, 19, 37–39, 42–43, 46, 52, 122–23, 143, 148, 154, 170, 172, 250, 292–93, 297, 299, 301–2, 304, 306, 309, 311–12, 316–17
imperialism: and natural teleology, 155n39; and religion in the public square, viii, 44, 64–65, 180; priestly, 215
Incarnation, doctrine of, viii, 68–70, 80, 187, 240–41, 283, 318, 324, 326
incest, 43, 49, 222
Inquisition, 207, 212, 214n58, 220n7
instinct, 56, 98
intermarriage (between Jews and non-Jews), 32, 50, 189
International Group of Orthodox Jews, 190
International Theological Commission of the Catholic Church, 99n29, 152n26, 215n62
Intifada of the 1980s, 189
Iran, 170, 179
Irenaeus of Lyons, 170, 318–19
Isaiah, 3, 86, 89, 133, 163, 188, 223, 227–29, 231n39, 233n47, 236–38, 250

Ishmael, 324
Isidore of Seville, 202, 230
Islam, xii–xiii, 4, 13n41, 18, 26, 68, 74, 77, 80–81, 85, 88, 179, 181–85, 187–88, 191–92, 208n41, 223, 323–25, 331
Isles of the Blessed, 259
Israel, modern state of, 9, 11, 13n41, 23–24, 26, 189

Jackson, Andrew, 91
Jefferson, Thomas, 30, 79, 250
Jerusalem, 148, 197, 236, 248, 320n12, 324; Athens and, xi, 9, 31, 160n1, 162, 252–61, 263–67, 276, 284–85, 288, 290–91; New, 3
Jesus Christ: and contraception, 305n38; and disagreement between Jews and Christians, 19–20; election of sinful followers, his, 215; and inter-religious dialogue, 187–89; Jewish reception of, 197; Jewish rejection of, 15–18, 86, 320; and justice in the Bible, 228–29, 233–36, 238–40; and law of Moses, 170; and Marcion heresy, 196; message of love, his, 183n6; and Mortara case, 211, 213n57; Muslim perspective on, 80n56, 324n17; neighbor-love commandment of, 142–43; and reason/revelation dialectic, 252, 283; and same-god question, 74, 76, 78–81; and secularism, 40, 331; and suicide, 96n20; and supersessionism, 5, 11–12, 86–87, 313, 319; as unifying figure in Christian-Jewish relations, xiii, 325–26
Jewish Theological Seminary of America, 29, 34
Jinping, Xi, 167
Job, book of, 90, 98n27, 104, 228n21, 231n39, 237n61
John, epistles of, 40, 136, 228–29, 238
John, gospel of, 40, 78–80, 213n57, 237n66, 239n82, 318, 326, 331
John of Damascus, 185
John Paul II, pope, 56n76, 119–20, 200, 234–36, 299n21, 305n38, 321, 328
John the Baptist, 238, 239
Jubilee Year, 233
Judaism: post-biblical, xii, 314, 319–20, 330
Judgment, Last, 19, 173, 239
justice: economic, 9; God's, xi, 10, 49, 225n1, 230, 235–36, 238–41, 259; natural, xi, 129, 151n21, 204–5, 208–9; rectifying, 234–37, 240–41; retributive, 225, 238; of due, xi, 206, 225–26, 230–32, 234, 240–41, 243–44; of right relationship, xi, 226, 228, 332–35, 240, 242–45

Justinian, 225n3
Justin Martyr, 318

kalām cosmological argument, 75
Kant, Immanuel, 137, 151; and anti-Semitism, 199n3; and autonomy, 102n37; and classical metaphysics, 89; and justice, 238, 248; and law, 126; and neighbor-love commandment, 310; and religious epistemology, 7, 291; and rights, 39, 232; and secularism, 171, 177, 323; and suicide, 2, 90, 92, 105
Kaveny, Cathleen, 110
Kerr, David, 188
Kertzer, David, 200, 211–14
Kierkegaard, Søren, 177, 289
King, Jr., Martin Luther, viii, 37, 49
Kingdom of God, 4–5, 8, 40, 65, 176, 179, 229, 235n54, 305n38
Koester, Helmut, 149–50
Koons, Robert, 153n31, 162
Korn, Bertram Wallace, 200
Kristol, Irving, 31

laïcité, 179
Latin Mass, 28
latitudinarianism, 324
law: divine, 18, 41–42, 100, 122, 126–33, 142, 149, 154–56, 161, 163, 172–73, 222, 312; eternal, 42n8, 128, 130; revealed, 41–42, 100, 142, 144, 163, 180, 222, 229, 263, 292–93, 303
Lawler, Justus George, 200n5
Lazarus, 234
Left, political, 24, 27, 179
legalism, 121–22, 126, 135, 139
Leirvik, Oddbjørn, 187
Lennon, John, 69
Lent, 134
Lessing, Gotthold, 173
Levenson, Jon, 182–83, 187
Levinas, Emmanuel, 296–97
Leviticus, 49, 118, 127, 142, 231n39, 237n62, 300, 310
Lewis, C. S., 75–77
lex talionis, 237
liberalism, viii–ix, 95, 101–4, 111n61, 167, 226, 323–24
liberal Judaism, 4, 24, 27, 63
liberal Protestantism, 4n12
Lieberman, Joseph, 24
Lincoln, Abraham, 49
Little Sisters of the Poor, 54
Lonergan, Bernard, 33

Lovejoy, A. O., 163
Luke, gospel of, 215, 234, 40
Lumen Gentium, 183–84

MacIntyre, Alasdair, 109n59, 150n19, 152–54, 162–63, 244n103, 290
MacLachlin, Beverly, 60n85, 164, 178–79
Mahoney, John, 121, 133n72, 138n102
Maimonides, Moses, 2, 4, 6–7, 9–10, 18n57, 33, 36, 43, 72, 77, 80, 88, 105, 125, 161, 222, 253n6, 263, 265–66, 328
manualist moral theology, ix, 121–22, 133, 138–39. *See also* scholastic moral theology
Marcionism, ix, 68, 70, 85, 121, 170, 196, 318, 321, 323–24
Marion, Jean-Luc, 291
Maritain, Jacques, 35, 211n50, 231n41, 249
martyrdom, 10, 96, 139, 298
Masada, 96n22
mass culture, 32
Massignon, Louis, 182n3
mass shooting, 94
material causality, 153n33
materialism: Marxist, 4n12; metaphysical, 317; secular, 206n35
Matthew, gospel of, 40, 135, 142, 228–30, 233–35, 238–39, 241, 321n12, 325
Mattison, William C., 121n3, 126n30, 133n70, 228n18
McGrew, Lydia, 69–70, 80–81, 87
McHugh, John A., 210–11
Mecca, 324
mediation: of the apostles, 215; divine-human, 267, 271, 274, 280, 283–85; hermeneutical, 262; of Jesus, 197, 313–15, 320, 325; of natural law, 179
Mendelssohn, Moses, 10, 105, 177
Messori, Vittorio, 200–201, 207, 210n48, 212
midrash, 125, 289
Mill, John Stuart, 171
mitzvot, ix–x, 154
monogamy, 167, 223, 323
monotheism, xii, 73, 149, 182–85, 188, 195–96, 275n85, 316, 318, 323
Moore, Roy, viii, 37
moral theology, 211n50, 228n18; Catholic, ix, 112, 120–22, 133, 135, 137–39, 143
More, Thomas, 178
Moreland, Anna, 188
Moreland, J. P., 76–77
Morgentaler, Henry, 39
Morisi, Anna, xi, 200, 208, 211, 213–14, 224
mortal sin, 15, 96n20, 112

Mortara, Edgardo, xi, 199–202, 204, 206–7, 209–15, 220–21, 223–24
Mosaic law, 4, 42, 143, 145, 170, 222, 260n32, 315, 317, 322, 324–25, 329. *See also* Sinai
Moses: covenant of, 16, 229, 314, 316. *See also* Sinai
Muhammad, x, 183n6, 185, 187–88, 331
Mundelein Seminary, xv, 22, 161
murder: and abortion, 57, 323; and capital punishment, 299, 301; divine prohibition of, 124, 135, 145, 222, 231, 233, 249–51, 292; and euthanasia, 91n4; and suicide, 92–94, 96n20, 99–100, 105–6, 115–17. *See also* homicide
Murray, John Courtney, 8, 35, 58–59
Muslims, viii, x–xi, 13n41, 32, 64, 68–75, 77, 80, 82, 86, 88, 181–88, 190–92, 199, 202n12, 223–25, 331. *See also* Islam

Nahmanides, 125, 129, 131, 139, 143, 221
Nardoni, Enrique, 228–29, 233, 238–39
National Association of Evangelicals, 183
Natural family planning (NFP), 56–57; Creighton and Marquette methods, 57
natural theology, 76–77, 87–89, 311
Nazism, 20, 191, 199, 215n64
Neuhaus, Richard John, 1, 29, 38, 164, 178–79
Neusner, Jacob, 149n8, 183n8
Newman, John Henry, 147
new natural law theory, vii, 293
Newton, Isaac, 89
New York Times, 56, 67, 112, 186
Nicaea, Council of, viii, 78–79
Nietzsche, Friedrich, 173
9/11, 10n31, 182
Nineveh, 237
Noahide covenant, 236, 316
Noahide law, 2, 10, 18, 42–43, 97, 105, 117, 144, 208n41, 222, 293, 300
nones, 32, 181, 191, 331
Nostra Aetate, x, xii, 29, 182–84, 186, 188–90, 197, 213n58, 314–15, 318n4, 320–21
nuclear war, 9
nuclear weapons, 8
Nutt, Roger, 207

Obama, Barack, viii, 53, 55
Ochs, Peter, 192
Ockham's Razor, 331
O'Donovan, Oliver, 169
olam ha-ba, 222, 331. *See also* eschatological consummation; eschaton
O'Neill, Colman, 207
Oral Torah, 13–15, 18

oral tradition, 43, 330
Origen of Alexandria, 31
original sin, 39, 129, 166
Orthodox Judaism, vii, x, 23–27, 30, 36, 190, 196, 315, 319
Otto, Rudolf, 124
Oxford Centre for Hebrew and Jewish Studies, vii
Oxford University, vii, 22, 25

paganism, xii, 31, 78, 129, 257, 266, 274–75, 289
pantheism, 75
papal police, xi, 199, 202, 212n53
Papal States, 199–200, 202–3, 206–8, 214
particularism, viii, 4, 35, 41, 44–45, 47–48, 316
Pascal, Blaise, 88
Passover Seder, 6n15
Patient Protection Affordable Health Care Act, 53
Paul, Apostle, viii, 12n38, 15, 77–79, 81, 209, 211, 215, 228–29, 231, 238–40, 318, 320
Pauline privilege, 203
Paul of Antioch, 185n14
Paul VI, pope, 29, 56–57, 213n58
Pelagianism, 131n57
Pelagia of Antioch, 97
persecution of Jews, Christian, 1, 12–13, 17, 20, 184n12, 209n44, 213–14
Peter, Apostle, 215, 320n12
Peter, epistles of, 229n23, 239–41
Peters, Nathaniel, 27, 207n35
Peterson, Jordan, 165
Peter the Venerable, 185
Petrus Alfonsi, 185
Pew Charitable Trust, 181n2
Philippians, epistles to, 40, 240n86, 326
Philistines, 164, 174
Philo, 4
philosophy, classical, 64, 99, 105, 252, 254n8, 257, 285
philosophy, public, 44, 48–51, 55, 64
philosophy, scholastic, 132n65, 153n23, 260
pilgrimage, 134
Pinckaers, Servais, xv, 121, 126, 135n84, 138n102
Pius IX, pope, ix, xi, 199–215, 220–21, 223–24
Pius XII, pope, 56n76
Plantinga, Alvin, 76–77
Plato: and divine revelation, xii, 2, 254, 258–60, 262, 267–73, 275–77, 279–83, 289–91; on justice, 248; and natural law, 125, 149–50, 152–53, 162; and Platonism, 252, 266–68, 270, 274–85, 289–90; and political philosophy, 166–67; and suicide, 90, 92, 105
plenitude, principle of, 270

pluralism, viii, 8, 10, 40–41, 58–59, 85, 148, 164, 177, 191
polygamy, 146, 223–24
polytheism, 18n57, 73, 85–86, 123, 146, 184–85, 284
populism, 102, 171
Porch of Solomon, 252
Porter, Jean, 120n3, 230n31
positive law, 144, 150–51, 173, 293, 312
positivism, legal, 36, 42, 102
Potiphar's wife, 300
practical reason, 39, 42–43, 46, 127–28, 162, 300, 303, 311
preambles of faith, 72–74, 88
pre-nuptial agreement, 146
presumption, sin of, 134–35, 139
pride, sin of, ix, 130, 213n57
Prime Mover, 153
Princeton University, vii, 22–25, 27, 38, 161–63
privacy, ix, 50, 95–96; right to, 47, 102–4
privatization of religion, 44, 52
procreation, 10, 49, 56, 168, 204n23, 305
Prodigal Son, 235, 240
progressivism, 27–28, 65
proselytism, 5, 8, 13n40, 48n43, 197, 330–31. See also conversion; evangelization
Proverbs, 227n7, 229, 231n39, 233n47, 237n61
Psalms, 31, 136, 227–29, 236–38
psychedelic drugs, 107
psychotic disorder, 104, 106–12, 118–19
puberty-blocking hormone treatments, 168
public prayer, viii, 24, 48–49, 88, 173

Québec, 179
Qur'an, 74, 77n45, 183n5, 188, 191n32, 323–24, 231

Rad, Gerhard von, 227
Radner, Ephraim, 199
rape, 49, 57. See also sexual assault
Rashi, 116
Ratzinger, Joseph, 200, 215n62, 314n1. See also Benedict XVI, pope
Rawls, John, 172, 225, 248
Raz, Joseph, 167, 171
Reagan, Ronald, 91
Reform Judaism, 23, 26
regula fidei, 256
relativism, 85
religious fear. See fear of God
religious liberty, viii, 9–10, 36, 47, 51–53, 55, 58, 60, 322, 325. See also rights
Republican Party, 24, 58

resurrection: general, 175, 317; of Jesus, 16,
    75–77, 215, 238–40, 242, 317, 331
retributive justice. *See* justice
revelation, general, 72, 161
revelation, special, 41, 48, 87, 160, 251
rights: in Aquinas, 230–31; and Bible, 225–26,
    231, 244–45; civil, 51; covenantal, 41n5,
    49–50, 73, 122–25, 128n45, 134n77,
    137–39, 149n8, 151–52, 155–57, 162,
    165, 169, 172–73, 208n41, 243; and
    duties, xi, 45, 103, 233, 243–44, 248–51;
    of God, 175, 201n9, 204n22; human,
    9–10, 43–45, 49–50, 148; individual, ix,
    323; language of, 66, 95, 101; to life, 174,
    294–95; nature of, 8; of parents, xi, 168,
    201n9, 224, 231n38; of the poor, 232–34;
    to privacy, 102–3; religious, 2n4, 53–55,
    95, 322, 326
Risorgimento (Italian unification), 206n35
robbery, 43, 222
Robeck, Johann, 304
Rockefeller, John D., 25
Roe v. Wade, 39
Roman law, 22
Romans, epistle to, 12n38, 15, 17, 40, 128, 130,
    184, 209, 211, 228n21, 231, 238–40,
    278n95, 314–15, 318, 320
Rome, 56n76, 203–4, 212–15, 248
Rommen, Heinrich Albert, 34
Rosenzweig, Franz, 2, 4n12, 9, 144, 178, 312
Rousseau, Jean-Jacques, 88, 177

Sabbath, 24, 39, 124–25, 132
Sacks, Jonathan, 2n4, 30, 38, 209n44
sacramental realism, ix, 207
sacramental theology, 201, 314
sacraments: in Aquinas, 204n22; of baptism,
    205, 207, 209, 211, 214, 221, 224, 217;
    doctrine of, 214–15; of the Old Law, 314,
    319
saeculum, 59
salvation history, 74, 138
Samaritan, Good, 234
same-sex marriage, 8–10, 49–51, 146, 165, 168,
    174n35
sanctity of life, xii, 38, 95–97, 99n30, 101–12,
    116, 292–308. *See also* dignity, human
Sanders, Bernie, 27
Sanhedrin, 33, 320n12
Sanhedrin (tractate), 33, 117, 222–23, 263–64
Santa Claus, 69–70, 81
Saudelli, Lucia, 274–75, 283n122

Saudi Arabia, 179
Saul, king, 172, 237
scandal, sin of, xi, 12, 112, 209, 221, 282
Schizophrenia, 106n51, 133
scholastic moral theology, ix, 144
Scotus, John Duns, 206n34, 214
Scriptural Reasoning Network, 192
Second Temple Judaism, 10, 13–14, 18, 30
Second Vatican Council, x, 28–29, 52, 56n76,
    64, 121, 126, 138, 182–83, 199, 245, 314,
    320–21
sectarianism, 63–65; non-, 88, 180
secularism: anti-religious, vii–viii, 23, 27, 30–31,
    44, 40–41, 51–52, 63–64, 180, 198, 221,
    323–25, 331; anti-semitic, 191, 321;
    definition of, 41n2; and Pius IX, 206n35,
    213, 221; and public ethical theory, 3, 8,
    9–10, 29, 44–47, 63–65, 95, 147–48, 165–
    66, 172, 243, 248; and Second Vatican
    Council, 28; and suicide, 97n24, 119; and
    supersessionism, xii, 323; universalism
    of, 47, 331
secular Jews, 24, 26–27, 44
secular religion, viii, 58–60, 88
secular space, x, 161, 170–73, 178, 197
secular state, 4, 45–45, 49, 177
sensus divinitatis, 76–77
Sephardic Jews, 26
Septuagint, 228, 290
Sermon on the Mount, 135, 228n18, 234
sex education, x, 168
sexual assault, 57n78. *See also* rape
sexual misconduct, 132
sexual revolution, 165
Shoah. *See also* Holocaust
Signer, Michael, 192
Sikhs, 181, 191
Simon, Yves, 1, 35
Sinai, 213, 229, 317; covenant, 42, 49, 236;
    revelation at, 89; Torah of, 69, 328, 331
Singer, Peter, 38
Sirach, 127, 234
Six Day War of 1967, 189
slavery, 49, 233, 282
Smith, Christian, 134
social contract, 9–10, 102n36; and fundamental
    communities, 167–72; and individualism,
    165–66; and rights, 225, 243
socialism, 167
Socrates, xi, 150, 257–60, 262–63, 267–269,
    271–73, 275n85, 279–282, 291
Soloveitchik, Joseph, 29–30, 187, 197–98

Sophocles, 151n21
Spinoza, Baruch, 2, 9–11, 88, 177–78, 261n35
Stalin, Joseph, 167
Stegman, Thomas, 240
stem cell research, 38, 292
sterilization (reproductive), 53, 55, 58
Stoicism, 99n28, 105, 111, 149–51, 248, 252, 258n21, 281n112
Strauss, Leo, 1, 35, 162, 253n4, 257, 261–63, 266
suicide bombing, 94
Superman, 71
supersessionism: Christian and Jewish, 11–15, 30, 89, 315–17, 323–24; five forms of, xii–xiii, 313–26; hard and soft, 15–20, 67n2, 86–87, 196, 329–31; in modern political philosophy, 173, 323
Supreme Court of the United States, 54n70
syncretism, 5–6, 19–20

ta'amei ha-mitsvot ("reasons of the commandments"), 123, 127, 163, 251
Talmud, 22, 30, 33, 108n55, 118–19, 139, 145, 163, 223, 330; Palestinian, 142–43
Tapie, Matthew, 201–4, 224
Taylor, Charles, 164
Taylor, Holly, 207n35
Tel Aviv, 26
teleology: Aristotelian, 7n20, 151–52, 162, 222; infused, 45; in Maimonides, 6; natural, x, 152–56, 162–63; and natural law, 161–63; neo-Aristotelian, 153, 163; of Old Law, 143; Plato's, 290
temperance, virtue of, 137n95
Temple in Jerusalem, 28, 197, 241n92, 319
Ten Commandments, 16, 37, 100n31, 116–17, 127–28, 132, 137, 251, 319
Ten Points of Seelisburg, 186
Teradyon, Hanina ben, 298
Tertullian, 31, 252–57, 262, 265, 276
theocracy, 179
theology: anti-Jewish, 199; of the body, 56n76; Catholic, 25; classical, 64; comparative, 181–82, 187–88; of contempt, 191; of creation, 126, 220; and ethics, 7, 198; Jewish, 2, 4, 8, 18, 126n30, 192, 198; and law, 115; and natural law theory, 88–89, 160–61; of Novak, David, 20, 63, 122–23, 126, 134, 137, 142; of Old Testament, 227–28; and philosophy, xii, vii, 42n12, 252–57, 261–67, 275n85, 285, 288–91; political, 9, 169, 172, 225, 243, 249; and supersessionism 11n35, 314, 316, 319, 321; Thomistic, 145; trinitarian, 78. *See also* moral theology; natural theology; sacramental theology
Thessalonians, epistles to, 228n21, 322n16
Thessalonica, 79
Thomas Aquinas: on capital punishment, 297–99; on Christ's atonement, 240–42; on divine commandments, ix, 122, 125–38, 142–43, 145; on forced baptism, 201, 203–10, 214; on Jewish people, 319, 322; on justice, 225, 228n20, 230, 235, 240–42, 248; on mercy, 234–35; on natural law, x, 36, 42n8, 155–56, 161, 221–22, 224, 251; on natural order, xi, 142; and natural science, 290; and preambles of faith, 72–80, 87–88, 311; and rights, 230–31; and sense-reference distinction, 70–71; on suicide, 2, 90, 92, 98, 100n32, 105, 116–18; on Torah, 319n6
Tikkam Olam, 190n30
Tillich, Paul, 8
Timothy, epistles to, 40, 132n67, 137, 142, 241n95
"To Do the Will of Our Father in Heaven," 190
Toledo, Fourth Council of, 202
Tollefsen, Olaf, 308
torture, 9, 233, 321
totalitarianism, 47
Trinity, viii, xii, 11, 16, 68–69, 74, 76–77, 80–81, 188, 318, 324
triumphalism, 19, 65, 86–87, 330–31
Trump, Donald, 54, 182n4
typological sense of scripture, 318–19, 323

Ulpian, 127, 225n3
United States Conference of Catholic Bishops (USCCB), 57n78
universalism, 4, 35, 41, 44, 47, 313, 323–24, 329, 331
University of Chicago, 25, 28, 34–35
University of Notre Dame, xv, 126, 192
University of Toronto, vii, 1, 31, 33–34, 142, 146, 165, 178, 199, 308
University of Virginia, 1–2, 22, 30, 35, 183n9

Vatican, 29, 56, 99n29, 187, 200–202, 204n22, 206–7, 212–14, 220
Vatican II. *See* Second Vatican Council
Venus, 71–72
Veritatis Splendor, 120–21, 208n41
via negativa, 291
Virgil, 273
virtue ethics, 121–22, 126, 162–63

virtues: acquired and infused, 129–33, 138; and justice, 225–26, 230–31, 234, 244; and natural inclinations, 98–99; and natural teleology, 152–53, 162–63; and philosophy, xiii, 151n23, 272–73, 281; of Pius IX, 210n48; relation of to commandments, ix, 110n60, 120–22, 126–28, 132, 135–37, 139, 142, 151–52. *See also* individual virtues
Voegelin, Eric, 163
von Bismarck, Otto, 4
Vulgate, 118, 142

Walls, Jerry, 69–70, 80–81, 87

Webb, Eitan, 38
Webb, Stephen, 93n10
Weinfeld, Moshe, 227n12, 237
Wheaton College, viii, 68–70, 183
William of Tripoli, 185
Williams, Bernard, 152, 154, 162, 230–31
Williams, Thomas, 249
Wills, Garry, 215
Wittgenstein, Ludwig, 88, 262
Wolterstorff, Nicholas, 225–26
Wright, N. T., 238–40

Zedong, Mao, 167
zionism, 9, 11, 20